Mary Elizabeth Braddon

**Belgravia**

Mary Elizabeth Braddon

**Belgravia**

ISBN/EAN: 9783742830548

Manufactured in Europe, USA, Canada, Australia, Japa

Cover: Foto ©Andreas Hilbeck / pixelio.de

Manufactured and distributed by brebook publishing software (www.brebook.com)

Mary Elizabeth Braddon

**Belgravia**

# CONTENTS OF VOL. LXXXVIII.

|  | PAGE |
|---|---|
| A Bitter Expiation. By A. M. JUDD | 149 |
| A Black Sheep. By K. D. K. | 39 |
| A Hum-Drum Girl. By JENNY WREN | 179 |
| A Mission in Life. By Mrs. EDWARD CARTWRIGHT | 277 |
| An Old Maid's Mistake. By MRS. CONNEY, Author of "A Lady Horsebreaker," "Gold for Dross," &c.:— | |
| CHAP. XXV. | 1 |
| XXVI. | 7 |
| XXVII. | 16 |
| XXVIII. | 113 |
| XXIX. | 121 |
| XXX. | 128 |
| XXXI. | 225 |
| XXXII. | 235 |
| XXXIII. | 241 |
| XXXIV. | 248 |
| XXXV. | 255 |
| XXXVI. | 337 |
| XXXVII. | 342 |
| XXXVIII. | 354 |
| XXXIX. | 360 |
| A Prosaic Idyll | 390 |
| A Tale of the Fens. By NEIL WYNN WILLIAMS | 431 |
| Autumn Clouds. By E. YOLLAND | 169 |

## CONTENTS.

|  | PAGE |
|---|---|
| A Victim of Circumstances. By KATHARINE F. HILLS | 303 |
| Eleanor and Arthur Plantagenet. By CHARLES BRUCE-ANGIER | 83 |
| Famous Poets.—VII. Percy Bysshe Shelley. By CHARLOTTE A. PRICE | 399 |
| Ivan the Terrible. By JOSEPHINE ERROL | 262 |
| La Bourboule. By E. C. VANSITTART | 197 |
| Late in Life. By A. PERRIN, Author of "Into Temptation," &c. :— | |
|     CHAP. XXV. What Might Have Been | 94 |
|     XXVI. Nina's Indisposition | 103 |
|     XXVII. Death | 212 |
|     XXVIII. A Meeting | 217 |
|     XXIX. Engaged | 323 |
|     XXX. Married | 328 |
| Patty's Lovers. By MARGARET MACKINTOSH | 380 |
| Poppies. By MARY S. HANCOCK | 74 |
| Sir William Gregory. By AMELIA AYLMER GOWING | 23 |
| The Art of Swearing. By EDGAR VALDES | 366 |
| The First Three Princesses of Wales. By CECIL LEIGH | 134 |
| The Provincial Doctor. By CHARLES EDWARDES | 66 |

# BELGRAVIA.

SEPTEMBER, 1895.

---

## An Old Maid's Mistake.

BY MRS. CONNEY,

Author of "A Lady Horsebreaker," "A Ruthless Avenger,"
"Gold for Dross," etc.

### CHAPTER XXV.

THIS was how it happened that as John and Adrian Lisle jogged homewards together across the fields—for Arnold and Lady Colthurst had at once dropped behind—they caught sight, in the distance, of the runaway, galloping madly down a steep, stony by-road, with the buggy bumping and jolting at her heels. Cicely, who, to do her justice, kept her wits about her, was holding on to the side. Her companion, on the other hand, had completely lost his head, and was making matters worse by dragging and tugging at the maddened animal. It was the first intimation Lisle had had of Cicely's escapade.

"Miss Denison!" he ejaculated, unable to believe his eyes. "Good God, John, look there!"

John looked, and took in the situation.

"The bridge," he muttered hoarsely, pointing to a corner a couple of hundred yards away, and putting his horse into a gallop.

Adrian knew the place. A sharp turn to the right, on to a narrow bridge, with a low parapet, and a drop of twenty feet into the stream beneath. He also remembered that whereas John was riding Arnold's park-hack, an animal which had probably never been out of a canter or jumped anything bigger than a hurdle in its life, he himself was mounted on a seasoned, well-bred hunter. And there was no time to be lost! As he set the chestnut going, he measured the distance to the fatal corner, turned away from the gate, and galloped straight for the big blind fence before him. The race was an exciting one. The Hackham waggonette appeared over the brow of the hill in time to witness it, yet too late to be of any use. John, pounding in the rear, held his breath, as the chestnut took off, and landed a couple of feet clear of the stake-and-bound fence and its ugly overgrown ditch.

By this time Cicely, stout-hearted as she was, was growing sick and dizzy. The landscape was whirling before her eyes, while the singing in her ears drowned even her companion's shouts for help. And then—— Well! she never quite realised what happened. There were at least a dozen eye-witnesses of the scene, but as they all gave different versions of it, it was hopeless to attempt to arrive at any clear understanding of it. All she personally recollected was the looming-up of something through a mist, a something which seemed to spring up out of the earth, and then a jerk, a crash, a shower of sparks before her eyes, a sensation of going down—down. . . .

Where was she? What had happened? Why was John bending over her, forcing something into her mouth, something hot and stinging, which made her cough and start?

"What do you want?" she asked pettishly, wishing he would leave her in peace.

"Try to get up," was his reply, in a voice which sounded strangely far-away and unfamiliar. He helped her to her feet. Yes. Notwithstanding a swimming head and shaking limbs, she could stand pretty well.

"That's right." John's voice had become his own again. "Now sit down, and don't move till I come back."

Instinctively she obeyed the authoritative accents, sat down with her back against the parapet of the bridge and surveyed the scene. A few yards away lay the buggy smashed in pieces; the cob, badly cut about her legs, her glossy coat all dripping and stained, was held by Aubrey Page, whose face was as white as the handkerchief with which, with his free hand, he was wiping the blood from a cut on his mouth. In the middle of the road lay something, she couldn't quite make out, John was standing in her light. Just as, in a vague, dazed way, she mastered these details, up dashed the Hackham waggonette. What a babel of tongues! What clatter! What confusion! The noise went through her head. What was it all about? If she hadn't felt so stupidly disinclined to move, she would have gone to look. And here was someone pushing through the little crowd. Esme! And looking ghastly!

"Oh, Cicely!" she cried, with a shudder, throwing herself down beside her. "My poor child! How terrible!" And then, taking her in her arms, she burst into tears.

Cicely laughed—such a poor, feeble ghost of a laugh.

"What is it all about?" she asked. "I feel so stupid. I don't understand. What are we doing here?"

Esme gulped down her tears.

"You have been run away with," she explained unsteadily. "We were behind, and saw it all. Mr. Lisle rode across country to stop you, got to the corner just in time, caught hold of the cob, and over you all went together. It was horrible!"

"And Mr. Lisle?" By this time Cicely had pretty well come to herself.

Esme shivered.

"He is there—in the road. He hasn't moved. He is insensible —badly hurt," she whispered.

Badly hurt! And by her fault! Cicely started up.

"How are you now? More yourself again?" asked John, coming up. "Lisle?" in answer to her breathless question. "Oh! he's coming round. Damaged his leg a bit, I'm afraid, poor chap. You see he fell under the buggy. No, don't go to him. You can't do anything. And we can't tell for certain till we get him home. Look here, Mrs. Blunt," turning to Esme, "Adams has taken the chestnut on to prepare your people, and Arnold is off in search of a doctor. He thinks we had better get Lisle into the waggonette, and back to Hackham as quickly as possible. It's the nearest place, you see."

"Of course," assented Esme, whose lips were so dry that she could hardly form the words.

"The only question is what is to become of you ladies?" John continued doubtfully. "The men can walk, but how about you?"

This question was answered by the reappearance of Mrs. Fulton and her brake on the scene. Having heard the news from the groom already sent on, she had hurried back to offer such help as she was able to give. Like the good-natured creature she was, she refrained from any reproaches or crying over spilt milk, and managed to find room for Cicely, Esme and a dowager with her. The other ladies elected to walk, as they were perfectly able to do. Cicely, indeed, only entered the brake under protest.

"I am not hurt," she declared, " I can walk quite well and would much rather do so," which was true, for she was ashamed to look Mrs. Fulton in the face.

"Get in," was John's reply to this remonstrance, "we don't want to have you too in the doctor's hands!"

Too crushed to offer opposition, the culprit obeyed meekly. She always looked back on that drive as one of the most humiliating half-hours of her life. Although shaken and bruised from head to foot, her injuries were not such as to excite popular sympathy or render others oblivious of the fact that she had brought them on herself. Mrs. Fulton realised only too well the horrible injustice, which had deprived her husband of a valuable animal he was in no position to replace, had seriously disabled a wholly innocent person, disfigured a second, and allowed the chief offender to escape scot free. For of course, young Page would never have dreamed of committing such an outrage on propriety without direct invitation, or at least most improper encouragement from the girl. Oh! Cicely deserved no pity; she certainly received none. Even Esme for once found it hard to take up the cudgels for her when attacked by Arnold on the subject.

"You're satisfied I hope with this bosom friend of yours at last," he grumbled. Naturally he was greatly annoyed at the incidents, and naturally was venting his annoyance on his wife. "A nice name we shall get for ourselves! What were you thinking of to let the girl go off with Page at all? I warned you. You can't say you didn't know. You know what she is, what her mother was. I must say, Esme, if you will bring such people to the house, the least you can do is to look after them."

"I'm very sorry," was all Esme could say. "No one, I'm sure, can be more distressed and penitent than Cicely is herself either. She meant no harm. She could not possibly foretell the accident, for which after all she was not responsible."

"I'm not so sure of that! How do we know what tricks she hadn't been playing? Old Fulton will have his knife into her, of that you may be sure. There's his buggy reduced to matchwood, and that nice cob, as good as fifty pounds in his pocket any day, won't fetch ten now."

"Couldn't we make it up to Mr. Fulton in some way?" she suggested.

"What? Give him a cheque to cover damages as if he were a cab proprietor? My good girl, Fulton's a gentleman. You can't offer him money. Besides, why should I pay for Page's cursed clumsiness? And how about Lisle either? Will he take a cheque as compensation?"

"How is Mr. Lisle?" she inquired, for Arnold had come to her after seeing the doctor.

"He's doing all right. It's just as we thought—a broken leg—a long business, but not dangerous, with proper precautions. It's a confounded nuisance for the poor chap, and for us too, but that can't be helped, thanks to Miss Cicely. By the way, what's she doing now in the hall? She was hanging about there as I came through. Why can't she go to her room, where she'll be out of mischief, which is more than she is anywhere else?"

In this, he was unjust to the poor criminal, who was lingering simply to satisfy her anxiety for the invalid. As he was carried into the house, she had caught a glimpse of a helpless figure, and drawn white face, and at once visions of a broken back, an injured spine, a fractured skull, every conceivable horror rose up before her. He was going to die. She was sure of it. And his death would lay at her door. To have killed a fellow creature, all to satisfy her miserable vanity and pride! Never never, *never* could she hold up her head again or know a happy moment. In speechless misery, a prey to every terror which an over-vivid imagination and disordered nerves could conjure up, she crouched on a seat in the corner of the hall, longing for certainty, yet lacking courage to put an end to her suspense. She watched the doctor come—what an eternity it seemed before he passed through on his way back to his carriage! In vain she tried to stop him, to ask for news. She dared not face the worst. As Arnold returned she started up. He brushed past her, ostentatiously ignoring her. Again she turned coward and fell back.

A long interval. Darkness deepened. A lamp was lighted in the centre of the hall, a spot of brightness, only accentuating the gloom reigning in her corner. In the distance doors opened and shut. Servants passed to and fro preparing the table for dinner, the dressing-bell clanged through the house. Life had resumed its usual routine, but Cicely did not stir. How could she endure the solitude of her own room? Here at least, she could catch occasional gleams of light, hear a murmur of voices. And to face her fellow creatures! Oh! impossible. She could only hide in her corner and wish with all the passion of her undisciplined nature that she were in the place of the sufferer upstairs. Why had she not been punished? she asked in a frenzy of impotent remorse. Let her get her deserts, and no one, not even Mrs. Fulton, surpassed her in the severity of the judgment she passed upon herself—she would not complain. Only it was cruel, unjust, monstrous, to make another suffer in her stead, and thereby double her punishment. At last, someone—by the tread she could tell it was a man—opened the library door and walked not towards the stairs, but to her hiding place. As he came near, she cowered back against the wall. It was John! The very last man she wanted to encounter! Stooping, he took up a coat from a number of wraps thrown down on the floor, felt in the pocket of it, and extracted a pipe. And then he glanced towards her corner.

"Who's there?" he asked sharply. "Cicely!" in a voice of astonishment, "what are you doing here? The bell rang ages ago. Dinner will be ready in ten minutes."

Dinner! Did he think her capable at such a time of thinking of *food*?

"How is he?" she faltered. "Will he die?"

"Die? Who? Lisle? Not a bit of it," was the cheerful rejoinder. "What put that into your head? He's knocked himself about a bit, and broken a leg, but that sort of thing doesn't kill a man. Tedious perhaps, but no danger. Why, what is it?" for, worn out with fatigue and suspense, Cicely had broken down and was sobbing hysterically.

John was really exceedingly kind, *how* kind she didn't quite realise till later. At the time, she was merely conscious vaguely that he soothed and reassured her, half led, half carried her to her room, sent for a maid, ordered her to bed, and arranged for the tray, which soon after made its appearance in her room, and for the contents of which she found herself vastly the better.

Once comfortably housed in bed, Cicely ceased her tears, and realised how she longed to pour into some sympathetic ear her self-reproach, her repentance of the silly pride and vanity which had prompted her to such lengths of folly. If Esme were only there! What a relief to confide to her lenient gentle keeping the story of the last few months, to gain strength for amendment, perhaps even to plead those extenuating circumstances which might surely be urged in her favour. But then Esme was not there. She didn't come up till after dinner, when she found Cicely fast asleep. It was a climax to the misfortunes of this most unfortunate day. Such a confession as Cicely's did not improve with keeping. To be made at all, it needed to be made at once. For what would have come so easily just then, became impossible twenty-four hours later, and in the end never came at all, which was a pity.

## CHAPTER XXVI.

WITH the following day came the inevitable reaction. Cicely woke up rested, refreshed, and, so to speak, in her right mind. As, by morning light, she reviewed her doings of the past twenty-four hours, she was amazed, not so much at her remorseful terror, exaggerated as she now considered it to have been, as at the stupendous folly and recklessness of which she had been guilty. Setting aside all question of the accident, she had coolly outraged propriety and compromised her reputation—for what? Not most assuredly for the sake of such a man as Aubrey Page, for whom she never entertained more than a moderate semi-contemptuous liking, a sentiment now transformed into absolute loathing. No. Any stick will do to beat a dog with. Aubrey Page had merely been used as a means by which she might pay John out, as she phrased it; might vex, spite and annoy him, might rouse his jealousy and gratify her own vanity. That was the truth.

How mean and contemptible it looked! For what had John done? Nothing at all, except refuse to comply with a demand, which, when she made it, she knew to be unreasonable. On the contrary, all her life he had been her most loyal friend and champion, while she had persistently contradicted and thwarted him, taking a malicious pleasure in setting him at naught. And why? Because he was generous and firm, because she could not despise and laugh at him, as she had done with other men, because he was immeasurably superior to the rest of his sex, because, in short, he was her master, and, rebel as she would, she knew it, and loved him all the better for it. For she did love him. Why should she deny it? She was conquered, was glad to lay down her arms, give up the unequal struggle and submit herself to the goodwill and pleasure of her lord and master. Even if he didn't care for her, or show his feelings just as she would have had him do, he was just ten thousand times better than any other man she knew, and she was proud to think she had had the good taste to bestow her heart upon him.

Having learned that Mr. Lisle was going on as well as could be expected, she dressed and went downstairs, feeling brighter and more contented with herself than she had done for a long while. She repented of her reckless indiscretion, but she no longer wanted to turn her face to the wall and die. On the contrary, she was eager to try and repair her wrong-doing and do better in the future. She would go to John, who would understand and help and protect her. True she had deeply offended him. But then he must know that she had not been in earnest. Besides, he never bore malice. And so, with a truly meek and chastened spirit, she descended. These good resolutions of hers were put to an early test, for the first person she encountered was Lady Colthurst, a lady whose powers of exasperation were of the highest order.

"You must be feeling pretty sick," was her elegant greeting. "How are you? Wishing you had taken the advice of your elders and betters, I should think."

Lady Colthurst, it may be stated, was thoroughly annoyed with Cicely. Such an escapade did harm to herself and everyone connected with her. Besides, her own reputation did not permit her to indulge in the luxury of charity towards others. Also she had had dunning letters from her milliner and dressmaker that morning and was generally out of sorts. And so, when Cicely, mindful of her resolve, suppressed the sharp retort on her lips, "I do hope this will be a lesson to you," her cousin went on sharply. "You want one badly enough, goodness knows. You can't afford these little games in your position, you know. With ten thousand a year you might carry it off. As it is, men fight shy of marrying a girl with such a reputation as you will get. Oh! I know what you are going to say," as Cicely opened her mouth and shut it again resolutely. "John is always there as a last resource. Always ready and willing to take you. Poor wretch! He must be. He can't help himself."

At this Cicely was unable to restrain herself.

"What do you mean?" she burst out angrily.

"Why, what I say," retorted Ada, delighted to have roused the sleeping lion at last, for it was poor fun hitting an adversary who wouldn't hit back. One might as well beat the air with a pillow.

"John *must* marry you; considering that he takes the place, which if you were a boy, would be yours, that he turns you adrift without a home or a sixpence to bless yourself with, what else can he do?"

"You are entirely mistaken," Miss Cicely declared contemptuously. "Where you get your distorted ideas from, I can't imagine. As the head of the family and my nearest relation, John is my guardian, that's all. He looks after my money, but it is mine. He is under no *obligation* to marry me more than any one else. I have my own fortune, and when I come of age I can take it and do as I please with it."

"My good girl, you're talking nonsense."

In her annoyance Lady Colthurst grew indiscreet.

"All that may impose on you, but it doesn't on anybody else. *We* all know that your father died in debt, which debt John has had to make good, and that the property won't be free from Uncle Richard's mortgages for ages. Where do you suppose then that the money you live upon now, and that you are going to live upon later, comes from, except out of John's pocket? Do you think Lady Louisa takes you for nothing, and that your clothes pay for themselves? And how, by the time John has settled money on you, and freed the estate, is he to keep a wife and live at Abbottsleigh, I should like to know?"

Cicely had grown first scarlet and then white. "I don't believe a word of it," she said defiantly, which was not true. A thousand trifles had returned to her memory in confirmation of the news. John's reluctance to enter on the subject of money, his calm, business-like wooing. Had it all been prompted by pity, or worse still, by a mere sordid consideration of money?

"Whether you believe it or not, that doesn't alter the fact. Uncle Richard hadn't a sou. He never had. To provide for your future, he was anxious that John should marry you. John consented. There's nothing to make a fuss about. It's quite a simple, sensible arrangement. John sees the force of it. If he were married so that you could live with him, or you were married, it would be all right, but then you're not. Therefore he must either marry you, or pay away a big slice of his income, because, you know, you have a very good notion of spending money. And so he takes you and puts up with you, and that's why I do think you might show a little gratitude, instead of attacking a man who can't retaliate. However, as your mother's daughter——" she checked herself hurriedly.

"What then?" demanded Cicely with ominous calmness. "Pray finish your sentence. Whatever insult you have to offer to my mother, let me hear it!"

For the first time Lady Colthurst exhibited signs of confusion. "It was nothing," she said hurriedly. "It slipped out unawares, I meant nothing."

"I know it was nothing," the other flashed out, "nothing but your vile tongue, which simply revels in slander. My mother, let me tell you, was a far better woman than you are or ever will be, and be careful, please, how you speak of her in future."

This was too much. Lady Colthurst lost her last remnant of self-control. "If you must have the truth, you shall get it," she retorted sneeringly. "Your mother, let me tell you, was one of the most notorious women of her day. She half ruined her husband by her extravagance, and then went off with another man."

"Silence!" cried the girl, "it is false."

"It is perfectly true. The story is common property. You can read it for yourself in the papers if you don't believe me. You will find a full account of the divorce. She went off with a Captain Armstrong, who would have married her if he hadn't died before six months were over. Her money, too, it was a trifle—about £100 a year, comes to you, just enough for you to starve upon. And now you know all about it, and I hope you'll think twice before calling me a liar."

There was no answer. The speaker's heart smote her as she looked at the white face, the rigid attitude.

"I'm sorry if you don't like it. It was all your fault. You would have it, you know. Come, don't be a goose. The thing is over and forgotten. It's no use crying over spilt milk." She put her hand on the girl's shoulder. Cicely threw it off with a gesture of repulsion. "Oh! very well! if you choose to show temper!" exclaimed her ladyship, with an uneasy laugh as she shrugged her shoulders and left the room.

Poor Cicely crept back to her own room. So this was the explanation of so much that had puzzled her. John was sacrificing himself, not from any consideration of money—oh, no! she knew him better than to believe that—but from a mistaken sense of duty, because she was poor and friendless, and no honest man would care to marry her mother's daughter. It was all from pure pity, from a Quixotic sense of his obligations to her as her father's daughter, that he had borne so patiently with her petulance, her sharp speeches, her grudging careless words of appreciation, without ever giving her a hint of her true position. Truly there was no one like John. And in her blind vanity she had fancied that he cared in his own quiet, undemonstrative way. She had laughed at him and his love, had twitted him with his coldness and backwardness in showing it, yet in her inmost heart she never doubted but that the love was there. And now she didn't know whether to adore him the more for his magnanimity, or to hate him for the intolerable obligations he had heaped upon her. All she did know was that there could be no appeal for forgiveness now to him. She would die rather than become a pensioner on his bounty, or accept a proposal dictated solely by a sense of duty.

Miss Denison remained invisible all through that dismally wet Sunday. Lady Colthurst, who was present during the delivery of a message to the effect that she had gone back to bed and would prefer not to be disturbed, rather wished she had held her tongue. One could never tell how Cicely would take a thing. Just as likely as not she would make a scene before a roomful of people, which would be a fatal blunder. She was reassured when the girl appeared at dinner looking rather pale and subdued, as was only to be expected, but otherwise much the same as usual. At the same time it seemed advisable to give her a word of warning.

"Don't talk, please, about what I told you this morning," she therefore said, looking rather awkward. "In one sense it's no secret, yet one does no good raking up old stories. And I wouldn't make mischief by mentioning it to John."

Cicely smiled contemptuously. "It was a pity you didn't think of that before," she answered cuttingly. "However, set your mind at rest. If ever I mention the subject at all, which isn't likely, it certainly won't be to John."

John, indeed! The one man who must never know the truth.

"I think, Esme, I will go back to Aunt Louisa to-morrow," Miss Denison observed in the course of the evening to her hostess. "She is back in London now and can take me in. I won't apologise for running away in a hurry, because it is evident just now my room will be preferable to my company."

Which was true. A masterly retreat on Cicely's part as Esme was aware would save a good deal of unpleasantness to all concerned. And so although she begged her guest to do exactly as she pleased, she was distinctly relieved when the latter stuck to her plan, and departed after an early luncheon the following day, John did not hear of his cousin's flight until it was an accomplished fact. He had spent the day at Abbottsleigh and only returned in time for dinner.

"What train did she go by?" was all he asked.

"The two-thirty," an answer to which he made no comment.

Nevertheless it had not escaped him that the Fulton carriage had been seen conveying Mr. Page and his luggage to the station to catch that same two-thirty express. From which coincidence he drew his own conclusions. How could he be expected to know, that, no sooner did the pair catch sight of one another on the platform than the one dived hurriedly into a smoking compartment, while the other sought refuge in the seclusion of a ladies' carriage?

Lady Louisa did not kill the fatted calf for the prodigal.

"Dear me, Cicely! This is an unexpected honour! What may I ask, has brought you back?" was her tart greeting.

Thereupon Cicely made a clean breast of the business.

"Aunt Louisa is certain to hear of it sooner or later," she decided, "so she may as well know about it at once."

Accordingly: "We had an accident the day before yesterday," she began. Was it really only two days ago? "Mr. Page, who was staying with the Fultons, drove me back from a pic-nic in their buggy. The cob ran away. Mr. Lisle tried to stop it; we were all upset, and Mr. Lisle broke his leg. He is laid up at Hackham. The party broke up, of course, and I thought it best to come away."

"Obviously," commented her ladyship, to whom the narrative naturally had not been pleasing hearing. "And how came you to be with Mr. Page, and alone—as I presume you were?"

"I thought I should like a drive in the buggy. He was ready to take me, and I went," which it must be admitted was a generous version of the affair so far as her fellow-culprit was concerned.

And then the storm burst. Lady Louisa talked herself hoarse, dilating on the enormity perpetuated by her niece. At last she stopped, puzzled by the ominous silence with which her censure was received. "Was the girl ill, or too hardened to care?"

She gained a clue to this strange conduct, when, the storm having raged itself out, Cicely quietly said:

"Tell me about my mother, if you please. I want to hear her history. Why do you never talk about her?"

"There is nothing to be said about her." Lady Louisa might be cross-grained, but she had her own notions of honour, and meant to play fair. "She was brought up as other girls, came out, and married your father at the end of her first season. In those days men did not require so much hunting down as at present. She lived at Abbottsleigh till after your birth."

"And then?"

Lady Louisa looked away. "She died," she answered constrainedly.

"But before she died. Did nothing happen?"

So the girl knew. The deception could no longer be kept up.

"Who told you?" came the irrelevant question.

"I found it out," was the evasive answer, "I heard things, and suspected it, and wanted to make sure. Is it true, then?"

Lady Louisa nodded. "I am afraid so," she said abruptly.

"It is true also, I suppose, that I have no money except what John chooses to give me?" was the next question.

Again her aunt recognised the uselessness of denial. "You have £125 a year of your own," she said drily.

"Which doesn't pay for my frocks."

Lady Louisa looked at the tea-gown the girl was wearing

"Coralie is a dreadful robber," she observed. "That tea-gown cost sixteen guineas."

Cicely stared at the fire. Crabbed old woman as she was, Lady Louisa felt quite a softening at her hard old heart-strings as she watched the set misery on the young face.

"Am I like my mother?"

The question was an inconvenient one. Her aunt hesitated. "In face, the counterpart of her," she said at last unwillingly.

"And in disposition?"

Another hesitation. "You have her love of admiration and impatience of control," was the reluctant admission.

A long silence. "Poor John!" the exclamation broke like a sob from the girl.

Lady Louisa got up stiffly and crossed the room. "Don't fret, child," she said. Who would have believed that so kind a tone could issue from those crusty lips! "Put the past behind you. Remember you have every prospect of happiness in the future, which is yours to make anything of you please."

Cicely's response to the advance was prompt. "Thank you, Aunt Louisa," she faltered. "I see now how much you have had to bear, and—I am sorry to have given you so much trouble," and then, for the first time in their respective lives, a kiss was given and received which was a caress, and not a perfunctory salute.

John made his appearance in Eaton Place the very next day. As he informed his cousin, Adrian Lisle was going on well, and every one had left Hackham.

"What made you bolt off in such frantic haste, Cicely?" he asked.

"Under the circumstances, it seemed the only thing left me to do," she answered.

"I don't see that. With Blunt away and Lisle laid up, this is just the time Mrs. Blunt would want a companion. Anyhow, what I came to say was that I want you and Aunt Louisa to help me entertain some people at Abbottsleigh next week."

Cicely flushed. "Thank you," she said quietly, "you are very kind, but I could not be your guest there now."

"Why not?" he asked bluntly.

Why must he make it so difficult for her, she wondered.

"Need you ask? Didn't we agree to separate? At least, if

you meant anything at all, it must have been that, when you told me to make my choice."

"But have you chosen Page—I mean are you going to marry him?"

It was impossible to doubt the sincerity of the "Certainly not" of the denial.

"Very well, then. We stand precisely as we were before," he observed, "and so—will you marry me?"

With perfect composure she looked him full in the face and answered—"No. You are very kind, but I cannot."

"Have you any special reason for your refusal?" he enquired. They were a quiet couple—judging by their looks they might have been discussing the weather.

"None, except that I am convinced we are not suited to one another, and should not be happy together," for which lie let us hope she received absolution.

"Your decision has nothing to do with this business at Hackham?" he went on searchingly. "Don't be afraid," as she hesitated. "Let me know exactly how things stand."

"It has nothing to do with that," she assured him.

"Then, excuse me, but is there anyone else?"

She dropped her eyes. "Don't ask me," she murmured.

John turned away and walked to the window, while she stood with her hands clenched, wondering how long she would be able to keep it up.

"Can I do anything?" he asked after a minute. "Is it a question of money?"

She shook her head. "He does not care," she said desperately. Had he finished at last? Did he never mean to go?

But John had not finished. "One more question," he said abruptly. "Is it an affair of long standing, I mean, are you certain of yourself?"

"Quite certain, but I only realised it myself the other day." This was the only perfectly honest answer she had given. It led poor John on to a false scent. He guessed her secret at once, or thought he did. It was Lisle, of course, a man she had known, more or less, for years, and who these last months had been thrown a good deal with her. An attractive fellow too. Insensibly, she had grown to care for him, and his accident had opened her eyes to the state of her feelings.

"Thanks. I understand," he said quietly. "I won't worry you any more. And—this need not make any difference. You will come all the same to Abbottsleigh, I hope?"

She shook her head. "I couldn't," she faltered brokenly. "Later on, perhaps. Not now. Do be generous. Leave me to myself now."

He went without a word.

## CHAPTER XXVII.

THE party at Hackham having dispersed, Arnold showed no disposition to fill the house again.

"I must be in town off and on during the next few weeks," he explained, "and Lisle won't want a lot of racket going on, so the fewer people we have about us the better." All the same he protested when Lady Colthurst promptly fled from the stagnation of unadulterated country life.

"My good man," she observed with the charming candour which was her chief characteristic, "don't expect me to do sick-nurse. Your wife is admirably fitted for that sort of thing. I'm not. It only depresses me, and no one is one ha'porth the better for it."

"Yet you might think of me a little," he remonstrated in an aggrieved tone.

"So I do," she retorted promptly. "It would be a thousand pities if we were to quarrel, which we certainly should do for want of better employment."

"We are too good and tried friends to quarrel at this time of day, I hope," he objected.

"Are we?" she laughed. "Just you see. I never met the man, woman or child either with whom I couldn't get up a row when I was in the humour for one. And you have been far too good a friend to me for me to seek a breach with you. By the way, can you put me on to any nice safe thing just now?"

"Never a one. We're doing badly ourselves," he answered gloomily. "Woods made a nice mess of those last Australian railways, and unless we bring off a grand coup soon we shall have to draw in our horns a bit. Things are deuced bad in the City now, I can tell you," and he sighed despondingly.

Lady Colthurst never encouraged long faces about her.

"Cheer up, dear boy," she said with a brisk laugh. "'Care killed a cat,' you know. Depend upon it, something will turn up, and, if it doesn't, you won't make things better by grizzling over them. And now, to change the subject, what do you say to a dinner and play in town Friday?" a proposal to which Arnold promptly assented. Long as he had known her, it was still a privilege and a pleasure to him to be permitted to swell her train of admirers.

In this way Esme was practically left alone—for Arnold when not in town was shooting—to undertake the entertainment of Mr. Lisle during his long and tedious convalescence. The task was easier than she had anticipated. To give him his due Adrian made an admirable patient, careful to run no risks, obedient to his doctor's orders, and never complaining at a confinement, which, restricted as he was to the society of a woman and a child, he must have found inexpressibly dull. Esme's last shred of prejudice vanished when she noticed his patience, his consideration to those about him, his gratitude for any trifling service rendered him, as well as the care he took to render his enforced presence as little obtrusive as possible.

Thrown together as they were, from acquaintances they soon became friends. Books and newspapers don't last for ever. Cards are all very well as a last resource, and music will do to fill up gaps. Still it was on conversation that they mainly depended to fill up the time. And although they conversed on every conceivable subject, they naturally found the topic of themselves the most engrossing. Finally, one wet afternoon, they drifted on to the threadbare question of the possibility of friendship between the sexes. It so happened that Esme, who in many ways was singularly guileless, had remarked of a certain couple that they were friends.

"Perhaps," he answered thoughtfully. "The only question is, can real friendship exist between a man and a woman? What do you say?"

"I say yes, most decidedly," was her verdict, given with some warmth. "It seems to be the fashion now-a-days to doubt it. There are persons I know, who seek and find evil in everything, who, incapable themselves of honour or loyalty, deny its existence in others. I do not think so poorly of my fellow-creatures. When I meet with true and disinterested friendship I accept it, with the gratitude it deserves, no matter whence it may come, without insulting myself or my friends by searching for ulterior motives."

"Have you frequently met with such friendship?" was all he said in reply to this outburst. He was rather glad when she hesitated.

"No, I cannot say I have," she finally admitted. "Still, I have lived so much absorbed in my home and my child. No doubt if I had tried to find friends I should have done so."

"No doubt," he agreed. "Still, if you will forgive my saying so, the word friendship is not often used in the sense in which you employ it. More frequently it is misapplied to some passing fancy, and so has come to be looked upon merely as a cloak for flirtation, deceiving nobody. Real disinterested friendship such as you have in your mind, I fancy, is rarely met with."

"I don't think so," she persisted. Then with a frank smile—"Our case surely is one in point. May I not say that we have become very good friends lately?"

Now no one knew better than Adrian did how practical a refutation of her theory he supplied in his own person. That however was beside the question. A man's feelings, as he argued, are entirely his own concern, so long, of course, as he keeps them to himself, as in the present case, he had every intention of doing. Accordingly—

"I am delighted to hear you say so," he answered with obvious gratification, "because, to tell you the truth, I have been dreading that your kindness might have only been extended to the cripple, and that, with my recovery, I should find myself dropped back into the ranks of your acquaintances. It is the best of good news to me to hear that such is not the case. And I can assure you that if you will honour me with your trust I will do my utmost to deserve it."

In this way a bond of friendship was signed and sealed between the pair, which, as Esme herself acknowledged, added considerably to the enjoyment of her life. Her friend too grew steadily in her estimation as a man whose good qualities were essentially his own, while his bad ones were chiefly the result of circumstances, training, and association. Realising this, she regretted especially that he should have wasted hitherto both time and money in a purposeless existence unworthy of him and quite unable to satisfy him. He was not happy. He was meant for better things than an aimless pursuit of pleasure, and so she told him frankly when he alluded regretfully, as he frequently did, to his empty, objectless life. Circumstances too helped her just then, for the local member having announced his intention of retiring, it had been intimated to Mr. Lisle that he would prove an acceptable candidate if he would consent to come forward. When mentioned to her Esme warmly took up the idea.

"It would be quite the best thing you could do," she declared enthusiastically, "that is, if you won't think me impertinent in seeming to dictate to you. You say, Mr. Lisle, you are tired of drifting about the world. You complain that your life is of no use either to yourself or to anybody else. Now here is your chance. It only rests with yourself to make it anything you please."

"I am too old," he objected, more for the pleasure of being contradicted than anything else. "My mission in life hitherto has been that of an idler, and I have filled it so long that all capacity and energy have deserted me."

"Nonsense," she declared stoutly. "Why make yourself out so much worse than you are? It would be different if you were satisfied with yourself. As it is you feel the want in your life, which after all is the first step towards satisfying it."

He laughed. "By religiously going to sleep on a back bench of the House, obediently recording my vote with my party, and making a rung of myself to hoist some political adventurer to the top of the ladder. Is that your specific for the satisfaction of every want in a man's nature, Mrs. Blunt?"

"Certainly not," she answered with decision. "You have influence, money, position. You have it in your power to do an enormous amount of good. I would have you lead, not follow."

He shook his head. "I have lost all belief in myself," he said gloomily. "The little ambition I feel does not lie in the direction of encouraging professional pauperism under the guise of philanthropy, or sharing in the greedy rush for power and self-advancement, which is dignified by the name of patriotism."

"You are wrong," she persisted. "For your own sake, if for no other reason, you ought to make all the use you can of your abilities and set yourself some object in your life."

"My constituents and fellow-members would not thank you for urging me to swallow them as a moral tonic," he retorted. "So nauseous a draught I fear would require a stronger effort than I am capable of to gulp it down. Besides, how can one work when no single human being cares twopence for one's success or failure?"

"Your friends care," she reminded him.

"Would *you* be interested, I wonder?" he asked abruptly.

"Of course I should," she answered warmly. "I should be delighted to see you what you ought to be, a power in the country, using your brains and wealth for good, instead of letting them rust away neglected."

"'Almost thou persuadest me,'" he quoted, watching her glowing face and glistening eyes. "Very well, Mrs. Blunt. You have stimulated me to some purpose. The least I can do is to make an effort to carry out the programme you have laid down for me. Henceforth my residence shall be at Lisle, my object in life the kotowing to and entertaining of my future constituents. Mighty dull work too for a lonely bachelor, I'm afraid."

She smiled. "You have the remedy for that always in your own hands. You have only to marry."

He looked at her. "Am I not in a matrimonial sense a pariah?" he asked slowly. "Many women, of course, as I know, would accept me as an appendage to Lisle, but then I do not choose to marry under such conditions."

"But why assume that because you are rich, you must of necessity be unlovable?" she asked not without diffidence, for she was treading upon delicate ground. "I see no reason why you should not find some nice woman for whom you could care, and who would care for you in return."

"You surprise me, Mrs. Blunt," he retorted bitterly, for this off-hand way of disposing of his affections was displeasing to him. "Have you changed then so much since the days when you taught me that any good and innocent woman must necessarily look on me with loathing?"

It was the first allusion he had ever made to the past. Esme would have dropped the subject, if she hadn't thought him unduly morbid over it. As it was she coloured and hesitated before answering.

"Not if she really cared for you," she reminded him gently. "She would be your helper then, not your judge."

"If she cared! Perhaps so. But then how can I hope to inspire any feeling of that sort?" he questioned sadly.

"Genuine feeling ought to call forth feeling in return."

"But then, if there be no genuine feeling. Consider what I have to offer. So much pin-money, so many diamonds, a big house, a name, the privilege of heading subscription lists, and figuring as lady patroness to every local charity, a certain modicum of liking and respect, and a fragment of heart so infinitesimal as not to be worth taking into consideration. No, Mrs. Blunt. Matrimony, I am aware, with you ladies is a panacea for every ill, but it will not apply in my case. I can offer nothing but externals. I can hope for nothing in return. And so as I require neither a housekeeper or a nurse at present, I must just remain as I am."

At which Esme smiled and felt more convinced than ever of the necessity of a wife for her friend. She mentally reviewed all the eligible spinsters of her acquaintance with an eye to their qualifications for the position. Yet curiously enough she never managed to fix upon any eligible candidate. One was too young, another too old, a third too worldly, a fourth a doll, a fifth lacking that knowledge of the world so indispensable to the wife of a public man, a sixth all grace and no virtue, a seventh all virtue and no grace, an eighth equally destitute of either.

In the meantime life of late had become very easy and pleasant to her. Delighting in the rest and freedom of the country, she laid aside all care for the morrow, and enjoyed to the full the era of peace which seemed to have set in. Her daughter was thriving, her patient gaining ground, while although she considered so much travelling undesirable for her husband, she saw no reason for anxiety on his account.

Still a broken leg, however carefully made the most of, must mend in course of time. Adrian Lisle awoke one morning to the fact that the very slight lameness from which he now suffered in no way warranted a further stay at Hackham.

His departure, be it said, was a source of unfeigned regret to all concerned. Arnold, who had become quite confidential with him latterly, and would sit talking with him on his return from business till the small hours of the morning, had the best of reasons for his lamentations on the subject. Dot too, whose heart he had completely won, was eager in her suggestions of a joint household, while Esme, although not so outspoken, was astonished to find the blank his absence caused in her life.

These regrets, to say the least, were fully reciprocated. Long ago Adrian had dismissed his last scruple. Whether wise or not, his friendship with the Blunts was now an established fact, from which he neither could nor would draw back. Whatever others might think, Arnold's confidences had shown him clearly enough the heavy clouds now gathering on the horizon. The day was coming when the Blunts would need the help of every friend they possessed to weather the storm which sooner or later must burst over their heads. Therefore it would be both cowardly and disloyal were he to allow any considerations of self at such a time to keep him from their side. In which plausible way he managed to justify a line of conduct, which in another man he would have been the first to condemn as both insane and wholly inexcusable.

*(To be continued.)*

# Sir William Gregory.

### BY EMILIA AYLMER GOWING.

ONE of the ablest Irishmen ever sent out to do the work of England—typical, racy of the land of Wellington and Tom Moore—passed quietly from the fretful stage of this world, early in the fatal time of death, 1892. Sir William Gregory went full of years, but, almost to the last, exempt from their common infirmities. In spirit, ever young; in heart, full of "the genius of kindness;" a bright, joyous nature, giving and receiving happiness. His were the power, the charm inherent in the best of his nation; must we say, too, the faults that so often mar what was created for the noblest ends of man? But if much was lost, in the morning of his life, much was redeemed as the evening shadows fell. By the regeneration of Ceylon, his memory will be perpetuated, and who shall gainsay the true and loving words appended to the records of his story by the young wife of his age?

"He has written so frankly and candidly of the errors and mistakes of his youth, that it is only just that this great success of his later days should be dwelt on—*On ne revient pas de si loin pour peu de chose.*"

Sir William Gregory's Autobiography, edited by his widow, one of the successful books of the past year, seems likely to prove a permanent contribution to the history of our Indian Empire. Such a record shows the man as a remarkable exception amongst his kind and origin. By right of birth he enjoyed the advantages—and disabilities—of an old-fashioned squire of the squirearchy of the distressful and belated Island, the race for whose eyes and ears the world stood still, at the precise moment when each one of them looked out upon it through the sunny windows of youth. Unfortunately, the poor globe went off spinning on its own account, faster and faster, in its mad whirl through the ominous decades of this fateful century. His forebears were of the breed of Tennyson's county magnate, who lived his life to the end, "Like an Aylmer in his Aylmerism," irrespective of all inferior folk.

The Gregorys owned as their common ancestor the worthy of Stephen's reign who acquired the seat of Styvechale Hall, in Warwickshire. In Cromwell's day, they took the Puritan side, and adopted "Love-is-God" as a family Christian name. One of them went to Ireland with the great Protector, and stayed there. In the middle of the eighteenth century, his descendant, "the son of Henry Gregory, who lived in Galway," ran away from home, made good his flight to India, obtained a berth under the East India Company, and amassed one of the great fortunes not uncommon among the "nabobs" of those palmy days of the Indian pagoda tree. In that land of the sun, he took a wife, who brought some Eastern blood into the vigorous race. He had three sons; Robert, disinherited for persistent gambling on cock-fights; Richard, a dashing young Guardsman, gayest of the gay, who allowed his life to be spoilt by certain unkind innuendoes against his personal courage. He renounced His Majesty's service, cut society and turned misanthrope. Finally, eloped with a school-girl, who lived with him secretly in man's clothes, under the name of "Jack the Sailor," in a small house upon the paternal acres. He honourably married her, when the fear of being disinherited was removed by his father's death.

That parent had followed the custom of the time, and sunk his moneybags in the "earth bank"—that "mine of wealth" associated in popular faith with the broad acres of Ireland ground. Thus he became "an estated gentleman, with hills and valleys, sheep and cattle, silver and gold"—the latter, in due course, to be absorbed into the former. Meantime, he lived in great state and wielded much political influence, till his death at the age of 83 in 1810.

Richard the prodigal, married to Jack the sailor, "reigned" at Coole Park as his lawful successor, but suffered social ostracism at the hands of his younger brother's spouse, the Lady Anne of the Clancarty Trenches. This couple rose in the world above the diminished head of the family. William Gregory became a Privy Councillor, and refused a baronetcy. He was Under Secretary for Ireland from 1814 till 1831; also Ranger of Phœnix Park, enjoying two official residences, in the Castle and Park. The latter was his home, much given to family hospitality. His son Robert was always welcome; his son's wife, perhaps less so; her beauty and extreme youth quite eclipsed her sister-in-law, the Lady Anne's own daughter. She came of the Liberal-minded stock of the O'Haras, to affright the old Toryism of the Trench connection. All the same, it was at Phœnix Park that she provided an heir to the old name, William, born 13th July, 1817, the future Governor of Ceylon.

With Phœnix Park, this remarkable boy's early years were associated, as scenes and events moulded his character for good and evil. The Park has a "genius loci" of its own, as the finest parade-ground in the three kingdoms; as the field most favoured by ambitious duellists in the "good old days" of fighting Irish gentlemen, whose doughty deeds were the height of fashion during the boyhood of this lad of promise. In recent times, the lovely pleasaunce has sustained its reputation as an Aceldama by the murder of Lord Frederic Cavendish, hacked to death by American knives wielded by assassins in whose mouths the consecrated elements of the blessed Sacrament had lain on the morning before. The event roused a spirit in England which, so far, has denied the claims of the American Irish party, although thirteen years ago, the new-made widow of Lord Frederic, an enthusiastic Home Ruler of English birth, could write that she did not grudge her darling's life to the "Cause of Ireland."

Young William, in his seventh year, made himself acquainted with the famous Marquis of Wellesley, when fishing in the pond of the Lord Lieutenant's lodge. His Excellency happened quietly on the scene of a stout conflict between the small boy and a large fish, which, being successfully hooked and landed, the child became aware "of the presence of a slight, short, elderly gentleman, who seemed to take the deepest interest in my doings." The youngster, fascinated by his pleasant manner, offered to reveal the piscatorial treasures of the pond—in strict confidence —to this new friend. Thence arose a fast friendship between the pair; Lord Wellesley gave "the little fisherman" a handsome copy of Walton's famous book, with the inscription under the Vice-Regal hand :—" 1824. To the Compleat Angler, from his obedient scholar, Wellesley." To this encounter Sir William attributes the influence that brought him to a love of classsic literature, and thereby tinged his whole after life.

To counteract any such bookish proclivities, the promising boy was subjected to the utmost severity of spoiling by a couple of doting grandmothers, both most anxious that he should do nothing but what he liked best; and naturally, in such case, no lessons whatever would be included in the young gentleman's curriculum. His disposition must have been singularly amiable, as he tells us both grandmothers were "very dear to him," and the remembrance of each "most sweet even to this day." Spoiling is usually repaid in very different coin by the wise young creatures marred by it. Little William, happily, had a mother, alive to the fatal consequences of no-work-all-play upbringing. She insisted, at least, on teaching her boy modern languages. French and Italian were imparted to him in native fluency, by one Madame Le Brun, daughter of an *émigré*; this instructress, unhappily, sowed other seeds, to bear deadly fruit thereafter, in the gambling passion instilled by the early habit of playing cards for sweetmeat stakes.

At the age of ten, he was sent to school at Iver, Bucks. Four years later, he went to Harrow. Here he gained the prizes for Latin Lyrics, Latin Hexameters, the Peel Medal, the Scholarship, and finally stood at the head of the school for a considerable time. His successes led to a reconciliation, of his own personal seeking, with the long-discarded great-uncle and family chief, Robert Gregory of Coole. The youth's graceful advance was cordially met and generously rewarded. By Dr. Longley, in whose house he was placed, William Gregory was described as "the cleverest boy he ever had under him." Such praise was hardly reciprocated by the over-ripe young scholar towards his instructors. Of Dr. Kennedy, his Greek tutor, his appreciation was high; but with this exception, he pronounced the masters "bad. The system was bad. I came there with a considerable knowledge of French and Italian; I left it having in a great measure forgotten both. I came thoroughly grounded in arithmetic; I left it without the power of doing a rule-of-three sum. Of Euclid and Algebra I was entirely ignorant. History was little more to us than a collection of dry facts and dates—the husks of history were thrown to us to digest as best we might, and we were punished if we did not digest them. We were not asked to think in our own language, or to write it with vigour and correctness."

This, the customary neglect of the Queen's English in most public schools, has not yet quite died out.

Withal, young Gregory's schooldays were occasionally varied by times of truant wandering, when shooting and fishing and other sportsmanlike dissipations were given the rein. At nineteen, he made acquaintance with the high breeding and stiffness—only tempered by an occasional matrimonial sensation in the family—which at that time pervaded the atmosphere of Garbally, the seat of his grand-maternal relatives, the Clancartys. Here he "chummed" with a daughter of the house, on escapades intent, in visits to country houses. They enjoyed some rollicking experiences of old-fashioned "wild Irish" fun, within the exclusive borders of the county.

The next move was to Christchurch, Oxford. Matriculation was happily got through without accident, but on the threshold of the college, the freshman's luck as a prize-winner deserted him—or rather, perhaps, was superseded by passions so often fatal to the ambitious aspirant. Among Gregory's fellow-students was one uncouth object known as Linwood; a born schoolmaster and annotator, but one who would never be anything else; a kind of modern Porson in Greek. This worthy carried off the first scholarship at Christchurch. To Gregory, "it was hardly a crumb of comfort to have got the second." The same year the twain went in for the Craven Scholarship, open to all the university. "Alas! it was again Linwood first, Gregory second."

Ill content with the barren honour of being the second best scholar of his year, the fated youth drifted into the quagmire spread ready to tempt his unwary feet—horse racing. The madness bit him on his first vacation, spent with old Harrow friends at Cambridge. They took him to Newmarket and his doom was sealed.

After outstaying the usual number of terms at Oxford, he just missed the object of his ambition, of which he was all but sure, a "first-class"; and ultimately left Oxford in broken spirits, without the heart to go in even for a common degree. So much for Newmarket.

But worse was yet to come. He joined his father and mother for a winter in Rome, travelling in great state, as befitted a family of rank. It was a grand time for the cultured, though defeated Oxonian, but somewhat marred by severe Roman fever. Rapturous was the return to health, as he was taken out, day after day, to sit on a cushion propped up upon the steps of St. John Lateran in the warm early spring; too weak to speak, but not to look at and drink in the soft outline of the Alban Hills, and the solemn beauty which gives to the mother of dead nations that indescribable fascination which ever holds captive those who have once come under its influence. "All the while strength seemed to be pouring in, and I gradually was strong enough to mount a horse and take a gallop with the hounds on the Campagna."

But long before his convalescence was established, the wayward patient tore himself away from his amazed parents, as if compelled by some mysterious spell to go back to England by a certain day. Though scarcely able to crawl, he started from Civita Vecchia, and passed through France—and certain appropriate adventures—to the Derby Day. There he stood to win or lose heavy sums on the favourite, Coronation, and persevered in backing the horse, even till he was saddled. By unusual luck, the favourite actually won, and Gregory—in an evil hour, netted £5,000. He was noted, as a very young man, lingering in the corner of the Jockey Club stand, to make up his book, and afterwards, saying half aloud to himself: "Well, I am sure I don't know how I shall spend all this money." What would our modern plungers say to a youth self-disciplined with so tight a rein? Ill news sped fast, meeting his parents on their way home, at a Frankfort *table d'hôte*. Somebody spoke of the recent Derby, and mentioned that one of the heaviest winners was a young Irishman, newly from Oxford, of the name of Gregory. This was but the beginning of sorrows, which bad training, rather than natural depravity, had entailed upon their gifted son.

In the course of the next year, 1842, he became a glory to the house. Kinsfolk, friends, and local public opinion conspired to thrust upon his youth precocious honours as M.P. for Dublin. Those were the palmy days of the "free and independent," 1,500 of whom had fixed their price at £3 a head. Others were to be conciliated by the prospect of more delicate, exalted favours. The candidate was to be kept pure from all bribery. £4,000 down were requisite; £5,000 more to be made up somehow. Where the balance came from, he knew not. But parents proud and fond, no doubt, could tell a tale. They would submit, with a light heart, to the process termed "dipping the estate," in such a cause.

The story of the election reads like a roaring farce of the Gilbertian school. Propped by the "Protestant Ascendancy," courted by O'Connell, the large-hearted, open-handed candidate was swept up to the top of the poll, by all the opposing winds of Irish faction. The great Liberator's life-long favour was won through a sharp wordy duel between the pair, in which the younger champion decidedly put the old parliamentary hand to the worse. Lord Morpeth, afterwards the popular Viceroy known as the Earl of Carlisle, was badly beaten from the field by "the whiteheaded boy" from Galway.

Thus, the new member was presented to the House "like a Roman conqueror." Ringing cheers hailed his entry; he was led forward to the Speaker by Sir Robert Peel, of old his grandfather's friend, more recently his own—since he won the Peel medal at Harrow. At the young Connaughtman's entrance into London life, all the doors of success flew open wide to receive him; fame, fashion, pleasure, "at his heels leashed in like hounds—crouch for employment;" the Marquis of Wellesley saw in him "the fulfilment of ardent hopes formed in your most promising childhood," and renewed past days in the company of his "dear fisherman." Great ladies of the stamp which, in Lord Beaconsfield's novels, take so prominent a share in the making of history, as well as the men they delight to honour, took up young Gregory; Lady Ashburton, Carlyle's philosophic flame; Lady Londonderry, of ultra-Orange exclusiveness; Lady Jersey, of strictest Tory *haut ton*, aptly blent with a touch of Russian and German *haute diplomatie;* these, and other high and puissant dames received the neophyte with open arms. Unfortunately, other doors than theirs made haste to bid him welcome. He was a favoured guest at houses "where the society was sure to be light and merry, though extremely ignorant and unprofitable. I am ashamed to say that I lived much in that class of company, having all the time the most supreme contempt for it." Worse than this, he was immediately elected a member of Crockford's, the great resort of youths like himself, bent on ruin to be achieved as gentlemen. Gregory tells us he did not suffer, owing to salutary precautions imposed on him by a friend; but the playing with fire was carried steadily on.

Among his fast friends were Lord George Bentinck and Disraeli. Of both he speaks with personal affection, but as a keen critic of their political defects. The former fares the better at his hands, painted to the life in a few rapid touches. We see the man of splendid physique, developed in the vigorous life of the shires; with a good sufficiency of brains blunted by disuse. Above all things a sportsman. Something of a dunce, "who scarcely ever read a book"—save a betting one—although he had been secretary to Canning, his uncle. For eighteen years he had slept soundly upon the back benches, every night the House of Commons was sitting, unless he was called elsewhere by a race. Absolutely devoid of personal ambition, yet stirred to a total change by strong resolve to rally the broken and dispirited forces of his party and order "to avenge the country gentlemen and landed aristocracy of England upon the minister who"—struck the first blow for Free Trade! Thus, Lord George braced himself for the championship with heroic scorn of nature and habit—with self-annihilation. He starved himself out of the custom of post-prandial sleep; pored over blue-books and statistics, and crammed his head with uncongenial facts and figures; grew eloquent upon the theme of which his heart was full, and never gave in till he fell, stone dead, upon the English earth he loved so well.

Gregory, in his own mind, had scant sympathy with the squires in the memorable contest. He recalls with some sly satire their resistance, and final subservience to the "d——d Jew, as they chose to call the man whose memory they now adore with primroses in their buttonholes." For himself, at the time, he elected to earn the distinction of being the first seceder from the Protectionist cause, voting in favour of the new Revolution. He saw at once the food-tax was doomed.

"There is a tide in the affairs of man——" it came now; the turning point of his life. One day in February, 1846, Sir Robert Peel made him an offer of the Irish Lordship of the Treasury—and more, to place the conduct of the Irish business in the House in his hands.

"To this day I bitterly regret that I refused Sir Robert's offer," wrote the repentant waverer, grown old and wise. He tells us the story: "Most unfortunately for me, my father and mother were passing through London at the time. 'Of course your father and mother will be only too glad that their son should get such an opening, but remember, my good fellow, that henceforth the days of Newmarket are over. You will have to give up racing. It will be hereafter a matter of pride to you to be associated with measures of a wide and generous character which may entirely change the aspect of Ireland to England.'"

And so "it might have been." He had his chance—and missed it. He could have counted among the young and brilliant band chosen by Peel as England's coming statesmen—Gladstone, Dalhousie, Elgin, Sidney Herbert. It was not to be!

"I went home and found my father so averse to my accepting the proffered office that I at once declined it. On the one side was the brilliant position; on the other was the speech I made advocating Protection at the hustings and the imputations that would be poured out on my head by the rabid Dublin press. My father was exceedingly sensitive, he could not bear that it should be said I had spoken and voted to obtain office."

And so the budding statesman was fain to eat humble pie in the presence of his critics. That he did so, surely he had a double excuse, being misled through his graceful act of filial duty. On such principles, no Irishman need ever hope to rise above his fellows—so long as they could find a hold to pull him down. To such extinguishment the "son and heir" is specially liable. Debarred from almost every wholesome field and outlet for his energies, he is too often given over, hands tied, to the power notorious for providing his kind with evil occupation. If by uncommon ability and some wonderful stroke of luck, he should come to the point of making a path for himself in the world, he is too often dragged back by family prejudice and pride.

Disaster followed upon disaster. Next year came the Irish Famine. The head of the house fell, laying down his life for his people during that terrible time when fever followed famine. In August, the young squire lost his seat in Parliament, mainly through neglect of his own business for the stronger attraction of Goodwood. Then followed six years such as, he tells us, he would gladly have blotted out of his life.

Frankly, he has recorded their errors and misfortunes in these autobiographical records set down for his son.

"These six years were a time of struggle and humiliation,

during which I abandoned society and public life for the turf only; during which I became deeply involved, chiefly through liabilities for friends, and during which I was forced to sell two-thirds of my ancestral estate. But at last, by a strong effort, I turned over a new leaf, and though a poor man, became a free man, and once more in my right mind."

He boldly proclaims the fatal motive—haste to grow rich—the true mainspring of the gambler's progress. Out of a turf brawl arose a duel: "An act so foolish, so wrong, and so contrary to public opinion, even in those days." For a whole year, he was bent on inflicting the retribution of death upon the man who had affronted and injured him; "in spite of culture, education, refinement, something of the tiger lingers in our blood." By such spirits, the pistol was regarded as the best peace-maker. Once fired, in this case, the burning of powder cleared the air of every particle of enmity; and the two mortal antagonists shook hands and made it up.

A sterner foe was found in Lady Jersey, upon whose domain of Osterley Park the battle field was chosen by the seconds, at the suggestion of her own son, Fred Villiers. Her grandchildren, on the terrace, witnessed with huge delight "some gentlemen shooting at each other in the Park." But for the lady, such a deed, without her permission, involved an irreparable breach of friendship.

But the unpardonable sin in the land of his birth, was the parting with so much of his portion in the soil of Erin, an act, second only to vulpicide, far more heinous than attempting the life of a mere human being; an act not to be atoned by any good wrought upon other portions of the habitable globe. There were two courses open to him. To pay off old "blisters" he was bound to sell a portion; the question was, as to more or less. More, to clear his own private debts; less, as urged by friends, "to cling to the land, looking forward to a great rise in value of it hereafter."

This was the strange superstition prevailing at that time, of a vast unearned increment to accrue, for the benefit of Irish landlords, in the course of the coming hundred years or so. Happily for him, his mother had the rare wisdom to embrace the course which promised immediate relief to her son—the object of her life's devotion. Through her jointure, and the large arrears due to her, she was able to protect Coole Park, with the more valuable part of the estate, for the inheritance, while the outlying lands were sold. This measure, so to say, of taking in sail before the storm, proved his salvation. The matter was not taken in that light by the dread Sycorax whose voice is all too potent in the Isle of Saints—Mrs. Grundy. His name became a by-word on her lips, and was handed down as an awful warning to any of the younger generation, slow to yield obedience to "her abhorred behests." The worst reproach cast up against the rash and wilful was, to be pronounced "as bad as Gregory of Coole."

After ten years came the turn of the tide. He was elected member for the county, by the united interest of landlords and priests: the former, in those days, having still a voice potential in the elections to Parliament; all changed by the new system, which practically disfranchises the classes, and endows Demos as sole lord, with the unmixed voting power.

"It seemed to me, from the minute on which I entered a fresh House of Commons and shook the Speaker's hand, that my former life had been shifted as a scene from the stage, and that I had become a totally different man in character, and objects and thought. . . . I had seen enough of the old Tories to be utterly estranged from them. . . . I began by being Conservative, and every day became more and more Liberal."

This time he proved a useful, no less than a brilliant statesman. But the golden opportunity once let slip, returned no more. He had to be content with promoting or seconding the measures of others, without much influence on his own initiative. The British Museum, the Scientific Societies of Dublin, and other national interests, profited by his good offices. Travels in many lands, far and near, added colour to his life and created a longing that grew by indulgence and could never be quite satisfied—the restless thirst of a maimed life. By and by his thoughts turned towards the desire of many an ambitious politician, with aims defeated at home, towards the broad domains of Greater England, the islands of the sun, where semi-royal state and almost absolute sway may be enjoyed by a duly-appointed ruler, as the Queen's Viceroy. Such an Atlantis existed in his mind's eye—"The glorious Island of Ceylon," the Serendib of the Arabian Nights, the "Gem of Paradise," the priceless pearl, hung as a pendant beneath our Indian Empire. To this haven of rest his troubled fortunes at last happily tended. In 1871 he bade farewell to Parliament. "I left the House of Commons, of which I had been fourteen years a member, and a popular member, both outside and inside its walls. I had worked hard and successfully, and had taken a prominent place, and when I quitted Westminster Hall for the last time, it was not without certain feelings of dejection. At the same time I clearly foresaw that I could not long look forward to hold the County of Galway without giving pledges which no inducement would have made me accept . . . and so I buried my dead, and turned from the West to the glowing horizon of the East, and to Ceylon, the object of my ambition and my day-dream for many a long year."

So he was appointed a Privy Councillor and Governor of Ceylon, and this time he no longer went out to far countries alone. In his 55th year was made his first venture in the deep sea of matrimony in search of the pearl of price—life's happiness. Strange, that it should have come so late to this man, who seemed born to make a woman happy. A true Irishman in susceptibility to the charms of the fair, as more than one chance record of his pen betrays. But in his circumstances poverty stood as a bar to free choice, and his was not a disposition to barter freedom for gold.

At last his time came. "In January, 1872, I married Elizabeth, third daughter of Sir William Clay, M.P. for Tower Hamlets, and a well-known public man in his day. She was the widow of James Temple Bowdoin, late 4th Dragoons. She was a woman of many accomplishments. I had been deeply attached to her for many years (of trouble to her), and she amply rewarded that attachment by her own. Through her liberality I was at once freed from every liability, and went out to Ceylon with a comfortable private income besides my official salary."

This big honeymoon trip was one of state importance; a gracious reception from the Khedive awaited the bridal pair in Egypt; honours by the way, and a great stir on taking possession of the Government of Ceylon. Very brief was their spell of mutual happiness. In little more than a year the poor lady succumbed to the burning sun of the tropics. "After a few days, first of anxious, then of hopeless watching, she passed away, conscious to the last." So he was left, with the greatest sorrow of his life, in a far-off land, alone. He fought it out like a man.

"My life was terrible for a time in the deserted, mournful Queen's House at Colombo. Work, however — incessant, slogging work, far harder than I would otherwise have undertaken —restored my strength of mind." Unflinchingly, he clung to the duties of his post, until five and a half years of his rule had changed the face of the island from ruin, decay and famine to a very overflow of prosperity. With the power of a Pro-consul to direct and govern the lives and fortunes of a subject race, he had a quick eye to discern the needs and capabilities of the land and people alike. He discovered the traces of ancient civilization, the remains of illustrious cities; the broken "tanks," or rather vast artificial lakes, whose decay meant the drying up of the very springs of human existence. He set to work with a will, and by influence and stratagem, became the cause of work in other men, from the Secretary of State at home down to the recalcitrant peasant at his door. The supplies of water were restored, pure and abundant. Vegetation and health revived. Ancient cities were explored, and their art wonders preserved with reverent care. The literature of antiquity was brought together in national libraries. Roads, railways, a magnificent harbour, and no end of other great public works were undertaken, achieved, or at least, far advanced towards completion; the whole face of the country transformed from a wilderness to a Garden of Eden— all during that brief reign of one lustrum of power for good.

The accounts, under his own hand, of this most brilliant period of his life carry away the reader with the fascination of an embodied dream. With all manner of men and beasts he made friends and acquaintances. Kandian chiefs, fair native princesses, toilers of the soil, tigers, mosquitoes, unruly horses, elephants with the breeding and magnanimity of forest kings. Then came the stirring events of the Prince of Wales's visit to India. Necessarily he spent some time in Ceylon, and, of equal necessity, a treat of big game hunting was to be enjoyed by His Royal Highness and his suite.

This could not be satisfactorily accomplished, with the sauce of danger cut out—a natural fact, which the Home Office failed to appreciate. Telegram after telegram was being forwarded, that, under no circumstances, was the Governor to permit the Prince to incur danger! *Quis custodes custodiet?* Set a Galway squire to control the sporting proclivities of the heir of England! It seemed too huge a joke. A better way was found by the sympathetic Governor. The two famous hunters, Messrs. Varian and Fisher, were told off to keep a watchful eye on the Prince, and coolly ordered not to scruple to lose their own lives in saving his. So the fun went on.

"To try and stop him would have been as futile as the Pope's bull against the comet." The guns were stationed on rocks above the jungle of canes, fifteen feet high, through which the elephants rushed madly about in terror. Failing to obtain a shot in this way, the sportsmen determined to leave their posts and go down into the jungle—a most rash proceeding. All at once, an elephant came right down upon, and as it were, over the Prince, who was as cool as a cucumber in the emergency, and brought him down literally at his feet. He shot another, and jumped on his carcase in triumph to possess himself of the tail. When this was effected, they saw that the courtier-like elephant got up and made his way to his friends, tailless."

A carriage-upset followed, Lord Aylesford holding the reins and landing the Royal party in a ditch. Happily, no one was the worse, and the Prince was quite unconcerned—save for the safety of his elephant tails!

On this visit the Prince, on behalf of the Empress of India, invested his host with the order of St. Michael and St. George, as Knight Commander. The new knight was invited to the Durbar held at Calcutta, the greatest spectacle ever seen in the Anglo-Indian empire. Here Sir William stood in the place of honour, next after the Prince and the Viceroy of India.

Then came the days when the loneliness of his life was unbearable, when he sighed for rest in the old home, among friends of youth, and to be the comfort of his mother's last years. He wrote:

"I shall regret the glorious climate and scenery and the occupation, but I cannot stay; nostalgia is too strong for me. Besides, I have done my work; I have set on foot all the great material improvements on which my heart was bent—a man with new ideas should now come, and ladies would do much to popularise the government. I say to myself daily, when I struggle to entertain, *Tempus abire tibi*, but I hope to live and be strong enough to come here once more, and see what my successor has done at the close of his reign. . . . With a companion, a wife, a sister, or even a very intimate friend, I should prefer Ceylon to anything that could be offered me."

But this being denied him, he chose to return—not knowing what was to come: the crown of his life's autumn. No mother met him on the threshold of his deserted house. But as the days went on, he met his fate in a fair daughter of the land, and renewed the story of Othello and Desdemona. In March, 1880, he was married to Augusta, youngest daughter of the late Dudley Persse of Roxborough.

The great tribe of the Galway Persses were of old his intimates. Their two chief branches, headed by two cousins, were known as Persses of Roxborough and Moyode Castle. Of the latter was the M. F. H. who for many years hunted the county with the famous "Blazers." His sisters, and latterly his daughters, took part in his sport, as dauntless Amazons; the light weights being ever in the first flight of the adventurous field. There had been an old kindness between their house and my father's. Writing these lines, I remember being sent out as a small child habited in black, on a tiny Shetland, to meet the Blazers and follow their renowned horsewomen—at a distance. The elder branch, of Roxborough, was fruitful in numbers I dare not state. They were one of the wonderful Irish "long families," ensuing on two marriages of the head of the house. It was notorious that the gap of years dividing the eldest and youngest was equal to that between most parents and children. First on the family tree was Captain Dudley, a Crimean hero in his youth; last, Augusta Lady Gregory. The ladies of this house were no Amazons: they went in for beauty. At county balls, they were represented by a few sisters at a time; tall and stately, or fair and slim, crowned with a wealth of hair, from dark with glints of auburn to pale shining gold. No fashion ever tempted them to add jewel, feather or flower to Nature's proud adornment.

Much to his own surprise, Sir William carried off his young bride, and to her he owed an unbroken spell of twelve years' happiness, and a son to continue his race. Just before their marriage he wrote her:

"I am very glad indeed that the country people are pleased. Whatever naughty deeds I may have done, I always felt the strongest sense of duty towards my tenants, and I have had a great affection for them. They have never in a single instance caused me displeasure, and I know you can and will do everything in your power to make them value us."

So, among those he thought "the most lovable and loving people in the world," the congenial pair spent their summers and autumns very happily at Coole, varied by travel, and some time each year in their London residence. Three times, Sir William re-visited Ceylon; once he took his wife to enjoy the happiness and pride of sharing in his reception by a grateful people, who looked upon him as one more than human—a living embodiment of a bountiful Providence. In 1890 he bade his enchanted Island farewell—his last look at his old "Raj" and the wonderful beauty of the East. He never would enter Parliament again, saying that "five years of despotic government had removed all interest in our wretched Irish squabbles, into which, however, I could not fail to be drawn."

More was the pity. Could such "despotism" have been exercised by him with a free hand at home, he would have brought the distressful country within measurable distance of Arcadia. But even he could not altogether escape the Land League troubles. His tenants, after paying the last penny of his just rents—less his generous return of ten per cent.—were driven by terrorism to join, nominally at least, with the faction of rebellion.

Life was dear to him, for the sake of his wife and boy, while death had no terrors; but, as he desired, he escaped the misery of a lingering death in life. "We are all God's children. We must do our best to help one another." These were his last conscious words to her he loved, before he fell asleep. His work was done. Much in itself, but much less than he might have accomplished, had his opportunities been more worthy of his natural powers.

# A Black Sheep.

## CHAPTER I.

### HOW THE BLACK SHEEP WENT FORTH.

THERE were the usual items in the scene outside the house in Park Lane—including carriages; the Force; footmen; more carriages; always carriages; the inevitable block; tantalizing glimpses of unrevealed splendour; still more carriages and still more; hopeless congestion of traffic; and the listlessly curious crowd. There were the usual items in the scene inside the house in Park Lane; and these included all the beauty, rank and wealth of London, and a divine dancing band. There was a dance at the Audleighs', to celebrate the coming-out of the youngest daughter of the House, and nothing, not even Royalty's presence, was wanting to make the dance THE "success" of the season.

It must have been long past midnight before the man who had been gradually elbowing his way through the carriages, and then through the little straggling crowd on the pavement, took up his final position on the base of that one of the pillars, running alongside the house front, that overlooked the interior of the house.

A limited portion of the interior, when all is said—but a distinct portion, nevertheless; and thus a position of unlimited advantage. For the man, perched not uncomfortably on the stone, could not only look straight into one of the rooms on the ground floor, where the windows were flung wide open, owing to the tropical heat of the July night, but could, by twisting backwards and an oblique glance, see what was going on in one of the inner halls of the house.

Risking a dislocated neck, the man on the pillar devoted his entire attention to the shifting scenes in the hall. Not a soul came into that room he could look into so easily; and he had not run the combined gauntlets of the Force and the footmen to stare at *nothing*. Yet the scenes in the hall were commonplace in the extreme as Society swirled through—chiefly in couples. The dancing rooms were beyond, into which his obliquest glances could not penetrate.

The man himself must also have found Society thus viewed dull and uninteresting; for after a while he lapsed from an attitude of eager expectation, to one of almost listless indifference. Yet the occasional recognition of an old acquaintance among the gay and smartly-dressed throng, within, brought, ever and anon, a renewed light to his eyes, and a flashing look—that was less smile than sparkle—to his handsome, slightly bored countenance.

The night was as intensely dark as it was intensely hot. The artificial lights marked out this house among its fellows; and there was no escaping the searching light of the large electric globe that hung over the hall door, and lit up the darkness less than it revealed the hopeless state of congestion on both sides of the road. But the man, twisted, half-impatiently, half-wearily, on the pillar base, just by the side of the open window, was hid in the midst of the blackest shadows.

"Or the police would have had me off my gallery seat long before this," thought he, shooting lazy glances inwards.

A light flared up into his eyes, and a faint smile played about his lips. A tall and majestically beautiful woman was passing across the hall, seven gentlemen waiting on her smiles, and each cursing the other six in their seven manly hearts.

The group passed out of the man's range of vision, but both light and smile stayed. Four years of married life and a baby had not altered that beautiful woman in the very least degree—he perceived that instantly. He had not seen her for over five years, but he had read in the papers of her marriage and the rest. She was his eldest sister, and her lord and master was one of his old college friends. Her little son would be heir to a dukedom. The man's smile deepened into grimness, remembering all these things.

A soft voice—it sounded almost in his ear—startled him out of an uneasy reverie into all but losing his balance and crashing forward, head-first, on the pavement. By a vigorous effort he pulled himself together and shot his dazed eyes round, into the light-and-shadow interior of the dim, deserted room.

Crouched up against the pillar, ear and eye set straight to the scene in that room he had been turning his back on so long, the man, himself, was only another shadow of the night, and was lost in utter darkness. The two who stood by the open window thought themselves entirely alone with each other and their thoughts. *He* saw *her* only. She looked out sadly, into the unreal world of shadows, seeing nothing of the noisy bawling crowd in the street below, but what visions rising before her eyes we can only guess at.

The man was telling her that which fills some men with such utter awe and wonder when told them in return by a woman. Five years ago, another man had told her the same thing, by that very window, on another such night as the present.

Between that time and this, more men than I dare tell had also said the same to her, with but slight variations. For the woman (who was but a girl, still) was as lovely as an angel. Also, hers was that spotless purity and goodness that does more to regenerate the world than all the sermons that were ever written; and it was of the kind that frightens men into vain repentance, less than it fascinates them into hopeless adoration.

Those men were different! But what that man had said to her, by that window, five years ago, she would never forget. Nor would he (though he should try to a thousand years) ever forget what she had said to him, in answer, before their first kiss burned down into their hearts, from their pressed, passionate lips.

The man, pleading his cause so earnestly this night, five years after, had not known this—else he had not hoped more than he feared, when he told her of his love, and asked hers in return. That other man, crouching in the darkness, on the pillar, bit his lips till the blood came out, drop by drop; but he could not bring to them to stay, nor to his ashen face at all, the blood that the first note of that soft, sweet voice had driven back to his throbbing heart.

He clung to the pillar, in the loneliness of his hiding-place. His breath came thick and fast. His whole body shook.

"No," said the woman's voice sadly, out of the quivering shadows, "no."

A loathing of himself for playing the spy, so, on *her*, seized him outside. But to slip down, and dive into the traffic was beyond his power. "No," said the woman again. It sounded like the sigh of a spirit, that soft sad "no" of hers.

She said other things, half-tenderly, half-sadly, and wholly pitying; for her suitor was not minded to give up hope easily, and was stubbornly desperate; nor shrank at last, from driving her to the confession that no generous man—unless he be in most desperate stress—would ever press home to the woman who has rejected him. But " No " was the gist of all she said, until finally —his importunity not ceasing—"Yes, I love One—One," she murmured.

What else was said by her, and the other's passionate reply, was not heard by the man hidden away among the shadows. There was a great throbbing at his heart, after those words— "Yes, I love One"; and this, rising to his head, deadened all hearing. He realized then, though he had half-known it for years, that he had forfeited all right to ever kiss again the lips that said that saying—" I love One." But he had never doubted that she would not be faithless to him, though he should forfeit his right a thousand times over.

They passed away as silently as they had come, and the window framed them no more. They too, might have only been shadows, so silent was their coming and passing, had they not left that throbbing pain in the heart of the man, left suddenly alone, a pain that was less triumph than a wild sore longing for impossibilities.

A voice clinked somewhere far away, from that dim interior: " My word! Craven's had his answer, I guess. Look at his face when he passes! "

And the reply:—" Fifth man that's gone over this season! By Jove! It's too hard on us! That little girl *ought* to marry!" struck harshly on the man outside, as if he had seen an altar profaned.

"It's the Black Sheep, you know," began the first voice; but the rest was lost in the murmuring distance. A great silence seemed to have fallen upon the world, though the clamour around continued unceasingly.

The man outside was remembering that Lord Craven was considered the most eligible *parti* of the year, when he knew him, five or six years ago. Since then he had come into his inheritance, and " Mamma " had not ceased from hunting him. Also, he was as fit to marry a girl as might be, since he was manly, kind-hearted, and not evil as men go. Though Mamma, in the exigences of the chase, had forgotten to consider this.

Outside, throughout the night of revel within, and tumult

without, the man crouched up against the stone, with bent head and face hidden by the shadows; not stirring from his position of advantage over the crowd, or looking up any more; though Society did not cease from circling where he could see her if he chose. He was thinking his long, hopeless thoughts, alone; and they were as lanes that have no end and no beginning.

Until dawn broke; when he slipped down, cramped and strained by his long vigil. He shivered as he went restlessly to and fro, among the carriages, though the air was already soft and warm.

The traffic was thinning every second, but the festivities within showed no signs of abating. Half working London was about its daily business of bread or money getting, before the last carriage wheeled away. Then the man, his face pale in the morning sunlight, sprang lightly up the steps of the house of late frivolity; and passing the sleepy servants, pulling in rolls of red carpet and bunting, stayed the closing of the front door, by an imperious gesture of his hand.

The old major-domo's gasp, in answer to his own grim smile of greeting, was less of wonder than of awe.

When the young man held out his hand to the old man, this one only bowed with the stateliness of a dignified humility. *He* was only the servant, in spite of his chain of office; and the other would be his master, though this house's door should be closed on him for ever.

"Will you tell my father I'd like to see him now, if convenient," said the younger man, sinking somewhat wearily into a seat. "Tell him I've been waiting outside, with that gutter herd since midnight, for the show to be over. I had that decency," he said, grimly. "No; don't tell him that, Noyton; only tell him I won't keep him long."

He stared round the familiar scene, with aching eyes, which the lights hurt painfully. The servants paid no attention to him at all. They were dead sleepy; and went out, like candles, one after the other, though the work of putting things to rights was not anyway completed. A lump rose to the man's throat. The inner hall, where he was stranded, at last, was so sorrowfully familiar; and yet he seemed to have no business there, at all; and to be committing an outrage by remaining there.

"His lordship will see you, sir, now." The major-domo's

voice called him out of one of those endless lanes of thought, into the bewildering present.

They went up the broad, shallow, velvet-carpeted stairs, along a great corridor ; and down a smaller one. The younger following the older, and wondering what it was that made the walls spin round him, and his thoughts so confused. "His lordship is in his own room, sir," said the major-domo.

The other came to his senses, suddenly, recalling a past shameful scene in Lord Audleigh's study, five years ago. He had not set foot in this, the house of his forefathers, from that weary time to this. He bit his lips, as some burning thought struck home—the hot blood flying over his cheeks in scarlet dashes. But his face had recovered its first calmness and pallor, and was not without a certain dignity, when (the major-domo opening the study door), he passed through, to the words :

"Mr. Francis Audleigh, my lord."

His flashing glance took in the whole scene, before the echo of his own name had died away. There was the master of the house, sitting bolt upright, at his study table; his kindly, old face hardened into sternness, a cloud of impenetrable pride drawn over his handsome brow. The heir, his eldest brother, framed gracefully by the window curtains, shooting half lazy, half apprehensive glances at himself and his father, alternately. The politician, the third son, leaning on the mantel-piece, having brilliant, eloquent, slightly sarcastic eyes for him, alone. Lastly the subaltern, home from India, on furlough, whom he knew only as a little Eton schoolboy. And on the downcast face of this one as he sat at the other end of Lord Audleigh's study table, lay the shamed consciousness that perhaps should only have showed on the face of the second son ; he who was showing a countenance as full of pride as his father's ; as impenetrable as the rest of the politician's face ; and its own added defiance.

The master broke the short silence. "Will you not sit down, Francis?" he said ; asking the question of his son, rather than pressing the civility.

"As the business I have come about, at this highly inauspicious time, may be rather long, I will, thank you, sir," returned Francis Audleigh, taking a chair with a coolness he was far from feeling. The old room, the sight of his father, of his brothers, brought a strange despair upon his soul he was steadily hardening for the interview. Not a muscle of his features betrayed anything but well-bred calm.

"Business," repeated the older man—the lingering inflection of his voice was very significant. "I cannot imagine what—*business* you have come to see me about, Francis."

The ominous silence of his brothers steeled the other man's heart more than the sudden thunder-cloud on his father's brow.

"Surely you guessed it was business I came to see you on, sir," returned his son. "You had else not called my brothers together, to be present at our meeting."

"Do you object to your brothers' presence? I meant to see you alone, till I remembered they were not present at our last interview——"

"When you turned me out of your house."

"With what in your pockets you have forgotten, Francis," said his father, more in sorrowful shame for the other's shame than in bitterness.

"I beg your pardon—I have not forgotten. Twenty thousand pounds it was; and together with what you had already paid me—an uncountable sum—my share of the inheritance," replied his son, with assumed lightness.

Movement, half of incredulity, half of surprise, ran round the rest of the group.

"Do you remember what you said then?" went on Francis, leaning forward, but with the same impenetrable mask of cool indifference before the older man's burning glances.

"Perfectly," replied Lord Audleigh, drily.

"But my brothers?" said his second son, turning round and meeting, with a dazzling smile, the half curious, half angry looks shot at him.

The subaltern met his brother's eyes with a kind of wildness in his own. The other two had nodded, one slightly shame-faced, the other only returning smile for smile. The subaltern neither nodded nor smiled. He was a very young subaltern.

"Because I would not keep you at home any longer, for your mother's sake, I sent you away," said Lord Audleigh, in slow measured speech; and rather as if he were recalling past events than retailing past reasons. "Because you would have spent your brothers and sisters' portion, as well as your own, on your lust, I gave you a limit in which you could indulge it.

"Because you would indulge in it till this very house came under the hammer, were it not checked, I told you then, I would not give you a farthing more, as long as we both lived—were you to come to me in beggary and rags, and ask my alms. . . . Because I was determined you should have all the chances that —that wealth and rank—apart from affection—could afford, I made provision for you to start a new life in a new world, where you could work honestly, in a way your hands or your head found best; and by the best, the only means, rid you of the curse of your life.

"That was five years ago, Francis. Since then I have not had word or news of you. You went out with a princely fortune and a new life before you; and chances such as few men ever get twice; and this was your fifth—your sixth.

"You left me, promising you would do your best, on your word as a gentleman and an Audleigh, to give up the curse of gambling, that had brought you, and myself, too, to such piteous straits more times than I will recall now.

"You gave me another promise. The young lady you loved was willing to wait for you, till you had shown yourself worthy of her hand. She would have gone to you, then and there, in your shame, five years ago. But she was my ward, and you my son. I could not let it be. You told me, and her, in my presence, you would show her you could be worthy, even of her love; and only a man who has utterly *killed* a lust such as yours, could ever dare to think he was even approaching worthiness to *her* love.

"She and I, we trusted you. You were my son and an Audleigh; and you had given me your word to try, honestly—to try——"

He rose from his seat, the cloud sweeping away, leaving only a great love and longing beneath. His hands went out to the young man, sitting in steady silence, a few paces off. This one neither moved nor looked up; not even his lips stirred, though the politician was as grave as the heir, and the subaltern had turned his head away.

"After five years," said Lord Audleigh, with a curious little catch in his breath, and coming a step closer, "you have come *home*, I hope, Francis."

But Francis Audleigh, knowing what that emphasized, almost

sobbing, word meant, put out his hand impatiently, with a half-muttered curse. If he had done less he had broken down.

"I've come to talk to you on business," he said roughly, the next second, and throwing back his head with harsh defiance, saw the swiftly changing tone of the startled, eager faces bent towards him. "I haven't come here to rake up my past misdeeds, or your past threats—and I have not come *home*, as I gather you mean it. I've come on business pure and simple."

"Well?"

The word clicked out, short and sharp, like the click of a pistol. The cloud had swung back as suddenly as it was swept aside, and had covered all the love and longing. The suspense in Lord Audleigh's eyes was less fierce than agonising.

"I'm stone broke. That's about the chief of what I've got to say, I reckon. I'm stone broke."

It was observable that this man adopted a roughness of tone and slanginess of language, that were wholly foreign to his tastes and nature. Such icy coldness froze every feature of his face as is impossible to describe. His left hand, playing aimlessly at the beginning of the interview with a jagged nail end, on which it had alighted, on the outer rim of his chair's seat, was cut through to the bone, and he pressed it harder still when the blood fell, unobserved, to the floor. Every muscle of his was under most perfect control; and his right hand lay relaxed and open on his knee.

"You had twenty thousand pounds then! I—I cannot believe it!—and the land—that was a fortune in itself! It is only five years," gasped Lord Audleigh, utterly shaken and dismayed.

"Well, I've gambled it away; money first, every chip, and then the land. I'm stone broke," said his son, slowly and deliberately.

Lord Audleigh's involuntary cry was hardly above a whisper. His face was blanched, and he looked, for the first time in his life, an old man.

"I'm stone broke, so I've come home," said his son in an indescribable voice.

Lord Audleigh motioned towards the door.

"You can go," he said, with what effort to speak quietly and keep from open despair can never be told. "Go, as you came, empty handed."

Francis met his father's blazing eyes; his own impenetrable as frozen waters.

"I'd better finish the tale first, sir. I'm in debt, too. When my money was gone, and the land with it, I drew on the—er—family name——"

"You dared!"

"I owe fifteen thousand pounds," said his son, returning glance for glance, steadily.

"Did you arrange to leave your promises behind you, as you left my threshold? Did you give them, meaning them to hold good only until you had got what money you could out of me?" asked Lord Audleigh, with passionate sarcasm, "or did you *forget?*"

"No; I never forgot. I remembered them all, even when I was drawing on the family name. And my promises were sincere, at the time," returned the young man, steadily, staring out before him with strange, sunken eyes.

"You would stake your mother's most sacred treasures! You would stake your dead brother's golden hair—the locket she wears round her neck, he gave her, to satisfy your lust when the devil possesses you!"

"I would stake my soul when the—yes, devil, possesses me," said the other, deliberately.

"You would have sold our Lord's life to His crucifiers, I believe, if you had nothing else to stake," muttered Lord Audleigh in a kind of terrible madness. "Oh, my God! My God! To think this man, possessed of such a devil, should be a son of mine—of his mother's! Brother of my good noble sons—of my innocent daughters! That he should be the little innocent child, Frank, I have seen pray at his mother's knees! I have——"

Speech failed him. He put his hands to his face; his head fell forward on the table. There was the sound of weeping.

"That is it," said his son, with ashen lips, but unshaken countenance. "I am possessed of a devil—that neither your prayers—the prayers of a good man, who has lived every second of his life cleanly and honourably—nor my saintly mother's prayers can ever exorcise."

By this time the subaltern had hidden his face in his hands. Lord Audleigh raised his. It was grey and worn, and full of bitterness and despair.

"Have you anything more to tell me?" he said in a frozen voice.

"I have nothing more to tell you."

"And I have nothing more to say to you. You can go, Francis Audleigh."

Their eyes met again.

"I cannot pay this debt," said the younger, doggedly.

"Neither can I."

"But it is disgrace to our name to leave it unpaid!"

"You have disgraced our name so much already, Francis, that any further shame can hardly disgrace it more."

"I cannot pay it," replied his son steadily, but white now as driven snow.

"Work! You have been shown how!"

He rose from his chair. Francis rose also. The heir and the politician came a step nearer. Only the subaltern stayed where he sat, his head resting on his hands.

"You promised me," said his father, "you would try to overcome that devil within you! You promised! I cannot think—I cannot think how you can look me in the face, Francis, when you remember you promised."

The old nobleman turned away. The heir stepped forward, his hand on the study door. His father passed through, his head bent on his breast, his face the face of an old, old man.

"If I had not tried to overcome that devil—and with what prayers of anguish you may never know—I could not have looked you in the face," said his son.

But Lord Audleigh was gone, and the other had not known he had spoken half aloud.

There was an uneasy pause. The subaltern looked up half eagerly, half in doubt.

"To be without a cent in your pockets is deuced awkward," murmured the heir, sympathetically, at last.

The tightening hands round the second son's heart loosened suddenly, and left him master of himself again. "Deuced awkward," he assented, with a grim smile. "And a fifteen thousand pounds debt is deuced awkward too."

"I'm going to be married this month," said the heir, with regretful apology, and the first glow of visible feeling in the eyes he turned quickly on his brother. "Large establishment—settlements on the young lady—provision for—er—possible family. Else, you're welcome to every penny of my share in the inheritance!"

"Thank you," replied Francis, gravely, returning the hand grip. It was easier to keep his self-possession when the silver head of the master was not there to add torture. "But I couldn't think of it, anyhow."

"You see I can't exactly put the wedding off, now; cards—er—out; and—er—presents coming in; and the rest of it. And I'm afraid—er—*she* wouldn't see it."

"That is my opinion also," returned Francis, without a smile. "Do you know your news is news to me? I wish you every happiness in your marriage."

"I'm only the third son," said the politician, grimly, "but——"

"You have constituents and a future before you," interpolated Francis, with a graceful wave of his hand. There was less mockery than restless despair in his eyes. "You must not think of it."

The subaltern darted out after his brother; banging the study door to, behind him, as he fled. The very air of the house was choking Francis; he hastened down, but his youngest brother caught him up, before he was half way down the staircase.

"It's all been so beastly expensive—India—the regiment—polo and the rest!" gasped the subaltern, with working mouth. "I've dipped pretty heavily into my allowance, I—I'm afraid. But Francis, do—do take what's left! God knows it's precious little! But it'll be something to go on with."

A tear was running down each of the subaltern's cheeks. Francis' mouth twitched, but he said nothing.

"Take it o—old man," sobbed the subaltern, clinging to his brother's sleeve. "Oh! Do take it! I wish to God it was more!"

"No, I won't take it," said Francis, wrenching himself away, and speaking breathlessly, with bloodless lips. "But I won't ever forget you wanted me to."

He was standing below, where he first had speech with his father's old major-domo, and shaking from head to foot. The subaltern had fled long ago. One dim light shone through the great loneliness of the hall. A touch fell on his arm. He trembled still more, knowing that touch. When he turned, she, who had followed him down, softly, as a spirit, whispered his name, "Frank," and put her arms round his neck. But he, with a most bitter cry, slipped from her embrace; and falling to his knees, laid his forehead upon her feet.

At that, she bent over him, laying her hands upon his bowed head.

"Oh, Frank! My love, my dear love," she said.

All the brazen self-possession that had stood him in such stead above stairs, had fallen from him, as a cloak, loosened by her presence. He sobbed at her feet like a child. She did not need he should tell her the shameful tale of the past five years. She knew all before he had first cried out at seeing her, and fell to hide his shame from her eyes.

What she said to him then, need not be written. She told him she trusted in him still, to free himself from the cursed thing that had ruined his past life. And that she would trust in him to the end. She renewed her troth, and bade him remember she was his, and would be his, only, always, and that he belonged to her.

She tied round his neck the diamond and ruby cross she always wore on her bosom. For she had no money to give except what her guardian gave her. *She* belonged to him always, she repeated; but the little cross would remind him of his promise to her, as it was almost a part of her. She had worn it so long.

He renewed his promise to her, humbly, remorsefully, promising that he would be overcome no more of evil, but would overcome it. The touch of her fingers on his neck thrilled down to his inmost soul. He was ashamed with a great bitter shame, and filled with more remorse than shame. She saw that his eyes had grown old and very tired.

"I think of you all day long," she said to him, "and every thought of you is a prayer to God for you. Won't you pray for yourself, too, Frank?"

"Yes," he replied, "I will pray."

He did not tell her he had prayed as his mother taught him in childhood, till he could pray no more, when the temptation assailed him—and that was more times than he had years to his life. He did not tell her he had fallen to his knees, many times, in mortal agony, when the devil stirred within him, driving him forth to stake recklessly all he had, and all that which he could never hope to have, and that he had risen from his knees, spent with prayer, and *then* gone out to do the evil thing he shuddered at in his sane moments. He did not tell her how often he had made the sacred sign, when he felt actual hands pulling him on to handle the dice, and to plunge his reckless fingers through the gold he did not care to keep, though he desired, with a most maddening, terrible desire, the chance to win it.

He did not tell her how many times he had prayed that he might be kept from the lust of gambling, and how that which was within himself, and yet not part of himself, had fought against him and prayer, and had been stronger than both.

He said:

"Yes," humbly, remorsefully, "yes, I will pray."

At that, she kissed him again, and held him to her breast. He prayed then, praying that he might die so that moment. Then she glided away, into the shadows, and he was left alone again. Fire on his lips and on his breast, where both those she had given him lay. He let himself out into the morning sunshine, and drew the door softly to behind him.

Outside, he turned, suddenly, and stooped, and kissed the stone at his feet. His face was very white and piteous, and his hands were clenched, as one wrestling with mortal agony.

Then a great surprise came to him. . . It was as if it had fallen from Heaven, so suddenly he found that envelope pressed into his hands.

But the heavenly messenger was of flesh and blood, as he soon saw, wheeling round, swiftly, in his amazement. Noyton, his father's major-domo, retraced a hurried step.

"My lord told me to give you this, sir, with—with his love, sir. I waited, but you slipped out. I did not see. I followed you. That is all, sir. And—and—excuse an old servant's liberty! God bless you, Mr. Francis!"

The old man's hand touched his, timidly, once, ere he turned back, down the street. When he was a tiny child, Francis remembered Noyton as a very old man. His wilful, boyish pranks had always found an exonerator in his father's major-domo.

Francis stared vacantly after him. "This" was clenched in

his hand, but he was not wondering what it could be. He was thinking; thinking that he had been speeded out into the wilderness again, with three blessings and his father's "love."

When he opened the envelope, he saw that it held a cheque for fifteen thousand pounds, on his father's bankers, and a letter.

"Pay your debts with the money I freely give you," began the letter. "But remember I would not pay, were the debt you owe ten times greater, did I not—caring for you still—believe you have enough honesty left to make a fresh start. And as much as my love for you is greater than my abhorrence of your sin, so much rise above your present self, to the Francis Audleigh I used to know—my clean-hearted, noble boy Frank, who had never felt the blighting touch of Lust and Sin, or known the bitterness of Shame."

Francis turned the leaf over, with trembling fingers.

"Oh, my boy!"—his father had written there—"Come home to me before I die, and tell me my prayers — your mother's prayers—are answered. We pray for you night and day, knowing what you have to struggle against; and what torments of flesh and spirit must be yours, before you finally overcome.

"You will overcome, Frank, I know it—I know it! I appeal to you now in great sorrow and love. I forgive you all your past—all this fresh, bitter blow. I will not tell your mother. You will come home to us both some day, Frank, with hands made clean by honest work, and with will to do good strengthened by honest resolve, and with soul sanctified by victory over sin. You will come home and tell us this is so, won't you, Frank? I, your loving father, am waiting for that day, even now! . . ."

A tear dropped on the signature, Cecil Beauclerk Audleigh, that followed those passionate, loving words. Then another tear and another. Francis was in the Park now, that was fast waking up into animated life and laughter. Society was beginning to feel the desirability of sunshine and the fresh air, and the mob of riders, driving folk, and pedestrians was overwhelming. Slipping to a seat drawn up behind a clump of bushes, this man—lonely, by reason of his sin, in the midst of his own people—sank down there, hidden from the eyes of the world.

His sorrow, in its immensity and bitterness, should be as a thing sacred, and not to be pried into by eyes which have not looked on another such lonely soul, fighting for its salvation against the hosts of hell.

"But I will come home," said Francis, crossing the Park, as the shadows lengthened, and Society swarmed out to tea, and talk, and drove up and down the face of Town, without rest or intermission. "I will come home as he said, with hands made clean by honest labour, with will strengthened to do right, with soul sanctified—Oh, God in Heaven, let it be so!—by Victory!"

## CHAPTER II.
### HOW THE BLACK SHEEP CAME HOME AGAIN.

TWO years later Lord Audleigh was sitting in his study, reading the *Times*. The return of a harassed look, that his friends knew once very well, had long since passed away, and on his face there was a great peace.

What Society said was this:

"No wonder Lord Audleigh carries his years so well! He is so fortunate in his family."

That fraction of Society which had a memory (it was so small a fraction as to hardly exist!) used to reply:

"But how about the Black Sheep?"

To which, Society proper would express amazement in the following terms:

"Good Heavens! The Black Sheep!!! Why, he's not been heard of or seen for seven years now! We've *forgotten* him!"

Reminding that part of Society that was afflicted with a memory, that to be forgotten by Society proper was to have no existence.

Therefore, according to Society in general, it was no wonder Lord Audleigh was the youngest, handsomest man of his age; since there was nothing to disturb his peace, either at home or abroad.

If you asked further, and there was no scandal Society particularly wanted to talk about, you would be told (until Society's breath ran out), how and why Lord Audleigh was so fortunate in his family.

You would be told his eldest son was following in his father's footsteps, and showing a career free from every stain of vice. You would be told, in gasps, his beautiful young wife's diamonds were such as to bring actual tears of envy to the eyes of a well-known Indian prince, noted for his diamonds, and that their establishments were the smartest in the country. You would also be told, indifferently, that his eldest son has an infant son and heir, himself, who is his grandfather over again, as tradition tells of him at that early age.

You would be told his eldest daughter had married an earl, heir to a dukedom. And that she was the most beautiful, popular woman in Society.

You would be told that his son, the politician, is one of the men of his generation, and will be leader of his party, when his party are next in office.

Society would tell you, frankly and truthfully, she does not understand politics, but she knows confidently, the Audleigh politician will be Prime Minister at the next General Election. Society does not care, but you may care to be told the politician's political life is as free from spot or stain as his private life, and that both are as clean as his father's.

If you are not tired, but would know Lord Audleigh's further domestic happiness, Society would tell you his youngest daughter is just engaged to the " catch " of the season, and that every Belgravian mother but one is inwardly—not outwardly! (for the Audleighs are a power in the land)—reviling that one mother, who does not care, knowing her youngest girl has won the man of her choice, and that that man is worthy to win and wear her virgin heart—innocent and pure as it is.

Lastly, Society would tell you that a little dull cross hangs, among other martial ornaments, on the subaltern's breast, and that Lord Audleigh's youngest son's name is a name to conjure up visions of valour and glory, wherever the English flag is flown.

Society would require refreshment after this exhaustive account of the family. Society would not be best pleased if you insist:

" Was there not another—the second son? A young man of more brilliant promise even, than those other brilliant sons? You remember something——"

That part of Society which has a memory would, if not too bored, tell you:

"Yes, there was a second son who gambled away princely fortunes, one after the other, from sheer wicked love of gambling. That some said he was possessed of a devil (but Society, herself, does not believe in devils), because his heart was originally clean and honest, and his life, save for this sin, as pure and free from stain as his father's himself, and even Society cannot take away Lord Audleigh's reputation. That every means had been tried to reform this Black Sheep, but that he had fallen time after time and was now . . . ."

Society would shrug shoulders at this point. You could settle for yourself into which particular circle of the Inferno the Black Sheep had fallen.

But one thing Society was sure of, and that was that the Audleighs were well to be rid of him. He was a Black Sheep, and would never be anything else. It was not likely he would ever return, after seven years of silence. It was less likely he would reform; wickedness was inherent in him. (*How*, Society could not tell, in the face of his mother's and father's inherent goodness! But it was!) And without reformation he could not return. Society, who couldn't commit herself to an opinion as to the Black Sheep's present whereabouts, was certain of that.

Neither Lord nor Lady Audleigh listened to what Society said. Life was easier to live in consequence. The shadow that had fallen two years ago on Lord Audleigh's face was already gone. The hot afternoon sun was streaming in, through all the available chinks of the lowered blinds, as he dozed over his paper; having read every word of his son's great speech in the House the night before. A knock at the door recalled him to himself. One among the pile of letters, brought in by a footman, with apologies for having overlooked it, in last night's delivery, flung him back, pale and trembling, into the Past.

"If it should be what we have prayed for so long, his mother and I," murmured his lips, blanched suddenly, as the blood in his body rushed back to his heart. His fingers trembled so that they could hardly tear the envelope open, or draw out the long letter it enclosed.

A few extracts only will be enough to explain the light that transfigured Lord Audleigh's face as he read:—

"Your own words, father,—By honest work I have, I hope,

kept my hands clean. By resolve I have strengthened my will. And I dare write to you and tell you I have won the victory!

"Your blessing and love and your prayers—my mother's prayers, and hers, who has been my guardian angel to drag me up to the light when I have fallen into the blackest hell, again and again; my own prayers, have conquered the wicked thing within me; and I am coming home to you, not only a free man, but one set on the path of work and duty; and who will, please God—I ask it in humility, knowing what my sin has been—stick to that path and fall no more.

"For two years I have not touched the cards. At first—oh! I can never tell you what the agony of the struggle was at first. Only the thought of you and my mother, and of her, and of you all at home, kept me from going over to the devil then and there. Had that happened I should never have come home to you again; I know enough of myself and the black depths within me to know that. But you all helped me; so by degrees the struggle became less agonizing, the straight path easier to go down; and I think—I think I can come to you at last and say I am a man free from that cursed thing.

"I know what God has done for me! And, oh, father, don't think I don't know all your goodness and great love; and I know myself, and in my freedom now, and the joy of looking forward to coming home, I know that I am utterly unworthy of it all. Only I will honestly try to make amends, by the rest of my life, for what has gone before. And though I know that what has been, has been, and shall ever stand, I know you have forgiven me now, and loved me always.

"And you don't know how I love you all at home and have loved you always, even in the midst of my misery and despair. . . .

"I am on my way home! I shall get home in the afternoon of the fifth. I have heard so little of you all. Oh! you don't know *what* it feels like to be looking forward to coming home now. . . ."

Lord Audleigh stared into the streaks of sunshine which had crept into his study. He was looking at a boy called Frank, who had great, pure, heroic eyes, and a noble forehead.

"My child that was lost has come back to me," he said

tremulously, tears of happiness standing out on his transfigured face.

If Society had been able to read his thoughts, and reading understand, she would have said that he was indeed blessed in his children.

But Society was very, very busy those days; and everybody, even the best, had functions to attend. With a sudden tightening of his fingers on the letter he held so lovingly and long, Lord Audleigh, realising that he was alone in the house, remembered that to-day was the fifth. To-day his son would come home! To-day!

The tremendous thought was hardly to be borne. He paced the room eagerly, restlessly, listening to every one of the thousand distant noises without; his heart racing round till the pain of suspense was almost greater than the gladness of anticipation. At last love would wait no longer, and he went downstairs wandering about the halls, saying over to himself, with lips pale through joy: "The fifth! This afternoon! This afternoon!"

He glanced at a clock. It showed after six. The shadows outside were growing less intense and longer, every throbbing minute. He found it very, very hard to wait.

Yet the far-off pealing of a bell, and approach of several footmen startled him when they came quickly, one after the other. Noyton stole past him. He waited in the inner hall, such emotions in his heart as can hardly be told. "My child that was lost has come home to me," he was saying; and did not have ears or attention for the sound of hurried talking and the slight confusion in the outer hall. Then the swing doors opened, and Noyton passed through with a troubled face.

But the visitor followed hard on his heels; a grave man, dressed in sober black; and before the major-domo could speak, stepped forward and delivered his own message to Lord Audleigh. He knew him instantly.

"There had been an accident," he said; "the Honourable Francis Audleigh had been brought into the hospital half-an-hour ago, and he gave this address. It was an accident; and Lord Audleigh had better come."

"What else?" Lord Audleigh thought he said; but he only opened his piteous mouth, and no word came out.

"I think it is serious, my lord. I did not hear particulars; I was sent off as soon as the gentleman was able to tell who he was and belonged to."

"What was it?" gasped Lord Audleigh, looking up painfully from the table, where he was writing two notes, with hands that trembled as if suddenly stricken with palsy.

"A dray, I think, my lord. Run-away horses, or a tipsy driver. I could not gather accurate information before I was sent off."

Giving orders that the two notes be despatched, one to the party at which his ward was; the other down to the country, where Lady Audleigh had taken refuge for a few days from the claims of Society; Lord Audleigh set off in the hansom the messenger had arrived in.

"It is not far, my lord," said that one, shooting curious sympathetic glances at his trembling companion. But to the driver he whispered, ere hurriedly stepping in himself, "Drive as fast as you can."

"I do not understand," said Lord Audleigh, tremulously, at last, staring at, but not seeing London pass him, as in a dream. "What did you say it was?"

"He was knocked down by a dray, my lord, and they carried him in; and he sent us to your house. I do not know any more, my lord. We are there now!"

Lord Audleigh found himself repeating those comforting words that his heart had framed earlier in the day. "This my child that was lost has come home again." He was saying this over and over, vaguely, with a numb, stony feeling at his heart, when he felt his hands seized.

"Ph—Phyling!" he stammered.

The great physician looked at him with twitching mouth. These two were old friends, knowing each a little of the other's heart.

"Your son is a hero," said Dr. Phyling quickly, a curious shadow passing across his face. "He saved an old woman's life, who would else have been trampled to death. He swung the horses clear, Audleigh, leaping forward to seize them no one knows how. For the driver had lost control over them. He swung the off horse aside, and the front wheel caught him."

"My God!"

"They went over him, Audleigh! Both wheels went over his poor body. You must be very quiet and calm."

"Yes, I know—I know I must. I am very quiet and calm. Feel my hand—there! Take me to him!"

"He is in great agony. I injected morphia at first, and would have continued it, but he would not let me. He wants to be entirely conscious when he sees you. You must be calm, remember! Yes, you are! That's right. Now I'll take you to him."

There were two hospital nurses in the room; but they slipped out as the men entered. The smell of drugs was almost overpowering. His body, who lay stretched upon the bed, was covered by a sheet; fastened so that the lightest linen-touch could not fall, to further torture what lay beneath. The two men stepped softly up to it, and one, touching it, stepped back again with a sigh.

Not death, nor agony, nor the soul's loneliness in approaching death (though all these were written there too) was what Lord Audleigh saw, as he drew near to that piteous bed. He was looking down on the face of his son; but despair stared back at him, and a lost soul, lost beyond hope of mercy or redemption, looked out of his son's eyes.

"My child that was lost—has come back to me!"

The words fell from his trembling lips, unconsciously, as he bent to kiss his son's forehead. "You got my letter?" was all Francis said.

Lord Audleigh began to fondle one maimed hand, oh! so gently and tenderly. But his son only looked up, with those tortured eyes of his, and repeated, hoarsely: "You got my letter?"

At that his father put his hand to his pocket in the breast of his coat, and bent afresh over the hand he held, touching it again with his trembling lips.

"My dear child—my good, noble son."

"Are we alone?"

But not hearing that cry that broke from his son's distorted lips, and very gently and quietly, because this poor shattered body must be kept so very quiet and calm, and with his heart breaking at every word, Lord Audleigh began to speak of that letter, and *What* he had thought and said when he had read it, and realised that his dearest son was really coming home again, a free man at last.

And to that, very slowly, and with steady eyes staring before him, and stony lips, Francis took up his father's broken speech, and told him how he wrote that letter five days' journey from home, posting it when he arrived in London. How he wrote it, honestly believing it to be true. How he had gone out to work, and had overcome the evil within him ; and how he had, by his own honest labour, got a small sum laid by, to show the trust placed in him had not been placed in vain. How he came home to London over-night. . . .

How, believing himself to be entirely free from the Lust that had dogged his path so long, he let himself be taken by an old acquaintance (the hated name Lord Audleigh supplied in his heart) into the place of temptation again. . . .

"Then that evil thing I thought was killed for ever sprang suddenly into life again within me. I can't tell you what the struggle was like! You could never know! It was between devils on one side, fighting to drag me down to hell again, and the angels on the other, fighting for my soul. Then I tried to pray, having overcome by prayer before.

"But I found I could not pray, for I desired *less* to be saved, than to handle the cards again! The devil took possession of me so suddenly, and so unawares, and I thought he was killed for ever! I hardly knew what had happened at first.

"Then I felt for the cross Lily gave me. It had helped me to conquer before. Holding it and saying *her* name, I have fought against Satan himself and won.

"But it did not keep my hands from the cards this time, and I lost all I had saved by that year's work."

The doctor returned, swiftly, and drew Lord Audleigh aside.

"You know it cannot be long now, Audleigh? One hour at the most. You have left word?"

"Ah! What? I—I beg your pardon! Yes, I have sent for Lady Audleigh and my ward. She will come ; but his mother cannot be here till midnight."

"She will come too late," thought the doctor, vanishing as quietly as he had come, and wondering, with a thrill of vain regret—recalling the brilliant promise of that sad, unfulfilled life

—what terrible and tremendous confession of the Black Sheep had set that piteous look on his father's face.

A corner of the sheet had been folded back against Francis's face. He caught it in his teeth, and had bitten it through and through before Lord Audleigh returned. He made no other sign of suffering. By the time his father was back by the bedside again, his lips were stonily reset, and only twitched ever so slightly when he began to speak again.

"I have sunk very low, have I not?" he said. "But I have reached a lower depth than that I have already told you of."

"No, Frank, dear, dear child! No, not any more. It—it is a dream—a mistake," groaned his father, in piteous excitement. "You are my boy, come home to me as you said, a free man—victorious! It—it is not true what you are telling me."

"When I had staked and lost all my money," said the remorseless, pitiful, twitching lips, "I drew out the cross Lily gave me. She tied it round my neck that night I last came home, two years ago; and I felt her hands there, softly, on my neck, as I held it in my hand, the good and the bad fighting within me, for its possession. I was hearing what she had said, all the while, and I wished God would strike me dead there as I stood there and struggled—struggled against myself now! For I wanted to go on, once I had handled the things, more than I wanted anything in earth or heaven. You—you don't know how I struggled, for I thought of you all; and her face was before me, and her voice was in my ears, and I felt her soft fingers about my neck, all the time.

"And yet I gave it up—that cross Lily tied round my neck; and with it my soul! I staked it and lost both.

"Don't you wonder at me, father? You say no word; and I can't see your face. Father, don't you wonder that such a devil as I am should be your son and my mother's? When I think of you and her, and then of what I was, I wonder at myself almost as much as I loathe myself. And that word doesn't tell *what* I think of myself! There is no word known to man that can express that. I was mad, I was possessed, when I was doing it, I know that; and yet I knew what I was doing. I couldn't have saved myself then, I had tried—tried my hardest and failed. *But I knew what I was doing!* I knew it was my soul I was staking as well as Lily's cross. I can feel her fingers round my neck now; they were so soft and she loved me so. But I do not pretend, even to myself, I did not know what I was doing all the while.

"Father, won't you turn your face to me? I can't lift my head. And you don't say anything. Let me see you. I had rather hear the curses on your lips than see them in your eyes. But I would rather read them there than feel them in your heart through this silence.

"Father!"

"Do you kiss me," whispered his son, in utter awe, "and not curse me?"

If tears can ever wash another's soul clean, those that fell from Lord Audleigh's eyes to his son's forehead would have washed every stain away.

"Was it madness? The devils were so strong."

"Yes, dear, yes; it was madness, Frank."

"But why couldn't I fight them? What else did I need? A mother's prayers alone can bring a son to God. My mother's couldn't keep me from falling to the lowest pit of hell. Nor yours, nor Lily's, who is as pure as an angel. Nor my own; and I tried to pray. What else did I need, father?"

"God Himself will tell you soon, Frank."

"You don't know how I loved you all! But I'm glad those wheels went over me for your sakes."

"You saved a woman's life!"

"Did I? Poor old soul! She was scared, I remember! I heard her screeching as the wheel went over me. I thought what an old fool she was to shriek so, as she wasn't hurt."

"You saved a life!"

"But I couldn't save my soul."

Lord Audleigh wrote something on a card and handed it through the doorway. "Lily will be here soon," he said, reseating himself by his son's side, to watch life die out from that drawn, colourless face, and death fill in her piteous lines.

"And mother?"

"She will not come in time."

"But mothers forgive everything. Mine will!"

"Yes—hush, keep still, dear! Mothers forgive all, and love."

"It follows us down to hell—their love! O, my mother! My mother!"

"You'll tell her how I love her, father, won't you? She'll believe that, even though I've broken her heart—and yours! But you forgive me, too!"

"I could inject morphia now," suggested the doctor's quiet, grave voice.

"But I will not have it," said the steady voice from the pillows. "Do you think I am suffering with my body? I do not feel it. And I will not be made unconscious."

Nearly every bone in his body was broken. From minute to minute his father bent over him, to wipe away the sweat of agony that streamed down his face and hands. "But I do not suffer with my body," said his son.

"Tell me of the others," he said, his voice failing, after a silent spell of waiting for her who must come very quickly now or she would come too late. Lord Audleigh was also waiting for something else, to get which he had written his name to a sum of money large enough to turn a poor man into a rich man. "Tell me of them all; I want to hear—Maurice?"

"He has a little boy. We have called him Francis."

"Ah!"

"Beauclerk—"

"He's leading the country, isn't he? I read of him in the papers. I'm glad he's successful; and Marie?"

"She is very happy and beautiful, and a dear good daughter and wife and mother," said Lord Audleigh softly.

"And Jack's got his company! For Valour—I read about that in the papers too. Dear old boy! And little Emmeline?"

"She is very happy too. She is going to marry Lord Craven."

"Three brave, good sons and two dear daughters. And I was always the Black Sheep. . . But I did try, father; you believe me, don't you—I did try!"

"Yes, I believe you. I know you tried! I love you!"

"It was very strange about that letter I wrote to you. I thought it so true as I wrote it. And you read it and believed it to be true, too, and find me *this!* It's so strange and sad, and hopeless."

"Not hopeless. We all love you."

A nurse ran softly in, with a parcel and the breathless, choking information (both for Lord Audleigh), "The young lady, my lord. Dr. Phyling is bringing her in."

"I think you'd better go and tell her," said Francis's unrecognisable voice to his father. "There's hardly time to tell all, but you'd better prepare her a little. She can't know I'm so utterly damned as this. And I've only a few minutes left for—everything."

The room was sunk in twilight, but another nurse, coming in as Lord Audleigh went out, brought in two lighted candles. . . .

"This side, dearest; he cannot see your face there. He cannot move."

Her lips met his, twisted in agony. "Lily," he said.

A sob broke from him. "I can see you love me still," he whispered.

And then:—"Your fingers are round my neck, as when you put that cross on! Lilly! *what* is it you are laying on my breast? . . . Did you know I gambled it away, Lily, though I cared for it as my very soul! Did you know I gambled and lost it?

"Did you get it, father, after I'd told you? Did you give it to Lily to give back to me before I die? Ah, father! . . . Put my fingers on it; I can't move them. And then yours on mine—so, and your head here against mine—poor Lily!

"Can you hear what I say? I can't speak louder. Shall I in the long Eternity ever get to Heaven, at last, Lily? Did you say you would meet me there?

"Are you praying, Lily? I can't hear. But I can feel your arms round me, and your kisses. . . .

"Is my father there? I cannot see; all the lights have gone out. Yes, that's his lips on my forehead! On my lips now, father, please. I'm not worth crying over. You'll tell mother I love her, won't you?

"And you, Lily! Kiss me, sweet—bless—me—Lily!"

With her name upon his lips and her face to his, the Black Sheep's soul went out into the dark.

K. D. K.

# The Provincial Doctor.

IT is a curious commentary upon human nature that young unknown doctors who immigrate into our town in quest of patients succeed in nine cases out of ten. Perhaps they have an uphill struggle for six months. It may even extend to a year or eighteen months. But, unless they are perfect brutes in manners, or otherwise ill-favoured, at the end of that time they are nearly sure to have blossomed into sweet success. They ride to hounds and have quite as many social cards as they can do with. Our provincial town, in fact, dear blind old community, receives them with open arms, and seems to regard their welfare as being no less bound up with its own than is the life of a child in its first week or two with that of its mother.

But there is one condition that these newcomers must not, for prosperity's sake, fail in. They must not presume to bring a wife with them. If they do, the cold shoulder is their portion. Not for them are portly patients with chronic diseases, and the suffering wives of such of our citizens as have three or four marriageable, yet unwedded daughters at home. They must be content with the poor and needy, who haggle about eighteenpenny visitations, whose domestic interiors are repellent to the refined, and whose numerous babies have a vile habit of entering the world at one or two o'clock in the morning—November, December, and January being the months most favoured by these irresponsible little mortals. It is just possible indeed that in despair they may have to compete with one another for the proud position of parish doctor—a position which lays them open to public enquiry if by chance they give a poor woman a wrong medicine, and which once or twice in the year brings upon them a vote of censure for neglect or waste of public money from those eminent persons the guardians of the poor, sitting in solemn conclave in the boardroom at the workhouse.

The young medical immigrant need have no qualities to recommend him except his bachelorhood and a quite ordinary measure of good manners. He may be as poor as the proverbial church mouse—which, by-the-way has, presumably, undisturbed access to the church money-boxes; and those who know may feel compelled to avow that he proved himself rather a duffer at Guy's or Bart's. No matter. These sole certificates of excellence shall suffice him. Mothers and daughters put pressure upon the nominal heads of their families. They are tired of their old family doctor. He has been married twice and could hardly now be considered an eligible "parti" were he to be widowed a second time. They undermine him in Paterfamilias's esteem; and so, when next Madame has a touch of neuralgia or one of the dear girls is oppressed by headache, young Mr. Novice is sent for and welcomed cordially. An hour suffices to set him at his ease with all the household—except perhaps papa, who clings fondly to his medical contemporary. If, six months or a year hence, the young man takes one of the girls to the altar, the crown is put upon his fortunes. All his bride's relations are then bound to call him in when they are indisposed.

On such a foundation it cannot be expected that our town's medical men are of the first rank. They develop into what are called "good all round practitioners," and presumably acquire consciences as indurated as those of the average advocate or the average statesman. When any of us astonish them with diseases out of the common, they are at first delighted, like children with a new conjuring trick. They enjoy themselves in a nervous manner for a day or two or a week, keeping their treasure quite to themselves. Then, however, if they do not seem like making a cure (and that can hardly be expected of them) they send for a specialist from town and take an expensive lesson (at the patient's cost) in the higher surgery or in diagnosis from the lips of the great man, in whose presence, if they will but have the grace to admit it, they are as the Liliputs to Gulliver. Speaking generally, they have two broad characteristics. They make light of all complaints in their initial stages. And when the patient is dead they exhibit no astonishment—however much they may feel. They have been taught to be cheerful in the presence of suffering humanity; hence they enter the sick-room invariably with a mirth-provoking jest and a demeanour of gallopping optimism. And they have learnt that the phrase "Death from natural causes" satisfies the laity to a marvel, even as a death certificate is a responsibility that must not (considering the number that have to be filled up in the year) be regarded too seriously.

We would not be hard on the average provincial medical man. He does not lay claim to be a genius or to work miracles. Indeed, there are times when he is more serviceable than the Harley Street gentleman whose very forehead suggests the midnight oil, and whose omniscience leads him to extravagant conclusions. When he doubts, he plays the trick of Nature— and really he could do no better. He just gives the patient a simple phial or two of coloured water tinctured with nastiness, and perhaps a box or two of paste pills, and backs up these potent agents with the set phrase, "Be regular in your habits, take plenty of fresh air, and let nothing trouble you." Nothing is more enchanting than the way in which the dear fellow takes all your anxieties, ties them up and shoves them on to the top of your wardrobe, or some place equally hard of access. "There," he says, "that's done. Now, you may get well." If, when he has vanished, laughing loud at his current joke of departure, you feel constrained to ring for the steps and recover the bundle of anxieties, how in the world is he to blame? The consequences will rest upon your own head, not his.

But, apart from his professional abilities, the lot of the provincial medical man seems as comfortable and bright a one as may be had. Of course, he soon acquires the necessary amount of philosophy to enable him to regard the troubles of others as a field for his skill rather than his sympathy to an immoderate degree. How, he demands, and reasonably, can I hope to be of use to my patients if I permit myself to be depressed by the sorrow it is natural for me to feel for them in their afflictions? He therefore cultivates the habit of keeping his sympathies under lock and key—for domestic use only. This explains his cheerfulness as he goes from a person dead of typhus to a person dying of peritonitis. You might, unless you understood him, suppose that he was, as far as his patients were concerned, quite of the opinion of the Greek sage who accounted no man happy while he lived. As touching himself, he enjoys the sweets of family life in his own house. He is also infinitely in the secrets, even as he shares much of the pleasure, of the family life of his patients. In Protestant England he is to the household what the confessor is to the wife in the Catholic south. He is a man to be welcomed and conciliated, since he carries life and death (or at least the latter) with him wherever he goes. And he could, if he would, say so much about his clients, of whose frail humanity he has such a cruelly exact measure. As he drives gaily through the highways and streets, he receives salutations by the hundred. One wonders how he thinks of us, in his mind's eye. Does he view us merely as a train of more or less affected anatomies? Yonder smug person, for example, with the elevated nose, righteous tread and the blue flower in his buttonhole—what of him? Is he Bright's disease or fatty degeneration of the heart? It is a pretty notion, in truth, and one which may go far to explain the smile which ever lurks about the corners of his lips.

This, his peculiar standpoint, seems to give him almost an unfair advantage as a municipal officer. It is not unnatural, however, that he should aspire in this direction; and hence his procession into full-blown mayoralty is also natural. But imagine what an influence he must have in the council chamber, surrounded by his patients! It is, in fact, little better than a terrorism. If Alderman B. proves annoyingly restive against a motion upon which Councillor Dr. C. has set his heart, what more easy than for the latter to whisper to the former that it is as much as his life is worth to become excited? It has happened that this course has not succeeded. Then an even worse method of procedure may be adopted. Even as perfectly sane men have ere now been incarcerated in lunatic asylums and retained there in spite of their most strenuous protestations of sanity, so a few words in season disseminated by the medical town councillor among his fellow councillors may prove a solid bar to the support which the obstinate alderman confidently relied upon. The gentlemen are conjured for the poor patient's sake not to humour him. There is no knowing what the consequences may be. He is thus regarded with a compassionate leniency while he is pleading his best against the medical gentleman's resolution, and when he sits down (patently exhausted and out of breath), after a magnificent peroration, it is as if he had not opened his lips.

As mayors our medical men shine. There can be no question about it. On the councillors' seats their dogmatism (a "you'll-die-if-you-don't-do-as-I-advise" sort of manner) is not always successful. It arouses the antipathy of commercial councillors who can afford to laugh to scorn the hint that anything is wrong with either their hearts, livers or lungs. But this very dogmatism, if tolerably bridled, gives a certain impressiveness and even sublimity to the doctor as chief magistrate. He, at any rate, is not embarrassed by overweening modesty, whether in the council chamber or on the bench of justice. Under shrewd guidance from the town clerk (a patient) he plays his part so as to compel admiration even from those who are not in accord with him on political and social questions. He has not felt pulses and looked at tongues for twenty or thirty years without becoming something of a humourist in spite perhaps of himself, as well as deeply versed in human nature and most of its foibles. Hence when he speaks at banquets and dinner-parties he coaxes tranquillising smiles to the lips of most men. And it is not a small matter to realise (as all the councillors and their constituents must do) that the doctor as mayor does credit to the town he represents when he journeys to London and in his civic robes and bullion gives the Lord Mayor the honour of his company at a Mansion House reception. If Her Majesty has a particular reason for knighting the mayor of the borough (be he whom he may), it is upon the whole distinctly a subject for rejoicing if the mayor for that year chance to be a gentleman of the medical profession. The other councillors do not feel jealous of the dignity bestowed upon him. They would mostly in such a case, their year of office being ended, lapse into objects of pity, if not of positive ridicule, with the responsible prefix of "Sir" to their honest, and perchance uncouth, surnames. Not so the medical man. He, as Sir Erasmus Galen, may be trusted to carry himself well; and they share in his glory in swallowing his potions.

One thing may be taken for granted. If two or more medical gentlemen are on the Town Council, these two or more medical councillors are at daggers drawn with each other. The laity may then enjoy some passable comedy in their exchanges. The gentlemen dispute heatedly, especially when sanitary affairs are discussed. The Borough Health Officer, for example, is backed by one of them and adversely criticised by the others. Interesting debates, acrimonious rather than mild, are started whenever the death-rate soars above five-and-twenty to the thousand. If there is even the ghost of an epidemic of anything in the town, argument is bound to wax to the verge of indecorousness, if not past it. The lay Councillors signify their opinions on these questions with a certain deference, as becomes them. Afterwards they loll back on their seats, and with their gowns cast free of their chests and their hands buried in their pockets, prepare for the passage of arms which seldom fails to follow. Assuming that there are three medical gentlemen in the Council Chamber, it may really almost be said axiomatically that two of them are in agreement only in one contingency. When the third dies, the other two in their hearts congratulate themselves and the town, while outwardly deploring his early demise as they stride solemnly in civic procession after his supine body (with the Union Jack over it and the volunteer band playing the "Dead March") to his comfortable grave in the gravelled part of the cemetery. Subsequently, without even winking, they support the motions of condolence formally initiated in the Council Chamber, and have much to say about the abilities and admirable parts of their lately deceased colleague.

But to revert to our doctor in private life. He is, as a rule, worth dining with. Whether he be a civic officer or a plain servant (and master) of the public, depend upon it he knows a great deal about sauces. Not for nothing has he made acquaintance with the domestic economy of a thousand households. From one house he culls a wrinkle about roasts, from another about boiled things; and it will be odd indeed if among his patients he have not two or three accomplished and travelled epicures, whose kitchens bear witness to the skill with which they have borrowed the choicest culinary ideas from four or five continents.

If you are brought into the mean clutches of dyspepsia after a hearty feast at the good doctor's table, you may feel assured that you were in a bad way before you there unfolded your napkin and complimented the soup.

As host, the doctor is as nearly perfect as anyone with ordinary senses and appetites need be—for comfort's sake. Of course it is after dinner that he grows most communicative. Though he has great faith in the superior secrecy of the ladies, he will not therefore whisper this, that and the other about his patients until they have gone to the drawing-room. But the blissful moment arrives when the door is gently (as if reluctantly) shut upon them. Then he expands like a filling balloon, beams upon you (as he would continue to beam upon your death-bed, if you only knew it), lights a cigar, touches a decanter of port in a caressing manner with his delicate sensitive fingers, and begins his piquant retail of gossip and his yet more piquant hints and anecdotes about his and your fellow townsfolk.

Breach of confidence! you exclaim. Stuff and nonsense. Of what value are confidences in any form or field unless they can be discreetly shared with another human being? Besides, of course, even the good doctor has his reticences. He will not wreck his self-respect and destroy his medical reputation and connection for the sake of an idle hour's pleasure. But as he sips his port (long in bottle) and breathes the faint eddies of fragrant smoke into the warmed air, his tongue must take exercise. And you and he, with no sense of guilt, are soon laughing the most delightful and intimate kind of laughter, inspired by the innocent weaknesses of your fellow creatures. Every other minute the dear man breaks out with another, " Between you and me and the port "—and so it would continue until midnight unless his wife interfered, or if that dreadful surgery bell did not sound at the very climax of your contentment, and the good fellow were not called forth (sighing heavily, but with no words of more than transient petulance on his tongue), to attend a poor woman in a fit some two miles away—in heavy rain.

With all his frailties, and he has his share of them, our provincial medical man, in his mellow prime, is a lovable object. There is proof of it (and of the good luck that has attended his physic and bandages) in the valuable collection of silver that adorns his buffet and his hall. Indeed, if you are behind the scenes, you may, in his dinner-table array, see memorialised an appalling number of dire diseases and accidents. That centrepiece, for example, was the gift of the county magnate. The county magnate's wife suffered long from cancer, and died of it. But our good doctor at least alleviated the poor lady's sufferings, in gratitude for which, after the funeral, the centre piece arrived. The four salts, again (of chaste design—each a nymph holding a silver shell), were a grateful acknowledgment of a clever amputation, whereby, in all probability, life was indefinitely prolonged at the expense of a limb. The tankards, biscuit box, claret jug, the superb silver tea-service and much else, are all in like manner suggestive of typhus, scarlet fever, a variety of tumours and so forth. Did not the doctor's jovial face bloom across these grim mementoes of the plagues that dodge (and only too often grip) us in our journey through life, it would be something of an ordeal to sit in the midst of this mortuary silver.

Our provincial doctor takes short views of things in general, including diseases. This is well, on the whole. It gives brightness to his own life, and enables him to bring sunshine into yours, even when you have the entire length of one foot and about half of the other over the edge of the grave. He does not perplex himself inordinately about science or theology. If a patient asks him for his opinion as to that other life to which death is believed to be the prelude, he turns the question aside with a hopeful little laugh, or answers it pat in some such manner as the following: "My dear sir, there's nothing in the world so stimulating as a knotty conundrum. For my part, I look forward to being able to solve the mystery of posthumous futurity as much as I look forward to anything!" After that he must indeed be a naughty or morose-minded patient, who will not consent to die as eagerly as a boy goes to his first pantomime.

It is easy to say and suggest hard things about all men who stand out conspicuously from the majority. Our provincial doctors are such men. They soon become callous of the quips and cranks they inspire, pass them on indeed with a disinterested sort of relish; and even originate others that are much more derogatory to them. As accomplished scholars in human nature, they know that these things cannot but be said of them, and so they start the laugh as often as not.

This it is, more than a sense of conviction, that makes us of the laity take up the jests and cavils against them and ring the changes on them. Even as I have done in this paper, we make fun of them (rather bitter and venomous fun sometimes); but in our hearts we know that they are of the salt of the earth. And the poor of our provincial towns know it with a surer knowledge than we possess.

CHARLES EDWARDES.

# Poppies.

BEHIND me was the sea, shining in all the glory and the beauty that an east wind, a clear atmosphere, and strong sunlight can give it; and in front, with a background of green fields and yellow "mustard" blossom, stood a girl crowned—covered—draped with glowing, vivid poppies that fell in showers over her, from the crown of her sailor hat to the long clover-laden grass at her feet.

The girl was a picture in herself. Her dark hair clustered in small curls above the oval face, and her darker eyes gleamed all the more brightly in contrast to the colour called into her cheeks by the touch of the keen fresh breeze.

Poppies abounded on that land, it could bring forth little else, said my brother-in-law with a groan every time he looked out over his crimsoning fields; but all the same, they imparted a glory to the landscape that nothing—save themselves, could give. I had told John so that morning, and been called a "Job's Comforter" for my pains; I told myself so *now* as I walked across the field to meet the poppy-laden Ailsa St. Ruth, my sister's friend—and *mine*.

"Look at me!" she cried, half in fun, half in protest. "And the children will not let me throw these things down."

"Not likely, when we have taken the trouble to make the garlands on purpose," said my nephew, Roland the second.

"I must sketch you—just so," I cried, pulling out pencil and sketch-book. "Stand as you are for a moment—the details can be added by-and-bye."

A faint tinge of colour swept into her temples, and played underneath her hair, yet she stood patiently to gratify my whim, while the children crowded round me to watch the process.

"You're making it very nice, Uncle Jim," said Monica, the youngest. "I want it when you's done."

"It shall be mine," said Roland the assertive.

"Indeed, I'm to have it myself," quoth Harold, whose impatience made him jog my elbow more than once. "Just be quick, Uncle Jim, will you?"

"And why are you going to have it, I'd like to know?" enquired Roland aggressively. "Ailsa——"

"I'm going to marry Ailsa when I grow up," he announced quickly, "and everything belonging to her will be mine also."

"There spoke the true man," said I with a laugh, as I calmly put both block and pencil into my own pocket again. "Harold, boy, others can play at that game—and, meanwhile, the sketch is *mine*."

Harold looked angrily at me, the intruder.

"I always intended to marry Ailsa," he began with a little plaintive ring intermingling with his anger; but Roland, who had been studying me attentively, put in his word.

"Uncle Jim means to marry her himself," he said, with the air of one who makes a discovery. "And so, of course, he wants everything——"

His words had taken away my breath, so that I could make no earlier protest.

"You young scamp—" I was beginning, when my second nephew interposed again in his clear, high treble.

"Uncle Jim *cannot*—he cannot marry any one. He's got a wife already—somewhere."

A look of pain shot into the girl's eyes for one moment; but I felt hot and angry, and I fear I hated this clear-voiced boy, Helen's favourite child— an *enfant terrible* to the household.

"I never jest about such things," I began slowly, but that boy interrupted me passionately.

"Who's 'jesting'?" he asked sharply. "I've heard all about your wife, Uncle Jim, and I'm very sorry and all that—but you ought not to take my sketch, you know."

"Is it not my own?"

"It is clearly Dr. Chester's, Harold," said Ailsa gently. "Come here, dear, I will give you a photograph when we go in—and it shall be your very own—with a little frame to put it in, so that it can stand on the table in your room."

"Then it'll be half mine," said Roland in huge content. "Let us go back at once, Ailsa."

She had turned while speaking, with her profile towards me; and I saw that she meant to give me time to recover my usual manner.

"His wife—his wife!" I could fancy she was saying. "I did not know—I never thought." And I, ah, what was I thinking? Better not ask. Better not know. Mine was no enviable lot. It had never been one.

All that life could give me of pleasure or gladness, was bound up in that poppy-crowned girl, who was only Helen's friend—and mine.

"The world has forgotten I have a wife," I said presently, in a tone that was half an apology for not acknowledging the fact before.

"Did you not forget her yourself?" she said, turning round in a momentary flash, which even I owned was justified, but I shook my head gloomily.

"I, forget?—I wish I could. My wife has been insane for many years. I think she must have been mad when we married. Three weeks after that event she was taken away, and has been shut up ever since. That is the history of my wife, Ailsa."

"Oh, I didn't know," she cried, stopping to put her hands in mine in token of her sympathy, while tears filled her lovely dark eyes. "I didn't know. It seems the saddest thing in the world."

"It is even worse," I muttered to myself. "She does not know that I married this woman because I was told she was breaking her heart over *me*. I did not love her; oh, dear, no. But I was not worthy of any woman's broken heart, so I married her, and took my misery on my own head." Aloud I said quietly—"We can always be friends, you and I—can we not?" and hand in hand, within sight of the silent sea, we made a compact of friendship—friendship to the end.

The children had raced on in front—little they recked how they had hurt—*us*. They raced on, trying to see who would get home first. We, with a world of sorrow between us, came soberly after, lingering in the faint sweetness of the fading day.

Somewhere out of sight in the borderland 'twixt Heaven and earth, a lark was singing, his song floating down to us in a sweet refrain of almost celestial hope and joy, and Ailsa lifted her head to listen.

"That song is full of hope," she said. "It is intended for you. Out of the gloom of your life something bright and good may come."

"Ah! *What?*"

There was a want of faith underlying my question, but the outlook before me was not inspiring, and I had seen nothing but misery for so long.

"When can anything different come to me? My life is forecast from the beginning to the end."

My poppy-laden friend turned quickly round, her flowers

falling gently on either side from the garlands which she still wore; although I believe she had forgotten their existence.

"Oh, hush!" she cried, her lips parting tremulously with her words. "I do not like to hear you speak so bitterly. To be able to endure is to show one's self victor over circumstances. Don't you remember

> "'How sublime a thing it is
> To suffer and be strong'?"

I almost smiled at the passion and the pathos she displayed. This was a new story to her. It was a fresh experience to come in contact with pain—with part of life's agony, even although the contact were but vicariously borne.

"Your poppies have faded," I told her as we neared the door of Cloudsley Manor. "How soon these wild things die!"

She smiled painfully.

"They are the flowers of the Garden of Sleep, are they not?—of sleep and forgetfulness. I don't want them to die just yet."

"Give me one," I pleaded, holding out my hand. "I want it for a memory."

She did not give it, but I took one—it had been hanging on the brim of her hat; it fell while we were talking—and I have it still.

"To-morrow I am going home," I told her. "I have much to do there before I am ordered abroad again. Perhaps you will think of me sometimes—as the most unfortunate man you know."

"I will think of you as they think of the brave who fight valiantly——"

"A losing battle," I supplemented when she paused. "Ah, Ailsa, you little know——"

Then the door was flung open, the three children stood framed in by the dark oak, and beyond were my sister Helen and her husband—Roland Cloudsley.

"What an age you have been! And what have you been doing to yourself, Ailsa?" cried Helen, drawing her friend's hand through her arm as she spoke. "The tea is nearly cold, too, I declare. Roland and I were tired of waiting, so we had a cup each by ourselves."

The tea-table looked very inviting, spread out daintily in the big hall, beneath the stag's horns, and the men in armour, and the children flitted about like tiny ghostlings, as they tried the merits of girdle-cakes and scones, while Ailsa sank down on the oak settee near the cavernous fireplace, and I lounged against the broad window-seat.

"And what did *you* do, my sonnies?" asked Helen of her sons. "Have you been good boys?"

"Very," they both replied in a breath. "We trimmed up Ailsa with flowers. And then Uncle Jim came and drawed her, but he won't give us his picture."

"He is selfish," added the younger Roland.

"All right, young man; I'll pay you out for this," I said grimly. "Just wait till I return from home."

"Are you going to see your wife?"

The question came from Harold, but it made Helen turn white.

"Oh, Harold!" she cried sharply, and then she turned to me as if to apologise for his words. "I am so sorry, Jim."

"It's all right, little woman," I replied. "I am going to see Grannie, Harold. Shall I give her your love?"

"Ask her to send me something nice," he rejoined, with the promptitude that distinguished the children of this household. "It is a long time since my birthday."

"When I grow old, I'll have a buffday *every* day," said the little Monica; whereat her father kissed her, and her mother laughed.

"When you grow old, you'll have no 'buffdays' at all, I expect," said Roland the elder. "That's one of the things that belongs to the days when we think 'as a child.'"

But this subject became fruitful of much controversy, and in the midst of it I slipped away. I had my packing to do, and we dined at seven.

I had not much time to spare. But when I reached my room I did not pack.

I sat down instead, and thought—a far more dangerous proceeding, and one that could not profit me at all.

The next morning I left the Manor very early, and three weeks later saw me on board a liner, bound for the East once more, for my leave was up.

I bade Helen farewell in a note that gave her much wise counsel concerning the way in which she was bringing up her children—the boys especially—but I said not one word about Ailsa St. Ruth.

Two withered poppies were lodged in my old note-book. Photographed on my mind was the figure of a girl standing in a clover field, with the gold and red background, and the setting sun in front; and in my desk was a sketch. These things went with me.

My wife lived on. They said she might live to be a very old woman, she was so well and strong. And I, with my spoilt life, was going alone to take up my work once more.

"You were too ready to listen to her father's story, dear Jim," said my mother wistfully, as we said "Good-bye." "She was not at all the sort of girl you could ever have loved. My boy, why were you so easily blinded? The man was a fortune-hunter; the girl was brought up in a dreadful school. It is a sorrowful bit of history for my son."

She was a clever woman—would God I had taken her advice long ago!

We make mistakes—we men! We must learn to live under the shadow of those mistakes.

This is life.

\*　　\*　　\*　　\*　　\*　　\*　　\*

Two years later I came home again—*free*.

My wife had died—no matter *how*—it was a gruesome story, and were better forgotten.

She was dead, and we do not say harsh things about the dead.

I came home, and the first person I met in Town was Lawton, whom I had known abroad, who hailed me joyfully.

"Chester, by all that's lucky!" he cried in an ecstasy. "Can you lend me a hand for a day or so? I am nearly dead with work—fever and so forth; my assistant is down with it too, and if I don't get relief I'll knock under also. You've nothing on earth to do, stay and help me like a good fellow. You like work, I know."

"I can give you a day or two, that is all," I replied. "Remember, I am on my way home, and my mother will be hugely disappointed if I don't turn up."

What was the good of talking to Lawton? He was the most obstinate donkey in the world, and he looked deadly ill into the bargain.

In five minutes he had convinced me that I should be doing the most virtuous thing I could if I went to his aid. So I went.

"I am an ass for my pains," I told him frankly. "It has been my ruin to be too good-natured, but you look ill——"

"Ill!—I believe I'm going to die," said the unblushing Lawton, like a second Ananias, as he carried me and my luggage off in a "growler." "You are a trump, Chester—you always were. Had you lived in the Middle Ages you would have been a knight errant or a creature of that sort."

Then he tucked himself and his long legs into the vehicle after me, and away we went, jogging as far in one direction as I had intended to go in another, while I wondered at myself for my folly.

Lawton was a man with a hundred and one fads. He had set up a private hospital arrangement, and run it pretty successfully, until his assistant fell out—ill. Hunting about for his successor, he came across *me*—worse luck!

This was what I learnt as we went along. In his hospital there were three nurses, a matron, and a staff of servants. Patients he seemed to have in plenty. The beds were seldom empty, and the cases interested him.

An enthusiast in his way, he took the most real pleasure in this kind of work, and, by degrees, he infused some of his enthusiasm into me.

By the time we arrived in Great Middleham Square I was almost reconciled to the capture, all I bargained for was one night's rest. Not one stroke would I do until the morrow; so, seeing I meant it, he gave me a decent dinner, a big smoke, and sent me to bed, where I slept peacefully.

The next day my duties were to begin.

Lawton's hospital was a cheery place when seen by daylight. Each patient had a room, and some of the "cases" were bad ones. The nurses were bright young women, carefully chosen, and full of unfailing good temper and energy, and their manner was perfect. Lawton introduced me to the matron and then went off.

"Dr. Chester has kindly promised to take care of the patients here," he told her in my hearing. "I have outside work enough on my hands. Good-bye, Chester; don't kill yourself."

"No fear of *that*," I retorted with a laugh. "Now, Mrs. Morton, I'll begin with the worst cases first; will you come with me to-day?"

She rose at once—a kindly, plump little woman, I wondered where Lawton had picked *her* up—and we went upstairs together, she talking all the way. At one door she paused.

"This is a very serious case," she said in a low tone. "I don't know how Mrs. Jennings is to-day, but last night she was restless, and that was a bad sign. Nurse Grace is sitting with her now."

The room was shaded by heavy curtains, and these were drawn. Evidently this patient wanted sleep and rest. A tall woman in a nurse's garb rose at our entrance, and moved to let me draw near.

"She is asleep," she whispered. "And Dr. Lawton thinks she is better."

"This is Nurse Grace," said the matron quietly in my ear. "Nurse Grace, you go with this gentleman to the others—you know them, and I don't. I'll stay here till you return."

There was nothing to be done for Mrs. Jennings but to let her sleep; so I moved on, following my new guide, who closed the door softly behind me, as we passed out of the room.

But as we stood in the corridor, with the light streaming in upon her, I started. There was something strangely familiar in her manner and figure. Her face was the face of my day-dream —of my most tender haunting memories.

"Nurse Grace!" I cried aloud in my astonishment. "You are——"

"Ailsa Grace St. Ruth—yes," she said in low, sweet tones—all the sweeter to the ears that had not heard them for so long. "You are home once again, Dr. Chester; I may say 'Welcome back to England,' I suppose."

I caught her hands in mine and held them fast.

"Ailsa," I cried, scarcely heeding what she said; "Ailsa, I came back to look for *you*. It is true, my love—my dear love."

"Dr. Chester!"

She drew away her hands, and her voice trembled.

"It is quite right, my darling," I murmured. "I am free to come here—to tell you of my love—to plead for yours in return. She is dead, Ailsa; and the unhappy past has gone for ever, thank God! But I did not expect to find you so soon——"

"Nor here," she added gently. "Yet I have been very happy in my work——"

"Ailsa—do you love me? Don't keep me waiting for my answer."

Her head fell lightly on my shoulder, her hands yielded to my clasp; I kissed them over and over again, blessing Lawton, in my heart, for the persistency with which he had brought me here to find my love at last.

I had found her in the midst of unselfish work for others—blessing the sick and sorrowful by her presence, carrying lessons of faith, and patience, and endurance wherever she went, and calming her own spirit into submission and peace. For all earth's heavy-laden ones may find comfort in such work, whereby their souls are soothed in soothing others, and they rise out of self into self-abnegation.

I think Mrs. Morton opened her eyes when at last we returned to her, we had been so long away; but, happily, Lawton found Mrs. Jennings a great deal better for her sleep.

To picture Lawton's face when I led Ailsa to him as my promised wife is delightful. Consternation, concern and anger struggled for mastery by turns; and only the poppy-crowned sketch showed him I had found her whom I had lost so long before.

"My best nurse! My most trusted ally," he grumbled. "I must say it is too bad of you, Chester — and I was so certain you were not a marrying man, or given to this kind of thing. I am not. I don't know why *you* should be."

"That is as we are made," I replied penitently. "My dear fellow, I must have married Ailsa, had I gone down into the very depths to find her."

After all the grumbler did not lose either of us.

I had come home "for good" this time; and when our brief honeymoon was over, Ailsa and I came quietly down to go on working in Dr. Lawton's hospital.

Why not?

The greatest happiness life can give comes from helping others. That is the lesson we have both learnt in the hard school of experience. But in our rooms you will always find poppies in the tall vases, and my wife's portrait that adorns my "den" is of her as I saw her that evening long ago, crowned with the flowers that belonged of old to the Garden of Sleep—the land where Earth's sorrows are forgotten.

We forget *ours* also in the larger love that makes the "whole world kin" to us.

The only disappointed people in this matter of our wedding were Helen's boys, but they find their revenge in favouring us with their company at stated periods, and I always take care to remember their "buffdays."

MARY S. HANCOCK.

# Eleanor and Arthur Plantagenet.

## By CHARLES BRUCE-ANGIER.

> Fair Pearl? Fair Eleanor Plantagenet
> Daughter to the elder brother of base John
> And rightful queen o'er him and all that he enjoys.

POSSIBLY the reader knows little of the hapless Princess Eleanor Plantagenet, granddaughter of Henry II., on whom the lineal right of the English crown devolved upon the death of her brother, Arthur Plantagenet, in 1203, *de jure* King of England.

In order to fully comprehend the extent and nature of this lady's claims, it will be necessary to trace the connection of English and French history during the 12th century.

King Henry II., not content with his already immense possessions in France, thirsted for an extension of empire, and by cajoling Conan V. the reigning Duke of Bretagne, who is described in Breton history as "L'Imbécile Conan," obtained such an influence over him that at last the weak prince was persuaded, under the pretext of betrothing his daughter and heiress Constance to Geoffroi of Anjou, the third son of Henry, to give up his dominions to the English monarch. This was in 1166. Geoffroi was then about eight years of age, and Constance, his *fiancée*, about eighteen months older.

Henry therefore having made most unjust seizure of Bretagne (for he only allowed the unfortunate Conan to retain the Comté of Guingamp and the Earldom of Richmond in Yorkshire, which ever since the Conqueror's day had been an appanage of the Ducal line), proceeded in the May of 1169 to send Geoffroi over from England to Rennes in order to receive, as Duke of Bretagne, the homage of the Breton lords and the acknowledgment of the bishops and other prelates. This ceremony was performed in the church of St. Peter. Subsequently the boy Duke joined his father at Nantes, where they kept the Christmas of 1169.

The New Year found the young usurper and his unscrupulous parent making a progress through the different parts of Bretagne in order to receive the homage of the seigneurs who had failed to attend at Rennes.

Thus was Geoffroi Plantagenet, a boy of eleven, recognised as

Duke of Bretagne. Thus was an English, or more correctly speaking a Norman, prince allowed to assume the crown of the Armorican kings. It is the more remarkable, as not only was Conan still living, for his demise did not take place till 1171, but Geoffroi was not married to Constance till 1182, thirteen years after his assumption of the sovereignty, at which time the princess had reached the—for those days—mature age of 24, while her husband was in his 23rd year. The death of his elder brother, Henry, which occurred the following year, placed Geoffroi a step nearer to the English throne, while about the same time the Duchess Constance gave birth to a daughter Eleanor, the subject of this sketch and so named after her paternal grandmother, the ill-famed Eleanor of Aquitaine, Queen Consort of England. Geoffroi was remarkable for his manly beauty and the agile grace of his figure, he was also—we are told—an eloquent speaker. Like his elder brothers, Henry and Richard, he resembled his mother, who was a Provençal, and had been trained in all the accomplishments of that fair and sunny grape and rose grown clime, where first the old chivalric lays were sung, and where, glittering towards its strand, the purple Mediterranean kissed the land. She had been very beautiful, having inherited the rich gold beauty of the South. She was moreover a woman of great talent and was by hereditary right chief reviewer and critic of the poets of Provence, and being a fine musician, composed and sang many *chansons* of Provençal poetry; indeed, like her son Richard (for it was from her that he derived his talent as a poet), she was a popular Troubadour poetess and her *chansons* were sung long after her death.

It will be remembered that she was in her own right hereditary sovereign of the Aquitanians, at that time the most polished and civilized people on the face of the earth. After the death of her eldest born, she seems to have lavished on Geoffroi all her love, and she looked upon her granddaughter, the infant Eleanor Plantagenet, with favourable eyes, perhaps seeing in her cradle the shadow of a future crown. But if Geoffroi and his brothers inherited beauty and talent from their mother, they probably also owed to her other traits of character not so becoming. Many sinister stories are current in old writings of these Plantagenet brothers. Henry, Richard, Geoffroi and John, when they were not in arms against their parents, were always quarrelling and fighting amongst themselves. One authority goes so far as to denounce Geoffroi as being "false and plausible, universally distrusted, and known as a mischief maker and a contriver of evil." You must know that his mother, though as a sovereign she ranks among the greatest of female rulers, pursued in her early days a guilty career as Queen of France. She was a woman they say of "exceeding levity," and her ideas of morality were of the wildest—but why recall the "*chroniques scandaleuses*" of French and English court life in the 12th century? Sufficient be it for me to state that she was divorced from her first husband, Louis of France, and six weeks afterwards was publicly married, and with great pomp, to the King of England. Such was the grandmother of Eleanor Plantagenet, after whom she was named, and though she did not inherit the vices of her grandam she probably derived her beauty from her Provençal ancestors. The Plantagenet ancestry of the young Princess Eleanor was by no means spotless; there is the story of Fulk the Red Count of Anjou, he who wore the sprig of broom, and was first to take the name of Plantagenet. Then there is the wonderful tale of the witch Countess of Anjou, Henry II.'s great grandmother, who seldom went to church and when she did always quitted the edifice at the elevation of the host, so that at last the Count, her husband, thought it high time to oblige her to remain through the service, and further made four of his esquires hold her forcibly by her mantle to prevent her exit. When lo! at the moment of consecration the Countess, untying the mantle by which she was held, left it in the hands of the esquires, and flying through the window was never heard of more. A great thunderstorm happened at the moment of her departure, while a strong smell of brimstone hung about, which "no singing of the Monks could allay," and overpowering the scent of the incense, that was hastily tossed in the air from out the fuming censers. No doubt, if the truth were but known, the poor lady was killed by lightning in a church injured by a thunderstorm. Her ungracious descendant Richard Cœur de Lion, Eleanor's uncle, used to tell this tale with great glee to his companions in arms. "Is it to be wondered," said he, "that having sprung from such a stock we live on bad terms with each other? From Satan we sprang and to Satan we must go." He referred of course to the dreadful quarrels—matters of history—

in which he, his brothers and his mother, indulged from time to time against their father, Henry II. It is said that during one of these filial rebellions, Geoffroi narrowly escaped being his father's murderer. The story goes that a conference having been called in the market place of Limoges for the purpose of discussing peace, Geoffroi in a fit of passion at the thought of his mother being kept as she then was in durance vile by his father, aimed from the château of Limoges a shower of cross bows at the royal person, which came so close as to shoot the king's horse through the ear. Henry afterwards presented the arrow to his rebellious son, saying with tears, "Tell me, Geoffroi, what has thy unhappy father done to thee to deserve that thou, his son, shouldst make him a mark for thine archers?" Geoffroi professed to be greatly shocked, and maintained that it was an accident, of which he declared himself to be wholly innocent. It seemed the fate of this family that none should love the rest. Hatred seems to have been their common heritage.

Just before the death of Geoffroi, his elder brother Richard invaded his dominions of Bretagne with fire and sword, to avenge some fancied affront. After this affair Geoffroi betook himself to Paris, where at a grand tournament he was either flung from his horse in the midst of a *mêlée* and trodden to death, or as some relate he died of a sudden complaint in the bowels which seized him—in retribution for his undutifulness and his threats against his father. This event occurred on the 19th August, 1186, in the twenty-eighth year of his age. Thus perished the father of Eleanor Plantagenet, who was now in her fourth year, and actually proclaimed heiress of Bretagne, and for a brief space held a momentous political position, for, failing her uncle Richard, she was regarded as next heir to the throne of England. But her "sun" was soon eclipsed by the birth of her brother the hapless Prince Arthur, which event occurred on 29-30th April of the following year, 1187. Queen Eleanor was perhaps not best pleased at this event, for she disliked her daughter-in-law, Constance of Bretagne, who never could be brought to bow to the will of the older woman, so that this haughty Provençal queen determined that neither Eleanor nor Arthur should be recognised whilst their mother lived. The Queen Mother never ceased to deplore the untimely death of her beloved Geoffroi: we have the evidence of her own most eloquent words contained in one of her letters to the Pope, in which she speaks of the death of her two sons Henry and Geoffroi. "The younger King," she writes, "and the Count of Bretagne both sleep in dust, while their most wretched mother is compelled to live on, though tortured by the ineffaceable recollections of the dead." Not long after the birth of Arthur "great scandal" arose regarding the Duchess Constance (whose disconsolate widowhood exists only in the pages of fiction) and her brother-in-law, John Sans Terre, who until his marriage with Isabella of Angoulême was constantly "haunting" the widowed Duchess, and as his attentions caused considerable comment it is supposed that on that account Henry II. compelled Constance to espouse *en secondes noces* the Earl of Chester. Constance, however, soon eloped from this husband, and next allied herself to a noble more to her taste, one Guy, Count of Thouars, by whom she had two daughters, Alice and Katherine, half sisters of Eleanor and Arthur. The childhood of the Princess Eleanor seems to have been passed in great obscurity, but in the year 1194, when only eleven years old, she accompanied her grandmother Queen Eleanor to Germany, whither the old and the young Eleanor journeyed to pay the first instalment of King Richard's ransom. In the ransom treaty the Princess Eleanor was promised in marriage to the heir of Leopold of Austria. But alas! it was never to be. At this time she was surnamed from her beauty "La Perle de Bretagne," and being fair must have favoured her father's family rather than her Breton ancestry. The birth of her brother Arthur had been hailed with enthusiasm by the Bretons, who, seeing in him the probable heir of England, insisted on bestowing the name of their national hero upon this last descendant of the Armorican princes. Meanwhile all things ran their course.

In 1189 their grandfather the old King Henry died, and Arthur and Eleanor were advanced to a critical position on the variegated chessboard of Anglo-French history. But one life, that of their childless Uncle Richard, stood between them and the succession. The year after his accession Richard, in order to repress the dangerous ambition of his brother John, assumed the guardianship of the royal children and asserted Arthur's claim. He even opened negotiations for the young Prince's marriage with the infant daughter of Tancred, King of Sicily, and received from Tancred 20,000 ounces of gold in anticipation of the Princess' dowry, and in a letter to the Pope Clement III. dated 11th November, 1190, he distinctly declared his nephew his heir in case he should die childless. From this date John, who was always plotting to supplant Richard, must have regarded Arthur and Eleanor as his most dangerous foes.

Six years afterwards (1196) King Richard, despairing of heirs by his consort Berengaria, the beautiful daughter of Sancho the Wise, King of Navarre, sent for his niece and nephew of Bretagne that they might be educated at his court as heirs of England. Arthur was then nine years old and his sister Eleanor thirteen. But their mother Constance, out of enmity to Queen Eleanor, unwisely refused this request, and in her folly placed them under the care of the king of France, then in the midst of one of his constantly recurring quarrels with Richard. This step cost her unfortunate children their inheritance ; for, smarting under this affront, Richard immediately acknowledged his brother John as his heir. But in the August of 1198 he was reconciled to his nephew. Eight months later the king died from a wound incurred while besieging the castle of Chaluz. It was the lively imagination of the poetical Richard, heated by the splendid pictures of Arabian romance, that hurried him to his end. A report reached him that a peasant ploughing in the fields of Vidomar, Lord of Chaluz in Aquitaine, had struck upon a trap door which concealed an enchanted treasure, and upon going down into a cave, he discovered several golden vases full of diamonds, all of which had been secured in the castle of Chaluz for the private use of the Sieur de Vidomar. Richard, when he heard this fine tale, sent to his vassal demanding as Sovereign of the Duchy his share of the spoil. Vidomar declared that no such treasure had been found, nothing but a pot of Roman coins which he was welcome to have. But the lionhearted Crusader was not to be put off thus and accordingly marched to besiege the castle of Chaluz, where he met his death. Arthur is said to have been with him when he died, and that the King ere he breathed his last recognised and acknowledged him as his heir. But his Queen, who was also at the deathbed, afterwards gave out that Richard had devised his dominions, and two-thirds of his treasures to his brother John.

At the time of King Richard's death, the historian, Matthew

Paris declares Queen Eleanor his mother was governing England, but would not recognise Arthur as the rightful heir for fear that Constance should become regent during his minority.

Arthur and Eleanor were now left face to face with John. Phillip II. could not be trusted to render them genuine assistance, as he was known to be willing to employ any means to injure English influence in France, yet outwardly he remained the friend of the House of Bretagne, and Constance sent the young prince to Paris, where he was placed under the care of Lewis the Dauphin, a lad of exactly Arthur's age. Meanwhile Eleanor remained with her mother at the court of Bretagne. On 27th May, 1199, John was crowned King of England, but the nobles of Anjou, Maine and Touraine immediately declared for the children of Geoffroi, John's elder brother. If we read with care the history of those days we shall see that had the mother of Arthur attempted to conciliate and gain over the aid of Queen Eleanor, there can be little doubt but that Arthur, and failing him, Eleanor, would have obtained the throne of England. For though now advancing into her eightieth year she still acted a queenly part in the arena of Europe.

At the Court of Bretagne the position of Eleanor could not have been a very enviable one; there was a stepfather and a stepsister Alice, a child of ten, who eventually became Duchess of Bretagne to the exclusion of the fair Eleanor, who was now old enough for her marriage with the heir of Austria to be consummated. The position of the princess was, however, considered so critical that Leopold of Austria did not scruple to break the marriage contract. After Anjou, Maine and Touraine had risen for these promising scions of Plantagenet, Philip took possession of several castles in Arthur's name, on the plea of protecting them from John. Shortly afterwards the French king knighted and formally invested Arthur with Bretagne, and all the late King Richard's French possessions, *i.e.*, Anjou, Poitou, Maine, Touraine and Normandy, but at the same time Philip's high-handed treatment of those who acknowledged Arthur's sovereignty soon led to an estrangement between him and the Bretons. The leaders of Arthur's forces, though outwardly arranging a pacification between uncle and nephew, seem to have in reality simply finessed to place the Plantagenet children and their mother in John's hands, who is said to have imprisoned and so ill-used them that as soon as they were able they fled in all haste to Angers, a town which was known to favour the cause of Bretagne. In 1201 the Duchess Constance died, soon after the birth of her fourth child, Katherine. The following year Philip of France, disregarding the fact that Arthur had for some years been affianced to a daughter of Tancred of Sicily, affianced him afresh to his own daughter, Marie, a child not six years old. Eleanor meanwhile remained neglected or forgotten either at the Court of Bretagne, or with her grandmother in Aquitaine. Before many months were over Philip forced Arthur not only to re-open the strife with John, but also to turn his arms against his aged grandmother, who, after resigning her vice-regency of England into the hands of John, had retired to her native dominions which she was governing in peaceful security, when her hot-headed grandson Arthur, then only in his 16th year, suddenly laid siege to her summer castle of Mirabel, where she was then residing.

It is said to have been a plan of Count Hugh de Lusignan's devising, who meant if Queen Eleanor had been captured to have exchanged her for his lost spouse Isabelle of Angoulême, whom John had carried off almost from under his very nose. But the intrepid Eleanor of Aquitaine, after they had stormed the town, betook herself to the citadel, from whose lofty heights she scoffed at her grandson's efforts.

Eleanor Plantagenet had also joined her brother and was in the camp before Mirabel. The Queen Mother sent for John, who, hearing of the prizes which now lay almost in his lap, traversed France at "lightning speed," and arrived unexpectedly before Mirabel on the night of August 1st, 1202, suddenly attacking and hemming in the forces of Arthur and Eleanor between the town and the citadel. He gave them fierce battle and overthrew them with an "utter defeat," taking prisoner his rival in Empire and the fair "Damosel of Brittany," as she is quaintly termed, with four and twenty barons of high degree and about two hundred barons and knights of inferior rank, twenty of whom are believed to have been starved to death in Corfe Castle.

It is said that the Queen Mother charged her son on threat of her malediction not to harm his noble nephew or his high-spirited niece, and while the ancient dame retained her faculties John was obliged to content himself with incarcerating Arthur in the citadel of Falaise, Normandy, and Eleanor within the donjon of Bristol Castle, in which place Count Hugh de Lusignan, Arthur's friend and adviser, had also to suffer a weary confinement. Eleanor was now in her twentieth year and her brother had attained his sixteenth birthday. Like his sister he appears to have inherited the Plantagenet beauty, being a prince of graceful figure and winning manners, and had aroused in the hearts of his Breton subjects memories of the prophecies of Merlin and the second "Coming of Arthur." He was removed to Rouen the following year, and there, on the night of 3rd April, 1203, this promising heir of Plantagenet is said to have been done to death, though great uncertainty exists as to the manner in which he came by his end. It is said that when his guardian, William de Braose, was ordered to give him up to be transferred to Rouen, de Braose led him out before the Norman nobles and called all men to witness that not a hair of the boy's head had been harmed. Beyond all is darkness. It is known as a fact that John was at Rouen on 3rd April in that year. Of the contemporary chronicles of the event, one states that John "in a fit of frenzy struck Arthur dead with a huge stone, and flung his body into the Seine," and that this Royal fish was subsequently rescued by fishermen and buried secretly in the Priory of St. Marie de Prez, near Bec. Another pathetic story relates how John had ordered that he should be emasculated and blinded, but that two of the three executioners slunk away for very shame on the way, while Hubert de Burgh proved incapable of executing his master's barbarous orders and sheltered the young prince under a false report of his death, his clothes being given to lepers, and the church bells tolling for him as for the dead.

Then when the cry of public indignation rose high against the uncle, it is said Hubert produced the young prince and that the King was not displeased at de Burgh's disobedience, though his penitence was short-lived, Arthur being subsequently placed under the care of Robert de Vipont, and 'tis further spoken how John, leaving his court secretly as if on a hunting party, came at midnight to the gates of Arthur's prison and stabbed the boy with his own hand and cast his bleeding body into the river some miles lower down. There are wild stories that the murder was preceded by an angry interview, John offering him his freedom and friendship if he would renounce his claims to England, and the young Duke haughtily and resolutely refusing.

In the absence of any official record, all that we can say is that the fact of a murder seems the only point certain. The Prince suddenly disappeared and his burial place is unknown, and the best proof of the crime is that John himself never professed when it might have done him service that his nephew died naturally.

The murder of Arthur placed Eleanor once more in a prominent position; for even if John's usurpation held good she was still the next heir, as at that time his consort Isabella of Angoulême had borne him no heir, so that the sole representative of the heroic line of Plantagenet after his dishonoured self, was his niece Eleanor. Yet she was kept shut up in rigorous confinement within the walls of Bristol Castle. She had now attained to womanhood and was in the full lustre of her beauty. We can fancy her pleading for her freedom in much the same words as Arthur, when pleading for his life, had said:—Ah! my uncle, spare the son of thy brother; spare thy young nephew; spare thy race." But in vain, for her sanguinary uncle was inexorable, fearing that if she were allowed to go free she might by marriage to a foreign prince raise up a new competitor for the succession of her father; and though the French King demanded that if Arthur were dead Eleanor should be given up to *him* with all the English dominions in France as her dower, yet John continued to keep her for the remainder of his life a state prisoner at Bristol. She had no one to help her, or defend or assert her rights. Poor hapless, lonely prisoner! and in the land which was hers by rightful heritage! Even her grandmother, who would at least have freed her from her weary confinement, was no more, having it is said died of sorrow when she found the depths of guilt into which John had plunged.

It is unfortunate that at this interesting crisis we are compelled to rely on the authority of writers who lived at a later period, and whose broken and doubtful notices cannot furnish a connected or satisfactory narrative. The Bretons swore to avenge the murder of Arthur and proceeded to settle the succession to the Dukedom. In their annals we read how Guy of Thouars entered the Council Chamber " carrying in his arms his eldest daughter Alice," though she must have been at that time fourteen years of age—and that he succeeded in getting this Princess acknowledged, "without prejudice to the right of Eleanor." Having once got the succession fixed on his own children it was not likely that Count Guy would do anything to advance the restoration of Eleanor to her French dominions. So we see that while it was the policy of John and his successor to keep Eleanor in durance, it was equally the policy of the Regent of Bretagne to uphold them in this for the benefit of his own daughter Alice, who in due course reigned over Bretagne in her stead. And so the years went by, till Eleanor, worn out by her long weary captivity, faded and withered and grew old before her time, till people failed to recognise in her grief-stricken appearance the lovely woman whom men had named "The Pearl of Brittany."

She was popularly supposed to have died in Bristol Castle in the year 1241, after an imprisonment of nearly forty years. But it is now ascertained that the unfortunate lady took the vows, probably after the accession of Henry III. From a bundle of charters belonging to the Abbey of Fontevrauld, it is evident that Eleanor Plantagenet was appointed by the Abbess Superior of the Nunnery of Ambresbury in Wiltshire, upon which King John is said to have conferred many important privileges. The Nunnery at Ambresbury seems during the rule of the Princess Eleanor to have increased in splendour and Royal favour, for with her advancing years and the Nun's habit, the children and grandchildren of usurping John ceased to regard her as a rival. Here it was that she died, in 1241, at the age of fifty-eight, having survived her brother eight and thirty years, and here it was that she was buried at her own request. For, strangely enough, our famous "Stonehenge" lies within the parish of Ambresbury, and those inscrutable stones doubtless reminded her of the avenues of Carnac, for which her native land was, and still is, famed, while the sombre wildness of the surrounding country may have recalled the days of her youth, in that weird and mystic land, full of legends and traditions of the old Breton saints and kings, the home of Arthur and Merlin and Launcelot du Lac.

Such are the facts that I have been able to collect relative to this ill-fated Princess, excluded Queen of England, who lived a captive, forsaken and forgotten by the English, though in Bretagne her people continued to mourn her, almost the last representative of their native line, so that even now after the lapse of so many centuries the name of Eleanor Plantagenet, "The Pearl of Brittany," is not forgotten.

# Late in Life.

BY A. PERRIN.

Author of "INTO TEMPTATION," &c.

## CHAPTER XXV.

### WHAT MIGHT HAVE BEEN.

"Thou shalt hear the never, never, whispered by the phantom years,
And a song without the distance in the ringing of thine ears."

FIVE weeks had passed swiftly away and Ella's wedding day drew near. She had stayed on at The Abbey for a short time after the evening on which she had so displeased Mrs. Hatherly by her nocturnal ramble, and had then contrived to make good her escape, but not before the date for the marriage had been fixed, the scene of the honeymoon decided on, and the trousseau practically ordered. Latterly Ella had helped to forward matters almost as eagerly as Cecil himself. She wanted to get it all over, to plunge into her new life without delay, and to feel that as another man's wife she would be committing a sin in allowing herself to think of George. She fancied that as Ella Hatherly she would have less difficulty in banishing him from her mind than as Ella Seton, and that, once married, her heart-ache would cease. Outwardly, she was almost herself again, though her eyes had lost their light-hearted expression, while her manner was more womanly, and she was far more considerate and affectionate towards Cecil than before. She had no notion of allowing the restless vexation of spirit that tormented her to gain the upper hand, or of playing the love-sick damsel in any way; on the contrary, she defied her feelings, forced herself to be bright and make the best of her life, and fought one continuous battle with her thoughts to keep George out of them. In this latter respect her sister unconsciously helped her. Emily had never mentioned George's name since the day she had heard of his having left the neighbourhood. She bore her trouble with quiet uncomplaining, and not even Ella could have guessed what a tumult of regret and baffled hope raged at times beneath her commonplace little ways and unattractive manner. Her sallow face became smaller and more pinched-looking than ever, and grey threads were permitted to increase and multiply in her abundant dark hair without any attempt being made to uproot them.

And now, though the wedding was to be as quiet as possible, "owing to the ill-health of the bride's father," Garthwood was in that inevitable state of discomfort and confusion which invariably attends an event of unusual importance in any establishment. Bustle and excitement reigned supreme amongst the servants. Emily fussed, cleaned, and tidied, with a vigour that was distracting to the household, and the Colonel's temper became more and more unbearable in consequence. This afternoon a general feeling of alarm and apprehension was added to the disturbance, for "Aunt Eliza" had just arrived on her long-promised visit, which was to include her niece's wedding and at the same time compensate the Colonel for the loss of his favourite daughter—a considerate thought which he by no means appreciated as he should have done. Indeed, the moment he heard the sound of approaching wheels, he had been seized with extra severe twinges of gout, and calling vehemently for the support of "that confounded ass William," had hurried to his bedroom, and given stringent orders that he was to be disturbed by nobody for the rest of the evening.

Though Aunt Eliza had been travelling all day she was in excellent spirits, brusque and energetic as ever and not in the least tired.

"Nothing ever fatigues me!" she explained, "for the simple reason that I have never worn stays in my life. That's the secret of my good health, that and eating and drinking as little as possible, and I defy you to find a stronger, hardier woman in the United Kingdom!"

She drained the cup of boiling water that she had demanded in place of Emily's proffered tea, and looked about her with triumphant satisfaction. She was a true Spartan in her habits. She slept little, rose at cock-crow, ate as sparingly as possible without actually starving herself, wore clothes merely for the purpose of warmth and covering, and never dreamt of indulging in such feminine weaknesses as gloves, veils, or parasols. Consequently her skin was hard and ruddy, her eyes bright and piercing, and her frame large and bony. She had the appearance of a middle-aged man in petticoats, and her contempt for luxury, ease, comfort, and other people's failings was as unbounded as it was disagreeable. She made her own plans without the slightest regard for anyone else's, and ruthlessly carried them out; her religious views were bigoted, intolerant, and extremely "low," yet in spite of all these shortcomings she did a great deal of good with her money in her own way, and real distress amongst the poor was never overlooked by her once it came under her notice.

After having finished her hot water she took off her clerical-looking black felt hat, rumpled up her short grey hair, and surveyed her two nieces critically.

"Well, Emily, so you haven't improved in appearance since we last met, but eight or ten months does make a difference at your age, though in my opinion the plainer a woman is the greater her advantage. If you had been good-looking, your soul would have suffered. As it is you're an excellent little creature, and your spirit is more attractive than your body, for which you ought to be very thankful."

Then turning to Ella—"H'm! So you're going to be married? Well, you were born to be married, for you're fit for nothing else, and it's lucky you got the chance before you had time to get into any mischief. Men are fools, as I've said many millions of times already. Emily here, is worth ten of you, and would make a much better wife, but fortunately for her the men haven't the sense to find it out. What are you laughing at, you little sinner?"

"Oh! I was only thinking of an old joke in *Punch*," replied Ella with haste.

"And I suppose," continued Aunt Eliza, ignoring Ella's flippancy, "that those two idiots Hope and Wanklin are going to perform the ceremony? Hope isn't a bad fellow, but like the majority of them he's afraid to strike out his own line. His surplices and cushions, and hangings and rubbish would clothe half the children in a London slum—which reminds me I've written a pamphlet against surplices which ought to convince anyone with two grains of sense. I particularly wish to read it to those two men and as many other people as we can collect together. You'd better give a tea-party, Emily. I suppose they will expect something to eat and drink, and then I can give my reading without opposition."

"Won't the Wanklins and the Hopes be enough?" asked Emily persuasively, for she had a lively recollection of a lecture delivered by Aunt Eliza a year or two before, under the guise of a tea-party, when half the neighbourhood had left the house in high indignation at the insults and insinuations hurled at them from her pulpit (improvised out of the music-stool and a strong oaken cabinet) on which she had thumped and pounded in earnest vehemence till the drawing-room shook again.

"No," she replied decidedly, "the Hopes and the Wanklins will *not* be enough. I wish to convince as many people as possible. You can ask the Barrows and the Walshes, and the Haigs and a host of others, and what has become of old Bennett Compton with his Bible quotations and dirty nails?"

"He's married, Aunt Eliza. I wrote and told you," said Emily eagerly, hoping to change the subject and drive the projected tea-party from her aunt's head.

"Well, at any rate I'd forgotten. Married? Who has he married?"

"A widow," said Ella, "with three boys and a friend."

"Very well, I have no objection. Ask them all, Emily, and do it at once. I hate delay."

"There's plenty of time, people are very seldom engaged about here," said Emily unwisely, who ought to have remembered that to oppose Aunt Eliza in anything merely had the effect of making her more determined than ever to carry out her intention.

"No time like the present," she said briskly; "come along now, and write to all these good people. Fix an early afternoon, and invite them to meet *me*, but don't mention the pamphlet. I'll spring it as a surprise on them!"

Much against her will, Emily was forced to sit down and write the desired invitations. She felt very much disgusted, for, added to her dread of the party, and her father's rage with her for consenting to it, she particularly disliked having to invite Nina Compton to the house. The latter had come over to Garthwood two or three times since her brother's departure with the intention of reasoning with Emily over her refusal to become George's wife, but Emily had been so extremely stand-off that she got no opening for a confidential conversation, or the chance of a *tête-à-tête*, and all her little informal invitations were quietly but firmly refused. Emily could not forgive Nina's behaviour towards her in the churchyard that Sunday morning, and under the circumstances felt most unwilling to ask her to tea, though she could not very well help herself, since it was impossible to explain the reason of the coldness to Aunt Eliza. So finally all the notes were written and dispatched by post, and highly satisfied, old Miss Seton announced her intention of paying her brother a visit.

"I think you had better wait," pleaded Emily; "he really isn't well enough to talk to-day, and he is always so much better in the mornings."

"Pish!" said Aunt Eliza, "he can't be too ill to see me; besides, if he was dying my place would be at his bed-side."

She strode to the door without further ado, and clattered across the hall in her thick boots with their iron-tipped heels.

Emily and Ella gazed at one another in silence, Ella with laughter in her eyes, and Emily with despair written on her features.

"What *are* we to do?" groaned the latter presently.

"Don't sink into the depths of misery, Emily! No one will come except Mr. Hope and Mr. Wanklin, who can't resist a skirmish with Aunt Eliza, and perhaps Mrs. Compton, who has never seen her. You said in your notes that it was to meet her, so we're all right. Of course dad will be furious, but that we can't help, and most likely he'll refuse to come down at all."

\* \* \* \* \* \* \*

Ella's prophecy proved fairly correct. Most of those invited declared they had previous engagements, but, in spite of this, the drawing-room became fairly crowded when the afternoon arrived. Mr. Wanklin's two daughters accompanied him; Mr. Hope brought his sister and a friend who was staying with them; Nina, Mr. Compton, and Lady Jebbs, all put in an appearance; and Cecil and his mother, the latter *en route* to pay a call some distance beyond Garthwood. There were also a few stray neighbours who anticipated a good cup of tea and a little amusement.

Aunt Eliza herself was late, for which respite Emily was truly thankful. She had gone out immediately after luncheon to make a round of the village, and was now upstairs changing her boots, having sent word that she would be down in a few minutes.

The afternoon was cloudy and dull, and the cheerful warmth and brightness of the drawing-room, together with the odour of tea and hot cakes, was particularly encouraging to conversation, and very soon the room was in a buzz. Lady Jebbs, of course, established herself in the largest and most comfortable chair, turned up her veil over her nose, and prepared to enjoy herself. She was looking a little worried and discontented, for Nina had been somewhat difficult to manage lately, and even a little trip that the two ladies had taken together for a fortnight, to a fashionable seaside town, had failed to improve her fickle little friend's temper, and render her more agreeable. Nina was very much disgusted at the failure of their plan to engage George to Emily, and also at his unshakable determination to return to India. She was unjustly inclined to blame Augusta for it all, and had begun to try and make the latter "feel" her kindness, which would have caused most women to pack up their boxes and depart with all possible speed. But Augusta was not sensitive, and now that George would so soon be altogether out of her way, she meant to cling to Nina, like a veritable old man of the sea, so long as there was anything to be got out of her.

Nina herself was looking prettier than ever. She was dressed more quietly than usual, and even Mrs. Hatherly's stony reserve could scarcely withstand her innocent, pleading expression as she fluttered up and sank timidly down on the sofa at her side.

"I never see you now, dear Mrs. Hatherly," she murmured plaintively. "We have been away, and you, of course, have been so busy with the wedding coming off; but I have been longing to ask you something ——I hope you won't think me a bother, but *would* you tell me if you think it is better to give away blankets, or food, or clothing to the poor people instead of money? I want to establish a little system of charity of my own, but I am so ignorant about these things, and I thought, perhaps, you would be so very kind as to give me your advice."

Mrs. Hatherly's heart began to melt. Perhaps, after all, she had been rather hard on the little woman who was apparently harmless and well-meaning enough.

7*

"Well," she began rather reluctantly, "you must take individual cases. Indiscriminate charity often does more harm than good. Oh! how d'ye do, Mr. Compton?" as the old gentleman hobbled up and took a chair next the sofa. "How are you getting on? And what kind of winter do you think we are going to have?"

Nina felt extremely cross with her husband, as he began an elaborate forecast of what the coming months were likely to bring forth in the way of weather. It was so aggravating of him to come and interrupt just as she was getting on so nicely with Mrs. Hatherly! She must get rid of him, or she might lose her chance of renewing the conversation.

"Bennett," she said, leaning forward to attract his attention, "have you made your peace over there?" nodding her head in the direction of the window where Cecil and Ella were talking to each other. "You know," turning gaily to Mrs. Hatherly, "he deserves to get into dreadful trouble. Weeks ago he took some letters into Yatebury to post, and forgot all about them! I only found them this morning in the pocket of the overcoat he was wearing that day, and which had been hanging up in the smoking-room ever since. The servants never dare touch his pockets! And there was one for 'Miss Ella Seton' from my brother. I hope it was nothing that mattered, as we expect him back this evening for a few days to say good-bye to us before he sails, and I shall be obliged to tell him."

"Yes, yes," replied Mr. Compton, who had been fumbling in his pockets, "thank you, my dear, for reminding me. I had forgotten again. My memory is getting very bad." He sighed tremulously and rising from his chair started off towards the window, whispering to himself.

Nina would dearly have liked to go with him, but much as she longed to discover what was in the letter, she could not afford to lose such an excellent opportunity of ingratiating herself with Mrs. Hatherly, and nothing short of reminding Mr. Compton of the confession he had to make would have induced him to relinquish his talk about the weather. Nina was eaten up with curiosity, she felt convinced that George had made a confidante of Ella, and probably the letter contained an appeal to the latter to use her influence with her sister and persuade her to think more kindly of him. If this was the case, how lucky that the letter had been discovered before George's return! Perhaps that, and the knowledge that he was coming back so soon might have some effect on the obstinate Emily. She took the opportunity, when the latter passed by the sofa a few minutes afterwards, to lean back and communicate the news of George's expected return as abruptly and suddenly as possible, and had the satisfaction of seeing Miss Seton grow scarlet and turn away without making any comment.

When Mr. Compton reached the window after many stoppages and promiscuous conversations on the way, Ella was in the act of smiling up into Cecil's face with pleased approbation. He had just told her that his particular wedding present to her, a miniature dog-cart, and pony, for her own special use, had arrived the day before, and that he had given orders to have the turn-out brought over to Garthwood this afternoon for her inspection.

"It ought to have been here by now," he said, unable to conceal the delight he felt at her evident pleasure, "I thought you might like to try the pony. He seems an awfully good-tempered little fellow. Do you think we could get away for a drive?"

"Of course we can, though it seems rather a shame to desert Emily. Oh! goodness, Cecil, here's old Mr. Compton making straight for us! Now we shall never get away."

"Good-day, Miss Ella," said Mr. Compton, approaching her and shaking her hand cordially, "we haven't seen you up at Undercliff lately. Been better employed, eh?" he glanced knowingly at Cecil; "you must both come over soon, that is, if you can forgive an old man whose memory is not to be trusted," here his hand dived in his pocket. "'I acknowledge my transgression,'" he continued, producing a letter and handing it to Ella, "you ought to have received this several weeks ago, and it has been in my pocket ever since. I regret my stupidity extremely, and I hope it is of no great importance. Nina advised me to make my peace as soon as possible, and that was really why I accompanied her this afternoon, for we saw that the letter was from her brother George, and we expect him home this evening to say good-bye before he sails."

Cecil's heart sank into his boots. He looked at Ella, who,

deadly white, was turning the letter over and over in her hands, and he longed to snatch it away from her and tear it into shreds before she could read it. But the strong instinct that rose in him to stand by her, and be ready to help her whatever happened, made him draw Mr. Compton into a conversation about the merits of his pigs and calves, so that she should have time to recover herself and feel that no one was watching her. Her pulses were throbbing wildly, and the address on the envelope danced before her eyes. What would the contents reveal to her? Setting her teeth she slowly opened the letter, feeling that she could read it more bravely in a room full of people where it was incumbent on her to retain her self-command, than if she took it upstairs to her bed-room as had been her first impulse.

"It was a wonderful harvest," Mr. Compton was saying, "the best we have had for years. I only remember one like it, and that was before *you* were born, my boy," he rubbed his lean wrinkled hands together and chuckled. Ella heard the words and Cecil's somewhat incoherent reply. She felt inclined to laugh hysterically because he said:—" Oh! yes, I remember it well," but she tried to stop herself, for she knew that if she made any sound at all it would be a cry of desperation. She had read the letter through and was realizing that she had misjudged the man who wrote it, that there had been some terrible mistake, and —that it was too late to put it right! She glanced at Cecil and saw intuitively the suspense he was undergoing. His long thin hands were gripped tightly over the back of a chair, and his sensitive mouth was twitching nervously, while the blue veins stood out more distinctly than ever on his white forehead.

Like a sudden blow there shot the conviction into her mind that she must allow this letter to make no difference between him and her. Did she not owe him more than she could ever repay? Had she not caused him suffering enough already? Was she not almost his wife? And for all those reasons there could be no drawing back, everything must go on just the same, and she must never let him know. Mingled with the confused voices of the people in the drawing-room came the rumble of wheels outside, and a smart little trap drawn by a pony with a shining coat, and stepping up to his nose, flashed past the window. Her wedding present from Cecil! Ten minutes ago she had been exulting in the thought that at any rate she would have something of her very own at The Abbey over which Mrs. Hatherly would have no control, and now the very sight of it brought her a still greater sense of her own helplessness, and the weight of her obligations towards Cecil. She summoned up all her courage and gently tore the letter into small pieces. She took them to the waste paper basket, dropped them in, and then returned to Cecil and Mr. Compton.

"I saw the pony and cart go by, Cecil," she said rather breathlessly. "I think we might go at once. I am longing for a drive and we shouldn't be missed."

Cecil eagerly assented, and managed to pass Mr. Compton on to a lady who was sitting alone with a desire for more tea written on her countenance. Then he turned to Ella and whispered anxiously:

"Was it anything, darling?"

She choked back the lump that rose in her throat at the tender loving sympathy in his voice, and smiled up at him.

"Nothing that mattered," she answered, keeping the smile on her face, and Cecil was too relieved by her manner to ask any more questions, for his fear and suspense during the last few minutes had been almost more than he could bear.

## CHAPTER XXVI.

### NINA'S INDISPOSITION.

*"I cannot say how the truth may be,
I say the tale as 'twas told to me."*

SCARCELY had Cecil and Ella left the drawing-room when Aunt Eliza entered, breathless from her rapid toilette and descent of the stairs, crimson in the face from stooping over her boots (for she scorned the attendance of a maid) and bringing a brisk disturbing atmosphere with her which penetrated into the midst of the assembled company like a blast of cold wind. She seized Miss Hope (who happened to be nearest the door) by the hand and shook it long and vehemently, crushing the gentle lady's rings into her delicate taper fingers.

"How are you?" shouted Aunt Eliza, her bright, piercing glance roving in every direction; "so sorry to have been late, but I walked across a ploughed field and got muddy up to my knees, and then I climbed a stone wall and tore a rent in my skirt, so I had to change that as well as my boots and stockings. Ah! Mr. Wanklin, so glad to see you again, and here are the girls too. What? neither of you married yet? Sensible creatures! And I declare there is my good friend Mrs. Hatherly—how are you? We have both changed a good deal I fancy since I was last down in this part of the world. I see a considerable difference in you, but of course we can't expect to remain young for ever, can we?"

Emily retired behind the tea-table in an agony of embarrassment, as her aunt proceeded round the room, making the most inappropriate remarks on all sides.

"Where's your father, Emily?" she demanded presently, pausing in the vicinity of Lady Jebbs' chair.

"He's not coming down to-day."

"Oh! nonsense, he shuts himself up a great deal too much. Go and tell him I particularly wish him to be present this afternoon "—she significantly tapped a roll of manuscript in her hand—" but wait a moment," waving her hand towards Augusta, " I don't remember ever having met this lady before, and am afraid I cannot lay claim to the pleasure of her acquaintance. Introduce me, please." She stood in an expectant attitude, with a broad smile on her face, disclosing the upper row of her strong yellow teeth.

"Lady Jebbs?" she repeated, as Emily made the desired introduction, "what a very curious coincidence! The only woman I ever knew that I could really call a friend was a Lady Jebbs! Now let us compare notes, for Jebbs is not a common name and there may be some connection. Emily, be off and fetch your father, I'll talk to this lady till you return." She looked about for a suitable chair, and having selected one with a high back, a hard seat, and no cushions, she settled herself by Augusta's side, who sat unmoved with absolutely no expression on her face, though it was flushed almost purple, probably from having eaten and drunk a great deal more than was good for her.

Emily escaped with alacrity. She was thankful for any excuse to get away and be alone, for she could scarcely retain her self-command after the news Nina had so suddenly sprung upon her. To think that George was coming back that very afternoon, was perhaps arriving at Undercliff that moment! When would she see him, and what, oh! what would be the result? Then, supposing Fate was against her, and she got no chance of meeting him? She was always so unlucky, everything was sure to go wrong, and most likely she would find herself obliged to sit quietly at home while the precious days of George's last visit to his sister flew quickly by. She felt almost beside herself, and having no intention whatever of delivering Aunt Eliza's message to the Colonel, made her way to her bedroom, where she indulged in a fit of helpless weeping, while her aunt was attacking Lady Jebbs on the subject of her name in the drawing-room below.

"Well, as I was saying, the Lady Jebbs I knew has been dead a good many years, and a merciful release for her, poor thing! Her husband was an old villain!" Her tone was loud and argumentative, as though challenging her listener to explain the fact of her bearing the same name as the defunct lady, and attracted the attention of everyone in the room, particularly Mrs. Hatherly, who broke off· her conversation with Nina, curious to hear the account Lady Jebbs would give of herself having often speculated as to the true origin of this extremely unsatisfactory person.

"Yes?" said Augusta calmly, drawing down her veil.

"Her husband died soon after she did, though he lived long enough after her death to disgrace himself by making a very low marriage. I must say I wasn't surprised when I heard it. A man will do *anything* in my opinion." Here she smote her leg with her clenched fist, and looked around for applause or contradiction, but receiving neither she again turned to Augusta. "He was only a knight, so his title couldn't go to any one else," she continued, evidently expecting her new acquaintance to explain whether she were any connection or not of the people in question; but Lady Jebbs was apparently not at all interested in the subject, for she only said "Yes?" again and brushed some crumbs off her lap.

Nina began to fidget, and glanced at her friend with heightened colour and arched eyebrows. What did this mean? Was it merely a coincidence, or could it have been *Augusta* who was the "low marriage" in question? The very idea made her tingle all over with rage and indignation. Had she been duped and deceived all along?—and if so would anybody in the neighbourhood believe for one moment that she had been ignorant of Lady Jebbs' past life? Suspicion became conviction in Nina's variable mind, and as she always judged other people by herself, she felt certain everyone else in the room must have jumped to the same conclusion, and her one desire was to prevent further confirmatory disclosures in Mrs. Hatherly's presence. She frantically endeavoured to draw the latter into a fresh conversation, by saying how much she missed the boys now they had gone back to school, but failed, and had to sit wretched and miserable while Aunt Eliza, who was not to be baulked of her say, continued at the top of her voice:

"There was a great scandal, and no end of stories at the time, though it was so long ago I've almost forgotten the details. I believe some people said he engaged the creature as housekeeper while his wife was alive, and that they worried poor Sophia Jebbs into her grave between them. However, as I saw nothing of Sophia during the last two years of her life, I'm not in a position to say positively what happened. Anyway, the woman got a lot of his money when he died, though his relations declared he never really married her at all. However, I don't know what was true and what wasn't, though there certainly was something queer. You must understand that I don't talk scandal as a rule. I merely mention the matter to see if you are any connection of the people I knew."

"And even if I were," said Lady Jebbs in her most refined, fastidious manner, "it is scarcely likely that I should be willing to discuss such a painful family episode in public."

Nina grew scarlet with vexation—she felt she could have shaken Augusta. Did not the woman realize the suspicion with which everyone must view her if she did not at once either deny having any knowledge of the matter in question, or explain what relation or connection she might be of the Jebbses alluded to? She tried hard to catch Augusta's eye, but the latter was engaged in drawing on her gloves, her back slightly turned towards old Miss Seton, as though to dismiss the subject, and a contented smile on her broad face. At that moment Mrs. Hatherly rose from the sofa and crossed the room to where Miss Hope was sitting, an action which poor Nina at once interpreted to mean that she objected even to sitting on the same sofa with a person whose bosom friend might be suspected of possessing a "past" of the most undesirable description. She longed to call out to Augusta to speak and clear herself without delay, and it was all she could do to keep from following Mrs. Hatherly and assuring her that she was absolutely innocent of any knowledge of Lady Jebbs' history.

Anger and mortification burned in her breast. Would Mrs. Hatherly ever speak to her again? Would she be laughed at, and cut by the whole neighbourhood for having such a questionable friend? How could she contrive to get rid of Augusta? What was to be done? and a host of other bewildering queries crowded into her brain. She saw the two Miss Wanklins giggling and whispering. This was nothing out of the common, but to Nina in her present state of mind, it meant that they were discussing her and her "housekeeper friend." Now Mrs. Hatherly was saying good-bye to someone, and preparing to leave, doubtless because she would not stay in the same room with herself and Augusta! She felt certain she could detect disgust and contempt written on the faces of Mr. and Miss Hope. Oh! it was more than she could bear, and all on account of this wretch, this viper, whom she had been so fond of and treated so well! Tears welled up into her eyes; anger, annoyance and disappointment gathered together in a lump in her throat, the room seemed to whirl round her, and at last, to the surprise and alarm of everyone, she gave way to a little hysterical burst of tears.

"Oh! poor darling, she is ill!" cried Lady Jebbs, rushing to her friend's assistance, while Mr. Compton tottered to his wife's side, and began patting the back of her smart bonnet in an agony of fright and distress.

"What's all this?" enquired Aunt Eliza, "hysterics? Rubbish! Throw cold water over her!"

"Oh! no, no, take me home," cried Nina in dismay, clinging to her husband.

There were murmurs of sympathy, and offers of scent-bottles from the ladies, and a tendency to huddle together in the furthest corner of the room on the part of the gentlemen, while Augusta took command of the situation, supporting Nina with tender care, sending Mr. Compton to order the carriage, and assuring everyone that dear Mrs. Compton had been doing far too much lately, and only wanted a thorough rest. Nina struggled bravely to recover herself, well knowing that her bonnet was awry, her fringe in hopeless disorder, and her smart appearance completely spoilt.

"The best way to treat hysterical people is to scold them soundly," declared Aunt Eliza, who had begun to fear that the little disturbance might interfere with, or delay, her lecture on surplices; "now get up and don't make a fool of yourself," addressing Nina in harsh, strident tones, "you look a most ridiculous object, and are causing the greatest inconvenience to everybody, particularly myself. There!" nodding her head triumphantly as Nina rose from the sofa livid with fury, "you see I cured her pretty quickly."

Luckily at that moment the announcement that the Undercliff carriage was at the door prevented a further scene, and Nina, escorted by Lady Jebbs, feebly made her way out of the room (Aunt Eliza speeding the parting guests), and managed to swallow her indignation and disgust until she was safely packed into the carriage.

Then she flew at Augusta.

"Why didn't you speak? Why didn't you deny that old creature's insinuations? I believe it's all true and that you are the woman, and I'm certain everyone else thinks so too, and now I shall be cut by the whole place. It's shameful! It's too bad after all I've done for you!"

"Tut, tut, tut, my dear!" put in Mr. Compton soothingly.

"I don't understand you," said Lady Jebbs, quite unruffled, "do you mean that you imagine *I* was the person alluded to by that unmannerly woman?"

Nina's courage began to melt away. Augusta was so terribly majestic in her injured innocence.

"People must have thought so," she faltered.

Augusta was silent for a few moments as though giving herself time to realise the accusation. Then she spoke calmly, but in accents of the deepest pain.

"It is very hard to believe that you should have thought this of me—the one person in the world whom I imagined was my true friend in every way. Nina," drawing out her pocket-handkerchief, "if I were not so devoted to you, and if I did not know that your over-sensitiveness is at the bottom of this I should say the sooner we parted the better; but as it is it would indeed be unkind of me to leave you now, for I fear you may have done yourself serious harm this afternoon."

"How? What?" cried Nina, rather frightened.

Lady Jebbs lifted her veil, and dabbed her eyes with her handkerchief.

"My dear, you are only a child" (Nina bridled and began to smile), "I am a great deal older than yourself and I naturally treated Miss Seton's remarks as they should have been treated by one who knew nothing of her disgraceful acquaintances. On the other hand you behaved—forgive me, darling, if I hurt your dear feelings—as though you were aware that there had been something discreditable in my past life and were overcome by the shock of its being revealed in public. I don't suppose any-one would have dreamt of such a thing if you had not put it into their heads, and now if you *are* cut you will have yourself to blame. You must not mind my saying that you hardly acted wisely, and the only way to stamp out any possible gossip is for us to be seen about together as much as possible for the next few weeks. You must give people to understand that any friendship you have chosen to make is entirely above suspicion."

Nina sat aghast at this turn of affairs. What if Augusta were right, and she had burnt her own boats? Oh! If she could only have the afternoon over again so that she might behave differently. Perhaps she *had* been the only person in the room to suspect Augusta, until by betraying her feelings she had suggested the idea to the others! Perhaps after all Mrs. Hatherly had only left the sofa because she wished to speak to Miss Hope!

She burst into fresh tears of vexation, for the knowledge that she had probably made a fool of herself, and done herself un-necessary harm, was anything but pleasant, and, added to this she had a secret conviction that now it would be useless ever to attempt to get rid of Augusta so long as she chose to stay, and the feeling exasperated Nina more than ever. She knew she did not possess the moral courage to make a determined stand and turn her ladyship out of the house, and besides she was somewhat averse to the idea of voluntarily giving up the daily flattery, and sense of self-esteem, which the presence of Augusta ensured her.

So, torn by conflicting doubts and fears, she alternately sulked and wept until they reached Undercliff, turning a deaf ear to her husband's and Augusta's anxious endeavours to console her. Altogether she was in anything but an amiable mood when she alighted from the carriage, and far from greeting her brother (who had arrived only a short time before) with the cordiality her letters might have led him to expect, she barely kissed him when he met her in the hall, and betook herself to bed forthwith.

As for Lady Jebbs she ordered a glass of peach-brandy to be sent up to her room, for the evenings were chilly and she had also slight indigestion after the amount of hot tea-cakes she had indulged in at Garthwood, and then sat over her fire in a comfortable dressing-gown, sipping her liqueur, and occasionally smiling to herself with the most intense satisfaction.

George lighted a cheroot and strolled out in front of the house. He was a little disappointed and distressed at the way in which his sister had received him, and he did not feel equal to a prosy conversation with his brother-in-law in his den, or a possible *tête-à-tête* with Lady Jebbs in the drawing-room. His return to Ella's vicinity had made him restless and heavy-hearted, and the necessity for movement was strong within him. How he hungered to catch another glimpse of her before he left! But he had no intention of indulging his longing, for he knew that she was going to be married very soon now, and the sight of him would only remind her of that episode in her life which she would naturally desire to forget, and which, alas! he must remember to his life's end. He put his fingers into his pocket, and touched the little leather case containing the pencilled words of her song, and continued his rapid pacing up and down the gravel, heedless of the chill white mist that was creeping into the garden from over the park and meadows.

Presently a quick rumble of wheels coming up the drive broke the train of his thoughts, and he watched the bright lamps of a trap approaching at what seemed an almost break-neck pace. He was only a few steps from the house, so he walked back and stood beneath the portico, wondering who could be coming with a strange curiosity that almost amounted to apprehension. The vehicle dashed up and halted before the door, the horse was blowing hard, and had evidently been driven at full speed, while the driver who jumped down at once and peered at George in the uncertain light, seemed agitated and almost equally out of breath.

"Is that you, Mr. Peek?" he asked hurriedly, apparently taking George for the butler; and then, seeing his mistake, touched his hat. "Beg pardon, sir, is Dr. Roseberry here?"

"No," said George, recognising William, Colonel Seton's man-servant. "What's the matter, William, no one ill at Garthwood, I hope?"

"Oh, sir!" said the man incoherently, preparing to get back to his seat, "there's been a fearful accident to Miss Ella and Mr. Cecil. I don't rightly know what happened, but they went out driving this afternoon, and Bradley, the groom, he came back after a bit on the pony's bare back to say there'd been a terrible smash-up. Miss Emily she sent off for the doctor, but he was out, so I came on here hoping to find him, as Mrs. Compton left Garthwood took ill this evening. I must go and look for him somewhere else, but he may be ten miles off for aught anybody knows."

"Wait," said George, as the man scrambled up into the trap, "I am a doctor, I will go back with you."

He gave Peek (who had been attracted into the hall by the sound of wheels) a message for Nina, explaining what had taken him away, and in another second they were flying through the park.

"Are they both hurt, do you know?" he asked, forcing himself to say the words and dreading the reply.

"I can't say exactly, sir, but I'm afraid it's Miss Ella. The groom as come back seemed that dazed, he could tell nothing rightly, but he said as how the new pony took a fright and bolted across the common, where there's no road, as you may remember, sir. The smash came just outside Bill Wattle's cottage and they're in there. Miss Emily and Miss Seton and me, we starts off at once in this trap after sending for the doctor, but we had to walk nigh on a quarter of a mile after we got to the nearest point to the cottage where we could drive——" William stopped for a moment to take breath, it was difficult work talking at the pace at which they were spinning through the air.

"Go on," said George thickly.

"Then, sir, when we gets to the door we meets the man as was sent riding for the doctor to say he was out, and they didn't know where he'd gone, and Miss Emily sent me straight off up here, so I never went inside the cottage, and I can't say what we shall find when we gets there," concluded William darkly, who, in spite of his anxiety and honest concern, could not conceal the love of his class for anything approaching to horrors.

"Oh! get along, drive quickly!" urged George, despairingly. "We shall never get there, and we've some little way to walk after we leave the road. What shall you do with the trap?"

"Oh, this 'oss he'll stand any time, tied to a tree or a hedge, and I'll send Bill Wattle out to mind him if he'll go; but he's such a disobliging, cranky sort of chap, likely as not he'll say no."

William flicked the willing little horse with the whip, and they sped on faster than ever through the gathering darkness.

*(To be continued.)*

# BELGRAVIA.

OCTOBER, 1895.

## An Old Maid's Mistake.

By MRS. CONNEY,

Author of "A Lady Horsebreaker," "A Ruthless Avenger," "Gold for Dross," etc.

### CHAPTER XXVIII.

To Esme, the first warning of rocks ahead came from her stepmother, to whom in November she paid a flying visit for shopping purposes. Considering the excellent control in which that lady usually kept her emotions, she found Mrs. Langley strangely nervous and preoccupied.

"I am specially glad to see you, dear Esme," observed the latter as they sat together over the fire after dinner, "because I don't feel very happy about Arnold, and I want a little chat with you about him. How is he?"

"Much as usual," was the wondering reply. What on earth was Mrs. Langley driving at? "I cannot think these constant journeys to Town good for him, but he doesn't complain. Indeed, he is so busy, that, except at dinner and for half-an-hour perhaps afterwards, I seldom get a word with him."

"Does he never talk to you of his money matters?"

"Never," Esme answered with decision. "He dislikes any allusion to business in his home—and for that matter so do I. It is so much better that he should get a complete rest out of working hours."

"No doubt," assented the other. "Still, you may carry your ignorance too far. I am no alarmist, but I think—I fear things have been going wrong with Arnold latterly in the City. Your father has heard a rumour that the firm has been indulging in foolhardy speculation, and is shaky." (Arnold, it will be noticed, was bold when he succeeded, foolhardy when he failed.) "He would have spoken to him himself, but I thought it best you should do so. Men always resent interference so much from their wives' relations."

"But what can I do?" asked Esme, looking bewildered. "I know nothing of business! My advice is not worth having, and if it were, I am sure he would not listen to it."

"But, my dear, the money is yours."

Mrs. Langley, who thought that Esme carried the duty of wifely submission too far, spoke rather sharply.

"You are responsible for it jointly with your husband. It is your duty to remind him that you can permit him to run no risks with it. And you manage him so well, you have so much tact and good sense, that you can easily make him listen to you."

"I will do my best," promised Esme, with a doubtful air.

The warning, however, came too late to do more than excite a vague sense of uneasiness, and prepare her in a measure for the catastrophe itself. For several days Arnold was detained in Town on business, and when he did return it was evident that the time for remonstrance had gone by. One glance at his face told his wife the truth.

"Arnold!" she cried in alarm. "What is it? What has happened?"

"Woods has bolted with every shilling he could lay his hands upon."

Arnold's face was ghastly, his lips twitching, so that he could hardly frame the words as he made the announcement.

"Mr. Woods! A man you trusted implicitly! How shameful! Have you any hope of catching him?"

"None whatever. I don't suppose we can touch him; and if we could that wouldn't bring the money back!"

A long pause.

"This is terrible!" faltered Esme. "Will it injure you personally?"

He laughed harshly.

"It will only ruin us, that's all," he said roughly. "We've been in difficulties for some time, and this finishes us up. Well, why don't you turn on me? I've played fast and loose with your money and beggared you. It's all my fault. Don't spare me, no one else will, so the sooner I get accustomed to abuse the better. It's damned bad luck for me, after slaving as I've done; but that don't count. Better be a rogue than a fool. Well, haven't you anything to say?"

"My poor Arnold!" She came up and put her arms round his neck. "It is all so sudden, so hard to realise. What can I say, except that I am deeply, terribly grieved?—for your sake, dear, chiefly. It is on your account that I regret the loss of the fortune, for, as you know, I never did care so much about money. Never mind, Arnold, so long as we are together to help one another, and keep Dot with us, nothing else matters very much!"

He kissed her.

"You're one of the right sort, Esme," he said hoarsely. "It's like you to put the best face you can on things. But you don't understand. Not matter! Good Heavens! When we must give up our home and friends, and horses and carriages and servants, must stint the child as well as ourselves, and vegetate in some out-of-the-way village or beastly Continental hole. Not matter! Why, it's death!"

"Don't say that," she pleaded. "Things will come right, believe me. When we get away from our old life and all its temptations to extravagance, we shall want very little, I assure you, to live upon."

"We shall be lucky if we manage to live at all," was the desponding retort.

In which despairing frame of mind he remained throughout the ensuing time of uncertainty, when every day brought fresh complications, fresh liabilities, until it seemed doubtful whether any means of subsistence would be rescued at all out of the general wreck.

At this juncture every one spoke of the courage with which Mrs. Blunt bore the reverse. While the Colonel fumed, Mrs. Langley wept, old Mr. Blunt seemed dazed, and Arnold brooded sullenly over the pass to which he had brought himself, Esme alone kept up her heart and spirits. No doubt she failed to realise the extent of their misfortunes.

What did she know of the grinding cares of poverty, of the worries of butchers' and bakers' bills, of cheap, ill-trained servants, of those thousand and one irksome petty economies in cabs, washing, gas, coal, all the details in fact of everyday life, so trying alike to the nerves and temper of those who are forced to practise them? All she understood was that she hated London, was indifferent to society, and saw no hardship in retiring to a modest home where she would be free to devote herself entirely to Dot.

To Adrian Lisle, with whom, after the crash she discussed the situation, she spoke freely of these feelings. She could do so with him, because he understood, and did not seem to think it would gratify her—as others had done—to hear her husband blamed, or to assume that life henceforth was at an end for her.

"Personally I don't mind so long as everything and everybody can be paid in full," she said frankly. "My only dread has been that others might suffer. However, they say that when everything is sold, the furniture, jewellery, carriages and all, we shall owe nothing, so I am comparatively easy in my mind. It is only for Arnold that I feel anxious. He will find it so hard to accommodate himself to a dull, cramped life."

"No harder than you will," Adrian could not help observing.

"Oh, yes, much harder!" she corrected. "Men, you see, want so much more than women do. I can assure you, the cottage he talks of with so much contempt, will amply satisfy me. You know"—with a laugh—"I am the most hopelessly petty-minded stay-at-home ever created. I haven't a single idea or a wish beyond my home, not one of those up-to-date aspirations and grievances and cravings, which seem *de rigueur* now amongst women."

"How about those ambitious views, though, you were airing to me the other day?" he enquired.

"Oh, but that was for *you*," she explained. "One may be totally devoid of personal ambition, and yet care very much for the success of one's friends. Yet now, so far as Arnold is concerned, my only ambition is that he should find congenial employment of some sort."

"Has he any plans?"

She sighed.

"None," she acknowledged. "It seems quite hopeless for a man to find work who has been brought up to no profession. He knows something of a land agent's business, to be sure, but there, as everywhere else, the market is overstocked."

Adrian said no more. At her mention of a small home, a

plan had suggested itself to his mind, to which no possible objection could be taken, and which, he told himself, he could honestly recommend to the Blunts without any suspicion of ulterior motives.

The next time he happened to be with Arnold he introduced the subject.

"Have you any preference as to locality?" he asked, when the latter spoke of looking out for some little country place to which, until something better turned up, he could retire.

"None whatever," was the answer. "I should prefer to be within reach of London, that's all."

"How would Hawthornden suit you, I wonder?" suggested the other. "It's a little place of mine close to the Court, in fact, looks into the park. The agent lived there at one time, until I put a working bailiff in at the home farm. It's rather pretty, a cottage *ornée* sort of affair, lots of creepers, thatched roof, bit of garden, orchard and paddock—rather a compact little box."

"How about rent?" asked Arnold.

Adrian shrugged his shoulders.

"That won't be much. You must settle it with the agent fellow in Wilburn," he said carelessly. "Personally, indeed, I shall be only too glad to get the place inhabited. It's out of repair, but that of course, could be put right for you."

"It sounds the very thing," said Arnold, who forthwith decided to speak to Esme, and take her down to look at it.

To his surprise she went reluctantly, neither did she share her husband's delight at what she saw. She admitted that the situation was charming, the cottage all that could be desired—small, but not poky, cosy, yet not stuffy, and, considering its dimensions, wonderfully convenient—and yet, she did not think it would do.

"I can't imagine what you want!" grumbled Arnold, a good deal put out at what to him appeared sheer cussedness. "You've raved about a cottage, and now that you can have one, which can be made simply perfect of its kind, you turn up your nose at it. What fault do you find in it? It's pretty, it stands on gravel, it's not too far from a station, and it's dirt cheap."

"I know it is," she admitted unwillingly.

"And then look at the advantage of getting so good a neighbour and landlord as Lisle."

"Will it be such an advantage?" she asked in a low voice.

For the first time almost on record Arnold found his wife absolutely unreasonable.

"So it's the old prejudice!" he exclaimed in an aggrieved tone. "I did hope you'd got over that by now. Really, Esme, I don't think this the time to pick holes in a man who has been an uncommonly good friend to both of us, let me tell you!"

"I don't want to pick holes in him," she rejoined. "No one can appreciate his kindness more thoroughly than I do, only that is no reason why we should take advantage of it, and place ourselves in a position where we must be for ever accepting favours from him, for which we can make no return."

At this Arnold lost all patience.

"What do you mean?" he asked angrily. "Who's accepting favours? Lisle lets us a house at a low rent, simply because he can't get anybody else to live in it. Beyond an occasional day's shooting, I don't suppose we shall ever be indebted to him for the value of a penny piece. And if it comes to that, how about the weeks he was laid up in our house at our expense? Do you think he minded? I wouldn't have believed you could have talked such nonsense."

"I may be wrong," was all she said, "but that's how I feel about it."

"Then the sooner you get over the feeling the better," retorted her lord, "because if you mean to see patronage in every simple act of kindness, you'll have a very poor time. We shan't find so many friends that we can afford to turn our backs like this on them."

Perhaps she realised the empty nature of her objections, perhaps she was ashamed of the ingratitude and false pride which shrank from any further obligation to one who had proved so true and good a friend—perhaps she simply yielded because she couldn't help herself. At all events she did yield.

Hawthornden was taken on a yearly lease, was papered, painted and put in order from top to bottom, during which interval of preparation, the Blunts removed into London lodgings.

Notwithstanding her determination to make the best of things, Esme undoubtedly found that winter a trying time. The dull, foggy weather, the dingy dreariness of the London lodging-house, Dot's fretfulness, for the child missed her airy nursery, her playthings and former luxurious surroundings, and didn't take kindly to the change, Arnold's depression—all combined to make the outlook peculiarly disheartening. She also felt her isolation. True, she had never cared overmuch for the shoals of acquaintances whom, at Arnold's desire, she had cultivated. She understood perfectly, that even with horses and carriages at command, the distances between Mayfair and West Kensington do not admit of frequent interchange of visits. Also it is a doubtful kindness to pay a call at all upon a person who can't afford a cab-fare to return it. Yet for all that she was but human, and she suffered from her condemnation to a solitude which, but for the constant visits of Cicely and of Adrian Lisle, would have been pretty well unbroken.

It was to Miss Denison that one dull February afternoon—

"The workmen are out of the house at last," she observed with an air of relief. "We are really off next week, I believe."

"I'm delighted to hear it," replied that damsel, who, though looking slightly older and graver, was prettier than ever. "How glad you will be to find yourself again in a home of your own! And Dot? What do you say to the country, eh, young lady? Green fields and daisies to make chains of, and dear little baa-lambs and great cows with big horns to frighten you, and all the little chickens and pigs and rabbits to be run after from morning till night."

Dot hugged her.

"Mr. Lisle says I've got a nice nursery and a garden all to my very own self, and a donkey and a swing same as at Hackham," she announced. "Will there be a swing?" in a crescendo of delight.

"I daresay. Wait and see."

"But I want to see now! Mumsey, when do we go? Soon?"

"Yes, very soon, darling."

"To-morrow?" impatiently.

"No, not to-morrow, but very soon."

"Why this frantic haste to be off, Dot?" enquired Cicely. "You needn't be so anxious to say good-bye to me."

"Oh, but you may come too, same as at Hackham."

"Indeed I can't," was the answer. "I'm going away myself, a long way from you and Mumsey."

"Going away!" exclaimed Esme, who happened to hear the remark. "Don't you believe it, Dot. She's making fun of you."

"Indeed I'm not," Cicely retorted quite seriously. "I've not said much about it lately, because you've had quite enough to think about with your own affairs; but I've settled to go to my old governess, Mrs. Barker, in Guernsey."

"In Guernsey? What for?" For once Esme was genuinely astonished.

"Because"—Cicely laughed in rather a forced way—"Guernsey is cheap, which, with an income of little more than a hundred pounds per annum, is the chief consideration. Mrs. Barker will take me for thirty shillings a week, which will leave me about fifty pounds for personal expenses, enough I should suppose for Guernsey. Anyhow I mean to try it."

"And what does Mr. Denison say to this scheme of yours?"

"He opposes it of course, says it can't be done, which is ridiculous. Other women do it, why shouldn't I? And then Guernsey is quite a gay place, lots of society, heaps going on, with plenty of soldiers to talk and dance and play tennis and flirt with"—with another forced laugh—"and Mrs. Barker, dear old soul, loves a little bit of fun."

"It will hurt his feelings dreadfully, I am afraid," observed Esme.

Irrelevant as the pronoun was, Cicely understood to whom it referred.

"I don't see why," she maintained. "John has done quite as much as could be expected of him; surely he can leave me with a clear conscience to take care of myself now that I have arrived at years of discretion. Come, Esme, haven't I grown discreet?"

"You have sobered down certainly, but I am not sure that you are fit to be left to your own devices, and I do think you ought to consider your cousin's wishes in the matter."

"So I do," protested Cicely. "Haven't I waited all these months, because John begged me to be sure I knew my own mind?"

"Lady Louisa will miss you terribly." Which statement, incredible as it may appear, was nevertheless quite correct. Lady Louisa had been laid up that winter with inflammation of the lungs, during which time Cicely had developed unexpected talents as a sick nurse, and by her cheerful good temper had made herself indispensable to the invalid.

"Nonsense! Now that she can get about again and see her friends she won't want me," was the careless rejoinder. "If I stayed we should soon be at it hammer and tongs again for want of something better to do. No, don't throw cold water on my plan, which, believe me, is far away the best for everybody, except, perhaps, that poor dear Barker, whom I pity sincerely."

"I don't at all," declared Esme. "In my opinion she is very much to be envied for getting so nice a companion to share her solitude."

"I never can make out why Cicely refused her cousin," said Esme, when informing her husband of the girl's plan.

"Perhaps he didn't give her the chance," suggested Arnold, who never lost an opportunity of girding at his wife's friend.

"Oh yes, he did. It was she who refused him, why, I can't imagine."

"Just cussedness!" he observed with a yawn.

"They are quite made for one another, and I can't help thinking with time and opportunity things might still come right," Esme went on, disregarding the interruption.

"Which means, I suppose, that you want to put your finger in the pie and try a little match-making," sneered her husband. "Take my advice then, and don't," which advice Esme was constrained to follow, for lack of opportunity to do otherwise.

## CHAPTER XXIX.

ONCE settled at Hawthornden Esme quickly lost her last remnant of prejudice against a place which, after her late troubled experiences, was literally a haven of rest to her. The peace so ardently desired seemed at last to have settled down upon her home. Arnold busy gardening, carpentering, arranging and disarranging, playing in short to his heart's content with his new toy, had thrown off his moody depression. Dot, ecstatic over her swing, her garden, and her donkey, ran about regaining in the pure country air the roses and the strength of which the

London fogs had robbed her. As for their landlord, Esme was ashamed of her ridiculous scruples, when she saw how simply and satisfactorily their relations with him were established.

What in the world could she have been afraid of? she wondered. Of patronage? Surely one may remain on good terms with a wealthy friend and yet retain one's self-respect? Of a rapidly growing intimacy culminating in the estrangement inevitable after such unduly close association? Absurd! Where was the unduly close association? As member for Wilburn—for Mr. Lisle had been returned for the place early in the New Year—his visits to his home could only be of a more or less flying nature, during the greater part of the year. When there, too, he could call very little of his time his own. Moreover, whatever his shortcomings, he possessed at least the saving quality of tact, and was the last man to wear out his welcome. In fact, Esme often wished he would come a little oftener than he did, for his visits formed a pleasant break in a life, which was not only one of peace, but also one of stagnation. And then his society was such a boon to Arnold. For as the novelty of his surroundings wore off, Arnold began to suffer terribly from want of occupation. First he grew dull, then discontented, then desperate. He could find no work, he equally lacked amusement.

Unhappily it chanced to be so hopelessly and thoroughly wet all that summer, that tennis and cricket, when possible at all, could only be played under difficulties. And so, for want of something better to do, he took to walking into Wilburn most mornings, and hobnobbing with the townspeople he met in the little club where he went to eat his lunch, read the papers, smoke and drink whiskey and soda. Esme was intensely relieved, when in July an invitation came for them, by telegram, to go yachting with the Colthursts.

"Do go, Arnold," she begged, too much gratified by the attention from persons who were not credited with over-long memories towards absent friends, to resent the short notice. "I won't come, because firstly I don't care to leave Dot, who hasn't been quite herself the last few days, next I'm a wretched sailor, and finally it will be far cheaper for one than two. Still I should really like you to go."

For form's sake Arnold protested, told his wife that Dot had only over-eaten herself, that a change would do her good, and that she ought not to drop her friends. Finally he bade her please herself, which she did.

The next day accordingly, he set off alone in the highest spirits for Southampton. He gave no address for the excellent reason that he didn't know where he was going.

"If I can I'll send word where to write," he said. "Don't bother though if you don't hear. No news, you know, is always good news."

Esme heard nothing, nor did she bother, for he had trained her to be "sensible" over his movements, until Dot, instead of mending, developed sore throat and feverishness, and the doctor, when called in, looked grave and hinted at scarlet fever. Scarlet fever! The very words sent a knife through the mother's heart. At best a long and costly illness, with Arnold away, and oh! so little ready money in the house. At worst danger . . . No, no. . . . She would not allow herself to admit the possibility of such a contingency.

Nevertheless Adrian Lisle, when he strolled down to Hawthornden the day after his arrival at the Court from town, found her terribly disturbed.

"Don't come too near," she said, standing in the doorway, and hurriedly waving him back. "Dot is ill, and Dr. Evans is afraid of scarlet fever."

"And you have been with her?"

"Naturally. I have just come from her."

"But the infection."

She misunderstood him.

"Don't be alarmed," she answered, "the infectious stage only comes later."

He let the mistake pass, and asked for her husband.

"Arnold is away yachting with the Colthursts," was the answer. "I do not know his address yet."

Mr. Lisle suppressed an exclamation.

"Then you are alone?" he asked shortly.

"Yes, but I do not mind. Dr. Evans is most attentive, and the servants are very good."

He said no more.

The only service he could render her clearly was to let her get back to her child, which he did.

The following day Dr. Evans on leaving Hawthornden encountered Mr. Lisle.

"Undoubtedly the little girl has scarlet fever," he said, in answer to the latter's enquiry. "A bad case too, no stamina, no constitution. However, she has the best of nurses in her mother, which after all, is half the battle."

"Ought Mrs. Blunt, though, to be allowed to do it?" asked the other. "She's a delicate woman, and with the risk of infection and everything."

Dr. Evans stared.

"My dear sir," he said shortly, "she'd be a most unnatural woman if she didn't insist on doing it. How can you keep a mother from her child? She mustn't overdo it of course. Later on she'll have to have a nurse. Now she may as well please herself by looking after the child and keep the money in her pocket."

To this Adrian could only reply that in such a case, expense he was sure need be no object, and beg that in Mr. Blunt's absence Dr. Evans would let him know if anything were wanted.

The latter's fears it may be said were justified. From the outset the case was a bad one, and as time went on it grew worse rather than better. For ten days Esme watched by her child's side, racked with agony at the sight of a suffering she was powerless to alleviate, seeing nothing but the tiny form, so wasted and shrunken, hearing nothing but the piteous moans to "Mumsey" to come and take the pain away.

And every day the doctor's face grew graver, while the distracted mother, when she could do nothing else, exhausted herself in frantic appeals to Heaven to spare her darling, entreating still more frantically that, if one were taken, the other might not be left. And all this time she was alone. Vaguely she was aware that Adrian Lisle was constantly at the Cottage, even that she had seen and spoken to him, looking with unseeing eyes into his gravely sympathetic face, listening with unhearing ears to such words of hope and encouragement as he could bring forward. Yet she barely realised his presence, any more than she asked or cared to know whence the ice, the grapes, the champagne came, with which the ebbing strength was kept up. Yet afterwards she was conscious both of the material help given her, and of the inexpressible comfort she had gained in her loneliness by the mere presence of so sympathetic a friend.

The end came quickly—suddenly. Days and nights of delirium, of piteous moaning, of restless tossing to and fro, and then the crisis. The fever left the child and she sank into a lethargic stupor. In it she passed away.

Nothing all this time had been heard of Arnold. It was Adrian Lisle who, with Dr. Evans, made the necessary arrangements for the funeral, and Adrian who broke the news to the bereaved father, who the day before the ceremony at last reappeared. He did it curtly. Any consideration for the feelings of a man who could leave his wife and sick child for a fortnight without a word of his whereabouts seemed quite superfluous. He was surprised at the emotion displayed by Arnold, who broke down and cried like a child:

"Good God!" he said with a sob. "Dot—Dot—I can't believe it. I never heard a word. I hadn't a suspicion she was even ill."

"She was sickening before you left," was the curt reminder.

"I never knew it, at least, her mother was fussing over her, but that she was always doing. She was with her, I suppose."

"She never left her."

"Poor girl! What a blow! What will become of her? How is she? Taking it pretty well, eh?"—nervously, for Arnold had a masculine horror of a scene.

"She's quiet enough, I fancy. Heartbroken, that's all."

Try as he would, Adrian could not keep the contempt out of his voice.

"Poor girl! poor girl! I must go to her." He walked to the sideboard—the interview had been held in the dining-room—and poured himself out a stiffish glass of brandy and water from the case standing there. "Such a shock," he muttered. "So sudden! My God! I can't get over it. Don't go, Lisle. I'll come back when I've seen her. There are several things I must ask you about."

He came back looking more unnerved than ever. "It's awful to see her," he whispered hoarsely. "There she sits by the bedside all day long—never speaks, or cries, or anything—took no notice of me. It's unnatural, too horrible—I can't bear to see her." It was also alarming, as Dr. Evans, who at one time feared for her reason, pointed out. The blank despair passed away, however, as all things, good, bad and indifferent, do pass after a time.

It was only when they covered the coffin with flowers, and she saw the waxen face, framed in snow-white blossoms, and wearing an air of serenity that no earthly happiness could impart, that something seemed to give way, and a merciful flood of tears came to relieve the awful oppression round the overcharged heart and brain. After that she mended and set herself to live her life apart from the one human being without whom she had declared life at all to be impossible. Like other people, too, she discovered "impossible" to be a merely relative term after all. In the meantime Mrs. Langley wrote her characteristic letters, dwelling on the necessity of submission to the Divine will, while Arnold went about, very subdued, evincing his sympathy for her by a show of awkward and rather wearying attentions towards his wife. Mr. Lisle went away after one painful interview when she insisted on seeing him, tried to thank him and broke down completely over the attempt. And then life dropped back into its usual groove—just the same with a difference, that was all. Esme did not break down again. Indeed, she managed to keep her feelings pretty well to herself. It would have been better for her perhaps if she hadn't. She merely drifted into what may be called moping ways, sitting for hours in the empty nursery, her eyes heavy with unshed tears, her lap filled with the child's playthings, her doll, her ball, her frock, her Noah's Ark.

Arnold, perhaps, under such circumstances, might be excused for finding his home depressing, with nothing to do and no one to speak to except on those red-letter days when Lisle was down. But then such red-letter days were not too frequent, and poor Arnold at other times sorely felt the need of companionship. He possessed no resources in himself, while unhappily his wife had long since ceased to amuse him. He admired her, he respected her, he trusted her, but he didn't make a companion of her. He never had done so. And so, as a man must speak to somebody, he acquired a habit of dropping in at a certain cottage on the Wilburn Road, tenanted by Captain Dixon and his pretty granddaughter. It was a harmless enough proceeding. Old Dixon certainly had no pretensions to gentility, but for all that he was an honest, well-meaning soul, and by no means a dull companion.

He had risen from the ranks, a fact of which he was justifiably proud, receiving a commission in consideration of his long and honourable career, had been adjutant of his regiment for two years, and had retired on his pension to his native place, Wilburn, where, with his granddaughter he occupied a neat little villa-cottage, midway between the town and Hawthornden. Arnold, who had come across him at the club, was amused by his talk, as indeed he might be, for the old fellow had seen a lot of service, had kept his eyes open during his wanderings, and loved nothing better than to dilate on his experiences.

Finally, as one cold evening they walked back together from Wilburn the Captain, with respectful hesitation—for he knew his place—asked if Mr. Blunt would be pleased to step in and try his whiskey. Why not? The offer was well-meant. Arnold was a man of sociable instincts. Besides, he was cold. And so he stepped in, and discovered that in addition to some excellent whiskey, the Captain possessed a cosy little parlour and an uncommonly pretty granddaughter. The ice thus broken, he became a frequent visitor at the Firs. A man would be a fool to trudge off to Wilburn in bad weather and short winter days when within a mile of home he could always find a warm welcome, a glass of first-rate whiskey, a comfortable chair, and a pair of bright eyes to look admiringly at him. And then to the Dixons their guest was a king, and as such they treated him with a respect not far removed from adulation. Arnold, to be sure, did not call it by this name. He merely thought himself properly appreciated. In return he appreciated his hosts. He liked the Captain and he liked Clara. He was also sorry for her. She was better dressed, better spoken, better looking than the other girls of the town, too good for the tradespeople, not good enough for the gentry, and therefore so far as society was concerned had fallen between two stools to the ground. And then consider the future of one who was neither fish, flesh, fowl nor good red herring. Her grandfather's pension died with him, so that unless she married she must be prepared one of these days to look for a situation as nursery governess or companion. And how was she to marry? Did her grandfather think she would look at such country bumpkins as Joe Hunt, or Will Philpotts, or any other of those well-to-do local beaux who, with the smallest encouragement, would have come forward to woo the belle of

Wilburn? Arnold, when asked this question by Miss Clara, who was not shy, and very speedily fell into the habit of discussing her prospects or want of them with her new friend, was prompt and vehement in his negative. She was fit, as he assured her, to adorn any station in life, which flattering decision she accepted, as she did everything else from his lips, without question as the verdict of an authority from whom there could be no appeal.

In this way, to the enormous gratification of its members, a mutual admiration society of two was formed, which, if it did no particular harm, was likely certainly to be of very little benefit to its foolish founders. It was all very silly but quite innocent, and in no way worth recording, except for the fact that silliness often may, and in this instance actually did, work a great deal more mischief than any intentional evil would have done.

## CHAPTER XXX.

WHILE Mr. Blunt with the best possible intentions was engaged in turning poor Clara Dixon's empty little head, Mrs. Blunt was spending her winter in a seclusion which might commend itself to her grief-stricken condition, but which was good neither for her bodily nor mental health. Her visitors indeed at this time were so few as to be not worth mentioning. Wilburn recognised the fact that she was not " its sort," while such of the county as realised her existence, were very well content to postpone the duty of calling till the days grew longer and the roads better. Adrian Lisle's visits therefore, and he was a good deal at home just then, formed her only link with the outer world, the sole glimpses she gained of light and life. He brought her books, flowers, newspapers, told her what was going on in the world, all that was thought of, read or talked about. He also discussed with her the line he himself contemplated taking in politics, which was an independent one, until to watch the career she had been more or less instrumental in shaping, grew to be a welcome distraction to her own thoughts, and the source whence her sole interest in life was derived. Was it wise or safe to allow a third person thus to usurp a husband's place, to become her confidant, consoler and stay? She never asked herself the question. She only knew that round Adrian Lisle were centred both the sweetest and bitterest recollections of her girlhood, that he was inseparably connected with the memory of her lost darling, a friend indeed such as in her loneliness she could not afford to turn her back upon.

Arnold, too, encouraged the friendship. To be sure he had the very best of reasons for declaring, as he frequently did, that Lisle was one of the nicest fellows going. But to specify the nature of these reasons would be unfair. Suffice it to say that the transactions which from time to time passed between them, were such as gentlemen by mutual consent invariably keep to themselves. No rumour of them ever reached Mrs. Blunt's ears. Why should it? It was not Arnold's habit to consult her over his money matters. She took her share of work in so far that with him she portioned out the slender income at the outset; so much for rent, so much for wages, for housekeeping, for personal expenses, so much too as margin for unexpected calls upon their purse. Having done this, she took the sum allotted to her for weekly bills, and dress, made it suffice with difficulty—and assumed as a matter of course that Arnold would cut his coat according to his cloth with equal care.

It was towards the end of January that the first break occurred in the monotony of her life.

"Can't I persuade you two to come over to the Court for a few days?" proposed Mr. Lisle one day. "Some people are coming to me next week for some shooting. How I came to ask them I can't imagine any more than I can say why they accepted. Anyhow, they are coming, and it would be a charity to me to help entertain them. It won't be a noisy party, either, just the Burtons, Kestertons, and a few other local folk, whom it's my duty to entertain, and whom you may as well know now as later."

Left to herself, Esme would probably have declined, but Arnold overbore her reluctance. "The change will be good for you, and there's no earthly reason why you shouldn't go," he declared. "Don't be selfish and throw away the only chance we have had of mixing with civilised people here. You might at least remember that I for one should be very glad to know the Burtons and Kestertons, who both have lots of shooting to give away, and might be very useful to me." Arguments which produced the desired effect.

9

Why, unless he wanted them, Mr. Lisle should have invited his guests to the Court it was hard to say. Why they came on the contrary was patent to anyone with eyes in his or her head. For the Kestertons, the big folk of the place, went wherever it pleased Lady Julia, their heiress and only child, to take them, the smaller fry following humbly wherever it pleased the Kestertons to go. Just now it so chanced that Lady Julia's pleasure took her in the direction of Mr. Lisle, and Lady Julia was both clever and handsome, the very wife for a public man, and was getting to an age to render matrimony desirable. Now a man cannot thwart a lady in his own house, especially one who never has been thwarted in her life, and who would neither understand nor submit to such treatment for a moment. And so, if such a lady should elect to claim one's time and monopolize one's attention, what can one do but submit with as good grace as possible to the inevitable? This at all events was what Adrian did with so good a grace that it seemed doubtful whether any effort of submission were needed on his part at all.

"I wonder whether Lisle means business this time?" Arnold was moved to ask his wife at the end of an evening spent by Lady Julia mainly *tête-à-tête* in the conservatory with her host; "looks uncommonly like it. He's seen a lot of the Kestertons lately too. They're all mixed up politically. And what do you think of the lady?"

"How can I possibly have any opinion about her, considering I never saw her till this evening?" Esme's voice was almost sharp. "She is good-looking," an admission made with an effort, "and she seems to have plenty to say to Mr. Lisle, at all events."

Mrs. Blunt, let us confess, was but human after all. Besides to be quite candid, she was not at all favourably impressed with the damsel, who by common consent had latterly been assigned to Mr. Lisle. She thought her both self-satisfied and self-assertive, loud and forward in her manner to men, supercilious and lackadaisical towards women. But then Esme was feeling too thoroughly out of sorts to be able to form an impartial opinion. For the time she and Arnold seemed to have changed places. Whereas he in the best of spirits found praise for every-thing—company, food, wine, cigars—she felt dull, lonely, dis-satisfied, and if the term may be applied to so essentially sweet-natured, amiable a woman, quite cross. The fact was she was out of her element amongst these smart folk. She looked at herself in the glass, so dingy, so insignificant, so shabby in her severely plain black dress, such a contrast to the other women resplendent in their silks and laces and jewels. No wonder no one cared to notice her. A lump of mortification came into her throat, as she wished herself back in her own home. Poverty indeed must have changed her. Why, a year ago would she ever have thought twice either of her looks or the attention she received? But then a year ago she still had everything she wanted; she had Dot—her darling—her treasure. Whereas now—she broke down, and cried until she fell asleep exhausted.

During her stay at the Court Mrs. Blunt played into Lady Julia's hands in a way which should have earned the gratitude of the Kestertons, as indeed it did. They showed their appreciation of her good offices by pronouncing her quite a nice little woman, and deciding to invite her and her husband to stay at the Castle for the next big Primrose League meeting. And Adrian, noticing the affability of these great ladies, congratulated himself on the success of his little scheme for drawing his friend out of her shell, and inducing her to mix once more with her fellow creatures. He also took credit to himself for the self-denying tact with which he had purposely refrained from exciting adverse comment on her by any marked seeking of her society, and had left her free to cultivate those women friends she so greatly needed. It was not till the last day of her stay that he happened to get a few words alone with her, and to learn by personal experience that, notwithstanding her manifold excellences, she was still a member of a sex proverbially uncertain and hard to please.

"Congratulate me, Mrs. Blunt," he said, coming into the library where she was reading, and sitting down with a sigh of satisfaction. "Pat me on the back. Say all manner of nice things to me. I'm sure I deserve them richly. Haven't I done my duty nobly, and been bored to extinction?"

Esme did not appear to concur in this view of the case.

"You have managed to conceal your sufferings with signal success," she observed drily.

He laughed. "Would you have had me yawn in the faces of my guests?" he asked lightly.

Whereupon, to his amazement, she took up a newspaper.

"Pray yawn if you feel so disposed," she said coldly. "I will go on with my reading so that you may do it unobserved and at your leisure."

He frowned, stared, got up to go, then thought better of it and sat down again.

"But this is absurd," he said. "I won't insult you by apologising for my thoughtless speech, which you know cannot possibly apply in the least to you."

"Why should I expect an exception to be specially made in my favour?" she retorted drily. She was telling herself either that Mr. Lisle was behaving unwarrantably in raising hopes he had no intention of fulfilling, or that he was showing scandalous disloyalty to the woman he intended to make his wife.

"Because," he answered with some warmth, "you don't rank with the common herd, because you have allowed me to talk to you and interested yourself in my affairs, or feigned an interest at least if you felt none, so kindly as to lead me to imagine we were friends and that I might speak freely to you without picking and choosing my words, a mistake on my part it appears."

"We are friends, I hope," she said, relenting somewhat at his evident annoyance. "Still that does not mean that others may not equally be your friends, and I have no warrant for dissociating myself from them, and therefore it is the poorest possible compliment to me to hear you speak slightingly of them."

He flushed and bit his lip.

"I am sorry you should think so badly of me," he began stiffly. Then "Frankly, Mrs. Blunt, what are you driving at?" he asked abruptly. "Does all this mean that I have managed to offend you? If so, all I can say is that I have done so quite unintentionally, that I apologise humbly for my sins of commission or omission, whatever they may be, and that if you will tell me my fault, I will do my best to repair it. . . ."

Esme drew back. She considered his language absurdly exaggerated.

"Why make so much fuss over trifles?" she said coldly, "and do not consider yourself answerable for your behaviour to me, I beg of you. . . ."

She broke off. Arnold had just put his head in at the door.

"Run you to ground at last, Lisle!" he cried out cheerfully. "Are you aware that Lady Julia is rampaging about in search of you everywhere? She declares you promised to take her to the home farm, and that she has been waiting for you at least half-an-hour."

Mr. Lisle muttered something uncomplimentary towards his guest, which luckily passed unnoticed, and got up unwillingly.

"Can't you take her?" he suggested. "You can do showman as well as I."

But Arnold laughed, and shook his head knowingly.

"Not I! I haven't the pluck to go and offer myself as a substitute, besides which, it would be no use, as I certainly shouldn't be accepted."

"Would you care for a walk, Mrs. Blunt, that is, if you are not afraid of a little mud?" Adrian then proposed, turning to Esme.

But Mrs. Blunt shook her head and declined the tempting offer. Mr. Lisle must kindly excuse her. She preferred her book and her fireside.

*(To be continued.)*

# The First Three Princesses of Wales.

By CECIL LEIGH.

## JOAN, FIRST PRINCESS OF WALES.

ALTHOUGH six hundred years have come and gone since the father of our first English Prince of Wales, and his faithful Queen Eleanor, reigned over Merrie England, there still linger, notwithstanding the practical spirit of the present age, some traces of the "halo of romance and chivalry" that once clustered so closely round their names.

Historians now assert that the story, so familiar to us all, of Queen Eleanor sucking the poison from the wound inflicted upon her husband by the hand of an assassin, is a mere romantic fable.

No doubt they are right, but still "we hope they are wrong," for we confess that we like to picture to ourselves the devoted wife kneeling by the sick bed of the Crusader Prince, heedless of danger and suffering to herself.

It is one of the many glimpses of womanly devotion and courage that lights up for us the dark pages of war and bloodshed that constitute so much of the history of olden times.

Some years later we again see the "faithful Queen" by her husband's side in warfare, the Welsh having invaded England in consequence, so it is said, "of some ambiguous words of a prophecy of Merlin," asserting that "a Prince born in Wales should be the acknowledged King of the whole British Island." A war which ended in the death of Llewellyn, last native Prince of Wales, and shortly after this the reputed prophecy of Merlin was really fulfilled, but in a manner little dreamed of by the Welsh people.

For when the chieftains of Wales implored the King to appoint them a prince "who was a native of their own country," and whose native tongue was "neither French nor Saxon," the astute monarch immediately promised to grant their request. The Welsh naturally expected that this promised prince must be a kinsman of their own royal line, and in their turn promised to "accept him as their Prince if his character was void of reproach," upon which the King presented to them his baby son, saying that "he was just born, a native of their own country, that his character was unimpeached, that he could not speak a word of French or English, and that if they pleased, the first words he uttered should be Welsh."

We can imagine the astonishment and disgust of the warlike chieftains, but true to their promise, indeed there was nothing they could do but submit. They kissed the tiny hand of their new prince, and swore fealty to the infant who, but a few days before, had first seen the light in the then newly-built Castle of Carnarvon.

The well-known motto of Ich Dien borne under the three feathers so familiar to us all as belonging to our Prince of Wales, is thought by some writers to have been adopted in connection with this episode. These assert that the King, on presenting his infant son to the assembled chieftains, exclaimed in Welsh "Eych Dyn," which being literally translated means "This is your man," though in the Welsh language it really signified "This is your countryman and King."

According to others the motto was only adopted in 1346 by the Black Prince after the battle of Cressy. The words "Ich Dien," or "I serve," being used, as the story runs, under the plume of feathers worn by the King of Bohemia in his helmet at that battle in which he served—and was slain—as a volunteer in the French Army. It is further stated that it was in veneration of his father, Edward III., that the Black Prince adopted this motto with the plume of feathers as his own, and which has ever since been borne by the heirs of the crown of England.

The young Prince Edward of Carnarvon, so styled from the name of his birthplace, did not marry until he ascended the throne as Edward II. It was however his niece, the beautiful Joan, daughter of the unfortunate Edmund, Earl of Kent, who became our first Princess of Wales by her marriage with that other Edward, the darling of his people, the valiant and heroic Black Prince.

In early youth a strong attachment sprang up between the young prince and his lovely kinswoman, who was four years older than himself. A love that on the part of the prince never seems to have wavered or faltered.

It is said that the great objection of his parents to this marriage was the flighty disposition of the fair Joan. However this may have been, the prince was firm in his determination that if he could not wed his cousin he would wed no other woman.

The Countess Joan is described by contemporary writers to have been a woman of rare beauty and sparkling wit, with fine eyes and luxuriant auburn hair; she was not, however, so faithful as her princely lover, for in her twenty-fifth year, despairing to gain the royal consent to her union with her cousin, she married Sir Thomas Holland, who was evidently a gentleman of but small means, for we are told that he was granted for the better maintenance of his wife, a pension of a hundred marks.

The bravery and beauty both of person and character of the Black Prince are too familiar to all readers to need much comment here. "Learned, elegant and brilliant," is he described by one historian. "A mighty champion in the field, courteous to his foes; true, faithful, and sincerely religious."

In the year following the battle of Poictiers, the fair Joan became a widow, and in the following year Princess of Wales.

Though the King and Queen had withdrawn their opposition to the marriage of their heir with his beautiful cousin, only the Queen was present at the wedding, which took place with great magnificence on 10th October, 1361, at St. George's Chapel, Windsor, and, strangely enough, since that day no other wedding was celebrated there until the 10th of March, 1863, when our own Prince—Albert Edward of Wales—was united to the "Sea King's daughter," our own fair and beloved Princess.

It was not only the nearness of kin between the Black Prince and his cousin that made the King dislike the union; other impediments existed, for "the prince had formed a still stronger relationship with his cousin—according to the laws of the Roman Catholic Church—by becoming sponsor to her two boys, and holding them in his arms at the baptismal font, and, above all, the divorce of Joan from the Earl of Salisbury was not considered legal."

It must be remembered that Joan had only been "contracted in her infancy" to the Earl of Salisbury, and that she obtained the divorce before her marriage to Sir Thomas Holland, who perhaps was not so particular about the legality of the deed that made the fair countess free to become his wife as was King

Edward. However, "all these impediments were legalised by a bull, obtained some years after the marriage."

Although the fair Joan was no longer in her first youth, and the mother of several children, a quaint old chronicler describes the bride of the heroic Prince as an "incomparable paragon of beauty."

The first months of their married life were passed at Berkhampstead Castle in Hertfordshire, and at the Prince's mansion in London, which was situated on Fish Street Hill, near London Bridge. At the former place they were visited by both King Edward and Queen Phillipa, who went there to take leave of the Prince and Princess on their departure for Aquitaine, the King having invested his son with the Duchy of that place, and to which he departed with his bride in an evil hour. In the summer following their nuptials the Prince and Princess sailed for Bordeaux, with a splendid fleet and a brilliant retinue.

The chroniclers of that time tell us much of the warm and deep affection of the princely couple, of their mutual happiness and of the glory and brilliancy of their court; but alas! these bright and happy days were all too soon brought to an end by the departure of the Prince for the war in Spain, from which he returned in broken health, and soon after, to add to their grief and trouble, their eldest son was taken from them by death.

Almost immediately after this sad blow they returned to England with their second son, afterwards Richard II., who had been born to them during their sojourn in Bordeaux. After four years of pining, decay, and suffering, the Black Prince was laid low by that mightiest of all conquerors, Death—and the fair Joan became once more a widow, and with her mourned a whole nation.

In the cathedral of Canterbury, where in celebration of his marriage, the reward of his true and faithful love, he had founded a chapel, the Black Prince was laid to rest.

The Princess survived her husband ten years, but though she saw her son seated on the throne and was herself beloved and revered by the whole people—a love and reverence given, not only for the sake and in memory of the departed Prince, but for her own gentle nature and kindly deeds—the last years of her life were full of trouble, much of which was caused by the illconduct of one of her sons by her first husband, and much from the miseries and dissensions which befell her country.

Not by the side of the heroic prince, the beloved both of her youth and later years, but in the little northern country church of Stamford, beside the remains of Sir Thomas Holland, was laid to rest—and this by her own request—the beautiful Lady Joan, Princess of Wales.

## ANNE—SECOND PRINCESS OF WALES.

THE second of our English Princesses of Wales was Anne, the younger daughter of Richard Nevill, heir to the vast inheritance of the Montagues, Earls of Salisbury and also Earl of Warwick, in virtue of his wife Anne Beauchamp, who was Countess of Warwick in her own right. Famous in history and romance as the "King Maker," the last, and it might with truth be added the most powerful of the Barons, Warwick, set up kings and put them down again—as if they had been mere puppets in his hands. One thing, however, was denied to the mighty Earl, he had no male heir to inherit his wealth and greatness, his family consisting of only two daughters—Lady Isabel, afterwards wife to "false, fleeting, perjured Clarence," and Lady Anne, who was born at Warwick Castle in the year 1454. The elder daughter is described as "very handsome," while the younger is spoken of as "the better woman of the two," though in what sense the word better is used we know not.

His castle of Middleham in Yorkshire seems to have been the favourite residence of the mighty Earl, when he was able to leave Calais, over which place he held the post of Governor, to reside in England, and it was during one of these visits to Middleham that the young Richard, Duke of Gloucester, was placed under his guardianship, and formed, as it is affirmed, a strong affection for his cousin, the Lady Anne.

As Richard was but fourteen and Anne only twelve at that time, the youthful duke must have been as precocious in his love affairs as he was in other matters, if we are to believe the account of Rous, a contemporary chronicler, who, writing of the birth of the future king, tells us that "he came into the world with teeth, and a head of hair reaching to his shoulders."

It is somewhat the fashion nowadays to speak of Richard III. as a much abused and calumniated man; the words that

Shakespeare puts into the mouth of Gloucester in the play that bears his name :—

> "I, that am rudely stamped,
> I, that am curtailed of this fair proportion,
> Cheated of feature by dissembling nature,
> Deformed, unfinished,
>     Scarce half made-up,
> And that so lamely and unfashionable,
> That dogs bark at me, as I halt by them"—

are undoubtedly a great exaggeration, are merely the outcome of that licence allowed to all poets and which, we must confess, ardent admirers as we are of that greatest of writers, Shakespeare, certainly strained to the utmost, when treating of historical matters, but with every allowance for this exaggeration, there can be no doubt that Richard of Gloucester was crooked in figure, for Rous, who knew him well and, as one historian tells us, "delineated him," not only "with the pen, but with the pencil," describes him as "small of stature, with a short face and unequal shoulders, the right being higher than the left," and there can be no doubt, judging him by his own deeds, that Richard was, if not very deformed in figure, decidedly crooked in character and actions.

Warwick was ambitious not only for himself, but for his daughters. After he had removed Henry from the throne he placed there his own cousin, Edward, son of the Duke of York with the evident intention that it was to be shared by his elder daughter Isabel, but Edward, instead of complying with these views followed his own inclinations and married the pretty widow of John Gray, Elizabeth Woodville.

In fierce wrath at this marriage, Warwick formed an alliance with George, Duke of Clarence, a younger brother of the King's, and bestowed upon him the hand of the handsome and well-endowed Isabel, and the marriage took place at Calais, but not until the Duke of Clarence had sworn on the sacrament, "Ever to keep part and promise with the Earl," his father-in-law. Shortly after this Warwick and his Countess, with the newly-wedded pair and the Lady Anne, returned to England, where Warwick and his son-in-law raised the banner of insurrection against the very king whom he had raised to the throne, but being defeated at the battle of Edgecote, they made good their escape to Dartmouth and took refuge on board the fleet of which

Warwick was still master. After terrible suffering they arrived safe at Dieppe, and from there "journeyed across France to Amboise, where they were graciously received by Louis XI. and that treaty was finally completed which made Anne the wife of Edward, Prince of Wales and heir to the house of Lancaster."

It seems almost incredible that the Earl should even think of proposing a marriage between his daughter and the son of a man whom he had deprived of his throne, of the woman on whom he had entailed such bitter poverty and humiliation, such terrible suffering and peril, but Warwick seems to have had but little delicacy and fewer scruples where his ambition was concerned.

When the King of France made this proposal, for no one but he would venture to make it to the brave and unfortunate Margaret, she refused it with ineffable disdain, though at last she yielded her consent, by the advice of her counsellors, and in the hope of thus regaining the kingdom for her husband and son. As Warwick had promised that "for the time to come," he would be "as much the foe" of King Edward "as he formerly had been his friend and maker."

According to some of the French chroniclers the young Prince of Wales was both handsome and accomplished and "very desirous of becoming the husband of Anne Neville, whom he had seen in Paris some time before," while another authority asserts that the marriage was "one of ardent love on both sides."

Before the marriage took place, however, Warwick "swore upon the cross that *without change* he would hold to the party of King Henry, and be a true and faithful servant" of not only the King, but also of the Queen and the Prince, their son. The wedding of the youthful couple—the bride was only in her seventeenth, the bridegroom in his nineteenth year, took place at Angers, in August, 1470.

A few days later Warwick and Clarence, for the second time, invaded England, landing at Dartmouth, from which place they had but a short time before fled in peril of their lives. In a few days Warwick found himself at the head of sixty thousand men. Edward fled to Holland, and a fortnight later Henry was taken from the Tower and "brought home with great reverence and rejoicing to his palace at Westminster."

The March following their marriage the young Prince and Princess of Wales set sail for England, but their passage was delayed by contrary winds, and it was only after a journey of sixteen days that they landed, on Easter Eve, at Weymouth. While the weary travellers were keeping their Easter festival at the Abbey of Cerne, their cause was receiving its death blow, for on that day the fatal battle of Barnet was fought. The mighty Warwick was slain and King Henry was once more a prisoner. On hearing these evil tidings the young Prince and Princess, and with them the unhappy Queen Margaret, fled to the sanctuary of Beaulieu Abbey. Unfortunately the Prince of Wales was persuaded by those still faithful to the cause of the Red Rose, to renew the conflict, and a fortnight later the gallant young bridegroom fell, fighting bravely, at the battle of Tewkesbury, May 4th, 1471, leaving the gentle Anne, the bride of scarce nine short months, a widow.

Poor, ill-fated Princess, a child in years, but a woman in sorrow, orphaned and a captive!

Numerous and contradictory accounts have been given as to the exact manner and date of the death of the young Prince. Some assert that he did not fall in battle, but was taken prisoner and brought before King Edward, and was slain in his presence by the Duke of Gloucester and other nobles, while others assert that Gloucester, out of respect for his cousin Anne, whom he still regarded with affection, "was the only person present who did not draw his sword on the royal prisoner." However, all authorities agree in saying that he was buried the day after the battle, "under the central tower" of the Abbey of Tewkesbury.

Almost immediately after the death of the young Edward, Prince of Wales, Richard petitioned the King for the hand of the newly-widowed Princess, but Anne had disappeared, and for two years Richard sought her in vain, for the Duke of Clarence, under the pretence of protecting his sister-in-law, had hidden Anne away, being anxious to keep for himself the whole property of Salisbury and Warwick, that at the death of the great Earl, had become the joint inheritance of his daughters. And this Clarence well knew would be impossible if Gloucester carried out his avowed intention of marrying Anne.

That the Princess assisted Clarence in his efforts to conceal her from her unwelcome suitor is proved by the fact that instead of taking refuge openly, and as befitted her rank, in a convent or holy place of sanctuary, she hid herself in the disguise of a kitchen maid, and in this guise was found by Richard, in a mean house in London, who at once carried her off to the sanctuary of St. Martin's, from which place she was removed to the care of her uncle the Archbishop of York, and in the course of the year was married at Westminster to the persevering Richard.

These facts entirely prove that the widowed Princess was no ready or willing bride, and the incidents so familiar to us all, as related by Shakespeare, of Anne attending as mourner the bier of her murdered father-in-law, and her ready acceptance of Richard, are mere fables.

His claim to the property of the Earl of Warwick, and the dispute between the two brothers, waged hotly for some years, and was then only put an end to by Parliament deciding that the whole of Warwick's property was to be equally divided by the two royal brothers, and that the Countess of Warwick was no more to be considered in the award of her inheritance, than if she were dead.

Strange justice this to the lady who was by right of birth sole mistress of the Warwick estates.

The year following her marriage with Richard, a son was born to Anne, who was named Edward, and who some years later was created Prince of Wales.

In June, 1483, during the minority of his nephew, Richard was offered and accepted that nephew's crown.

On hearing this news Anne hastened with her little son from Middleham Castle to London, arriving in time to share her husband's coronation, which took place at Westminster with great splendour.

But sorrow was following fast upon the heels of all this royal show and glitter. The spring following their coronation, an insurrection headed by Buckingham, broke out after the murder of the Princes in the Tower, and Richard, accompanied by Anne, left Edward at Middleham and hastened south, but they were fated never to see this son they both so fondly loved. The child was taken ill and died after a very short illness.

Poor Anne of Warwick never recovered from this last blow, and her last year was further saddened by the knowledge that Richard had grown so weary of her, that it was her fast-declining health alone that prevented him getting a divorce from her, and rumours of her "speedy death" were spoken of so openly, that they actually reached the ears of the poor unhappy Queen who, in dread of a sudden and violent death, rushed in agony to her husband and asked with piteous sobs, "What she had done to deserve death?"

Richard, with smiles and fair words, soothed and bid her "be of good cheer, for in sooth she had no other cause."

Report also had it, that Richard was impatient for Anne's death, as he intended to take for his second wife his niece Elizabeth of York.

Within a year of the death of her son the broken-hearted Anne of Warwick breathed her last and was laid to rest with much pomp and magnificence in Westminster, but no memorial marks the resting place of the unhappy daughter of the proud and ambitious King-maker.

## KATHARINE—THIRD PRINCESS OF WALES.

WHEN Spain was in the full tide of her victorious campaign against the Moors, there was born to the renowned Isabella, Queen of Castille and her consort Ferdinand, King of Aragon, during a temporary sojourn at the Holy City of Alcala, a daughter who was named Catalina, though better known to history as Katharine of Aragon, third English Princess of Wales, and afterwards first Queen of that royal Bluebeard, Henry VIII.

The infancy of the little Katharine was passed amid the din and turmoil of camp life, her parents being lodged with the army that for so many years beleaguered the beautiful Granada, that strong and magnificent capital of the Moorish Empire in Spain, a life this that was not unknown to danger for our future Queen, for we are told how, in one particular instance, during a desperate sally of the besieged, the pavilion of the Queen was set on fire, and that it was only with great difficulty the children were rescued from the flames.

When Katharine was four years old beautiful Granada fell into the hands of the conquering Ferdinand, and we read that the little Catalina accompanied her parents in their triumphal entry into the conquered town; from that time her home was to be no longer in camps, but in that most famous and exquisite of palaces the Alhambra.

Here under the sunny southern skies and amidst the fair groves of orange and myrtle, where fountains played and pomegranates ripened, the childhood of Katharine was passed.

According to Erasmus, the little Catalina was "imbued with learning from her infant years." It is certain that she could both read and write Latin in her youth, for when in the year 1497, when she was but twelve years old, she was betrothed to the youthful heir of the English crown, the little Princess and her *fiancé* corresponded with one another in Latin. Probably, however, these letters, which were couched in most affectionate terms, were written, or corrected by some of the many tutors and governesses who superintended the education of the youthful pair.

The following extract from a letter that was written by the young Arthur, Prince of Wales, is interesting as a specimen of a royal love letter of the fifteenth century, and it touches us with a feeling of sadness when we remember how short-lived was the joy to which he looked forward with so much eagerness.

The letter is dated from Ludlow Castle, 1499, and is addressed:

"To the most illustrious and excellent Princess the Lady Katharine, Princess of Wales, Duchess of Cornwall, and my most entirely beloved spouse.

"I have read the sweet letters of your highness lately given to me," writes the Prince in Latin, "from which I easily perceived your most entire love to me. Truly those letters traced by your own hand, have so delighted me, and made me so cheerful and proud, that I fancied I beheld your highness, and conversed with and embraced my dearest wife. I cannot tell you what an earnest desire I feel to see your highness, and how vexatious to me is this procrastination about your coming."

Fancy a schoolboy of thirteen, for that was the age of the youthful scribe at this time, he being ten months younger than his "entirely beloved spouse," writing such a letter as the above nowadays, and yet quaint and old-fashioned as it reads, there is a certain boyish ring about it, that makes one fancy that it could not have been written altogether from the dictation of a tutor.

Not until two years later, however, did the fair-haired young daughter of Spain leave her beautiful Southern home for England. Katharine embarked at Corunna, but contrary winds soon drove her back and "occasioned so great illness" to the Princess, that she was unable to start again for some weeks. When she was sufficiently recovered to travel the weather was fortunately more favourable, and the fair bride made a good voyage to Plymouth, where she was welcomed to her new country with "much feasting and rejoicing." By easy stages the Princess journeyed towards London with her Spanish retinue, among whom both an archbishop and bishop were numbered, and with them were a large number of English nobles whom King Henry had specially appointed to attend the young Spanish Infanta.

At Dogmersfield in Hants she was met by the king and the young bridegroom Arthur, Prince of Wales. An incident that occurred on this occasion amusingly shows the ceremonious but etiquette-loving nature of the Spaniards. On the royal party nearing Dogmersfield, they were met by a group of Spanish cavaliers, who solemnly forbade the bridegroom and his father to enter the presence of the Princess, for according to the fashion of their country, the bride was not to be looked upon by her betrothed until they met at the altar. Indeed, it would seem as if this punctilious ceremony were to be observed by the father as well as by the bridegroom, for the king, after a few minutes' surprised hesitation, called those nobles in his train who were of his privy council, round him, and laid this matter before them. Heedless of the heavy rain that was falling and the chill and rawness of a wet November day, the council consulted together, arriving at the opinion that as the Spanish Princess "was now in the heart of this realm, of which King Henry was master, he might look at her if he liked."

And the King did so like, for leaving the bridegroom behind him, to wait with what patience he had, he hurried forward—but the Spaniards still made a fight for the observance of their country's fashion, and the King's entrance to the Princess's room was barred by "an archbishop, a bishop and a count," with the intelligence that "the Princess had retired to her chamber."

But both the wrath and curiosity of the Tudor king were aroused by these excuses, and he protested that he "meant to see and speak with her," even "if she were in her bed," which was actually the case, but so determined was Henry that the Princess was permitted or obliged to rise, dress herself and give the King an audience, though neither of them could address the other except by signs and through an interpreter. Not only once, but thrice did the King and his future daughter-in-law meet that evening, for when the Prince of Wales arrived, the king presented the youthful couple to one another and made them "pledge their troth in person." This done His Majesty withdrew to supper, and again after that meal was ended, he and his son "most courteously visited the Infanta in her own chamber." The King evidently was determined to show the Spanish magnates that he both could and would do what he pleased in his own country. The next day Katharine continued her journey towards London which, after a sojourn of some days at the palace of Kennington near Lambeth, she entered in great state, riding on a mule, beside her, attired "all in black rode her governess, behind her came four Spanish ladies, who were also on mules, which were each led by an English damsel," riding on a palfrey and dressed in cloth of gold.

On the Sunday following her entrance into London Katharine and Arthur were married in St. Paul's, the youthful bridegroom being attired in white satin, the bride in a white hooped gown, and a veil of white silk, "bordered with gold and pearl and precious stones."

After the wedding there followed some weeks of gaiety, feasts, and tournaments, after which, in the early spring, the marriage having taken place on the 14th November, the Prince and Princess of Wales set off for Ludlow Castle in Shropshire. The journey was made on horseback, the Princess "riding on a pillion behind her master of horse."

At Ludlow the young couple kept their court—loving and beloved. The young Prince was devoted to his fair young bride and treated her with the chivalrous courtesy worthy of his namesake, "the gentle and blameless King Arthur."

But the wedded life of this third Princess of Wales was to be of even shorter duration than was that of her predecessor Anne, for ere Katharine had been a wife five months, Prince Arthur died, not having yet completed his sixteenth year.

The years that followed her husband's death were sad and trying to the poor little widow. As only half her marriage portion had been paid King Henry determined to keep his daughter-in-law as a sort of hostage for the remainder due, but the Spanish sovereigns objected to pay this further sum, so the King proposed a marriage between the widowed Princess and his only other son Prince Henry, who was nearly five years younger than his sister-in-law.

To this marriage the parents of Katharine agreed, when a dispensation should be received from the Pope.

Little more than two years after the death of Arthur, Katharine was betrothed to his brother, Prince Henry, and the Princess of Wales left her dull palace at Croydon and once more appeared at court and tasted of its pleasures and gaieties, but the following year brought another change to the Princess—for some reason the King became as averse to the fulfilment of the marriage as he had before been anxious for it, and poor Katharine returned to her lonely life at Croydon.

Poor and alone, the years that followed were full of sorrow to the Princess. Her own mother had died in Spain, her mother-in-law, the good Queen Elizabeth dead also, Katharine had not a friend to whom she could turn for help and advice. Her Spanish ladies, six in number, continued with her, but so poor was Katharine, that not one of them were paid any of their fees. She complains to her father, who seems to have done nothing for her—"Since I came to England I have not had a single maravedi, except a certain sum which was given me for food . . . that which troubles me most is to see my servants and maidens so at a loss that they have not wherewith to get clothes."

This was the treatment received by a foreign Princess, widow of one Prince of Wales and betrothed to another, in our country in the good old times, but notwithstanding this evil treatment, Katharine was determined to remain in England, for she truly loved Prince Henry, and felt sure that she was beloved by him. And in this her woman's heart told her nothing but the truth, for when Katharine had been a widow seven years Henry VII. died, and the June following Katharine became the wife of Henry VIII. and in the same month was crowned Queen of England.

For many years Katharine's married life was happy, but when the beauty which had won the heart of Henry, began to fade, he grew weary of his "haughty Kate," as he once fondly and proudly loved to call her, and with a pitiful pretence of acting for conscience sake, divorced the mother of his child—the wife who for twenty years had been faithful, loyal and forgiving.

Surely never were words more pitiful and humble than those which Katharine addressed to her faithless lord, as she knelt before him in the presence of the court, who had assembled to decide the divorce.

"Take of me some pity and compassion, for I am a poor stranger, born out of your dominions . . . . I flee to you as to the head of justice within your realm! I take God and all the world to witness, that I have been a true, humble and obedient wife, ever conformable to your will and pleasure. . . . It is a wonder to me to hear what new inventions are brought up against me, who never meant aught but honestly."

To this piteous appeal and prayer for justice Henry, after his Queen had left the court, lamented "that his conscience should urge the divorce of such a Queen, who had ever been a devoted wife, full of all gentleness and virtue."

But all her entreaties, like all her love and devotion, failed to win her justice. The decree declaring Katharine was not the King's wife was delivered, and in future she was to be styled as before her marriage to Henry—Princess of Wales.

Not satisfied with this indignity and injustice towards his Queen the further cruelty of taking from her her only surviving child was done, and never again—not even when near her death she entreated to be allowed to see her child once more—were the mother and daughter permitted to meet. But even this last act of cruelty was forgiven by Katharine.

In a letter of farewell dictated on her deathbed, to the man she still styled "my lord and dear husband," are the words:

"For my part I pardon you all—yea, I do wish and devoutly pray God that he will also pardon you."

Katharine died at Kimbolton and was buried, not as she expressly desired in her will, "in a convent of Observant Friars," but by order of the King, in the Cathedral of Peterborough.

# A Bitter Expiation.

### By A. M. JUDD.

"EARTH to earth, ashes to ashes, dust to dust," the solemn words were uttered as the clods fell with a dull thud on the coffin that had just been lowered into its last resting place, and a man who was standing by the side of the grave turned his face away with a convulsive shudder, as though the quiet inmate of the coffin could feel the blows of the earth that was rattled unceremoniously on the lid.

"How he do take on, to be sure," said a common, but good-natured-looking woman, who formed one of the small group around the grave. "He were devoted to him, and what he'll do now, I can't tell. His own mother couldn't have nursed him with greater tenderness, and he that helpless, poor chap."

This somewhat involved sentence seemed to be perfectly clear to the woman's companions.

"He were just that, helpless as a babby, poor fellow, for nigh a year, and must have cost Joe Mason a lot of his salary for doctors and dainties, and he'd no call neither, he were not to blame in the least for the accident," said another.

The man called Joe Mason moved a little away from the group, as though the snatches of conversation that reached his ears galled him.

He was a striking contrast to the majority of his companions, who were of the ordinary type to be found in a travelling circus company. Tall and finely formed, with an athletic frame and handsome face, he seemed to be of a different rank from those with whom he associated. Indeed, he was often called "Gentleman Joe" by the other members of the company, though they knew nothing as to his original station or rank in life. From the time he joined the troupe, some five years before, he had never opened his lips about his past life. They even did not know whether the name he was known by was his own or an assumed one. They could tell he was different from themselves, but that was all.

When first he came there had been many conjectures as to

who he was and where he had come from, but he never satisfied any of them, and they had long ago found out that the only thing to do with Gentleman Joe was to leave him to his own devices.

He was a daring rider, he would mount the most vicious brute and master it, he had no fear, and animals that no one else could ride had to own him master.

He seemed utterly careless about risking his own life, and only laughed when anyone warned him of the danger he ran. "The horse is not born that could kill *me*," he would say, adding as an afterthought, "unless I permitted it to do so, and there is not much likelihood of that."

Proud and cold, Joe Mason made no friends among the troupe; though he was polite to them all, he never drank or smoked with the men, or flirted with the women, though there were two or three among the latter who showed very plainly their preference for him, and would have been proud to have had so handsome a cavalier.

But their wiles fell harmless, their witcheries had no effect upon Joe Mason, and they had to content themselves with less aristocratic sweethearts.

So it came to be thought that the daring rider was minus the possession of one essential particular in his anatomy—a heart. Yet the persons who thought so were wrong, for all his icy exterior, Joe Mason had a heart, and one that beat in response to very varied passions. Love, rage, jealousy, hate, all in turn had been felt by this outwardly seeming non-impressionable man, and they had left their mark upon his life.

Just a year before this story opens there had been a terrible accident at Jewel's circus, when a young man named Ralph Hargreaves had been frightfully, and, as it eventually turned out, fatally injured.

Then it was that Joe Mason had astonished everybody by acting as he did. He had never, as it appeared, before that taken more than a casual notice of Ralph Hargreaves, but now he constituted himself nurse and guardian in one. Poor Hargreaves was dreadfully shattered, and his spine was injured; he would never ride a horse again.

Jewel, the proprietor of the circus, was not a hard man, but he could not afford to pay a member of his troupe for nothing; as it was, he could only just make the two ends meet, and, but for Mason, Hargreaves would have been left behind in the workhouse infirmary. But Joe had his way and Ralph remained with the troupe, under his care.

Hargreaves was of a hopeful nature. He did not believe his injuries were fatal, and often talked of the time when he should be well and strong again, and making money enough to realize the dearest wish of his heart and marry pretty Mina Jewel, the eldest daughter of the proprietor of the circus.

Mina was very pretty, and a good girl, too. She used to perform acts on a bare-backed horse, jumping through hoops and over flags held by the clowns and ring men, but though she appeared in the shortest and stiffest of muslin petticoats, she was a modest girl withal, and no one ever heard a coarse word from her lips or had breathed a syllable against her fair fame. She had been as it were born in the sawdust and from her earliest infancy had been accustomed to the glare and sounds of the ring.

It is scarcely necessary to state that all the young men of the troupe, and, for the matter of that, some of the old ones too, were in love with pretty Mina; but though she had a smile for them all, there was not one of them who could honestly declare that he was preferred above his fellows.

But this was somewhat altered after Ralph Hargreaves met with his accident. With a true woman's tender pity, Mina tried to soothe his pain. She would read to him and bring him flowers, which attentions made the poor invalid's eyes brighten and set him thinking and longing for the time when he could ask her to share his lot.

I said that *all* the young men of the troupe were in love with Mina; there was, however, apparently an exception. Gentleman Joe never made any attempt to win her regard. He was not of the number of those who laid offerings at her feet. He was polite to her when his duties brought him in contact with her, as he was polite to the other female members of the circus, but he never placed himself in her way or sought her society as the others did.

And yet little Mina, though she scarcely acknowledged it to herself, felt strangely attracted towards the stern, cold man, of nearly double her age. She was only a child when he joined her father's troupe, yet she instinctively went to him, in spite of his somewhat repellent manner, when in some childish scrape or trouble, and though outwardly cold he never repulsed her.

But as she grew to womanhood she became shyer in her manner towards him, and did not go to him with her troubles as she had in her childish days.

He took no notice one way or the other, but went about his duties in his usual cold fashion.

Apparently it did not matter to him whether Mina gave or withheld her confidence, she was no more to him than any other female member of the troupe.

Then Ralph Hargreaves joined, and at once singled out Mina as the object of his adoring attentions.

Mina laughed at him and gave him no opportunity for declaring his passion, but being young she could not be quite insensible to such marked adoration from a good-looking specimen of the opposite sex, and occasionally relenting somewhat after having administered a severe rebuff, she was kinder in her manner towards him, and the young man would be raised from the depths of despair to the heights of bliss.

It was somewhat odd that Joe Mason, outwardly so unobservant, should see so keenly the apparently good understanding on which Ralph Hargreaves and Mina Jewel were. It was nothing to him, as he told himself savagely over and over again; if the girl had the bad taste to fancy that popinjay, what possible interest could it have for him? Yet he ground his teeth as he furtively watched them and once, when Ralph attempted to put his arm round Mina's waist, he rapped out a furious oath and walked headlong away from the spot as one possessed.

Had he only waited an instant longer he would have seen Mina indignantly wrest herself free and bestow upon Ralph such an angry rebuke as instantly to bring him to his senses, and make him most humbly apologise for the liberty he had dared to take.

But Joe did not see this, and striding away with a fierce, muttered imprecation, he mounted one of the most unmanageable horses in the stable and went across country at a pace which would have ended in disaster for most riders, but which seemed to agree with both him and his mount, as the pair returned in an equable frame of mind, if one was to judge by their calm bearing.

Joe Mason was the only man that Jewel would allow to mount any horse he chose. He was a past master in the art of equitation, and several of the other members of the troupe were decidedly jealous of his superiority over themselves in that respect, though they had nothing to complain of with regard to his success with the fair sex.

He might have been a marble statue for all the notice he took of women.

Love and Love's ways seemed to be a sealed book to him.

So does the world judge from outward appearances.

Who would have thought that that icy, indifferent exterior concealed a very whirlpool of passion?—a lava stream of love, hate, jealousy, and a mad, wild desire for revenge—that was hurrying the man on to inevitable destruction?

Yet so it was, and the torch that fired the flame had been kindled by the light from Mina's blue eyes.

No one knew this, however, least of all the girl to whom the mischief was due.

She never dreamed that Mason regarded her in any other light than that of a friend, and if sometimes she half sighed to think that Ralph showed all the devotion and Joe none, she loyally tried to prevent herself wishing that their positions might be reversed.

But a young girl's thoughts are errant things; she could not help longing, even while she blushed at the thought, that Joe Mason would address such impassioned words to her, and look into her eyes, with the love-light shining in his own.

Poor Ralph, his honest affection touched her not one whit, while she sighed for that which was apparently out of her reach.

It was the moth and the star over again.

Then came Hargreaves' terrible accident, and a flood of tender pity came over Mina as she saw his shattered frame, and she tried everything in her power to assuage his pain, thereby increasing, if that might be, the love he bore her.

She knew, though Ralph did not, how futile were his hopes of once more being strong and well, and able to provide a home to offer her.

The doctors had said, even should he live, of which they had but faint hope, he would be crippled for life; the spine being injured he would never walk again, but she had not the heart to tell him this, or the fact that her love could never be his.

So he lay, weaving bright romances for the future, while each day wafted him nearer to the Unseen, and the Angel of Death hovered near ready to strike.

Then it was that Mina marvelled at the conduct of Joe Mason, conduct which made him more than ever a hero in her eyes. No woman could have been gentler with the invalid than he was. No trouble was too much for him to take on Ralph's behalf. He denied himself that he might get luxuries for the sick man. He sat up with him night after night, trying to assuage the terrible paroxysms of pain which racked his shattered frame. At his own expense he brought a celebrated physician to see him, and when the great man's verdict was that all was hopeless, no human power could save Ralph Hargreaves' life, he reeled and seemed as though he were about to faint and only by a strong effort recovered himself.

No heart?

Why, Joe Mason showed that he was possessed of almost too much.

It was the wonderment of the whole circus.

In the parlance of those about him, "Why should he 'take on so' about one who was neither kith nor kin to him? What 'call' had he to do it? It was the fortune of war, Ralph Hargreaves' fate might be his own any day."

So they wondered, but little Mina set him up on a pedestal in her heart. He was her Bayard, the knight *sans peur et sans reproche*.

## CHAPTER II.

AND now they were all grouped round the grave of poor Ralph Hargreaves, who was thus cut down in the prime of his youthful manhood.

The burial ceremony was over, the clergyman had hastened away to another funeral, most of the members of the circus had moved off; though Death was in their midst, life's daily duties had to be performed as usual; yet still Joe Mason lingered by the grave of the comrade to whom he had been so devoted a friend.

There was a look of stony despair upon his face as he watched the grave-digger leisurely filling in the earth. It seemed as though he could not tear himself away from the spot which held the remains of Ralph Hargreaves.

Suddenly he started violently, as a soft voice fell upon his ear.

"You here still, Miss Jewel?" he said.

"Yes," she answered; "the others have gone, but I waited for you."

"It is very kind," he said mechanically.

"Will you not come home, Mr. Mason?" the girl asked timidly. "You can do no more good now. You—you have been so kind, so very good to poor Ralph."

"Kind, good?" he echoed, with a dreary laugh. "You little know what you are saying."

"But you were, everybody says so," she persisted.

"And of course 'everybody' must be right," he said bitterly.

"Mr. Mason," she said gently, "poor Ralph's death has upset you, and——"

"Child," he interrupted her almost fiercely, "if I had ten lives, I would give them all if only Ralph Hargreaves might be restored to life sound and well as he was on the morning of that fatal day."

"I never thought you cared for him so much before—before the accident."

He turned suddenly as if he had been struck.

"Nor did I," he said. "I—I think I almost hated him."

"Mr. Mason!" in surprise.

"Yes, I——what need to speak of that?" he interrupted himself, to say more quietly, "but when it happened I would have done anything if only I could have restored him to you."

"To *me*?" opening wide those blue eyes of hers in astonishment.

"Yes; did you not love him?"

Mina turned away without answering, a slight blush rising to her face.

"You loved him?" the man said wildly, coming after her, and laying a detaining hand upon her arm.

"No," she said. Then, shyly, "I liked Ralph Hargreaves, but I never loved him."

"My God!" It was like the cry of a creature in direst agony, and Joe Mason reeled back, clutching at a tombstone for support.

"What is it?" Mina exclaimed in alarm. "You are ill; let me help you home."

"No, no," he cried, waving her off. "Do not touch me. That is," he added, recovering himself by a desperate effort, "you are very kind, but I am quite well now."

Mina looked at him doubtfully, but did not offer to go near him again.

After a moment or two, Mason said, "I thought you loved him. I know he loved you, and the dearest wish of his heart was to marry you."

"Yes, he loved me, and after the accident I had not the heart to undeceive him, he seemed so happy when I was near, but had he never been injured——"

"Well?" as she paused for a moment.

"I should never have married him."

"You love someone else?"

Again the soft colour flew to her face, but she said gently: "You have no right to ask me that, Mr. Mason."

"I have not the slightest right. Forgive me, child, but, whoever it is, I hope he will prove worthy of you."

Mina did not answer, and together they left the cemetery, the girl remarking that the man walked heavily, as though he had aged suddenly.

Joe Mason did not perform that evening in the circus; another item was put on the bill instead of his daring act on the "wild, untamed steed," as the programme always had it, nor for several nights after were the audience gratified by a sight of "Signor Mazzoni's" world-famed equestrianism.

Jewel, who knew what a valuable member of the troupe he was, said nothing about such unwonted idleness on his part.

There was some strange, indefinable change about the man, that all who were in the habit of coming in contact with him felt. He had never been communicative or sociable, but now no one dared to break into his solitude when in this mood.

There were nights when he sat up writing as if for dear life. His companions opined that he must be writing a novel, and they were certain that it would be one that would make a stir in the world; he was clever enough to become Prime Minister if he chose, and they hoped to have some inkling of what it was he was writing about.

But in this they were disappointed, Joe Mason carefully locked away the sheets covered with writing, and when one or two bolder than the rest hinted they would like to know what engaged his time so much, they were met with such a haughty rebuff that no one cared to repeat the experiment of prying into what he wished to keep secret.

There were nights and days too when he seemed possessed with a fever of unrest, when to stay still was positive torture. Then it was, that coming in after a long day's riding he would go out on foot and not return till early morn, haggard, footsore and completely exhausted in mind and body.

But even then, tired out as he was, sleep would only come in fitful, unrefreshing periods induced by opiates.

Jewel shook his head gravely as he noticed Joe Mason's downward career. He had no wish to lose so valuable a performer, but he did not like to do more than faintly remonstrate with him.

"Flesh and blood can't stand the way you are going on," he said to him once when he met him returning from one of his nocturnal rambles wet through. "If you don't pull up short you'll be having rheumatic fever or something of that sort."

"What does it matter?" Joe asked recklessly.

"Oh! well, of course it's no business of mine," the proprietor answered, more carelessly than he felt, "if you choose to court serious illness in that way. You must have been in the rain for hours."

"I never felt it," Joe Mason said, and with perfect truth.

Jewel shrugged his shoulders.

"Queer!" he muttered under his breath, "I wonder if his brain is giving way." Aloud he said, "I know this, a man can't stand long burning the candle at both ends, and that's what you've been doing pretty freely of late."

"The sooner the better," Joe said doggedly.

"As I said before it's no business of mine, only remember this."

"Well?"

"There's no one here to nurse you and pay attention to you if you fall ill, as you nursed Ralph Hargreaves."

A spasm of agony contracted Joe Mason's face at this mention of his dead friend. He seemed as though he were about to speak, then, altering his mind, he turned away without a word.

Jewel stood looking after him with a strange expression on his countenance.

"Curious," he muttered, "how any reference to Hargreaves seems to upset him. Yet they were not much of friends, if I remember rightly, before Ralph met with that accident. I don't deny that after it no brother could have done more for him, not half so much probably, but why he should take his loss so to heart is what puzzles me." And the worthy proprietor betook himself to the stables, for he made it a rule to see after the well-being of his animals himself.

On the way he encountered Mina, looking fresh and rosy in the early morn.

"Well, my buttercup," he said pausing, for he was very fond of this pretty daughter of his, "you are up betimes this morning. I suppose you find the dew beneficial to your roses," and he patted her soft cheek lovingly.

But the girl took no heed of his compliments, there was a troubled look on her fresh, young face.

"That was Mr. Mason you were talking to, was it not, father?" she said, a little abruptly.

"Yes, child," he answered, slowly.

"And he has been out all night again?"

Her father started and looked at her keenly.

"How do you know that he stays out all night?" he asked.

Mina looked a little confused under Mr. Jewel's searching gaze.

"I—oh, I heard them talking about it," she stammered.

"Don't you trouble your pretty head about Joe Mason, my girl," he advised, "he is very well able to take care of himself."

"Yes, but, father," she said, "it must be very bad for him getting no sleep, being drenched through and tired out."

"I suppose he likes it, he wouldn't do it else," Jewel returned in a matter-of-fact tone.

Her interest in the daring rider roused her father to the knowledge that she was no longer a child, but a woman with a woman's heart, capable of forming a romantic attachment, and somehow he felt that Joe Mason, though he was among them, was not of them, and that there would not be much prospect of happiness for his daughter if she set her affections upon him.

"It cannot be good for him," she persisted.

"He's right enough," answered her father; "he's been over most of the world and camped out in many queer spots, I'll be sworn, a little wet won't hurt him. You put him out of your head, and come along and see the new piebald I've bought on purpose for you; it is such a beauty, with flowing mane and tail."

Mina dutifully followed her father, admired the piebald and tried its paces, but it is to be feared she did not take her parent's advice and think no more about Joe Mason; on the contrary she was always thinking of him, and his handsome haggard face was constantly before her mind's eye.

The sleeplessness, the wettings, and the want of proper food, for it was with the greatest difficulty Joe Mason could force himself to eat, at last told upon his vigorous frame, and one day he found himself unable to move hand or foot without excruciating pain. Acute rheumatism had seized upon him.

He fought against it at first, but soon had to give in and take the remedies Jewel pressed upon him.

"Why don't you send me to the local hospital?" he said one day to the latter. "I am only a log upon your hands."

"Don't you bother yourself," Jewel replied, "and don't you think anything of what I said before. You'll soon get right, this ain't much this time, and if you're too proud to take assistance, why, you can pay me when you're in work again. I tell you I'd rather lose any member of my company than you, there ain't one as can rival you. Only you be more careful in future, that's all. I told you flesh and blood wouldn't stand the way you were going on, and I was right; but this will be a warning to you. You give up those tricks for the future."

"I am not worth the trouble you are taking!" Joe said faintly.

"Yes, you are," Jewel said heartily, "it's all in the way of business I'm doing it. Why, the circus would go down without Signor Mazzoni. Isn't there a falling off in the receipts already? You get well quickly, that's the best way to pay me."

"I will," Joe said.

"That's right, lad, no use crying over spilt milk. You look forward, not back."

Joe felt there was truth in the showman's homely words, but alas! he could not profit by them. There was a worm gnawing at his heart of which the worthy proprietor knew nothing—the undying worm of remorse.

Still in spite of everything he grew better, though as yet he was unable to take his place in the ring.

## CHAPTER III.

DURING Joe Mason's convalescence, Mina offered to read to him as she had to Ralph Hargreaves.

Jewel did not half like her doing so, he had a sort of indefinable feeling that sorrow would come to his child through this man, yet he felt he could not very well refuse. He had made no difficulty about her reading for Hargreaves, and it would look odd if he raised objections now.

So in spite of his misgivings Mina often sat with the invalid and read to him in her soft voice.

One day he was so quiet that she thought he was asleep. She stopped reading and looked at him. He was lying back in an armchair with closed eyes, and she noted how ill he looked and how much he seemed to have aged since Ralph Hargreaves' death. He was handsome still, but his face was haggard and lined, and the hair above his temples was rapidly whitening.

As she looked at him a lump rose in Mina's throat and a mist swam before her eyes. She scarcely realised how dear this man had become to her.

Without knowing it a sob escaped her.

Joe Mason opened his eyes.

"Miss Jewel—Mina," he said, "what is the matter?"

"There is nothing the matter," she asserted in spite of the evident fact that tears were trembling on her eyelashes, at the same time turning away her face to hide the tell-tales.

"You were crying, Mina," he said quietly.

"And if I were," she responded half defiantly, "what does it matter to you?"

"Were you crying about *me*?" he said in wondering tones.

There was no answer from the girl, who kept her blushing face averted.

"I am not worth one tear of yours, little Mina," he continued, "such a blackguard as I am——"

"You are not a blackguard," she interrupted him to say vehemently, "you have no right to call yourself that."

"I am one," he returned, "a worse scoundrel than you have any idea of. It would have been better had your father left me to die. The sooner the grave closes over me the better."

"Why do you talk like this?" the girl cried passionately.

"What use am I in the world?" he answered bitterly. "It would have been well had I died years ago. I wish to Heaven I had, then I should not be——" he paused with a shudder and then added, "what I am now."

"But surely," Mina said, half frightened by his manner, "there is somebody in the world who loves you, who would regret your death?"

"No," he muttered more to himself than to her, "I am utterly alone."

"You have no mother?"

"Oh!"—starting—"do not talk of her! I—I cannot bear it!"

"Forgive me," Mina said. "I did not know that she was dead."

"Dead to me," he murmured, but so low that Mina did not catch the whispered words. "Dead to me—and by my own act!"

"But there are others," she said gently.

"Others?" he echoed. "I know of none who would care were I to die this minute, and I would not have it otherwise."

"You are unkind. We, that is father, would care and——"

Joe Mason started as if he were shot, as his eyes fell on the downcast, tearful face.

"You!" he cried, seizing her wrist in a grip that all unconsciously hurt the tender flesh. "You! Oh God! I never dreamed of this. You—you care for me?"

"I think I have loved you always, Joe," she said in faltering tones. "Ralph never touched my heart, but you——" her eyes spoke the rest which her tongue could not put into words.

With a heavy groan Joe Mason dropped his head upon his hands.

"Retribution has come!" he cried hoarsely. "Ralph Hargreaves, you are terribly avenged!"

Mina was alarmed.

"You are ill!" she exclaimed, "let me call some one to your help."

But he stayed her with his hand.

"Call no one," he said. "I deserve my punishment; but you—you—when I think of you, it seems more than I can bear. The innocent must suffer for the guilty."

Mina looked at him doubtingly. She thought he must be delirious to talk in this strange fashion.

"I am sure you are worse," she said.

"I am sick at heart, would that I were sick unto death. Pray for me, child, pray that I may be soon released."

"I do pray for you always," she answered simply.

"The prayers of the innocent may be heard—as for me I dare not pray."

"I must go now," Mina said, "it is time to dress for the circus. Lie down, rest and sleep, you will be better after it, and these morbid fancies will fly away," and she laid her hand gently and soothingly on his bowed head.

"May God bless you, Mina," he cried brokenly, "though the blessings of such a wretch as I, can be of little avail."

Slowly and lingeringly Mina left him after looking back, but he never raised his head from where it was bowed upon his arms till the door had closed behind her.

Then with a heavy groan he dragged himself up. "I must go away," he cried in despair, "away, anywhere from her pure presence. She loves me, and the love that might have been my salvation comes too late. Oh! my punishment is heavy, bitter, yet it is not greater than the crime. If I could only end it all. Ralph Hargreaves, how gladly would I change places with you. If giving my life would restore yours, I would give it ten times over were it in my power. But it is useless, you are in your grave and I must live on, accursed. Doubly cursed now in the knowledge that she loves me."

Joe Mason was quite sincere in his resolution to go away, but Fate was against him.

In the first place the illness had pulled him down more than he had any idea of, and any prolonged exertion fatigued him so that he was forced to remain inactive where he was for some time longer.

In the second place, when the old strength began slowly to return to him, and he broached the subject of leaving to Jewel, the latter would not hear of it. "It was preposterous, what reason had he for wanting to leave? None, of course, therefore he, Jewel, wished to hear no more of it."

In spite of this, however, Joe determined to leave as soon as he was able. "I must go," was his constant inward cry. "I have brought harm enough on her innocent head already, no further harm shall come to her through me. When I am away, she will soon forget her fancy for me. She does not know, she never shall know that I love her, that it was that love drove me to crime. I will go away lest more evil befal her. I cannot, I dare not, stay near her lest I should betray my secret. And knowing what I know I could never clasp her in my arms. I have forfeited the right that might have been mine to kiss her on the lips. If I could only roll back Time and stand where I did two years ago! But it is useless, I must accept the inevitable, there is no one to blame but myself. Yet how shall I bear with the horror of my life? It is maddening, and it may last for years. Never that, rather than that would I take my own life. Moralists may prate about the sin of so doing, but surely one has a right to end one's life when it becomes as burdensome as mine."

One of the reasons why Jewel was anxious to retain Joe's services was, that some of the local magnates had signified their intention of patronizing his show on a certain date, and the proprietor wished to show off all the talent of his establishment, but he felt a certain hesitation about asking "Signor Mazzoni" to take his accustomed place in the bill, as he was scarcely recovered yet.

However, before the performance, Gentleman Joe announced his intention of performing.

Jewel was delighted that he was spared the necessity of asking him to do so. "By the way," he said, "which horse will you have for the fire trick? Blueskin is lame, and it will not do to put him in the ring. I think Gladiator will be the next best, he is quiet, but of course if you wish Firefly——"

"I will ride none of those."

"But they are the only ones that will stand the flame. Firefly is the most dashing, but then he is hard to manage; however, you can easily master him."

"I shall not ride Firefly."

"Then it must be Gladiator."

"It will *not* be Gladiator. I shall ride the Fire Demon."

"What?" said the proprietor, as though he could not believe his ears.

"I shall ride the Fire Demon—or none."

"But—but," stammered Jewel; "you know he is a veritable Demon if he but smells fire, he will never face the blaze."

"He shall, for once in his life. To-night he shall in truth be a Fire Demon."

"Are you mad?" gasped Jewel, "already he has cost one man his life, with my consent he shall never kill another."

A spasm crossed Mason's face at this allusion, but there was a glitter in his eyes as he said, "I ride the Fire Demon to-night," and turned away without another word.

"It is suicide," murmured Jewel to himself. "He could manage him straight enough except for the fire, the other was not a patch upon him for horsemanship. I should not fear but for the blaze. I wonder what's made him so set upon riding the Demon to-night, he seemed scarcely able to bear the horse since it threw poor Hargreaves. I know what," as a sudden thought struck him, "I'll tell the men to wet the furze so that it won't light, he'll be obliged to go over the hurdles without it. I wish I'd had the brute killed. I had a mind to, only he cost a mint of money and is such a perfect specimen of horseflesh; however I'll tell the men and make it all safe," with which comforting reflection Jewel went to superintend the various arrangements for the evening.

That was a memorable night for Jewel's Circus, every seat was taken and each member of the troupe outvied himself and others in his efforts. The applause was loud and frequent as, one after another, daring feats were performed. Mina came in for her share of approbation when her graceful act on the bare-backed steed was over.

Then came "Signor Mazzoni's" turn. Never, in spite of recent illness, had he ridden as he rode that night. Man and horse formed a picture, so perfect were they at all points, so wonderfully matched, though, as it was afterwards remembered, in the eyes of both glittered a demoniac glare.

The applause was more frantic than ever, as dangerous feats were performed by the pair with most consummate ease. It seemed as though one spirit pervaded them both, the magnificent animal obeying the slightest hint from his rider, and behaving in most perfect fashion. Even Jewel breathed more freely; he had never seen the Fire Demon in such a complaisant mood, and he hoped the last feat of all would be as safely got through as the others.

High hurdles were placed at distances apart, then were covered with furze and brushwood, which was to be set on fire, and horse and rider were to jump in succession through the blazing flames.

To Jewel's consternation he saw that the furze ignited readily. In the hurry the men had forgotten his instructions about damping it.

It was too late to do anything now, and it was with trepidation that he watched to see the result. For the first time that evening the Demon showed temper; he refused to go near the blazing furze. Then began a struggle between man and beast for mastery that held the audience spell-bound.

With dogged determination, Mason made the horse approach the nearest hurdle, but just as he reached it the animal either swerved aside or reared on its hind legs, pawing the air with its front ones and snorting with rage and terror.

Still the fight went on, and bringing down his heavy whip upon the Demon's head, Joe by a mighty effort almost lifted the animal over the first hurdle and, before it could recover its astonishment, over the second one likewise.

A most deafening round of applause greeted this feat, but at the third hurdle the Demon reared straight up, and with a sickening thud fell over backwards with its rider beneath it.

For one moment there was an appalled silence, then shrieks, cries and groans rang out, women fainted and strong men turned sick as they looked at that sight in the arena, the brute struggling to rise and falling back again and again upon its luckless rider, while the flames cast a lurid glow upon the scene.

With a wild scream, a white figure, still in all its bravery of satin skirts and pink tights, rushed into the arena. It was

Mina, who, regardless of her own danger from those iron hoofs, strove to drag the motionless figure to a place of safety.

In an instant, all was wild confusion, a doctor sprang into the ring and laid his hand upon the heart. "Dead," was his verdict after a very brief survey, and with a sobbing groan, Mina fell senseless across the lifeless body of Joe Mason.

Poor little Mina, her love-dream was ended.

The Fire Demon's back was broken; he was put out of his misery before he was dragged from the ring.

When they were looking over Joe Mason's effects they came upon a packet of manuscript labelled: "To be given to Mr. Jewel after my death." Inside it was headed: "My confession."

It was Jewel who opened and read it, and who when he had finished it put it in the fire.

"No use making it known," he said sorrowfully to himself, "it would only add to her pain. My girl is young, she will get over the fancy in time. To think that he should have done that. Ah! well, jealousy is cruel as the grave. Poor chap, he has gone to his last account and his family will never know. I always thought he was a gentleman. Who was he, I wonder?"

But conjecture was of no avail, Joe Mason had taken the secret of his identity with him into the other world.

Though Jewel burned his confession we are privileged to read it. This is it:

"I am a murderer! Yes, the hideous word is written on my heart as well as on this paper, and cannot be erased. I murdered Ralph Hargreaves as surely as though I had shot or stabbed him, and jealousy drove me to do it. No matter now who I was, suffice it to say that my family hold up their heads with the highest in the land—or did, till I disgraced them. But into that I will not, I dare not, go. I changed my name and sank my identity in that of Joe Mason; they will never know that my nameless grave covers one of their race. But this is digressing. I tried one thing and another till I fell into a groove which suited me. I had always been the crack rider in my regiment, and that was a crack cavalry one, so the life in the circus suited me. I went on very well till Hargreaves joined, and then suddenly I awoke to the fact of what a lovely girl Mina Jewel was. I had not thought much of her before, she was only a child when I joined, but when I listened to his ravings about her, I knew that I loved her myself. I sometimes laughed grimly as I thought of what my proud old father would say if I presented a circus-girl to him as his daughter-in-law, but I had done with the old life for ever; if I married Mina it would be as Joe Mason, one in her own rank of life. Then jealousy took hold of me. I saw how she laughed and joked with him, and I thought she loved him. I was wrong, terribly wrong, but I did not know this till we stood by his grave the day he was buried. She shall never know of my love for her and how it made me a murderer, that I swear. I was driven nearly mad by Hargreaves' ravings about his love, and how he thought it was returned, and then one day the Devil tempted me and I fell. Ralph was not much of a horseman, though he thought he was, and something put it into his head that he could ride the horses reserved for me. I pretended to dissuade him from the project, but only in such a way as to make him more determined to do it. On that fatal day he gained Jewel's consent to his riding the Fire Demon, but only on condition that he did not attempt to jump him. I knew it was murder—I knew that horse would acknowledge no one but me for his master, yet I let him mount without a word of warning. I felt a kind of exultation that my enemy would be removed from my path. Oh! God, that day—shall I ever forget it? I see his white face constantly before me, drawn and pale with suffering. The moment the deed was done a revulsion of feeling took place, and I would have given worlds, had I them, to undo the past. You know how I tended him, but you do *not* know that your praises burned me like red-hot fire. In my heart I knew I was his murderer. What I suffered during that year none can tell. Perhaps my punishment will form some little expiation for my sin, and now lately I have learned that she, Mina, cares for me, and I—I dare not look into her pure eyes knowing what is in my heart. Surely the torments of the damned cannot be worse than those I suffer. Sometimes I had a faint hope that he might recover, that the horrible curse of murder might be lifted from me, but it was not to be, and in my own eyes I stand a convicted criminal. But this torture will not last much longer. Last evening I dreamed of him, he did not look stern, only sorrowful. 'I am waiting for you,' he said, and I know it is my summons. I only pray that little Mina may never know what kind of a man it was upon whom she bestowed the treasure of her love."

Here the document ended, and those last words had much to do with Mina's father committing it to the flames.

\* \* \* \* \* \* \*

In the cemetery, not far from where Ralph Hargreaves rests, is a simple cross, but simple as it is, persons often stop and wonder at the inscription upon it which reads as follows:

J. M. Aged 31,
Died, July 25th, 18—.

" Priez pour lui."
"Qui a beaucoup souffert,
Sera beaucoup pardonné."

## Autumn Clouds.

THE cloud angel sighed as the order reached her to let the grey clouds go free! It was always a trial to her gentle nature to see the wild havoc they wrought, when with the fierce wind as coachman they swept in swift flight along—for four-and-twenty hours, and then the sky was to be dressed in blue, with tiny flecks of white.

Out they came, in size and colour varying according to age, and carefully the angel examined their water reservoirs, and saw all the syringes were in working order. Right in the middle of the powerful dark grey masses moved the thunder-car, and when disputes arose around as to their speed or height, these heavy bodies flew at each other to such purpose that out flashed the bright, wild lightning's flame, and the angry roar of the tempest's voice.

With what a rush and spring they bounded forward, rejoicing in their much-prized liberty. They had not had a good race for many a long day; indeed they had only been exercised once or twice for nearly six weeks, and it was no pleasure to the stormy greys just to be driven wildly forward and round home again, without pause or rest. No! what *they* enjoyed was the angry clamour of an awful storm, when they had dropped so low they hung like a great pall over the earth beneath, and drenched the land from end to end with their great squirts; watching with keen pleasure the oceans rise to meet them, with crested waves and thundering surf, and all the forms of life below, animate or inanimate, bowing in dread and fear. Often and often when so engaged in real sport and pleasure to them, the recall had sounded most unwelcomely, and very, very reluctantly had they ceased their pleasant game, and in disjointed groups mounted slowly and lingeringly to their home above, meeting half way their white-robed brethren, with their edges tipped with sunlight, carrying warmth and hope to the drenched land below.

So on this glad day to them, out they came, passing the angel 'n splendid order, with all their torn ·edges mended, and their colours smooth and unblotched. The last to sally forth was a tiny soft grey, who bowed joyously to the sad-faced angel. "You said I should go to-day, dear friend; I have been looking forward to my trip so long."

"Remember you keep the sun on your edges as long as you can, and never do any needless harm! You are very young to go on such an errand. I shall keep an eye upon you, and in four-and-twenty hours the recall will sound!"

"Am I to have any peep-holes?" said the sun as the clouds swept over his face. "Let me know when a rainbow is required."

"Part in sunder, kind friends, now and then, that I may touch up your sharp edges for you; the effect will be all the greater, and I hate being out of the fun," whispered the sleepy moon. On, on in mad joy raced the storm's messengers; and then the wind relaxed the reins, and down lower and lower they dropped. The little cloud felt giddy and breathless at first, and got left a trifle behind. "Now I must leave you," whispered the last sunbeam. "You have your work to do. Farewell."

Slower and slower the rate became, and the ranks began closing up in a hurry; the little cloud caught hold of a friend, and waited for what would happen.

Below lay a large and populous town, whose streets were full of evil smells, and where water had long run short. The poor and the feeble had suffered greatly; the rich could still buy their water, and the strong fetch it from afar, but in the poor courts and rookeries, fever was raging terribly, and in the last few days an awful whisper had spread that dread pestilence in the shape of cholera had broken out!

Strikes were everywhere about, want and misery frequent household guests.

In the church of "All Saints" day after day the prayer had gone up for the blessed rain, and only this morning as he went his round old Mr. Fortescue had scanned the blue ether above, and his brave heart had sunk in fear as he watched that Italian sky, as to what would befall if the drought lasted much longer. To him his people looked for help for body and soul, and all honour be to him!—so far they had never looked in vain, but at what a cost God and himself only knew!

His only daughter lay ill—dying—they said of the awful fever, and as she tossed from side to side, and moaned in her weakness and pain, the father's heart felt broken, for money was very scarce, he could not provide her with the comforts she really needed most.

The room was hot and stifling, and yet if the window was opened the smells from the ill-drained streets adjacent were so offensive they dared not run the risk.

On a stipend of £150 and no private means the margin in case of need could but be small, and of late, with starvation around, the reserve, and more, had long been exceeded. There was not much of luxury in the home, and the larder was painfully bare.

"I shall not be in for lunch," said the vicar as he left his home. "Miss Irene will like a little soup; can you manage it?"

"Certainly, sir, we had a sheep's head yesterday, and I can taste it up nicely for her, never fear. How bad your cough is; must you go out?"

"Indeed I must, old Granny Hughes is passing fast, and they have just sent from the Smiths' to say the poor baby is dying for want of nourishment."

"Sir, would it be any sin to use a bottle of the communion wine? We have but a wine-glass of brandy left. I *must* keep that for Miss Irene."

"No sin in dire need, Jane, perhaps, but unless absolutely compelled, I must not do it; there, my good soul, don't fret, with you to nurse her, Miss Irene is well off."

His hand was on the latch when again Jane stopped him:

"For the love of heaven, don't go fasting into the Friar's Court; they have fires at each end now, and a black flag flying —for Miss Irene's sake."

"Jane, I am *surprised* at you—would you have me turn coward? Nay, nay," as he saw the worn face quiver, "I am as safe in Friar's Court as here! *I* will sit up to-night, you are tired out!"

"Dr. Hunt said he expected the crisis to-night, sir, I meant to tell you."

"Fetch me a crust of bread, pray, if it will make you happier."

Out into the street passed the old man with shabby coat and frayed linen indeed, but a heart as brave and true as ever beat in human frame.

With a start he saw the clouds were gathering up—nearer and

nearer they came—surely the rain was coming. Into his church he stepped as he passed the ever open door, and there at the altar rail, asked for help in this hour of need.

Then down that poor narrow court, with policemen on guard at each end. Not him would they dare to stop, as they touched their helmets in salute, and watched his unfaltering steps.

"It is a spasm of the heart, I fear, sir," said heart-broken Mrs. Smith; "if I had but a drop of brandy, I think I could save her yet."

Was it the tempter's voice that sounded so loud in his ears? "You have but the one wine glass—keep *that* for your daughter's need."

Five minutes later, Constable Burns of the "A" division, handed Jane a small folded paper, and then in another five, a grateful mother looked up in her vicar's face and blessed him for the life preserved!

\* \* \* \* \* \* \*

"You are the youngest—begin." The whisper travelled along until it stopped at the little grey cloud. "Yours can be only summer rain; we will back you up well—make haste."

Gently the soft drops fell, hardly touching the old man's coat, as he went farther down the court, and in a very few minutes, jugs, basins, pots, kettles and cans—chipped, ugly and old, were put out from every door and window to catch the pure drops as they fell. Lower and lower dropped the clouds, as one by one their fountains began to play on the sun-baked earth below.

"It may save us yet," the doctors said, "if only it lasts long enough—a week's rain would be the thing!"

"A week," whispered the tiny cloud, "dear, dear, I must take a message back when we go home, and pray to return again."

His neighbour gave him a slight jostle.

"Hadn't you better wait and see?—these mortals can't judge for themselves, and in the meantime, your spray wants seeing to; you had better hold firmly on to me when we move on, or you'll get yourself badly torn."

"Move on—oh, mayn't I stay here and help these poor creatures?"

"What nonsense you talk, to be sure! Don't you know we go on expanding and spreading until we hear the recall from above, when we drop quickly apart, and hasten above as fast as the wind permits?—*what* a baby it is, to be sure."

The poor cattle below were licking the damp shrivelled grass with hungry pleasure, and the mist was now so thick, it was difficult to see anything clearly. Presently it lifted a little, and the young cloud saw they were playing over a vast stretch of country right in a hop-growing county. . . . . Crouching under a dripping hedge, a wretched and miserable group of hop-pickers paused on their weary tramp till the worst of the storm should be over. What dirty, depraved-looking creatures the *best* of them were, and the *worst* looked of the very lowest scum of the people—coarse, ignorant, friendless, homeless—tramping from day to day in search of their daily bread, sleeping at night in unions and shelters, and often out in the open.

Is it their fault they grow up brutal and ignorant? Have they had their chance of better things?

"It's going to rain all night; come, father, we must push on for Worcester at once. We have none too much time already."

"My limbs ache so sadly, I shan't get far," moaned the wretched old shivering creature, "best let me stay behind."

"A likely tale *that*, to be sure, at this time of day; there's my arm to help you and a stout stick to lean on, and as we are now all soaked, it's safer to move along."

"How is Tom to-night, Susan?" she asked, as the poor draggled group began to start. A sad look answered her, and the shivering young mother opened a fold of her shawl to shew the ashen white face of a child of five, who might have been only three from his tiny size and light weight. "He has done nothing but talk about his Robin dinner last Christmas, he will have it he's going to one to-night."

A low, hacking cough interrupted her, and she pressed her hand hard on her side.

"I think I have done my last hopping, I feel quite worn out and so weary. What a noise our boots make, now they are soaking wet!"

"Boots," thought the little cloud, as he looked at the shapeless bits of sodden leather, gaping wide in the front, and bulging in holes at the sides, only however in keeping with the rest of the garments of rags. . . . . "Is there no one to help the poor hoppers, to give them a meal and a shelter and to wash the dirt off the roads? Why, the gipsies are rich compared with them, for *they* have their caravans! Can't we stop raining now?—see, we are drowning those poor souls."

"How inconsistent you are," scoffed his friendly comrade, "did I not tell you to wait? Dear, dear, what *is* the matter?" as a dull sullen roar began.

"It's only a dispute on the road, I felt we should soon come to blows!"

Out flashed the weird lightning's flame, zig-zagging in all directions—crash!—bang!—came the thunder's answer, and the shock was so strong and long, the little cloud felt dazed and had quite a job to hold on to his neighbour; and now the fierce whistling wind caught up his reins again, and urged on his willing steeds, at a very rapid rate. And the wild ocean's voice, thundering on shore and rocks, joined in the din of the storm—higher and higher rose the dashing crested waves tossing in gleeful play the cockle shell boats of men up on to the top of the billow, and down in the trough beneath.

Curiosity made our young friend peer close through the gloom below, and he saw the poor fishers' wives in crowds on the stormy beach, straining their eyes into the grey distance and watching the boats struggle in.

Then in the shades of evening a rocket's wild gleam went up, and he saw on the cruel rocks a vessel fast going to bits. But with a rush and a cheer out sprang the life-boat, her crew firm lashed to their seats, and with their lives at their brothers' call. And the cheer from a hundred hearts brought hope to the drowning crew.

"Room for one more," was shouted hoarsely, "we'll soon be back for the rest."

The captain turned from the bridge, and signed to a man standing near with grizzled hair, and furrowed face, "Now, Mike, your turn."

"I'd rather stop with you, sir."

Too late for either, the chance was gone, the boat was well on her homeward way—would she return in time?

Only a few stood on the sloping deck, and the grinding, grating noise of the poor ship on the rocks, warned them their time was short. The captain did his best, the belts were all served out, and the men lashed to floating planks, and then they could do no more, but peer with their eyes into the darkness, and strain their ears for the life-boat's cheer.

Captain Fortescue's heart was heavy, as he thought of his much-loved home, his father's voice of welcome sounded *so* near at hand and he felt the warmth of his sister Irene's arms around his neck? A sob rose up in his throat as he knew he should see them no more! Never repay his father's care, and all his self-denial!

Close home on Old England's shores, the Master's call had come; in the simple discharge of his duty, he should pass to the Land of Rest—thanks to his father's teaching in humble faith and fear.

Higher and higher rose the mighty crested waves, lifting the ship like a child in their arms, and throwing her down broken and smashed on the cruel rocks beneath.

The little cloud felt so sad, he tried to stop off his rain and dropping his comrade's side, pressed his damp edges together; for one minute there was a lull, and in the small rift thus made the moon sent her silvery beam right through to flash on the scene below.

Only a swirl of water bubbling and circling round in a whirlpool marked the grave of a gallant ship, whilst here and there tossed about the helpless form of a man. Above rose the beetling cliffs, below, the jagged rocks, far in the distance a speck struggled across the huge waves, the life-boat again to the rescue.

"Catch hold of me, you stupid, and don't play such a prank again," hissed an angry murmur around; gone was the silvery light lost in the deepening gloom.

All of a sudden a great hush fell—the like of which can only be felt—and a silence that could in the darkness almost be seen, when the tumult's wild rage was still and the powers of the air hung waiting.

Frightened at the awful pause, the baby cloud gave a grip to his friend, "What is the matter now?"

"HUSH!" came the answer back, "the angels of Life and Death are passing through us to the earth, to gather the golden grain."

"May I not see them pass, and who will they fetch to-night?"

"Only the Good God knows, you can ask when we get home. Now we're off again, and there comes the morning light—dear me, what a mess you're in, pull yourself well together, and overlap some of your edges; how did you tear yourself so?"

"I am sure I don't know," sighed the cloud, "I feel very much knocked about, " and I don't like the work at all—must I always remain a storm cloud?"

"Yes, if you've any constitution you must; it's only the weakly one, the wadding clouds, as we call them, that get off the ranks of the storm masses—then when you are old and weary, in the sunset's golden army a niche will be found for you, and robed in beautiful purple, you'll watch the angels dressing and painting the heavens. Do leave off sighing, child; our work is by no means done."

"Shan't we soon go home?—I do feel so very sad."

"No, our time is extended for some hours, but the wind has altered his course and is driving us now from the opposite quarter, so we really are on our homeward way, and I must to work again."

All day long they rained, spreading a covering of grey, whilst from the earth beneath heart-felt thanksgiving rose on its heavenward way.

Then the clouds lifted a trifle and eagerly peered the little cloud, through its soaking mantle of grey, to see any familiar faces below, but at first he looked in vain, all seemed strangers to him.

He saw in the colliery districts the starving women and children, whilst groups of stalwart men lounged and smoked the day away, standing out for a better wage, and a fairer share in the profits.

Were they right or wrong?—the little cloud wondered. He tried to linger to see some more, but the others would not wait, and off he had to go. His body was feeling so light he felt sure the cisterns must be low, and he noticed it was a steady downpour that fell from his comrades around; the fierce storm and bluster was over, gone with the light of day.

The sun was sinking fast, as they passed over the fishermen's cove, the shore was thick with wreckage, boxes, and barrels. A group of men bent over a lifeless form just thrown up by the tide. All the earth lines were gone from the face, sealed with the peace of God and a smile on the silent lips.

The sailors who stood around drew their hands across their faces, as they told in disjointed whispers, what a friend he had been to them, in helping them all to do right. And then as the question came, why *his* was the only life lost, old Mike in faltering tones explained that the lifeboat's crew could have picked the captain up one of the first, but he would not have it so ; he refused to be taken in until all the crew were safe, as he said there was not room, and just as again they neared him, with all the others aboard, a plank was dashed by a mighty wave against his head, and to their regret and sorrow, he had sunk like a stone at once in the powerful swirl of the sea.

In vain they waited about, till the danger for all was so great, overcrowded as they were, they were obliged to give up the search and make for the shore.

The old man lifted the curly hair, and showed a long purple scar, that told its own tale to all.

"We can't rain any more without a fresh supply of water," said the little cloud's friend. "See, the big blacks have parted asunder, and the moon is lighting them up ; now look out for our orders, our flight is nearly over."

The clouds paused in their steady pace, and the silvery light of the moon fell like a ladder to earth, making a path for the angels' feet.

Vainly the little cloud peered, in hopes of getting a sight of them, only the light shone clear on land and sea below. Illuminating for a minute's space a large infirmary ward, where in a clean white bed, a poor young mother lay, whose sands of life were so low, the sun would find her gone—gone up the silver track, helped by the angels' hands. Beside her sat watching a friend, who yet in her heart of hearts, could not wish for the struggle to last.

"My child," came faintly from the white lips, and the pitiful eyes were wide open, " who will take care of him ? "

"You won't have to part from him," sobbed poor kindly Susan, "he's only a little ahead, and you'll soon overtake him, poor lamb! He's gone to his Robin dinner to-night, as he always said he should."

Oh! what a look of peace fell on the dying face.

"Thank God for his great goodness, he knew what was best for us, and if he had lived to grow up, he might have been like the others."

Again an upward flight, and now to the cloudlet's pleasure, through a wide open window he looked in on Irene's face. Sleeping like a little child, she lay, with the flush of fever gone, and very close beside her, her father knelt in prayer.

God in his Infinite Mercy had spared him the light of his home.

A poke in the tiny cloud's shoulder startled him from his pitying gaze. Across the great vault of Heaven, a shooting star was rushing, leaving a trail of glory, as his message he carried afar.

It was the clouds' recall—they must hasten at once to obey, now they were in the way when the sky was required clear—so up jerked the wind his reins in a hurry, and away higher and higher mounted the clouds; the little one was so light he went up just like a bird, straining his eyes to the ground, all the time with an eager, wistful gaze, but now in his rapid race he could not distinguish clearly and needed his breath to keep steady, and clear of the beautiful stars.

"You didn't give *me* much room," grumbled the moon as he kissed her. "I have had a dull time of it behind your backs, and now I'm going to bed."

The cloud angel stood waiting the return of her regiment with a smile on her patient face, and as she held out a hand to steady the baby cloud as he reached the clouds' great home, wondered to see such a shadow on the fleecy robe of grey.

"What is the matter, my child, are you quite worn out with your journey?"

"My heart is so very sad with the woes of the earth beneath and the unfinished lives of men."

"Only our own Great Master ever sees the whole of a life; it is but a few stray bits that shew to the world at large, each works out a portion of the design, that forms in the end a perfect whole. Now hurry to rest, the others are close behind. Be content, my child, you see such a little way. Remember the Lord of All holds the clouds and the winds in the hollow of His hand, and He doeth all things well!"

E. YOLLAND.

# A Hum-drum Girl.

### By JENNY WREN,

Author of "LAZY THOUGHTS OF A LAZY GIRL," "A BUNCH OF VIOLETS,"
etc., etc.

## CHAPTER I.

WINIFRED LOVELL was described as a hum-drum girl—that is to say in the rare moments in which she was discussed at all. There are some people who do not need to be pushed into the background; they go there of their own free will, and Winifred was one of these.

How it was that she had gradually become a person of so little consequence in her family and the neighbourhood, she would have found it hard to say herself. Being the eldest daughter of Mr. Lovell of Lasworth Park, she ought, on once coming out, to have taken up a position for herself and kept it.

But there were too many treading on her heels. One by one her four sisters followed in her footsteps and came out, taking society by storm with their beauty and wit and totally eclipsing their quiet and less brilliant elder sister, who sank into insignificance by their side.

Not that she minded, indeed she accepted the background as her natural position, and from that standpoint admired her lovely sisters and took more pride in them than any of the people round about.

And this adoration was very acceptable to the younger Miss Lovells. "Poor Winifred," they would say, they always spoke of her as "poor," "was so good-natured, she would do anything she was asked—they really did not know what they would do without her."

And people came and went at Lasworth and admired the tasteful draperies, the charming recesses formed by the quaint corners of the old house, that, decorated so artistically, broke up the square look of a room and formed such delightful recesses for *tête-à-têtes*. Yes, they admired it all and the arrangements of the flowers and different coloured foliage with which the whole place was so lavishly filled, and all the credit of it fell to the lovely quartette, Lily and Mary, Olive and Rose; no one would have imagined that the effect was solely produced by Miss Lovell's tasteful fingers, that quiet Miss Lovell who was not up to anything and could never be made to see a joke.

But after all, Winifred was not quite forlorn, and there was one person at least who appreciated her to the full and who would rather be in her company than in that of any of her noisy, laughing sisters—and that person was Mr. Lovell. Many hours would the two spend together going round Lasworth—his ancestral home which he loved—discoursing on the advisability of taking a tree away here and so obtain a peep through at the lovely valley below, or planting another where the gale had torn its predecessor up, roots and all, for Lasworth Park lay among the Cotswold Hills and there was but little soil for the roots to take hold. Winifred's decision weighed more with her father than that of the greatest landscape gardener in the world.

Changes had lately taken place in the county, for old Lord Cranby, the largest landowner and richest man round about, had died, and his grandson had come to reign in his stead.

Perhaps the excitement was greater because the present earl was so little known—for he was of a roving disposition, and had spent at least a third of his life in foreign countries—and everybody was on the tip-toe of expectation to find out what he was like. That he was thirty-six years of age and unmarried was the utmost they could glean about him. All around conspired to bid him welcome.

The news of his advent did not much affect Winifred—why should it? What difference should a man more or less in the neighbourhood make to her? She listened as her sisters discussed Lord Cranby and smiled to herself as she saw the extra care with which they adorned themselves before starting for the garden-party where they were to meet him for the first time. But when the carriage drove off she dismissed all such trivial matters from her thoughts and turned and wandered into her beloved flower-garden, now one blaze of colour and filling the whole air with fragrance.

The "Lovell Quartette," as the girls were invariably called, returned from the garden-party in even higher spirits than they had gone.

"Lord Cranby was there, Winifred," cried Lily, as she stood arranging her pretty fair curls in the glass and examining herself to see if she had looked her best this afternoon. "And oh! such a good-looking man—very dark eyes, a bronzed face, and his hair nearly grey! He asked," with a little gratified smile at her reflection, "he asked to be introduced to me."

"He asked to be introduced to us all," broke in Mary sharply. "One would think Lily was the only one he spoke to. Why, he and I played croquet together for a long time."

"And you *did* play badly," cried Rose, laughing. "I was ashamed for the credit of the family that he should have seen such a shocking specimen of Lasworth play. Why, you missed a ball every time!" and Violet joined in her derisive laughter too.

Mary turned round hotly and Winifred hastened to intervene.

"And what did you think of the new comer, Olive?" she asked.

"Oh, Olive!" struck in the sharp-tongued Rose again, "I don't suppose she even saw Lord Cranby. She was not visible the whole afternoon, and, funnily enough, Mr. Shepherd was missing too!"

Winifred smiled at Olive's blushing face. She was perhaps her favourite sister, being less selfish than the others and more in accord with her own nature. To be sure Mr. Shepherd the curate would not be a very brilliant match, but if Olive liked him, what did that matter?

The weeks rolled on; August took his departure and September was growing old. Winifred had had plenty of opportunities for studying Lord Cranby, for he was in and out of Lasworth very often, but she reserved her opinion, for she could not exactly make him out.

She spoke to him very little, for as usual when any stranger was present she effaced herself and took up her old position in the background—a standpoint nevertheless from which she could perceive most that was going on.

And Lord Cranby puzzled her. That some attraction drew him to the house was obvious, but then who was the magnet? He seemed to treat all her sisters alike and paid one no more attention than the others—what did it all mean?

And now his visit to Cranby Towers was narrowing to a dreadfully short space of time. It was the 23rd of September, and in two days he was going north to spend two or three weeks visiting, preparatory to wintering in Ceylon.

He was dining with them to-night, and Winifred half unconsciously watched him with anxious eyes. But two or three times, whether by magnetic instinct or not, he had looked up and caught her glance, and ashamed of her scrutiny she had turned her eyes away in confusion.

"It is the Houghtons' dance to-morrow," said Lily, as they were all sitting after dinner in the drawing-room, "you are going of course, Lord Cranby?"

"Eh?" he answered, starting from a reverie, "the Houghtons' dance. "Oh, yes, I received an invitation. You will be there?"

"Oh," struck in Mary, emphatically, "we are all going," she would not allow Lily to take the pronoun in the singular. "We have been asked to drive over after lunch to-morrow, and to stay the night. It would be such a long way to come home and so dark too."

"*All* going? Miss Lovell too?"

Winifred shook her head and Mary laughed.

"Winifred never goes to dances," she said in rather a slighting tone.

"Lily, I cannot find that book on fossils I was reading," said Mr. Lovell, turning the volumes over on the table. "I want to show Lord Cranby a passage. I wish you would see if I left it in the library."

"Oh, bother!" cried Lily, *sotto voce*. She was sitting next the guest and did not wish to vacate her position. She knew she would find Mary in her chair when she returned.

"Winifred, father has lost his book, do go and look for it, he will never leave off worrying until it is found," and Winifred rose and went at once.

"I can't stand fussy people, can you?" went on Lily, turning to Lord Cranby. "They always get on my nerves."

"Are you talking of your father?" surprised.

"Yes," laughing. "I can never stay in a room long when he is in it. He nearly drives me mad!" And she glanced archly at her companion, expecting a vigorous disclaimer that she could ever be put out, and her pretty brows met in a frown when no answer came.

It took Winifred some time to find the book, and when she returned everybody in the drawing-room seemed to have changed places. Rose was at the piano playing soft dreamy music and Lord Cranby sat silent by her side, Lily and Olive were having rather a noisy discussion the other side of the room, and Mr. Lovell lay in his easy chair nearly asleep.

"Here is your book, dad," said Winifred going up to him brightly. "I found it under a pile of papers—you really must learn to be more tidy," and she looked up laughingly as Mr. Lovell thanked her and patted her hand, but she started and her smile died on her lips as she caught Lord Cranby looking at her across the room—regarding her with intense scrutiny through half-closed eyes. She was not used to being stared at, and she began wondering why she should so often find his glance wandering in her direction. She peered in the glass when she went up to bed that night to see if she could find anything wrong—a hairpin out of place or a lock of hair uncoiled—something to justify that piercing scrutiny. But no—the small pale oval face looked just the same as usual and the abundance of dark hair had kept within its proper bounds.

And so Winifred went to sleep still mystified.

## CHAPTER II.

WINIFRED stood in the porch watching her family as they drove away *en route* to the Houghtons'. She was left all alone in the house, for much against his will Mr. Lovell had been dragged off too, to be present at the festivities, and so Winifred had the whole afternoon and evening to herself. She leant against the stone archway and wondered what she should do.

It was a glorious September afternoon and a sense of drowsiness pervaded the air, but Winifred threw off the feeling, and fetching her hat, determined to wander off to the woods which covered the uplands opposite. Down into the valley she wended her way, startling the sheep into a sharp run as she drew near, while numberless rabbits scurried away at her approach.

The hill was very steep and the sun beat down fiercely on

her head, but still Winifred persevered—she felt that the delicious coolness of the shady woods was worth any trouble to reach. She paused for breath when she got to the top and sat down and rested on a trunk of a tree which lay alongside the drive. Far down below was the valley from which she had come, looking blue and hazy in the distance, and on her right were the woods—her much-desired goal — where the leaves were already beginning to turn, and shone gold and red beneath the afternoon sun.

Winifred was tired, and perhaps the soft cooing of the wood-pigeons acted as a lullaby—anyhow she drifted off to sleep unawares, and awoke with a start to find she was not alone.

Someone was standing over her and looking down at her with a smile.

She rubbed her eyes in astonishment as she met Lord Cranby's eyes. "How ever did you come here?" she said, hastening to rise from her lowly position.

He assisted her with one hand, while with the other he still held his horse's reins.

"Have you had a nice sleep?" he asked, smiling again, "you seemed so tired I did not like to disturb you."

"Have I been asleep long?" she asked.

"Ah, that I cannot say. I have only just come up myself, and I could not resist dismounting when I saw you. You see I am going north to-morrow—so I came to say good-bye."

"Oh," she cried, "what a pity the others are all out; they will be so sorry to have missed you. They have gone over to the Houghtons' for the dance—I thought they told you they were going early last night."

"Did they? Then I suppose I was not attending properly, so you see it is my own fault."

"But I am so sorry," in a voice of concern, "that you should have ridden over for nothing."

"For nothing? Do you mean then that I am to go back again? Go home without my tea? You cannot surely be so inhospitable?"

She laughed nervously and looked away.

"I did not think you would care to come," she said. "I shall be only too delighted if you will stay for a little while, for otherwise I shall be all alone."

They walked on together slowly down the drive, Lord Cranby leading his horse. A horrible feeling of shyness had descended on Winifred, which struck her dumb. What should she talk about to this man? She hoped—oh, how she hoped he would not stay long. Oh, for one of her sisters' ever-ready tongues, which never in all their lives had experienced such a sudden stroke of paralysis as hers was afflicted with now.

"Why have you not gone to the Houghtons' to-day?" he asked suddenly.

"I? Oh, I never go to dances now."

"Don't you care for it?"

"Yes," regretfully, "I used to be very fond of dancing, but it is a long time since I went to a ball."

"Why have you given it up?" with a quick frown.

"You see," she sighed, "there are so many of us, we could not go out five."

"But *you* always stay at home," impatiently. "Why don't you take it in turns?"

She looked surprised.

"Oh, I don't mind—the girls enjoy themselves much more than I ever should. I am quite happy here alone."

Lord Cranby checked his stride—it had grown so quick that her faltering footsteps could scarcely keep up with him. He checked his tongue too—he would have liked to have said something, but forbore.

Again silence fell on the two. The drive was a mile in length, but to Winifred it seemed double; she could think of nothing to say, and he too remained dumb.

But when they had arrived at the house and tea was brought in, matters grew better. Lord Cranby threw himself into a comfortable chair and appeared so much at home that Winifred, perforce, felt more at her ease, and her tongue was loosed.

"There is quite an excitement in our lower regions to-day," she said. "The housemaid was married to the head gardener this morning, and there have been great festivities up at his cottage."

"Indeed. And did you see the wedding?"

"Yes," smiling, "and some of the costumes were so funny. But," with a little sigh, "I don't think I ever saw two people looking more happy."

Lord Cranby helped himself to a cucumber sandwich.

"I wonder how long it will last?" he said dryly.

"Don't," she cried, "you are horrid when you talk like that. Why should not their happiness last?"

He looked at her for a few minutes through half-closed eyes in the characteristic way he had.

"Do you believe in the immortality of love?" he asked incontinently.

She wrinkled her brows.

"People have different ideas about falling in love," she answered gravely. "With some," thinking of her sisters, "it is only a question of a few weeks, and then they prefer another person better. But I do not call that love, do you?" looking up at him with serious eyes.

He shook his head.

"It is only base metal," he said, "not the true gold. But you haven't answered my question yet."

"Whether I believe in the immortality of love? Well, yes, I suppose I do—at least, I think if I were to love anyone at all it would be for always."

He leant his face on his hands and looked across at her over the table.

"And have you ever loved anyone at all?" he said, and his voice dropped his careless tone, and he waited eagerly for her answer.

But she laughed in amusement.

"I? No, I am twenty-eight, and am too old for such frivolities. Have you?"

Her question startled him, but he saw it was asked in all sincerity—there was no coquetry in her tone.

"Ten years ago," he answered thoughtfully, "I imagined I did, but the fit only lasted a few months, so, you see, as it will not stand your test, it could only have been base metal."

The hours flew on and the evening drew in. Winifred looked at her guest in perplexity as he still lingered on.

Perhaps it was the entrance of the man with the lamps which suggested to Lord Cranby that it was getting late, for he took out his watch directly the butler had left the room.

"Seven o'clock," he said with rather more than necessary astonishment. "I shall never get home in time for dinner."

Winifred laughed.

"You are your own master," she said. "I don't suppose there is anyone to mind if you are late?"

He looked at her whimsically.

"As you won't take my hint," he said, "I suppose I must ask for an invitation outright. May I not stay and dine with you?"

Winifred did not respond with any heartiness.

"But the Houghtons' dance?" she suggested, "you will never get there in time."

"I am not going to the Houghtons' dance," he answered offended. "I never had the slightest intention of going, but," rising, "as you are evidently anxious to get rid of me I will say good-bye."

"No, no," cried Winifred in confusion, "you know it is not that. I should like you to stay—of course I should, only—well, I will tell you the real truth. You see, there is a dance at the gardener's cottage to-night, and all the servants are going. Of course they will get dinner ready beforehand, but it will be all cold—there will be no one to wait, no one to——"

"Do you mean," quickly, "that you and I should be in the house alone?"

"Yes. It would be horrid for you, and that is why I did not like to ask you to stay."

Lord Cranby laughed aloud.

"It makes no difference if you ask me or not," he said firmly. "I mean to stay, and you can't turn me out!"

And dinner passed off gaily enough. Under Lord Cranby's influence Winifred's shyness quite wore off, and by the time they had finished she was chatting away volubly.

The glorious harvest moon was rising in the heavens and shedding her radiance around.

"Let us come out," said Lord Cranby. "It is wicked to keep indoors on such a night," and he caught up a light shawl from the hall, and wrapped it tenderly round Winifred.

They wandered down the old-world walk that looked as if it should have been peopled with ladies in powder and patches, and gallants with their white queues. On the stone seat at the end, moss-grown and stained by years, how many Lovells had sat and told their love-story? Round about strutted peacocks, breaking the soft silence with their shrill voices. Opposite rose the undulating hills, now bathed in a flood of moonlight, broken up here and there by the long dark shadows of the trees. And away in the distance the sound of the fiddles from the gardener's cottage fell gently on the still night air.

"Let us come and see them dancing," said Lord Cranby presently, and the two wended their way in the direction of the music.

It was a pretty scene, the figures dancing on the lawn, silhouetted and transfigured by the moonlight and apparently in the height of enjoyment. It had the appearance of some weird midnight revels.

Lord Cranby caught the excitement.

"Come and dance," he whispered eagerly to his companion. "You say you like it—we will have a dance all to ourselves," and catching her slender figure round the waist, he started off on the soft springy turf.

On and on went the fiddles, the wedding guests paused a moment for breath, but the two on the lawn below still kept on, on and on they danced, until at last through sheer exhaustion Lord Cranby stopped. He looked down into Winifred's face bathed in moonlight and flushed with exercise, but he did not at once remove his arm.

"Did you enjoy it?" he asked in his quick whisper. "Do you think the gardener's wedding dance is better than the Houghtons' ball?"

But she turned her eyes shyly away. Somehow she did not wonder now if there was anything wrong with her hair to make him look at her so.

She pointed to the hills sloping up before them.

"Isn't it lovely—lovely?" she said.

"Lovely!" he echoed. "How fond you are of Lasworth! Could you ever tear yourself away, I wonder?"

"How do you know," she asked, "that I love the place so much?"

"Child, every thought is mirrored in your eyes—I know exactly what you think."

They strolled back to the house.

"This really is the end," said Lord Cranby regretfully. "I suppose it must be good-bye now."

They went into the stables and he saddled his horse himself and brought it out into the grounds. He stood by his horse's head before he mounted, and looked intently at Winifred.

"I am going north to-morrow," he said, "and then afterwards I am obliged to go to Ceylon—I promised my sister long ago, or I would not go. It will be many months before I see you again, but I shall never forget this night and—I am going to ask you to remember it too. Will you promise to think of me sometimes when I am away?"

Winifred looked at him with her soft grave eyes.

"It is not necessary to promise," she said simply. "One does not easily forget the happiest time of one's life."

And as the rider disappeared in the distance, a little fleecy cloud floated across the face of the moon and a sudden darkness fell around. Only Winifred's eyes had caught a gleam that had nothing to do with borrowed light and that would take years and years to extinguish.

## CHAPTER III.

THE months rolled away, winter came and went, and now spring had begun and the trees and hedges were bursting out all around.

Winifred's eyes grew brighter and her heart beat quicker every day.

"A few months—only a few months, he said," she would repeat to herself, "it cannot be very long now before he is here."

And meantime changes had occurred at Lasworth, for one of the young birds had already flown and left the parent nest. Mr. Shepherd had been presented with a living in the south, and he had taken Olive with him to his new home.

And so it was that when the Towers was once more thrown open and everything hurried into preparation for the Earl's return, Winifred had left Gloucestershire and was staying with her sister in the Isle of Wight.

But she heard the news of Lord Cranby's return with composure. True, she had pictured herself as being one of the first to welcome him home, but what did a little delay matter? She would be back at Lasworth in three weeks' time, and then they must meet, and—did he remember she wondered anxiously, did he remember that evening spent together under the harvest moon?

Little scraps of news came to her in her mother's letters, telling her how much greyer Lord Cranby had grown, how that they had met him here or there, how he was always in and out of Lasworth as of yore, and how he was giving a dance at the Towers in a month's time and insisted that they all should go. "Even you too, Winifred," ended Mrs. Lovell, "are to be there; he will not let you off."

"Even you too!"

Winifred had treasured the words up. He had given her a special invitation then, he had not forgotten after all.

But gradually an anxious look grew in Winifred's eyes and her spirits slowly sank. Mrs. Lovell's letters had become full of one topic—one topic only, which burnt into her daughter's heart. It was Rose who was the attraction, asserted the writer, pretty blushing Rose was the one to whom Lord Cranby's visits were wholly due; wherever she went, Lord Cranby went too. Lord Cranby and Rose seemed never apart, and so on and so on, until the words danced about in front of Winifred's eyes and the letter fluttered to the ground.

Was it not only the natural course of events after all? Charming, lovable Rose, just twenty-one—who could help being fascinated? What was she, Winifred, with her quiet, shy ways and her nine-and-twenty years, by her side? Oh, of course it was only to be expected, and she ought not to mind. And she clasped her hands together tightly and forced back the smarting tears.

And on her return home she had to go through it all again. Mrs. Lovell was growing excited over the affair and rejoiced to have a sympathizing ear in which to recite her anticipations. But Winifred bore it all without a word, and no one knew that she suffered.

And in the evening Rose came into her room. The girl was looking pale and sad, and not at all happy. Winifred wondered at her appearance.

"What is the matter, Rose dear?" she asked, sitting down beside her. "You are not looking well."

Rose tapped the carpet nervously with her feet.

"I am unhappy, Winifred," she said, "and I don't know what

to do. We have quarrelled—that is to say—he—he—oh, you know what I mean—he said something I did not like, and—and I grew angry and said I would never speak to him again until he apologised, and he—he is so proud, I know—I know he never will." And Rose burst into tears.

Winifred put her arms round her and soothed her.

"Poor little girl," she said. "Don't cry, it will sure to be all right. Take the initiative and go and talk to him yourself, he —he is so good, he will be certain to meet you half-way."

Rose dried her eyes and sat up.

"Yes, I will try," she said, "and Winnie, dear, it is so nice of you to call him good. I am so glad you like him."

"Rose," said Winifred slowly, and her voice sounded far away, "do you love him?"

"Love him?" cried her sister with emphasis. "Oh, Winnie, I couldn't live without him. I have been simply miserable these last two days. He has not told me so yet, but I think—I hope he loves me too." She paused for a moment by the window and looked dreamily out into the darkness. "He is coming to our garden-party to-morrow, and I will take your advice and talk to him. Thank you so much, Winnie dear." And she tripped out of the room with a lighter heart, while Winifred still sat on in the silence alone.

There were all sorts and conditions of amusements at the garden-party at Lasworth Park—lawn tennis, badminton, golf, croquet, in fact, everybody was able to indulge in his favourite pursuit.

Lord Cranby went about from court to lawn scanning the assembly—was he never to find the face he sought?

At last, on one of the distant croquet grounds, he caught sight of Miss Lovell's tall slender figure and hastened at once in her direction. She had just finished a game and had thrown her mallet aside.

"I told you I could not play," she was saying to her partner apologetically. "I have only spoilt your game."

"How do you do, Miss Lovell?" said Lord Cranby, and Winifred started round at the well-known voice, and all the colour left her face.

"How do you do?" she repeated mechanically, and he thought

she might have been more pleased to see him when he had been away so long.

"You have finished your game? Will you come for a walk?" he said, and Winifred silently acquiesced. Why did he want to walk with her?

Once out of sight of the rest he turned eagerly towards her. "How are the bride and bridegroom?" he asked smiling. "They must be an old married couple by this time."

"They have only been married ten months," she answered slowly.

"Only ten months?" he echoed, "and it has seemed centuries to me! Winifred, what has come to you? Why are you so altered? All the time I have been away I have been hungering for a sight of your face; longing for the sound of your dear voice, Winifred——"

But she put up her hand to stop him with a little deprecating cry.

What did it mean? Did he then love her after all—love *her*? and her heart beat quickly, noisily—surely he must have heard it. But then Rose, poor Rose loved him and thought he loved her. She could not live without him, she had said. Winifred caught her breath. How could she destroy her sister's happiness? No. She must stop him—keep his words back at all hazards—fling back his love. Oh, misery! before he began to tell it.

And meantime, while these thoughts passed as lightning through her brain, Lord Cranby went on.

"You promised," he said, "promised to remember that night —that lovely moonlight night——

"I have not forgotten—it was cold—and chilly," she broke in abruptly, in a voice she did not recognise as her own.

"What! You found it cold when we wandered down the terrace walk——"

"And the peacocks made our heads ache with their loud, shrill noise."

Lord Cranby stopped and looked at her. "Winifred," he said, and all the life had gone out of his voice, "have you forgotten when we danced together on the lawn—just you and I— and the fiddles——"

Winifred caught her breath and her words fell from her lips in harsh, irregular jerks.

"The grass was damp—and heavy," she said, "and the fiddles—out of tune."

Lord Cranby was silent—at last he understood.

"And that is all you remember?" he said, after a while, which had seemed to Winifred as an eternity in which she had tasted the bitterness of death. But his cold unfamiliar tones brought her sharply back to life; she tried to answer him, but the words would not come.

He waited a few moments for her to speak, but as she still kept silent—"Had we not better go back to the croquet ground?" he said, and this time the harshness had left his voice and only a weary apathy was to be heard out of which all heart was gone.

## CHAPTER IV.

"Winnie! Winnie! it is all right. We have made it up and—and he has asked me to marry him," and Rose's appearance as she danced into the room was very different to that on the previous evening.

And so her sacrifice had not been in vain—and he had asked Rose. But, oh! he might have waited a little time.

Winifred steadied her voice. "I am so very glad, Rose, dear," she said. "I know Lord Cranby will make you happy."

Rose looked at her in perplexity.

"Lord Cranby!" she exclaimed. "Why, I am engaged to Cyril Norwood—I thought you knew Cyril Norwood?"

Was Winifred going mad or had she heard correctly?

"You told me last night," she faltered, "that—that you loved Lord Cranby."

"Lord Cranby! Oh, you must have misunderstood me. I love Lord Cranby, when his heart is full to overflowing of *you!* Why, even last year he would sit and look at you for hours together when the girls thought he came only to see them—it often made me laugh. And now ever since he has been home he has haunted my footsteps—was that why you made the mistake?—Oh, Winnie dear, it was only to talk of *you.*"

Winifred suddenly burst into tears.

"Oh, Rose, if I had known—if I had only known!"

Rose looked at her in perplexity, then a sudden glimmering of the truth dawned upon her.

"Winifred," she said, "you strolled off together this afternoon, did he—did he propose?"

Winifred shook her head.

"No—he—he was going to, but I stopped him because—because——"

"Because you thought I loved him, and you sacrificed your happiness for—me?" the tears sprang into Rose's eyes. "Winnie dear," and she threw her arms round her sister's neck, "thank Heaven, it is not in my power to accept your sacrifice even if I would. You cheered *me* up last evening, now I am going to cheer you. Don't grieve over it, Winnie, for I know it will come all right."

\* \* \* \* \* \* \*

Lord Cranby had chosen a lovely night for his dance, everybody seemed to be enjoying themselves, and it bid fair to be a great success. Only the host looked weary and depressed.

"Are you not going to ask me to dance to-night?" said Rose, tripping up to him.

He shook his head dismally.

"I am not going to dance at all," he said.

"Then let us come outside and have a talk. What is the matter—you are not looking at all well?"

"No. I am going away soon. I should have gone earlier but for this dance."

"Going away? That is very sudden, isn't it?"

"Yes," he answered, and looked up at the star-lit sky. Every beautiful thing seemed to have disappeared out of his life, even the moon had gone.

"Would it be very impertinent to ask you why you are going away?" asked Rose in a low voice.

He did not answer at first, and then said without turning:

"It is not necessary to tell you—I think you must know."

There was silence between them for a few minutes, and then Rose spoke.

"I am going to tell you a tale," she said, and without giving him time to answer she began:

"There was once a garden in which grew all the most beautiful flowers of the earth—a garden full of colour and sweet scents.

"And some one came into that garden, and he wandered

round and round looking at this flower and that, but did not admire one. At last he came to a group in a corner and he stopped before it. There was a tall lily, a hollyhock, a dahlia and a rose, all flowers vivid in their colouring and conspicuous from afar. But it was not these which had attracted his attention. Over-shadowed by the tall plants and nearly out of sight was a single violet — a violet which would never have been noticed but for the fragrance it shed around.

"And the stranger stood and looked at it, and the more he looked the more he coveted that flower."

Lord Cranby's eyes had left the stars, and Rose knew he was intently listening.

"And it came to pass," she continued, "that the rose fell a-sighing, for one that she loved had passed her by, and she stooped and whispered her troubles to the little violet. And the violet, though it cheered the rose, hung its head and drooped, for no names had been mentioned and it thought that the stranger was the one whom the rose had loved.

"And thus it was when the stranger came to pluck his cherished flower that the violet hid under the leaves and turned away. It hoped if it could not be found that the stranger would take the rose instead, and so in its unselfishness it turned away from the hand it—loved."

Lord Cranby started to his feet.

"Loved! Rose," he cried, "do you know what you are saying? Do you mean that she *loves* me?"

"It turned away from the hand it—*loved*," continued Rose, as if he had not spoken, "but the other came back and plucked the rose, and then the violet found its sacrifice had been in vain, and —and——" Rose left her seat and stood before him. "I do not know the end of the story, Lord Cranby—you must finish it for yourself," and she turned and went back to the house.

\* \* \* \* \* \* \*

Winifred was standing by a window looking out at the spangled sky; she did not hear Lord Cranby's footsteps, and started at the sound of his voice.

"Winifred!" he had said.

"Did you call me?" she faltered, looking round.

"Winifred," he cried, "Rose has been opening to me the gates of Paradise. She says it has all been one great mistake. Winifred,

Winifred," and he came nearer, and took her in his arms, "she has been saying that you—love me."

He held her closer still, and kissed her pale face.

"Put your arms round me, my dearest," he whispered, "so that I may know it is true and that I am not dreaming. Let me hear you say that you have not forgotten after all."

And Winifred's white arms stole round his neck, and her head drooped upon his breast.

"Forgotten!" she repeated softly. "How is it possible when the remembrance has been always with me?—the remembrance of a still, beautiful September evening, when the harvest moon was holding her court in the heavens, and all the world appeared to me to be enchanted; when even the peacock's shrill cry seemed as music, and the fiddles were not really out of tune."

# La Bourboule.

### By E. C. VANSITTART.

"Une rivière au fond ; des bois sur les deux pentes."
—Victor Hugo.

## PART I.

MANY now doubtless know the sunny little watering place of Royat, one of the health-giving springs of Central France, as it nestles in a green valley, with a glorious view over the town of Clermont-Ferrand in the great plain of the Limagne below, over which the ever-changing play of lights and shadows is beautiful to watch; but few English people have penetrated farther into this strange volcanic country of Auvergne, or become acquainted with La Bourboule, not to be confounded with the better-known Mont Dore.

It is reached in two hours by train from Clermont to Laqueuille, where the rail ends, followed by a two hours' drive across country. It is a unique railway line running through a hilly district where walnut, apple, pear, apricot and other fruit-trees, together with vineyards, occupy the level ground, while woods of fir, oak, chesnut, and beech cover the lower slopes of the mountains; picturesque villages appear embedded among the trees, and a general look of prosperity prevails till Volvic is approached, where the country grows wilder, and passing by the great lava quarries of the Puy de Nugère; the peculiarly sombre appearance of most of the houses and churches of Lower Auvergne is due to the use of this dark-coloured building material.

After this, the cultivated land gives way to wide moors covered with broom and heath, or strewn with rocks and boulders, the scene grows more and more desolate till the dreary-looking station of Laqueuille, standing in the open country neglected and forlorn, is reached. Here we left the train, and got into the *diligences*, or rather public omnibuses, which convey travellers to La Bourboule.

Far away before us stretched a strange country bounded in the distance by the beautiful blue peaks of the Monts Dore. The first part of the drive was not unlike some portions of

Switzerland; midway we rattled through the pretty village of Saint Sauves, buried among trees, with a tapering church spire, and soon after entered the valley of the Dordogne (the Dore and the Dogne, two rivers, uniting form the Dordogne), where the fine high road has been traced on one side of the valley, wide here, but soon closed in amongst mountains and hills of the most fantastic shapes, either standing isolated or in groups, till it becomes a cutting between magnificent beech-trees growing down to the water's edge below, where the river wound and twisted, now rushing noisily over stones and boulders, now flowing crystal clear over a sandy bottom.

Every moment the scene changed and grew more lonely; peeps were caught of large stretches of short grass, where fine herds of cattle grazed, as we entered the shade of fir woods where the golden sunshine filtered through the trees, and the air was scented with the turpentine; then we descended into a deep ravine where great masses of granite and basalt lay in wild confusion, to creep once more into the open, where fields of yellow corn shimmered in the quiet sunlight. There was no sign of a human habitation, and we felt far from the haunts of men, when suddenly, at a turn of the road, the valley widened out, revealing a mass of houses and buildings, and our horses clattered gaily into the principal "*Place*" of La Bourboule, and deposited us at the *Bureau de la Poste*. Here we were besieged by a noisy crowd of porters and *commissionaires*, all shouting out the merits of their respective hotels and pensions, producing a very Babel of sound, confusing in the extreme to the bewildered traveller, and the illusion produced by our drive was roughly dispelled, as we were rudely brought back to the present of a nineteenth-century French watering-place.

The first impression of the actual village or town of La Bourboule is decidedly disappointing, consisting as it does of a number of second-rate hotels all close together, a badly-paved road lined on one side with dusty trees, on the other with rows of wretched shops and booths, and dignified by the title of *Boulevard*, two modern casinos, many unfinished houses, the great *Établissements*, and a general look of newness and untidiness, contributing a whole at which the newcomer's heart is apt to sink, and he is tempted to exclaim: "What a mixture of squalor and pretension."

Nor is this estimate altogether wrong. The hotels leave much to be desired on the score of comfort, while their prices are decidedly high ; the roads, even in the town itself, are in a disgraceful condition, and almost impassable for pedestrians in bad weather; in the Dordogne, which flows through the town, clothes are washed, notwithstanding its being made a receptacle for stale fish and rubbish of every kind, and the price of the commonest necessities of life is exorbitant. On the other hand, we must remember that the season is very short, lasting only from June 15th to September 15th, that the place is of mushroom growth, for though in the fifteenth century a hospital for poor patients was founded by the Vicomte de Turenne, La Bourboule was unknown and unvisited except by a few peasants from the neighbouring country, and was a mere hamlet till a few years ago. Even now, on September 15th the doctors depart, hotels close, shopkeepers return to Clermont, and La Bourboule is left to sleep its long winter sleep ; life seems suspended, communication with the neighbourhood, such as Mont Dore and Laqueiulle, is rendered difficult by the snow, and not till spring once more wakes new life in Nature, is La Bourboule too restored to activity in making preparations for the reception of summer guests, who now number nine thousand per annum, but increase year by year.

In spite of jerry-builders' unlovely improvements, the situation of La Bourboule remains unspoilt ; nothing can take away its charm as it lies there in its green valley 2,811 feet above the level of the sea, catching every ray of sunshine at the foot of an immense rock of granite which shelters it against the chill north wind. All round rise the strange forms of extinct volcanoes : the *Banne d'Ordenche* (*banne* in the patois of the country meaning " horn ") ; the *Puy Gros*, with its wide serrated profile ; the *Pic du Sancy*, at whose foot the Dordogne takes its rise ; the *Pic du Capuchin*, so called because the craggy rock on its summit resembles the figure of a cowled kneeling monk ; the beautiful outlines of the Monts Dore standing out against the sky, and many others, whose red-brown sides form a vivid contrast to the rich vegetation at their feet ; little villages are perched on the hill-tops. One of these, Murat le Quaire, seems actually to overhang La Bourboule.

The air is delicious, for the absence of snow-mountains

renders it soft and warm, though bracing, and never does one here feel that cold nip which Swiss air carries with it from icy peaks, and which even in the height of summer is so pernicious to delicate lungs; it blows fresh yet soft on this tableland of Central France, where in August itself the thermometer indoors, before the sun's rays become potent, rarely marks more than 58 degrees Fahrenheit, and though the middle of the day may be hot for a few hours, the freshness of the mornings and evenings and constant thunderstorms keep the atmosphere cool. Crowds of French people with delicate children frequent La Bourboule, but few English as yet give the place a thought, though the fame of its arsenical waters is spreading rapidly, and the presence of an excellent English medical man will doubtless induce many more to give this health resort a trial. An English church service is occasionally held on Sundays in one of the *salles* of the Établissement, and funds are being collected to build a church where, in turn, both French and English Protestants may hold their respective services. The new Roman Catholic parish church which has just been erected is of yellow stone picked out with grey lava, and, though still wanting its tower, is a remarkably fine specimen of the modern Romanesque.

The name of La Bourboule is derived from the old word *borbola*, meaning boiling or bubbling water, and is most suitable to its therapeutic springs. They are the strongest arsenical waters known, and excavations made in sinking foundations for modern buildings have revealed signs that they were used by the Romans. There are now three établissements; the Grand Établissement, commonly known as *les Thermes*, will be an immense and very handsome building, though now only half completed, with wide halls, luxurious bath-rooms, and *salles de pulvérisation* (spraying), *aspiration* (inhalation) and *humage* (vapourizing), douches, fitted with the best and latest appliances for hydropathic treatment; Choussy is a smaller establishment on a simpler scale, where the water seems hotter, perhaps because it is nearer the fountain head; and Mabru, where poor patients are treated free of charge. These three establishments are all supplied from the same spring, which discharges at the rate of 400 litres, or 88 gallons, an hour, equal to 2,112 gallons in the 24 hours. The water, which issues from the ground at a temperature of 60° centigrade (140° Fahrenheit), is clear and colourless, with a slightly saline taste; it has been likened to veal broth, and after the first taste is not in the least unpalatable; amongst its chemical ingredients are arsenic, chlorate of sodium, bicarbonate of soda, chlorate of potassium, magnesium, chalk and sulphate of iron. Besides this principal spring, there is the Source Fenestre on the left bank of the Dordogne, whose water is cold and contains iron; this sends up 140 litres, or 30¾ gallons per minute, and the Source Clémence, which has only lately been discovered, and is situated on the same side of the river in a bit of waste land nearly a mile out of the town. The sum of 400,000 francs (£16,000), has already been refused by its owner on the ground that the water is likely to become very valuable, containing, as it does, carbonic acid and iron in addition to arsenic. A touch of romance also hangs round this spring, as the owner is a lady named Clémence, who, though wealthy and young, is unmarried, and heiress of her millionaire uncle; she is therefore the *parti* of the neighbourhood, and many speculations are abroad as to the likelihood of this or that one of her many suitors being accepted. The complaints treated most successfully at La Bourboule are anæmia; scrofula in all its forms (the waters in the case of delicate children producing the same effect as cod liver oil; skin complaints (such as eczema and psoriasis), throat and chest affections (asthma, chronic bronchitis, laryngitis and consumption in its early stages); intermittent fevers, diabetes, gout and rheumatism, the waters affording a strong fillip to the nervous system and the circulation, besides acting powerfully on the skin. One patient gained six pounds in three weeks, another — a consumptive case—three pounds in the same period. More than 40,000 bottles of Bourboule water are exported annually. Perhaps I cannot better close this part of my subject than by quoting the following note kindly sent me by Dr. Gilchrist, the resident English physician. He says:

"For many years, during which the waters of La Bourboule were supposed to contain only a certain quantity of ordinary saline constituents, the springs were frequently resorted to for skin diseases; scrofula in its numerous forms, asthma and bronchial affections. The hot springs attracted sufferers from rheumatism, while La Source des Fièvres enjoyed the reputation of being particularly efficacious in malarial fevers. With the discovery that the waters contained arsenic almost in medicinal doses (there being the equivalent of twenty-one drops of "Fowler's Solution" to each 1¾ pints of liquid), the secret of their wonderful success was in a great measure explained, and the sphere of their therapeutic usefulness extended. More recent investigation attaches some significance to the fact that their other saline ingredients are almost identical in composition and proportion to those contained in the serum, or liquid portion of the blood. The waters may be employed for their general tonic and strengthening qualities, or for the specific action of arsenic; they can be recommended in cases of chlorosis and anæmia, especially in those refractory to iron. In most lymphatic and strumous affections, children, who bear arsenic so well, being especially benefited. It may here be remarked that a mountain climate is similar in many respects to that of the sea, a fact which may explain in part the results attending the treatment of these cases at La Bourboule."

Though sad enough scenes meet the eye on every side, there are equally comic ones ready for such as have the appreciative faculty; first come the blanket-swathed mummies peeping through the half-glazed door of a sedan-chair, which two porters bear along with more or less exertion; then, within the precincts of the establishment the inhaling room (*Salle d'Aspiration*) has fully earned its title of *Séance des Spectres*, for there, on raised benches, rising in a semicircle from floor to roof, sit silent, phantom figures in loose white flannel dressing-gowns, with towels arranged more or less fantastically round their heads, breathing in with all their might the thick steam which fills the apartment. Next door is the spraying room (*Salle de Pulvérisation*), here, a ledge runs round the walls, and at regular intervals sit the patients with an oil-skin bib and a towel (in the case of ladies an oil-skin cap in addition), tied round their necks, their mouths wide open to receive the tiny jet of spray which plays down their throats from the miniature hose placed in front of them; conversation is naturally impossible, and to the onlooker the grunts of assent or dissent in reply to the attendants' enquiries as to the comfort or otherwise of the victims are most entertaining, as, assisted by pantomime, they try to explain that the jet is too strong or too weak, its level too high or too low; at such times the possibility of ape ancestors comes home to one with cruel force!

Two Casinos already cater for the amusement of the bathers, and a third is in course of construction; the oldest, distinguished by the emphasis always laid on the definite article THE Casino, has a theatre attached to it, is provided with games of all kinds in the grounds, and plenty of chairs hired by the French ladies who sit with work, while their husbands smoke and read their papers, and the children play about. The second, Casino Fenestre, is pleasanter and quieter, standing in a pretty shady park, where an ornamental sheet of water is crossed by rustic bridges. Fireworks are constantly let off in the evening from both, and the effect of the rockets going up like fiery snakes high above the tree tops is very pretty: one night we watched a zig-zag line of coloured lanterns, carried up a hill side, and Bengal lights illuminating the summit with weird crimson and green glow. Sometimes a *quête* is got up in the hotels for some charitable purpose, when, notice having been previously given, young ladies go the round of the *table d'hôte* with a plate or salver; once during our stay it was the *Petites Sœurs des Pauvres* themselves who collected for the old people under their charge, but there is little real poverty among the thrifty Auvergnat peasantry, who, it must be said, are a singularly unpleasing people. Far from welcoming the visitors from whom they annually reap so rich a harvest, they scowl silently at the stranger, and do not put themselves out in any way for his convenience; amongst their own compatriots they are a proverbially grasping, miserly race, who make it their business to fleece, or, to use their own expressive word, "*plumer*" the unfortunate travellers. The hotel keepers carry this out even towards their poor servants, whom they overwork like the Egyptian taskmasters of old, grinding them down to the utmost. The three principal hotels are kept by brothers, all wealthy, yet their old uncle, a reputed millionaire, whose heirs they are, works in his fields among the cabbages like any day-labourer, and will go on toiling to add one *sou* more to his already ample store. The peasants all wear wooden *sabots;* the men blue linen blouses and wide-brimmed felt hats, while the women affect the universal white muslin cap of France, with an embroidered crown and stiff lace frill; widows present a curious appearance, owing to a long black crêpe veil depending from the ordinary cap, the effect being singularly incongruous. Their Romanesque patois is unintelligible ; though it has many words of Spanish and Italian origin, it is singularly unmusical, lacking the dignity of the former and the polish of the latter tongue.

Excellent, sure-footed little donkeys are to be had by those who cannot climb the mountain paths ; in the morning the *Place* is lined with as many as a hundred donkeys and their drivers, but by twelve o'clock often none are to be had. It being the custom for the countrywomen to sit astride like men, the side saddle is reserved for strangers only, and is consequently often of strange construction. Riding horses and carriages can also be hired, but the charge for the latter is high.

The great charm of La Bourboule lies in the lovely country around, with its endless and varied walks by the riverside, through the birchwood where the branches sometimes dip into clear brown water in whose depths every stone and pebble is seen ; invisible streams gurgle through the meadows with a delicious purling sound ; fir-clad hills and magnificent basaltic rocks rise on every side, while the rich Subalpine Flora is a source of ever fresh delight to the botanist ; bog-cotton grows in the fields, together with golden gentian, pink mallow, and yellow poppies. The river banks are fringed with forget-me-nots growing down to the water's edge ; tall plumes of meadow-sweet wave in the breeze, and the purple heather on the downs vies with that on the Scottish moors ; wild strawberries, raspberries, filberts, and whortle-berries grow in profusion in some spots: the " Noli-me-tangere " (or wild balsam), with its delicate yellow flowers and drooping green leaves carpets the shady sides of the banks ; oak and beech ferns flourish in the limestone, and those who choose to stoop low enough will find exquisite cup-moss like miniature goblets containing tiny silvered seeds, fit only for the fairy queen to drink from.

Lovers of Nature might spend hours in the silence of the woods, watching the life of beetle, ant and spider, or listening to the hum and whirr of bees, crickets, cockchafers, and other woodland denizens. One strange fact struck us ; during our stay at La Bourboule, we did not see a single snail in spite of damp weather, though one of our party was collecting land-snails, nor did we come across any snakes, vipers, or adders, only once a slow-worm lay dead on the road, having evidently been killed by a passer-by; on the other hand, slugs abounded—jet-black or brown—longer and larger than we had ever seen; also wondrous green, gold and bronzed beetles shining like jewels when the sun touched them. Every valley had a rushing mountain stream whose clear water dashed sparkling over the rocks and under primitive bridges, sometimes merely a plank laid across, or a felled tree without any railing; oftener still, rough stepping-stones alone led to the other side.

If weary of the woods, you may turn into the cornfields where blue corn-cockles and scarlet poppies stand among the full ears swaying in the gentle breeze, follow a narrow track which leads to the hamlet of Prégnoux, where the thatched cottages seem as if roofed with green velvet, so thick is the growth of moss and lichen. It might be Goldsmith's "Deserted Village," for there is no sign of life in the roughly-paved street, not a sound but the barking of a half-starved dog or the cackle of a startled hen breaks the silence. Or you may struggle up the winding path which zig-zags along the granite *Rocher de la Bourboule*, at whose foot the springs have their rise, and which is specially interesting to geologists as representing a fragment of the earth's primitive crust. The summit is covered with short grass, and commands a glorious view over La Bourboule lying in the valley below, the river winding through it, and the hills rising around, while beyond are range upon range of volcanic formation, an indescribable picture, and everywhere the same delicious life-giving air.

## PART II.

LITTLE by little we forgot the discomforts and drawbacks which at first impressed us so disagreeably. The fascination of this wonderful country grew upon us, and we realized its charm more keenly as we learnt more of the beauties hidden away in its depths.

Of the many easy walks round La Bourboule itself, I would give the palm to the following:—first to the Ravin de l'Eau Salée, an offshoot of the lovely valley of Vendeix on the south side of La Bourboule, along whose fine high road we wandered, through sweeping green fields with fir-clad hills beyond, and the strange pile of the Roche de Vendeix in front; this is a mass of columnar basalt whose sides, where not precipitous, are richly cultivated. In the fourteenth century it was the home of the robber chieftain Lymerigot, whose castle crowned its height, and who made raids from thence, striking terror into all hearts. In the summer of 1888 excavations made on the summit of the rock disclosed fragments of spears, swords, and other articles buried at a considerable depth, the last relics of the robber and his band. One of the legends of the country tells how this district was formerly inhabited by beneficent fairies who took the whole valley under their protection. At a stroke of their wand the granite rock divided, and from it flowed the waters of a hidden lake, which afterwards enabled the valley to be cultivated ; to these fairies was also due the discovery of the health-restoring springs, whose properties they taught the villagers to appreciate, and in which they themselves were wont to bathe. La Roche des Fées is still pointed out, on which they are supposed to have left the imprint of their dainty feet, but the depredations of Lymerigot and his evil life finally drove them away, never to return.

Turning off the high road abruptly to the left, we enter the *Ravin de l'Eau Salée*, and find ourselves transported into a miniature gorge: a streamlet once said to have been salt (whence its name), but which now retains no particle of saline matter, flows between great masses of granite, gneiss, and basalt, interspersed with hoary fir trees, twisted and gnarled in their conflict with the storms of centuries; the grass at our feet is starred with delicate pansies, forget-me-nots, and wild pinks, while dog-roses and honeysuckle fling their shackles over low-growing shrubs, and the air is fragrant with the scent of herbs crushed by our own feet; up in the sunlit air a hawk is poised on outspread wings, every now and then the fir trees sigh in the summer breeze as if weary of the ceaseless hum of insects and twitter of birds.

If, on the other hand, we turn to the North, and go up to Murat le Quaire, we find ourselves on another extraordinary mass of columnar basalt facing the Roche de Vendeix, with the valley of Bourboule intervening. This square rock was also once crowned by a fortress owned by the Lords of Murat, the hereditary and deadly enemies of the owners of Vendeix. Like two eyries, the castles were perched on either side of a chasm, frowning at each other across the deep shadow, their halls resounding to the clang of arms and the cry of war, and many a scene of bloodshed and cruelty did their walls witness. Now but a handful of crumbling ruins remains, scarce traceable under their cloak of coarse grass, on which goats browse peacefully, undisturbed by the hawk soaring aloft in the blue, or by passing cloud-shadows on the wooded slopes and swelling lands below, whence rise the sounds of distant village bells. We felt as though we were poised in mid-air, as, standing on the edge of this precipitous rock, we drank in the brisk invigorating air and enjoyed the panorama. Below, halfway to La Bourboule, lies Murat, now a mere collection of cottages, but formerly the principal village in the valley, containing the parish church and the communal hall; the castle of Murat le Quaire on the rock above fell into ruins, as I have said, but there remained the castle chapel nestling in the shelter of the great basaltic mass. There a few houses sprang up, and as years went on, the Murat family lost interest in the place, left the neighbourhood, and the chapel went to ruin. Twenty years ago, when the parish church of Murat became too dilapidated for use, the heiress of Murat presented the commune with the ruined chapel of her family, aided it substantially in repairing the edifice, and now the off-shoot eclipses the original locality. Murat has become a churchless hamlet, and the hamlet of Murat le Quaire an important village; a picturesque one it is too, with its thatched roofs, mellowed by exposure to wind and weather, grouped round the little *Place*, a fountain in the centre, and sheltering trees all round.

Another favourite walk was to the cascades of La Vernière and Plat à Barbe, by a stony path along the ancient river-bed, with the modern Dordogne flowing in a very much narrower channel, passing the Source Clémence, and after crossing the river by means of stepping stones, stretches of green fields, where the soft grass was grateful to tired feet; the grasping Auvergnat exacts a toll of two *sous* a head at the entrance to three different fields, which tax is levied on the passers by an urchin in *sabots*, a girl and a woman in turn; finally we reached the shade of pine-trees, whose coolness struck pleasantly after our long hot walk, for the pitiless rays of the western sun had beat on our backs all up the river-bed. The path wound through lovely woods, where tall fox-gloves, pink willow herb, wild geranium, and delicate quaking grasses grew among the brown and rugged rocks; the ground was thickly carpeted with fallen pine needles, and the dark green of the firs was here and there relieved by the lighter tints of the birch. In the depth of the forest, where the shade cast a chill, we suddenly came upon the beautiful Cascade de la Vernière, a truly sylvan scene, the semi-gloom being accentuated by the white gleam of water pouring down and filling the air with its roar. The second waterfall of Plat à Barbe is smaller, but rather more interesting, as instead of merely falling over the face of the rock, it rushes down a steep, self-cut channel between two boulders, hits the rock opposite, falls back into the basin hollowed by the swirl, and flows off at right angles down an incline to form the Vernière Fall a short distance lower down.

Of longer excursions the well-known watering place of Mont Dore is one of the commonest; the pleasantest way of accomplishing the intervening five miles is to drive there, and back by another route through the forest of Bozat. Having followed the course of the Dordogne for some distance, and passed the hamlet of Genestoux, we came to the *Salon de Mirabeau*, a kind of natural amphitheatre, whose greensward was enclosed by rocks where the echo is perfect. This place derives its name from the fact that Mirabeau, elder brother of the famous statesman, used to picnic on this spot; on one side is a wild ravine, bounded by a suddenly-arrested stream of lava, the picture of desolation. At intervals along the roadsides we came upon water troughs, formed out of hollowed tree-trunks, and wayside crosses, with faded wreaths lying at their feet, were frequent; further on the village and Fall of Queureille is reached, the water rushing and foaming furiously, from a height of ninety feet, over a perpendicular rock of black basalt, whose summit is crowned by some firs outlined against the blue sky. Shortly before reaching Mont Dore we passed the little cemetery on a hill-side, with a tall crucifix standing in the midst, the bronze figure on an iron cross, with outstretched arms relieved against a background of green hills. Mont Dore, though situated 656 feet higher than La Bourboule, strikes the visitor as confined and shut in, for it lies in a narrow valley between bare stony hills blocked at the south by the Pic de Sancy, the highest mountain in Central

France. Its hot springs, six in number, emerging from the soil at a temperature of 112° Fahrenheit, are very efficacious in all affections of the throat and lungs, as well as articular rheumatism; the Romans used them in days when Auvergne was under their sway, but they were abandoned as far back as the fifth century, till ages later some workmen, as they dug, came upon the ruins of the "Baths of Cæsar," with the shafts, capitals and entablature of a Roman temple, which were removed to the public promenade, where they still lie in a confused heap. The *Établissement* is much more primitive than at La Bourboule; generous provision is, however, made for the poor, a third of the patients annually treated being gratuitously received into the Hospital and tended by the Sisters of Charity. Many singers and actors come here for their throats, and when, as often happens in the course of the season, a charity concert is given, one may chance upon an assemblage of the greatest celebrities of the musical and dramatic world. Mont Dore itself is by no means an attractive place, with a Cockneyfied public park, bad band, and numerous bazaars and stalls, where walking sticks, articles of clothing in Pyrenean wool, and trashy trinkets, set with imitation gems, are displayed to tempt the unwary. So stifling was the atmosphere of the valley on the day we visited it, that we were glad to leave it behind, and wind along the south-west side till we reached the high lands which form the watershed between the Mont Dore and Vendeix valleys, and are in great part covered by the splendid old forest of Bozat; exquisite was the sunlight on the tips of the fir-trees; on all sides streams like silver threads meandered through fairy dells and miniature ravines, where dock-leaves and fungi of all shapes and colours formed tents and umbrellas for elves and fairy folk. As we penetrated deeper into the heart of the forest, it grew sombre and gloomy in the afternoon light; the giant fir-trees were hung with fine specimens of the grey lichen familiarly styled "old man's beard"; each depression of the ground seemed the bed of a tiny stream almost hidden by delicate ferns and forget-me-nots and the plumes of white spiræa. At last the forest cleared, and we emerged into the full glare of the setting sun slanting across the wild and lonely *Plateau de Bozat*; thence, as if raised on a central mound, we saw weird mountain forms; not a tree, not a shrub within a mile of us which could afford shelter when one of the pitiless storms of the district sweep across this desolate moorland, but lying as it did then, steeped in the golden light of an August afternoon, it was grand and beautiful: a herd of cattle was browsing in the distance, a bird of prey hovering high up overhead, otherwise there was no living creature in sight, no human beings beyond our own party. In spring, when the short springy grass of this district is one sheet of colour with wild flowers, it must be a still more gorgeous sight; we longed ourselves to pick the *Spergularia marina* and *salina*, *Trifolium maritimum* which, by some unexplained means, have forsaken their usual seaboard habitat, and are now exiles in a strange land, or the *Saxifraga hieracifolia* now commonly associated with Greenland and Spitzbergen, the much-admired *Edelweiss* of Swiss renown, or the delicate *Capillis Veneris*, always connected with warmth and moisture, not to mention hundreds of other lovely blossoms, an unrivalled medley of botanical specimens which are all to be found in this wonderful Province of Auvergne, but more especially in the stretch of land between the Mont Dore range and the Cantal.

Another afternoon was devoted to a drive of five or six hours to the Lac de Guéry; as far as Mont Dore it was familiar ground, but instead of entering the little town, we turned our backs to it and crept along the eastern face of the valley skirting the base of the *Plateau de L'Angle*, a lava stream whose suddenly-arrested progress has left a precipitous promontory, round which the road to Clermont *viâ* Randanne is engineered at a stiff gradient. Once round the projection, it meanders, always steadily ascending, through luxuriant beech and pine woods, passing the *Saut du Loup*, a cascade which falls over a rock of columnar basalt into a wooded gorge; mountain ash, hawthorn, and holly trees covered with scarlet berries glowed among the green. It was all peaceful and calm, but gradually the character of the country changed, growing wild and desolate, as the road grew black or reddish-brown with lava and dust from the scoriæ, and the very stones were coated with oxide of iron. The lake, high up on a flat table-land, lies in a hollow like a cup, the bottom of an extinct crater, with the chain of the Mont Dore rising behind; it glistened like a polished mirror in the sunshine, its surface unruffled, save when a silvery trout leapt out of the water. A sudden turn of the road lands us on the edge of another of these wonderful valleys; at first, a glen thickly covered with copse wood, then two huge masses of rock rise like giant sentinels on either hand, the *Sanadoire* on the right, the *Tuillière* on the left; from their bases the valley widens ever more and more, till its lines are lost in the great plain of Rochefort stretching away as far as the eye can reach into Northern France; green and golden patches of corn fields, fruit gardens, purple cloud-shadows, and silver streaks marking the course of some distant river, mingle into one harmonious whole framed by the two magnificent phonoliths, as they stand, grim reminders of past ages. The shape of the *Sanadoire* is by far the most picturesque, its pointed summit, as yet unscaled by human foot, offers a coign of observation to the eagle as he rests on its crags. The *Tuillière*, on the contrary, resounds to the pickaxe and hammer, for it is formed of closely-packed basaltic prisms which are easily split transversely into rough slating stones for cottage roofs, hence its name. The loneliness of the Lac de Guéry, with the solitary inn on its further shore, the rough moorland, clothed with juniper, heather, and the coarse foliage of *Gentiana lutea* on which we stood shivering in the keen breeze, notwithstanding the hot sun that poured down as we gazed spell-bound on the scene at our feet, made up a picture which would require a master-hand to do it justice, so extraordinarily do the weird and the beautiful, the delicate and the powerful, aspects of Nature intermingle.

The above only represent a few of the many excursions round La Bourboule, but suffice to give an idea of this wonderful country; many other places might be visited, such as Murol, St. Nectaire, Issoire, Besse and La Tour d'Auvergne. At the last, an annual fair takes place towards the end of August, to which the peasant girls come to sell their hair, exchanging their long plaits for so many *mètres* of linen or so many cotton handkerchiefs!

To the artist, the photographer, the geologist, and the botanist, this corner of France is a very treasure-trove; to those who enjoy that "keenest pleasure of travel, getting off the beaten track," Auvergne is full of charm, combining in itself every variety of scenery, from the ordinary sylvan, to wild rocky passes and ravines, which rival many a Spanish Sierra and defile, but always instinct with a character all its own.

# Late in Life.

BY A. PERRIN.

Author of "INTO TEMPTATION," &c.

## CHAPTER XXVII.

### DEATH.

*"The sad vicissitude of things."*

THIS was what had happened. The new pony had conducted himself admirably after Cecil and Ella left Garthwood. He trotted out in his best style, with his little pointed ears pricked forward, hoping to catch sight of some object that might justify his indulging in a mild shy. He was very fresh and rather inclined to be nervous, so Cecil spoke to him occasionally in a coaxing, encouraging tone, and all went well until the outskirts of the common were reached.

Then a difference of opinion arose. Cecil wished to continue straight ahead along the Yatebury road, while the pony took a fancy to the short cut across the common used only by riders or pedestrians. The smooth springy turf looked to him very tempting, and such a delightful contrast to the hard dusty road! He snuffed the fresh breezy wind that swept over the gorse and bracken, wakening recollections of the days of his youth, when he could kick up his heels and gallop at will with no tiresome vehicle behind him. He stopped resolutely when Cecil opposed his desire to cross the common, and began to back into the hedge. At the first touch of the whip he reared, and then laid his ears back as though contemplating a kick next time for a change.

"Little beast!" said Cecil impatiently, "what can have come over him? I hope I haven't been stuck—I bought him as being absolutely free from vice."

"He's only very fresh," said Ella, who was not in the least nervous, "give him time. Let Bradley go to his head, he only wants coaxing and soothing."

On receiving the order the groom sprang to the ground, and the sudden movement was too much for the excited little animal.  Before Bradley could reach his head he had taken advantage of a momentary slackening of Cecil's hold on the reins, and bolted full tilt across the common, regardless even of the pathway.  Had he only followed that, Cecil might have managed to pull him up before any harm was done, but the jolting and bumping of the trap over the hillocks in the ground maddened him still further, and taking the bit between his teeth, he positively tore over the uneven ground, leaving the terrified groom running far behind.

"It can't last much longer," said Cecil breathlessly, as one of the wheels rose over a grassy mound, all but upsetting them; but still they sped on, bounding over hillocks, swaying and swinging from side to side, and expecting the final crash every moment.

"Look!" gasped Ella, "there's the Wattles' cottage.  Try and head him for it, it may stop him."

She and Cecil seized the left rein together, and pulling with all their strength, managed to turn the pony's course in the direction of the dwelling.  Another desperate haul at the reins and the mad gallop seemed about to slacken, when the figure of a woman rose from behind a clump of gorse and waved a shawl wildly to and fro.  It was Sally Wattle, who had been sitting on the ground a few yards from the cottage, awaiting Bill's return from work, and on hearing the rattle of the approaching trap had sprung to her feet, moved by a crazy impulse, and waved her ragged shawl, at the same time yelling at the top of her voice.

The pony swerved violently, the wheel rose high over one of the many knolls that dotted the common, there was a sickening lurch, a noise of splintering wood, the thud of hoofs against the splash board, and Cecil found himself shot head foremost into the middle of a furze bush.  He was on his feet again in a minute, shaken, dazed, and scratched, but otherwise unhurt, and then he saw a sight that afterwards haunted him to the day of his death—the trap upside down wrecked and broken, the pony struggling on the ground, entangled in the harness, and amongst it all, close to the kicking, fighting heels, lay Ella, helplessly doubled up and unconscious.

Cecil hardly knew how he got her out, and laid her, white and still, upon the grass; how he kept his presence of mind and carried her into the cottage with the help of grinning Sally Wattle, whom he frightened into bringing a ricketty bed into the kitchen, and fetching some water. Or how when the horrified breathless groom arrived on the scene, he helped him to free the pony, and started the man off to Garthwood post haste on its back.

The interval during which he was forced to wait till help could come seemed to him an eternity. Ella lay on Sally's shaky, squalid bed, as though she were dead—she never moved or even sighed, and Cecil sat rubbing her hands and bathing her face with water, feeling half-mad with terror and apprehension. Bill Wattle returned from his work, and Cecil sent him off to the doctor's, with orders to stay there until he came in, if he should happen to be out, and the weary watch continued until Emily and Aunt Eliza appeared with pillows, rugs, brandy, and everything they thought might be useful. But almost simultaneously with them came the man whom they had despatched for the doctor to say that the latter was out. Then Emily had sent William on up to Undercliff, remembering that Nina was not well, and in the meantime every effort was made to restore Ella to consciousness, but without success.

At the moment that George entered the cottage Cecil had gone out at the back-door, thinking he heard the sound of hoofs in that direction, so that all George saw at first was the red countenance of Aunt Eliza, shining in the flickering light of the candle as she sat bolt upright, with her bushy eye-brows drawn into an anxious frown, and her grizzled hair in wild disorder. He wondered who she was, and then Emily's face caught his eye, white and small with fear, as she knelt beside the low bed, on which lay a form in that helpless attitude that betokens unconsciousness. A glint of yellow hair in the faint candle light told him only too surely who lay there.

"Oh! you've come?" cried Emily, as George's tall figure crossed the threshold, and thinking at first that it was Dr. Roseberry, then recognising George, she gave a start of surprise and relief.

"Oh! you will know what to do," she said, with involuntary confidence in her tone. "Look! she has never moved—we can't bring her round! Aunt Eliza, this is Dr. Barr." Then turning to him again, "You will do all you can? Don't say she is seriously hurt—don't let her die!" Emily's voice rose to a wail, and she wrung her hands despairingly.

"Hush!" said George quietly. "If you want to help me you must keep your presence of mind."

He could see that Emily was over-strung, that her nerves were giving way, and he wanted to summon her natural command over her feelings to her aid. She had been through a terrible strain during that helpless time of watching. The fruitless efforts to bring her sister round, Cecil's despairing anxiety, and angry impatience for the doctor's arrival, and Aunt Eliza's noisy ways and repeated declarations that it was nothing but an ordinary faint, added to George's unexpected appearance, had been too much for her, and when she rose from her knees to go and call Cecil, she would have fallen had not George caught her in his arms.

"There!" said Aunt Eliza, hastening forward, "now *she's* fainted. Give her to me, I'll take her outside into the air; she'll only hinder you here, and I'll soon bring her round."

She seized Emily in her muscular arms and half carried her out of the room. As she did so Cecil entered, his face drawn and grey, and a look of terrified dread in his eyes.

"Thank God!" he began in a tone of relief, then in angry surprise, "Where is the doctor? What are you doing here? You of all people?" He spoke roughly, almost brutally, and glared savagely at George, who explained his presence clearly and quietly, and added:

"I am only a doctor now, so put personal feelings out of the question. I may be able to save her life."

Cecil drew back with a groan and watched George kneel down by the bed and tenderly feel the helpless limbs. There was a minute's absolute silence, and then he rose from his knees. He opened his mouth to speak, and a queer, dry, muffled sound came from his throat. He waited for one moment, his large, firm features growing hard and set, and then said:

"She is dying—nothing can be done."

The two men looked at one another until the meaning of the words had driven itself into Cecil's brain, who called out: "You liar! you liar!" and flung himself down by the little still figure, pouring out his grief in tearing, heart-rending sobs. George stood by the table and looked on, he envied Cecil the right to show his sorrow, also the power of shedding tears. His own eyes were clear and glittering as steel, and he looked almost impassive by the side of poor Cecil's passionate grief.

Just then Ella stirred very slightly and moaned. Cecil leant over her as if he wished to be the first her eyes should rest on. George did not move, he knew what was coming, that the poor little back was broken, and that this was the end, and he meant to let her rightful lover have her last moments. The blue-grey eyes opened slowly, and the scene of Bertie's death-bed came back to George with startling distinctness. He could almost hear the punkah creaking, almost fancy he was listening to Bertie's weak, tired voice speaking of "the governor and sisters." She looked at Cecil wearily, unknowingly, and moaned a little again, then she gave a slight shiver, hardly more than a sigh, and then the two men who loved her so dearly knew that she had gone from them to the arms of Death, who was her lover now.

George watched Cecil pressing his lips to the little dead girl's forehead, muttering sobbing, incoherent words, with a bitter envy at his heart. He himself had no right even to kiss her hand! The candle guttered and spluttered in the neck of the broken bottle that held it, the strong stuffy smell of the cottage rose in his nostrils, Cecil's sobs of misery rang in his ears, and also another sound that suddenly cut through the stillness :

"Of all the girls tha—hat are so smar—hart,
There's none like pretti—hee Sally !"

There, unnoticed in the corner, Sally Wattle had been crouching, frightened and subdued, and now, unable to keep quiet any longer, she had begun to croon her favourite song gently to herself.

Good Heavens! How it brought back that balmy summer afternoon to George, when the squalid cottage had been flooded with the clear sunshine and the golden-haired child, radiant with life and spirits, had stood looking up at him with her sleepy blue-grey eyes full of mischievous laughter. And now—oh! now!
—He turned abruptly to Cecil and said hoarsely :

"Shall I call the others ?"

Cecil did not answer at first, then he looked up and said :

"Yes. You are not wanted here any longer—you had better

go. You did not help to make her life any happier, so perhaps it is as well you could not save it."

There was a hopeless, sullen animosity in the tone that cut George to the quick, for he felt that Cecil was in some manner justified in speaking as he did. Ella must have told him of the scene on the terrace, and of her own subsequent repentance of her folly, and naturally he regarded himself (George) with feelings of anger and hatred.

George hesitated as to whether he should reply, and then the hopeless knowledge of how futile any explanation would be, closed his lips. What defence could he make? After all he could only own that he had taken advantage of Ella's youth and susceptibility to betray his love for her! It did not matter how Cecil felt towards him; nothing in the world could ever matter again. In a few days he would be going back to his old life to face the remainder of his existence as patiently as he might.

He went to the door, and found Emily and old Miss Seton just entering the cottage, the former white and shaking, but more or less herself again. He prepared them for what they would find inside and then watched the first shock of their grief with a hardness and a lack of sympathy that surprised himself, and made him wonder if his heart had been turned to stone.

A moment afterwards Dr. Roseberry arrived and George left the cottage without another backward look within.

## CHAPTER XXVIII.

### A MEETING.

*"Who does the best his circumstance allows,
Does well, acts nobly; angels could no more."*

BUT, after all, George did not leave England so soon as he had intended, for when he got back to Undercliff that terrible night, weary in body and soul, feeling stupid and bewildered, and scarcely able to realize what had happened, he found Nina distinctly ill. She had worked herself into a high nervous fever, and was almost delirious over the events of the afternoon, and having really a somewhat delicate constitution, George was afraid she might be in for a nasty attack unless she was kept very quiet and free from all excitement.

She was furious with herself for having betrayed her feelings at Garthwood, and furious also with Augusta, all the more so as she was doubtful what attitude to assume—whether to attempt explanations with Mrs. Hatherly, or carry matters with a high hand and follow Augusta's advice by going about with the latter in public as much as possible. She insisted on her brother sitting up with her, and also listening to a rather incoherent recital of her troubles which lasted the greater part of the night and so occupied her mind that she was quite satisfied with the purposely vague replies George made to her questions as to the consequences of the accident.

By the time the morning came he deemed it advisable to send for Dr. Roseberry, who immediately responded to the summons, and, being a hopelessly loquacious old man, utterly unable to hold his tongue, proceeded on his arrival to furnish Nina with full details of the accident and its fatal results, of which George had been carefully keeping her in ignorance while in her present nervous excitable state. The old fellow was full of the topic, and could talk of nothing else, until Nina became hysterical, when he advised perfect rest, and took his departure after prescribing a cooling dose and a sleeping draught, both of which his patient flatly refused to swallow. She was the most trying and exacting of invalids, and took it into her head that George and no one else should sit with her and look after her. She would not see her husband, declaring that the noise of his boots drove her mad, and she declined to allow Augusta into her room, querulously asserting that she was too ill to talk to her, a decision that by no means hurt that lady's stolid feelings, or even affected her appetite, and during Nina's illness she passed the most comfortable time she had yet spent at Undercliff. She drove about in the carriage both morning and evening, enjoyed the most *récherché* meals, which she ordered herself, and often partook of in bed, opened and read all the papers first, and altogether had a very good time of it, while poor Mr. Compton creaked sadly about the house, haunting Nina's door at intervals and whispering unhappily to himself.

Nina's one idea and desire seemed to be to persuade George to delay his departure from England. She implored him not to leave her, and besought him with floods of tears to extend his leave if only for a month, vowing she could never recover her health unless he yielded to her wishes, all of which finally ended in communications with the India Office, and a transfer (after a good deal of trouble) of his passage to a steamer starting a few weeks later. Then, once Nina had accomplished her desire, she permitted herself to become gradually better, and was rather less exacting in her demands on George's time and attention. Also she received Lady Jebbs back into favour on hearing that Mrs. Hatherly and Cecil had gone abroad for an indefinite period immediately after Ella's funeral, reflecting that she might just as well retain Augusta's friendship now that there was no danger of losing Mrs. Hatherly's.

The result was that George found the time inexpressibly weary, and very much repented of having indulged his sister's whim. He was terribly miserable, depressed and restless; all interest in life seemed to have left him, his face looked older and more lined, his blue eyes graver and more stern. Twice since Nina had given him back his liberty he had started for the churchyard where the love of his life was lying, and each time he had turned back. He longed to see her resting-place, and yet he so dreaded the anguish of mind that he must suffer, and the bitter heart-ache with which he must view her grave.

At last the longing became too strong for him, and one mild hazy afternoon he left the house on foot and walked rapidly in the direction of the Branthorpe churchyard. It had been at Cecil's desire that she was laid there; she had once told him half laughingly that when she died she should like to be buried on the little green slope dotted with crosses and stones, old and new, shadowed by the thick clipped yews and melancholy cypress trees. Her words had come back to him with bitter distinctness after her death. George felt glad they had put her there as he entered the silent little "garden of God," and became conscious of the rest and peace that filled it. The solemn hush and stillness calmed his aching soul, and softened the awfulness of her death and the cruel suddenness of her loss. He knelt down and laid his hand tenderly and lovingly on the withered grass that covered the little newly-made mound, and then that subtle sense stole into his mind which might perhaps be called prayer without words.

On the grave was laid a mass of beautiful white, waxy flowers, sent daily from the Abbey gardens and conservatories (Cecil's last order before he left), and amongst their fragrant, delicate petals, George saw a few tiny daisies struggling to raise their heads for a glimpse of light and sunshine. He picked one of them, and placed it carefully in the little leather case that contained the pencilled words of the song that Ella had given him. Then he rose from his knees and stood motionless for a moment; the constant gnawing sorrow in his breast was soothed, and as he turned to leave the churchyard, the hard light in his eyes was softened, and the lines on his rugged face were smoother than they had been since that awful night in Sally Wattle's cottage.

When he got outside the little iron gates he paused. It was still fairly early, and he felt the need of a long walk before returning to the house, so he looked about him for a second, and finally started down a green lane that skirted the village, with his eyes bent on the ground, and his thoughts behind him in the churchyard.

He had not gone more than a quarter of a mile when a sudden exclamation startled him, and looking up quickly, he found himself face to face with Emily Seton. She was dressed in heavy mourning, which seemed to drag her spare narrow shoulders down, and accentuate the angularity of her figure, and her woe-begone face with its deadly pallor and red eyelids, struck a thrill of pity through George's kind heart. Poor thing! how she must feel her sister's loss! Her life must be a thousand times more dull and cheerless now, with that ray of sunshine gone out of it for ever! All his old compassion for Emily came doubly back to him, and sympathy for her sorrow obliterated his own for the moment.

In truth she was sorely to be pitied, for her life was hopelessly grey. She had lost her only sister, of whom she had been very fond in her own common-place, unemotional way; her father had collapsed entirely after the death of his favourite daughter, and now rarely left his room, where he railed unceasingly against Providence, and frequently informed Emily that had she been killed instead of her sister, nobody would have regretted it—least of all himself. Still she nursed and tended him untiringly, but with a patient resignation that enraged and maddened the unhappy old man, and made him throw books and papers at her, call her every name he could think of or invent, and generally lead her the life of a dog. Aunt Eliza had departed, so Emily had not even her companionship; but apparently she did not mind, her feelings seemed blunted. She accepted her hardships without complaint or rebellion; but nevertheless they were leaving their mark on her tired little face and form, and Emily was growing an old woman before her time.

When she saw George her whole expression changed. Her dull sad eyes lit up with hope and joy, she smiled—wistfully it is true—but very sweetly, for love will beautify even the plainest face, and when she smiled she showed her small, regular white teeth, which were one of the very few good points in her appearance. She flushed crimson, and when she put her hand out in answer to his friendly greeting, it was trembling visibly.

Then a thought shot through George's mind that made him redden in his turn to the roots of his hair, for he suddenly remembered Nina's words one night in the drawing-room, when she had asserted her conviction that Emily Seton cared for him. He felt heartily ashamed of himself for harbouring such a suspicion for a moment, and the embarrassment he showed was delightful to Emily, who did not know its true cause, for it revived her deadened hopes and brought back possibilities to her which she had quite given up for lost. She was sure he was glad to see her! His hand was shaking like hers and his face was flushed—oh! *dared* she let him see that he might speak? dared she give him any encouragement? It was so hard, standing there alone in the lane with the man whom she adored and admired above all other human beings, to control her feelings and keep them to herself.

"Where are you going?" enquired George, when they had gone through the usual enquiries as to health, and he had explained his altered plans.

"To the churchyard," she answered, holding up the basket of flowers she was carrying.

"I have just been there," he said softly; and then, as he looked at Emily, a sudden impulse came over him to confide in her and tell her all his trouble. He felt that her friendship would be valuable to him, and that making her his *confidante* would create a bond between them which might last all their lives.

He liked her, he saw the excellent traits in her character; he honestly admired her for her patience and unselfishness, and he knew he could trust her. Also, if any mistaken ideas regarding his feelings towards her had grown up in her mind—much as he loathed himself for the thought—well, his confession would place their friendship on a sounder and surer footing.

"Can you spare me half an hour? Will you turn back with me a little way?" he asked appealingly—he felt he could not retrace his footsteps towards the churchyard—"I want so much to talk to you."

"I will come," she said simply, and they walked on slowly together, both their hearts beating very fast.

"Emily," he said, unconsciously using her christian name in his agitation, "I shall be going back to India a great deal more miserable than when I left it. I don't know what you will say when I tell you the reason, for I tried very hard to hide it, and I think I succeeded. There was only once when I gave way to the hope that came so suddenly to me, and then it was shattered almost as soon as it was born."

Emily bent her head, and her breath came thick and fast. She could not speak, she could scarcely step firmly and steadily, and she clutched her umbrella and the basket of flowers in her thin hands with a desperate grip. George found it difficult to go on. He suddenly realized that she might blame him as bitterly as he had blamed himself for his behaviour to her sister, might treat him with contempt for not having been man enough to control his feelings, and for having given Ella an experience which she must always have remembered more or less with shame.

"I know I made a grievous mistake——" he began, and had meant to continue—"in not leaving the place when I found I was in love with your sister"—but the latter words were never uttered, for a sob from Emily had stopped him. She had turned and faced him, her two hands held out, and the umbrella and the basket—with all the flowers scattered—lay on the ground.

"No—it was not a mistake!" she cried desperately, "it was I who made the mistake—I cared all along—I do care—oh! I didn't know what to do or how to act."

Her eyes were full of tears, her face was white and quivering with the intensity of her feelings, she stood before him overcome with her great love—and he? He saw that Emily had misunderstood him, and had taken his words as a declaration of love for her, and at that moment he thought far more of her than he did for himself. He realized what she was feeling, he could see her overwhelming happiness, and he shuddered to think of the reaction when she knew the truth.

How was he to explain? What was he to say? Could he bring himself to let her keep her happiness? Ought he not to do so, since his own life was now of little or no account to him? No, he could not do it, he must tell her. He took her shaking hands in his, gently and firmly, and waited till she should have recovered her self-command, and then, as they stood there hand in hand in the middle of the deep lane, with its high banks shutting out the world on either side, the flowers, basket, and umbrella lying neglected in the dust, and Emily looking tremblingly up into his eyes—the two Miss Wanklins suddenly turned the bend of the road and came full upon them!

"Oh!" they cried in a breath, stopping short, hardly able to believe their eyes. Then they looked at one another and smiled meaningly, as George, it must be confessed, stooped down to pick up the basket and umbrella to hide his confusion. Here was an excitement! Here was the event they had made so sure of, and over which they had been so disappointed. Emily Seton engaged to be married! What a piece of news to go round with, and what honour and glory would be theirs as being the first outsiders to know of it!

The elder Miss Wanklin, who was the more prudent of the two, then began to think it might be as well to make sure of the fact before spreading the news. It would never do to announce the engagement and then find there was nothing in it! Men were such base deceivers, she thought, with an angry remembrance of her own numerous disappointments, and perhaps this one was only making a fool of old Emily Seton after all.

"Oh! Emily," she giggled, looking from the latter to George's stooping figure, "I'm afraid we came round the corner too suddenly! But we really didn't know you and Doctor Barr were here. I am so sorry! But won't you——? mayn't we?—you know we're such old friends—and we should be so glad if we might congratulate you!" The last sentence was spoken in a loud whisper, and George straightened himself quickly, looking at the two odious girls as though he could have slain them then and there.

"I am sorry to say that you did come round the corner rather too suddenly, Miss Wanklin," he said, in an icy, contemptuous voice, "and as it does not seem to have occurred to you to pass on as most ladies would have done under the circumstances, I will confess that I was just asking Miss Seton if she would do me the honour of becoming my wife, and perhaps, if you would continue your walk, I might have a chance of receiving her answer."

He burned with indignation for Emily's sake. He could not have stood by and seen her humiliated, and made a laughing-stock of, by these two detestable women. He felt he could not have acted otherwise under the circumstances, and yet—*what* had he done?

The two Miss Wanklins stood for a moment speechless with astonishment, and half frightened at George's angrily severe manner, then they muttered some incoherent apology, and hurried on their way, though they looked back several times, bitterly regretting that the bend in the lane hid the two figures from their inquisitive view.

George and Emily took a few steps in absolute silence till the corner of the road was turned. Then the former braced himself up, the die was cast, his fate decided, and henceforth he would have a great duty in life—that of making this poor, plain, trembling little woman's existence a happy one.

"What is your answer, Emily?" he said, looking down into her face.

There is no need to tell it. Emily returned to Garthwood that evening George's promised wife, and there was one person at least in the world who was so supremely happy that she could almost fancy herself in Heaven.

*(To be concluded.)*

# BELGRAVIA.

*NOVEMBER*, 1895.

## An Old Maid's Mistake.

BY MRS. CONNEY,

Author of "A Lady Horsebreaker," "A Ruthless Avenger," "Gold for Dross," etc.

### CHAPTER XXXI.

BOTH Mr. and Mrs. Blunt returned from the Court thoroughly out of sorts. Esme, who had parted coldly from her host, reproached herself one moment for having thus wounded the best and most generous of friends, and the next, devoutly hoped she might never see or speak to him again. Arnold for his part found the simple surroundings of his own home doubly distasteful after his late experience of luxury. Also he hadn't done himself justice with his shooting, and the Kestertons, although civil enough, had shown no eagerness to cultivate him, while he had fallen completely out of touch with the world of fashion. Especially too he missed the flattery to which in his prosperity he had grown accustomed, and felt himself overlooked, poor and of no account. Naturally he didn't like it, and could hardly help drawing comparisons between the manners of his little friend Clara Dixon and those of Lady Julia for instance, which comparisons were by no means to the favour of the latter. It was curious indeed how much he missed his visits to the Firs, in which direction he turned his steps half-an-hour after his return to Hawthornden. He found Clara alone and delighted to see him.

"So your fine friends haven't made you forget us," she said flushing with pleasure. She had a pretty complexion, and a trick of colouring vividly, which he at all events found most attractive.

"No. And they're not likely to either," he answered gloomily. "If adversity does nothing else, it teaches a man where to look for his real friends, and that isn't amongst smart folk. You wouldn't turn from a man because he happened to be down in the world, would you, eh, Clara?"

"Indeed I wouldn't," she assured him, and it was obvious that she spoke nothing but the truth. "You'll never find friends who'll think more of you than grandfather and me would, no, not if you were to search the whole world through."

"I'm sure of it," he agreed heartily. "You're true and good, and worth a hundred of these dressed-up painted dolls, who call themselves leaders of fashion. And you were a little bit glad to see me, weren't you?"

"I was—I am indeed," she answered with a glance which emphasised her words. For indeed to her Arnold was very little less than a demi-god. As though they were the utterances of an oracle, she hung on his words, while he enunciated various truisms on the heartlessness of a time-serving world, and the hard treatment meted out to deserving poverty. Poor Arnold! It was a necessity to him to be a hero to somebody, even if that somebody were only a little underbred girl with a pretty face, red hands, restless movements, and a nervous giggle. "I know where I'm happiest, at Lisle Court or here," he finally declared, at which Clara tittered delightedly.

"Oh, Mr. Blunt," she protested. "You can't expect me to believe that. With the powdered footmen, splendid dinners, and beautiful ladies."

"There wasn't a single woman there to compare with you," he answered with the air of an authority. "Put you into an evening dress, rig you out with plenty of diamonds, and you'd take the shine out of any one of them." If Arnold were greedy of flattery, he was equally lavish of it in return.

Clara's cheeks grew pinker and her eyes brighter than ever at this gratifying assurance. "Oh, Mr. Blunt! What nonsense!" she cried.

"It's very good sense," he declared. "I never flatter. I've got eyes in my head, that's all, and I know a pretty woman when I see one." And then he changed the conversation by asking her what she had been doing with herself during his absence. His question recalled the trouble overlooked for the time in the pleasure of his visit. Her face clouded over, the corners of her mouth began to droop as "It's been dreadful," she said dolefully, "not a soul to speak to, and grandfather nagging at me from morning till night. Says I've got to marry Mr. Westerton from Mill Hill, and I won't, a nasty, coarse, vulgar creature."

"That brute Westerton!" ejaculated Arnold. "What cheek!"

Quite an angry thrill ran through him at the bare suggestion. Westerton, it must be explained, was a local miller and corn-dealer. He had a shop in Wilburn, owned land in and about the town, was an advanced Radical, a member of the County Council, and it was reported cherished an ambition not only to become Mayor of Wilburn, but also some day to write the magic letters M.P. after his name. For the rest he was a hard, pompous, overbearing person, and was disliked almost as much as he was feared and envied. Nevertheless he was honest, respectable and prosperous, and, so far as manners and appearance went, in no way inferior to those other suitors from whose ranks Miss Dixon must eventually select a husband.

But this Arnold did not stop to recollect. And so when Miss Dixon with a pout declared that she wasn't going to marry a man old enough to be her father, "I should think not indeed," he was injudicious enough to reply. "Whatever his age may be, you shan't throw yourself away on a man who isn't fit to black your boots."

"I won't," whimpered Clara, "if I can help myself, but grandfather likes him, says he's just the husband for me. And if I won't say Yes, I'm to be turned out to earn my own living."

"How abominable!" The threat uttered when Captain Dixon was more or less under the influence of whisky, had been an empty one, as both threatener and threatened were aware. However, it served the purpose. In a white heat of indignant sympathy, Arnold fumed up and down the room. "He can't, he daren't," he declared. "Oh, you poor little girl! How I wish I could help you, but I can't. That's what it is to be a penniless devil. A year ago, it would have been different, but now. . . . Never mind though. I'll see you're not bullied into this monstrous marriage. Trust me. I'll speak to your grandfather about it."

He was given an early opportunity of carrying out this intention, for, just as he was leaving the Firs, having exhausted himself in sympathy for this luckless victim of parental tyranny, Captain Dixon himself appeared.

"I'll walk a step back with you," said this brutal oppressor of helpless innocence, "if you'll excuse the liberty, for I've something to say to you, and I hope you'll not take it amiss if I speak out plain what's in my mind."

"What is it?" asked Arnold, who, ready as he was to take offence, could find no fault with the man's respectful manner.

"Well, it's this way," began Captain Dixon in some embarrassment. "You see, sir, you've been very kind coming in to see us, and treating us like the gentleman you are, as if we were friends and equals, which we're not and never can be, and that I know as well as ever you do. But my girl, she don't understand it. She's lifted above herself by your notice, and discontented with folk in her own rank of life. Now there's a good well-to-do man ready to marry her to-morrow, can give her a comfortable home and everything of the best, and she turns up her nose at him, calls him rough, can't abide his manners at table and such-like nonsense. Now she thinks a deal of you, and what I want you to do is to talk to her and show her where her duty lies."

"That's impossible," retorted Arnold. "From your point of view this man Westerton may seem suitable enough, but I'm not in the least surprised that your granddaughter should object to him. I tell you plainly, to me it seems nothing more nor less than a crime to sacrifice Miss Clara to a surly brute without an idea in his head beyond hay and oats. She's a thousand times too good for him, and if she asks my opinion I shall tell her so."

"I hope you won't do that, sir," begged the old man with the same respectful earnestness. "Don't think I'm blaming you, for I know you've meant well, but to my thinking you've done Clara harm already, filling her head with notions above her station, and I hope you won't take it amiss if I tell you that if you won't help me teach her sense, you mustn't come upsetting her with nonsense. For marry Westerton is what she's got to do."

"It seems to me you are talking nonsense now and nonsense of a most arbitrary and unjustifiable kind," was the lofty rejoinder.

"The days are past for forcing a girl to marry a man she hates and despises.

" Hates and despises ? " loudly repeated the Captain, who was losing control of his patience and temper. "And what call has she got to hate and despise a steady, hard-working feller like Westerton ? I'll tell you what, Mr. Blunt, I'll trouble you to leave my girl alone in future. You—a gentleman and a married man—you ought to know better than to go against lawful authority, and come making mischief between me and my child."

" Thank you, Captain Dixon," rejoined Arnold in a white heat of rage. "That will do. Pray settle your affairs in your own way. I can assure you it will be a long time before I lower myself by associating with you again."

" Serves me right for forgetting myself so far as to have anything to do with the man," reflected Mr. Arnold as he strode off. Yet, ready as he was to wash his hands of the Captain, Miss Clara was not to be so dropped so easily. In the first place, honour and humanity forbade him to leave her in the clutches of a brutal tyrant. Besides, he was interested in her, and had promised to stand by her. Above all, he liked her. Clearly, it would be impossible to withdraw without a word of explanation. And as he sat in the drawing-room that evening revolving plans for the rescue of beauty in distress, Esme startled him a good deal by saying :

" Do you care much for this place, Arnold ? I mean, would you have any objection to going elsewhere ? "

" Does that mean that you want to leave ? " His voice was impatient. The question he felt was ill-timed.

" I think I should be glad to get away for a time certainly," she replied.

" I daresay. So should I," he retorted sharply. "Unfortunately, my dear, going away costs money, which we haven't got, so I regret that, not being millionaires, we must just make the best of it and stay wherewe are."

" We might let Hawthornden and go abroad," she suggested.

" To some beastly fifth-rate hole, without a soul to speak to ? No, thank you. That's asking a little too much of a man. Besides, I thought you liked Hawthornden so much. But then one can't expect a woman to know her own mind.

There's no knowing from one day to another what you do want."

Her lips quivered. "I don't think the place suits me very well," she said slowly. "And now since Dot went—I've——" Her voice broke. To his surprise she got up, threw her arms round his neck, and burst into tears. "Take me away," she sobbed. "Please, please—take me away"

He was most kind and forbearing with what was palpably the unreasoning caprice of a hysterical woman. "My dearest girl," he said, patting her head soothingly, "you're out of sorts, that's what it is. I'm awfully sorry. I'd willingly send you away if I could, but I can't. And if we did move altogether, how do you know you'd be happier elsewhere? You've grown fanciful from being alone so much, that's all. Try to rouse yourself. Go out more and see a few people. You might get Mrs. Langley to take you in for a few days' change, and then, why not ask someone, Cicely Denison, for instance, to keep you company for a bit? And I'll see Evans, too, and get him to give you a tonic."

By the time he had finished his string of remedies Esme's outburst had spent itself.

"Thank you, Arnold," she said, quietly withdrawing her arms and drying her eyes. "I suppose I am unreasonable and out of sorts. I'll try a few days' change of air."

In which way the storm passed as quickly as it came, and was speedily forgotten—by Arnold, at all events.

But to return to Clara, for whom he lay in wait the next day, on her return from her weekly marketing in Wilburn. Her pretty eyes were red and her air dejected, but she summoned up a watery smile as she caught sight of him in the road. "Oh, Mr. Blunt," she faltered. "I am so glad to see you. I was afraid after grandfather's behaviour you would never come near me again."

Arnold pressed the hand—a substantial one—he was holding. "Did you think so badly of me as that?" he asked reproachfully. "Why, if your grandfather should be unjust and cruel, all the more reason that I should stand by you. All the same, I'm afraid I can't come to the Firs again. You see, he actually expected *me* to press Westerton's suit, and when I refused coolly warned me off the premises."

"I know," she whimpered. "He forbade me ever to speak to you or to let you into the house again."

"And do you mean to obey, to submit blindly to such unreasoning tyranny?"

"What am I to do?" she asked helplessly. "Mr. Westerton's coming this afternoon. I shall go out. I said I would, and he declared if I did I needn't trouble to come back."

"Nonsense! He dare not turn you out of your own home. If he did, come to us. We'll take you in, and if there's anything at all in public opinion we'll raise such an outcry that he'll be forced to behave decently to you. Be firm, that's all."

"I will," she answered him, "so long as you don't desert me."

"That I'll never do," he emphatically retorted. "I'll stand by you through thick and thin, and even if I am forbidden the Firs, that's no reason why we shouldn't meet elsewhere. When you go out—and you won't be kept under lock and key, I suppose—you might walk through Red Copse occasionally, couldn't you?"

He made the suggestion with a hesitation, which proved uncalled for. Clara, it appeared, was ready to walk in that or any other direction. She saw no harm in the clandestine turn thus given to their intimacy. Indeed, it lent a flavour of romance which to a mind nourished on cheap and highly-flavoured fiction vastly added to the piquancy of it. If Arnold felt any qualms of conscience he silenced them by the recollection that Captain Dixon's harshness alone had necessitated this secrecy, so that the blame, if blame there were, rested solely upon him.

Accordingly day by day Miss Clara would hurry off to the Red Copse, a wood which skirted Mr. Lisle's park palings, and there pour out her woes, her grandfather's cruel obduracy, her lover's persistence, his low notions, his rough speech, his want of refinement. And there day by day Arnold would uphold, cheer, pity and flatter the girl till she felt quite like one of the persecuted heroines of her favourite romances. It was idle, silly, mischievous talk, yet devoid of intentional harm. Intentional, however or not, the harm was done. The inevitable crisis came at last. Clara one fine spring afternoon had been unusually doleful. Her grandfather, urged on by her impatient suitor, had attacked her with absolute ferocity, so she said. Her life had become unbearable. She would die if she married the detestable brute . . . and. . . Her pretty brown eyes swimming in tears met his. Arnold lost his head. In a rush of pity, he stooped and kissed her. He meant no harm. How could he suspect that just one single kiss, given on the spur of the moment, would call forth a betrayal of the girl's feelings?—how foresee, that carried away by this open display of affection, he himself would be drawn into a similar avowal?

Naturally, in the excitement of the moment he said a good deal more than he meant, when he swore he loved her dearly, and regretted the bonds which forbade him to make her his own. Well! it was nothing much, just a kiss and a score of pretty speeches, no more, still the scene was such as neither the gentleman's wife nor the lady's guardian would have cared to witness. The gentleman this time too, had some difficulty in silencing the voice of conscience. In vain he told himself that no one but a scoundrel would take advantage of an innocent girl's artless self-betrayal to lead her astray, and that from him, not being a scoundrel, she had nothing to fear. In the meantime it was more than flesh and blood could stand to see her distress without making some effort to console her, also under no circumstances could he desert one who trusted so implicitly in him. Nevertheless, he was uneasy, and it was with a guilty sense of wrong-doing that he presented himself the next day at the usual trysting-place.

Now such meetings in a country neighbourhood clearly were not likely to remain unnoticed. Arnold may have flattered himself that the voluminous Inverness cape he habitually wore rendered him invisible to the naked eye. Clara may have considered her sudden craze for fresh air a sufficient cloak for her lengthy absences from home. Her neighbours thought otherwise. In course of time it began first to be whispered, then openly asserted, that Clara Dixon was going wrong; thanks, however, to the cape, there were doubts as to the identity of her companion. In the meantime, a kind friend, justifying her interference on the score of a friendly interest in a motherless girl, made Captain Dixon acquainted with the condition of things.

"You're a long while getting that girl o' yours married," she said, meeting the Captain on the Wilburn road one afternoon. "Which of 'em is it hanging back, Clara or Westerton?"

"Westerton's ready enough," growled the old man. "No shilly-shally about him."

"Then it's Clara. I tell you what, you're too easy with her, you let her gad about too much. Keep her at home and out of the way of her gentlemen friends if you want her to come to her senses. It don't do her no manner o' good to be carrying on in the woods every day."

"Who says she's carrying on?" interrupted the Captain, purple with rage. "It's a lie."

"Everybody says so. Go and see for yourself if you don't believe me. You can meet her comin' out o' Red Copse any afternoon."

Hardly were the words out of her mouth, when the Captain started off. Now Red Copse was a biggish wood, in which he might have wandered for hours without coming upon the culprits. As ill luck would have it, however, he chanced to take a path which led him direct to the spot where, with their heads suspiciously close together, the guilty pair were engaged in earnest conversation. So absorbed indeed were they in one another that neither noticed the approach of the intruder. The first warning received of his presence was when Clara found herself seized by the arm and swung round so violently that in her fright she stumbled and nearly fell.

"Hussy!" panted the Captain, raising a threatening fist.

"How dare you?" shouted Arnold, rushing forward to protect her. "If you lay so much as a finger on her. . . ."

"Hands off!" Captain Dixon's voice shook with rage. "Look to yourself, Mr. Blunt, for I tell you, if I catch you tampering with my girl, by God, I'll shoot you down like the cur you are. We're honest folk, and honest we'll keep, so long as I'm above ground."

"You are insulting Miss Dixon," began Arnold fiercely. His words were unnoticed. Gripping his granddaughter by the arm, the Captain was dragging her away.

What was to be done? To argue with the man in his present frame of mind was impossible. To use force towards a man of sixty and more was equally out of the question. With all the will in the world Clara's protector realised the impossibility of interference. And therefore—it was not a very dignified proceeding, but he had no choice left him—he simply picked up his hat, which had fallen off, and walked away, looking rather like the whipped schoolboy he felt.

## CHAPTER XXXII.

ESME had duly followed her husband's advice. She had spent the inside of a week in London with her stepmother, who, charmed to give her sweet child a little amusement, had taken her to seven teas, an evening party, two bazaars and a charity concert. Nevertheless, so singularly constituted was the sweet child that even this round of dissipation had taken as little effect on her as had the tonic which at Dr. Evans' bidding she swallowed so obediently. Yet who could blame her because her life remained as it had been before—utterly flat, dull, stale, and unprofitable? Such a condition of things was clearly her misfortune, not her fault. No matter. Fine weather was coming. Already, it was marvellously warm for the middle of April. And Cicely had fixed her visit for the beginning of May. Her cheery presence no doubt would help to shake off the intense weariness and depression from which the bereaved mother suffered so terribly.

In the meantime so far as Mr. Lisle was concerned she might dismiss him from her mind. He was away, and likely to remain away. In fact she hadn't even seen him since her visit to the Court. To be sure, he had called at Hawthornden three times. On the first occasion, moved by some unaccountable impulse, she had said—not at home; on the second, she really had been out; on the third, she had been away in town. And now he happened to be staying with the Kestertons, and as Parliament was reassembling after the Easter holidays, would naturally go direct to London from thence. Having arrived at which decision, she heard a ring at the door bell, and a minute later Mr. Lisle was ushered into the room.

"I thought you were away," was all she could find to offer her visitor in the way of welcome. It was an inauspicious beginning, for it confirmed him in his determination to find out the cause of her change towards him.

"I came back last night," he said shortly. "When one has the blues badly, one is fit for no one's society but one's own." He sighed as he spoke. How haggard too he looked! Esme's heart softened. Was it, could it be possible that Lady Julia had refused him?

"You don't seem to have enjoyed yourself at the Kestertons?" she observed.

"I didn't in the least," he admitted.

"Lady Julia was there, I suppose?"

He looked up, but failed to follow her train of thought. "Naturally," he said indifferently.

There was a pause. She wondered why the silence should suddenly have become so awkward, and wished he would exert himself to help out conversation. "You leave the Court for good, I suppose, to-morrow?" she asked at last for want of anything better to say.

"Thursday morning," he corrected. "I had thought of running down off and on for the next few weeks, but now it seems to me that I shall be better away for a time. Don't you think so, Mrs. Blunt?"

"That is a question entirely for you to decide," she replied. "Luckily you are able to come and go as you please. I only wish we could do the same."

He was surprised to notice how feelingly she spoke.

"Are you already so tired then of Hawthornden?" he asked.

"Tired?" She laughed drearily. "Tired is not the word. I hate this place. Can you wonder that I should, when everything here reminds me of my loss, when all through the endless days I sit and sit, surrounded by memories of the past, without enjoyment in the present, without hope for the future? Oh! it is driving me mad."

This passionate outburst from a woman of her reserve and self-control, came upon him like a thunderbolt.

"If you were to go away for a change," he suggested lamely.

"No, no." She waved the proposal aside impatiently. "Half measures are worse than useless. It must be for ever. I cannot live at Hawthornden. It is unendurable. If only I might get away, forget, find fresh occupation, fresh interests amongst strangers, who will not remind me of the difference between what I was and what I am."

Notwithstanding his sympathy, he was only human, and her allusion to strangers hurt him horribly.

"And has everybody connected with Hawthornden become

equally hateful in your sight?" he was stung into retorting. "Your old friends for instance—are they to be banished? Because—pardon me if I seem selfish—in that case what becomes of the plans we have so often discussed together, in which you were pleased to profess at least an interest? Is our friendship, with everything else, to go by the board?"

She smiled in a conventional way, which to him was simply maddening. "You have so many friends to interest themselves in your doings," she murmured with pretty insincere civility. "How can I flatter myself that my movements should affect you and your plans in any way?"

It was the last straw. The bitter jealousy, the soreness, the unsatisfied cravings of passion, repressed for so many months, rose up in a mighty flood, sweeping away as though they had been so many straws, those barriers of conventionality, expediency, nay, of honour itself on which he had relied so over confidently.

"If you really think that, you must be strangely mistaken in your estimate, Esme. I am not so constituted as to be able to take up and throw away my friends as I would an old glove. Your definition of friendship differs radically from mine when you talk so glibly of a separation which to me means the loss of all that makes life worth living." He spoke quietly enough, but Esme looked at his set white face and blazing eyes and trembled.

"Mr. Lisle, you are speaking at random," she began with a desperate effort at self-possession.

"I beg your pardon if I offend you, but you try me too far."

The flood was surging on in overwhelming force. Notwithstanding his solemn vows to the contrary, he was uttering words he had sworn should never pass his lips, was offering to the woman he professed to reverence beyond all others the deadliest insult it was in his power to offer her. He knew it. He knew too that he was working his ruin, undoing the patient self-control of months. What of that? As well have stayed a torrent with a piece of stick as have attempted to stem the tide of passion which now possessed him.

"I have given you my whole life," he went on, speaking in the same low, level, concentrated voice. "You know it. You must know it. You can't help knowing it. From the beginning you were my ideal of womanhood. Oh, yes! You may not believe it, but in my worst moments I had an ideal, and you fulfilled it. To me you were all that was good, pure, desirable in woman. From the beginning I worshipped you. I worship you now. Does it surprise you that I should? Am I a man to love and unlove to order? Are you less worthy of worship, less likely to inspire it than you were years ago? Is it so strange, that what I felt *then* I should still feel now?"

"Mr. Lisle," she interrupted passionately, "you forget yourself, and insult me."

"Insult you!" He laughed harshly. "God forbid! Insult you! In what way? Is the sun *insulted* by the adoration of the savage? I expect nothing. I ask for nothing in return beyond permission to serve you in such small ways as I may. Never in my wildest madness, have I dreamed you could feel anything beyond mere liking for me. Oh! I have no reason, Heaven knows, to feel proud of myself and my past, but the one thing I am not ashamed of is my feeling for you. If there be any good in me at all, it is all bound up in, and connected with my love. . . ."

"Oh, stop, stop—" she entreated, "why say all this?"

"Because I can't help myself, because to me your presence is everything, because—God help me! I cannot live without you, and *you*—you care nothing at all whether you ever set eyes on me again or not."

He stopped abruptly. There was a pause. Once, twice, she tried to speak and failed. "Mr. Lisle," she began at last in a low, hurried voice, her eyes cast down, her fingers nervously clasping and unclasping themselves. "We are greatly in your debt, and I do not wish to hurt you. All I beg of you is to say no more. I do not wish to hear about your feelings. They do not concern me. You insult me by any mention of them. Every word you speak shows me the hollowness of the friendship on which I relied. It has all been false—a horrible sham. Go—go—at once—before I forget the past, my obligations to you."

He moved to the door, then stopped. "Have I offended beyond hope of forgiveness?" he asked in a low voice. "Mrs. Blunt, you are strong. You can afford to be merciful. Have you no word for me?"

"Not a word," she answered with sudden passion, "except that I never wish to see your face again. As we must meet—for I am tied here—the only kindness you can do me is to make our meetings as few and brief as possible."

"I accept my sentence. You shall not see me again unless you send for me. But remember if ever you need me I am there absolutely and entirely at your orders."

He waited a moment, but she never stirred. Then slowly he left the room. He was gone. With an immovable face she heard the hall-door shut. And then she stood and stood, as if turned to stone, her hands clenched, her face rigid. At last with a shiver, she roused herself.

"Strong! My God! If he only knew. If he only knew!" she muttered, as slowly she dragged herself upstairs and into her bedroom where she locked the door upon herself.

Arnold dined alone that evening. Mrs. Blunt he was told had gone to bed with a bad headache. He was sorry for the headache and told her so—through the keyhole, but he found her absence a relief. It left him free to think of Clara and devise plans for her benefit. Not that, think as he would, he could hit upon any satisfactory course of conduct. He couldn't desert her, he was unwilling to enlist Esme on her behalf. He shrank from the risk of a brawl with her grandfather, and a public scandal. For the girl's sake; not his own, for to do him justice he was no coward, he felt the imperative need of care.

And while he sat racking his brains for some safe and speedy means of communication with her, Clara was taking a simple and direct if somewhat extreme step towards this end. After an exceedingly bad quarter of an hour with her grandfather, who hadn't minced matters in speaking of her conduct, she rushed to her room beside herself with shame and anger; she was silly, but not bad, and Captain's Dixon's plain-speaking had outraged her beyond bearing. She could never face her grandfather again, she could never endure a repetition of the awful, horrible things he had said to her. She had done no harm. Why should she stay to be insulted and despised? She would not stay, she'd go. She'd not wait to be turned out of the house. Grandfather perhaps would be sorry when he found he'd driven her from her home. So much the better. She'd go—to Mr.

Blunt, who'd promised times out of mind to stand her friend He'd protect her against insult and persecution... With shaking fingers, giving herself no time for reflection, she crammed into a bag a few necessaries, with such odds and ends of lace and cheap jewellery as constituted her treasures. There! she was ready. Now to go downstairs, proclaim her intention to her unnatural grandparent, and march out of the house—let him stop her if he dared. It was only when she tried to leave her room that she discovered she had been locked in. The commotion she had made rattling the door brought Captain Dixon up to her.

"It's no use," he told her gruffly, "if you want food I'll bring it you. If you want to go out I'll take you, but you shan't be free to bring me to shame. I'm going to send for your Aunt Eliza to help look after you. Till she comes, you must stay up here. And your banns, I tell you, will be up next Sunday."

Well! that settled it. Clara was woman enough to feel it a point of honour to outwit him. She soon made up her mind. She must just wait till her grandfather was in bed, and then, well! the window was not far from the ground. Of course she couldn't rouse Mr. Blunt and his household so late at night. No matter, she had money, she would go direct to London, send word to Arnold, and wait for him there. A train left Wilburn at eleven, arriving some time in the small hours of the morning. She would be in safe quarters before even her flight from home had been discovered, and then—well, Mr. Blunt would look after her, put her in the way of getting her living, as numbers of other women did. And she would be free, able to live her own life, and make her own friends. This last consideration quite decided her. No sooner had Captain Dixon gone to his room—fortunately he kept fairly early hours and was a sound sleeper—than she began her descent, which to an active country girl, accustomed to birds-nesting, presented no great difficulty. Then seizing her bag she tore into Wilburn, arriving at the station at a run, just as the night mail steamed into it, and was bundled into a third-class carriage where she dozed uncomfortably through the journey.

A good deal of her courage had oozed away, when, in the small hours of the morning, she reached King's Cross. She was cold, tired, hungry, and absolutely helpless. What could she do?—where go? Must she tramp the streets until she found a lodging; or if she took a cab, what address could she give? As she stood irresolute, a gentleman, one of the few passengers, passed her, glanced at her, struck by her forlorn, dejected attitude, then looked again. "Old Dixon's pretty granddaughter!" What in Heaven's name was the child doing alone in London at two o'clock in the morning?

"How are you, Miss Clara?" he asked. "Where's the captain?"

It was Adrian Lisle, who had elected to travel as the best means of passing the weary watches of the night.

Clara started, crimsoned, stammered, and finally said almost inaudibly—" He isn't here, Mr. Lisle, I've come up alone."

Now no penetration was needed to see that something was amiss. In some perplexity Adrian wondered what he should do. It was no business of his of course, and yet when it came to his finding an inexperienced girl he had known from her childhood, living on his land at his very gates, wandering about the streets of London at night—

"Are you going to friends?" he asked abruptly. "Can I do anything for you? Let me call a cab and find your luggage."

At which suggestion the girl looked more and more confused. Oh, how could she explain? What must Mr. Lisle think of her? If the earth would only open and swallow her up.

"I have no luggage, thanks," she faltered timidly, "and I'm looking for a lodging."

"Looking for a lodging! But what was the captain thinking of to send you off alone at this time of night?" he went on.

"Grandfather didn't know I was coming," she stammered. "We had a quarrel. He was very unkind, and so I've left him."

So the foolish girl had run away in a fit of temper. Great Heavens! What madness. Of course she must go home. In the meantime, until her grandfather fetched her back, she must be placed in the care of some respectable person. With some relief Adrian bethought himself of an old nurse and housekeeper of his own who now lived somewhere out at Holloway, in a ridiculous stucco villa she had christened Lisle Lodge.

"I'm sorry to hear all this," he said kindly. "However, if you want a lodging, go to the address I'll give you. Mrs.

Watkin is a Wilburn woman. She'll take you in, and give you food and a bed."

Clara looked doubtful. A Wilburn woman! Someone from home! The idea was tempting, but then, how about the danger of discovery?

"Thank you very much," she began hesitatingly. "Only, Mr. Lisle, you won't let grandfather or any one else know."

He hesitated. What he had meant to do was to send a telegram to the old man as soon as the office was opened. Only—well! the child had piteous eyes, and Captain Dixon's tongue was notoriously a rough one.

"Your grandfather cannot be left in ignorance of your whereabouts," he said gravely. "You need not live with him unless you choose, but he ought at least to know where you are, and what you are doing."

In reply to this Clara bundled out of the cab in which he had just established her. "I won't go unless you promise to keep my secret," she declared tremulously.

He thought she was going to cry. What man could stand and argue with a hysterical girl on a London platform at two in the morning? Anything to get her safely under a respectable roof. And a few hours more or less would make no difference to Captain Dixon. Of course he temporised.

"Get in again," he said hastily. "Promise me to go quietly to Mrs. Watkin, and wait there till I come, and I promise to hold no communication with your grandfather until I see you again. I'll be with you during the morning." It was a compromise which seemed to satisfy her, and with exceeding great relief he saw her drive away.

## CHAPTER XXXIII.

By morning light Captain Dixon was disposed to regret his harshness towards the offender. To place her under lock and key had certainly been an extreme step, and he was beginning to regret it. He regretted it still more when he saw the untidy room and slovenly meal served for him by the girl, who, under Clara's superintendence, "did" for them. He realised that, notwithstanding her giddiness, Clara was a careful housewife, whose presence was needed in the house. And so he took her some breakfast, prepared, if met with proper humility, to relax the severity of her imprisonment. No notice was taken of his knock, whereupon, assuming her to be either asleep or sulky, he retired. This manœuvre he repeated three times at intervals, until, discovering that her bedroom window was open, a suspicion of the truth dawned upon him. He quickly made it a certainty. Clara, the child of his old age, the pride and darling of his heart, had left him! His first thought naturally was of the scoundrel who had brought her to ruin, and in a frenzy of rage and horror he started off post haste for Hawthornden.

In this way it happened that as Mr. Blunt, with a pipe in his mouth and his hands in his pockets, was taking a morning stroll, he saw his enemy of the previous evening advancing towards him. Pride forbade any step which savoured of flight, or Arnold would have turned aside to avoid an encounter only too likely to lead to unpleasantness. As it was he kept on his way. "Is the old brute mad or drunk?" he asked himself, noticing the Captain's livid face and uncertain gait. A little of both, he decided, when, with a threatening gesture, the old man literally rushed upon him.

"Where is she?" he asked hoarsely. "You—scoundrel! What have you done with Clara?"

"Cla—Miss Dixon? What do you mean?" Either Arnold's surprise was genuine or his powers as an actor were of the first quality. "Damn it, man, keep your hands off and explain yourself."

With an effort the Captain controlled his passion. "My girl has left me during the night," he said, more intelligibly. "This is your doing!"

"That I swear it is not." The contradiction came short and sharp.

"Dare you deny that you know where to find her?"

"Most certainly I do. I give you my word of honour I know no more of Miss Dixon's movements than you do."

In spite of himself the Captain was staggered. His arms dropped to his side. "Where is she, then?" he asked with a helpless air.

"God only knows," said Arnold roughly. "At the bottom of the nearest pond most probably, thanks to your brutality. But

I can't stand arguing here. You've driven the unfortunate girl to desperation. If it be possible, I must find her and repair the harm you've done."

With this Mr. Blunt hurried away. As to his anxiety for the missing girl, there could be no possible doubt. The unhappy grandfather at all events, completely broken down by the suggestion of suicide, could only totter home, renounce all thought of vengeance, and spend his day in an agony of impotent suspense and remorse. Not so Arnold, who, making enquiries on his own account, soon discovered that a young woman answering to Clara Dixon's description, and carrying a bag, had taken the night mail the previous evening to London. This information, however, he kept to himself. "Serves the old curmudgeon right if he does get a bit of a fright," he reflected. "He'll treat her better next time."

With this idea he also kept his own counsel, when, the following morning, as he had rather expected to do, he received a letter from the fugitive, giving her address, which on no account must be divulged, and begging him to come and see her. He obeyed her instructions. He was not blind to the compromising position in which she had placed both him and herself, yet what could he do? It was not for him to betray her confidence. Without her permission to open them, his lips were sealed. Accordingly, without a word of his errand he took the early morning train to London. For his part, poor Captain Dixon barely moved all that day from the chair into which, on his return home, he had dropped. He never even roused himself to go to bed, he barely touched the food at intervals placed before him, but sat on in a sort of stupor of despair, occasionally raising his fist with a threatening gesture, yet for the most part remaining unnaturally quiet, looking at the picture before his mental eye of a woman's white face floating on the surface of the mill-pond not a mile away, listening to the awful despairing death-cry, which rang out as the waters slowly closed over her.

All this time Adrian Lisle had not been unmindful of his self-imposed mission. To Mrs. Watkin's delight and astonishment he duly appeared at Lisle Lodge in the course of the morning, and in the presence of that worthy dame exerted all his powers of persuasion to induce the fugitive to return to the safe shelter of her home. He was unsuccessful. Clara, fortified by food and sleep, obstinately refused to see or hold any communication with her grandfather.

"I've written to my friends," she declared. "They will look after me and help me to get work. I'm quite safe. Mrs. Watkin has been very kind. She says I may lodge with her for the present at all events. It's no use asking me to go home, to be locked up and scolded and bullied into marrying a man I detest, for I won't do it," a resolution from which it was impossible to move her. "To-morrow—not before—you may let grandfather know if you like that I'm alive and well and in good hands," was the utmost concession she could be induced to make.

Mrs. Watkin, in a private explanation with Mr. Lisle, advised him to accept these terms. "Don't contradict her, Mr. Adrian," urged the worthy dame, "you'll only drive her out of the house. And what for? Just for the sake of a single day. And when she's that excited and upset, and so I'll be bound is the Captain. They'll be none the worse, I tell you, for a little time to think things over in. And as for getting her own living, Lord love you, work is just what she wants to teach her the value of a good home and a husband. Don't you trouble yourself, sir. Just you let the Captain know there's no call to be uneasy. He'd better let things be. I'll see that she keeps herself quiet and respectable as she should do."

To these arguments Adrian yielded. "You must have your own way, I suppose, Miss Clara," he said not over graciously, for her obstinacy had annoyed him, and he was anxious to wash his hands of the whole concern. "To-morrow by mid-day Captain Dixon will know that you are with Mrs. Watkin. I shall advise him not to interfere with you in any way. Still, if he should insist on seeing you, I neither can nor will prevent his doing so."

With this declaration Clara professed herself satisfied, and on it he acted. In going down himself to Wilburn the following morning, he conceived himself to be taking not only the safest and quickest means of communicating with the Captain, but also the one least likely to excite comment. He was glad to have done it, too, when, arrived at the Firs, he saw the wreck which twenty-four hours of suspense and remorse had made of the poor man. Unwashed, unshaved, his face an ashen-grey, his eyes bloodshot, his gait stumbling and uncertain, the hale old soldier was hardly recognisable.

"Is it about her?" he began. The words were barely audible, but his eyes asked the question.

Lisle nodded. "She's quite safe," he said reassuringly. "Sit down and I'll tell you all about it."

And so he did, while the Captain, in the revulsion of feeling, broke down and cried like a child. Finding a lamb where he had been led to look for a lion, Adrian took advantage of his softened mood to urge him to leave the girl to herself. But here the Captain displayed unexpected firmness.

"I don't mean to be harsh," he declared, and he certainly spoke in the most temperate, kindly way. "I won't say a word of blame or reproach. This has been none of her doing, I know that well enough. Don't be afraid, I'll not hurt or frighten her. But I've got my duty to do by her, and there are things I must say to her before I leave her to herself."

All this seemed so reasonable that Adrian saw no reason to gainsay the old man's resolution to go up to Town by the next train and seek out his granddaughter. Indeed, it seemed to him that the sight of him so aged and broken, might exercise a salutary effect on Miss Clara's obdurate temper. And so the two travelled back to Town by the very next train. Both at Wilburn and King's Cross Mr. Lisle saw enough of Captain Dixon to feel very uneasy about him. He seemed quite dazed and feeble, dozed most of the way to London, and could hardly be persuaded to leave the railway compartment, while he hardly seemed to grasp what was said to him. His condition was possibly only the result of sleeplessness and want of proper food. However that might be, he was clearly in no condition to wander about London alone. His companion accordingly saw nothing for it but to get him into a hansom, take his own seat in it and drive with him to Lisle Lodge. On the way he received a considerable shock, as meeting a hansom coming from the opposite direction, he caught sight of its occupants as they were whirled along—Arnold Blunt and Clara Dixon! Oh, impossible! Absurd! He glanced at the Captain, who was leaning back apparently half asleep, and decided his eyes must have deceived him. Nevertheless, his eyes had not deceived him, for in answer to his enquiry for Miss Dixon,

Mrs. Watkin, looking perturbed, curtly announced that she was not there.

"How's that?" he asked sharply.

Mrs. Watkin drew herself up, while Captain Dixon looked with a puzzled air from one to the other.

"Indeed, Mr. Adrian," she said, and her voice was respectful but injured, "it's none of my doing. I'm willing enough to put up with Miss Clara for all her hoity-toity ways, but when it comes to her shutting herself up with a gentleman visitor, and as good as telling me to mind my own business when I ventured to ask a question or two, not liking such goings on, as was but natural, I had to tell her my house was not the place for her, and with that she flounced off and took her fine gentleman with her."

"Has she gone altogether?" asked Lisle.

"That's more than I could say," was the answer. "She's left her bag with a few odds and ends of trash in it. She may come back for it, but I have my doubts. I think she's off for good and all with her gentleman friend."

"What's the matter?" Captain Dixon, who hardly seemed to have taken in the foregoing conversation, now suddenly woke up. "Where's Clara?" he asked impatiently. "I want her. I want to see her. You told me I should see her. What's become of her? Out is she? and with a friend? A gentleman friend?" raising his voice and growing quite excited. "What gentleman friend?"

Mrs. Watkin tossed her head.

"I'm sure I don't know," she began.

"But I do," he interrupted angrily. "It was that smooth-tongued villain from Hawthornden, Mr. Arnold Blunt. Oh, I know. Don't try to contradict me. He's been after her these six months; used to come and drink his glass of whiskey and smoke his pipe with *me* every evening last winter, pretending to be my friend, and all the time he was turning her head and setting her against the honest man who would have married her." The old man's voice was thick with passion, his face aflame, his eyes suffused, the veins in his temples swelled to bursting. "I found out his game and stopped it," he went on thickly. "I shut her up out of his way, and she left me for him. And yesterday he swore he knew nothing of her. And I believed him. Thief!

Liar! Curse him, I say—curse——" His voice broke. With a strangled cry, he staggered and fell heavily to the ground.

"It's a stroke," announced Mrs. Watkin with mournful exultation, as she helped to move the unconscious man into the best bedroom. "It's my belief he'll never move again, and if he doesn't, his death will be at that hussy's door. A fine lot she'll have to answer for."

In this cheering prophecy she was mistaken. By the time a doctor had been found and brought to the bedside the Captain had rallied, very slightly certainly, yet sufficiently to be pronounced in no immediate danger, so long of course as a second and necessarily fatal stroke could be averted. As to his permanent recovery, it was impossible to hazard an opinion. He would never be the same man again, so much was certain. Either his bodily or mental faculties, both possibly, might be affected in a greater or lesser degree; to what extent time would show. And Adrian, remembering the trouble which awaited him with his return to consciousness, could not honestly look upon a loss of memory as an unmitigated evil. For himself, having done all that could be done, he went home to reflect at leisure on the last development of affairs.

Whether Captain Dixon lived or died after all was to him a matter of secondary importance beside the fact that it was Arnold Blunt who was responsible for this terrible tragedy. It was Blunt who had broken up a happy home, enticed an innocent girl to her ruin, and brought down an old man's grey hair in shame and sorrow to the grave. And this was the man who had been preferred before him, into whose careless keeping had been given the treasure of which he himself had been held unworthy, who held in his hands the happiness of the woman to whom he himself might not presume to speak a word of love while the husband to whom she clung so loyally might outrage, betray her and go scot free. A crooked world indeed! Adrian surely might be pardoned for remembering that whatever his own faults, he would have been incapable of such a betrayal of trust. An old man and a young girl living under the very shadow of his own home! Faugh!

"He shall answer to me for this!" said Lisle to himself, who felt that as *his* tenants it became both his duty and his privilege to avenge the Dixons' wrongs. A privilege, indeed! What keener satisfaction could life give him than to expose this heinous offender against the laws of hospitality and good feeling, to hold him up to the scorn and derision of the world at large? Or, stay! Why not take the law into his own hands? A vengeance swift, secret, summary, sure! To seize the criminal by the throat, and at one stroke avenge the broken-hearted grandfather, the injured girl, the outraged wife! Pleasant as the thought might be, he very soon dismissed it. Of course there must be no scandal. No one was better aware of that fact than himself. Captain Dixon would not thank him for spreading abroad his granddaughter's shame, while Esme—would not her loyal soul shrink in loathing from the man who exposed in all their hideousness the idol's feet of clay, and robbed her of the last support, which, however inadequate, was all she had to cling to? Would she think the better of him for thinking the worse of her husband? For her sake Arnold must go free. Such reparation as could be made he must be forced to make, but let him do it without publicity or noise, so that no hint of the disgraceful truth should ever revolt and pain his wife's ears.

## CHAPTER XXXIV.

When a disagreeable has to be faced, the sooner it is over and done with the better. On this principle Adrian Lisle lost no time in accomplishing the distasteful task thrust upon him.

His knowledge of Arnold's habits enabled him to find his man that same day about dinner-time at the club, of which the latter was a member.

Mr. Blunt looked a trifle conscious, but made no effort to avoid an explanation he foresaw to be inevitable. On the contrary, he agreed promptly when the other proposed an adjournment to his own rooms. "I was coming anyhow to look you up this evening," he said. Also it was he who, as soon as they were alone together, broached the subject of the Dixons.

"About this Dixon business," he began, with an affectation of ease which, if not absolutely successful, was yet creditable enough under the circumstances. "I should like to have your advice, if you don't mind giving it me."

"By all means," was the curt rejoinder. "Drop the whole concern at once. Don't see or speak to the girl again."

Arnold flushed.

"That's out of the question," he said quickly.

"Not at all," responded the other with equal promptitude. "It's the only decent or possible course you can take. You've made quite enough mischief already by taking the girl from her home."

Arnold started up.

"It's a lie!" he exclaimed violently. "I beg your pardon, Lisle, but whoever told you I had anything to do with Clara Dixon's flight from Wilburn, uttered a most malicious and wilful slander."

Lisle shrugged his shoulders.

"I may as well tell you, Blunt, I saw you driving with Clara Dixon myself this afternoon," he observed drily.

"Very likely. She wanted a companion and escort. I took her out and showed her a little of London. I also sent her back in a cab to that old watch-dog of yours an hour and more before I met you. Look here, Lisle," with some heat, for the incredulity so plainly written on his companion's countenance exasperated him, "you've only heard that old rascal of a grandfather of hers, who of course tries to make out the best case he can for himself. Be good enough, please, to listen to my version before you cast these aspersions on as good a girl as ever lived."

"I'll hear what you have to say," was the rejoinder.

"Miss Dixon has been treated shamefully," Arnold began hotly. "For months her grandfather has been trying to bully her into a marriage she detests. Now from dropping in occasionally last winter for a smoke and chat with the old man, I came to know the girl and see what was going on. Naturally I was sorry for her."

"So it appears," interpolated the other, unmoved.

Arnold bit his lip and suppressed the angry retort on the tip of his tongue. A quarrel with Mr. Lisle was a luxury he was unable to afford himself at present.

"She told me her troubles," he went on defiantly, "and begged me to put in a word for her with the old man. I did so with the result that Dixon flew into a passion, insulted us both, and forbade me the house."

"And then?" as the explanation hitherto so fluent came to an abrupt halt.

"Well! what was I to do?" demanded Arnold in an injured tone. "How could I desert her when her life was made a burden to her, and she hadn't a friend in the world beside myself?"

"Does Mrs. Blunt know her?" Mr. Lisle enquired thoughtfully at this juncture.

The question was a poser. Arnold began to hum and haw. "She has met her," he finally explained in some confusion. "I did try to get her to take an interest in Clara Dixon, but—somehow it didn't work. For one thing, she's been too much taken up thinking of poor little Dot to bother about strangers and then, well! I don't know how it is, but no woman is ever fair towards another woman. Anyhow, I soon saw it was no use, so I gave it up."

"Yet you met."

"We saw one another occasionally." Arnold's tone grew more and more defiant. "There was not a shadow of harm in our walking at times fifty yards in the same direction. And if harm came of it, old Dixon has no one to thank but himself for forcing his granddaughter into a compromising position. Some of these village fools I suppose got cackling together, and the gossip reached his ears. Anyhow he did find us together the other day, and made an outrageous scene. I believe he would have struck Clara if I hadn't interfered. At all events he dragged her away, locked her up in her room, and swore she shouldn't leave it till she went to church with Westerton. He terrified her so much by his violence, that she got out of the window, walked to Wilburn, took the train to London, arriving there homeless, friendless, almost penniless. I shudder to think what might have become of her if you hadn't met her. The first I heard of her flight was from Dixon himself, who came down raving to know what *I* had done with her, as if I were responsible for the straits to which his own harshness had reduced her. Naturally I was horribly anxious about her, and it was a great relief to me to get a letter from her this morning, giving her address, and begging me to come to her at once, which I did. And that, whether you choose to believe it or not, is the true story of my relations with Clara Dixon."

Adrian Lisle would have liked to disbelieve it. Being, however, a just man, he was forced to confess, which he did with an effort, that so far as it went he did believe the story.

"Oh, I believe you," he said grudgingly, "but it's more than nine people out of ten will do, for, if you'll excuse my saying so, you've played the fool all through, if you haven't played the villain. Anyhow you don't want to do any more mischief, I suppose. The girl is compromised, her grandfather at death's door. . . . ."

"What do you mean?"

"What I say. The shock pretty well did for old Dixon. He insisted upon coming to London to see his granddaughter, although he was in no condition to travel. When he reached Mrs. Watkin's and found Clara had gone with you, he naturally concluded the worst. That finished him. He had a sort of stroke, was insensible for a bit, and although he was rallying when I left, he knew nobody, and most mercifully seemed to have no recollection of what had happened."

"I'm awfully sorry," murmured Arnold, looking disturbed. "I had no idea of all this."

"No doubt. And so under the circumstances as a man of the world, Blunt, you'll agree with me as to the necessity for saving appearances and separating yourself once for all from the young lady. Understand me," he lifted his hand as Arnold tried to protest, "I don't question your statement. All I say is, whether intentionally or not, you have done Clara Dixon harm in getting her talked about, and I tell you plainly I shall not allow you to injure her any further."

Arnold, who was exceedingly angry, would have liked nothing better than to tell this high-handed meddler to mind his own business and be d—d to him. But then how can one quarrel with a man to whom one owes money one is not in a position to repay? He therefore swallowed his resentment as best he could, sulkily muttering something to the effect that he desired nothing but the girl's good, and was perfectly ready to co-operate with him or any one else to that end.

"Very well then," was the reply. "Drop all communication with the Dixons. At present the girl will have plenty to do in helping Mrs. Watkin to nurse her grandfather. Should she wish later on to take a situation, I will do my best to place her in one. I make myself responsible for her welfare. I give you my word she shall be forced into nothing distasteful to her. You haven't the shadow of a cause for interfering with her any further."

Little as he liked them, these terms were such as Arnold could not afford to reject. For which reason, not over graciously, he signified his acceptance of them, and took his departure.

"I wonder what makes me saddle myself with all this trouble and responsibility just to save a couple of fools, who don't want to be saved, and to bind a woman all the more closely to a husband who isn't fit to black her boots, and whom I'd give ten years of my life to see her rid of," reflected Mr. Lisle when left alone. "It wasn't that I didn't realise how I was cutting my own throat. No fear of that, with the devil at my elbow all the time whispering, 'Leave him alone. Why meddle with what doesn't concern you? Give him rope. He wants to hang himself. Let him. A word, a hint, will be enough to spread the scandal at Wilburn. Let it spread. Retire into the background. Do nothing while the storm rages. Then when the storm is over, the law has been appealed to, the guilty husband discarded, the injured wife set free, then your turn will come.'" He shrugged his shoulders. "What a temptation! I wonder why I didn't yield to it. My good angel," with a cynical smile, "must have been particularly active to-night, making up for years of indolence and neglect. Adrian, my boy, allow me to congratulate you. For the first time in your life, you've stood up to the devil and got the better of him. Make the most of your victory though, while you can, for I tell you, you were a fool to let your opportunity slip, and you'll live to repent your folly."

Whether he repented of the line he had taken or not, he certainly adhered to it. He went to Lisle Lodge the following day, heard that Clara, very subdued and conscience-stricken, was devoting herself to her grandfather, who, although stronger, still recognised no one. He then gave some much needed attention to his own affairs. One of his first steps was to go down to Wilburn for a few hours to arrange for a political meeting he was expected to attend, and also to find out how the land lay with regard to the Dixon pair.

The information he gained was of the most meagre kind. Yes. Certainly, the cottage was empty. The Captain, they'd heard tell, was away, and his granddaughter? Well, yes! She was away too. Mr. and Mrs. Blunt were not at Hawthornden either. They had gone away that morning to Devonshire for change of air. So far, so good. Adrian rashly concluded he had heard nothing, because there was nothing to hear, under which pleasing impression he retreated. This illusion he was not suffered long to cherish. A few days later the *Wilburn Sentinel*, a local paper of pronounced Radical opinions, published a leading article inveighing in the strongest terms on the selfish profligacy of the so-called upper classes. It pointed this invective by alluding in no obscure terms to a certain shameless case which latterly had excited the utmost scorn and indignation amongst all honest folk. For, it asked in virtuous horror, by what name can we designate the conduct of a man of high station, wealth and influence, who, occupying a position of trust, deliberately uses that trust to enter a happy and honoured home, bringing shame with him, betraying a young and innocent girl for the amusement of an idle hour, and striking at the unhappy guardian, a blow which had shattered his health and affected his reason. A marked copy of this effusion was forwarded anonymously to Mr. Lisle, who quite by accident, for he was accustomed to political personalities, and rarely noticed them, chanced to open and read it through. He did so carefully and deliberately from beginning to end. And then, with a shrug of his shoulders, he laid the paper down. Well! it was not his fault. It merely proved what he had been aware of before, namely that one invariably suffers more for one's good deeds than for one's faults? And after all, what did it matter? He never had cared for the public opinion. He didn't propose to consider it now. If people liked to talk at him, it didn't signify. Nothing indeed signified much now-a-days—which meant that Mr. Lisle just then was suffering more acutely than ever from the profound *ennui* and self-disgust to which at all times he was so subject, and from which one presence, henceforth forbidden to him, could alone rouse him.

Lightly however as he might treat the utterances of the *Sentinel*, others did not follow his example. The very next day about lunch time, lo and behold! John Denison strolled into his rooms.

"I'm just up from Wilburn," he proceeded to explain, coming straight to the point as usual; "was at a meeting there last night. People were talking about you. Do you know what they said?

"I daresay I can guess. Someone was thoughtful enough to send me a copy of the *Sentinel* yesterday morning."

John deliberated. "Scurrilous, lying, little rag!" he observed with some warmth. "I should like to have a half-hour's private conversation with the editor, I confess."

"A waste of time and trouble," Adrian observed indifferently. "Such gentry should be left to wallow in their own mire."

"There I don't quite agree with you," objected the other, whose usually impassive countenance looked almost anxious, "because you see however contemptible such lies may be, there are always people who'll believe them."

"Quite so. The majority of my constituents, I am aware, will lend a ready ear to the utterances of the *Sentinel*," was the tranquil rejoinder, "and that, notwithstanding the fact that for once there happens to be a good deal of truth in them."

John smiled incredulously. "My dear fellow! Don't ask me to swallow that cock-and-bull story, for I couldn't do it."

"All the same," retorted Adrian, "Clara Dixon and I did travel up to London by the night mail, I did meet her on the platform, send her off in a cab to an address I provided, while Captain Dixon's stroke has certainly been the result of the anxiety he suffered over his granddaughter's disappearance. Those are the facts, from which you and the rest of the world are quite at liberty to draw your own conclusions."

There was a pause. "You ought to bring an action for libel," John finally announced.

Adrian frowned. "On no account," he retorted decisively. "Understand me, John. I utterly and absolutely decline to move in the matter. What is it? You don't seem satisfied," for indeed John looked anything but pleased.

"Oh, I'm satisfied," he said hastily, emphasizing the pronoun, "but then I should never have wanted or thought of asking for any denial or explanation of the thing. It's only that politically this sort of story may be so injurious to you that we thought— that is, a number of your supporters came to the conclusion—some steps should be taken to contradict the slander."

"I see. And you have been sent as ambassador to see how far I am prepared to pander both to the curiosity and the scruples of the free and independent electors of Wilburn. Well! it so happens that I can pander to neither one nor the other of these sentiments. If my supporters no longer consider me fit to take care of their interests, they must withdraw their support, that's all."

"That's nonsense," protested John. "We shall all stand by you of course, only——" he hesitated, "your attitude will complicate matters most infernally, there's no denying."

"And lose a lot of votes I can't well spare," concluded Adrian. "I quite understand. Personally, I should prefer to let things slide and take my chance, not because I'm particularly enamoured of political life, but because one naturally doesn't care to turn tail before a lot of curs. Still I'll do nothing to split up the party or endanger the seat. Politically I place myself unreservedly in the hands of the wire-pullers. The other thing is a personal matter upon which I can submit to no dictation whatever, not even from you, John," he added with a smile.

Whereupon John, seeing that further remonstrance was useless, got up, lamented that what he bluntly characterised as pig-headed pride should be allowed so to mar a man's career, and took his departure.

"Behold the result of a meritorious action. The resignation of the honourable member for Wilburn, which I fancy will be the next move in the game." Mr. Lisle smiled as he made the reflection. "Well, no matter. The whole business has become a tie and a weariness and I don't care, I'm sure, how soon I get rid of it."

Which was not true. He did care very much.

## CHAPTER XXXV.

"You dear thing! How delightful it is to see you again!" was Cicely's enthusiastic greeting on her arrival at Hawthornden.

"I am so pleased you were able to come at last," was the no less fervent rejoinder.

"I have such heaps to talk about, and am simply longing to hear all your news," announced the one.

"I'm delighted to hear it," replied the other, "for we shall have ample time for conversation. Arnold will be away all this week, so you will have to put up with my unadulterated society."

"I ask for nothing better," declared the over-candid Cicely.

"Not of course that I am not exceedingly sorry to miss Mr. Blunt," she hastened to add, becoming aware of the somewhat left-handed compliment to her host, "but I *shall* enjoy having you all to myself for a whole week. How we will talk! And now let me see the house, which is perfectly sweet. How pretty you have made it. But then, you couldn't help making any place nice."

Praising everything indiscriminately, chattering nineteen to the dozen, asking innumerable questions at random, to be answered equally at random, Cicely made her tour of inspection of the house and garden, and all the time her heart was aching as she noticed Esme's sunken cheeks, worn face and drooping figure.

"Poor thing," she was saying to herself while engaged in pouring out a flood of inconsequent nonsense, "what a wreck!"

For her part, Esme was equally busy lamenting the change in the pretty piquante face before her. Pretty and piquante it still was, and probably always would be, but the laughter sounded forced, the eyes were unnaturally bright, the colour painfully fleeting, while when her face fell into repose there were shadows round her eyes, marks about her mouth, which showed that for all the good face she put upon things, Cicely's lines had not been cast in quite as pleasant places as she represented them to have been. This, however, she was not disposed to acknowledge.

"I like my life," she declared in answer to Esme's enquiries. "Mrs. Barker is the best creature in the world, and she bears with me with a patience which is quite sublime. Then it suits my purse and my tastes. One can live there on twopence ha'penny a year, and," with a slight smile, "in a mild way I can get plenty of that frivolity which those who know me best tell me is a necessity of existence to me. Of course it means separation from one's own belongings, but then, if one misses one's friends, one avoids equally a good many persons one doesn't care to meet, so it cuts both ways."

"Have you seen Mr. Denison lately?" asked Esme rather irrelevantly.

"Oh, yes, several times while I was with Aunt Louisa in London." Cicely spoke with ostentatious carelessness. "Do you see much of him here?"

"Not so much as one could wish. He has been very kind in coming over, but the distance is so great and I have been so much shut up, that we seem to have lost sight of everybody. No doubt though we shall see him while you are here."

"I don't think so. He's away from home, staying with some people in Wales" (here she laughed rather consciously) "called Anstruther. He's going to marry the daughter."

If she wished to create a sensation or provoke a denial of the statement she was signally disappointed.

"Indeed!" Mrs. Blunt observed composedly, "I had not heard the news."

Again Cicely laughed. "You're behind the times," she said flippantly. "I hear it spoken of everywhere. An excellent thing too. John may be permitted surely to enjoy domestic bliss just the same as any other man."

"Certainly," acquiesced the other. "Are you sure though that he proposes to enjoy domestic bliss in this particular way with this particular lady? I mean, is the engagement given out?" Whereupon Cicely confessed that it was not. "He hasn't confided in me either so far," she added, "but then I don't suppose he would. However, it seems to be looked upon generally as a settled thing."

"What sort of a girl is this Miss Anstruther?" was the next question.

"Charming, I am told," with exaggerated emphasis. "What Aunt Louisa would call a thoroughly nice, ladylike, well-brought-up girl, with money too. John, I assure you, is a very lucky man."

"I am glad to hear that. He certainly deserves his good fortune," was Esme's disappointing response.

A pause. "And how is Mr. Lisle?" asked Cicely. "You see a lot, I suppose, of him?"

Esme bent down and took up a piece of work.

"He is not often at home," she said evasively. "Being in the House, he is a good deal tied to London, still, we see him of course when he is here."

"How quickly he seems to be coming to the front," Cicely observed thoughtfully. "John was talking about him the other day, and saying he was certain to make his mark. You must feel quite proud of so distinguished a friend."

"He is very clever," Esme smiled constrainedly.

"He is going to speak at a meeting on Monday," Cicely went on. "I should so like to hear him!" ("So should I," assented the traitor in Mrs. Blunt's fastly beating heart). "Couldn't we manage to go?"

Esme's fair head bent lower over her work.

"Impossible, my dear Cicely!" she said hurriedly. "Arnold will be away. We couldn't go without an escort."

"Why not? Send a line to Mr. Lisle and ask him to reserve a couple of seats for us."

"On no account." Miss Denison found herself pulled up quite sharply. "I could not think of troubling Mr. Lisle. He will be busy. It will be impossible for him to take the charge of two women upon him. If you really wish to go," more gently, "Mr. Denison will probably be back for the meeting, and I am sure will escort you."

"I wouldn't think of suggesting such a thing." Cicely's protest was equally emphatic. "John has been victimised sufficiently by me. He has other claims upon him now. But, after all, why shouldn't we go alone? These things are quite quiet. I've been to them before. We could put on old frocks with thick veils, go early, get seats near the door, and slip out before the crowd. No one would notice us. Would you dislike it?"

"Dislike it!" Esme shivered. "Dislike it?" when, worthless, disloyal wife that she was, degraded for ever in her own eyes—every pulse was leaping for joy at the mere chance of the sound of his voice, of the sight of his face. And after all, it would hurt nobody. It was Cicely's idea too—entirely her suggestion. No one would ever know. She shut her eyes.

"I couldn't go," she said faintly. "Don't ask me, please. I have been nowhere since——"

She got no further. Distracted with remorse, Cicely had rushed to her side, flung her arms round her, begged ten thousand pardons, called herself all manner of names, and vowed she would never so much as mention the subject again—nor did she, which doesn't mean that it was forgotten. To one of the pair at all events, it returned for the next six days with a maddening persistency, torturing, tantalising the unhappy woman, who, bent on keeping her marriage vow both in letter and spirit, was battling with all her might against the intruder, who, thanks to her own treacherous frailty — unintentional perhaps, yet none the less shameful—had gained a footing in what should have been her husband's sanctuary. No wonder that engaged in such a struggle, she made but a dull companion, gentle, amiable, but *distraite*, dejected, and bearing in every line of her face and figure the evidences of a mental burden too heavy for her strength.

"She is heart-broken," decided Cicely. "She will never get over the death of the child. Oh dear! why is it that being good pays so badly? The better you bear your troubles the more you get laid upon you."

She ended with a sigh for which Esme's misfortunes were not entirely responsible. It was dull work at Hawthornden. Not that she was in a mood to complain of dulness. A reputation for high spirits must be an inconvenient one at times to sustain. Cicely, who, like other folk had her little anxieties, was perhaps not sorry for a little breathing time, during which she might lay aside her own armour, take off her mask, and mope as she pleased.

At the same time, after six days of absolute unbroken *tête-à-tête* with her hostess, it was only natural that when on the afternoon of the seventh—a Sunday—the doorbell rang, she should have started up flushing violently.

"A visitor!" she cried quite excitedly. "Who can it be?"

"I can't imagine."

Esme too had risen and was looking round apprehensively as if meditating flight. Were ever two women set in such a fluster by so ordinary an event as an afternoon caller?

"I can't imagine," she repeated helplessly, when—

"Mr. Denison," announced the maidservant, and John walked into the room.

Cicely had quite recovered her composure as she shook hands with her cousin.

"You here, John?" she observed coolly. "Where have you sprung from? I thought you had gone to Wales."

"I came back yesterday, and am staying with Lisle for this function to-morrow. By-the-bye, Mrs. Blunt, he begged me to make his excuses. He would have come with me to-day, but was detained by a number of letters which had to be answered."

To which Esme murmured something to the effect that she quite understood, as she did.

"What a politician Mr. Lisle has become," Cicely chimed in. "A prelude I suppose to his settling down, getting married, and doing his duty in that state of life, etc."

John shook his head.

"That's just what it isn't," he said regretfully. "I'm sorry to say he's talking of giving up his seat already, and setting off on his travels again," an announcement which called forth Miss Denison's unqualified disapproval.

"Dear me! the man must be mad. Never knows his own mind for two hours together," she cried. "Esme, you are on the spot, talk to him, show him the folly of throwing up his future the first time he happens to get a fit of the blues," and then she turned to John with a question as to his doings in Wales.

While the two cousins conversed in their usual half-sparring, half-chaffing fashion, Esme sat in silence. Going away! Throwing up the new plans and ambitions, returning to the old purposeless existence, to the old waste of time and abilities, ruining a life—God help her!—which was dearer, far dearer, to her than her own! Did he think to please, to propitiate her by so wholesale a sacrifice? Surely not. Why should she punish him for a fault for which she herself was chiefly responsible? For dared she hold herself blameless? No, no, a thousand times no! He would never have forgotten himself if she had not set him the example by forgetting Arnold. She let him see her weakness, her coldness, her indifference, her forgetfulness of her wifely duty. Why then blame him for having taken advantage of it? Why then should he suffer while she went free? It was not just, not right. He should not go. He must not go, ruining himself for what, after all, was but a passing madness. Oh! he should not go. And yet how *could* she ask him to stay?

Occupied with such thoughts, it was not strange that her contributions to the conversation should have been few and irrelevant.

Mechanically she found herself at last standing up, wishing John Denison good-bye, and agreeing with him when he told Cicely she had better walk part of the way back with him.

"You don't get half enough air and exercise nowadays," he said, "it will do you good."

"It's so late and so cold," she objected.

"Nonsense. It's barely six, and a lovely evening," he retorted, while Esme, thankful for the chance of solitude, chimed in:

"You would find it pleasant, I think, and, except to church, you haven't been out to-day."

At this Cicely yielded with some reluctance.

"You fool!" she muttered angrily, as she put on her hat. "What is there to make a fuss about? As if you couldn't walk a hundred yards with a man who's been like a brother to you all your life."

Notwithstanding her own preoccupation, Esme smiled to herself as she watched the two set out.

"I have a notion that Cicely at last is getting tired of cutting her own throat," she reflected.

*(To be concluded.)*

# Ivan the Terrible.

THIS imperial demon, the last but one of the race of Rurik, the pirate chief of the Varangians, who subdued the Novgorodians, and was virtually the first king of Russia, becoming the ruling prince in 852 on the death of his brothers, Seniaf and Trouver, was the grandson of Ivan the Great, the third of that name, and son of Vassili Ivanovitch and the Princess Helen, a woman who seems to have been profligate and abandoned to the last degree, even for those times, and quite unfit for the office of regent, which she assumed and shared with a paramour.

Vassili Ivanovitch had been declared heir to the throne of Russia, to the exclusion of Dimitri his nephew. Ivan the Great married twice. His first wife, Helen, had a son, who died early in life, leaving the child, Dimitri, heir-presumptive to the throne; but Ivan's second wife, the Princess Sophia of Byzantium, daughter of Thomas Paleologas, Prince of Achaia, the last princess of the Greek Imperial family, a woman of ambitious and imperious temper, became jealous of Dimitri, thinking that he ought not to inherit the rich succession of the Emperors of Constantinople in preference to her own son; and her jealousy caused domestic feuds in the family, until Ivan, to obtain peace, declared Vassili to be his heir, and exiled Dimitri and his mother.

It was also owing to the Princess Sophia's ambition that he adopted the title of Tzar, an old Sclavonic word which the Russians interpreted as "autocrat" or "emperor"—a word well calculated to convey the immensity of the authority to which he undoubtedly aspired. In the oldest Sclavonian translations of the Bible, Saul and David are called Tzars, and it was very probably taken from thence by the Emperors of the East, and the Khan of the Tartars. "Tzarstovovat" signifies to reign, "Tzaristvo" kingdom or realm. This ruler likewise was the first to assume the insignia of the Greek Emperors, the double-headed black eagle, which was incorporated with "St. George on horseback," the insignia formerly adopted in Russia. This Princess introduced into Russia those arts and graces which the barbarous invasions of the Turks had banished from Constantinople, and the luxurious habits of the East and the grand ceremonies were soon adopted by the Boyards or nobility, while the crafty sovereign managed to get himself acknowledged as representative of supreme power, then only known to the sovereigns of the East, but by which the sovereigns of the North have ever since been distinguished.

After a brilliant, if somewhat brutal, reign of forty-three years, Ivan the Great died in 1505, and was succeeded by the son of the Tzarina Sophia of Byzantium, Vassili Ivanovitch, while the unfortunate young Dimitri died in captivity, no one troubling themselves about his sad fate. Vassili consolidated the conquests of his father, but did not seek to be engaged in fresh wars. Still, when he died, twenty-eight years later, he bequeathed Russia improved and enlarged to his infant son.

Ivan IV. was three years of age when his father died, and the education and bringing-up he received during his minority helped to form his brutal and ferocious character, which in later years won him the title of " The Terrible." " He was led," says a historian, " to the commission of the most horrible atrocities, even in his youth. He was taught that the only way of asserting authority was by manifesting the extremity of his wrath, and that power consisted in oppression; his pupilage was one continued scene of horrors, the recital of which only serves to stain the historic page." Others say that he was subjected to gross insults, that his education was purposely neglected, and, that he might be rendered unfit to assume the hereditary power, he was kept in total ignorance of affairs of state ; while Prince Schuisky, one of the Boyards, whose race had been injured and humiliated in common with most of the other noble Russian families, by Ivan the Great, revenged himself for these injuries on the grandson of the man who had inflicted them, never losing an opportunity of insulting his young sovereign, whom he uniformly treated in a degrading and contemptuous manner. It is said that on one occasion, " he stretched forth his legs and pressed the weight of his feet on the body of the boy." The privations to which he was condemned, the insults he endured, the evil amusements provided for him, no doubt produced terrible after results in the child's nature, and generated that fiend which lived in his soul, and wreaked itself in terrible outbursts of fury upon his victims.

Prince Belsky, a wise and far-seeing man, in vain urged prudence and moderation; the Boyards, headed by Schuisky, would not listen to reason, continuing their hideous orgies, until awakened to a sense of their own peril and insecurity by an invasion of the Tartars, when they rallied, faced, and overcame the danger. But no sooner was it over than they returned in all their strength, seized upon Moscow, and dragged the young Ivan from his couch in the dead of night, with the idea of making him an idiot through fright. However, they failed in this. He was naturally brave, if headstrong, and retained his senses unimpaired, despite the shock and fright. Belsky, who seems to have been the only decent member of the Court, was murdered about this time, and Ivan was left surrounded by artful and ferocious counsellors, who provided amusements of a horrible description for him. It was their habit to take him to the top of his palace and induce him to fling live dogs and cats from the summit, to precipitate huge stones upon the heads of the passers-by below, while they constantly had wild animals tortured in the most abominable manner for his diversion, and they told him he had every right to ride or drive over tottering old men and women who could not get out of his way with due celerity.

Prince Schuisky was one of his worst advisers, and by a curious retribution was the first victim of his sovereign's terrible temper, and it must certainly be admitted that, amongst all those surrounding the boy, he best merited the punishment.

When Ivan was about thirteen, he went out hunting with a party at which Prince Gluisky, another quarrelsome lord, and the President of the Council were present. Gluisky, a rough, murderous man, violently jealous of Schuisky, incited the prince to insult him grossly. Schuisky, taken unawares, and surprised at his tool's boldness, replied insolently. That was enough; his fate was sealed! Ivan opened the floodgates of his wrath, and at a preconcerted signal, the miserable Schuisky was dragged out into the streets, and worried alive by huge, savage dogs, in broad daylight. He expiated by unspeakable agonies a life of guilt.

Though Ivan was thus rid of one tyrant, he was soon destined to find others in the Gluisky, who urged him ceaselessly to commit acts of blood, only too congenial to his sanguinary nature. Under their advice, Ivan commited the "most extravagant atrocities." These wretches applauded each bloodthirsty act, and initiated him into a summary way of relieving himself of any enemy who displeased him, by sacrificing the victim on the spot. This went on for three years more, then, after a "minority of blood," he took the reins of the Empire into his own hands at the age of sixteen, was proclaimed and crowned at Moscow, 10th January, 1546, Tzar and Autocrat of all the Russias.

About this time he married Anastatia, daughter of the Roman Ivanovitch, a beautiful and extremely amiable princess, who gained great ascendancy over her ferocious husband, and gently persuaded him to be more humane and forgiving than he had hitherto been. But the improvement which took place in him at this period was supposed to have been brought about as much by terror. The citizens, trembling and desperate under his despotism, fired the city in several places one night, and surrounded his palace, howling and imprecating. Awaking suddenly to this scene of tumult and horror, he was alarmed, and the monk Sylvester, seizing upon the opportunity, suddenly appeared before the terrified despot, with one hand raised as if in the act of prophecy, and in the other a Gospel, and telling the Tzar that the heavens prognosticated evil to his dynasty if he did not abandon his evil courses, worked so powerfully upon his fears, that he gained a complete ascendancy over him, and as a result an entirely new system of government was inaugurated. The corrupt and cruel counsellors were replaced by able and upright men; a new organisation of the army took place, proprietors of estates were compelled to contribute to the maintenance of the military strength of the country according to their means, and the available force was raised to the number of 300,000 men. He established the "Strelitz," or regular militia, and they were disciplined according to European fashion. A guard for the prince was formed of them, whilst the others were distributed amongst the irregular troops, and Russia for the first time possessed a fairly well-disciplined military force, who were paid regularly when in the field. Then, at the head of a powerful army, he marched in the depths of winter to the siege of

Kazan, which he captured by springing a mine, a mode of warfare unknown to the Russians at that time, and which filled them with astonished admiration. He completely subdued the Tartars of Kazan, and after taking their city, he turned their mosques into Christian temples, and obliged the Khan to be baptised, no doubt greatly to the barbarian's disgust.

Some of the old Russian chroniclers assert that Ivan wept upon entering Kazan, at the sight of the numbers of dead bodies strewn about the streets. "We certainly cannot," says a historian, "put in any evidence in disproof of this apocryphal assertion, but the picture of 'Nero fiddling while Rome was burning,' is even more probable"; which is certainly true when one considers the character of this Tzar. Ivan was also successful in the kingdom of Astrachan, which he afterwards annexed to the Russian empire, it being a valuable acquisition, the vine and other productions of the soil growing luxuriously there; and while he was pursuing his victories in other places, the Turkish army, consisting of 80,000 men, despatched by Selim II. against Astrachan, perished miserably on the desolate Steppes.

The wars thus gloriously and successfully terminated, laid the foundations for greater commerce, and rendered illustrious the reign of one of the greatest monarchs the world has ever seen.

A very important event for Russia occurred in or about the year 1560. It was the discovery of Siberia, an empire of great magnitude, studded with inexhaustible mines of gold, silver, platina, copper and salt, and producing the richest and most valuable kinds of fur. The discovery was accidental, but very fortunate for the country. The Tzar took possession of his new kingdom, and the whole of Siberia, from Europe and from the frozen ocean to the Chinese frontiers, was annexed to Russia.

In the same year, 1560, the gentle and amiable Anastatia died, after having restrained the fury of the imperial fiend for thirteen years, and after her death the slumbering demon within his heart woke, a series of sickening crimes being the result.

He banished his prudent counsellors, replacing them by wretches, who studied to betray their predecessors by false stories of their treachery to the dead Tzarina, whose death they accused them of. Ivan hunted the partizans of his late ministers with ferocious cruelty, putting some to death, imprisoning and banishing others, torturing many, on the most frivolous excuses. One prince he stabbed with his own hands while at prayers in church, and another because he remonstrated with a new favourite.

Prince Andrew Kurbsky, who had rendered important services, getting a hint that a similar fate awaited him, withdrew into Lithuania, and joined Sigismund, King of Poland, at that time one of Russia's most formidable enemies. This revolt maddened Ivan, and when a messenger had the temerity to deliver a letter from Kurbsky, the Tzar struck him across the legs with an iron rod, which he always carried in his hand, and while the blood poured from the wounds thus inflicted, he read the letter unconcernedly.

He grew to distrust everyone, and redoubled his fury against his subjects, while when remonstrated with by some of the clergy he withdrew in a rage with his family to the fortress of Alexandrovsky, situated in the depths of a gloomy forest. His subjects, alarmed at his departure, thought they were deserted by heaven itself, and when, after the space of a month, two letters were received, one addressed to the Metropolitan, and the other to the people, complaining of the interference of Athanasius and the clergy, and bidding them farewell for ever, they shut up their shops, closed the tribunals of justice and public offices and exclaimed:

"The Tzar has forsaken us; we are lost. Who will now defend us against the enemy? What are sheep without the shepherd? Let him punish all those who deserve it; has he not the power of life and death? The State cannot remain without a head, and we will not acknowledge any other than the one God has given us."

The political creed of those days of absolute sovereignty was slavish obedience.

A deputation of prelates and nobles hurried off to Alexandrovsky, where they prostrated themselves before Ivan, striking the ground with their heads and entreating him to return to Moscow. He pretended to be moved by their prayers, and with feigned reluctance consented to return, provided "the clergy pledged themselves not to interfere whenever he found it necessary to punish those who engaged in conspiracies against the State, or against him or his family. This artful condition was immediately granted, and the magnanimity of a tyrant, who thus entrapped the people into an admission of the necessity of his despotic proceedings, was extolled to the skies."

On his return to Moscow the Muscovites were astonished at the alteration which had taken place in his appearance. In a month his powerful body, muscular limbs and broad chest had shrunk, his luxuriant hair was gone, he was quite bald of his flowing beard, there only remained a few ragged stumps, his eyes were bleared and dull, and his features disfigured by an expression of ravenous ferocity. Yet the infatuated citizens were excited to expressions of deep sympathy by these changes, the results of the ceaseless torture of a mind bewildered by its own rage and lust for blood.

He chose a body-guard of 1,000 men, afterwards increased to 6,000, from amongst the Strelitz, the ranks of which were composed of infamous wretches, ready and willing to execute his merciless orders. To show their office they suspended from the saddle-bow a dog's head and a broom, the head to show they worried their bloodthirsty master's enemies, the broom to signify that they would sweep them, if necessary, off the face of the earth.

Armed with hatchets and long, thin, keen daggers, they went from street to street searching for victims, a score or more of whom were despatched daily. The slaughter was indiscriminate; the roads were strewn with dead bodies. Amongst the first victims to this monster's insatiable lust of blood were Prince Gluisky and his son. When they arrived at the place of execution the young man wished to be beheaded first, but his father, unable to endure the sight of his child's death, insisted upon being executed first. His son, as his head rolled off, embraced it passionately, and while the living lips yet clung to the quivering face of the dead, the executioner's axe severed the young man's neck. On the same day another prince was impaled and four others beheaded. Several Boyards were exiled, and several forced to embrace monastic vows. The universal terror was so great, that the relatives of the murdered men did not dare to appear and give the dead the rights of burial, so the streets and squares remained encumbered with putrefying dead bodies.

For a time he employed himself in building a new palace, outside the walls of the Kremlin, driving out the inhabitants of the surrounding streets, and to furnish funds for this unnecessary building, and to enrich his favourites, twelve thousand of the richest inhabitants were dispossessed of their estates. The palace was to all intents and purposes an impregnable fortress, but the guilty soul of the Tzar, full of the horrors engendered by his murderous course, made him think it insecure, and he retired once more to Alexandrovsky, where he built a town, fortified strongly, and made a rule that no person should enter or leave the town without his express permission, while a patrol was constantly on the alert to see that this law was not violated.

While here he was struck with a new idea, and turned his palace into a monastery, assuming the style and title of Abbot, turning his favourites into monks, and his bodyguard ruffianly legionaries into brothers. He made them all wear black vestments, over splendid habits of satin or velvet, embroidered with gold and trimmed with fur, while he instituted a code of rules as austere as it was inconsistent.

The matin service began at three o'clock in the morning and went on until seven; at eight mass recommenced; at ten the whole brotherhood, with the exception of Ivan, who stood reading aloud from a religious book, sat down to a grand repast. Afterwards the remnants were distributed amongst the poor, Ivan always aiming to win the favour of the multitude. After the others were finished the Tzar dined, and then went down to a noisome, underground dungeon, to see his victims tortured, a proceeding which used to fill him with extraordinary delight. In the evening, at eight, vespers were read; at ten Ivan retired to his own chamber, where three blind men lulled him to sleep, but by what process history recordeth not. He diversified this monotonous life by visiting monasteries, hunting wild beasts in the woods, and issuing his cruel and sanguinary orders.

Horrors increased daily. The murder of individuals ceased to satisfy him; he lusted for massacres on a large scale, and would order wholesale butcheries of an entire town. He sought for excuses to slaughter hundreds.

Some of the inhabitants of Porpok happening to quarrel with his legionaries, he caused them instantly to be drowned, or tortured to death *en masse*, while the inhabitants of Kolumina were similarly disposed of. These atrocities, were, however, but a prelude to crimes of such enormity that we in this enlightened nineteenth century can hardly realise that they took place, and that a slavish people submitted to them.

"His march of devastation to Novgorod may be considered as the grand act of his career of blood. The provocation which led to the sanguinary punishment of that city was a falsehood invented by a profligate fellow who wanted to escape justice, and to take revenge upon the authorities who had found him guilty of the commission of some offences. This criminal, knowing that Ivan rewarded all those who came before him with charges of disaffection, wrote a letter in the name of the archbishop and inhabitants of Novgorod to the King of Poland, offering to put the city under that monarch's protection. This letter he carefully concealed behind an image of the Virgin, in the Church of St. Sophia, and then laid before the Tzar at Moscow a private revelation of the conspiracy which he had himself invented. Ivan despatched a trusty messenger to Novgorod, who discovered the letter in the spot to which the informer had referred, and upon this evidence the city was denounced to the vengeance of the select legion. But as it was likely that the sight of this dreadful deed would be more exciting than any he had hitherto witnessed, Ivan put himself at the head of his guards, and, accompanied by his son, departed from Alexandrovsky on his mission of destruction." *I* should rather call it total annihilation, for on his way he exterminated the whole population of Klin, Twer, and all the towns that lay on his route to the banks of the Ilmen, his advance guard arriving on the 2nd of January before the doomed city of Novgorod. Here his savage leaders ordered all the churches and convents to be closed, and demanded from the monks a temporary levy of twenty roubles a head. Some of these unfortunate ecclesiastics being unable to comply with these exorbitant and unfair demands, were brutally thrashed from morning till night. The inhabitants were loaded with chains, their houses seized and closely guarded, but this was only a preliminary. Four days later, when Ivan and the remainder of the demons of the Opritshnina arrived, all the monks who had been unable to pay the tax, were taken out into the streets, beaten to death in a savage manner, and their mangled bodies sent to their respective monasteries to be buried. The archbishop and clergy of Novgorod, bearing their miraculous crosses, met the tyrant on the bridge, and began to utter the accustomed benediction; but Ivan interrupted them with a volley of horrible curses. After which he ordered the crucifix and images to be carried to the church of St. Sophia, exclaiming, as he cast a ferocious look at the trembling archbishop, "Traitor, thou hast conspired to deliver this town to Sigismund, my enemy; thou darest call thyself the pastor and guide of the people, whereas thou art only a wolf, a robber, and a brigand!" after which he ordered him to celebrate mass, then retiring to the Archiepiscopal Palace, where a grand feast had been prepared for him and his Boyards. In the midst of this he uttered a cry which was a signal to his lawless crew to begin operations.

First the archbishop, his officers and servants, were arrested; then the palace and cloisters, with their holy treasures, jewelled and embroidered vestments, were given up to the plunder of the tyrant's satellites. Not a thing escaped the thievish hands of these impious spoilers. Every church and monastery was pillaged of its precious accumulation of treasures. The Tzar with his son on horseback retired to a small fort especially constructed for the butchery of his victims, and with his lance gripped firmly he rode after the trembling victims, prodding and piercing them with his deadly weapon, until he was too fatigued to continue the ghastly sport.

The massacre of the inhabitants came next. Every day from 500 to 1,000 Novgorodians were brought before this monster, and killed in the most revolting manner. Some were burnt, some were tortured by rack, fire, and weights, until they gave up the ghost; some were dragged into the Volkhof on sledges, others tossed over the bridge, while to insure their not escaping his soldiers, armed with spears, hewed and hacked to death those who attempted to escape by swimming. Infants of tender age were torn from the arms of their shrieking mothers and impaled before their eyes; husbands were butchered along with their wives; and for five weeks these bloody tragedies were daily enacted until, glutted with massacre, he went off and visited some monasteries in the neighbourhood, pillaging indiscriminately; burning corn, killing cattle, levelling houses; then, returning to Novgorod, he inspected, personally, the work of destruction, looked on while his myrmidons plundered the shops of rich silks, furs, jewels, which they were permitted to divide amongst themselves, while such goods as wax, tallow, hemp, etc., were burnt or flung into the river, crowded with the gashed, disfigured bodies of his victims, 60,000 people having been sacrificed by this monster in this once proud and flourishing city.

Having exhausted every form of torture and horror, and satisfied his terrible vengeance, he issued a pardon to the few wretched Novgorodians who survived, and commanded them to appear before him, when "a ghastly assemblage of skeletons, motionless and in despair, stood in the presence of the murderer like ghosts invoked from the grave. Untouched by the appalling sight, he addressed them in the mildest language, desired to have their prayers that he might have a long and happy reign, and took his leave of them in the most gracious words. The miserable inhabitants were smitten with delirium; they looked around them in vain for the friends that had been sacrificed, for the houses and wealth that had been laid waste. To complete the melancholy doom of the city, pestilence and a famine succeeded, sweeping off nearly all those who had survived the extermination of the less merciful Tzar. The city was now entirely depopulated, and presented the sepulchral aspect of a vast cemetery."

Once the capital of Russia, Novgorod in the present day has not even a ghostly semblance to its old, proud self.

On his return march to Moscow, he graciously spared the city of Pskof, only plundering the wealthiest inhabitants, but he carried with him the Archbishop of Novgorod and some distinguished men, whom he had reserved for public execution in Moscow. The Muscovites trembled at his approach and well they might, for to augment the number of wretches to be put to death he had several of his favourites arrested on the mere ground of suspicion, and then in the Market Place made extensive preparations for a general execution. No less than eighteen gibbets were erected, and in their midst a huge copper cauldron was suspended over a peat fire, while numberless instruments of torture were displayed. These preparations so terrified the inhabitants that they fled from the spot, abandoning their possessions to the hands of his Strelitz. In a few hours Moscow was deserted save by some of the Opritshnina, who were ranged round the great blazing fire and the ghastly gibbets.

Presently drums began to beat, and the Tzar, accompanied by

his favourite son, appeared, surrounded by his guard, and in the rear crawled a spectral troop of three hundred wan, bloody victims, already more than half dead, and enfeebled by horrible tortures. Ivan ordered his guards to bring the people to this "theatre of carnage," and the miserable Muscovites, not daring to disobey his commands, came hurrying in terror from their hiding-places, and soon the houses were filled, even to the roof-tops.

The dreadful rites began with the mutilation of a secretary of state. While one of the tyrant's myrmidons cut off his lips, another gouged out his eyes, and a third slit his ears; he was slashed and hacked to pieces, until at last he ceased to live. Many of them were hung up by the feet, and pieces cut from their bodies, after which, while still alive, they were plunged into the boiling cauldron. Women and children did not escape, but were subjected to a variety of tortures; and a poor old white-headed man was brought before the Tzar, and pierced through the heart with his own hand. Over two hundred victims, entirely innocent of the crimes of which they were accused, were executed in about four hours. One wonders that such a monster as Ivan the Terrible was permitted to live.

In spite of his bloody tyranny historians aver that Ivan's reign was marked by a great advance in civilization, and a regular intercourse between Great Britain and Russia was set on foot somewhere between the years 1559 and 1566, which formed the basis of the "Russian Company," and Queen Elizabeth sent an ambassador in the person of Thomas Randolph, esquire, and by him a present to the Tzar of a silver bowl curiously engraved. It is said that Ivan sought Elizabeth's hand in marriage, notwithstanding that he had already outraged and trampled on Russian customs by wedding *seven* wives—a heinous crime, according to the tenets of the Greek Church—but she declined the doubtful honour, whereupon he sent another ambassador to England to demand the hand of Lady Mary Hastings, or "one of the noble ladies of England"; the "noble ladies," however, like their queen, had too much sense to trust themselves to the tender mercies of such a ferocious fiend.

Russia became a prey about this time to some "unwearied foes," who took advantage of the country's internal distractions to wrest provinces from the Tzar. The Swedes took Esthonia, Kettler, the "last grand master of the Livonian Knights," helped himself to Semigallia and Courland, and Battori, the successor of Sigismund Augustus to the Polish throne, deprived him of one of the most important points in his dominions, Livonia.

"Battori terrified Ivan in the midst of his tyrannies, and the monster who could visit his people with such an example of cruelties, crouched before the King of Poland. His fear of Battori carried him to extremes. He not only supplicated terms at his hands, but suffered him to offer personal insults to the officers who represented the Tzar at his court."

During these wars, in most of which he was shamefully beaten, he committed the wildest excesses when he was victorious; robbing the captives of their wealth, condemning prisoners to be flung into boiling cauldrons, roasted over slow fires, spitted on lances, cut into small pieces, and tortured in every imaginable way.

To support his profligate and extravagant mode of life, he levied exorbitant taxes on his subjects, and if they refused to pay, revenged himself by horrible cruelties, making one man kill his brother, another his father, while he had eight hundred women drowned on one occasion *en masse!* His excesses carried him beyond all bounds, beyond all laws, human or divine. He is said to have sacrificed more victims than even Nero or Caligula, and Fowler asserts that he exceeded in refinement of horrors Agha Mahomet Khan, who built up the heads of his victims into pyramids, some remains of which are to be seen at the present day in Persia.

In the midst of his cruelties he *amused* himself by having savage bears brought from Novgorod, and he would let a brace or two of these slip when he saw a group of citizens collected near his palace, or a poor old man or woman tottering across the road. The flight of the terrified Muscovites, and the cries of those who, unable to escape, were seized by the wild beasts and torn, afforded him the greatest amusement, and elicited bursts of laughter, loud and long-continued. A company of jesters were also kept for his entertainment, to divert him before and after the executions. One of these, Prince Goosdef, the most distinguished of the court mimics, failing to please him with a joke, he poured the contents of a basin of boiling soup over his head, and when the unfortunate joker, in his agony, attempted to leave the table, his brutal master struck him in a vital part with a knife, and he fell to the ground, and lay there motionless.

"Preserve my faithful servant," cried the Tzar to the doctor, who had been sent for, when he arrived. "I have jested a little too hard with him."

"So hard," replied the doctor, "that only God and your majesty can restore him to life. He breathes no more."

Calling the prince a dog, Ivan cast a contemptuous look at his dead body, and went on with his dinner.

On another occasion he was visited by a Boyard, who, as was customary, bowed reverently.

"God save thee, dear Boris," exclaimed the monster. "Thou deservest a proof of my favour," and snatching up a knife he cut off one of his ears.

The poor wretch, such was the slavish obedience of his subjects, gave no sign of the agony he endured, only thanked the Tzar for his gracious favour, and wished him a happy reign.

The measure of Ivan's iniquities was not yet full, incredible though it may appear. The young prince, his eldest and favourite son, one day came to him, and begged permission to take a few troops to the assistance of Pskof, which had been placed in a state of siege by the Poles. Ivan, imagining he could detect in this proposal the germ of an insurrection against himself, exclaimed furiously, "Rebel, you are leagued with the Boyards in a conspiracy to dethrone me," striking him as he spoke with an iron rod he usually carried. He inflicted several severe wounds, and at last a violent blow on the head stretched the unfortunate youth on the ground, weltering in his blood. The monster seems to have been seized with instant contrition, to have realised the enormity of his crime, for he flung himself upon the body of the murdered youth, calling upon Heaven to give back the life he had so ruthlessly extinguished. But in vain. The hour of his retribution had arrived. The dying Tzarovitch clasped his father's hand, and with tears in his eyes besought him tenderly to be patient.

"I die," said he, "an obedient son and faithful subject."

He was carried off immediately to the monastery of Alexandrovsky, where he expired four days later, while his wretched crime-stained parent abandoned himself to despair. "The wretch, who had committed so many blasphemies against the moral justice of God, was now a terrible example of the power of conscience. He abandoned himself to the visions of a disturbed imagination. He often arose at midnight, filled the air with his cries, and only gave way again to repose when nature was exhausted. So fearful was his alarm, that he resolved to fly from Moscow, and bury himself in a monastery, but his subjects, fascinated by the very cruelties that appalled them, unanimously entreated him not to desert them."

He attempted to stifle the stings of a too-late awakened conscience by giving monasteries and other religious houses large grants of money and lands, and to induce them to pray for the repose of his soul "to the God of armies, who has so visibly protected me in the different wars which I have undertaken; to expiate the inevitable errors of princes charged with a vast empire, my desire is to render up my last sigh under the venerable habit of St. Basil and under the name of Jonas."

There was, however, no repose for the soul of such a monster; remorse devoured him. His health declined visibly, and in March, 1584, he was attacked by a dangerous illness. His approaching end was predicted by some astrologers, whom he threatened to roast alive. But on the same day, 17th March, that they were to be "roasted," he expired, with all his crimes and misdemeanours on his head. He was one of, if not *the* most extraordinary monarch the world has ever seen, for he combined in his nature more of the attributes of an infernal being than of a human creature. His atrocities, exceeding those of any other tyrant, of either ancient or modern times, stand unparalleled in the annals of history.

JOSEPHINE ERROL.

# A Mission in Life.

### By MRS. EDWARD CARTWRIGHT.

AT the age of twenty-eight Cecilia Banquet felt an irrepressible longing for a mission in life. It came to her suddenly in the very act of being bridesmaid to one of her younger sisters, and whilst Bessie was modestly promising to honour and obey the irreproachable young man at her side, Cecilia formulated a scheme of existence that should render her for ever independent of such subservience to the opposite sex. It was such an exciting occupation that she forgot to kneel down at the same time as the rest of the congregation, and was left standing up alone in the crowded village church, a somewhat conspicuous figure. Coming to herself with a start and a blush, she caught the eye of a sallow, middle-aged man, who was contemplating her meditatively. This was very annoying, because he happened to be the only person present in whose direction she had not intended to look during the progress of the wedding service. There was a certain fear that he might even interpret her blush as indicating embarrassment at his presence. To obviate this danger Cecilia calmly fixed her eyes on the unhappy man until he fairly wriggled with nervousness. Then, feeling her honour vindicated, and the other bridesmaids having again risen to their feet, she resumed her pleasing day-dream, which lasted all through the wearisome signing of registers, and the feeble frivolities of a wedding-party.

The unfortunate sallow man did not again offend after the broad hint conveyed by Cecilia's merciless stare. He was just home on a holiday after a prolonged absence in India, and was sensitively conscious of many changes.

Among others he had lost one of his oldest friends in Cecilia's father, and though Mrs. Banquet had sent him a cordial invitation to her daughter's wedding directly she heard of his return to England, he almost wished now that he had not accepted it. In the first rush of affectionate feeling towards his old friend's family, Richard Powell had taken rooms at the village inn for a week, meaning to stay on after the wedding and renew his acquaintance with them all. He had been very fond of them once; in fact ten years before, on the occasion of his last visit to England, he had made Cecilia an offer, which she had declined with barely concealed merriment. She was eighteen then, and just starting on a successful career as the pretty daughter of the popular county member. It is only fair to add that almost before the words were uttered he had himself seen the absurdity of the suggestion that she should throw over everything and accompany him to India. The funny part of the business was that he had altogether failed to recognize Cecilia at first when he saw her in church with seven other bridesmaids, and it was not until she stood up alone that he had been quite certain of her identity. Even now he could not help feeling far more familiar with the face of a merry, little, younger sister, just out of the schoolroom, than he did with the well-featured young lady who stared him so calmly out of countenance.

Cecilia had never been excited by Mr. Powell's attentions at the best of times, regarding him only as a benevolent but somewhat uninteresting friend of her father's. Of late years she had almost forgotten his existence, and she would have heard of his return to England, and her mother's subsequent invitation, with the utmost indifference excepting for a single reason. The very mention of his name, and still more his presence, reminded her of one unpleasant little fact, namely that his was the only offer she had ever received. Nobody would have suspected it, for she was constantly quoted as a girl who had been a good deal admired, and though no longer excessively pretty she was still regarded as an acquisition at parties. But a knowledge of the truth rather embittered her recollection of Mr. Powell, and covered her scornful rejection of him with a tinge of ridicule which it was unpleasant to dwell upon.

All that afternoon Miss Banquet mechanically offered coffee and ices to relays of country neighbours invited to inspect the wedding presents. "I can stand anything," she remarked, "so long as I am not expected to tell each visitor individually who were the givers of the pepper-pots and butter-knives." However, three younger sisters took this task willingly off her hands, and positively gloried in giving the required information.

But no sooner had the last guest left the house, than Cecilia rushed up to a bedroom where Mrs. Banquet had retreated to rest for half an hour before the large family dinner-party, with which the day was to close.

"Mamma!" began the girl impetuously. "I must tell you something at once!"

"Yes, my dear. Sit down and let us talk it over," responded Mrs. Banquet from the depths of the sofa cushions. "Dear Bessie looked very sweet, didn't she?"

"Oh, very. But——"

"There were just a few tears on her veil in church. Did you notice? So touching——"

"Yes, yes! But——"

"And Harry is such a handsome, manly young fellow! I thought the way he made the responses so——"

"Of course! But——"

"And dear Rosie," continued Mrs. Banquet, with a sigh of maternal contentment. "Who would believe she and Charlie have been married a couple of years! It seems only yesterday that I was pinning on her bridal veil—the same Bessie wore to-day, you know; it was my own first of all, and then——"

"Mamma!" interrupted Cecilia, in despair. "I don't think we shall have time before dinner to enter into the details of all the family weddings for the last thirty years, shall we? And what I want to say is so very important."

Mrs. Banquet's mind jumped at a conclusion. She could only imagine one subject of sufficient importance to take precedence of the description of a wedding on such a day.

"You are engaged yourself?" she gasped. "Oh, my dear, come and kiss me! I do congratulate you from the bottom of my heart. I had almost given up——"

"What are you talking about, mamma!" broke in Cecilia, sternly.

"You don't mean to say it isn't that?" murmured Mrs. Banquet, quailing before her daughter's indignant glance. "Oh, my dear, I am not mistaken, am I? How I did hope you were going to be as happy as you deserved."

"And do you suppose it would be any happiness to me to be the heroine of a prosperous, common-place wedding-day?" cried Cecilia, irritated beyond measure by her mother's assumption. "It may do for Rosie and Bessie," she continued violently. "I suppose it's about all they are good for! But I can tell you it will require something very different to satisfy me!"

"I am sure I don't see what fault you can find with the matches your sisters have made!" exclaimed Mrs. Banquet indignantly. "Charlie has been promised the family living directly the old incumbent dies, and now that Harry's father has taken him into partnership——"

"You don't understand me a bit!" interrupted the girl. "I wouldn't have a fat rectory or a prosperous young tea merchant at a gift! What I want is a mission in life!"

"A mission!" fairly screamed Mrs. Banquet. "Oh, Cecilia! To think of your taking up with the blacks after all, when you always pretended to hate poor people."

"Blacks indeed! Who said anything about blacks?"

"I never should have thought you were the sort of girl to trouble about zenanas and Siberian lepers," continued Mrs. Banquet, with her mind still running upon missionary sermons. "Now, if it had been Bessie or Selina, who were always good in the parish, it wouldn't have seemed so odd."

"Mamma, you are labouring under some extraordinary delusion." Cecilia spoke with laboured calm, befitting one who is patiently explaining palpable facts to a mental inferior. "I had never thought of those sort of good works," she continued. "At least, of course, I shall do an immense amount of good incidentally. Train people's minds and taste, you know, and, above all things, find an object myself worth living for. I had rather thought of taking up acting, or going in for public recitations."

Mrs. Banquet's response to this statement was a shriek of hysterical laughter, which so annoyed her daughter that the discussion threatened to become unpleasantly heated, when fortunately it was interrupted by the ringing of the dinner-bell.

Three months later, however, Cecilia got her own way, although in a somewhat modified form. Mrs. Banquet, backed up by a host of uncles and aunts, had remained absolutely obdurate to her entreaties for permission to become a public entertainer, either on the stage or platform. And Cecilia being entirely dependent upon her mother for money, this opposition was necessarily fatal to her scheme. She did not give it up without a murmur, but after making a magnanimous offer of her services to innumerable theatrical managers she gradually realized that to be penniless was equivalent to closing her career upon the stage, and she was forced to accept a compromise. Some old family friend discovered a philanthropic lady in London requiring a secretary, and though the pay did not quarter defray the girl's expenses living in a boarding-house, yet the once popular Cecilia had by this time contrived to make herself so disagreeable at home that it was considered advisable to get rid of her at any price. Miss Banquet herself naturally took a very different view of the situation. She talked largely about earning her livelihood, and having an independent position in the world.

" If another of us takes to earning her livelihood, there won't be money enough left to keep the rest out of the workhouse," murmured her younger sisters, as they looked at the boxes of new clothes that Cecilia had ordered for her London campaign. Two or three neat tailor-made dresses, and dark costumes with bonnets and hats to match, seemed the absolutely indispensable equipment for a secretary who wished to look her part ; and anything Miss Banquet did she prided herself upon doing thoroughly. The idea of earning her living in the same dress in which she had led a mere pleasure-seeking existence was too incongruous to be entertained for a moment.

It was with the fullest sense of her responsibilities that Cecilia took possession of her small bedroom in the highly respectable London boarding house which had been strongly recommended as a desirable residence by the same family friend who had unearthed the secretaryship. Mrs. Banquet had suggested sending up the maid to help her daughter unpack and settle in her new dwelling, but Cecilia negatived the idea at once. From the moment that she left home she intended to be entirely independent in thought, word and action, and that is an impossible feat under the eyes of the lady's maid who has done one's hair for the last ten years.

" Alone in London !" she exclaimed with a sort of ecstacy as she sat on her bed surveying the bare little room encumbered with luggage. " Alone in London !" she repeated, flinging open the window and getting a fine view of sundry smutty roofs and discoloured walls—the phrase pleased her ; it was dramatic and seemed well suited to the inauguration of a new unpacking. This gave her a delightful feeling of independence. For the first time in her life she was able to do things in her own way, without being subjected to family criticisms.

Cecilia was not an early riser, and it also took her several minutes to extract an appropriate secretary's costume from the bottom of one of her large boxes, so that by the time she reached the dining-room most of the other boarders had dispersed. Mrs. Brown, the owner of the establishment, was obviously impatient to go off to her household duties, a fact which Miss Banquet, completely absorbed in her own affairs, failed to notice for some time.

"This tea is very cold," remarked Cecilia calmly, when at last she looked up from her letters. "Can't we ring for some fresh? It's so nasty, isn't it?"

"Breakfast is supposed to be at half-past eight," replied Mrs. Brown evasively. "So many of the ladies who live here have a settled occupation, that I find it suits them best to keep early hours, and myself, I am glad of a long morning."

"Of course! Of course!" repeated Cecilia absently, as she returned to her letters.

"I think you will have a more comfortable breakfast if you join the other ladies another morning," continued Mrs. Brown.

"More comfortable what? I beg your pardon; I wasn't attending."

"I am sorry your breakfast has been so hurried," repeated Mrs. Brown impatiently, "but you see it's nearly ten o'clock, and things are apt to get cold if——"

"Oh, don't apologise," said Miss Banquet, drinking down her tea with great good temper, as she suddenly remembered that this fragmentary breakfast marked a new era of liberty. "I had an appointment myself," she added pleasantly. "How long will it take me to get to Sloane Street? I want to be there about ten."

"Dear me! You ought to have been off half-an-hour ago!" replied Mrs. Brown fussily. "You'll be late even if you catch a 'bus at the corner."

Miss Banquet, whose acquaintance with London did not extend to the quiet corner where she was now boarding, had previously contemplated finding her way to Sloane Street in a cab. But at Mrs. Brown's suggestion she instantly saw that such a course was inadmissible for a secretary. However late it might make her, the journey, to be in character, must be accomplished in an omnibus.

"You ought to be off at once," urged the landlady, breaking in upon these meditations. "It's full ten minutes' walk to the corner, and as likely as not you'll have to wait another five before you see a 'bus going in the right direction. I know this clock is a trifle slow by railway time. Oh, dear, you'll be terribly late, I'm afraid."

Cecilia swept together her letters which were lying scattered over the breakfast-table, and sauntered off to her room, calmly wondering how people like Mrs. Brown contrive to work themselves into a fever of apprehension lest other people should be late for trains or miss appointments. The idea that a philanthropic lady was at that moment expecting her new secretary in the neighbourhood of Sloane Street did not hurry Miss Banquet in the least. To speak accurately, she did not give the subject of punctuality a moment's thought one way or the other. She was far too intent on considering whether she would make her first appearance in a new character wearing a bonnet or hat. She decided at last in favour of a bonnet as being more business-like. It was also far from unbecoming.

Of course Miss Banquet did not carry out her landlady's parting directions to the letter. This was only to be expected, seeing that her attention was occupied wondering who was Mrs. Brown's dressmaker all the time that the excellent lady was giving minute directions as to which side of the crossing to stand in order to catch the Sloane Street 'bus. The consequence was that for about a quarter of an hour she occupied her time fully in climbing into omnibuses going in the opposite direction, and being pulled out again by the ever-vigilant conductors. However, with the help of a friendly errand boy, who witnessed her struggles and appeared to think her an object of compassion, she was at last safely started on her journey.

Now, Miss Banquet was bent on two very incompatible courses—she wished to enjoy the novel excitement of living like an independent worker, but at the back of her mind there was an unacknowledged desire that people should recognise she was only masquerading all the time. In the present instance she was divided between the desire to look the part of a secretary to perfection, and the instinctive wish to let it appear that she was not in the habit of rambling about alone in omnibuses. But after a time, observing that her eight fellow-passengers did not waste a glance upon her, and were evidently not absorbed in speculating on her private history, she relapsed into a day-dream which lasted until the conductor shouted to her that it was the place to get out.

Just as Cecilia was stepping on to the pavement she became aware of a clamour of voices arising from her late fellow passengers. She did not take much notice of it, concluding that the rumbling of an omnibus probably produced correspondingly discordant tones in those who habitually travelled by them, but when someone roughly seized her arm it was impossible to ignore the disturbance any longer. In a moment the omnibus seemed to have become the centre of a crowd, in which Cecilia, a policeman, and a fat woman with a bundle, occupied the places of honour. It appeared that the latter had just missed her purse, containing, as she was careful to explain, a half-crown, sixpence, and several pennies ; and she somehow connected its disappearance with Cecilia, who happened to have been sitting next her and to have left the omnibus at that precise moment.

"What a ridiculous person," observed Miss Banquet to the policeman, who prudently abstained from giving any opinion, and limited his efforts to keeping a large circle of street boys at bay. The confusion was now increased by the conductor pointing out that he could not keep the omnibus waiting any longer, and that the fat woman must either get in and continue her journey, or pay her fare if she preferred alighting and fighting it out on the pavement. This last suggestion added fuel to the flames, for the purse being gone precluded all possibility of paying even a penny fare. At this point somebody in the crowd started the theory that it was all a dodge on the fat woman's part for getting off without paying, which remark stirred her to such wrath that she threatened to become violent.

It happened that Mr. Powell was walking down Sloane Street that morning looking out for an appropriate christening present for a friend's eldest child. He was the sort of lonely man, with a reputation for saving, who is always in great request as a god-parent. A crowd across the pavement blocked his path, and he tried to step aside and avoid it. Great was his surprise when a clear voice rang out from the excited throng, calling him by his name. He was not an imaginative man, and it took him a long time to understand how Miss Banquet could be alone in the midst of a street row, when he had fancied her safe in a country house surrounded by relations. However, he did not wait to understand before extracting her from the crowd by a few quiet words to the policeman.

"Then I suppose I am not to go to prison to-day!" said Cecilia, laughing rather nervously as they walked away together. She was a good deal frightened by her late experience and most anxious not to show it. "Dear me! What will that unfortunate fat woman do if she hasn't a penny to pay the omnibus?" she added, stopping suddenly. "Oughtn't we to go back and lend her something?"

"Oh, no! Quite impossible. She'll do well enough," and Mr. Powell, seized with a dread that she would insist upon returning, quickened his footsteps.

"Are you going in this direction?" enquired Cecilia presently.

"No, not exactly—why?"

"Because I'm not, either! So hadn't we better turn round?"

Mr. Powell's sallow face flushed. For the second time it occurred to him that Cecilia had not turned out as sweet a girl as she gave promise of being ten years ago. Yet she could be a very agreeable companion when it pleased her, and for the next few minutes she entertained him with a vivacious account of her new career. She was absolutely candid about her motives, and soon fell into the confidential strain natural between old friends.

Mr. Powell was a good deal puzzled by these confidences. He had fallen sadly behind the times during his sojourn in India. Hitherto he had broadly divided all the girls of his acquaintance into two classes—those who flirt, and those who don't. It was a discovery to him that there was an additional subdivision who leave comfortable homes to live in boarding houses, for the simple satisfaction of feeling that they have a mission.

"I hope you will find it pleasant," he said, as they parted.

"Pleasant? Oh, no! I don't expect that," replied Cecilia

modestly. "But one likes to feel one is some good in the world."

"Ah, yes, of course," stammered Mr. Powell, who had hardly grasped this high motive with the distinctness it deserved. "Yes, it's always nice to feel useful. Can I give your people any messages? You know Mrs. Banquet has asked me down to Lea Home for a week? No? I am starting in a day or two, and no doubt they will be glad to hear the last news of you."

"Now why has mamma asked him down, without saying a word to me?" pondered Cecilia, as she knocked at a door and enquired for the philanthropic lady whose secretary she was about to become.

Her reflections were cut short by the appearance of a servant with the unexpected bit of information that Mrs. Lane, having awaited her secretary's arrival in the study for an hour, had started out at eleven o'clock to attend a meeting, and was not expected to return until the afternoon. Even Cecilia's self-assurance was slightly disturbed by this news. She had counted so confidently on getting to work that day, that it was a disappointment to be compelled to postpone her series of novel sensations. However she forgave Mrs. Lane with the good-natured magnanimity which she always extended to other people's little frailties. It was tactless and fussy of this philanthropic lady to hurry off in that breathless manner. Miss Banquet had read somewhere that really clever people manage to get through an incredible amount of work without any apparent effort. That was the kind of person she meant to be. It would be amusing for Mrs. Lane to observe the contrast. Cecilia determined to give that good lady every opportunity of realising the difference between real ability and a fussy assumption of fruitless energy. The idea put her into such good spirits that she determined to go straight back to the boarding house, change her clothes, go to luncheon with an aunt, and finish the afternoon by seeing what sort of a tea-party her friend had scraped together in October. This programme fully occupied the rest of the day, and deprived her of the distressing necessity of settling down to unpack her clothes by way of an employment.

On the following morning at ten o'clock precisely, the new

secretary entered Mrs. Lane's business-like study. The first impression Cecilia's appearance produced was usually good. The girl's marked features, and well-defined eye-brows, gave promise of a considerable amount of decision. Her smile was humorous, but rather destroyed this impression of firmness. However, fortunately, few acquaintances have time or inclination to analyze these subtle shades of expression, and Cecilia was generally credited with great abilities and an iron will. All that Mrs. Lane saw was a well-grown girl, in a beautifully-fitting suit of grey cloth, who proceeded to introduce herself without a shade of embarrassment.

"I was so sorry you were obliged to go out yesterday," observed Cecilia pleasantly. "So vexing just missing each other like that, wasn't it?"

The elder lady remained speechless before this strange substitute for the apology she had been confidently expecting.

"You can't think what a struggle it is to get here in time," continued Miss Banquet. "I have made a vow in the interests of economy not to get into a hansom more than twice a week, and I've used up my allowance already. So what I am to do for the rest of the week I can't imagine! It's nearly an hour's walk, and when I try an omnibus I excite instant suspicion as a pick-pocket. It's a funny thing why people who have nothing at all to lose, instantly think you are going to take it."

"I am sorry that your experiences have been so unpleasant," said Mrs. Lane stiffly.

As a rule, her secretaries commenced work after a brief greeting, without any preliminary conversation, and she dreaded creating an inconvenient precedent by encouraging Cecilia's philosophic reflections on men and manners.

But it takes a great deal to put out of countenance a girl whose lightest remarks have always commanded a certain amount of polite attention from a large circle of relations and friends. The pretty daughter of a popular county member is a sufficiently important personage in her own home seldom to encounter these rebuffs that render girls shy and self-conscious. Cecilia talked on brightly, just as long as it suited her humour; then she wandered up to the writing-table and began examining some antique seals with profound attention.

"I say! These are really good, aren't they?" she broke out.

"Genuine antiques? I thought so! And I have gone in for that sort of thing a good deal. I took it up once, and haunted the British Museum all one season. I must look them over. But any day will do. Perhaps you are in a hurry to get to business now," she added magnanimously.

Mrs. Lane did not immediately reply. She was wondering whether a lunatic asylum was not the only fitting destination for the mutual friend who had recommended Cecilia as a suitable secretary.

The particular form of philanthropic work in which Miss Banquet's services were now enlisted consisted of bringing meritorious servants and deserving mistresses into contact, without the intervention of a regular registry office. It entailed writing endless letters of a somewhat monotonous description, just such letters as Cecilia had rebelled most decidedly against ever being expected to write for her mother. But of course the motive with which a work is undertaken makes all the difference in its acceptability. Enquiries after servants' characters, when dignified by the name of a mission in life, assumed quite an interesting aspect. Cecilia worked away with a will, evolving elaborate letters out of the brief directions which Mrs. Lane jotted down on a piece of paper.

There was a short interval when luncheon was brought in on a tray, and then the secretary resumed her task without interruption until late in the afternoon.

From time to time Mrs. Lane appeared with enquiries as to whether the letters were finished. Cecilia gradually gathered that former secretaries had completed their work sooner; but then she had the comfortable conviction that they had probably done it in a very inferior manner. Now some of her notes were quite epigrammatic, and in spite of the sameness of the subject she prided herself on having expressed her ideas differently in every instance. With justifiable pride she read over several of her compositions which were really perfect little essays on the relative duties of servants and mistresses.

"Are not those letters ready yet?" interrupted Mrs. Lane, entering the room with her bonnet on. "It's absolutely necessary that they catch the country post. Please fasten them up at once. No, I haven't time to took through them"—waving aside a masterpiece that Cecilia held up for inspection—"but I trust"—and she looked critically at the addresses—" I really trust that they are legibly written. That is of the very greatest importance. Another time I should suggest a finer pen, and somewhat smaller writing. But the carriage is waiting for me; pray post them at once, Miss Banquet, and I will give you more detailed directions to-morrow."

For a moment Cecilia felt profoundly disappointed at her literary efforts meeting with such slight recognition. Then she remembered that Mrs. Lane was probably one of those commonplace souls who value mere mechanical labour beyond any ebullitions of genius. The contempt for her employer's intellect induced by this reflection quite restored her good temper. She made a rule of being magnanimously tolerant towards her mental inferiors; it had, she believed, saved much friction in a family whose ideals were deplorably conventional and old-fashioned. But this morning's work strengthened her in the belief that she had made a grave mistake in not absolutely insisting upon the stage as the scene of her labours. She already foresaw that a secretaryship might become insufferably monotonous before long. However, one must be grateful for even small concessions from a prejudiced parent, and the first assertion of independence was a great step gained.

After a few days Cecilia fell into a sort of routine, arriving at Mrs. Lane's with fair punctuality, thanks to entirely abandoning her rule of not employing hansoms, and fulfilling her duties creditably, but without enthusiasm. After all, as she soon realised, there are some works that can best be performed mechanically, so, flying rather from one extreme to another, instead of devoting much time and attention to the composition of her letters, she now carefully detached her mind from the matter in hand, and deliberately indulged in day-dreams, whilst outwardly engaged in tracing the characters of domestic servants up to their source.

Things had gone on in this way for a week or so, when Mrs. Lane one morning entered the study with a perturbed face. She seated herself magisterially at her desk, put on her spectacles, and requested the favour of Miss Banquet's attention.

At this formal address Cecilia recalled herself with a jerk from an imaginary voyage in the tropics, on board the yacht of a man whose name she often vowed she wished never to hear again.

She often yielded to the incomprehensible fascination of brooding over subjects that it would have been wiser to forget.

"There has been some inexplicable mistake," said Mrs. Lane severely. "The only manner in which I can account for what has occurred is on the supposition that you have put some letters into wrongly-addressed envelopes. Even that would not explain the obvious confusion you have fallen into between Emma Hazell and Emma Hunton. Here I find you have been recommending the former as an experienced lady's maid, when she is a girl of seventeen just out of a reformatory school, whilst on the other hand I have an indignant letter from the latter, saying that it is useless my sending her to situations where she is expected to clean the boots and knives for eight pounds a year. The very essence of my work being accuracy and punctuality, this is naturally very annoying. Have you any explanation to offer?"

Cecilia had none. It was not the first time in her career that she had left letters lying in blotting books, or slipped them into the wrong envelopes. The novelty lay in the blame attaching to this little oversight. However, she determined to be patient, and put up with the inevitable annoyances of her position, so she attempted no excuse, and preserved her mind free from irritation by not listening to what Mrs. Lane said.

"Well, yes, it is vexing," remarked Cecilia blandly when the lecture seemed finished, " I suppose I shall have to write at least four long letters of explanation, shan't I? However, it's not so bad as when we were giving a dance once, and I dropped a whole pile of invitations down behind a cupboard, and they weren't found for weeks, not until at least half the neighbours were mortally offended——"

"You will please be exceedingly careful to make the matter perfectly clear to all the people concerned," interposed Mrs. Lane, cutting short these reminiscences. "The whole utility of my undertaking will be impaired if these mistakes are repeated."

To Cecilia the whole affair appeared contemptibly trivial. Why some people should attach as much importance to the character of a housemaid as if she was going to be their inseparable companion for life, passed her comprehension. However, in a spirit of noble self-abnegation she sat down to repair the mistakes. It involved considerably more writing than she had anticipated, and she remained on long after her usual hour, doggedly fulfilling the required task.

About six o'clock a heavy step was heard in the passage, accompanied by an unmistakable whiff of tobacco. The same odour had greeted Cecilia's nostrils that morning on entering the study. Now, Mrs. Lane was an elderly widow, and the few visitors she entertained had hitherto been ladies of a mature age. Cecilia suspended her labours, and awaited developments with some interest.

Her patience was not put to a severe test. The next moment the door was flung violently open, and a young man appeared, closely followed by a fox terrier.

"Oh, I say!" he exclaimed, stopping suddenly, "I didn't know there was anybody——No!—It can't be Miss Banquet! How on earth did you get here?"

"The same way you did, I suppose," replied Cecilia promptly. She had recognised in the intruder a favourite partner at Christmas dances, a delightfully friendly boy a few years younger than herself, and her spirits had revived at the sight. A mutual explanation followed. It appeared that Mr. Fred Grainger stood in the position of godson to Mrs. Lane, and was paying her his annual three-day visit.

"It's probably the most uncomfortable house in London," he went on to say. "Jack is my only solace. They can't abide my bringing him, but I couldn't survive the ordeal otherwise. The servants here are always finding particles of mud they swear he has brought in on his feet—So absurd! Only Mrs. Lane can believe anything of a dog. This is the one room he is allowed in. His mud and my smoke are supposed to deteriorate property in the other parts of the house."

"I am afraid it must have given you a horrid shock to see a secretary established in your private smoking-room," observed Cecilia.

"Well, it did—at first—I have got over it though, since I recognised you. Not that you look quite natural. Perhaps it is your bonnet, and then there's a kind of stiffness about your manner. What they call the dignity of labour, I suppose——"

"Oh, shut up!" interrupted Miss Banquet, relapsing suddenly into her most familiar phraseology. "I can only tell you it's no joke prosing on about the most boring topic under the sun to correspondents who manifest their gratitude by writing to Mrs. Lane complaining of the way I discharge my duties."

"Why, have you made a mess of it already?" enquired Mr. Grainger, lightly seating himself upon the corner of the table on top of some freshly-addressed envelopes.

"I should rather think I had! An imperial mess, as one might say!" Cecilia laid aside her pen, and with it the last vestiges of her official manner. "Picture to yourself," she said excitedly, "two fussy old frumps, one requiring a confidential maid to watch over her declining years, and in the meantime take charge of the household linen, the other looking out for a stout scullery-maid, with an endless capacity for doing hard work on low wages. Then picture me successfully muddling up the supply and demand——"

"And what did my excellent godmother say?"

"Well, she didn't actually *say* much, but she inferred that she had had better secretaries."

"By Jove! Did she though? That old woman's equal to anything!" shouted Fred Grainger hilariously.

His voice died away in a feeble quaver as the door opened, admitting Mrs. Lane. The guilty start with which he rose to his feet dragged the table-cloth on to the carpet, and upset the great cut glass ink-stand, which slowly discharged its contents over the numerous letters around.

Mrs. Lane regarded the black pool on the floor with a sort of grim satisfaction, feeling that from a dramatic point of view the situation was now complete.

"No, it's useless spoiling your handkerchief, Fred," she said deliberately. "Even your ingenuity will not suffice to wipe up half-a-pint of ink with six inches square of fine cambric. Miss Banquet, will you have the kindness to ring the bell? And then I think if no more ink is trodden into the carpet the servants may be able to partially clean it. Personally I shall be occupied most of the evening re-writing these letters, which I see are absolutely illegible. No, there is no need for you to stay, Miss Banquet. I much prefer doing it myself."

There was nothing more to be said. Cecilia put on her cloak and left the house, trying hard not to look like a naughty child sent away in disgrace.

"You are the lucky one. You can go," whispered Fred

Grainger, opening the hall door for her with a very inky hand.

"Don't despair! I shouldn't wonder if it were your last visit," returned Cecilia, as she waved good-bye from the pavement, a little more effusively than she would have done if Mrs. Lane had not been watching her out of the study window.

"I shall have to be extra careful to-morrow to make up for this little mishap," she thought, as she reviewed the events of the day. "Really it isn't as easy as it seems even to make a conventional secretary. At any rate it isn't work that is congenial to me at all, and directly I come across anything more interesting, I shall drop it. This constant mechanical writing is really destructive of all originality."

Miss Banquet's release came sooner than she anticipated. A formal letter on the following morning informed her that her services as secretary would no longer be required. Her indignation and astonishment at this intimation knew no bounds. Naturally her first step was to rush off in search of the mutual friend who had procured her the secretaryship.

"Read this!" she cried, producing the dismissal with a tragic gesture. "Explain that woman's conduct if you can!"

There was no difficulty about the explanation, Mrs. Lane's account of the proceedings upon which her conduct was based having arrived by the first post.

"Of course you may have had your own reasons for pelting her godson with ink-bottles and pen-wipers," said the mutual friend diffidently. "But surely under the circumstances it was rather indiscreet?"

"Ink-bottles, indeed! He sat on it himself. And as for the pen-wiper—did she tell you he laughed at my bonnet? Have you ever known a time when I would have stood that?"

"No—possibly not—before. But surely you must recognise that when you accepted a secretaryship you forfeited your right to throw pen-wipers at your employers' godsons?"

"She's a pompous old prig, and as dull as ditchwater," said Cecilia conclusively. It was obviously easier to be epigrammatic about Mrs. Lane than to defend her own behaviour on abstract grounds. "Really clever people have a certain breadth of view," she continued. "They don't expect even their secretaries to be made by machinery. At the same time I shan't be sorry for a change, as the work was singularly distasteful. What shall I do now?"

As it happened the mutual friend was a lady of wide and varied experience. She had often successfully mediated between factory girls and their employers, and exerted a beneficent influence over washer-women on strike. On more than one occasion she had been subjected to long and harassing examinations before Labour Commissioners, anxious apparently to ascertain the exact limits of feminine patience. But she subsequently confessed that all previous trials dwindled into insignificance compared with the mental strain of a morning spent in evading Miss Banquet's demands for further employment. Feeding the starving, and providing homes for the destitute, was simplicity itself by the side of discovering a suitable occupation for a very inefficient worker, who objected on principle to coming into contact with any form of disease or squalor, and also declined all routine as savouring of what she termed mere mechanical labour. Cecilia was at last bribed to leave with a vague promise of recommendation to some post in connection with a Home for Lost Dogs, and she then hurried off to her aunt's house to inform her, as the nearest representative of the family, of her threatened change of plans.

Mrs. Vivian received her niece's disclosures with the most gratifying amount of emotion. It is true she had never smiled on the secretary scheme, the search after missions in life being the outcome of a wave of feeling by which her generation had been untouched; but at the same time she had shared the tacit belief of all Cecilia's relations that the services of a young lady of good family, who voluntarily descended into the labour arena, would be unusually sought after, and highly paid.

"I really wonder what the world's coming to if the prettiest and cleverest of all my nieces isn't considered good enough for a secretaryship!" And gentle Mrs. Vivian trembled with indignation, as she carved the roast pheasant at luncheon.

"I shall not be discouraged," observed Cecilia, "although I must say nobody would believe the difficulties all charitable institutions and people throw in our way directly one tries to do anything. And as for expense, of course much the cheapest thing is to live at home and do nothing. One requires a good private income to start as an actress, or a dressmaker, or even a hospital nurse."

"Oh, my dear! Don't tell me you are going to take up nursing!" cried Mrs. Vivian in dismay. "It's so terribly overdone. To be sure they are very nice when one is ill, but nowadays one can never be certain that half the people one meets at parties aren't hospital nurses in disguise, spreading all sorts of nasty germs and microbes."

Cecilia calmed her aunt by the assurance that she herself had a rooted antipathy to all aspects of medical work.

"Besides," she added, "I wore the dress once at a bazaar, and I wasn't one of the rare people who contrive to look pretty in it. And if you don't, it's quite too hopelessly dowdy."

"Do you know, my dear child, I sometimes think you are getting rather—well, just a trifle tired of your notions," remarked Mrs. Vivian tentatively.

"My notions, indeed! That's just how mamma talks! It's odd that people can never be just to a younger generation. But you must admit that girls are much better educated, and cleverer, and have many more interests now than they had in your time."

The elder lady confessed humbly that the girls of her youth had been mainly ruled by one idea. Then she looked from the anxious, discontented young face beside her, to her own placidly well-preserved reflection in the looking-glass. And she smiled with a dim recollection of a certain fable telling how the fox had a hundred resources and the cat but one; yet how nevertheless that one simple expedient availed pussy better than all the clever tricks of her highly-accomplished friend. "Your younger sisters seem to like the old way best," she said after a pause.

"The old way? Oh, getting married and all that! But one couldn't expect any originality of Rosie and Bessie."

"Violet is growing a very pretty girl, I hear," continued Mrs. Vivian. "The very image of what you were when you came out."

Miss Banquet felt unreasonably annoyed, and was about to disclaim the likeness with some energy, when she reflected that such an expression of impatience was open to misunderstanding. Besides, to the merely superficial observer Violet was undoubtedly an exact reproduction of her elder sister's features and colouring, with ten years' advantage in the matter of age. But Cecilia confidently hoped that to anyone of the slightest discrimination her own countenance must betray various subtle signs of the fire of suppressed genius which it was vain to expect from poor little Violet.

"I hear Mr. Powell is still staying at your mother's," remarked Mrs. Vivian rather inconsequently.

Miss Banquet did not even trouble to acknowledge this remark, considering the lack of sequence in her aunt's ideas to be amply accounted for by the deplorably illogical education of the last generation.

"It would be funny if little Violet made the best match of you all," continued Mrs. Vivian pleasantly.

"More funny than likely, seeing that she was in the schoolroom till Bessie married!"

"Exactly. Many of the best matches are made straight out of the schoolroom. Mark my words," she continued, "your little sister will be lording it as a queen of society in India before another year is out."

"What do you mean? Oh, I see! My dear Aunt Emma, what an ultra-ridiculous idea!"

But in spite of her loud expressions of incredulity Cecilia had received a distinct shock. The idea of Mr. Powell as an aspirant for her little sister's hand had never occurred to her before; and now she had no hesitation in characterizing it as ridiculous.

"Well, I don't see where the ridicule comes in," observed Mrs. Vivian with mild dignity. She would have placidly endured any reflections on her abilities and accomplishments; but to cast a doubt on her perspicacity in detecting the premonitory symptoms of a wedding was to wound her tenderest susceptibilities.

"And even if by any chance there is a grain of truth in it," began Cecilia, "his age——"

"Now don't go running away with any foolish ideas of that kind," interrupted Mrs. Vivian, quite sharply for her. "If Mr. Powell wants to marry your sister she will be a little fool not to have him. She won't get another chance of such a good match. Why, you don't understand what that man's position is in India. Always entertaining royal dukes and foreign princes." And she proceeded to expatiate at some length on the social aspects of an important Anglo-Indian official's life.

"It's very curious," reflected Cecilia, as she walked back to her boarding-house, "how with the best possible intentions people never tell one anything that is of the slightest importance until it is too late to be of any use. Here I have been all these years regarding Mr. Powell's offer in the light of a bad joke, when apparently it was the chance of my life! If my poor dear father, instead of always calling him 'good old Dicky,' and making jokes about his complexion, had only——But there! Life's made up of that kind of stupid mistake."

Once more, as on the evening of her arrival, Miss Banquet threw open her window, and gazing over the smutty chimney-pots indulged in a long introspective meditation. But she no longer repeated " Alone in London ! " with a species of rapture ; neither were her thoughts wandering longingly after any obdurate individual who had passed out of her life without making a sign. In point of fact, she had come to consider London an over-rated place of abode, and was already contemplating a distinctly retrograde movement back into the country. And with regard to men, she was entirely preoccupied with shamefaced regrets for the stupid indifference with which she had treated the only one who ever seemed alive to her merits. By the light of Mrs. Vivian's glowing encomiums she now for the first time realised that Mr. Powell's offer, instead of being a subject of ridicule as she had at one time imagined, was probably the greatest compliment she would ever receive. This discovery, coinciding as it did with the total collapse of her self-ordained mission, filled her with regretful disappointment. Curiously enough the upshot of her meditations was a resolution to return home on the following day. There seemed nothing left for her to do until such time as the mutual friend should bestir herself in earnest to find her an occupation ; and in the interval, there was a kind of painful fascination about seeing with her own eyes the development of Violet's triumph. Besides she had a strong feeling that she owed Mr. Powell a certain reparation for ten years' mental ingratitude, and indistinct visions of wise counsels given to a hesitating younger sister flitted through her throbbing head.

Early on the following day Miss Banquet was seated in the train on her homeward journey. She was feeling unusually inert and low-spirited after spending half the night laboriously re-packing clothes, many of which had never properly been taken out of their boxes. On looking back it almost seemed as if the creases in her frocks, and the ink-stains on Mrs. Lane's carpet, were the only tangible results of her mission. She was haunted also by a disquieting suspicion that her family might be inclined to receive with a tinge of ridicule her speedy return home, after the elaborate preparations made for her departure only a month previously.

After being for some time overshadowed by the dignity of a mission, it is a sad descent to again walk the earth as an ordinary mortal, liable to be judged by commonplace standards.

It is hard to say whether Cecilia experienced more relief or vexation on finding nobody at home to receive her. It is true her mother had left a host of messages with the servants explaining how the telegram announcing her return had not arrived until after all the plans for the day were made. It was all literally true, and full of good sense; yet Cecilia knew perfectly that at a not very far distant time, the plans for the day would have been entirely subservient to her own arrangements. It was evident that she had ceased to be the motive power of the family. A still more bracing experience was presently encountered when, on going to her bedroom to take off her wraps, she found that it had been appropriated by a younger sister, whose ornaments and books now occupied all the shelves and tables. For a moment she felt irritated past bearing by this impertinent usurpation; then justice re-asserted itself, and she had to admit that it would have been unreasonable to keep one of the most comfortable rooms in the house unoccupied when she had so constantly stated her intention of leaving home for good. And yet it was with rather a sore feeling of having been supplanted, that she rang the bell and asked the maid where she could put down her cloak.

For some time after this Cecilia sat alone in the drawing-room, brooding moodily over the wisdom of an experiment which, if it had done nothing else, seemed to have reduced her to the position of a stranger in her own home. The sound of wheels slowly coming up the drive at last roused her to look out of the window. It was only the pony carriage returning home, with its two occupants so absorbed in conversation that they allowed old Tommy to crawl up the hill exactly at his own pace.

As Cecilia watched she was forced to acknowledge that Mrs. Vivian had been quite right about the strong family likeness between the sisters. The bright-faced young girl who was chattering away without a moment's pause was an exact reproduction of herself ten years before ; and as for the grave-looking man who listened with such incongruously serious attention to his companion's childish talk, there was nothing new about him !

Now it so happened that both Tommy and the pony carriage had once been birthday presents to Cecilia from her father, and although she had hardly ever used them the last year or two it nevertheless gave her a distinct pang to see them taken possession of by the others. The circumstance was trivial in itself, but taken in conjunction with other things it brought home to her the feeling that her place was filled up. She also suddenly discovered that she had over-rated her philosophy when she projected giving wise counsels to her younger sister on the value of realizing her luck in time. Theoretically she still wished Violet every happiness, but all desire to witness her felicity had now completely departed.

Between irritation and unhappiness Cecilia's habitual composure deserted her more completely than it had done since she was a child. She turned and hurried out of the room, seizing the handle of the door just as someone was in the act of entering ; there was the usual slight awkwardness engendered by all similar collisions in doorways, which was rather intensified on the present occasion by Mr. Powell peering forward in a shortsighted way, and exclaiming :

"What, Violet, come in already ! I thought you were going to——"

"Oh, it isn't Violet—it's only Cecilia !" returned the girl sharply.

"Why, so it is !" Mr. Powell was a deliberate man, and it took him some time to get over his surprise, and shake hands in the manner demanded by custom after a separation of several weeks. But like most deliberate persons he was also very tenacious of an idea. Consequently, after slowly closing the door, and moving a couple of comfortable chairs nearer the fire, he seated himself in one, and waiting patiently until his companion was established in the other, enquired soberly, "Why do you say 'only Cecilia' ?"

"Oh, I don't know!" said the girl impatiently. "It was nothing—only an expression. No, it wasn't, though!" she added with a sudden, inexplicable desire to unburden her mind. "It's the simple truth. It never was before, but it is now. Well, you remember what I used to be in this house—they all petted me and believed in whatever I said. They did really, funny as it seems." She paused with a little hysterical laugh which didn't quite come off.

Mr. Powell gravely nodded to her to proceed.

"Of course it's all my own fault!" she continued passionately. "I ought to have been contented, but I wasn't. I got tired of them all, and now they all seem to have got tired of me. Everything that belonged to me has——Well, it's no good boring you with the whole story, but the fact is I've lost my place at home—it's filled up, and the worst is I haven't found another."

"But how about the thing in London?—the mission, you know, that you told me your life was consecrated to in future?"

"It's collapsed. Don't mind laughing, please—it's already passed into the regions of a family joke."

But Mr. Powell did not even smile. His mind had slowly reverted to an earlier stage in the conversation.

"As far as I am concerned there has always been only Cecilia," he remarked, paraphrasing her hasty words. "And you have not altered——"

"Oh, but I have!" she interrupted with such impetuosity as startled her companion into beginning again exactly where he left off ten years before.

"No, it isn't that I can't make up my mind!" Cecilia was tearfully protesting some quarter of an hour later. "And I am grateful to you—I should rather think I am—for caring about me all this time. And it's almost too good to be—but I can't give you a definite answer directly—I must ask—well, I can't explain."

Mr. Powell's former apprenticeship in patience enabled him to wait quietly in the drawing-room, and even to read the newspaper with tolerable success, whilst the girl hurried away, as he imagined, to consult her mother. But without waiting for Mrs. Banquet's return, Cecilia ran out into the garden, where she could see her younger sister throwing crumbs to a circle of friendly robins and blackbirds.

This slight, pink-cheeked young girl, entirely absorbed in feeding and recognising her birds, scarcely looked sufficiently formidable to be the arbitrator of another's fate. Yet, in this light she now appeared to Cecilia, whose whole life hung on the first words that should pass those rosy lips. For if her own happiness was only to be secured at the price of Violet's, she felt that justice and honour alike forbade her to snatch the prize that she had once abandoned. Far too nervous for any preliminary greeting she walked straight up to her sister.

"I came home just now," she began abruptly, "and—oh, yes! your robins are wonderfully tame, but do listen to me for a moment. You were out driving with Mr. Powell—what do you think of him?"

"What do I think of him?" Violet paused one long minute so as not to disturb an unusually tame guest who had actually hopped on her boot. "What do I think?" she reiterated carelessly. "Oh, of course, I think he is a good old soul—nobody could help it."

Cecilia drew a long breath of relief as she found Violet's judgment was an exact reproduction of her own at eighteen. Then she kissed her young sister with an amount of effusion for which the latter was quite unable to account, and which vexed her sadly, as it effectually frightened away all the birds.

# A Victim of Circumstances.

## I.

"I'M miserable—perfectly miserable! I wish I could get away somewhere and never be heard of or seen again!"

"But, Sylvia, you surely can't care for this man, who has treated you so outrageously! You, of all people——"

"Oh, of course, like all the rest, you think I'm absolutely heartless! I tell you—I did care—I do care—I never knew how much until he went away! I came down here to get out of it all. I couldn't bear the whispers and smiles that went round when I appeared, and the other girls watching to see how I took it! Everyone thought we were engaged; his going off like that made me a laughing stock to all my friends. Oh, I wish I had never been born!"

She broke down completely, and flung herself on a sofa, burying her face in the cushions. Nell Derwent looked at her with tears in her own eyes.

"A man who could behave like that is not worth caring about, Sylvia," she said.

"You wouldn't say that if you knew him!" with a half-angry sob.

"If I knew him, I would try and punish him somehow! I would revenge you, Sylvia; I would flirt with him, and make him fall in love with me, and then—depart as he did."

"You would do no such thing, you dear little innocent!" said Sylvia, emerging from her cushions. "You couldn't flirt to save your life, and he's a very fascinating man. You would fall in love with him yourself directly, and forget all about me."

"Sylvia, how can you say such things? You know I would do almost anything for you, and—oh, Archie, what a fright you gave me!"

"Talking about your swains as usual?" said the young man, who had just strolled in at the open window. "Why, what's wrong with Sylvia?" as that young lady, conscious of presenting a somewhat disordered appearance, hastily departed.

"She's very unhappy, I'm afraid," answered Nell, in a distressed tone. "I've been feeling quite anxious about her ever since she came down. She hasn't seemed a bit like herself."

"Don't you worry yourself about Sylvia's troubles. She's probably more out of temper than anything else. This is her fifth season, and she hasn't succeeded in bagging an eligible yet, so she comes rushing down here and makes herself out a martyr to you. I know her little ways of old."

"What horrid things you say sometimes, Archie!" exclaimed his sister angrily. "I don't believe she's capable of behaving like that!"

"All right, old girl, don't get mad. I don't want to insinuate anything against Sylvia, if you're fond of her, but I've known her longer than you have, and all I say is, don't take her too seriously. She's just the sort of girl, if she feels a bit out of sorts, or if her dressmaker's bill is bigger than she likes to think about, to get regularly blue and think the whole world's against her. Probably her latest man has got tired of her a little too soon. She's dull too—there's no one for her to flirt with in this house—all right, don't rush away, I've done, only you're most likely taking her griefs to heart a great deal more than she is herself. Look here, I want you to come out, and tell Jones where to put those new flower-beds. The work must be done, we're off to Switzerland in a week, and there's no end to arrange. Put on your hat and come out, Nellie."

And Archie Derwent, who was devotedly fond of his little sister, arrested her attempt at a dignified exit and carried her off to the garden.

Meanwhile, the subject of their discussion stood before her looking-glass upstairs, wishing she had not made her eyes so red. She was a tall, dark, handsome girl, and her eyes were her great beauty.

"I can't imagine what came over me," she said to herself. "It isn't like me to break down, and make a fool of myself in that way. But I really feel the better for it, and Nell is a dear sympathetic little thing. I'll just lie down and rest till tea-time, all this worry is making me look quite old. What *could* have made Jim go off in that sudden way, just when I was perfectly certain he was going to propose! He would have suited me so well. It's *too* annoying! By the way, I never told Nell his name. Perhaps it's just as well, and she didn't ask."

She flung herself down on the sofa, and was soon lost in the depths of a French novel.

A month later, a lady and gentleman were sitting on the terrace of an hotel, looking out over one of the loveliest of the Swiss lakes. The lady was the type of the fashionable young married woman in appearance, and was holding forth with great emphasis and vigour. Her companion wore a resigned, long-suffering expression, mingled with an amount of passive resistance, which suggested that it was not by any means the first time that he had been attacked on the same subject.

" But really, Jim, you know you *ought* to marry. Here you are, nearly five-and-thirty if you're a day, no ties to speak of, plenty of money, a good position—and your worst enemy couldn't call you plain! Yet instead of settling down with some nice girl, you go flirting round with one after another, never meaning anything serious all the time. You haven't the shadow of an excuse for such conduct. I don't believe you really enjoy it either. A man gets tired of that sort of thing after about twelve years of it. Why don't you marry?"

" Nobody would have me," said the object of this tirade lazily.

" Now you're talking nonsense. You don't mean what you say. I never flatter you, but you know perfectly well that half the girls in your set would be only too glad to be given the chance. There was that pretty little Kitty Sale, you were running after her last season. She would make you a charming wife."

" So she would if all I wanted were a doll, to sit still and smile and say Yes or No when I spoke to her. I could have a mechanical toy made which would do that equally well—and be less expensive."

" Don't be cynical, Jim, it doesn't suit you. If you want a clever girl, there are any amount about. That Miss—Miss—I've forgotten her name, but she's taken no end of degrees and things," vaguely. " A tall, thin girl. I saw you with her at the Leytons' dance."

" Her genius wouldn't seem to have made much impression upon you if you don't remember her name. I know who you mean though, I had the—er—pleasure of waltzing with her twice. It was exactly like dancing with a triangle. I took her to sit out, and when she found that I didn't understand Anglo-Saxon and was misty on the subject of the Heptarchy, she hardly deigned to bestow another syllable upon me."

"I confess I hardly thought she was your style," laughed Mrs. Templeton, dropping her rôle of Mentor for a minute, then returning to the assault with new vigour: "But there are lots of girls who are pretty and clever both——"

"Now, look here, Alice, once for all, I'm perfectly sick of the conventional society girl, with her everlasting talk about theatres, dances and scandal, or racing and the last new novel, according as her tastes may be. They're all alike on one point, their desire to marry 'up to their form,' and meanwhile fill up their time with as much flirtation as possible. And when they do marry, most of them forget to leave it off."

"And who's responsible for that, I should like to know? You men, of course! You lead a girl on as far as she will possibly let you go, and then despise her for it. I never knew anything so unreasonable!"

"Well, when one sees that a girl expects to be made love to, it's only polite to oblige her."

"If you are going to say such abominable things, I shall leave you," said Mrs. Templeton, rising with indignation.

"Don't run away in a rage, Alice. You know very well there's some truth in what I say, though perhaps I put it too strongly. You're right when you think I'm tired of the life. I shall go and shoot elephants in South Africa, and get out of it all."

"Yes, I do know, and I only wish some of the girls who have flirted with you could hear what you've just said, it might open their eyes a little. But women talk men over just the same when they're alone, you must remember, and, now I come to think of it, I've heard some rather harsh things said about you lately."

"What have they said?" demanded the young man quickly.

"That you didn't behave too well to Sylvia Burke, and—who's that?" breaking off abruptly as an unmistakably English couple went past, and Blake raised his hat.

"Archie Derwent, a fellow I know a little in town. He's a very decent sort of chap. I see him sometimes at the club. That's his sister with him, no doubt. He told me he expected her to-day."

"I used to know some people of that name down at home before I was married. I must find out if they're the same family. It's an uncommon name. What was I saying? Oh, about Sylvia Burke. You know everybody thought you and she were engaged."

"Then everybody was wrong. No, I shall never marry—unless I can find someone like you, Alice. What a pity I didn't meet you before you were irrevocably tied to my respected uncle."

"You impertinent man! As if I should have *looked* at you when Harry was about! And I wish you wouldn't talk as if he were about a hundred! You know very well there's only five years between you. Harry dear," as a tall, soldierly man strolled up to them, "here's Jim actually venturing to suggest that I should have preferred him to you if I had met him first!"

"Like his cheek. Don't mind him, Alice, he doesn't know any better."

"I shall go and see if there are any letters," announced Blake, rising rather abruptly. "See you again presently."

Mrs. Templeton's eyes followed him somewhat anxiously.

"You look worried, little woman; what's the matter?" asked her husband, taking the vacant place by her side.

"I don't understand Jim," she said. "He was talking just now quite bitterly, so unlike his usual easy-going way. It really seems as if he had met with some disappointment lately. It *was* odd, his going off like that and leaving Sylvia Burke so suddenly. I wonder whether he was really in love with her after all. Certainly there was nothing wrong between them up to the night of our dance, in fact, I thought he would probably seize the opportunity to settle it, but he went away before the evening was half over, and I don't believe he saw her again before he left town. The whole thing is a mystery to me."

"I think I may be able to throw some light on the subject, if you really want to know. But don't repeat it on any account," said Captain Templeton, smiling down at her.

"Oh, Harry, do you really mean it? Do tell me, I won't mention it to a soul."

"Well, it was like this. I had been dancing with Lady Leyton and she asked me to find her fan for her, said in her delightfully vague way that she believed she must have left it in one of the sitting-out places somewhere. Of course that entailed going into all of them to look for it. I never wish to have another such time. I kept rousing up couples at every step. And in the darkest corner of the conservatory, who should I come across but Miss Burke and a man? I couldn't see his face, but his arm was round her, and her head was on his shoulder, so they must have been going the pace."

"Harry! How *could* Sylvia have been so silly? But are you sure it was she? And perhaps the man was Jim himself?"

"I know it wasn't, because I met him directly afterwards and he said it was his dance and asked if I'd seen her. He went into the conservatory and I expect he found them. There was no mistaking that yellow gown of hers, it was the only one in the room. Old Jim's particular, and I daresay it fairly put him off her."

"I should think so, indeed. Sylvia ought to have known better. Of course that accounts for everything. She really is the most incorrigible flirt I ever met. Even when it's most to her own interest, she can't resist temptation, and then she loses her head and never knows where to stop. Well, she's thrown away the best chance she'll ever have."

"Miss Burke was never a favourite of mine, and if you want my opinion I consider that Jim is well quit of her. Also, my dear, if you don't want to be late for dinner, you had better come in and dress."

Jim Blake, coming in to table d'hôte that night, was most agreeably surprised to find that instead of the unprepossessing and dingy lady of German extraction who was his usual vis-à-vis, Nell Derwent and her brother were established opposite to him. His first impression was of a piquante little face, not the least beautiful, hardly pretty perhaps, but eminently attractive; a small head, daintily set on the shoulders, and a slender rounded figure, encased in a frock which compelled even Mrs. Templeton's admiration.

"What a sweet little girl, Jim," she whispered. "I shall lose no time in making her acquaintance."

Miss Derwent was quite unconscious both of Blake's admiring glances and Mrs. Templeton's criticisms. She seemed to be enjoying herself enormously, and divided her attention between her brother and a small French child who sat on her other side. They left the table before anyone else, and Mrs. Templeton followed them closely. Blake, strolling on to the terrace a quarter of an hour later, found them all in animated conversation.

"Miss Derwent and I have discovered that we are almost old friends, Jim," called out his charming relative as soon as she saw him. " Our families have known each other for ages, though we've never happened to meet. Miss Derwent, may I introduce Mr. Blake—my nephew, though you might not think it."

Blake bowed, and promptly took possession of the nearest vacant chair.

"I don't think I've ever had the pleasure of seeing you in town, Miss Derwent," he said, "though I've often met your brother."

"Oh, it isn't likely that you would," said the girl with a quick smile. "I'm very little in town. I live with Archie, you know, and I've 'done' a regular season. I was presented, of course, when I was eighteen, and I go up now and then on visits, but most of my time I'm down at Fairfield."

Blake vaguely remembered having heard that young Derwent had lately come into an ancient and encumbered family estate, and that money, in consequence, was none too plentiful with him.

"Don't you like London?" he enquired tentatively.

"Oh, yes," she answered brightly, "I'm awfully fond of it, it is so delightful to be within reach of good concerts and the galleries and all that. And I like going out, I just adore dancing. Only I shouldn't care to do nothing else for three months at a stretch, like some girls I know, though my friends don't believe me when I say so. They declare it's a case of 'sour grapes!'"

Blake thought what a charming voice and manner she had, there was a degree of animation and life about her not usual with the girls of his set. He began to think it would not be very difficult to enjoy himself for the next fortnight.

"I don't think you'd look as you do if you had been through the London season," he said. "Most girls are more like washed-out rags just now than anything else."

"'Le jeu ne vaut pas la chandelle' in my opinion," said Nell decisively. "I like it for a time and it prevents one from getting rusty, but I'm always glad to get back to my own little room at home and gather my books and music round me again."

"Are you talking about music?" broke in Mrs. Templeton. "It's getting very damp out here; let's go in and have some."

A general move was made to the *salon*, and, the piano turning out to be somewhat above the average Swiss hotel article,

Blake sat down to it. He was a cultivated musician and played well, after him Mrs. Templeton produced her banjo and gave them several stirring plantation ditties, then someone asked Miss Derwent to sing. Nell had a sweet, sympathetic voice, and she sang two or three modern ballads with much artistic finish, ending with a quaint old-fashioned air seldom heard in these days, but which was full of pathos that went straight to the hearts of her listeners and produced that hush which to a true musician is the greatest of all compliments.

After this, Mrs. Templeton forcibly broke up the meeting, remarking "that nobody would get any beauty sleep, and the Swiss thought late hours positively improper."

Blake sat out on the balcony of his room, smoking a last cigar. The pathetic notes of Nell Derwent's song still rang in his ears; he leaned over the balustrade and gazed across the moonlit lake to the shadowy mountains beyond, humming them to himself.

"She has lovely eyes," he said, as he finally roused himself and went in. "Was it my fancy, or were they really wet with tears while she was singing?"

## II.

BLAKE saw a great deal of Nell Derwent during the next few days. The morning after her arrival, he was lounging lazily by the lake, trying to decide whether it were too warm to go for a row, when he became aware of a girl, cutting rapidly through the smooth water in one of the gaily-painted boats belonging to the hotel. A graceful woman never looks more graceful than in the act of rowing, and he regarded with admiration the elastic swing of her body as she bent over the sculls, and the long, steady strokes with which she sent the little craft swiftly along. She stopped when she saw Blake, and rested on her oars.

"Good-morning, Mr. Blake," she called out. "Do you happen to have met my brother anywhere? He promised to take me on the lake this morning, but he disappeared directly after breakfast with some one or other, and I got tired of waiting."

Blake saw his opportunity and seized it.

"I haven't seen him," he said, "but perhaps you will allow me to take his place, if you want an escort?"

"If I want some one to row me, would be nearer the mark," laughed Nell, directing the boat to land. "I feel lazy, and I should be glad of a rest."

A few minutes later they were floating gently out over the blue water. The girl leaned back in the cushioned stern and shut her eyes. Blake wondered if she knew how long and curly her dark lashes were, and whether she wanted to show them off, but the expression of her face was one of such exquisite enjoyment that such a suspicion seemed unworthy. Suddenly she looked up.

"Did you ever see anything so beautiful as the Jungfrau this morning?" she asked. "It looks like silver against a sapphire sky. Archie thinks mountains are all alike—he says when you've seen one, you've seen all—but to me they never look the same for five minutes together. They change with every change of light and atmosphere. I believe I like them best in cloudy weather, it leaves so much to the imagination. Don't you think so?"

"I'm afraid I don't appreciate the clouds," said Blake, smiling a little at her enthusiasm. "I've had bitter experience of them on many an unsuccessful expedition. I suppose this is your first visit to Switzerland?"

"Oh, no, I've been several times before, though never to these parts, and I love it more every time I come. These Swiss hotels are so amusing too, the people who come to them, I mean; I often wonder why they do come, some of them. There was a lady sitting next to me at breakfast, who was holding forth to a friend on the subject of health; her one idea seemed to be to avoid getting wet feet. She had evidently come from some high mountain place, and I heard her say with great emphasis, 'I assure you, my dear, I found the *only* safe way was to wear goloshes *continuously*.' Fancy going on a glacier in goloshes!"

Blake laughed. This girl was distinctly amusing. It was a very long time since a morning had passed so quickly with him, and he made up his mind that he should probably do a good deal of boating in the course of the next week or so. Circumstances favoured him.

Mrs. Templeton took an immense fancy to the two Derwents, and many were the joint excursions undertaken under her able management. In a very short time Blake had constituted himself Nell's acknowledged cavalier. He walked with her, talked with her, gathered flowers for her collection, found points of vantage for her sketching stool, played her accompaniments, monopolised as many of her dances as possible, and conducted himself in every way as her devoted admirer.

At the same time, he was conscious of a something in their relations which baffled and puzzled him. Nell's attitude towards him was one of pure friendliness and nothing more. She received his attentions with the utmost calm, she was used to them and had come to consider them almost as a right. But she appeared perfectly unconscious of the fact that he was an eligible *parti*, and would turn from him to talk to Captain Templeton, or anyone else whose conversation happened to interest her more for the moment. This was naturally annoying to a man as unaccustomed to such treatment as Blake. His attempts to draw her into anything approaching a flirtation were quite unavailing. She laughed at his neatly-turned phrases, or retorted with little shafts of sarcasm, which went straight to the mark and somehow made him feel rather a fool. She tantalised and irritated him; he began to wonder if the blue eyes that looked so straight at him, had ever known what it was to soften with a tenderer light, and to be unreasonably angry because he could not make them do so.

But the days flew by, and one afternoon Nell announced to him that they had decided to leave the next day. It was as if someone had thrown iced water in his face. He had grown so accustomed to being constantly near her, in the intimacy of hotel life, that he had never realised that there must be an end to such intercourse. He felt suddenly that he should miss her more than he would have believed possible. But it was not by any means the first time he had experienced this sensation; he knew it would probably pass off in a week, and he resolved, meanwhile, to make the most of the time that remained to him.

There was dancing that evening, and after a waltz he took Nell out to the terrace and ensconced her in a secluded corner.

"What a magnificent night," she began. "I shall be so sorry to leave this lovely place to-morrow. I don't think I ever enjoyed myself more anywhere."

"And I," said Blake, leaning forward a little to be able to see her face. "Do you know this has been the happiest fortnight of my life?"

"Really?" she returned rather sarcastically. "I should have thought it was not nearly exciting enough for you."

Her tone annoyed him, and he cast all scruples to the winds.

"I am glad you are going away to-morrow," he said abruptly.

"Even if you are, it isn't polite to say so. Shouldn't we be going in? It's getting chilly."

"You have stayed here too long already," he went on, taking no notice of her words. "Do you know what you have done to me? You should have gone away before——"

"I don't think you quite know what you're saying, Mr. Blake," interrupted the girl gravely.

He could see that she had coloured faintly in the moonlight.

"I think I had better go in."

"How hard you are," he pleaded. "At least give me something, some little remembrance, of the happiest days I shall ever know. You won't be so cruel as to go away and leave me like this? Let me have one of those roses, it is such a small thing."

He had said very much the same to many women before; but to-night, carried away by the magic of the time and the surroundings, he was more than half in earnest. He bent forward and looked into her eyes. For a moment she seemed to be hesitating, tearing nervously at the flowers in her lap with one hand, the other rested on the arm of her chair. Blake thought she was going to yield, he took the little fingers in his own.

"Don't refuse me," he murmured. "It is very little I ask, and you are going away to-morrow!"

At his touch she sprang to her feet.

"No!" she exclaimed, flinging the roses far away from her into the garden beneath. "You're only amusing yourself, and trying to flirt with me. You may think you are paying me a compliment. You'll excuse me if I say I don't regard it as such. I had thought better of you. Good night."

She swept away, leaving Blake thunder-struck.

"By—Jove!" were all the words he could find breath for, as he sank back into his chair. He made no attempt to follow her.

"Who'd have thought she'd take it like that? I might have been the dust beneath her feet. No woman ever treated me like that before! Well, it served me right."

He was so dumbfounded that he went straight to his room and lay awake half the night, trying to concoct some form of apology which should not have the effect of enraging her further. He was down betimes the next morning, for he knew the Derwents were to leave by an early boat. As good luck would have it, while he stood hesitating at the foot of the stairs, wondering where he should find Nell, the door of an adjoining room opened and she came out. She bowed coldly, and was passing on, when he stopped her.

"Miss Derwent, I must speak to you," he said hurriedly. "I don't know what you must think of me after last night——"

"I fancy it doesn't matter much," she interrupted frigidly.

"It matters to me what you think of me, for you have made me respect your opinion." He could hardly have said anything to please her more. "May I hope that you will try and forget my——that you won't regard me quite as——"

He stopped hopelessly, for once in his life at a loss for words. Nell looked at him for a minute, and then broke into a charming smile.

"Don't say any more about it," she said. "You made a mistake, and I'm afraid I was rather rude, but we won't part enemies after having had such a good time together."

He took the hand she offered.

"You're quite sure you forgive me?" he asked.

"Quite sure," laughed the girl. "Don't look so dreadfully solemn over it. There's Archie shouting for me, the carriage is waiting. Good-bye."

Blake stood watching their departure until they were quite out of sight; then he turned away, and spent the rest of the morning rowing vigorously, if somewhat erratically, about the lake, after which he returned to the hotel and announced to the Templetons his intention of starting at once for the High Alps. Alice cast a significant glance at her husband as she received this information.

"Well, we shall be sorry to lose you, Jim," she said, "but I can't consent to be dragged up to any more of those inaccessible places even for the pleasure of your delightful society. We shall go to Interlaken, and you can join us later at Lucerne and travel home with us if you feel inclined. We've arranged to meet the Derwents there," she added as if by an afterthought.

Just about the same time, Nell, being whirled away as fast as a very slow train would carry her, was thinking to herself:

"It was very nice of him to try and apologise, though how awkwardly he did it! I think I gave him a lesson, and made him see that there are some girls in the world who don't care to be treated as playthings, to be made love to one minute and forgotten the next! I wonder if I shall ever see him again. How silly I am! I don't suppose he'll ever give me another thought, except as a prim little country girl who couldn't understand a bit of fun. Yet, when he said good-bye he looked——"

But here she brought her meditations to an abrupt close and buried herself in Baedeker.

Blake, on his side, plunged with energy into the sea of guides, ice-axes, ropes and alpenstocks, which surges around the great mountaineering centres during the month of August. He made several very satisfactory ascents, came once or twice perilously near losing his life, and was aware that he ought to be enjoying himself extremely. But the image of Nell Derwent was too persistently before him. She haunted him—he could not forget her. He fought hard for his independence, was somewhat reckless in his climbing, made himself unusually agreeable in society, and even tried to get up a flirtation with a pretty American, on the principle of "Like cures like." But it was of no avail, and there came a day when, walking up a sunny slope near Zermatt, he flung himself down under a pine-tree and owned to himself that he was hopelessly and helplessly in love.

Having once acknowledged the situation, he proceeded to face it with characteristic energy. He had no cause to believe that Nell cared in the least for him, rather the reverse, but that was no reason why she should not learn to. Alice Templeton had said that they would all be at Lucerne together for a time, before returning to England. He would go there at once and get the question settled at once. Having arrived at this conclusion, he descended to his hotel, packed his bag, paid his bill and started.

### III.

THE next evening, Nell Derwent, going in to dinner, was accosted in the hall with a cheerful "Good evening, Miss Derwent," in well-known tones.

"Mr. Blake!" she exclaimed. "You here! Mrs. Templeton said you were somewhere in the Engadine."

The colour had flown to her cheeks, her eyes sparkled, her pleasure was unconcealed. Blake thought he had never seen her look more charming.

"She ought to know by this time that I'm generally to be found in the place where I'm least expected," he said. "How are you, Derwent? Well, Alice, here I am again. Couldn't get on long without you after all, you see."

He dropped quite naturally into his old position with Nell, but there was a slight difference. She was now and then a little shy with him, had lost some of her look of frank indifference, and was careful to keep more with her brother or Mrs. Templeton. A week, ten days, went quickly by, then Blake, coming in one afternoon with his hands full of flowers, found Alice lounging in a chair on the verandah.

"Do you know where Miss Derwent is?" he asked, stopping when he saw her.

"She's just gone out. Sit down, Jim, I've got something to say to you. I daresay you won't like it, but I *must* speak. Jim, I don't want you to flirt with that little girl. She isn't quite the sort you're used to, and I think she might take it in a way that would surprise you."

Blake thought the warning came rather too late. Nell certainly had surprised him, though not quite in the sense intended by the speaker. But he simply said:

"How do you know I'm only flirting with her?"

Something in his tone made Mrs. Templeton look up.

"My dear boy!" she exclaimed. "Do you really mean it? Oh, I *am* glad! She's the sweetest girl I ever met, and I think you're worthy of her! But are you really in earnest?"

"The fact is, Alice," began Blake, glad of a chance to unburden himself to his faithful confidante, "I've gone a regular cropper. I can hardly believe it myself, but that girl can simply turn me round her little finger." He laughed rather awkwardly. "Do you think she cares about me in the least? I've fancied perhaps she did, since I came down here."

"I'm sure of it," said Mrs. Templeton, with enthusiasm. "I more than half suspected it before you came, and now I'm certain. She tries to hide it, but her eyes betray her. That was why I spoke just now. I was afraid you were only amusing yourself. Do get it settled before we leave, and be married as soon as possible."

"That's going rather fast," said Blake, "but it's what I should like. I'm afraid, though, she'll say we haven't known each other long enough. But I can't stand the suspense much longer; I must know my fate in a day or two at the outside."

Events developed themselves somewhat more rapidly, however. That afternoon, as Blake returned from a walk, a telegram was brought to him, summoning him back to England on urgent business. He read it with an exclamation of annoyance.

"Can't start now before the evening, any way," he said, glancing at the clock. Then the thought of Nell flashed into his mind. He went across to where she sat, the centre of a laughing group on the verandah. Seizing the first opportunity to do so unobserved he said in a low tone:

"Miss Derwent, I am called home unexpectedly. I needn't tell you how sorry I am, but it's perfectly unavoidable. May I hope to find you in the summer-house at the end of the garden in half an hour's time? I have a very important question to ask you. I think you can guess what it is."

The girl's eyes fell.

"Yes," she said simply.

As soon as she could, she slipped away from her friends, and made her way into the garden. Passing through the hall, she met her brother.

"Here's a letter for you, Nell," he said, handing it to her.

She took it mechanically, and went on. Her thoughts were rather in a whirl, and she wanted a few minutes to compose herself before Blake should come to her. She knew very well that he loved her, and was now willing to confess to herself that she loved him. She sat down on the bench that fitted into an angle of the low stone wall, under a canopy of late roses, and leaned her head on her hand, looking out over the sunshiny expanse of lake and mountains, and wondering if there were another girl in the world as happy as she. Her eyes fell on the letter in her lap; it was from Sylvia Burke. She tore it open.

"Poor Sylvia!" she thought. "I wish I could know that her affairs were running more smoothly."

The letter was very much in Miss Burke's usual style—an account of some visits she had been paying; a few bits of gossip; descriptions of two or three new frocks, and that was all. No—there was a postscript on the back of the last sheet.

"If you meet a certain Mr. Jim Blake in the course of your travels, remember your promise to revenge me. I know he is in Switzerland."

A sudden darkness swam before Nell's eyes. The blow was so utterly unexpected, that for a moment it stunned her. Then the scene in the morning-room at Fairfield rose vividly before her; Sylvia, with her pretty eyes full of tears, Sylvia's voice owning to her love for a man who had deserted her, and her own half-laughing words to her friend. She had thought it quite natural that Sylvia should not wish to tell her his name, and had asked no questions. So it was Jim Blake—who in another moment would be there to ask her to become his wife. Only one idea was impressed upon her bewildered brain, he must not find her waiting for him. She rose to her feet, feeling a little sick and giddy, with the intention of making her escape; but it was already too late. She heard his approaching footsteps, and almost directly he stood before her.

Nell sank down again, and faced the inevitable. Neither of them spoke at first, but she could feel his eyes upon her, and made a feeble effort to put off the crucial moment by murmuring something incoherent about the view. Blake did not answer; he did not even hear her. Suddenly he bent down, and caught hold of both her hands, looking straight into her eyes.

"I love you," he said. "Will you marry me?"

In his intense earnestness, the simplest possible form of words seemed to come most naturally to him. For one awful moment, Nell sat as if paralysed, struggling with an irresistible temptation to sweep away all barriers, and grasp the happiness one word would bring within her reach. It was only for a moment.

"For Sylvia's sake, for Sylvia's sake," she repeated to herself. Then she spoke, in a dry, strained voice, forcing her lips to form the words.

"You have made a mistake," she said. "I cannot marry you."

Blake dropped her hand, and turned pale.

"Nell, you can't mean it!" he exclaimed, in a tone of deep distress. "Don't play with me, my dearest. I love you. Surely you can try and care a little bit for me?"

Then, as she did not answer, he went on:

"I have spoken too soon. I have frightened you. Don't give me your answer now. Take a day or two to think it over."

"You have made a mistake," she repeated hoarsely. "Neither a day nor a year will make any difference."

Blake's face grew stern.

"Do you mean to say that all this time you have been flirting with me?" he demanded. "That you let me come here this afternoon, knowing very well what I meant to say, only for the pleasure of seeing me humiliate myself? I can't believe it of you!"

"I mean what I said," returned Nell, feeling she could not hold out much longer. "Let me go, please. You must think what you like of me. I can never give you any other answer."

Nell never knew how she reached the safe shelter of her own room. She had a dim recollection of meeting Mrs. Templeton on the stairs and of her surprised glance. She locked her door and flung herself on her knees by the bed, burying her face in the coverings and clutching them in both her hands. Her breath came in deep, quivering gasps; she was conscious only of one all-absorbing fact, that she loved Jim Blake with the whole force of her being, and that she had sent him away for ever, thinking her a heartless coquette. The bright afternoon faded into twilight, and twilight into darkness, but she did not stir. Her brother came to the door and asked if she were ill; she satisfied him with some excuse, her only desire was to remain undisturbed in her misery.

And Blake, on his side, sat in a corner of a first-class carriage, staring out into the darkness, as they whirled through France, sleepless, angry and miserable. He, who had always been proud of his invulnerability, had fallen in love like a boy at last, and this was the end of it. He had trusted the girl, he had fancied she was different to those others that he knew, he had been tricked and made a fool of, and he wondered bitterly if he should ever believe in a woman again.

Verily, Sylvia was revenged!

Mrs. Templeton sought her husband that evening, greatly perturbed in spirit.

"Harry, I can't imagine what has happened!" she exclaimed. "I heard Jim ask Nell Derwent to meet him in the garden this afternoon, after he got that telegram calling him home. An hour later I met her on the stairs, looking like a ghost; and when I went to his room to see if I could help him, he was almost as bad, and was throwing his things into his portmanteau in a furious rage. She wasn't at dinner, and he departed without saying good-bye to anyone. She *can't* have refused him!"

"Looks very like it," said Captain Templeton. "I'd have sworn she was completely gone on him too. But you never can tell in these things."

He puffed thoughtfully at his cigar.

"Well, I was never so disappointed about *anything*," declared his wife. "I had quite set my heart on it. Jim is a dear fellow, with all his faults, and she's a sweet girl. I shall see if I can't set things to rights."

It was easy to say this. But Nell Derwent avoided *tête-à-tête* conversations with Mrs. Templeton with the most anxious care, and with such success that the morning of her departure arrived without a chance having presented itself for any explanation. Then Mrs. Templeton took the bull by the horns and went boldly to the girl's room.

"Nell, dear," she said, closing the door, "don't think me impertinent or interfering, but I can't help seeing that something has gone wrong between you and Jim, and I *am* so sorry. I want you to tell me what it is, and let me try and help you."

"It's awfully good of you, Mrs. Templeton," said Nell, fighting bravely to keep the tears from rising to her eyes, "but there's nothing to be done. Mr. Blake asked me to marry him, and I refused, and it's all over."

"But, Nell!" cried her friend. "Didn't you care for him, after all? Couldn't you *try* to? He is so nice. I am sure he would make you happy. There must be some mistake! We all thought it was a settled thing, and he is head over heels in love with you. Do think it over and change your mind. You don't know what you're throwing away!"

"I can't change my mind," said Nell, with a pitiful little smile. "You're very kind to take so much interest in my affairs. I wish I could be more satisfactory."

"I've managed to get very fond of you, and Jim has always been a great friend of mine," said Mrs. Templeton. "I won't say any more to you now, but I hope you will come and see me at home. Here is my address, and remember, I shall *always* be glad to hear from you." This significantly.

"I can't understand it," she said, despairingly to her husband, later on. "There's a mystery at the bottom of this, I feel sure. It wasn't just an ordinary flirtation; I believe she meant to accept him up to the last moment. What *could* she have heard?" But she racked her brains in vain for an answer to this question.

One day, towards the end of November, Nell Derwent sat again in her pretty room at Fairfield. She was not much changed to outward appearance—she had lost a little of her animated look, her pretty colour had faded slightly, and her face, when no one was looking, wore a rather tired expression.

She had been entertaining a visitor, who was just departing with many voluble farewells.

"Well, good-bye, my dear, I really must be going. So glad to have seen you again. Oh! by the way," turning round at the door, "I met your friend, Miss Burke, when I was in town the other day. She was walking up Bond Street with her *fiancé;* they both looked radiant."

Nell turned pale. Then her sacrifice had not been in vain.

"I hadn't heard of her engagement," she said.

"You surprise me, I always thought you were such great friends. But it is only just announced, and I expect she's very busy, as the wedding is to be at Christmas. Her mother told me Sir Arthur refused to wait a week longer."

"Who—who is she going to marry, then?" asked Nell faintly.

"Sir Arthur Newby, a very good match, I believe, no end of money. She only met him this summer in Scotland. Is that five o'clock striking? I must fly."

Nell threw herself on the sofa as the door closed, and tried to think. Sylvia engaged, and not to Jim Blake? She could never really have cared for him, to forget so soon! And by the light of this discovery, Nell's eyes were opened to several little traits in her friend's character to which she had hitherto been blind. She began to think that Archie's estimate of Miss Burke was probably the most correct. So she had gone through two months of misery, such as she had never before experienced, merely for the sake of an idea! And now there was no barrier between herself and Blake. But how to let him know?

Nell was unusually silent that evening, though her brother noticed that she looked better and brighter than for some time past. As she was undressing, a bright thought flashed across her brain; she would write to Mrs. Templeton. On the strength of this resolve she went to bed.

The next morning Nell went straight to her writing-table after breakfast. The composition of the letter took some time, but as she sealed it she congratulated herself upon having said exactly the right thing. When it lay stamped and addressed before her, she leaned back and lost herself in day-dreams for a few minutes. Mrs. Templeton would understand, she would say something to Blake, would arrange for them to meet, perhaps he would come down to Fairfield, and then . . . . the colour rose slowly to her face, and Nell's thoughts faded in a golden mist. She roused herself with a little laugh. It was a perfect day, frosty and sunny; everything looked more beautiful than usual, she thought. The *Morning Post* lay at her elbow; she took it up carelessly and ran her eye down the list of Society notices, wondering if she should see the announcement of Sylvia's engagement. Yes, there it was, and next to it the name of Blake caught her eye:

"A marriage has been arranged and will shortly take place between Mr. James Harold Blake, of Thorne Park, Berks, and Marion, only daughter of the late Charles Fraser, of Palace Gate, W."

The paper fell from Nell's hands. She remembered Miss Fraser, they had met at Lucerne, and she had discussed her with Blake, who knew her well. He had said that her great and almost only merit was that she was "genuine." A curious feeling of unreality crept over Nell; as the irony of the situation dawned upon her she laughed a little. She felt as though she were an onlooker at the sufferings of another person. Her glance fell upon the letter addressed to Mrs. Templeton, which lay upon the table ready for the post.

There was a fire in the grate. She crossed over to it and dropping in the letter, stood watching it burn to ashes.

KATHARINE F. HILLS.

# Late in Life.

BY A. PERRIN.

Author of "INTO TEMPTATION," &C.

## CHAPTER XXIX.

### ENGAGED.

*"What's done is done."*

MANY and various were the comments in the neighbourhood over Emily's engagement, which became known at once, for the Miss Wanklins spread the news abroad without delay, agreeing cordially with those who considered such conduct shamefully heartless coming so soon after a death in the family, and backing up others strongly in their opinion that the match was a very suitable one and the pair quite justified in being precipitate over the marriage, considering that Dr. Barr was returning to India so soon.

In justice to Emily it must be confessed that George was to blame for the precipitancy. In answer to her timid suggestion that he should extend his leave in order to delay the wedding until three months had elapsed after her sister's death, he became almost impatient with her, saying that though, of course, he would not hasten matters if it was really very much against her wish, yet he should infinitely prefer to be married as quickly and quietly as possible and leave England on the date he had arranged for previous to their engagement. The fact was he felt it impossible to remain on, under his altered circumstances, where he had known and loved poor little Ella; he wanted to bring that chapter of his life to a close, to leave it behind him without delay, and endeavour to bury the past in his new duties and responsibilities as Emily's husband.

Luckily she deferred at once to his wishes, as she invariably did to the least desire expressed by him, and in this instance he was thankful for it, though as a rule her slavish adoration and entire self-effacement was somewhat trying. She would fly to do his bidding, or to carry out any suggestion he might make almost before the words had left his mouth; she anticipated his inclinations, agreed with everything he said, and thought of absolutely nothing but how she could best please him. His undemonstrative manner towards her, and the quiet gentle way in which he kissed her whenever they met or parted—just as he might have kissed Nina—did not strike her as being in any way cold or out of the common, she was only too grateful to him for the unvarying consideration, attentive kindness, and chivalrous respect with which he treated her. She was continually embarrassing George by asking him "what he could have seen in her," and telling him she "knew she was not half good enough for him," all of which often caused him a pang of shame and remorse, knowing as he did that he could never return her abject love as it ought to be returned. Still he did his utmost to make her happy, no lover could have been more thoughtful or conscientious in his attentions, and Emily remained secure in her paradise of ignorant bliss.

At first there had been one very big shadow on her sunshine, and that was the torturing thought that she ought not to leave her father. She could not feel now that Ella would be near him at the Abbey, and even if he could be persuaded to have any one of his relations to live with him, would it not be cruel to leave him to the constant irritation and discomfort of having someone about him who did not understand his ways and who would probably never dream of bearing with his ill-humour? So strong was Emily's sense of duty that she would probably have sacrificed everything and allowed George to return to India alone, had her father made the least sign that he would miss her, or suffer in any way from her going.

"So he has proposed at last?" he had said, with an exasperating chuckle, on hearing her confession, "and your efforts have been crowned with success? Well, allow me to offer my congratulations," he watched Emily out of the corner of his eye to mark the effect his words would have on her, "I am inclined to think the fellow must be a bigger fool than he looks," he added venomously.

"Father!" cried Emily, flaring up at the faintest hint of abuse of her beloved, "how can you say such things? and after all he did for poor Bertie too! Have you forgotten the debt of gratitude we owe him?"

"And which you have tried to repay by bestowing on him your hand and heart, eh? After such an overwhelming return I think I may feel myself free of any obligation."

Emily stared at her father with angry reproach. He was sitting up in bed, and his wrinkled ivory skin, and sunken glittering eyes shining on either side of his enormous nose, made him look scarcely human. There was something pitiable in his helplessness, coupled with his fierce indomitable spirit, and Emily softened at the sight, her unaccustomed anger giving place to a rush of remorse. She went quickly up to the bed and laid her hand on his.

"Father," she said gravely, "if you think you would miss me ever so little I will not leave you."

Her voice shook, and she turned very white, for she had offered to make a great and terrible sacrifice, and the happiness of her existence hung in the balance. The Colonel drew his hand away with a contemptuous jerk.

"Don't be an idiot and make a scene," he snarled, "and for Heaven's sake take the last chance you will ever have of becoming a married woman. You may relieve your mind of any fear that I shall miss you. I am still capable of giving orders, and of asking for what I want, and as I have frequently told you before, you are not indispensable to my comfort. Where's that ass William? Call him here at once. He's a great deal more use to me than you ever were or ever could be. Go out of the room and don't stand snivelling at me in that way!"

So Emily said no more; but had she only known it the Colonel began to miss her even before she had been a week engaged. He found she was no longer at his beck and call, or perpetually within easy throwing distance, and moreover when she was with him, his abuse and fault-finding seemed to fall perfectly harmless, and had no longer the pleasing effect of making Emily more humble and miserable than ever. He saw that her engagement had given her an unpleasant and surprising kind of independence, and as he would not for the world have even pretended he was sorry to lose her, he was forced to be content with making himself as disagreeable as he possibly could.

However, retribution fell on the Colonel's head, for Aunt

Eliza, on hearing of her niece's engagement, at once wrote and declared her intention of taking up her abode at Garthwood "with her poor misguided brother." This relieved Emily's mind to a great extent, for she knew that, much as her father disliked his only sister, he would be well and conscientiously taken care of by her, though he himself was furious at the bare idea and did all in his power to prevent it. But arguments, entreaties and assurances were of no avail, neither was his absolute refusal to either see or speak to his sister so long as she remained in the house. Aunt Eliza calmly ignored his threats, made her plans, fixed the date of her arrival, and adhered to it punctually. She gave Emily a substantial cheque as a wedding present, accompanied by several hundred copies of a tract entitled "Are you clean?" which she requested her niece to distribute amongst the heathen the moment she landed in such an idolatrous country as India. She also accompanied these offerings with a little piece of news, delivered with the utmost solemnity—*i.e.* that she had made her will, and bequeathed everything she possessed to Emily.

"You're a most excellent creature, my good Emily," she concluded, "though I maintain that you are a fool to marry. However, since you will do it, I must own that I think you have got hold of a nice man, though how he will turn out remains to be seen. Perhaps he will drink and beat you—you are just the sort of woman that a man would beat—but of course we must hope for the best."

George and Emily had many other wedding presents besides Aunt Eliza's, including one from Lady Jebbs (paid for by Nina), and Mr. and Mrs. Compton gave them a well-filled plate-chest, a grand piano, and a drawing-room carpet, which, George reflected, no doubt the white ants would enjoy immensely once it was laid down on the floor of a "kutcha" bungalow in India.

Nina's delight at the whole affair knew no bounds. She nobly fulfilled her promise to Augusta to give her "whatever she wanted most," being more than half-convinced by that lady's declarations that the success of their cherished plans was entirely due to her—Lady Jebbs'—exertions. The only thing that marred Nina's pleasure was George's obstinacy in going back to India in such a hurry, and also the thought that there could be no "show," no bridesmaids, no wedding-breakfast or smart dresses, and above all, that she could give no ball or any sort of entertainment. Augusta comforted her with the reminder that now Mrs. Hatherly was not at the Abbey to be made jealous, it did not so much matter, and Nina also found a good deal of consolation in taking Emily in hand with regard to her personal appearance and wardrobe. She found the latter a willing pupil, who eagerly obeyed her future sister-in-law, so anxious was she to find favour in George's sight, and as Nina's taste was perfect, wonders were soon worked, and George himself was astonished at the change in Emily's looks.

Her hair was no longer dragged painfully off her face, but was artistically waved and arranged in neat shining twists at the back of her head. The grey threads suddenly disappeared, and what happened to them probably Nina's clever French maid could have told had she not been the very soul of discretion. The dowdy, shapeless hats that Emily had always contrived to possess no longer flopped over her eyes, but gave place to the most stylish and becoming of head-gear—black, of course, but in exquisite taste, and not too juvenile in appearance—though when the colonel saw her in them he made unpleasant allusions to "mutton dressed up lamb-fashion." Her dresses now fitted her nicely and were properly put on, instead of hanging helplessly on to her figure and clinging round her feet, while the knitted slippers never by any chance made their appearance as they had been wont to do formerly on occasions. Emily was so delighted with the result of all this, and with the knowledge that she was looking a good deal younger instead of far older than her age, that she implored Nina to undertake the choosing of her trousseau, which the little lady was only too pleased to do.

"It is a pity," remarked the latter, "that you are in mourning. Couldn't you go out? Nobody in India would know what had happened."

"I shouldn't like to yet," answered Emily with a faint hesitation, for she was keenly alive to the fact that black did not suit her, "and I think George will agree with me."

George did agree with her with a tightening of his heartstrings as he thought of the reason of her mourning, and finally it was decided that Emily should only provide herself with a modest supply of clothes for the present, and that Nina was to despatch an abundance of "new things," as pretty and suitable as could be got, a few months later.

So the preparations went on, the time flew swiftly by, and soon the day arrived that saw Emily Seton converted into Mrs. George Barr.

## CHAPTER XXX.

### MARRIED.

*"Splendide Mendax."*

THE cold weather was creeping on at last. People who had stayed in Janwapur throughout the hot weather and rains began to appear in warmer garments that smelt of camphor and neem-leaves, and showed by their folds and creases that they had been carefully "put away" during all those weary interminable months. There was a delicious little bite in the morning and evening air, when thick smoky mists rose and hung in low heavy lines above the fields. The snipe and teal were in early, long V-shaped flights of cackling geese passed over the little station at dusk, and everything gave promise of a good shooting season, a prospect that gladdened the hearts of those whose lot it would be to dwell in tents for the next few months. Punkahs had been taken down, punkah-coolies dismissed to disappear mysteriously and be no more seen until the following hot weather, and doors had to be shut, and extra blankets added to the beds at night.

The only place that never seemed to get really cool was the ladies' room of the little club. There the mosquitos lived as happily in the corners and under the tables, and bit as venomously in January as they did in June. There it was always more or less close, stuffy, and depressing, rendered doubly so by the dingy cretonne curtains, baggy covers to the straw chairs, the round table in the middle of the room which always would lean down helplessly to one side for no discoverable reason, the hot odorous wall-lamps, and dusty book-cases filled with volumes of bound magazines and tattered rubbish in the way of fiction. The club was in debt, why, nobody seemed to know exactly, except that in remote ages it had been very much mismanaged and had never been able to right itself, so that there was no spare money wherewith to purchase new curtains, or recover the chairs, or do anything towards making the place a little more attractive to the ladies who came and sat there night after night listlessly turning over the pages of the English papers, while their husbands clicked the billiard balls in the adjoining room, or played whist silently in a corner.

To-night there were only two ladies seated at the sloping table, and they were not reading, though each held a paper in her hand—they were talking and they had a good deal to say, for one of them had been to the hills for three months and had only just returned, while the other had "stayed down," and was therefore highly virtuous and inclined to blame those who went away and left their husbands! This was far more sensible than grumbling and being discontented, seeing that her husband could not afford to send her away this year. Still the sight of the other, cool and blooming, with a stock of new clothes, and an air of commiseration for those who had not been away, was a trifle trying, and the poor little plains-lady, whose temper had not been sweetened by prickly-heat, fever, and many long hot, sleepless nights, felt decidedly cross and irritable.

"Yes," she said peevishly, as she continued her narrative of the sayings and doings of Janwapur for the past three months, "the MacDonalds took to giving dinner parties after you left. We went once, and then Frank declared nothing would ever induce him to go again. He said it was a dinner he'd have refused to pay for at a dâk bungalow!"

"Good gracious!"

"But I'll tell you where we did get a good dinner, and that was at the Barrs' last night."

"Oh! The Barrs! Do tell me about *her*. I was so surprised when I heard he had come out married. I suppose she's got money, you remember how close he always was, and I'm sure he'd never do such an expensive thing as to marry unless he gained something by it."

"I believe she will have money when her father, or her aunt, or somebody dies. At least so I heard."

"Oh! I don't think much of that! Why, my dear, people never die—my grandmother's ninety! But what is Mrs. Barr like?"

"Old," conclusively, "she was that poor Seton boy's half-sister. Dr. Barr was awfully good to him, and I suppose that's how the marriage came about. She's not good-looking, but she has a nice face and dresses beautifully. Last night she had on a lovely black velvet with valuable old lace all over the body, and—*oh!*—" for the lady from the hills had given her companion a sharp kick on the ankle, just in time to interrupt the latter's speech as two people entered the room. They were George and Emily, who had been for a walk and were now looking in at the club for a few minutes before wending their way home.

George had not been surprised, when he received his orders in Bombay, to find that he was to return to Janwapur. He was well aware that he was known to Government as a man who did not grumble or apply for transfers, therefore he was clearly the very person to go back to this unpopular station, especially as the inhabitants were indulging in one of their periodical petitions for a European civil surgeon. However, for once the authorities had reckoned without their host, for George now intended to change his tactics, and though he proceeded to Janwapur without any immediate expostulation, he meant to apply for a better station before the hot weather came on, for Emily's sake, in spite of her fervent assurances that so long as she might be with him she did not care where they were stationed.

She was looking marvellously young and happy as she entered the stuffy reading-room by her husband's side. The walk, and the cold sharpness in the air had given her a brilliant colour, and her neat felt hat, well-fitting tailor-made dress, fur boa, and silver-handled walking stick gave her an appearance of extreme smartness, for which Nina was to be thanked, since Emily did not possess a single garment that her sister-in-law had not chosen for her.

"Good evening," said the virtuous hot-weather lady pleasantly, bearing the pain in her ankle with admirable fortitude, as the pair approached the table, "been for a walk? How energetic! A sure sign that you've only lately come out from home! Mrs. Barr, let me introduce Mrs. Drew," indicating her companion, "she has just come back from the hills, and you are near neighbours."

Emily sat down at the table after the introduction, and

George, when he had exchanged a few words with Mrs. Drew, sauntered into the billiard room, leaving the ladies to themselves.

"Well, and how's the housekeeping going?" enquired Mrs. Smithson (the owner of the smarting ankle) with an indulgent smile which had just a tinge of patronage in it. For Emily was a person who invariably gave others a feeling of superiority to herself, which was perhaps the reason why almost everybody liked her. She was so deprecating, so humble, so grateful for any kindness, or interest taken in her concerns.

"Oh! very badly, I'm afraid," she answered distressfully, "I don't seem able to manage the servants at all."

"That will all come," said Mrs. Smithson encouragingly, "only don't let them cheat you now even in little things, or you'll find it impossible ever to beat them down afterwards."

"It's just the little things they do cheat in so," put in Mrs. Drew, "and there are so many odds and ends you can't prevent their stealing. I told my bearer in the hills that I believed he made a curry out of kerosine oil, dusters and matches."

"Oh! What a mixture!" said Emily, and all three ladies laughed.

"I hope," said Mrs. Smithson, turning to Emily, "that if there is anything you want to know you will come to me. I don't suppose you require any help, as you seem to be getting on so well, judging by last night. I think it's wonderful, considering you've been barely three weeks in the country! But still you know if you should want help you know where to come. I owe Doctor Barr a life-long debt of gratitude for his goodness when my baby was ill last cold weather. He saved the child's life." Tears came into Mrs. Smithson's harassed brown eyes, and she turned away to hide them.

Just then the club bearer, an old fellow with bow legs and a blue cloth coat several sizes too large for him, entered the reading room with a bundle of unopened papers in his hands.

"Oh!" cried Mrs. Drew, snatching them from him, "the English papers! I'd quite forgotten we should get the mail tonight—how nice!"

She and Mrs. Smithson promptly buried their noses in the new papers, and Emily began to feel restless. She wanted to go home and see her letters. She was anxious for news of her father, for Aunt Eliza wrote a few hasty lines every week, and last mail she had said that the Colonel was not quite so well. Emily timidly approached the door of the billiard-room, and peered round the curtain.

"George," she called softly.

"Yes," was the prompt reply, "I'm coming."

"The mail is in, dear," she said as he joined her, "and I should like to get home and see the letters."

"Of course," he answered; and then after bidding Mrs. Drew and Mrs. Smithson good-night, they left them waiting patiently for their husbands, and stepped out into the moonlight.

"Are you sure you were quite ready to come, George?" asked Emily, slipping her hand through his arm, as they walked briskly along the hard white road, "I didn't mean to drag you away if you were playing anything."

"Certainly I was ready," he said, giving her hand a little reassuring pat, "I'm always ready when you want me."

She smiled up at him with happy contentment, and they walked on in silence till they reached the house—not the low-rented, bat-smelling bungalow of George's bachelor days, with its walls and floors rotten with white ants, and its vermin-infested roof, but a substantial, solid building, that had once been the judge's dwelling before Janwapur was defrauded of that official, and it looked very massive and imposing as the white-washed balcony surrounding the flat roof gleamed in the moonlight, and the pillars of the verandah cast deep black shadows on the walls. The drawing-room had a tempting, cosy appearance as they entered, lighted by rose-shaded lamps, and adorned with the lately unpacked wedding presents, and on a small carved table lay the post, which Emily pounced on eagerly.

"Nearly all stupid official letters for you, George," she said, handing him some long brown envelopes, "and only one English letter for me—from Aunt Eliza," tearing it open, "shall I read it to you?"

"Yes, do," answered George lazily, and Emily seated herself near him and began.

"DEAR EMILY,—You will be glad to hear that your father is better than when I wrote last week. The doctor thinks he is going on very well, which may be, but I am of opinion that he may be taken any moment——"

"Oh, George!" said Emily, looking at her husband with a sudden rush of tears to her eyes.

"Aunt Eliza always makes the worst of everything, and you see the doctor evidently doesn't agree with her," he replied hopefully.

"Yes," admitted Emily, a little doubtfully, and then went on with the letter:

"——I try to impress this on your father's mind, for it is sad to think how unprepared he is, and I am inclined to believe that my words are at last taking root, for he is far less violent than when you were with him. I always considered that you did not know how to manage him. He never enquires for or talks of you, and apparently he does not miss you in the least—I think it my duty to tell you this. I have rather more leisure than usual to-day, so I am sending you a longer letter than I have done hitherto, though I have little or no news to give you. Mrs. Compton and her friend came over to call last Tuesday—your having married Mrs. Compton's brother is no reason why I should not say what I think, *i.e.*, that I do not approve of either woman, and I gave them to understand as much. One is a fool and the other a knave, or whatever is the female equivalent of the latter. I have a very strong suspicion that *the knave* is none other than the creature who was at the bottom of the Jebbs-scandal I have so often told you about. I am making it my business to find out, and if I am right in my surmise, I shall have no hesitation whatever in exposing the person. You know, my dear Emily, that whatever I set my mind to do, is invariably carried out——"

Here an interruption occurred in the shape of a servant with a note, which proved to be a summons to George to attend a child that had been suddenly taken ill at the other end of the station. He ordered the trap to be got ready at once, and hastened into his dressing-room to change his coat and waistcoat for warmer ones. Then telling Emily not to wait dinner for him, he drove hurriedly away.

She went back into the drawing-room after watching the trap disappear into the shadow of the trees, and finished reading her letter. There was very little more in it except details of the ungodliness of the servants, and an enquiry as to whether the bundle of tracts had borne any fruit, so that she soon put it down and lay idly on the couch thinking of her father. She suffered some sharp pangs of remorse for having left him, as she thought of his helplessness and angry irritation with Aunt Eliza. Still he had never asked for her, he had never written to her, he did not seem to miss her, and perhaps he was happier without her.

And she? She was so absolutely and entirely happy in her present life, and her only fear was that such bliss might be too great to last. Emily gave a little shiver as the idea crossed her brain, and she rose restlessly from the couch. Supposing anything were to happen to George to-night? If the pony shied into the ditch and upset the trap? If the child should be suffering from some infectious disease, and he should take it and die? She caught her breath and clasped her hands in an agony at the bare notion. She went out into the verandah and peered into the mysterious haze of the moonlight. The watchman prowled past, wrapped up in his wadded quilt, with his long staff thumping on the ground, and the low murmur of voices and twanging of some native instrument sounded faintly from the servants' quarters. The moonlight depressed her. She turned and wandered through the dining-room into her bedroom and from thence into George's dressing-room.

It was in dreadful disorder, with the things flung about just as he had left them in his hurry. The bearer had not been in yet to tidy up. Emily began to gather the clothes together, fingering them tenderly and with almost a caress as she put them away. She gave the waistcoat a little shake before she folded it up, and one or two things fell out of the pocket. A pencil which Emily put carefully on the dressing-table, an empty envelope, and a small leather case which she had never seen before. What a nice little thing! Just what she wanted to keep stamps in. She must ask George to give it to her. She opened it carelessly and seeing that it only contained what, to her short-sighted vision, looked like a piece of blank paper for memoranda, she took the case into the drawing-room and laid it on the writing-table. Then she went to her room and changed her dress for a comfortable tea-gown, after which she sat down to read in the drawing-room until her husband's return, as she had no intention of having dinner without him. Her eyes followed the words on the pages for nearly half an hour, and then she gave up trying to fix her attention on the story, for she had been thinking of George the whole time and nothing else; wondering when he would be back, straining her ears for the sound of wheels, frightening herself with imaginings of what might have happened to him, longing for the deep tones of the familiar voice, and the sight of the grave handsome face. Then at last came the rumble of wheels and the noise of fast-trotting hoofs, and in another few minutes he was back in the drawing-room.

"Ugh!" he said, with a shiver, as he unbuttoned his overcoat "how cold the nights are getting. The room looks so warm and comfortable, especially after the dreadful house I've been to! The Pogson child was ill, nothing serious, only over-eaten itself. But upon my word the mother is a terrible woman. I'm thankful I'm not Pogson."

Emily flushed with delight, she took this as an indirect compliment to herself.

"I haven't had dinner," she said, cheerfully, "but I ordered it directly I heard you coming; you must be so hungry, dear. Oh!"—taking up the case from the table—"this dropped out of your waistcoat pocket when I was tidying your dressing-room. Do you want it? Or can I have it to keep stamps in? There seems to be nothing in it but a piece of blank paper."

She handed him the case, and instantly the vision of a lovely childish face crowned with glinting golden hair, rose before his eyes. He felt the warm soft touch of little fingers thrusting a scrap of paper into his hand. Flower-scented night air seemed to be blowing round him, the measure of a wild Hungarian dance beat through his brain, the sound of a voice that still was in his ears, and a great love surging in his heart. He almost gave a cry of agony as it all came back to him so vividly.

Then he looked and saw Emily's expectant face, her hair a little unwaved by the damp night air, her colour gone, her tea-gown rather untidy at the neck from having hooked it wrong. He saw the happy confident love shining in her eyes, saw for the hundredth time, but now more forcibly than ever, that he was the whole world to this adoring, devoted woman, and that he had his part to play, which must be played well or not at all.

"Yes," he said steadily, "of course you can have it if you like." He opened the case, drew out the paper, with the faint pencil marks now scarcely visible on it, and tore it, and the little dead daisy within its folds, into fragments with strong resolute fingers. Then he handed the case to Emily.

"It's rather large for stamps, isn't it?" he said huskily.

"Oh! dear no. It's just the thing. Thank you so much, dear. Oh! George," suddenly coming close to him and lifting her face to his, "you are so good to me, and I love you so! Tell me that you love me too?"

George took her face between his large brown hands and kissed her on her lips.

"Yes, my darling," he said slowly and clearly, "you know I love you."

We are told that in the sight of Providence there is nothing that can justify a lie, but surely—*surely* George must have been pardoned for this one even before the sound of the words had died away?

THE END.

# BELGRAVIA.

### DECEMBER, 1895.

## An Old Maid's Mistake.

### By MRS. CONNEY,

Author of "A Lady Horsebreaker," "A Ruthless Avenger," "Gold for Dross," etc.

### CHAPTER XXXVI.

For a chatterbox Cicely was strangely silent during the walk. As a matter of fact she was preoccupied, turning over in her mind the best method of gaining a certain piece of information she wanted to acquire. The silence was getting awkward when John broke it.

"Haven't you had about enough of this last freak of yours?" he asked abruptly.

"What freak?"

"Well! Separating yourself from all your own people and starving in that out-of-the way hole of an island!"

"Don't insult the island. It's a charming place. You can live on the fat of the land for next to nothing, and you have no idea how sociable people are there. I consider myself most fortunate."

"You've lost about a stone in weight since you've been there," he observed, "and I haven't heard you laugh once—naturally."

"My dear John, would you have me a prize pig or a Cheshire cat? And if I don't laugh it's your fault for being so dull. And anyhow it's absurd to abuse a place when you've never so much as set foot in it."

"Oh, yes, I have."

She stared. "When?" she asked sharply.

"I've been over twice, once about this time last year, a month or so after you went there, and again in the autumn."

"And you never came to see me?"

"Wasn't asked," he reminded her curtly.

She laughed. "Don't you know me well enough to be able to pay a morning call without a formal invitation?" she asked.

"I know you much too well to come after I'd been ordered to stay away," he retorted.

"Which you never were by me, I'm sure," she declared warmly.

"I beg your pardon. My mistake, no doubt. Still I certainly understood you to say you would prefer we should not meet again."

Cicely crimsoned and made no reply.

"May I come and see you next time?" he went on.

She laughed. "How absurdly you do put things," she said constrainedly. "Of course, if you did happen to be on the island I should expect you to look me up, but then I don't suppose you will be coming there again."

"Why not?"

"Why not?" She paused. How tiresome John was getting. "Oh, well! Your time may not be your own much longer, you know," she explained.

John looked a little puzzled. "Why do you say that, I wonder?" he observed. "I have no special calls upon my time that I'm aware of."

She raised her eyebrows. "Haven't you? I should have said you had been a good deal taken up lately with your friends in Wales—and elsewhere."

The speech was a silly one. She would never have made it if the words hadn't slipped out unawares.

John looked quickly at her and a ghost of a smile flitted across his face. "I have been a good deal taken up with the Anstruthers lately," he admitted imperturbably, "but then there were special reasons why I should be. I can't say much at present, but Miss Anstruther——"

Cicely cut him short. "My dear John," she cried, with an airy laugh. "Not another word. I quite understand, and I won't ask a single indiscreet question. Let me know, that's all, when I may offer my good wishes and congratulations, which, you may be sure, I shall do with all my heart."

John listened very coolly to this masterpiece of histrionic talent. "Much obliged. Awfully kind of you, I'm sure," he observed. "But what have I done that you should say all these nice things to me?"

She thought it unkind of him to misunderstand her so wilfully. Surely things were hard enough for her already.

"When one's friends get married, one usually offers them one's best wishes for their happiness," she said shortly, "but perhaps with your peculiar views on matrimony, you don't consider it a subject for congratulation."

"On the contrary," he retorted with emphasis. "If I *were* going to be married I should expect the very heartiest congratulations."

"But haven't you as good as told me you *are* going to be married?" she asked impatiently.

"I am not going to be married yet," he objected.

Cicely stamped her foot. "How provoking you are, John! At all events you are thinking of getting married, which comes to the same thing."

"Not at all. I wish it did. I've been thinking of getting married for a long while, only I needn't tell you that it takes two to carry out an arrangement of that sort."

She smiled—disagreeably. "If report is to be believed, you need apprehend no difficulties on the lady's side," she reminded him.

"Report lies then as usual," he retorted drily, "for the lady will have nothing whatever to say to me."

"How do you know that? Have you asked her?"

"Certainly. Several times."

"Nonsense! Why, you haven't known her two months yet."

"Known who?"

"Miss Anstruther."

"But what has Miss Anstruther got to do with it?"

"Everything. Haven't you been telling me that you want to marry her, and that she won't have you?"

"Certainly not. Miss Anstruther has been as good as engaged for years to a particular friend of my own, and if they weren't both as poor as rats, they'd have been married long before now. As you know perfectly well, I never asked but one woman to marry me and I shall never ask another. Oh, don't be afraid," as she started and half turned away, "I'm not going to bring the subject up again. I shouldn't have alluded to it except for this extraordinary delusion you seem to have taken into your head."

"Why should you call it a delusion?" persisted Cicely in what she flattered herself was a perfectly natural, unconcerned manner. "It seems the most natural and suitable thing in the world that you should find some nice girl and settle down with her——"

He cut her short. "Look here, Cicely," he said roughly. "Leave that alone. I don't mean to make a nuisance of myself by crying for the moon, but that's no reason why I should be expected to accept thankfully the first piece of green cheese you choose to offer me."

Cicely's colour rose. It was cruel to talk like that, as if he cared, when she and everybody else knew the formal matter-of-fact nature of their relations.

"Don't be a hypocrite, John," she cried indignantly. "You know perfectly well you never cared one rap for me—not at least in that way."

There was a pause.

"How do you know I never cared for you?" John then asked slowly.

"Because"—Cicely's voice was unsteady, she was struggling with her tears—"you told me so yourself. You wanted a wife. I wanted liberty—at least, you thought so. It was a suitable arrangement, that was all. You never made any pretence at all at being in love."

"No pretence was necessary," he said gravely. "It was the real thing with me. If you ask me why I never talked about it, that's easily explained. You see, I knew you would only laugh in my face if I did. Of course, I very soon saw that a man of my age and appearance, and a bad hand at society and talking and that sort of thing, wasn't likely to take your fancy. I knew I should only make a fool of myself, bore and worry you and get sent at once to the right-about like you did those other fellows, if once I attempted anything in the way of love-making. Still, as I explained to you at the time, I didn't see why we shouldn't marry. I knew you. I thought just as a heavy father you were rather fond of me. I knew the kind of things you liked and could give them to you, and it seemed to me you would have as good a chance of happiness with me as with any one else."

"And how about your own chance of happiness, John?" she asked with a little catch in her voice. "Did you never think of that when you proposed to burden yourself with a frivolous, indifferent wife, whose mother had disgraced herself, whose father had calmly shifted the care of her on to your shoulders, and whose flirtations had made every decent man fight shy of her?"

"My dear," John answered with a smile which made him absolutely good-looking, "I knew, that if only I could get you, my own happiness was quite certain. Please understand the truth once for all, which is that at any time, on any terms, I would have taken you only too thankfully, if you would have had me. . . ."

He broke off. Cicely had burst into a flood of tears.

"What is it? I didn't mean to distress you. Do stop for Heaven's sake. I wish I hadn't ever said a word."

"I'm very glad you did," she sobbed, "I never understood."

"But the other man!" John had taken both her hands, and his clasp tightened on them. "The other man you told me about?"

"There was no other man," she whispered. "A man. Not 'another' man."

And then he too understood.

"We have been such a pair of fools." Cicely confided this fact to Esme's long-suffering ears somewhere about midnight, after an evening spent exclusively in dilating on John's perfections. "Think of the trouble we might have saved ourselves if only we had known the truth. He was the worst of the two, for I'm sure no one would ever have guessed he cared the least little tiny bit about me, would they?"

Esme smiled.

"I always thought he cared," she said gently, "and if you had given him the chance I think he would have told you so. But you know you were hard on him. You used to snub him unmercifully."

"I know I was horrid, but his indifference made me so mad," pleaded Cicely. "Besides, I couldn't say anything until he spoke first. How could I tell he would be so idiotically and unnaturally modest and unselfish as to say nothing because he wouldn't put his own feelings forward. As it was I thought he never would see. I almost had to ask him in so many words to marry me. Anyhow, it's all right, and Esme"—hesitatingly—"about to-morrow? He says he will look in some time in the morning. If you find us in the way, you can send us out for a walk. After lunch there's the meeting. I wanted him to take me, but he seems to think there may be a lot of roughs and a row, and that I'd better stay here, which of course I shall do."

With which announcement, singularly unlike the old wilful, headstrong Cicely, the happy *fiancée* betook herself to bed, to dream of her lover.

## CHAPTER XXXVII.

CICELY had gone, betaking herself and her radiant face under her *fiancé's* escort to London. Her smiles, her excitement, her rhapsodies over her lover might be fatiguing, but they left a decided blank behind them. Esme, after longing for solitude, was horribly oppressed by it. If only Arnold would come back! She simply counted the hours till his return, looking forward to the mere fact of his presence as a stay and protection against the demons by which she was tormented. But then Arnold's return was doubtful. He might be back that evening or the following morning, or even the next day again. In the meantime Adrian Lisle was there at the Court, not a mile away. The mere thought of his vicinity made her shiver with fright. Not that she anticipated any intrusion on his part. He would never dare, and if he did, her servant had strict orders to admit no visitor. It was just the knowledge that he was there, ready to come to her at a word, a sign, which tormented her so unendurably. She could settle to nothing. Her fingers trembled, her heart beat, her uncontrollable restlessness wouldn't allow her to sit down in peace, and finally drove her from the house.

"I'll go over to Allerton and home by the Wilburn road. By tiring myself out thoroughly I may at least be able to get a night's rest," she told herself as she started on a tramp, which, to a poor pedestrian like herself was a sufficiently fatiguing one.

So fatiguing did she find it, that by the time she reached Allerton her restlessness had worn itself out, and on the plea of wanting stamps she turned into the post-office and general emporium in the hope of getting a rest there. As thankfully she accepted the chair offered her by the woman in charge, her eye fell upon a pile of newspapers heaped on the counter. The very thing! An excuse for prolonging her rest, and a refuge from the loquacious civility of the post-mistress. She took up the paper—it was the *Sentinel*, and enjoyed a wide circulation in Radical Allerton—unfolded it and glanced languidly at it. What was this in the biggest, most obtrusive of type? "Grand Demonstration! Cooking of the Unionist Goose! Tory M.P. in Trouble! Bravo, Wilburn! Revolt of the People!" What, indeed! An account, written *con amore*, of the glorious stand made by the citizens of Wilburn in the cause of honour and morality against vice in high places. An appeal to every man of decent feeling to submit no longer to this shameless violation of hearth and home at the hands of a heartless libertine, to follow no longer the unworthy guidance to which unknowingly he had submitted himself, to rebel effectually against representation in the person of a hardened profligate. Then followed an account of the hisses, cat calls, shouts for the unhappy victim by which the populace had so plainly expressed their just indignation against the offender, who met them with a callous effrontery only to be characterised as unparalleled. All this and more Esme read to the running accompaniment of the remarks of a couple of red-hot Radicals who were eagerly discussing the savoury topic.

"A good plucked 'un though," said one determined, however grudgingly, to give the devil his due. "Never so much as moved an eyelid when they went for him. And without the police, he'd ha' come off badly."

"Serve 'im right if he had," growled the neighbour. "How dare he show his face amongst decent folk with that poor gal looking fit to break 'er 'eart and old Dixon not able so much as to put one foot before another? Look at the gal—a nice gal—a pretty gal—might ha' married anybody—and now the poor, pinched, broken-down creature. And what'll he do? Give 'im money—curse him!—to bring 'em back."

"Are they back?" came the eager question.

"Come back yesterday, saw 'im myself. My fine gentleman wants to smooth things down, afraid o' losing our votes. But it won't do. They won't take us in. Curse him, I say, and all the brood!"

Esme pushed her way into the open air. Adrian Lisle guilty of this abominable act! Adrian Lisle, who professed for herself an attachment of the loftiest and purest nature, an ideal sentiment, which, let her conscience reprobate it as it would, her treacherous heart accepted greedily. Oh, incredible! Yet why so? A man will woo women of different classes in different ways, that's all. She knew the stamp of man he was, she had had ample warning of his real character. Oh, what a fool! what a vain, presumptuous blind fool she had been. To imagine that such a man would voluntarily sacrifice his prospects, while all the time he was merely flying from the consequences of his wrong-doing. As for his much-vaunted devotion to herself? Bah! It was pollution to think of it. A madness of rage, self-contempt, self-loathing possessed her. On and on she wandered, where or how far she had no idea. Some instinct must have led her to the Dixons', for halting at last she found herself in the high road not far from The Firs. Such a pretty haven of domestic peace it looked, the house so trim, the strip of garden so gay with spring flowers, steeped in brilliant sunshine. Could it be possible that so bright an exterior should cover so much dark shame, and sickness and sorrow, dealt by the hand, which of all others, should have been extended in help and protection? Surely not! She stopped. Why not go in and judge for herself of the truth of these accusations?

As she hesitated a man came out of the little villa, pausing to speak to someone inside the door. Adrian Lisle! The man himself. And he would be upon her, must meet her! She turned and fled along a footpath, across a field, over a stile, and into a narrow strip of wood.

"He will not see me," she told herself, "I can wait till he has passed."

But he did not pass, he was coming after her. Oh, how dared he inflict the crowning insult of his presence upon her? Very well, it was not for her to run away, to hide from him. Let him take the consequences of his intrusion, see himself for once as every right-minded person must see him. And this was how it happened that as Mr. Lisle, immersed in thoughts already sufficiently unpleasant, got over the stile and turned into the wood—which happened to be a short cut to the Court — he found himself face to face with the woman of all others he would most willingly have avoided. Without the evidence of the newspaper she still held crumpled in her hand, a glance at her face told him he was in the presence of a relentless judge. So she believed the worst of him. It would be idle to attempt to defend oneself when one has been condemned without a hearing. He made no such attempt, but merely lifted his hat and stepped aside to let her pass, which had she been herself she would certainly have done without a word; but she was not herself. Something outside, stronger than herself, stopped her against her will.

"So you have been to gloat over your handiwork," she said cuttingly. "Poor old man! Unhappy girl! Have you not injured them sufficiently? Could you not leave them one day in peace? Oh, don't explain"—as he seemed about to speak—"don't attempt to invent excuses. I saw you leave the house myself. You can't deny it."

"I had no idea of doing so," he answered coldly.

Looking at him it was easy to understand how the term "callous effrontery" came to be applied to his demeanour. His unconcerned air maddened her.

"Then this story is true?"

She pointed to the newspaper in her hand.

He bowed.

"*You*, Mrs. Blunt, of all women should be able to decide that question for yourself," he said quietly.

Her eyes flashed. How dared he drag her name into such an affair?

"That is so like you." Her voice was low and bitter in its concentrated scorn and contempt. "To offer to me, a defenceless woman, this crowning insult, this coupling of my name with that *girl's*. I have to thank you also for a host of similar benefits. It was you who robbed me of my trust in my fellow creatures, who taught me my first lesson in my knowledge of good and evil, who did your best to spoil my life and very nearly succeeded. And when we met again, under a hollow pretence of friendship, you wormed yourself into my confidence, you came between me and my husband, you made pensioners of us, dependents on your bounty. Oh, I know how skilfully you played upon Arnold's failings to further your own designs. You took advantage of my loneliness to insult me. You robbed me of all happiness in my home life, of my peace of mind, my self-respect. You found me a contented woman, contented in my home and child. You leave me a despairing wretch, with neither present nor future, tied in chains from which I cannot free myself, and which make existence insupportable. This is the result of your boasted devotion. I thank you for it, I thank you for it."

Without waiting to see the effect of her words she turned and left him. Had she remained she might have had the satisfaction, such as it was, of seeing that her shafts had gone straight home. For a long while Mr. Lisle stood staring before him. A series of pictures, conjured up by her words, were passing before him. They were not pleasant to contemplate. An innocent, light-hearted girl standing by the shrubbery-gate; again the same girl, entrancing in all her youthful freshness, blushing, conscious, timid, with the love-light dawning in her eyes, love inspired by him—yet again a pale, serious, saddened vision, bereft for ever, and by his doing, of the frank light-heartedness of youth. Finally the woman, a graceful, dignified figure, a devoted mother, dutiful wife. He saw her gradual yielding to his advances, her gradual abandonment of her cold reserve, her gradual destruction of the barriers between them, her gradual transformation into the white-faced, haggard, despairing creature, burdened with the consciousness of guilt, held in chains from which escape and in which existence were alike impossible. And this was his handiwork. For her taunts had shown him the truth as no demonstrations of friendship could ever have done. He derived no gratification from the discovery, he felt not even a passing throb of satisfied vanity. He knew her too well for that. She was a good woman. That meant, not that she was insensible to temptation, but that she would fight till she died before she yielded to it, that she had put into the hands of an implacable conscience an instrument of torture which would be used unsparingly against her. And he, to whom her welfare was dearer than anything on earth, had inflicted unintentionally, but none the less surely, this last supreme humiliation, had deprived her of the last chance of peace and happiness left her, injuries by the side of which her loss of money, friends, position, were the merest pin-prick. He knew this, and the knowledge was very bitter to him. Verily, the day of reckoning had come to him. He was paying the price of those light, careless sins of former days down to the uttermost farthing.

It was getting on for dinner-time at Hawthornden. Nothing had been heard of Mr. Blunt, who, it was assumed, would not return that evening. Mrs. Blunt, who had come in looking more dead than alive, had just countermanded dinner, and ordered a cup of tea to be brought to her, when a ring at the bell startled her. Up she jumped, her shattered nerves all ajar. A telegram, no doubt, from Arnold. If so, why not bring it in? Why this sound of whispering, this fuss and confabulation on the doorstep?

"What is it?" she called out, coming into the hall. The sound of voices ceased at once.

"Nothing, 'm," said the little maid, who looked confused and flurried.

"But who is there?"

"Only Captain Dixon's granddaughter asking for Mr. Blunt. She thinks the Captain must be here," answered the girl in an off-hand voice.

"Captain Dixon here? Certainly not. What should he come here for?" Esme was puzzled. She went to the doorstep, where Clara, tearful and agitated, was shrinking back. "What is it, Miss Dixon?" she asked coldly. "Can I do anything for you?"

"Thank you, Mrs. Blunt. It's nothing." Clara spoke in a low, nervous voice, "only that grandfather's out, and I thought I was afraid—because of him meeting—Mr. Blunt, perhaps." She brought the words out with a gasp.

More puzzled than ever, Esme took her by the arm, drew her into the drawing-room, and shut the door. "Explain yourself," she said quietly. "Mr. Blunt is not at home. He has not yet returned from London."

She was interrupted by a cry of terror. "But he has come back," Clara shrieked. "I saw him myself, passing the door more than two hours ago—grandfather saw him too, that's what upset him. He's followed him. There'll be murder done. . . He swore he'd kill him. . . . He'll do it. Oh!" again her voice rose to a shriek, "what shall we do?"

As in a flash of lightning, the truth came to Esme. She caught Clara by the arm, who uttered a cry of pain. "What do you mean, girl?" The sound of her own voice startled her. She did not recognise it. "Was it my husband, Mr. Blunt—who was—your——" The word stuck in her throat. Clara shrank away as though she had been struck.

"No—no!" she wailed. "Don't look at me like that. I'll tell you everything. There was no harm. We were only friends, that was all. He was lonely, so was I. I swear it. Only grandfather wouldn't believe it, but turned him out of the house, and locked me up and frightened me so that I ran away."

And then, between her sobs, she poured out the whole miserable story of selfish vanity and mischievous folly, mean, paltry, despicable, yet stopping short of actual sin.

With tightened lips and averted eyes, Esme listened to her. "Does Mr. Lisle know?" she asked abruptly at the end.

"That grandfather is out? Yes; I sent a message to him at once. I dared not wait till he came. I was so afraid what might happen."

"You must go home at once, then," was the decided rejoinder; "your grandfather must be found. You can do nothing here. Go home and get Mr. Lisle's advice and help."

"I can't—I daren't go alone. I am so frightened," sobbed Clara, who had completely lost her head.

"I will go with you then," said the other.

Together they hurried down the little avenue, out at the gate, and were turning into the high road, when a brougham, dashing round the corner, very nearly ran over them. With a cry, Clara sprang on one side, as the horse was pulled up short on its haunches. Mr. Lisle jumped out and went up to the girl, while Esme drew back under the shadow of the hedge.

"What were you doing at Hawthornden?" he asked, and judging from his voice, he was extremely angry. "Were you mad, to go there, of all places in the world?"

"Grandfather slipped out," she faltered, "and I was afraid."

"Why not then have come to me?" he interrupted sternly.

"I thought grandfather had gone after Mr. Blunt."

"Nonsense! Mr. Blunt is not even here. He is in London. Besides, Captain Dixon is perfectly safe. He was found by a keeper wandering about the park, and brought up to the house.

I have just taken him back home. You had better hurry back as quickly as possible. You will find him just the same as usual, quite gentle and harmless."

"Yes, yes. Pray let us go. Come at once," urged Esme.

"You can be of no use, Mrs. Blunt," interposed Lisle. "Captain Dixon has a nurse as well as his granddaughter. He will be well looked after. My carriage is quite at your service, if you will allow me to send you home in it."

"No, no, thanks. It is no distance," she protested quickly. "Send Miss Dixon. She is anxious to get home. I will walk. You will perhaps see me as far as the house?"

At this astounding suggestion he could only bow in silent assent. Unceremoniously Clara was bundled into the brougham and driven off, and then Esme turned to her companion.

"I wanted to tell you," she began abruptly in a hard, unnatural voice he would hardly have recognised as hers, "that I know the truth. I have to beg your pardon. I know now that it was to my husband I should have addressed my speech this afternoon, not to you. I must apologise for my mistake, which, as I should have known both you and him better, was all the more inexcusable on my part."

"Don't say that," he protested earnestly. "Besides, Mrs. Blunt, you are entirely under a misapprehension. Believe me, there has been imprudence, nothing worse all through."

She smiled. "You are magnanimous, Mr. Lisle," she said bitterly. "You heap coals of fire on my head. A pleasanter process to you than me. Coals of fire burn."

"I did not mean to hurt you," he persisted, "and I must repeat that you are unjust to your husband now as you were to me. It was all a piece of folly, which is over and done with. All you can do is to forget it."

"Forget it!" she repeated scornfully. "Forget the old man, reduced to helpless imbecility, the wretched girl with her prospects blighted, yourself with your career in jeopardy, and all for a piece of folly! I could have forgotten more easily had there been the excuse of overwhelming temptation to urge, some all-absorbing passion, a momentary slip, but to break up a home for the amusement of an idle hour, to gratify a paltry vanity! Oh! shame. . . . But after all perhaps you are right," she suddenly reverted to her former reckless flippancy. "What does it matter? As you say the best thing to do is to forget it. We are at home, Mr. Lisle. You will come in and wait for your carriage?"

He hesitated. "Go home," urged his better angel, "she is mad, utterly reckless. She doesn't know what she is saying." "Stay," whispered his evil genius. "You have your chance at last. Take what the other has forfeited." The hesitation was but momentary. His face lighted up. "May I?" he asked. "The sentence of banishment is remitted?" His better angel was retreating worsted.

She shrugged her shoulders. "Why not? Why should we look on your piece of folly as different from that other piece of folly, which we are agreed is not worth remembering? Who cares? Not Arnold most assuredly. Why should I be less sensible over my friend than over my husband? Having swallowed the camel shall I strain at a gnat? Oh, come in, Mr. Lisle, by all means, I am charmed to see you."

He had gained the desire of his heart, yet as he followed her into the drawing-room he wished it had been given him in any other way. Silently he watched her as she moved about the room, turned up the lamp, which the maid had just brought into the room, straightened a table-cloth, unfastened her cloak, and finally sat down in a low chair near the fireplace. He came and stood over her on the hearthrug. He hardly recognised her, this woman with the glittering eyes, the brilliant colour, the restless manner. Oh, she was infinitely attractive, almost beautiful, but she was not the woman who had won and kept his heart all these years. Yet what she was now, he had made her. Perhaps he remembered this when he made a final effort at self-mastery.

"I wonder whether you realise all you have been saying, Mrs. Blunt," he broke out hoarsely. "You are not fair to your husband—to yourself—or to me."

She burst out laughing. "Is Saul among the prophets?" she cried mockingly. "Is it for you, Mr. Lisle, to remind me, Esme Blunt, of my duty? How strange that sounds. Quite of a piece with everything else in this topsy-turvy world. Never mind, Mr. Lisle, I have systematically belittled you, thought the worst of you, accepted benefits innumerable at your hands, and repaid them with scorn and abuse. You have your revenge.

Take it upon me, miserable woman that I am, helpless, alone "—with a sudden change of manner—" with everything gone, friends, husband, child, everything, down to my very self-respect, no hope, no future, nothing to live for. Oh, my God! how can I bear it?" With a moan she dropped her face upon her hands.

Adrian came nearer. He had done with struggling at last. "You cannot bear it." He spoke quietly, but his voice was unsteady and the hand he laid on her chair trembled visibly. "You have tried long enough to achieve the impossible. Give it up. Leave a husband who is not and never has been anything but a husband in name. Break a bond which is a merely nominal one and come to me. You have proved me. For years my love has never faltered. Body and soul I am yours. My life, myself, everything I have, I lay at your feet. Come to me, and never while I am there to shield and care for you shall you suffer another moment's uneasiness. I swear it. You cared for me once." His voice dropped to a whisper. "Except for your aunt, you would have been my wife long ago. Is that not so?" (She did not contradict him). "And no other man has supplanted me? Esme, this is not a time for subterfuge. You are not a woman to change. You do care for me—still—a little."

She looked up at him. "Why ask me?" she said dully. "Would you have been saying all this to me if you didn't know that I cared? Of course I love you. I have always loved you, I believe, since first we met. Why should I deny it? What difference does it make except to add to my misery and degradation?"

"You are wrong," he said earnestly. "The degradation lies not in your love for me, but in your marriage with a man as far apart from you as the poles. Oh! I am not tempting you from your duty to your husband. You owe him none. God knows I would sooner cut out my tongue than utter a syllable to disturb the happiness of your married life. But there is none to disturb. Had I found you a contented wife, had your husband been to you in the smallest degree what a man should be to his wife, I would never have approached you. But he was not. He was absorbed in money-making, society, meaningless flirtation, thinking only of himself and the gratification of his miserable vanity. Surrounded by friends of his choosing, your welfare subordinated to his amusement, you were as isolated as though you lived in a desert. Even now if there were a chance of happiness for you with him I would be content to stand aside and do my best to promote it. But there is none. You are wretched. He has forfeited every claim on you. And so I say come to me."

She shuddered. "You don't know what you are asking of me," she whispered. "To make myself a mark for scorn and insult, to perjure myself before God!"

"There is no perjury," he interrupted. "You are no longer your husband's. He has only the shadow, the husk, the setting. The substance, the kernel, the jewel are mine. He is the interloper. Before Heaven, you are mine. As for society? What has society done for you that you should bow before it? Why sacrifice happiness to conventionality, to a mere meaningless form and ceremony?"

She wrung her hands. "It is not conventionality," she murmured brokenly. "It is the sin, the shame, the falsehood, the breaking of my marriage vows."

"Which are already broken in the spirit," he retorted boldly. "Do you keep them any the better for bearing one man's name when you yourself belong to another? My darling, throw aside these scruples. Trust to me. Leave it to me. You shall not repent it, I swear. There will be a wrench, but only for a moment. We will go abroad, see no one, hear nothing, forget entirely that the world contains another human being beside ourselves. I will make up to you for everything you lose, and in a few months you shall be my cherished wife, your welfare and pleasure the end and aim of my life."

"And your position—your property—your career—Parliament?" she faltered. "You could not give them up."

"I would give up Heaven itself for you," he answered passionately.

"I could not bear to injure *you*," she protested.

"You can only injure me by giving me up. You are my good angel, my better self. You and you alone can call forth all that is best in me. Without you I sink back to a mere selfish idler. With you I become another and a better man. Have pity on me, Esme, if you have none on yourself. Do not sacrifice me, I entreat, to a mere fetish, a creation of your fancy."

She pushed herself away from him. "Why do you tempt

me like this?" she murmured distractedly. "I am not myself. You take advantage of my weakness. "Oh, what am I to say?"

She was yielding. He played a bold stroke.

"I will not try to bias you," he said, stepping back and folding his arms. "It shall be as you will. I offer you myself to take or leave. Tell me to stay, and I will be your faithful husband and lover until death, so help me God! Tell me to go, and I leave you for ever, only it must be all or nothing. If you send me away now, you send me for ever to my ruin."

A long pause. Once, twice she tried to speak.

"I cannot say it," she moaned. "My God! I cannot. I know what I ought to do. I want to do it, I cannot. I am so horribly weak, so lonely. I long so for peace—and happiness. I cannot let you go. It would be death. Oh, I am in your power. I cannot fight against you!" She lifted her streaming eyes imploringly to his face, her voice was broken with sobs. "Be strong for us both. If you love me as you say you do, help me to do right. Don't lead me into wrong-doing. For it would be wrong. And out of wrong no good can come. I know that too well. Every word you said about my marriage was true, more shame to me. I was wrong to marry, still two wrongs never made a right. Don't ask me to do it. You are a man, strong, noble, generous. Don't drag me down. Give me the happiness of knowing that I have done you good, not harm—been a blessing, not a curse to you. You have a future before you. For my sake make something of your life. Let it be my pride to feel that I have loved a man worthy of respect, stronger, better, nobler than myself, and you will give me the only happiness still possible to me; you have taken all the sting and bitterness away, and made my love my glory, not my shame."

Adrian held up his hand. "You shall have your way," he said between his teeth. "No—no—don't speak—don't come near me," as she moved. "I am going now at once—while I can."

The door closed behind him. She lifted her head and saw she was alone. She had conquered. With an exceeding bitter cry she tottered forward and dropped huddled up to the ground.

## CHAPTER XXXVIII.

It was dusk when Adrian Lisle, at a pace literally suggestive of flight from the powers of darkness, set off on his homeward way Once he stopped short. Was his resolution faltering already? Was he a child or a fool to change his mind with every half-hour? He set his teeth, gripped his stick, and tramped on resolutely down the road, in at a side gate of the park, across a hundred yards of grass, and so into the long narrow plantation leading straight to the house. Here, under the trees it was pitch dark. Once he stumbled and nearly fell over the root of a tree. A second time his foot struck against something in his path, not a stump or projecting root this time, but a heavy yielding lump. Looking down he saw something dark in front of him. What was it? A sack, a beast, a tipsy man? He stooped, put out his hand, and felt something warm and sticky. He struck a match, knelt down, and by the flickering light made out the outlines of a man lying on his face, in a pool of blood. With a sickening presentiment of horror he moved the body so as to get a sight of the face. Just as he had expected. It was Arnold Blunt. Captain Dixon had kept his word after all Arnold Blunt lay dead before him. Yet no—not dead, for the body was still warm, the heart still beating, and as he touched him a low moan escaped the stricken man's lips. He lived—most assuredly he still lived, although, looking at the gaping wound in his head, it was doubtful how long he would survive the exposure and loss of blood.

Adrian scrambled to his feet. "He must get out of this at once," he muttered, "old Dixon has done his work pretty well. Another hour or two of lying here would certainly have finished him off. Lucky that I happened to pass this way, for no one else would be likely to find him."

Was it lucky though? Lucky perhaps for Arnold himself, but for others? The thought arrested his footsteps; his shout for help died away unuttered on his lips. Where would have been the harm if Arnold *had* been suffered to slip quietly out of a world to which most assuredly he had been neither of use nor ornament? Why therefore interfere? Why attempt to frustrate the designs of Providence? Why shut the door of freedom thus miraculously opened to himself and the woman he loved? For this was what it amounted to. Arnold's death gave his wife peace, freedom, delivery from a bondage worse than death. To himself it meant the realisation of his wildest dreams. No more conflict between love and duty, no scruples, no sacrifice, no disgrace; just a future of absolute, blissful serenity. Why hesitate? What was it after all? Just one life against another? On the one hand that of a contemptible, weak, selfish creature he despised too thoroughly even to hate, on the other, that of the women he worshipped so madly—for was she not killing herself by inches by thus sacrificing herself, her youth, her strength, her happiness to the fetish she called her conscience. Why hesitate?

To pretend to any scruples on Arnold's account was absurd; nothing would have pleased him better than to meet the man in open fight and kill him. And what he had to do now was so simple, such child's play. No danger, no risk of detection, nothing even to detect. What was it? Just to walk on, hold his tongue, shut his eyes to the helpless figure, the staring eyes, the ashen face, the life-blood slowly oozing from that awful gash. She need never know. Her tender heart, her over-scrupulous conscience need never be troubled by any questions.

Such a little thing to do as it was. Just to raise up a shameful secret between himself and his wife prohibiting from the outset that perfect confidence which is the one essential to domestic happiness. Just to break the solemn oath he had sworn to himself not half-an-hour ago, that henceforth in all things he would make her standard his rule of life, and so order his life as to justify the unselfish love he had inspired. What had she asked of him? That her love might be a blessing, not a curse—that it might raise, not lower him—might help him to do his duty, and live his life as it should be lived—and he proposed to inaugurate this new life by an act of murder. For murder it was. He could have killed the man in fair fight and thanked God to have been the means of ridding the world of him, but to deliberately leave him to die!

As he stood irresolute a sound of footsteps struck his ear. Some one, a workman, a groom, a gardener, was going down to the village, not through the wood which was rarely entered, but by the carriage drive which ran about thirty yards away parallel to it. Help was at hand if he cared to summon it. The footsteps grew more distinct. The man was coming near. He was passing. Could he—dared he—hold his tongue? Just for another moment. The man was passing. Another moment, and he would have gained his heart's desire and taken the blood of a fellow-creature on his hands! Could he do it? No—no! He stepped forward.

"I hope to God you'll die," he said, grimly apostrophising the fallen man, "but I'll save you if I can."

And then he shouted.

Mr. Lisle was a man of his word. Having made his choice, he didn't try to cheat his conscience and shuffle out of it by any deliberate delay or neglect of proper precautions. No time was lost in getting the sufferer up to the Court, installing him in a bedroom, sending for a doctor and applying such simple remedies as his housekeeper could suggest. Dr. Evans, indeed, when he did arrive, was loud in praise of the promptitude and forethought the former had displayed in his care for the invalid.

"If Blunt recovers," he said, "which, mind you, I don't say for a moment he will do, for he's about as badly knocked about as any man could be to be still alive—however, if he should get over it, it's to you, Mr. Lisle, and no one else, that he'll owe his life. By the way, does Mrs. Blunt know?"

No. Mrs. Blunt did not know, and in Mr. Lisle's opinion it was just as well she should not—for the present at all events.

"Let her have her night's rest in peace," he said, "she can do nothing for him, and by the morning you will be able to judge how things are likely to go with him."

Dr. Evans looked serious.

"Twelve hours won't make much difference in his condition," he said gravely, "and in so serious a case as this I don't feel justified in leaving her in ignorance one moment longer than is necessary."

"But she can do nothing for him," urged Adrian. "She's looking wretchedly ill. I saw her myself to-day. It would kill her to attempt to nurse him."

"Not a bit of it," corrected the other. "My dear sir, you don't realise what these delicate women are capable of, especially when they happen to show the breeding Mrs. Blunt does. For all her fragile appearance she's got the pluck and endurance of ten men, and there's no earthly reason why she shouldn't look after her husband. Do her good most probably. Give her something else to think about except the poor child she's breaking her heart over. I'll go down and break it to her now. She needn't disturb herself to-night unless she likes, but depend upon it, she'll be here as quickly as my horses can bring her."

And there, sure enough, half-an-hour later, she was. Neither then nor subsequently did Mr. Lisle see her. On her arrival he retired to his own quarters, leaving his housekeeper in attendance in the sick room. He also carefully timed his visits there later on to fit in with those intervals of repose on which Dr. Evans insisted as indispensable both for the sake of patient and nurse. He heard enough, nevertheless, of her patience, her composure, her self-reliance, her unceasing devotion to the sick man to know that, from whatever source she gained her strength, it was sufficient for the burden put upon it.

"A woman in a thousand," declared Dr. Evans, when after days of suspense the verdict was pronounced that Arnold would live. "Her devotion to that husband of hers has been something astounding. Because, you know, without wishing to say one word in disparagement of Blunt, he's not fit to be named in the same day with his wife. Indeed, I always thought them rather an ill-assorted couple, which only shows how one may be mistaken. I was never more glad in my life to be the bearer of good news than I was this morning to that poor little woman."

"How did she take it?" asked Adrian, who himself had taken it with an unmoved face. He expected nothing else. He never had deluded himself into the belief that the sacrifice once made would not be accepted. It is only in story-books that a man reaps the reward of performing a disagreeable duty by the convenient removal of that duty. He knew that well enough. In real life the accomplishment of one task, however hard, is merely the prelude to the setting of another and a harder one. There is no royal road to salvation. And climbing is hard work, especially to a man who all through life has been accustomed to saunter down a gentle easy slope. Mr. Lisle knew what was before him, when before Arnold's body he deliberately began to climb. He didn't pretend to like the exertion, but he was prepared for it, and he didn't flatter himself that any exception would be made in his favour, or that one single stone would be removed from his path, one single rough place made smooth. And so he listened to Dr. Evans' jubilant confidences with an impassive and slightly-bored air which drew from his companion the mental observation that if he hadn't known from personal experience what a thorough friend in need Lisle had proved himself to be, he should have set him down as a thoroughly hard, cold-blooded, supercilious beast.

"How did she take it?" he repeated cheerfully. "Just turned as white as a sheet. I thought she'd have fainted, but she didn't, only sat down and said nothing. Seemed stunned. Couldn't realize it, you know. I've sent her to her room and she'd better have a sleeping draught later on. Now that the strain is pretty well over, will be the time to guard against a break-down. Luckily she's the most docile patient I ever had to do with."

Deluded man! If he could only have seen his docile patient at that moment, as she paced up and down her room in a frenzy of abasement and misery.

"Make me glad," she was praying. "My God, make me glad! Change this wicked, false heart of mine. Oh, was there ever any woman so lost, so degraded as I am? I wanted him to die, I hoped he might die. I wonder I didn't kill him as he lay there, murderess that I was. Teach me to copy Adrian's example. He has been strong. He has conquered his madness. Enable me to do the same. Teach me, my God, how to make amends for the past, and do my duty by Arnold. . . ."

Prayers after all are usually answered as they deserve to be. These petitions were, apparently, for Mrs. Blunt continued to tend her husband during his long and tedious convalescence with a solicitude beyond all praise. To both of them it was a trying time, for Arnold made the worst of patients, rash, careless of his doctor's orders, yet exaggeratedly nervous at the least sign of a relapse. With the frequent changes of mood, the alternate fits of recklessness and depression, the petulance, the weariness, the insisting on doing too much, the reluctance to do anything at all, all the ups and downs in fact which mark convalescence, Esme bore with exemplary patience. She bore the brunt of them too alone. Old Mr. Blunt came down to the

Court, but he bored and irritated his son so much by improving the occasion, and preaching homilies against extravagance, that all were thankful when he was gone. Colonel and Mrs. Langley limited their sympathy to a cheque for five-and-twenty pounds to help defray the cost of the illness and a weekly letter of consolation and advice. Cecily Denison, notwithstanding her honest affection, was just then too much absorbed in her lover to be of much use to the outside world, and besides would never have been tolerated by Arnold, with whom at no time was she a favourite.

As for Mr. Lisle, no sooner had the sick man been pronounced out of danger, than he betook himself to London to look after the interests of his constituents. For Mr. Lisle had retained unmolested possession of his seat. Not that the scandal had ever died a natural death. On the contrary, it seemed to be thriving merrily, when, to the chagrin of those opponents who were making such excellent political capital out of it, it effectually received a quietus by Clara Dixon's marriage to her original suitor Joe Westerton. How the two came together, how the gentleman was induced to renew his courtship, how the lady managed to overcome her former repugnance, and to convince him of the cruel and unfounded nature of the accusations brought against her, no one ever knew. Perhaps he was moved in the first instance by pity for a woman, left helpless to fight the world alone, for Clara, since her grandfather had developed the homicidal tendencies which necessitated his removal to a lunatic asylum, had been without a friend in the world. Perhaps she simply told him the truth, which perhaps he had the good sense to believe. If so, both were wise in abstaining from an explanation, which no single inhabitant of Wilburn would have been likely to believe. At all events marry her he did, and promptly made it plain that whoever spoke against his wife would have to reckon with him. Behind his back, he might be and indeed was universally called a deluded old fool for his pains. No one, however—such is the power of him who holds the purse strings—ever hinted as much to his face. Neither did any member of that Radical party, of which he was so staunch a supporter, henceforth ever venture to breathe so much as a word against the wife of the man, who, it was expected, would defray nine-tenths of the expenses of the Radical candidate at the next election, if he didn't stand himself. For the rest Clara Westerton developed into a very different woman from what Clara Dixon had been as a girl. Her misfortunes had exercised a most chastening and salutary effect on her. She eagerly threw herself into all her husband's schemes for social advancement, she also proved a devoted mother to a numerous and promising troop of boys and girls, and, so far as anyone is aware, neither husband nor wife have ever had the slightest cause to regret their marriage.

## CHAPTER XXXIX.

"Are you there, Esme?" She was sitting in the dusk by the armchair, in which Arnold, after an afternoon of incessant fault-finding at his food, his clothes, his cushions, the want of air, the horrible draught, varied by intervals of exaggerated penitence, had, finally, to the relief of his harassed wife, fallen into an uneasy doze.

"Are you there?" he repeated.

"Yes, Arnold. Do you want me?" came the prompt gentle answer.

"Of course you are," he added with a sigh. "I might have known you would be there, always patient, always thoughtful, always at hand when you're wanted. No, you can't do anything for me. Sit down. I only want to talk to you." His fingers closed tightly over her hand. "Do you know you've been awfully good to me?" he went on in the weak voice which contrasted so oddly with his wasted but still powerful frame. "Don't think I haven't appreciated it, for I have. I'm not the ungrateful beast I often seem. Not one woman in ten thousand I know would do all you've done."

"No, Arnold, no. Don't think that," she protested.

"'Let him die, and a good riddance to him,' is what I'd have said in your place." He was working himself up into one of those fits of excitement so injurious to him. "But you've waited on me hand and foot, putting up with my cursed temper, making a slave of yourself without getting so much as a 'thank you' in return. Why do you do it, I wonder? It must be because you're a saint, for God knows, you've no great cause to want to keep me. I've spent your money, spoiled your life, and been nothing but a trouble and a nuisance to you."

"No, no," she protested again. "Never that—never that for me one moment. Believe me, I have never harboured one single unkind feeling towards you in my heart."

"But you might have," he retorted gloomily, "for more reasons than just for the loss of the money. I've been thinking a lot since I've been here, Esme, and I can see now how I've failed towards you. I didn't mean it, but, somehow or other, I seem to have let you drift away from me, entirely by my fault."

"No, Arnold," she interrupted eagerly. "Indeed, if any one has been in fault it is I. At the beginning you did love me truly and honestly. But I was absorbed in the child. I see that now. I was cold and indifferent. I made no return for your affection. I never exerted myself to be a companion and helpmeet to you."

"Indeed, you've been the best, the most loyal, uncomplaining wife any man ever had," he declared. "It was I who let myself be led away by a lot of silly women who played upon my vanity, and made a fool of me. I neglected you, Esme. I see it now, and I'm heartily sorry for it. If I had my time over again, you shouldn't have such cause to complain of me. Not that I ever really forgot you for a moment. In my heart of hearts I always knew you were the only woman I ever really cared for, but I did play the fool. I acknowledge it—not meaning any harm though. But you don't know what some of these women are. However, I don't want to excuse myself; one ought to be able to resist temptation, only somehow one can't, at least, hardly anyone does. Besides, you never seemed to care—in short——"

"I know, I know," she murmured soothingly. "I quite understand. If I had been more to you, it would have made things easier for you. Let us say no more about it."

"Ah! but there's something I must tell you." His face was flushed, his eyes bright, and his manner painfully excited. "About the Dixons I mean. You thought his attack, of course, the act of a madman, and so it was; but he knew what he was about all the same. He swore he'd kill me, and he did his best, because——"

She laid her fingers on his lips. "Not another word," she insisted softly. He couldn't see her face, but there were tears in her voice. "You are only making yourself ill, and it is not necessary. I know. I have known all about it from the beginning of your illness. If I have anything to forgive, believe me I forgive freely, fully, as I hope you will forgive my shortcomings. If you have been foolish, you have suffered cruelly for it. I too have been wrong, and have been punished. Let bygones be bygones, and we will start afresh."

"Just what I long to do, only I didn't feel justified in asking so much of you," said poor Arnold. In the fulness of his repentance tears were running down his cheeks. "We'll start afresh, no more each going our own ways, but keeping together, always together. I'm not strong by myself, I know. Alone, I am bound to get into mischief, but I shall be all right if you are with me to help me, and keep me straight. And you will help me?"

So her hardest task was yet to come? The future would demand far more of her than the past had done. For merely wifely duty? What was that? A trifle, a nothing, a flea-bite compared with the tender affection he now seemed disposed to exact; and which, if she meant to play her part loyally, she must give him as his right.

"We will help one another," she murmured brokenly. "Oh, Arnold! If you only knew, you make me feel ashamed. I promise I will do my best. I will never fail you—God helping me!"

A smile stole over his face. He drew her face down to his and kissed her, a caress which, after a hardly perceptible pause, was returned. "God bless you, Esme!" he whispered contentedly. "I shall get well quickly now—I've something left to live for."

And then with a satisfied smile he fell asleep.

"Mrs. Denison? How do you do? This is, indeed, an unexpected pleasure. When did you get home?" The speaker was Mr. Lisle, who, bored and listless, was fighting his way through the crush at a big political reception he had felt it his duty to attend, when suddenly, to his manifest gratification, he ran up against Cicely, now a smart young matron of several years' standing.

"We only landed last week," answered the latter, who looked in radiant health and spirits.

"And John?"

"John is flourishing. I left him at Abbottsleigh. Wild horses wouldn't drag him away again from his beloved pigs and cows."

"But you had a pleasant trip, I hope?"

"Delightful!" was the enthusiastic rejoinder. "We saw and did a heap, and what in itself was well worth the voyage to New Zealand, sea-sickness and all, we spent a week with the Blunts."

"And—you found them well, I hope?" Mr. Lisle's voice never varied in its tone of polite enquiry.

"Quite flourishing on the whole." Cicely's expressive face had grown rather grave, and she spoke deliberately. "The life, I am sure, suits them both as well, if not better, than any other would do. He seems perfectly happy. He has just enough work to give him occupation without being a worry or a tie to him. Then he farms a lot, loafs a lot, fusses rather over his food—he is getting so fat—gets as much society as he can, flirts away in a perfectly mild and proper way, for he's devoted to Esme—and is the life and soul of the set who are always wanting to be sociable and get up things. Oh!" with an impatient shrug of her shoulders, "you know what he is—very popular, quite harmless, and hopelessly commonplace."

"And Mrs. Blunt?" asked Adrian, forbearing from any comment on a description, which he knew was probably coloured by prejudice.

Cicely sighed. "I can't say there's anything amiss with her," she declared in a dissatisfied voice. "She's well enough, looks better indeed than I ever saw her do before, which shows that the climate agrees with her. Then the boy is an enormous source of gratification to her—such a dear little chap, and as strong as a lion. In his way, too, Mr. Blunt is very fond of her and as good to her as he knows how to be. She declares she's happy, and she looks and seems contented enough, but, oh, it is such a pity. Well," breaking off abruptly, "I suppose I mustn't say too much, as I know you were chiefly responsible for pitch-forking Mr. Arnold into that berth, and of course it's been a tremendous help to them, and just what they wanted. Still, to see Esme wasted there stuck down in that out-of-the-way hole, amongst a lot of trumpery little nobodies, who haven't even the wit to see her superiority and understand that she's miles and miles too good for them and the twopenny-ha'penny society they think so much of. Oh! it drove me wild. I couldn't bear to see her thrown away amongst all those people who could neither appreciate nor understand her. You'll tell me I'm unreasonable, I know," with a vexed laugh, " and so I am, perhaps, but I can't help it."

He told her nothing of the sort. On the contrary, he didn't speak at all for some time, but stood staring in front of him, abstractedly stroking the moustache, which these last few years had grown so grey.

"We talked a lot about you," Cicely continued. She was as fond as ever of the sound of her own voice. "I told them all about your triumphs, and what a personage you had become. They were tremendously interested, I assure you. Esme bade me tell you that she reads every word of your speeches with the utmost attention. She's no end of a politician, you know, devours the papers and asks all sorts of questions. Really, she knows a heap more at the other end of the world of what is going on here, than an ignoramus like myself does on the spot."

"There is no chance, I suppose, of their returning to England?" he asked.

"Not at present. Their idea is to live quietly, and to put by money, which they are doing now steadily. Then, in ten years' time or so when the boy is ready for a public school, they will come home and settle near Torrington, and in time go back to the Manor, which with care they ought to be able to do. Why don't you combine business with pleasure, and take a trip out there, look them up, gather information on the spot and come back a walking encyclopædia on every colonial question?"

He smiled. "Not just at present, "I think," he said. "Some day, perhaps—later, but not yet."

"Of course—you must be too busy now. Ah, Mrs. Langley, how do you do? We have just been talking about Esme. John and I only came back last week from our New Zealand trip."

"And you saw dear Esme?" Mrs. Langley, stout and grey, but as polite and polished as ever, smiled her sweetest smile. "How did you think her looking? Quite herself, I hope. Dear child! She seems so happy. It is such a delight to us to get her letters, so full of praise of the splendid climate and their pleasant neighbours, the peaceful life too—quite idyllic it sounds. And it is all thanks to you, Mr. Lisle," turning to that gentleman, "we owe you quite a debt of gratitude for procuring for my son-in-law a post which so thoroughly suits him."

Whereupon Mr. Lisle, with a hasty and unintelligible disclaimer, made his escape.

"Poor, dear man!" murmured Mrs. Langley. "Such a pity it is he doesn't marry. With all that money and that splendid position, he really wants a wife. A public man ought to entertain, which as a bachelor he can't do. And with his talents, his money, his name, he might pick and choose anywhere. Especially now that he has steadied down so admirably, as I was always confident he would do. And he has such a future before him. I heard only yesterday, that when his party come in, as they are certain to do before long, he can rely on being given some office. Really," she concluded reflectively, "I don't know any man in London with such prospects as he has."

And as he walked home, "I suppose it's all right," this enviable individual was reflecting. "A woman manages to extract an amount of comfort out of self-sacrifice, which a man doesn't happen to be able to do. And then there's the boy. That's something I never could have given her. And health is half the battle. Oh, yes," with an impatient sigh, "I suppose I did the right thing and if I could feel sure all was well with her I shouldn't regret it—but the time hasn't come for a trip to New Zealand—not yet. Luckily"—another sigh, "the years go quickly, and such a life as I lead doesn't give one much time or opportunity to think of anything but the day's work."

He had reached home by this time and letting himself in with his latch-key went straight to his den, and sat down at a big writing-table, on which lay a pile of letters and papers, which for the next few hours claimed his whole attention.

Every lot, after all, possesses its compensations. Even if he have the inclination, a man who has thrown himself heart and soul into public life, and has become known as one of the rising men of his day, doesn't often find the leisure to sit down and indulge in sentimental yearnings.

**THE END.**

# The Art of Swearing.

"Procul, O procul este, profani!"—VIRGIL.

LONGINUS has commended timely oaths as not only a useful but sublime figure of speech, and the old Scotch lady who owned that "our Jemmy swears awfu'," added, on reflection, "but to be sure it's a great offset to conversation." Whether these or other apologists show reason enough for profanity, it is certain that it continues to retain a very firm hold on our vigorous English tongue. According to Calverley, "Sikes, housebreaker of Houndsditch, habitually swore," and there be those that are still of the same persuasion. Many of us have voluble friends and acquaintances, and some, perhaps most of these, "weave a glittering streak of profanity through their garrulous fabric" that is refreshing to a spirit weary of dull verbal neutrality. The imprecation, as a pastime, the missing word, a refuge in time of need, a fire-side companion, an inexpensive luxury, a mental safety-valve, a pretty piece of Paganism, is immortal, and goes on its way defiant and undisturbed.

This is matter for surprise in an age devoted to complacent crusades against human weaknesses. Why are not the Professors of Strong Language driven by repeated persecution into temperance of speech, as the drinkers of "stimulants" are into "winterine," and other delightful fluids resembling cherry tooth-paste with hot water poured upon it? As it is, the long reign of imprecation seems likely to last for ever.

There is always a sufficient stock of oaths, though "the individual," to quote the Laureate, "withers"; for swearing, like hosiery and philanthropy, is swayed by fashion; certain forms become obsolete, whilst the fundamental ideas remain the same, and "a good mouth-filling oath" is as popular in the England of Sir Augustus Harris as it was in the Athens of Pericles.

The study of oaths affords some interesting problems even to one who can make only a cursory survey of this wide-spread and vigorous habit. Why is it that such calm and such satisfaction succeeds an especially pungent execration? Why do some callings, and even some games, make such a "blastophone" of a man? Why do all the oaths of one age, with the exception of a very few fixed favourites, lose their point and aroma for the next? Damns have their day: "the best terms," as Bob Acres, that first-rate authority, remarks, "will grow obsolete." For one crowded year of glorious life, they fly, like Ennius in his epitaph, "lively o'er the lips of men," and then fade away into the limbo of forgotten things, as ephemeral as the music-hall ditty, and as secure for a time with the public.

The word "swear" was apparently colourless in meaning at one time; etymologists assure us that to swear was but "to buzz," or "to talk," quoting from Othello:

"She swore, i' faith, 'twas strange, 'twas pitiful."

Though this seems to prove but little, as ladies in Shakespeare were not free from this taint. Hotspur says, for instance:

"Swear me, Kate, like a lady as thou art."

To answer is also said to mean "to swear against"; are there then some who, if offenders, are better etymologists than they know?

The various kinds of swearing may be divided roughly into three classes—(1) asseveration, (2) denunciation, (3) interjection.

The asseverative class is usually not "swearing" in the general acceptation of the word, that is, not profanity. It is commonly represented by the process of swearing in before a court of law; it is a showy form of imprecation, but not used in private life; often the speaker employs some visible object, such as the Bible, in order to clench his statement with due solemnity. One of the earliest things on or by which oaths were made, was doubtless the sword: it was specially prominent at the time of the Crusades, when it bore a cross, but the usage goes back far earlier. The Scythians had the same custom, and with all primitive races might was right, and the sword, or weapon of destruction, the chief helper and punisher, and, therefore, the natural thing by which oaths were made. We find "Swear by my sword" in Shakespeare (*Hamlet*, i. 5; *Winter's Tale*, ii. 3); and, to give a modern instance, Mr. Rudyard Kipling speaks, in the "Barrack Room Ballads," of "the oath of the Brother in Blood . . . on the hilt and haft of the Khyber knife."

This class of asseveration invokes in its formulas perdition on the swearer if he fail to keep his bond. The Old Testament will suggest many instances of this sort, and the Greeks and Romans called down awful penalties on their heads; Aristophanes has frequently comic exaggerations of this character; in *The Knights*, Cleon and the Sausage-seller open a wordy war with such asseverations; the former wishes that, if he fail to do all that is best for Demus, he may perish and pine, have his carcase dried and curried, and his hide made into leather straps for harness; the Sausage-seller retorts by the prayer that, if he does not dote on Demus tenderly, he may be stewed in a dish, sliced, minced and hashed, and the pieces left by the cook dragged out to the grave with his own flesh-hook.

But our modern linguistic artists despise circumlocution; they have no time or patience to employ a form so indirect, so that, except in a few phrases, such as "Blow me tight if I do," "S'welp me Bob," these conditional formulas are not much employed.

Of the second or denunciatory class the Commination service of the Prayer Book is an example, and the awful eloquence which Lear pours out on the heads of his ungrateful daughters. Nothing again can be more sweeping and complete than the severe digest of curses by Ernulphus, which Uncle Toby so disliked in "Tristram Shandy"; another instance is the denunciation of the unknown thief by the Abbot of Rheims in the "Ingoldsby Legends," which fell with such force on the jackdaw as to reduce him to a mere shadow of his former self.

But we must leave this class to deal with the third—the interjectional—into which it merges; here we enter on profanity proper, with which this paper, as this is the most popular form of swearing, chiefly deals. Here, either in form of ejaculation or epithet, are the most striking and brilliant varieties; a copious glossary would be needed to record a tithe of the phrases of this most universal habit. Dealing, then, chiefly with this class, we now proceed to give a roughly historic record of oaths, going in one case to the root of the matter in its beginning and derivation.

In Greece and Rome, though one of the *obiter dicta* of the wise men was "Do not swear," the custom was common in every-day life. Everybody swore in Greece, and everybody in Rome, except the flamen Dialis and the Vestal Virgins, who were not allowed to indulge in that privilege on any occasion.

Legislation did not, as in England, attempt to taboo profanity altogether, but Draco, Solon, and other law-givers restricted the people to three deities for the purpose of obtestation, and even this mild attempt to control them seems to have failed as absolutely as the current English law.

The chief difference between these times and ours was that both sexes swore, for ladies in modern England, with the brilliant exception of "Dodo," do not do so. Consequently custom ordained curious special restrictions; women never swore by Hercules, and men never by Castor. Juno and Venus were mostly reserved to the use of the fair sex, and, if invoked by a man, indicated effeminacy.

The Greeks seem to have had a nicer sense of what was proper for each special occasion than the modern performer. We may be sure that the caution of Swift ("Polite Conversation") that "the same oath or curse cannot, consistently with true politeness, be repeated above nine times in the same company with the same person," would not have been necessary to this artistic and brilliantly gifted people. They had a whole circle of gods and employed all their names at the proper times: thus Menelaus bids Antilochus swear by Poseidon, the equestrian god, when horses are in question, and Aristophanes shows a remarkable fertility of resource and invention, only paralleled by the efforts of the ingenious Bob Acres; his oaths always fit the occasion, and often contain special personal hits.

In the public speeches of the orators oaths to emphasize statements are very common; Demosthenes at the beginning of his speech on the Crown seems determined that his oath shall not miss fire, swearing as he does, not by a single deity, but by all the gods and goddesses!

The desire to swear and yet not run the danger of mentioning a heavenly name is curiously exemplified in Greece. Aristophanes and Plato both have the oath μὰ τὸν ("By the ———") with the name of the deity suppressed, and the swearing by the goose or dog, which Socrates practised, was doubtless a substitute for more offensive expletives.

Herodotus mentions perhaps one of the earliest instances of swearing on record—among the Abarantians, who were primitive enough to have no separate names; "these people," he says, "utter curses against the Sun, when his heat is excessive, and, moreover, revile him with all manner of foul terms, because he oppresses them with his burning heat, both themselves and the land." (Bk. iv. 184.) Such an occasion for blasphemy would be only too gladly welcomed by many who live in England.*

It is interesting to note that among the Romans a special class held the pre-eminence in the matter of swearing; for from a passage of Petronius it appears that weavers (*textores*) were as proverbially strong in their vocabulary as troopers or bargees in modern times.

Mediæval blasphemy stands recorded in a curious place—the proper names of the day!

In the Battle Abbey deeds appear a "John God-me-fetch," and the surnames "Blood," "Death," "God-salve," "Godsall," "Pardew," "Pardoe" (forms of "*par dieu*"), "Godbeer" ("God be here"), are referred to the same source.

Later, a glance at the "Canterbury Tales" will show the enormous prevalence of oaths at that time, and many writers declare that this was the peculiar vice of the Anglo-Normans, who used the most violent imprecations (as they nowadays appear to us) with the same facility and want of ceremony with which the German lady raps out her "Ach! Gott."

There is much in Shakespeare on the subject of oaths; he reflects that "there are liars and *swearers* enow to beat the honest men, and hang them up," and that "it is not the many oaths that make the truth." Brutus will have no swearing a compact among his conspirators, for swearing is for "priests and cowards and men cautelous." From *Henry IV.* it appears that there were correct and vulgar oaths in these times: Hotspur says:—

> "Swear me, Kate, like a lady as thou art,
> A good mouth-filling oath; and leave 'in sooth,'
> And such protest of pepper-gingerbread,
> To velvet-guards and Sunday citizens."

Hamlet swears "by Saint Patrick," "by our Lady and the Rood"; Richard III. "by Saint Paul," and "by my George," meaning the figure of Saint George on the badge of the Knights of the Garter; "i' fecks" and "God's sonties," are both puzzles to the ingenious reader; "'slid" (God's eyelid) is hardly recognisable in its present shrunken proportions. "Zounds!" is "God's wounds." And "Snails" has deceived a lexicographer.

* Not written in 1895.

Richardson in his "Dictionary" gives the following quotation for "Snail" from Beaumont and Fletcher:

> "Oh! Master Pompey! How is 't, man?"
> *Clown.* "'Snails, I'm almost starved with love and cold, and one thing or other."

It is really of course "'Snails," *i.e.*, God's nails.

The oaths in diminutives such as "odds lifelings," and "by'r lakin'" ("by our ladykin"), are noticeable. The *Merry Wives of Windsor* is very full in its swearing vocabulary. Here Mrs. Page swears "by the Dickens"—a form of expression still current without the preposition, and possibly a perverted version of Old Nick, who is good for many disguises. Shallow and Page swear by "cock and pie" (which may be an ale-house sign); Parson Evans "by 'od's plessed will," and "by the devil and his dam," Nym, "by the welkin and her star."

An oath like "God's sonties" mentioned above suggests the question—why is it in its present corrupted and meaningless form? It may have meant "God's innocencies," but nobody can be certain about the matter. The reason for these odd forms, disguised past recognition, which appear also in other languages, is not far to seek. Sacred names and attributes, by means of these distortions, are so disguised, that the speaker and the hearer do not imagine that there is any profanity. Thus the speaker gets rid of the idea that he is using sacred names in vain, and manages, as it were, to sup with the Devil with a long spoon. To give a foreign instance, the German "Potz" in "potz-tausend," "potz-vetten," is a corrupted form of "Gott." The same feeling is responsible for many mild paraphrases, such as the French "*foi de petit bonhomme.*"

Shakespearian oaths generally have acquired a certain sense of solemnity—a glamour of antiquity, which mellowing time has not yet shed upon our own efforts. Modern blasphemy is much less artistic and picturesque, and much more limited in range of expression. Such impressive oaths as that of William I., who swore "by the splendour of God," are out of fashion, and the man in the street concentrates his powers mostly on the adjective of blood, for certainly this is the derivation of the word according to the indefatigable Murray. It is found in general colloquial use from the Restoration to *circa* 1750. Now, it is constantly in the mouths of the working classes, but is considered by respectable people a "horrid word." It is merely the adjective of "blood," which was used (much as in the Cambridge slang of to-day) for a man of spirit, "a fiery spark" (Johnson: Dict.) at the end of the seventeenth century, when aristocratic rowdyism was in fashion. It was confined at first to the phrase "bloody drunk," which meant as drunk as a "blood," or, as the proverb says, as drunk as a lord. The earliest use recorded is in Etheridge (1676), "not without he will promise to be bloody drunk." Later, as in Fielding, who has "a bloody positive old fellow," its sphere was extended to other expressions, and its imagined connection with bloodshed and murder recommended it to the rougher classes, who enjoy the use of similar violent words, such as "ripping," "tearing," "thundering," "stunning," etc. As to "thundering," Lowell conjectures that the use of the word is derived from the belief, common formerly, that thunder was caused by the Prince of the Air, and considers it an euphemism for "devilish," but this is hardly necessary, when we consider that other words describing violent or destructive action are so common in this connection. This craving for strong words is, as another American author remarks, a characteristic of the English, who compare in the matter of forcibility very favourably with the Germans; their words are so feeble and inexpressive, their sound so poor an echo of the sense, that he suggests that they should borrow the innocuous English word "tooth-brush" as more than an efficient substitute for their strongest efforts at imprecation. It is fairly certain that the word "bloody" has nothing to do with the oath "'sblood," and, therefore, though it is now tabooed by ears polite, it has no offensive associations. The claims of the derivation from "by'r Lady" (the Virgin Mary who appears in "Marry!") are also poor.

The very general use of this word amongst the lower classes is an excuse for this somewhat long discussion of it. It certainly demands a wider recognition, if, as the story goes, it plays a part as an explaining medium. A working man is said to have been unable to realise the meaning of the political catchword "One man, one vote," but when it was repeated to him with the insertion of this adjective before the two nouns, all difficulties of comprehension vanished, and the full force of the maxim shone on that intellect, which nowadays goes far to rule our country, and choose those legislators whose earnestness, if not their English, is their strong point.

It is a difficult question to decide how far the consciences of those who use the word are shocked by so doing, or whether it is so meaningless as to be harmless, especially when one considers its value as a safety-valve to the emotions.

And here we must pause to record our admiration for those persons who compromise matters with such expressions as "What the mischief!" "Drat it," "The deuce," and the like. "Deuce!" is correct for these precisians, but "God!" which is "Deus"—the same thing—would be a profanation. There are many oaths of this milder sort, such as "by Jingo!" (representing "by the Saint Gingulphus"). The soldier is ever "full of strange oaths," and one may trace to him the expressions "you be blowed" and "like blazes." The sailor prefers to take his "Alfred Davy" (Affidavit); one hears of being "jiggered" commonly, but the word "jigger" has in slang so many meanings, that it would be difficult to say what the verb formed from it precisely denotes.

Two other instances of words really harmless, which are popularly supposed to be otherwise, are found in the expressions not to care a "dam" or a "curse." Dam (not "damn") is according to its original derivation a small Indian coin, and used in this connection just as "not worth a rap" is—a rap being a base half-penny once issued in Ireland. So such a passage as Fuzzy-Wuzzy's view of the British soldier:

> "'E's the on'y thing that doesn't give a *damn*
> For a Regiment of British Infantree!"

is a misuse of the word.

Not worth a "curse" in the same way is probably not worth a "kerse" (wild cherry—German, *Kirsch*) a synonym for anything worthless; other writers say "curse" is "cress" (a weed), and an early book on "Names of Herbes" (1548) gives two forms, "cresse" and "kerse," while Chaucer has:

> ". He raught (recked) not a *kers*."

Foreign oaths do not differ materially from English ones. It has been noted above that German oaths are usually mild; what seems to a foreigner the strongest ("Ach! Gott!") is daily on the lips of the ladies, whilst the men content themselves with expressions as harmless as "donner wetter!" The French are not more vigorous with their "Sacrés" and "Sacre mille tonnerres"; the Italian swears regularly by Bacchus ("Corpo di Bacco"); it is curious that all the heathen gods, except Jupiter, curtailed into Jove, should have gone out of favour as references in England, for Shakespeare has, in King Lear alone, "by Apollo," "by Jupiter," and by "Juno."

A few specimens of Oriental oaths show that the Eastern world is more flowery and inclined to figurative language than the western, but not less vigorous. Thus the Persian swears "by God's heart," "by your death," "by your father's tomb," "by your head's sacrifice," but may also denounce you in such unmeasured terms as "Be strangled, you son of an ass!" "May my father's salt blind you," "May you choke, son of a dog-parent!"

In Arabic we find the comparatively mild "Allâh karim!" "G(o)od gracious," and "ya rabb" "O Lord," but also "gatalak allâh!" "Iá únak allâh!" (God kill you! God condemn you!) and the agreeable prayers "fudda fuka," "I ágran laka," meaning respectively, "May your teeth be broken!" and "May you be hamstrung!"

Hindustani has, like Persian, "the oath of your head," with which we may compare the words of Ascanius in Virgil (Æn. ix. 298), "per caput hoc iuro, per quod pater ante solebat," "Balâ sê" ("confound it!") and "râm râm" ("good God") are both western in expression.

There is also a delicate appreciation of our Teutonic neighbours in the Turkish imprecation: "May your soul have no more rest than the hat of a German!"

In the matter of printing oaths in literature, all times have been very free, but the dash with the initial and final letter is surely one of the poorest attempts at reconciling the conscience, and sparing the weaker brother. The author means to get, and does get, the full effect of his oath on the reader, but he will not be so wicked as to print it in full! This is stealing a march on Satan with a vengeance! Who does not know what "d——n" means, and who gains by the affected prudery of those who mean the word, and as good as say the word, but would not for worlds print it in full? It is surprising to find that even that most honest and healthy-minded of authors, Walter Scott, affected this literary prudishness. But the question occurs—should oaths be mentioned at all in literature? The realist replies "Yes," and one is inclined to agree with him; at any rate let us be consistent; Rudyard Kipling's stories have been described to the writer as "sadly marred by oaths," by one whose conversation on the same scale it would be difficult to describe. Perhaps oaths should be used sparingly for literary purposes, and not scattered at random. Some will prefer not to have them omitted from a man, when they form a part of him as he was; thus Canon Ainger has cut out some oaths from Charles Lamb's works; we should have liked to see them there, as every man's conscience is his own, and not his editor's. We may perhaps mention some of the most famous and felicitous passages which deal with swearing in literature, and a few opinions and paraphrases by well-known writers, but before we do so we must not fail to mention the swearing story, told as an easy method of gaining a reputation as a humorist, and stereotyped as one of the attractions of the Socialist lecturer; many of these are well known, but one or two, which are perhaps less familiar, are here given.

Sheridan Knowles was angry with his publishers, Saunders and Otley (who were then apparently no less black than Mr. Besant* paints them now); he did not know them personally, so, when he called and found one of the partners at home, he began: "If you are Saunders, damn Otley; if you are Otley, damn Saunders."

Charles Lamb wrote to Wordsworth (who was superfluously solemn): "Some d——d people have come in, and I must finish abruptly. By d——d I only mean deuced."

Macready was a great swearer, and his stage-manager, a recent book informs us, once rebuked him at a rehearsal for his unseemly language, but he added somewhat inconsistently: "It's such a d——d bad example."

Perhaps the most celebrated of oaths in literature is the imprecation of Sterne's Uncle Toby with its fanciful commentary: "He shall not die, by G——, said my uncle Toby, and the accusing spirit which flew up to heaven's chancery with the oath, blushed as he gave it in, and the recording angel blushed as he wrote it down, dropped a tear upon the word and blotted it out for ever." This is very pretty, but the authority of the sentimentalist is not that of the professor of dogmatic theology. We may note that

* Written before 1895; now "Sir W. Besant."

though clergymen are supposed to have no dealings with this verbal vice, Sterne and Swift both used oaths frequently in their works, and one of the most spirited and successful efforts in this way is a poem by the Dean, containing sixteen oaths in the same number of lines.

Bob Acres, with his "odds whips and wheels," "odds blushes and blooms," "odds tabors and pipes," is a very ingenious performer in a talented company, for all the characters in *The Rivals* swear without blanks. Fag says, "Damn the place!" Lucy, "O, gemini!" and Thomas, "odd rabbit it!"

We can surely well pardon a character his oaths when they serve to round off the man before us. The old Squire in Mr. Meredith's "Harry Richmond" would not be the successful portrait he is without his violent language. From the same book we gather the statement that "The Romans had a religion that encouraged them to swear," and that it is a necessity to "rap out an oath here and there."

Mr. Hardy's rustics think the same as Mr. Meredith's gentlemen; at the farmer's party in "Far From the Madding Crowd," Master Coggan complained that there was "not a single damn allowed; no, not a bare, poor one, even at the most cheerful moment when all were blindest, though the good old word of sin thrown in here and there at such times is a great relief to the merry soul."

"True," said the maltster, "Nature requires her swearing at the regular times, or she's not herself; and unholy exclamations is a necessity of life."

"There is, or rather *was*, one oath in the poems of Wordsworth, and surely though "Peter Bell" has been derided, the description of

> "The party in the parlour all silent and all *damned*"

is enough to make the poem immortal; would any other adjective have been so descriptive? We venture to think not, and whoever has removed this stanza from the popular edition of the poet's works has not deserved well of him.

Charles Dickens' novels also supply many felicities. The improvident Mantalini suggests at once the "ha'penny" he wished to be "dem-d." Mr. Peggotty is peculiar with his "I'm gormed," and what could be finer than Mr. Pell's story of the "Chancellor in "Pickwick," the objection of the elder Mr. Weller to that high functionary's language (when he damned himself), his opinion that, "if he had been a poor man, Parliament would have took it up," and his final satisfaction, when assured that the chancellor had "damned hisself in confidence," which was "quite another thing."

We add here a paraphrase of one of the commonest of oaths by Dickens, and put by its side another by the other great novelist of his time. Thackeray's is the neater of the two, Dickens' the more ingenious. Dickens in "Oliver Twist" speaks of "a very common imprecation concerning the most beautiful of human features, which, if it were heard above, only once out of every fifty thousand times that it is uttered below, would render blindness as common a disorder as measles." Thackeray in "The Newcomes" says: "The famous English monosyllable, by which things, persons, luck, even eyes are devoted to the infernal gods, we may be sure is not wanting in that Babel" (the gambling houses of Baden).

The door of Thomas Hood cannot be omitted from any anthology of this subject, that door that shut with such a slam, "it sounded like a wooden damn," and who can fail to appreciate the innocent and delicious strong language of Marjorie Fleming, the pet child of Water Scott? Her diary says: "I am now going to tell the horrible and wretched plague that my multiplication gives me you can't conceive it the most devilish thing is eight times eight and seven times seven is what nature itself can't endure." There is something exquisitely straightforward in the same gifted child's description of the turkey, who was a bereaved mother:

> "But she was more than usual calm,
> She did not give a single dam."

American oaths, like American humour, differ from the English variety, but are not wanting in force and ingenuity; there is a pathos about the miner's oath, which strives to conceal his tears for the man who died for him.

> "Here in the damp,
> Out of the sun,
> That 'ar *derned* lamp
> Makes my eyes run."

"Derned," we may notice is the favourite American form; the

pages of Artemus Ward, Mark Twain and Bret Harte are studded with it; there is something very comic about "Jim," who hears of his own virtues from the friend, who imagines him dead, is gradually recognised and finally dismissed with:

> "Why, you limb!
> You ornery,
> Derned old
> Long-legged Jim!"

And Mark Twain is quite as ingenious and humorous as Bret Harte; the "dog-my-cats" of "Tom Sawyer" is good, and no reader of the doings of the Mississippi pilots can fail to admire their gifts of vocabulary; one of them is recorded as never venturing nearer to the luxury of swearing than "Dod dern," but most of them were great linguists, and one envies the old hand who could say without apparent effort, "you dash-dash-dash-*dashed*-split between a tired mud-turtle and a crippled hearse-horse!"

But though there is still much worthy of record, we must hasten to conclude with some remarks on modern everyday swearing. A theatre-goer cannot fail to perceive how much more the characters of our present stage plays swear than they used to. This is due to the type of man who at present is popular on the stage—the man of one virtue and a thousand crimes—the man who has, if we wait till the third act, some good about him after all, though his earlier career makes him a fit companion for the soiled dove, who is at present the favourite type of the other sex on the boards.

In private life strong language is, we imagine, neither stronger nor weaker than it used to be. Whether the Teutonic need of a dental, which has been suggested as a palliation for the practice, is an excuse, it is certain that most men cannot restrain themselves from swearing. The Bible (Matthew v. 34-36.—James v. 12) is quite clear on the subject, and so is the law. By 19 George II. cap. 21, "every labourer, sailor or soldier profanely cursing or swearing, shall forfeit one shilling; every other person, under the degree of a gentleman, two shillings; and every gentleman, or person of superior rank, five shillings, to the poor of the parish wherein such an offence was committed. Any justice of the peace may convict on his own hearing on the testimony of one witness."

Now that the unemployed are so rampant, the law, if enforced, would give not only employment but a fine harvest to the collectors, but it is practically a dead letter. It has, far from killing, not appreciably scotched the snake. Many respectable members of society, men of good repute, who return a borrowed umbrella, undeterred by moral and legal restrictions do swear freely, yet they manage to do without this verbal luxury in the presence of ladies. Are they so free because they know really that their oaths are *vox et præterea nihil*, winged words, which break no bones? When they consign their neighbour to perdition, they do not wish their fulminations to be carried into effect, for they are often the kindest-hearted of men.

The most frequent class of anathematists are those who swear on special occasions of trial, such as the loss of a train, a breakage, or a bad stroke at golf. Then the expletive appears in full force, and, acting as a safety valve to resentment, restores the ejaculator to good temper. This is certainly an advantage, and no other process seems so effectual to achieve these results. Thus the explosion has a real value to set off against the disgust of the onlookers, and horror of the other sex; and surely a momentary phrase is better than a sullenness of a quarter of an hour. As for the infringement of the rules of correct conduct in society, oaths come fairly under what an authority calls "the supreme code of the natural sympathies," which are "above the provincial bye-laws of etiquette."

We do not know that any satisfactory substitute has been suggested, which would take the place of imprecation; a writer indeed in the *Spectator* some time ago recommended "eloquence and blank verse" as the natural outlet of the feelings "among more highly developed human beings," but many will consider this remedy worse than the disease. If, then, we cannot do away with swearing, let us improve our current code—let us be more picturesque and less inclined to follow the common track. Swearing is an art; as Scaliger said, "*Ars est etiam maledicendi.*" Anything that is worth doing, is worth doing well, and the linguistic artist should compromise between the claims of the imagination and the understanding, combine solid sense with fancy, and remember that success depends as much on conscientious finish as native endowment.

EDGAR VALDES.

# Patty's Lovers.

### By MARGARET MACKINTOSH,
#### Author of "Miss Stilt's Suspicion," etc.

"THERE! It's done! And I don't think I could do it over again."

So intense and heartfelt was the relief expressed by Patty's tone, that, if any uninitiated mortal had heard her, he would straightway have jumped to the conclusion that the enterprising young person had just performed some such feat as crossing the Falls of Niagara on a tight-rope.

Whereas—she had only been trimming a bonnet!

Or, to be strictly accurate, a hat; a little, artless-looking, pancake-shaped affair, giving not the slightest indication of the awful tension involved in its make-up.

"No! I *don't* think I could do it over again," repeated Patty emphatically, holding her handiwork out at arm's length, trying to view its glories with a stranger's eye.

"And *I* don't think it would matter very much if you couldn't," retorted her cousin Ann grimly.

This unfeeling remark elicited a reproachful glance from Patty as she stepped to the old-fashioned mantel-mirror to try on the "dainty confection"—that is the orthodox expression, I understand.

Ann was really getting very cranky, she thought. Of course everybody knew that her bark was worse than her bite. But her bark had certainly been rather biting lately.

This was true—undeniably true. But there were extenuating circumstances.

Ann Flack, bordering on fifty, severely practical and strong-minded, had just had a disappointment.

What? In *love?*

Yes, in love.

Ann had been jilted by——Patty!

Sixteen years ago, Patty, then a dark-eyed dimpled baby of two, had taken by storm the heart of the brusque angular old maid, the only relative willing to fill the place of mother to the poor little orphaned mite.

They had been all the world to each other until that never-to-be-forgotten day when pretty, blushing, happy Patty had shyly whispered "Yes" to a certain mysterious question put to her by handsome Miles Grimond.

To think of it!

For the first male wretch that asked her, the little ingrate had deposed faithful Ann to the second place in her affections. It was horrible—*horrible*.

To see her toiling and moiling too, like a galley-slave, making new changes of raiment, and altering old—all to look charming in *his* eyes, the villain!—was almost more than human flesh and blood could endure.

There now! What was the meaning of that lovely smile dimpling her velvety cheek? She was anticipating the raptures *he* would go into over her new finery!

Bah! it was sickening. Ann hastily resumed her darning, with as much vicious energy as if the obnoxious Miles himself were at her mercy instead of an unoffending stocking.

"Well, how do you like it?" asked the vain little puss, thirsting for appreciation of her labours.

"I daresay I've seen you with worse," admitted Miss Flack grudgingly. "There's nothing notorious about it except these feathers sticking up into the air like horns. Could you not get them to lie down?"

"Ann!" Get them to lie down! Did ever anybody hear the like? When it had taken a blessed hour to coax them into their perpendicular position. "*Ann!* don't you know that's the very tip-top of the fashion?"

"I could well believe it"—sarcastically—"and I suppose if people *had* horns, and the fashion was to cut them off, you would be one of the first, you little goose——"

"Come, come! no disrespectful language, if you please," suddenly broke in a masculine voice from the door.

"Miles, oh, Miles!" exclaimed Patty, a radiant, beaming, transfigured Patty, "you bad boy, what a fright you have given us!"

"Well, I'm sure Ann deserves it," returned the newcomer, shaking his head at her in mock indignation. "Little goose, forsooth."

"Whatever I deserve, so do you, and worse," retorted that

lady drily. "Haven't I heard you call her a darling duck a hundred times? And a goose is better than a duck any day, and dearer too, as you'll find if you go to buy one."

"All right. We'll accept the ingenious apology," laughed Miles. "But "—slily—"don't you think that it's somebody else and not me, that you should be instructing in such details of household economy?"

"Don't be foolish," interposed Patty hastily. "I've got years and years to learn everything before———"

She broke off in such deliciously charming confusion that her lover, moved by an uncontrollable impulse, drew her towards him, and before Miss Flack's looking, not to say glaring, eyes, snatched one, two—ay, a dozen kisses from the sweet red lips.

"Miles, oh, how *can* you!" remonstrated Patty shamefacedly, pushing him away with both hands, and blushing rosy-red all over to the nape of her dear little soft white neck.

"I'm awfully sorry. I won't do it again—till the next time." This cool effrontery brought Ann nearer breaking the sixth commandment than she had ever been in her life before. "The fact is, I'm half beside myself to-night. Guess what has happened? You can't? Well, then, ladies, allow me to introduce you to the new manager of Hill's Printing Works."

"The new manager?" echoed Patty in blank astonishment.

Ann, with a swifter comprehension, turned pale. If he had been so promoted, there would no longer be any pecuniary obstacle to his setting up house immediately. Like a prisoner awaiting sentence she hung breathlessly on his reply.

"Yes! You've the honour of beholding in the flesh the new manager. Mr. Hill called me into his private room to-day and offered me the post. Three hundred a year. There's riches for you, Patty. We can get married now as soon as we like."

"As soon as *I* like," corrected she, her dark eyes sparkling mischievously.

"You little despot!" said Miles fondly.

Even his worst enemy (who shall be nameless), could not deny that this stalwart lover of Patty's worshipped the very ground on which she trod.

"You little despot! I see you mean to rule with a rod of iron."

"I wonder you would be in so great a hurry to get into a state of bondage," snapped Miss Flack, vindictively.

"Isn't it an astonishing infatuation! The moth and the candle over again. Seriously, though," lowering his voice tenderly, "what do you say, darling, to June?"

June! Of course the girl cried out at the bare idea. June! did he know that was only four months? Four *years* would be more like the thing. And so on, and so on.

With an awful sinking of the heart, Ann listened in silence. She knew the matter would end, as it did, by the happy day being fixed for the first of June.

Happy day, indeed! The thought of the impending separation was *too* much. While the lovers were taking a prolonged farewell at the door, Ann's overcharged feelings gave way.

No doubt this was most unheroic conduct. She should have been filled with nothing but joy at Patty's happiness if hers had been the unselfish affection one meets with in books. That self-abnegating devotion, for example, which enables a man not only to resign the girl he adores to a supplanting rival, but to idiotically — no! romantically — endow the pair with all his worldly goods, and, invoking blessings on their undeserving heads, sail as a missionary to Timbuctoo or Kamschatka.

A sacred regard for the truth compels me to confess that Ann's sentiment was not of this lofty order. It was, alas! of a more common, a more human, description. Her own loss bulked so much more largely in her mental horizon than anyone else's gain, that, instead of rejoicing, she had never, never felt so miserable.

When Patty, a tender smile still hovering about her lips, quietly re-entered the room, she was amazed and startled beyond measure by the unprecedented spectacle of her cousin in tears.

"What is the matter? Oh, *what* is the matter? Are you ill, dear?" swiftly springing to her side and dropping on her knees.

"No, no, it's nothing," quickly averting her face in order to surreptitiously wipe away the big drops with a stocking. "I—I —ran the darning-needle into my finger."

"Oh, you dear, story-telling old thing," reproved the girl, half laughing, half crying. "Would you try to deceive me? But it's no use. I know what you've been thinking. That I am going away to leave you here all alone. How could you think that? Leave *you*, who took me a little helpless child——"

Here an irrepressible sniff from her companion changed Patty's half crying into whole. And for full five minutes these two foolish creatures wept in each other's arms as if they had anything to weep about. Which of course they hadn't.

This outburst of emotion, however absurd it may have been, cleared the domestic atmosphere wonderfully. The knowledge that Patty loved her as much as ever and wanted her to form a third in the new home—although Ann herself never dreamt for an instant of doing so—tended greatly to reconcile her to the inevitable.

Indeed, as time passed, one would almost have imagined that the elder lady was more interested in the manifold preparations for the wedding than the younger; more bent on lavish expenditure, at least.

Where the necessary funds came from, she kept a profound secret from Patty. Although old Flack had left his only daughter the whole of his accumulated savings the worthy baker had not realised a fortune, and Ann's limited income could stand no unusual strain. Accordingly she had paid her man of business a private visit. The result being that the sum requisite for the present emergency was placed immediately at her disposal.

What though it would take many a year of the strictest economy to pay back the loan? Wouldn't there be one the less to keep? she asked herself with a mirthless laugh. And what in the world would she have to do but hunt after her little maid and nip in the bud the slightest tendency to waste? The *cinder-mavises* (tattered old dames whose morning avocation was rifling the buckets set out on the street for the dust-cart), shouldn't make rich off *her* in future. Stale bread, cold meat, scraps of soap, and candle-ends would all be looked after with a lynx eye. People said inferior articles were the dearest in the long run; she didn't believe it for her part. Just take tea, for instance. Didn't she see it the other day in a shop-window at one and fourpence a pound? And what she used was half-a-crown. Nearly double! Oh, it was wonderful, *wonderful* what saving could be effected in a house by really making a study of it.

So Ann determined to make a study of it. And meantime the spare bedroom grew fuller and fuller every day of the trousseau.

"It's only once, isn't it?" she replied briskly, in answer to Patty's remonstrances at the unheard-of extravagance. "You're not going to be a female Bluebeard. Moreover, I can assure you that you couldn't get things too grand for Miles' taste now."

"He's in a different position, you know," Patty, ever loyal to her absent lover, reminded her with a touch of dignity.

At the same time a momentary shadow clouded her bright face. Miles' ideas *had* become extraordinarily high-flown. The consequence no doubt of his being so often at Roselea, Mr. Hill's suburban mansion.

The girl smothered a half-sigh as she recalled the early halcyon days of their engagement, when rarely an evening passed without Miles' presence transforming the plain little sitting-room into a paradise on earth.

Again she chid herself, with quick self-reproach, for her unreasonableness. Was it not a matter for thankfulness that his master had taken a fancy to him?

Besides—and the blissful thought thrilled her with a rapturous happiness that made her soft eyes shine like stars—was not the time fast approaching when they two should be always together, to be parted nevermore!

"How much she cares for him," mused observant Ann with a feeling akin to awe. "I believe if he were ever to change, it would just break her heart. But, thank God!"—fervently—"there's no chance of that."

Say you so, faithful Ann? Could you but see at this moment on the lawn at Roselea, under the pale crescent moon, a pair of lovers arm-in-arm, the one handsome as Apollo, the other a graceful vision of golden hair and blue eyes, you would change your opinion.

It was the old story. Not of man's fickleness—Miles did not admire blonde beauties, moreover Edith Hill was ten years his senior, and owed her lovely complexion and the sheen of her golden locks to art—but of worldly ambition proving stronger than love.

A few evenings spent in the society of his employer's daughter had sufficed to show the new manager that she regarded him with no common favour. Had he been free to climb the ladder of fortune, it stood alluringly within his reach. Edith was an only and idolised child. The man of her choice would have brilliant prospects, for her word was law to her indulgent parent.

On the other hand, Miles Grimond gauged her shallow, selfish character well enough to guess that she would resent, nay, *revenge*, any slight put upon her. Once let her discover that her affection was unrequited—it would instantly turn to hate. In which case his post wouldn't be worth a day's purchase.

With the bewitching glamour of Patty's sweet presence upon him, he was strong to resist the temptation to be false to her. Give his own little darling up! Never, *never!* And in a passion of remorseful tenderness he would strain the slender figure to his breast with a vehemence that half frightened her.

Away from her, however, the evil spirit returned with redoubled force. Many a morning, the grey dawn stealing into the eastern sky found Miles sleepless, haggard, traversing his room with hurried strides, worn out with the mental conflict.

So the struggle went on, until the crisis came.

It happened in this wise.

One evening, on accompanying his employer home to dinner, Miles met with a markedly cold reception from Miss Hill. His uneasy speculations as to the cause of her altered demeanour were not set at rest till, the constrained meal over, she proposed an adjournment to the garden, ostensibly to admire the beds of hyacinths which were filling the air with their fragrance.

Out of earshot of the library window where her father sat reading his newspaper, Edith turned with a forced laugh.

"I suppose I must offer you my congratulations, Mr. Grimond, although it is rather mean, don't you think, to have kept it such a secret from your friends?"

"I beg your pardon. I don't know what you mean," rejoined her companion stiffly.

"Oh, yes, you do," significantly. "You can't deny that you are going to be married."

Miles started in spite of himself, and the light blue eyes fixed on him flashed dangerously.

"I know all about it. Smith, the house-agent, was here to-day on business, and he told me you were going to rent a cottage from him. Now a bachelor doesn't set up housekeeping unless——"

"Unless his mother is going to stay with him," interposed

Miles huskily, his ready wit rising to the occasion. The unequal battle between his good and bad angels was over. Overweening ambition had trampled love and honour in the dust.

"Your *mother?*" faltered Edith, scarcely daring to believe her ears.

"Yes, my mother thought of coming to town," repeated Miles, more boldly. Then with a world of tender reproach in his tone, he added, "Surely *you* might have known it could be nothing else."

"I—I—didn't think," stammered Edith confusedly.

"If it had been otherwise—would you—would you have *cared?*"

"Y—es," was the faint reply, and the brilliant colour flooding her cheek for once rendered rouge superfluous.

For one brief instant Patty's lover hesitated. Then, bending his handsome head, he sealed his perfidy by kissing the lips of another woman.

Rat-tat! the postman's double knock.

"A letter for you," announced Miss Flack, appearing immediately thereafter in the parlour, where Patty sat weaving sweet dreams of the future into a brilliant-hued sofa-blanket destined to adorn her own house.

"It's from Miles," she murmured, lingering fondly for a moment over the clear, bold writing. Then tearing it open with fingers trembling with happy excitement, she began to read.

"MY OWN PRECIOUS LITTLE DARLING,

"Can you forgive me for calling you by that dear name once more? It is the last time. Patty, I am no longer worthy of your love. For the sake of worldly advancement, I have become a liar, a coward, *the promised husband of another.*

"Never again may I look in your dear face. I *dare* not.

"My only prayer is—but what avails the prayer of such as I?—that you may soon learn to forget the most miserable wretch that walks God's earth."

"Well? What is the news?" asked Ann cheerfully, bustling in again.

Patty, bending over her bright blue and orange wools, did not speak. The other, struck by a sudden chill presentiment, intuitively lifted the fatal missive. A glance brought home to her the cruel truth.

"My poor darling," she burst forth pitifully, pressing the dear head to her bosom in an agony of grief and compassion. "Oh, if I could have saved you from this, my poor, poor, suffering darling."

Patty gently extricated herself from her embrace.

"Ann, how queer you are to-day!" she said, looking up with a smile.

A *smile?* Ay, a smile! A smile that drove the blood from Ann's heart in a tumultuous rush, and froze the words on her lips with a horrible fear.

A smile that, God forbid either you or I should ever see on the face of one we love.

\* \* \* \* \* \* \*

Three times the June roses had bloomed and faded. On the fourth anniversary of what should have been Patty's wedding-day, Ann Flack sat in the shabby parlour *alone*.

In the early dawn of the fair summer morning the gentle life had flickered and gone out. Not in darkness, thank God. At the end, what had been in truth a merciful veil hiding the past, lifted for a brief space.

"You will give Miles my message, dear Ann?" was her last weak utterance.

True to her promise, Ann now awaited his coming. Her hands lay idle in her lap. Her life-work was ended. No more tending of her precious, afflicted charge. No more amusing of the poor, clouded brain. Nothing but a dreadful, *dreadful* blank.

On the little empty rocking-chair in its accustomed place lay, as Patty had left it, what had once been the gay sofa-blanket. Though the nerveless fingers had lost the trick of knitting, the poor girl, associating it somehow with happier days, had never been so content as when trying, hour after hour, to recover the lost art.

The sight of it now, a faded, tangled mass of dropped stitches and broken threads, only served to intensify Ann's bitterness of spirit. With tearless, burning eyes she sat like a stern Nemesis, preparing herself to meet him who had broken her dear one's heart.

The hard, implacable resentment she had cherished against him all these long years was but feebly shadowed in the look of abhorrence with which she regarded him, when, at length, he was shown into her presence.

"So, Miles Grimond, you have come to see the result of your work——"

A low groan interrupted her—a groan that will haunt Ann Flack to her dying day.

On entering the room—the old, familiar room—his eye had gone straight to the *empty chair.*

Patty, dear, little, loving, tender Patty, was dead! *Dead*, and *he* had killed her. And, oh heavens, for what? For the ceaseless torture, night and day, of that remorse whose worm dieth not, and whose fire is not quenched.

An ashy greyness crept into his face, as he stood in silence, his head sunk upon his breast.

The harsh words of recrimination died on Ann's tongue, the harsh judgment in her heart.

This haggard, despairing, prematurely-aged man was not the prosperous, heartless worldling she had been ready to denounce. Leaning suddenly forward, she laid her hand gently on his sleeve.

"This is the message she left for you." Her tone was strangely softened. "'Give Miles my dear love, and——'"

"Stop, for God's sake, stop," cried the conscience-stricken listener hoarsely. "I—I—can't stand it."

"'Give Miles my dear love, and tell him not to be sorry,'" resumed Ann, after a pause, in a choking voice. "That was all. She passed peacefully away this morning. Come," rising to her feet, a divine, compassionate forgiveness transfiguring her homely features, "come, you may see her if you will. She lies with the same innocent, childlike smile on her face that it wore —the first time she fell asleep—in my arms—my poor—little— motherless—lamb——"

She motioned him to enter the darkened chamber, and with eyes streaming with blessed tears, softly closed the door.

# A Prosaic Idyll.

HERR SCHWANK'S manners were certainly wonderful. He was the admiration of all the guests when he entered the *salle à manger*, and, putting his heels together, bowed to each person in turn with such a charming smile that the shyest of Englishmen had to respond, and the most *gauche* of English girls give a little blushing inclination of the head in recognition of his greeting.

He was one of a little colony in a Swiss hotel high up in the Alps, consisting chiefly of English people, with a sprinkling of Germans, and a few Italians.

The air was invigorating, the scenery glorious, the hotel was clean if not luxurious; and, above all other attractions, there was a beautiful crystal lake close to the windows, on the calm surface of which were painted such lovely reflections of pine wood and snow peak, that it was a satisfaction to sit and gaze and be thankful for them.

Herr Schwank was the latest arrival of the guests at the Hotel Blanc, but he knew it well, as he came every summer to enjoy the air and rest his brain after a busy life in Berlin. He was elderly, with bristly grey whiskers, a little tuft beneath his under lip, a neat, upright figure, and the kindest grey eyes in the world.

Beyond his bows on entering and leaving the table d'hôte room, and a remark now and then on the weather, which he always described as "*wunderschön*," he had little intercourse with the other inmates. They used sometimes to wonder, as he was not a botanist, nor an artist, nor a great mountaineer, how he managed to pass two or three months each year in such a very isolated spot. However, when it became known that the Herr possessed five sisters, who kept house for him in Berlin, wonder at his evident enjoyment of his holiday ceased.

Soon after his arrival came two more English guests, a young girl and her father — Mr. and Miss Temple by name. The former was a man of small speech but much action. Climbing mountains appeared to be his chief delight, and wearing hygienic boots his first duty.

His daughter Betty was as pretty as a young girl need wish to be, and was at the delightful age of twenty-one, full of buoyant life and energy, and prepared to enjoy and do everything possible to a young woman on her first visit to Switzerland.

To begin with, she said, it was necessary to find out all about the other people in the hotel, and for this reason she permitted her father to start alone on some long expeditions, while she studied her surroundings.

"Oh, yes, I like walking," she answered the inevitable English lady full of curiosity and questions, "but just at present I want to look at everyone and see whom I shall like best. But," she added, "it is a bore that I have to sit next that funny German. I speak his language so badly, and yet of course I can't let dinner go on without saying something to him."

Accordingly, she used blushingly to venture short remarks, chiefly questions, to Herr Schwank, who, after the manner of his kind, answered her single remark with floods of guttural German and much gesticulation.

The Herr, however, understood English perfectly, and could speak it well; it was only his extreme politeness that made him treat the language in which Miss Betty Temple made her halting little advances, as the only medium of conversation.

Betty discovered this ere long, and as she was a sociable young woman, she soon drew her neighbour out, and they became great friends.

Betty Temple certainly was most attractive. Her great simplicity and freshness led strangers to think she was younger than she really was, and by the unobservant she might have been considered childish and unformed.

But she had plenty of character and a real charm which never failed to impress those who came to know her well. In certain ways she resembled a nice boy, in her absence of self-consciousness and girlish vanity, and she was often a puzzle to some of her friends who could not understand a companion who neither cared about the fashions, nor considered her complexion, and was bored alike by tea-parties and best frocks.

As neither of these last were necessary at the Hotel Blanc, there was nothing to mar her enjoyment. Yes, Betty was happy in the present, she had nothing but bright recollections of the past, and she had her private reasons to look forward with a thrill to something that promised to be happiest of all in the future.

There were not many people at the hotel that she cared much about. There were some strong-minded walking ladies, who, however worthy of respect, were not attractive. Their complexions of brick dust, the deer-stalker caps they wore, and their most unbecoming dresses, were a terror to the less strong-minded, and as they rose before dawn and passed most of the day in climbing mountains, they were reduced to such a state of exhaustion at night that the less energetic, but more conversationally-inclined guests, found little pleasure in their company.

There were some delicate people, ordered up to the heights for the sake of the pure air, and there were several young men from the English Universities, spending the Long Vacation in the wholesome recreation of mountaineering, tempered with study.

Betty accompanied her father on a good many long walks, but as he liked rather more than she could do without fatigue, she usually contented herself with rowing about on the lake, in the very unwieldy and flat-bottomed boat which belonged to the hotel, or taking solitary little walks about the mountainous paths.

The Alpine rose was in its full glory, also the gentian, St. Bruno's lily, and the brilliant blue aquilegia that grows like a weed amongst the stones on the mountain side, and which Betty saw, with anguish, eaten so remorselessly by the cows.

She used frequently to come across Herr Schwank on these scrambles, and soon the two became good friends. The stiff, middle-aged German, who for so many years had preferred solitude, was glad to meet her, and became quite light-hearted and sprightly under Betty's influence, and the two used to walk and chat and laugh together as if they had been acquainted for years instead of weeks.

He told her of his quiet life in Berlin, how fond he was of his little garden, and what an excellent housekeeper his sister Amalie was, how fond Hermina was of her chickens, what splendid needlewomen were Dorothea and Lieschen, and in fact, how fortunate he was to have such good sisters.

"German ladies always seem so clever," sighed Betty. "I am dreadfully ignorant; I wonder what they would think of me."

Their brother apparently did not think her much amiss, and he would find himself studying her and looking at her with more interest than he could have believed himself capable of feeling for any young girl, and all she said was invested with a charm in his eyes.

One day several of the English visitors and also Herr Schwank were sitting in the glass Rauchzimmer, the only fair-sized sitting-room in the hotel, when Mr. Temple mentioned that he had heard that some more visitors were about to arrive.

This was always rather an event, as the Hotel Blanc was cut off by three and a half hours' steady walking from the more populated world, and there was usually a certain amount of discussion and guesswork concerning the new arrivals.

"Oh!" cried the unguarded Betty, "I do hope they will be nice English people and not stuffy Germans; their women are generally so frightful, and the men eat with their knives!"

There was a sudden pause of horror and she caught her father's significant glance. In a moment she perceived her blunder.

Herr Schwank had meanwhile walked to the door, and passed out as though he had not heard the unfortunate remark. Betty stood thunderstruck for a moment, then she rushed after him, and down the little path that wound towards the lake.

She came up to him breathless, and caught him by both hands.

"Herr Schwank, forgive me, please, please do," she cried. "I always say the stupidest things without thinking, but really and truly you are so nice and delightful, and exactly all that a man ought to be, that I entirely forgot you were not English too."

Now this was scarcely a tactful speech, and Herr Schwank might well have been justified in thinking she had made matters worse, but no, though patriotic to the core, he appeared proud, joyful. He made one of his deepest bows, and taking Betty's hand he kissed it and said:

"Dear Fraulein, you do me too much honour!"

Surely this was not a consistent speech for a man who had always prided himself on belonging to the Fatherland? Take care! Take care! Herr Schwank! Betty is fascinating, you are by no means old. There is danger ahead!

Their intimacy increased each day, and Betty began to take

the German to task and to lecture him about anything in him she considered amiss and not up to her standard of the ideal Englishman. A pair of elastic-sided boots, with mother-of-pearl buttons, which he had considered very smart, had brought on him deep disgrace, and he was begged never again to wear such shocking things in civilized society (by which Miss Betty, of course, meant her own). Herr Schwank next day gave them to the good-looking Italian boatman who lounged about the boat-house.

This individual appeared to spend all his time in smoking and setting his nets in the lake for trout, which, as the less credulous of the guests affirmed, existed only in the advertisements issued by the hotel proprietors. It was indeed suggested that the nets were set, not so much to catch fish as men, in the persons of certain gentlemen who appeared from time to time with rods and tackle, and disappeared, leaving behind them maledictions on the lake, the hotel and its owners. The placid boatman, however, still smoked on and set his nets, and Herr Schwank and Betty Temple sauntered amongst the sweet-scented fir woods and made bouquets of the Alpine rose.

Herr Schwank began for the first time in his life to study his appearance, and many were the minutes he spent looking in the narrow little glass which hung above his wash-hand stand. He left it each morning more dissatisfied:

"Wrinkles! *many* of them; of grey hairs? *hundreds!* Pouf!" he would say to himself; "who would look at such an old stick except the kind sisters at home?"

But in spite of the kind sisters at home who were perfectly satisfied with him, Herr Schwank did try to make himself look nice. During the periodical visit of the barber to the hotel he had his hair cut as short as the closely-trimmed locks of the young English officer who sat opposite him at table d'hôte. He endeavoured to tie his ties as much as possible after the same model: he entirely discarded the services of a napkin which, formerly, he had so carefully tucked into his collar and round his neck.

Finally he made an expedition down into the world, and bought himself a straw hat. Now, he thought, he would be quite English, and all kinds of happy thoughts came into his mind as he slowly ascended the steep path to the hotel, wearing his new purchase set jauntily on his head.  His mortification was great when he met Betty, who burst out laughing on seeing him.

"Dear Herr Schwank," she cried, "why are you wearing a bee-hive on your head?  Where did you get such a funny hat?"

He took it ruefully off and asked if it did not resemble the "Herr officier's?" but he now noticed it was rather higher in the crown, though the plaiting of the straw was so quaint and clever, and the coloured silk tassel with which it was adorned, had seemed to him so exceedingly tasteful, that he had counted on Betty's unqualified admiration.  But no, she implored him to put it away and to wear the familiar grey felt once more. She then kindly cut holes in its crown with her own little scissors, because, she said, felt hats were so bad for the hair, and it would be a pity for him to become "more bald than he already was."

Unfeeling Betty!  What would the sisters at home have said had they seen their well-beloved and much-revered brother having his good hat cut recklessly to pieces for ventilation by a mere slip of a girl, and then a sprig of Alpine rose stuck into each little hole by way of a joke, while the well-beloved brother stood by looking delighted?

Mr. Temple was amused at Betty's friendship with the elderly foreigner, and rather congratulated himself that she preferred the latter's company to that of any of the younger men.

"Dangerous work, philandering with young University men," said Mr. Temple to himself; "one does not know who they are at home, and if a girl does fall in love, it generally is with the undesirable man."

That the German could ever dream of losing his heart to Betty had never entered her head or her father's, nor did Herr Schwank himself realise his predicament until one day when Betty had a headache and remained invisible till the evening.

Then he began to see that the joy of life had disappeared with her.  He tried to go for a walk as usual, but with no success. His feet were like lead, everything was dull, and his thoughts continually reverted to his last walk with her for his companion.

He remembered how pretty she had looked, what she had said, and how inanely he had answered her.  At this point he sat down and looked wistfully homewards.  What was the use of going on? He then began to wonder whether disparity in age was a drawback to connubial happiness—and how old Betty was? Here he rose and began absently retracing his steps to the hotel.

Continuing his train of thoughts, he asked himself when a man ought reasonably to cease falling in love, and did it make a difference whether he had never been in love before? Was he himself too old to think of being in love — and was Betty? Here he dropped his stick and wrung his hands together.

"Betty! Betty! always Betty," he cried. "Can it be, is it possible that I *am* in love? No, it cannot be so, it *must* not. Fool! idiot, that I am! such folly must be crushed down and not thought of." And picking up his stick, he turned sadly from home once more and started afresh up the mountain zig-zag path.

But his thoughts were beyond his control. Instead of the lake beneath, the sky above, and the flowers around him, he saw but one thing, a young English girl with laughing violet eyes, clad in dark blue, with a blue ribbon in her hat, and a bunch of wild flowers at her waist.

He tried to laugh at himself for his weakness, his madness, his infatuation, but again and again he paused, and thought of what might be. Yes! he was picturing his home with that bright vision in it. Someone beside the five sisters was now necessary to his happiness. Someone with rich curling brown hair and a figure that no German girl could ever possess (but then who in the whole world was like Betty?), with a voice whose distant ring made his heart beat, and with a presence that diffused happiness around her. Here he thought of his grey hair and inclination to baldness, and sighed.

What a dull miserable walk he was having! He must turn back, such solitude was insupportable. How could he have liked this place before, and come to it year after year before he had known her? What would it be like after she had gone? Ah! Now his heart stood still. That must not be, he must see her, ask her, question her, implore her to stay if necessary, but let her go he could not.

He hastened back to the hotel, only stopping to gather some aquilegia which he knew Betty loved.

On approaching the hotel he saw her familiar figure on the

grass plot in front of the door. Betty was leaning back in her chair and greeted him with a beaming smile.

"Welcome back, Herr Schwank. I suppose you have had a charming walk, and of course these flowers are for me?" (taking them gratefully from him). "But surely you are tired, you look so pale?"

"No, I am not tired, but tell me how you are," he answered, wondering if she could hear his heart which was beating so fast that it seemed to take away his breath.

"My headache is much better, I feel as happy as possible," said Betty; "we had some good news to-day, a friend of ours is coming out to join us here, and may arrive to-morrow. Father is so much pleased, and so am I; of course one is always glad to see one's friends," she hastened to add.

But Herr Schwank took no notice and was looking at her strangely. He cleared his throat——

"Miss Betty," he said, "you have made me very happy here, and I cannot think what this place would be like without you. Tell me——" but here he stopped. Why had Betty risen? What? *Who* was she looking at, and why had she so suddenly grown pale? He turned and saw that a tall, square-shouldered young man in a Norfolk jacket had come round the corner of the hotel behind him, and was advancing rapidly towards them.

"Miss Temple! Betty!" he cried, and then there was a pause.

Betty dropped her flowers and went forward to meet the newcomer with a look on her face Herr Schwank had never seen there before. The young man took her outstretched hand.

"I have got my First Class," he said, "and now will you give me your answer?"

Herr Schwank turned away with a sick feeling at his heart. After he had walked some distance he looked back once more. They were still standing as he had left them, and Betty was putting an aquilegia into the young man's buttonhole.

* * * * * * *

Herr Schwank took a real walk this time and only returned to the hotel when everyone had gone to bed. Next morning it seemed to be a generally-known fact that Miss Temple was engaged to a young Mr. Gascoyne who had come out to Switzerland on purpose to settle matters with her.

The young couple had started off for an early ramble, and only came back just as Herr Schwank's baggage was being strapped on a stalwart porter's back, preparatory to being carried down to the world of stations and steamers below.

The German stepped up to Betty with a smile, in which she saw nothing but his usual kind expression, and offered her his congratulations. He then told her that sudden business called him back to Berlin, and how much he had feared having to start without giving her his felicitations and bidding her farewell.

Betty looked genuinely grieved. "How can you think of going?" she exclaimed. "Fancy leaving these beautiful mountains, and the lake, and US in this glorious weather, just to muddle your brains with stupid business, when you ought to be having a holiday! However, it is not good-bye, it is 'Auf Wiedersehen.' Remember, Herr Schwank, we must meet here again next summer."

But it *was* good-bye, and he knew it, and as he walked away, and descended the steep mountain path, his heart felt very heavy. He was not only leaving the mountains and the lake that Betty spoke of, and which he had so loved, but he was leaving behind for ever something even more beautiful and precious, the brief and only romance of a simple chivalrous heart.

The Hotel Blanc saw him no more, and Betty never knew how nearly she had two proposals on that happy summer afternoon.

mentally restless child. Trifles unnoticed by most children seem to have made keen and permanent impression upon him— the sound of wind, the leafy whisper of trees and running water. The imaginative faculties came so early into play, that the unconscious desire to create resulted in the invention of weird tales of legendary creatures, tales sometimes based on remote fact; in attempted delusion of neighbours; and in the experience of more or less positive hallucinations.

We owe much of our scanty knowledge of this period of the poet's life to the fragmentary information in the letters of his sister Hellen; information, however, the value of which has occasionally to be somewhat discounted as not being distinctly reminiscent. It is clear that he was invariably a kind and gentle brother, displaying a consideration for his younger sisters which contrasts favourably with the conduct of most lads during the early years of the schoolboy stage. The little girls at Field Place loved his company, and when he was at home for the holidays he would walk about with them, and tell them many wonderful things; he would take one of them on his knees and thrill the soul of his listener with awful tales of wizards, hobgoblins and secret passages. The "Great Tortoise" was long a theme of endless fascination. This strange creature, unseen of any, abode in Warnham Pond; many a romance concerning it was told by the inventive Bysshe, and if a bull roared in a distant meadow, if a tree fell in the woodland, if midsummer thunder rumbled mysteriously, the sounds were always accounted to the "Great Tortoise."

In later years the "Great Old Snake" usurped its predecessor's place—an interesting circumstance to close students of Shelley's poetry, where serpents are frequently and most effectively introduced. The "snake" in question had a genuine existence, and met an accidental death through the scythe of a gardener.

Shelley from his early boyhood seems to have puzzled his worthy father, a choleric, narrow-minded, but excellent-hearted squire, who has been absurdly abused because he happened to hold radically different views from those of his son, and because that son went contrary to his desires in many things. It is suggestive that Bysshe's indoor tales, narrated in the grim hours of shadow, were grotesque or terrifying; and hardly less

26

so to them were the games in which he induced his sisters to take part. The children would be robbers, led by a daring chief; discoverers in some terrible land where awful revelations lurked in store for them; they would even personate spirits or fiends, the illusion being intensified by the blue flame which Bysshe would light and carry about in a small fire-stove. Even as a very young boy he took the keenest interest in chemical and electrical experiments; and while—as his sister Hellen has recorded—his sisters would sometimes tremble with fright when he called upon them to assist him, he never persisted in any experiment if he saw that he was causing pain or real fear. There was nothing of the cold-blooded experimentalist in Shelley at any time of his life, and it was in all sincerity that, in the beautiful opening of "Alastor," he wrote:

> "If no bright bird, insect, or gentle beast
> I consciously have injured, but still loved
> And cherished these, my kindred."

The poet's memory even as a little boy was remarkable. When a small child, Gray's lines on the "Cat and the Goldfish" were repeated by him word for word after a single reading. Shelley's earliest instruction commenced when he was six years old. Till his tenth year he remained under the educational guidance of the Rev. Mr. Edwards, of Warnham; though these four intervening years were mainly spent in gaining bodily vigour. It is a common mistake to suppose that the poet was an ethereal being from his infancy onward; at no period was he too far removed from common humanity to be other than a genuine creature of flesh and blood. He was naturally of a vigorous constitution, though he had always more or less of that appearance of delicacy which is so far from rare among emotional and imaginative young folk of either sex. That he suffered considerably in later years is undeniable, but certainly the mysterious pains which affected him in Italy were for the most part the penalties incurred by his habitual neglect of the body, by his occasional use of narcotics, and by a fitful asceticism, which was undoubtedly the shadow of the spiritual and intellectual light in which he habitually lived.

Every student of Shelley's poetry must remember his love of making fragile craft out of paper or iris flags, and setting them a-sail on stream, or pond. How early this sport, for a sport of irresistible fascination it always was with him, was habitually indulged in is uncertain ; but the poet certainly had himself as a very young child in view when, in " Rosalind and Helen," he wrote :

> " He was a gentle boy,
> And in all gentle sports took joy ;
> Oft in a dry leaf for a boat,
> With a small feather for a sail,
> His fancy on that spring would float,
> If some invisible breeze would stir
> Its marble calm."

When Bysshe—the name always used by his relations—was ten years old, he was promoted from Mr. Edwards' care to that of Dr. Greenlaw, at Sion House, Brentford. There he certainly was not happy. For one thing, the mental stimulus too strongly dominated the physical energies for him to care much for the ordinary sports of boyhood. Again, Sion House was frequented by the sons of tradesmen, between whom and Shelley there was the shadow of a mutual antagonism. Genius cannot always free itself from conventional bonds, and the fact is evident that Keats undoubtedly resented Shelley's superior birth, when circumstances brought them together, although, while still a youth, Shelley lost all perception of class distinctions, and gladly took for granted the essential equality of all men who could meet on common intellectual ground.

At Sion House fagging was in full force, and the almost feminine beauty, and look of innocence and gentleness of the boy, tempted his schoolmates to affront and torment one whom they at first considered a milksop. Every spare moment Shelley could gain was spent in solitary reading or musing, and no doubt his early days at Brentford and Eton had a great effect upon his character, emphasizing what was noble in his nature, and developing certain traits which, without being good or evil in themselves, were later in his life to cause both him and his friends real distress.

The narrative of Shelley's early boyhood may be closed with Medwin's description of his cousin's personal appearance at this time. " He was tall for his age, slightly and delicately built, and rather narrow-chested, with a complexion fair and ruddy, a face rather long than oval. His features, not regularly handsome, were set off by a profusion of silky brown hair, that curled naturally. The expression of his countenance was one of exceeding sweetness and innocence. His blue eyes were very large and prominent. They were at times, when he was abstracted, as he often was, in contemplation, dull, and as it were insensible to external objects, at others they flashed with the fire of intelligence. His voice was soft and low, but broken in its tones—when anything much interested him, harsh and unmodulated; and this peculiarity he never lost. He was naturally calm, but when he heard or read of some flagrant act of injustice, oppression or cruelty, then, indeed, the sharpest marks of horror and indignation were visible in his countenance."

At the age of twelve Shelley was removed to Eton, and the change was not one that brought happiness to the thoughtful, imaginative boy. He was placed in the house of Mr. Bethell, a tutor who was the butt of the whole school, and apparently deserved the ridicule bestowed upon him. The head-master was a Dr. Keate, distinguished among his compeers for pugnacity, vigour, and self-assertion, and among Etonians for his brutality. Shelley received many floggings, besides the innumerable fag-thrashings from older schoolfellows, but to corporal chastisement he finally became indifferent, and even endured it with courageous defiance. The lad's life was rendered miserable to him. He was baited, worried, jeered at, and tormented till he gave way to paroxysms of rage, which "made his eyes flash like a tiger's, his cheeks grow pale as death, his limbs quiver." His fury when roused to extremes of anger and indignation, his reckless denunciations of those in authority, his wild language, his love of reading and solitude, his experimental antics, and his often eccentric demeanour, earned him the name of "mad Shelley."

The poet's literary life may be said to have budded at Eton. It was before his departure therefrom that he began the poem of "Queen Mab," though its composition, as we now know it, must be set down to the winter of 1812-13; that he wrote some short poems, and in collaboration with Medwin, composed a romance entitled "Nightmare," and that he finished his much-discussed boyish effort in fiction, "Zastrozzi." He left Eton abruptly, for what reason has never been made clear, though most probably his full expression of his views, his persistent studies in branches of knowledge tabooed at school, and his defiant attitude against what he considered oppression, invited the ill-will of Dr. Keate and others in authority.  When he left it was with the affection of his comrades, and he was frequently visited in Oxford by those who had been attracted to him during the turbulent years of his schoolboy life.

Shelley was an apt scholar, and gained a great deal of classical and miscellaneous knowledge while at Eton.  He translated in his leisure hours several books of Pliny's "Natural History," being especially impressed by the chapter "De Deo," in which the Roman philosopher censures superstitious myths of the loves and wars of anthropomorphic deities.

It was while at Eton that Shelley's liking for a girl-cousin, Harriet Grove, ripened into real sympathy and affection.  Miss Grove was exceedingly pretty, was of an ardent temperament, and treated orthodox religions and social opinions in a way that wholly charmed her unconventional cousin.  When Bysshe took up his residence in Oxford he continued to correspond at great length with Harriet, and gradually the young girl and her friends became alarmed at the advanced and extravagant opinions expressed in the young undergraduate's epistles.  There was at this time no definite engagement, but Shelley undoubtedly loved his beautiful cousin with sincerity, and their marriage was looked upon as a foregone conclusion by everybody.

Shelley's love of nature, always keen, became intensified during the season he spent at Field Place before he went to Oxford.  Long walks in the early morning, rambles by night, and solitary musings in lonely places, at once soothed and stimulated his mind.  The young poet entered University College as a Leicester scholar; the nomination to which was due to an influential family connection.  According to Hogg—the friend whose record of Shelley's Oxford life is more interesting than any other, Bysshe during his first term was more occupied with chemical and scientific pursuits than with literature; yet it is clear from what we know of his productions at this time, that he dabbled considerably both in prose and verse.  Few visitors to Oxford with any interest in literature, fail to see the rooms in University which Shelley occupied: but the poet's training, bent of mind, his rapidly increasing revolutionary ideas, along with his inherent indifference to what was clothed with the veneration of age and even of romance, wrought against his perception of what was lovely and of good report in the ancient city and its still more ancient institutions; he felt only its intellectual stagnation, its spiritual torpor, its bondage to the most wearisome conventionalities.

Shelley now published his second novel, "St. Irvyne," or, "The Rosicrucian": it is in some ways an improvement on "Zastrozzi," but it is equally morbid, unreal, grotesque, and inflated. About this period Shelley also published a third novel, in conjunction with Hogg, called "Leonora." The printers who began to set it up refused to proceed on account of the "free notions" which were interwoven with the narrative, and Shelley took it to a printer at Abingdon named King; the latter had nearly completed the printing of it, when the premature extinction of "Leonora" occurred, owing to the abrupt expulsion of both its authors from Oxford on account of Shelley's famous tractate on the Necessity of Atheism. This famous tract was printed at Worthing, and sown broadcast. Shelley enclosed it in envelopes to dignities and persons of repute. He was remonstrated with, but remained obdurate; and finally all the copies of the obnoxious tract which were readily procurable were destroyed. The authorities, however, took the matter up, with the result that the college life of Percy Bysshe Shelley and his friend Thomas Jefferson Hogg came to an abrupt termination.

Shelley felt his expulsion keenly, was almost prostrated by the sentence, when he found it irrevocable, and was only saved from utter wretchedness by his growing anger and indignation at what he considered gross injustice on the part of the authorities. While we may reprobate the severity of the college council, we must in justice admit that it acted quite within its rights. It is useless to speculate on what did not happen, yet one cannot but wonder how very different Shelley's life must have been had he remained at Oxford for the usual period. He would almost certainly not have married Harriet Westbrook, an event which was the beginning of much sorrow, transitory happiness, and intransient pain — one which also ushered in years of splendid, and in some ways unparalleled, achievement in literature.

The final blow to Shelley's heart in his expulsion from Oxford was the termination of the definite or understood engagement between himself and Harriet Grove, but his sufferings were transient. It was not long afterwards that his fancy was taken by the pretty face of another Harriet, aged sixteen, whose father was a well-to-do coffee-house keeper; in addition to his functions as tavern host he was wont to add those of a money lender, hence his sobriquet of Jew Westbrook. The family lived in Chapel Street, near Grosvenor Square, and besides Mr. and Mrs. Westbrook consisted of Miss Elizabeth (the "Eliza" of the Shelley letters and biographies) and of Miss Harriet—the elder sister a sour, affected, interfering, and troublesome woman; the younger full of spirit, and at once charming and comely. Partly from romantic sentiment, partly from genuine affection, Harriet Westbrook discovered that she cared for "Mr. Percy Shelley," poet and reformer. Her elder sister would fain have won that young gentleman for herself, but when she realised that he was indifferent to her charms, she did her best to ensure a union between him and her sister.

When Harriet Westbrook first knew Shelley she held, as was natural, no pronounced views of any kind. Whom the poet loved he proselytized. When she first learned that Percy was an Atheist she was shocked, but to his religious, philosophical and social views she ere long lent a ready ear. She was a lovely and clever girl, more intellectually inclined and more widely cultured than the majority of young ladies at that period, and in these respects she was doubtless a fitting mate for Shelley; there were radical differences of nature, however, which were of more vital import than any similarity of views upon mental problems. The young people saw more and more of each other, and, when they were separated by Harriet's father, an active correspondence was maintained. The outcome of the tragi-comedy which began with the elopement of the young lovers was sad enough to invest any recital of their brief married life with an ever-imminent shadow.

It was mainly owing to the kindly mediation of Shelley's maternal uncle, Captain Pilfold, that father and son were so far reconciled as to permit of the latter paying a visit to Field Place. The result of this visit was an arrangement whereby Mr. Shelley agreed to allow his son an annuity of £200, with full permission for Bysshe to reside wheresoever he chose, and to pursue his own way of life, but on the understanding that though he might correspond, he was to have no personal communication, with Hogg. The terms were reluctantly accepted, but the young poet rejoiced at the comparative freedom he could now enjoy. Bysshe was quite aware that he was heir to a large fortune, but he also had no expectation of ever enjoying it. The fear, or rather the conviction, of early death had taken possession of him. Like many young men of imaginative bent, he was more conscious of the shadow cast by the beauty of life than of its exceeding brightness. With the conviction that he had but a year or two, at most but a few years, to live, Shelley naturally thought little of his possible future wealth, and was content to have an adequate income meanwhile.

After his reconciliatory visit to Field Place, he yielded to one of those attacks of nervous unrest to which he was subject throughout life, and spent the ensuing weeks, now at Field Place, now at his uncle's house at Cuckfield, now in London, and for a brief while at Cwm Elan, near Rhayader, in North Wales. It was during this visit that Hogg received a note which astonished him. He learnt that his friend would probably, ere long, be in York with *Harriet Westbrook*, that the latter's father had persecuted her in a most horrible way by endeavouring to compel her to go to school, that Harriet had appealed to the writer, whose advice was to resist such tyranny; that she had written to the effect that she threw herself upon his protection, and would fly with him, and that "gratitude and admiration demand that I should love her for ever."

Shelley determined to reward Harriet's trust by a legal marriage. He made hurried preparations for an elopement. To the social distinction between the heir to a baronetcy and great wealth and the daughter of a tavern-keeper, Shelley was from his convictions wholly indifferent. He admired and sincerely liked Harriet Westbrook, and he would not have been the youth he was had he not been keenly sensitive to her charms of mind and body, her accomplishments as a musician, a reader, and a good listener; but it is undoubted that Shelley did not return her affection as a lover. He expressly spoke in one of his letters to Hogg as being actuated more by will than by "inspired passion."

Keen suffering and remorse would have been avoided had

Mr. Westbrook been able to prevent the elopement of his daughter with Percy Shelley. However, as they had sown to reap the whirlwind, they had, by the laws of nature, to realize its violence when the time came.

Early one morning towards the end of August, 1811, Shelley and his cousin, Charles Grove, met Harriet and drove to the inn in Gracechurch Street, whence the Edinburgh coach at that time departed. The fugitives waved good-bye from the top of the coach to young Grove, who went home with probably the lightest heart of the three. By the time the coach reached York, a night and a day after leaving London, the bridegroom designate had realized that no one can get on without money. He had borrowed £25 from his Uncle Medwin, but this seems to have almost disappeared by the time the borrower had reached York, and had it not been for the aid obtained from his friend Hogg, the straits to which the youthful pair would have been reduced would no doubt have been serious. At last Edinburgh was reached, and there the runaways were quietly married on the 28th August, when Percy Bysshe Shelley, ætat 19, became the lawful husband of Harriet Westbrook, ætat 16. Shelley was set down in the books of the registrar as a Sussex farmer!

When the poet's father heard the news of his imprudent marriage he stopped all supplies, even the quarterly allowance then due was retained, and "all was at an end."

It would have gone badly for Shelley had it not been for Hogg, and, in a greater degree, for his Uncle Pilfold, who had taken a fancy to his enthusiastic, wonderful, eccentric, puzzling, loveable nephew, and who in time of need behaved in a most generous way.

Some weeks passed happily enough in Scotland, though Shelley was often bored by the placid pleasure Harriet took in reading aloud certain highly intellectual and ethical classical works; the poet was wont to fall asleep, much to his young wife's disapproval. Even at this early period of her matrimonial life, and when she was undoubtedly happy, Harriet frequently spoke of suicide, not only as a justifiable act under certain circumstances, but as permissible in most cases—nay, further, of the possibility that she would herself at some future date put her theory into practice. If Hogg's account be credible, Harriet even attempted suicide while at the seminary at Clapham Common. Harriet Shelley was without doubt abnormally insensitive to certain matters to which most men and women are keenly alive, that, in a word, she had either an exceptional stoicism or a bluntness of feeling germane to—if not the symptom of the condition of—a partially diseased brain. It would be unjust to her, however, not to concede that in the ordinary course of life she was a cheerful, clever, and amiable person, and that as a wife she was as sympathetic as her nature permitted, and in all things dutiful and loyal.

Cities which have charmed and fascinated many true poets did not enthrall Shelley. He was more keenly interested in Irish politics and philosophy than in any beauty of ancient days or picturesque aspects of ruins. Thus it was that five weeks in Edinburgh more than sufficed for him, and he moved to York, the journey occupying three days. Shelley determined to make a sudden journey south, and see if he could not soothe the paternal wrath, and obtain the necessary means of living, the absence of which was daily becoming more serious; but, unhappily, he was unsuccessful in his endeavour. The young couple, accompanied by Eliza Westbrook, now moved to Keswick, where they resided in a small house called Claremont Cottage, from the garden of which could be seen a lovely view of Derwentwater and Bassenthwaite, and the lofty summits of Hindsgarth, Skiddaw and Scawfell. Here Shelley enjoyed, as he had never hitherto done, the ever-varying loveliness and wonder of mountain beauty. While in the Lake country he came to know Southey. Between them there was only a superficial literary sympathy, and a very real social and political antagonism; as a man, however, Southey had the young poet's warm regard. Wordsworth, the most ungenial of bards to brethren-in-song, paid him no attention, and Coleridge was not then in the Lake country. Besides the production of a variety of short poems, Shelley spent part of the early winter in the composition of a volume of essays, presumably on political and ethical subjects, and of a romance entitled " Hubert Cauvin," which has never been discovered in manuscript or in any other state. Under the most favourable circumstances Shelley could never have become a great writer of fiction; his insight into ordinary humanity was slight, he had too little sense of humour, and mere abstractions were too real to him.

In December Shelley heard of a scheme at Field Place, whereby he was to be offered at once a handsome sum in the event of his consent to entail the estates on his male heir, or failing such, upon his younger brother. This bribe, as the poet believed it, was to amount to no less than £2,000 a year. Nothing more vividly shows Shelley's high moral resolve in a good cause than his indignant refusal to entertain the proposal for a moment. Poor as he was, he was not going to perpetuate by a selfish action what he considered to be the great evil of the law of primogeniture. It is to the credit of Mr. Timothy Shelley that, though hurt and disappointed by his son's refusal, he agreed to grant the allowance of £200 a year, to which Mr. Westbrook added another £200 a year; this sum was not increased by any literary labour on the part of Shelley, but was considerably diminished by printers' bills and charitable deeds.

On leaving Keswick Shelley took up his abode in Dublin. Here Eliza Westbrook acted as dispenser of the funds, keeping all the cash "in some nook or corner of her dress." The poet's aim in coming to Ireland was merely to "effect a fundamental change in the constitution of the British Empire, to restore to Ireland its native Parliament, to carry the great measure of justice called Catholic Emancipation, and to establish a philanthropic association for the amelioration of human society all over the world." His "Address" was sown broadcast.

"I stand," writes Shelley, "at the balcony of our window and watch till I see a man *who looks likely*. I throw a book to him." But Shelley, though his frequent phrase was "for ever," had no intention of remaining "for ever" in Dublin. He realized in less than two months that his mission in Ireland was over. The unhappy nation had not risen *en masse* on the publication of the "Address"; the authorities had not prosecuted "the young English gentleman"; and the world went on very much as before.

Shelley had another motive for returning to England. The divine Miss Kitchener, the schoolmistress of the Sussex village of Hurstpierpoint, longed to see her ardent correspondent and friend, even as that individual yearned to see "the soul of his soul." Like Miss Westbrook, this highly intellectual woman rejoiced in the name of Eliza, therefore Shelley substituted therefor the more euphonious "Portia." In a short space of time

Shelley found it expedient to change this Shakespearian designation to the "Brown Demon." Ere long she was hated by Eliza Westbrook, disliked by Harriet Shelley, and finally repelled by the "soul of her soul," and had to be bribed to take her departure. Yet this experience did not cure the poet of his tendency to invest every new and sympathetic correspondent with hues of ideal glory.

After leaving Ireland the pair settled in Wales for a time, and then moved to Devon. The late summer of this year was one of the comparatively serene periods in Shelley's life. He was happy with his wife, and above all, he was beginning to realize that he was indeed a poet, though even yet he had written little or nothing on which to base a claim so often unjustifiably put forth; but in a short space from this time he placed in the hands of Mr. Hookham, the publisher, the manuscript of "Queen Mab," and arranged for its publication in a limited edition. A little girl was born to this young couple, and Shelley, not yet of age, realized that he was not only a husband but a father! The baby was christened Ianthe, possibly after the violet-eyed lady of "Queen Mab," though, poor child, it was destined to bring, not happiness, but grief, to its parents. That he loved the little one is beyond doubt; and though it is by no means always safe to accept a poetic record as a strictly veracious statement, one cannot read his touching and beautiful sonnet to Ianthe without realising his absolute sincerity. In this sonnet there is unmistakably set forth his love for his wife and child:

> "Dear art thou, O fair and fragile blossom;
> Dearest when most thy tender traits express
> The image of thy mother's loveliness."

In the first beauty of motherhood, Harriet seemed more closely drawn to Shelley than ever. It was not long, however, before he noticed with pain and sorrow—what was evident to Hogg and others as well as himself—that his wife betrayed a strange and growing insensibility to her child and even to him; that she lost her interest in those matters of the heart and mind which were to him far above all mundane circumstances, and that she was no longer the Harriet whom he had known and loved. Maternity seemed to have been the spell which resolved the angel into the commonplace woman. To be ideally loved by a man like Shelley is to court sorrow and disaster. As the divine Portia, "the soul of my soul," passed away from the poet's life as the "Brown Demon"; as Eliza Westbrook, once intelligent and amiable, awakened in her brother-in-law "an inexpressible sensation of disgust and horror to see her caress Ianthe," and even "sometimes made him feel faint with the fatigue of checking the overflowings of his unbounded abhorrence for this miserable wretch," so poor young Harriet was to pass out of the valley of enchantment. That she was in some ways to blame for the estrangement is unquestionable, but it is with pity we read of her life from this time forth. On the other hand, again, it must not be forgotten that Shelley married his wife, not from love, as commonly understood, but out of chivalrous generosity. Love, the overwhelming love of a man for a woman, was lying in wait for him, but the time was not yet come.

The winter of 1813 was spent in Edinburgh, so far as Shelley was concerned, mainly in arduous and abstruse study; but he produced little literary work beyond the prose dissertation, entitled "The Refutation of Deism." From thence he wrote an urgent letter to his father about his pecuniary troubles, but failed to obtain any assistance. It was suggested to him that if a son and heir were born, Sir Bysshe and Mr. Shelley might seek to bring forward a claim of illegitimacy, on account of his marriage in Scotland as a minor. To prevent any trouble in this direction he re-married Harriet at St. George's, Hanover Square, on the 24th of March. This re-marriage is, to us, the seal upon Shelley's early happiness. Want of sympathy and other alienating influences had now set in clashing currents from either side. Harriet became hard and indifferent; her husband grew more and more disappointed and disenchanted. Ianthe was but a frail bond of union; her mother's refusal to nurse her still further exasperated Shelley. In April Eliza took her departure, and with her went Shelley's wife and child, while he remained in the congenial household of the Boinvilles, some friends whom he had met in Berkshire.

It was while conscious of his ruined love and vanishing affection, and while suffering keenly from Harriet's indifference to his appeals that Shelley met Mary Godwin. Love arose, nay, love enveloped them both ere they were aware of their position; like a fiery wind, it consumed and swept away all obstacles to their passion. Mary was then in her seventeenth year, but had the carriage and demeanour of one accustomed to womanly ways of thought and action; she was fair to look upon rather than lovely, of an intellectual type; of a calm and apparently passionless exterior, she had an ardent nature, and was, in a word, just such a child of William Godwin and Mary Wollstonecraft as the theorist might have prophesied. By training, by temperament, by imagination —in all things she was fitted to mate with such a one as Shelley. She could be to him all that Harriet had been, and infinitely more, as he could be to her an ideal, a friend, and a husband—a triune creature beyond the conception of the girl-wife who had voluntarily left him, though without thought of definite separation.

Peacock, who at this period was closely intimate with the poet, says:

"Nothing that I ever read in tale or history could present a more striking image of a sudden, violent, irresistible, uncontrollable passion, than that under which I found him labouring when, at his request, I went up from the country to call upon him in London. Between his old feelings towards Harriet, from whom he was not then separated, and his new passion for Mary, he showed in his looks, in his gestures, in his speech, the state of a mind 'suffering, like a little kingdom, the nature of an insurrection.' His eyes were bloodshot, his hair and dress disordered."

It was almost accidentally that Shelley and Mary Godwin learned the secret of their love. The following verses are the poetic record of this period of passionate uncertainty, but though touching in sentiment they are juvenile in expression for so consummate an artist as Shelley was soon to become:

> " Upon my heart thy accents sweet
> Of peace and pity fell like dew
> On flowers half dead; thy lips did meet
> Mine tremblingly; thy dark eyes threw
> Their soft persuasion on my brain,
> Charming away its dream of pain.
> We are not happy, sweet! our state
> Is strange, and full of doubt and fear;
> More need of words that ills abate;
> Reserve or censure come not near
> Our sacred friendship, lest there be
> No solace left for thee or me."

From a pathetic letter written by Harriet from Bath early in July it is manifest that she had no idea of the permanency of the separation. Four days' silence had been sufficient to break down her reserve. Not having heard from Shelley for this brief period, she feared that some misfortune had waylaid him, and therefore she wrote a letter of anxious enquiry to Hookham, the bookseller, as one certain to be acquainted with Shelley's whereabouts. But by this time the latter was persuaded (on evidence very dubious even when most convincing) that his wife had been unfaithful to him; that, in a word, Harriet's as yet unborn child would not be of his parentage. Later he came to believe absolutely that in this point, at any rate, he had wronged his wife, and that Charles Bysshe was veritably his own son. With his peculiar views on marriage—views, it must be remembered, shared by his wife—the contract between a man and a woman was one dissoluble at will, on proven incompatibility of mind and tastes, and still more imperative seemed disunion when married lealty no longer existed.

When Shelley realized that in no case could he again regard Harriet as his wife, and that Mary Godwin had won his love, he determined to offer Harriet his friendship, and incredible as it may seem, he even urged her to live with him and Mary. It may be as well to give here the record of Harriet Shelley's after-life. She continued to correspond with her husband after his departure for the Continent with Mary Godwin, and hoped against hope that he would tire of her as he had of others, and return to her. She retired to Bath, and there her boy was born. On his return to England Shelley visited his wife and they agreed to name the child Charles Bysshe. He died in boyhood, some four years after the Spezzian Sea had calmed for ever the passionate unrest of his father's life. When at last Harriet realized the finality of her disunion with Shelley, she gave way to bitterness of heart. If her love had been lasting she would have yielded to despair; that this was not so is to be inferred from the fact that she formed a new connection. This resulted unfortunately, and then poor Harriet saw nothing worth living for. The reader will remember that she had always maintained not only the inviolable right of every human being to end at will his or her life, but had also again and again, at long intervals and before various witnesses, declared her intention to put her theory in practice the moment the burden of life should become too great for her to endure. In no fit of despair, but unable to bear her anguish, she left her lodging near her father's house one day early in November, over two years after Shelley's departure with Mary Godwin, and found rest from her grief in the waters of the Serpentine.

To narrate the incidents of Shelley's life impartially it is necessary to avoid the language of unqualified approval or of condemnation. It is better to leave readers to form their own conclusions on the poet's separation from his wife, her subsequent course of life, and her suicide. Shelley seems to have been guiltless of wrong intent, and to have believed that he was acting not only consistently, but wisely and even justly, and his sorrow and life-long regret for the unfortunate outcome of his action were genuine. It is doubtful if his philosophy brought him any comfort—the philosophy that told him he could in no wise be held responsible for what had occurred. It is a sad story whichever way we look upon it.

Mary Godwin shared her father's and her lover's views on the subject of marriage. When she and Shelley left London on the morning of the 28th July, 1814, they were accompanied by Miss Clara Mary Jane Clairmont—by her relatives called Jane, but to the Shelleys and their friends known as Clare or Claire—the daughter by a former marriage of Godwin's second wife. Mary was fair and suave, Claire was dark and extremely vivacious. Both at this time were young girls, and were affectionate companions, if not friends. There is some uncertainty as to whether or not Miss Clairmont left Godwin's house with Mary with knowledge of what was about to take place. Her own account (but she was by no means always a reliable authority concerning herself) was, that she left the house in the silent summer morning, believing that she and Mary were only going to indulge in an exceptionally early walk; and that when they met Shelley at the corner of Hatton Garden he begged her to accompany him and Mary to France, as she was a good French linguist, and they were unfamiliar with the language. The three journeyed to Paris, and thence with little delay to Switzerland, and finally settled at Brunnen on the Lake of Lucerne. Here Shelley began the last of his prose tales; it is well written, and the finest portion of it describes the beautiful valley of Beltrzatanai. Want of money caused an abrupt return, and the homeward journey was made by way of the Reuss and the Rhine. This trip gave Shelley the greatest part of the material wherefrom he extracted the glorious lines of "Alastor."

Early in January of 1815, Shelley's prospects materially improved, owing to the death of his grandfather, Sir Bysshe. By an arrangement with his father, now Sir Timothy, he found himself in possession of a yearly income of £1,000. Of this allowance a fifth part went to Harriet and the children, and no inconsiderable portion of the remainder was charitably expended. Many hours weekly were spent by Shelley in assisting the needy, and it is said (though on no good authority) that he even walked a hospital, in order to acquire sufficient medical knowledge to be of real service to the poor, whom it was his wont to visit. Shelley was very fragile in body and frail in constitution, but did not suffer from any organic complaint; most of his symptoms could be traced to the nervous disorder which naturally ensued from his habits of fasting, from insufficient nourishment, and excessive mental excitation. At all times from his boyhood he consciously dwelt in the shadow of early death; a fact which must be remembered when we come to consider his poetic development, powers and achievement.

In the month of February, Mary gave birth to a girl-babe, a delicate infant, which only lived for twelve days. The grief experienced by both parents at its death was poignant.

Shortly afterwards Shelley took a cottage at Bishopsgate, on the eastern borders of Windsor Park. Here he passed many happy days, and at this time "Alastor" was written, the poem wherein he first rises into the realm of absolute poetry. A delightful water excursion was planned in August, in which Peacock and Charles Clairmont were of the party. At Oxford they disembarked, and Shelley showed Mary his former haunts, and the rooms he and Hogg had occupied when the fiat of expulsion had gone forth against them. From thence they proceeded to Lechlade, and here he was touched with the pathos and mystery of the scene. The Thames near Lechlade has inspired at least two great poets since Shelley's time, but none has written lovelier stanzas than those composed by the youth of twenty-three.

"Queen Mab," and its heterodox notes have been frequently republished in this country and in America, and have undoubtedly had a wider circulation than any other of Shelley's writings. It is asserted that the poem, with its voluminous notes, has had a very considerable influence upon the working classes in the direction of free thought. It is in no sense a great poem; herein all qualified judges agree. But it has passages of considerable beauty, and is distinctly a noteworthy production, however regarded.

"Alastor" is a Greek term, signifying an avenging spirit. Alastor is, as Mr. Symonds has well put it, the Nemesis of solitary souls. The narrative relates how the poet leaves his home, and wanders far abroad through the Empires of the East, where he has a vision of a veiled maid, a vision which causes the fire of deathless yearning to arise in his heart. At length, in pursuit of this phantasmal beatitude, he embarks in a little shallop, and is at last stranded close by the verge of a great fall of water. The poet then roams through a primeval forest, in a remote corner of which he finds Death. The allegory is easy of perception; "the veiled maid" is the ideal love unattainable in mortal guise. This passionate quest of ideal loveliness haunted Shelley's dreams by day and night. Again and again he has uttered something of the pain at his heart—in "Alastor," in the hymn to "Intellectual Beauty," in "Epipsychidion," and in many of his short poems. In "Alastor," Shelley passes from apprenticeship to masterhood. His blank verse is at once beautiful and majestic.

On January 24th, 1816, Mary gave birth to a son, the son to whom the name of William, in honour of Godwin, was given, and who a few years later was buried in that lovely Roman cemetery where lie the remains of two of England's greatest poets.

Shelley now determined to go to Switzerland again. This trip was urged by Claire Clairmont, who had another aim in view than the wish to see Geneva. In London, she had become acquainted with Lord Byron. She had called upon him to solicit his interest in obtaining a post for her in a certain theatre, but from the first moment she saw him she fell in love with him. Byron was conscious of her infatuation, and took advantage of it. Claire knew of his intention to go to Geneva, and, aware of the fact that he did not mean to burden himself with her company, she urged Shelley to make that Swiss town his goal, in order that she might meet her lover. The Shelleys did not even know that she was acquainted with the name, much less the person of "Childe Harold."

The Lake of Geneva was full of fascination for Shelley, haunted and hallowed by the memories of Rousseau, Gibbon and others, who had dwelt by its shores. The boating, too, promised to be a source of delight, and there were prospects of infinite charm in nature. About the same time, Byron arrived at the hotel where they had taken up their quarters, and an intimacy soon arose between the poets. Ere long they left the hotel. Byron and his physician, Polidori, occupied the Villa Diodati (where Milton had visited a friend on his homeward way from Italy), and Shelley, Mary and Claire, the Villa Mont Alégre. The two poets became joint owners of a boat, and many were the excursions which were made, including one round a great part of the lake, to Chillon and Lausanne. Whether or not the intrigue between Byron and Miss Clairmont was a thing of the past ere the former and the Shelleys met at Geneva, is uncertain ; but it was not until the knowledge could no longer be kept from them that Claire Clairmont confessed that in her reckless passion she had given herself to Byron—"Count Maddalo." And many of Shelley's letters show how just and discriminating was his estimate of his brilliant friend ; he recognised the fact that Byron made himself out much worse than he in reality was, and regretted the selfish, unlofty ideas that obscured his good capacities. That, on the other hand, Byron recognised the fineness of Shelley's nature is clear, from his emphatic statement made after the latter's death. "He was the most gentle, the most amiable, the least worldly-minded person I ever met ; full of delicacy, disinterested beyond all other men, and possessing a degree of genius joined to simplicity as rare as it is admirable. He had formed to himself a *beau ideal* of all that is fine, high-minded and noble, and he acted up to this ideal to the very letter."

Like many ardent worshippers of nature, Shelley often found himself mute in her presence. He wrote in the after-glow of memory, not in the full light of the moment's enjoyment. The beautiful lines to Mont Blanc were an outcome of his emotions as he lingered on the Bridge of Arve on his way through the Valley of Chamouni, whither he had gone with Mary to inhale the pure air of the greatest of the Swiss mountains. On their return to the lake-side they found another visitor in the person of "Monk" Lewis. Naturally, now, the evening chats resolved themselves into ghostly discussions, and to pass the time, they indulged in the perusal of a book of ghastly narrations, entitled "Fantasmagoriana." On Byron's suggestion each member of the party undertook to write something weird or ghastly. Shelley began a story which came to nought. Byron commenced a tale called "The Vampire," but only wrote a fragmentary portion. Polidori indulged in an absurd narrative more fantastic than impressive, and Mary Shelley produced an extraordinary romance called "Frankenstein," a book which has made a permanent mark in the literature of the West.

In the early autumn, Shelley and Mary returned to England. This year, 1816, proved a tragic one to the poet. Godwin was hard pressed by poverty, and Shelley could not relieve him. Gentle, affectionate, unhappy Fanny, the daughter of Mary Wollstonecraft by Mr. Tunlay, had long been subject to dire dejection. One day she left home, and having reached Swansea, put an end to her life by poison, and was found dead in her hotel.

Shelley, who on behalf of Godwin had returned to Bristol in pursuit of the unhappy girl, felt the blow so keenly that his nervous system almost gave way, and while he was on a visit to Leigh Hunt, he received a letter from Hookham conveying the tragic news that "Harriet Smith" had drowned herself in the Serpentine. He had now two duties to perform without delay; to take his children by Harriet under his protection, and to marry Mary Godwin. On the 30th December in this eventful year, he and Mary were legally wedded at St. Mildred's Church in London.

To Shelley's reiterated demands for the custody of his children, their maternal grandfather, Mr. Westbrook, turned a deaf ear. This gentleman instituted a Chancery suit which was decided against Shelley, and the children were placed under the care of a Dr. Hume, to be educated in principles which their father considered mistaken and harmful. To add to the poet's troubles, Claire Clairmont in January gave birth to her and Byron's illegitimate child, afterwards known as Allegra. Shelley needed all the rest he could obtain to enable him to bear up against his recent sorrows. He even feared his own imprisonment on account of his avowed opinions. His anxious hours were cheered by the kindness of friends, especially by Leigh Hunt. At the latter's cottage in Hampstead he met Keats, and in the ensuing months, the two poets saw each other at intervals, but circumstances prevented their becoming really intimate.

Shelley had now in very truth entered the sphere of poetic creation. At all times he was wont to compose in the open air, by river, sea, mountain, or amid the vernal and autumnal woodlands. His last great poem was written in his boat upon the Bay of Spezzia; the Pisan pine-woods, the heights of the Euganean hills, the Venetian lagoons, beheld the birth of some of his most famous lyrics; fronting the sea at Livorno was the Villa Valsovano, on the windy roof of which most of "The Cenci" was written; and the greater part of "Prometheus" was composed amid the gigantic ruins of the Baths of Caracalla, less desolate then in their lovely grandeur than now in their tourist-haunted "picturesqueness." And amid scenes as lovely, if not so immediately impressive, Shelley's second great poem was written. "Laon and Cythna," or "The Revolution of the Golden City"—usually known as "The Revolt of Islam"—is not a popular poem, though in merit not inferior to "Alastor." It is said that early in the year of its composition, Shelley and Keats each agreed to write a long work in verse, and that the results of this undertaking were "Laon and Cythna," and "Endymion." Among the shorter poems written by Shelley at this time may be specially noted the sonnet entitled "Ozymandias," and the lyric "To Constantia, Singing." The latter is known to have been addressed to Claire Clairmont, whose voice was of surpassing sweetness. In "Rosalind and Helen," as in "Alastor," "The Revolt of Islam," "Prince Athanase," etc., the dominant theme is Love. As a poem it is the least successful of Shelley's longer productions, though it has some fine lines.

Throughout the autumn of 1817, Shelley's health deteriorated, and after one specially severe spasmodic attack, he came to the conclusion that a change to Italy was the only chance whereby his life might be prolonged. It was with little belief in ultimate recovery, however, that he made final arrangements for leaving England. His irregularity in his hours of eating, his inadequate diet, his prolonged fasts, the fire of his mind for ever consuming his excitable body, his swift and ardent emotions, his over-keen susceptibilities, all combined to increase the frailty of his physical health.

When Shelley left Marlowe, he must have been sorely missed. He was ever wont to practise as well as preach the Christian ideal. Not only did he give largely of his means to all whom he considered had any public or private claim upon him, and expend much upon the poor in the neighbourhood, but he also devoted many hours weekly to visiting the sick and infirm. He would even, on occasion, give needy wayfarers articles of his own apparel. One day he returned home shoeless, having met some weary vagrant whose wants he could not alleviate, having no money with him, and to whom he had given his boots, so that the toil of the journey might be mitigated. It was not his habit to carry money about with him, but this was no bar to his ever-ready charity. If he met someone whom he desired to help, he would tear out a leaf from a book, or a blank page from a letter, and write upon it a succinct cash order to be discharged by Mary on presentation. During part of the stay at Marlowe, there was great distress among the lace-makers, who then congregated in the old river-town, and during his visitations to those in dire need, Shelley caught a bad attack of ophthalmia.

Shortly before the travellers left England, their two children were duly christened at St. Giles'-in-the-Fields with the names of William and Clara Everina. On the same occasion, Miss Clairmont had her child baptized by the name Clara Allegra, the father's name being duly entered in the register as Lord Byron. The Shelleys had not yet lost faith in Byron, and believed that he would act honourably by the mother of his child if the twain could be brought together.

On the 11th of March, 1818, Shelley watched the shores of England fade slowly from his view. He did not surmise that he should never see them again, nor did Mary dream that when she should recross those narrow seas it would be in loneliness and grief.

The travellers made direct for Milan, through South-Eastern France and Switzerland. The summer was spent at the Bagni di Lucca. The weeks passed delightfully. In the early mornings and in the star-lit evenings, the young people would ride through the alleys of chestnut and beech, for while others drowsed in the heat of the day, Shelley disappeared to a loved haunt in the forest, where a mountain torrent fell into a basin. Here the poet took a bath, and dreamed away the hours.

Claire had, against Shelley's advice, sent Allegra to her father at Venice; she was much pained by the rumours that reached her of Byron's reckless life, and determined to set out to see him. Shelley, with his usual unselfishness, agreed to accompany her, and on their arrival at Venice, went alone to visit Byron. The elder poet took his friend's pleadings and remonstrances in good part, and half scornfully agreed that Claire might have her child again if she wished, but dropped a vague hint that if she thus acted, she might find herself absolutely discarded by him. From this time Shelley could no longer esteem or even care for the man whom, with justice, he then and always so much admired as a poet. When the painful interview was over, Byron took Shelley in his gondola across the lagoons to the wave-washed Lido. There the former's horses were in waiting, and, to Shelley's delight, he found himself riding along that magic strand which he afterwards immortalized in song.

There was one practical outcome of this visit. Byron then temporarily owned a lovely villa, "I Cappuccini," at Este, high up among the Euganean hills, and this villa he offered to the Shelleys and Miss Clairmont; an offer which was willingly accepted. Shelley at once wrote to his wife to join him with the children, but on this journey sorrow waited for them, the baby Clara was attacked with dysentery, and died at Venice in her mother's arms.

It was at this villa that the wonderful melodies, the splendid harmonies, all the music and magnificence of Shelley's greatest production, "Prometheus Unbound," began to haunt his spirit, and the famous poem "Julian and Maddalo" was mainly written in a summer-house adjacent to the villa. It contains the portraitures of two great poets. Both are idealized, yet each is recognizable—Byron as Count Maddalo, and Shelley as Julian. This poem contains one often-quoted line, and one famous passage, "Thou paradise of exiles, Italy!" and the pathetic lines setting forth how some unhappy men

> "Are cradled into poetry by wrong:
> They learn in suffering what they teach in song."

Before October had passed away, it was found advisable for

Shelley to seek a warmer clime, and Naples was finally chosen. Before the departure Allegra was (to Claire's passionate grief) returned to Byron's care, for the unfortunate mother could not but see that she might wholly ruin her child's prospects if she went against the wishes of Allegra's father. When Naples was reached a deep melancholy settled upon Shelley. All that he wrote through the rest of the year was tinged with sadness. He composed, among other mournful lyrics, those exquisite stanzas "Written in Dejection, near Naples." The pathetic music of the following lines is unequalled:

> " Yet now despair itself is mild,
>   Even as the winds and waters are ;
> I could lie down like a tired child,
>   And weep away the life of care
> Which I have borne and yet must bear,
>   Till death-like sleep might steal on me,
> And I might feel in the warm air
>   My cheek grow cold, and hear the sea
> Breathe o'er my dying brain its last monotony."

In 1818 the Shelleys went to Rome, and he strove to finish his greatest poem, "Prometheus Unbound," among the ruins of the Baths of Caracalla. As the season advanced their little boy felt the debilitating effects of the climate; the parents exhausted themselves in nursing, but after sixty hours of sleepless watching, Shelley saw the beloved little face suddenly pale and the eyes, which everyone had noted as of so rare and beautiful a blue, lose their soft light. The calamity almost broke the hearts of father and mother. He was laid in that lovely Protestant burial ground at Rome, of which, some months before, Shelley had written to a friend, "It is a green slope near the walls, under the pyramidal tomb of Cestius, and is, I think, the most beautiful and solemn cemetery I ever beheld."

After this sad event the Shelleys visited Leghorn and the drama of *The Cenci* was begun and finished at their villa near the busy Tuscan town. From Leghorn they went to Florence, but the cold proving harmful to the poet, they moved to Pisa, where he wrote his famous and lovely little poem "The Cloud." Here are the first and last stanzas of this exquisite lyric :

> " I bring fresh showers for the thirsting flowers,
>   From the seas and the streams ;
> I bear light shade for the leaves when laid
>   In their noonday dreams,

> From my wings are shaken the dews that waken
>     The sweet buds every one,
> When rocked to rest on their mother's breast,
>     As she dances about the sun.
> I wield the flail of the lashing hail,
>     And whiten the green plains under,
> And then again I dissolve it in rain,
>     And laugh as I pass in thunder.
>
> \* \* \* \*
>
> I am the daughter of earth and water,
>     And the nursling of the sky;
> I pass through the pores of the ocean and shores;
>     I change, but I cannot die.
> For after the rain, when with never a stain
>     The pavilion of heaven is bare,
> And the winds and sunbeams with their convex gleams
>     Build up the blue dome of air,
> I silently laugh at my own cenotaph,
>     And out of the caverns of rain,
> Like a child from the womb, like a ghost from the tomb,
>     I arise and unbuild it again."

The "Ode to a Skylark," "The Sensitive Plant," and "The Witch of Atlas," were all written about this time, and many more poems to which we have no space to refer. There is more than enough of criticism — good, bad, and indifferent — upon Shelley's poetry, and therefore we have endeavoured to do little more than recount the narrative of his life. Many of his poems are obscure, and can be only understood by those who know the secret of spiritual passion. But there can be none who fail to appreciate the beauty of the following words. Is it to a woman that these passionate lines are uttered?

> " Seraph of Heaven ! too gentle to be human,
>     Veiling beneath that radiant form of woman
>     All that is insupportable in thee
>     Of light and love and immortality !
>     Sweet Benediction in the Eternal Curse !
>     Veiled glory of this lampless Universe !
>     Thou Moon beyond the clouds ! Thou living Form
>     Among the Dead ! Thou star above the Storm !
>     Thou Wonder, and thou Beauty, and thou Terror ! "

Or what love is this which would fain annihilate individuality, so that spirit in spirit might merge, and in their supreme height of passion be veritably as one?

> " One hope within two wills, one will beneath
>     Two overshadowing minds, one life, one death
>     One Heaven, one Hell, one immortality,
>     And one annihilation. Woe is me !

> The wingèd words on which my soul would pierce
> Into the heights of love's rare Universe,
> Are chains of lead around its flight of fire—
> I pant, I sink, I tremble, I expire!"

Shelley was wont to horrify the Pisans by his excursions along the Pisan canal in a frail, flat-bottomed boat. On the occasion of the trial trip Williams and another friend were with the poet; suddenly rising and steadying himself by the mast, the former overturned the boat. Shelley, though unable to swim a stroke, behaved with his usual courage and self-possession, and Williams found no difficulty in towing him ashore. Life became a dream to the poet when he could lie in his frail craft drifting along, watching the clouds trailing their shadows over water and hill, or when in the cool of the evening the boat set towards home adown the picturesque *canale*.

Early in 1822, another friend was added to the Pisan society of which the Shelleys were members. There is no more striking figure among the poet's friends than Edward John Trelawny, and he is one of the most entertaining and reliable biographers of Shelley's latter days. Trelawny narrates how one fine spring morning he went with Mrs. Shelley in search of the errant poet. "As we advanced," he says, "the ground swelled into mounds and hollows. By and bye, an old fellow who acted as guide, pointed with his stick to a hat, books, and loose papers lying about, and then to a deep pool of dark glimmering water, saying "Eccolo!" I thought he meant that Shelley was in or under the water. The careless, not to say impatient, way in which the poet bore his burden of life, caused a vague dread amongst his family and friends that he might loose or cast it away at any moment.

"The strong light streamed through the opening of the trees. One of the pines, undermined by the water, had fallen into it. Under its lee, and nearly hidden, sat Shelley, gazing on the dark mirror beneath, so lost in his bardish reverie that he did not hear my approach. There the trees were stunted and bent, and their crowns were shorn like friars, by the sea-breezes, excepting a cluster of three, under which the poet's traps were lying; these overtopped the rest. To avoid startling Shelley out of his dream, I squatted under the lofty trees, and opened his books. One was a volume of his favourite Greek dramatist, Sophocles, the same that I found in his pocket after his death, and the other was a volume of Shakespeare."

The poet had been writing that dainty lyric "Ariel to Miranda take," and Trelawny tells how he gazed in amazement at the frightful scrawl—"a marsh overgrown with bulrushes, and the blots for wild ducks," as he describes it.

It was about this time that the friends talked over the scheme of a yacht to be jointly owned, and about a fortnight after the Shelleys had settled at Casa Magni, the small schooner-built craft arrived from Geneva. Though fast, strongly-built, and not deficient in beam, she was, as Trelawny remarked, very crank in a breeze; two tons of iron ballast, moreover, were required to bring her down to her bearings. On Byron's initiative, though rather against Shelley's approval, she was christened *Don Juan*, but this title was ere long changed to *Ariel*. The owners of the yacht were on the water morning, noon, and night. The evenings were generally passed in conversation, reading, and music.

One or two strange incidents occurred at this time. One of these was the supposed apparition of Allegra, who, a short while before, had fallen a victim to the malarious fever which, arising from the marshes of Ravenna, had reached the Convent of Bagnacavallo. On the evening of the 6th of May, Shelley and Williams were walking on the terrace of the villa, when the former suddenly grasped his companion's arm, and seemed violently excited as he stared seaward. "There it is again—there!" he exclaimed, pointing across the moonlit surf. The vision he thought he saw was that of Allegra, who had risen from the sea, clapping her hands and laughing joyously, and beckoning to him.

On another occasion, one of the household dreamed that Shelley was dead. Once, later, the poet was supposed to have been seen to walk into a little wood near Lerici, when he was indubitably in an opposite direction. One night, everyone was aroused by screams proceeding from the sitting-room. Shelley was found rigid with the horror of a vision which had just appalled him. A cloaked figure, he said, had come to his bedside and had beckoned him to follow; when they had reached the sitting-room, the figure had withdrawn the cloak from its features, and in them Shelley beheld his own. "Siete soddisfatto," the apparition said, and vanished. The origin of this vision has been supposed to be a drama of Calderon's, which Shelley was reading at this time.

On the 1st of July, Shelley and Williams left in the *Ariel* for Leghorn, where the former hoped to meet Leigh Hunt and arrange with him and Byron for the publication of their projected newspaper, to be called *The Liberal*. Before Shelley started he was engaged upon the composition of a poem which, fragmentary as it is, ranks among his best achievements. "The Triumph of Life" is the triumphal procession of the powers of Life dragging captive the spirit of Man. The poem closes abruptly with these words: "Then what is life? I cried——" A sentence of profound significance, when we remember that the questioner was now about to seek its answer in the halls of Death.

At Leghorn Shelley met the Hunts and went with them to Pisa, where they had anything but a cordial welcome from Byron. As soon as it was practicable, he prepared to return. Mary was anxious about him, and Williams was fretting to be back again with his wife.

The painful story has been told so often that it will be best narrated here with the utmost brevity. "On the afternoon of Monday, the 8th of July, Shelley and Williams, with the boy Vivian, set sail from Leghorn. Trelawny, who was then taking charge of Byron's yacht the *Bolivar*, was unable to accompany them. The glory of the day had changed. An intense sultry furnace glow had replaced the flood of sunlight; the thunder brooded among the jagged clouds, which gathered above the horizon. From the top of the lighthouse Captain Roberts uneasily watched the progress of the *Ariel*. On the *Bolivar*, the Genoese mate remarked to Trelawny, 'the devil was brewing mischief.'"

Ere long a sea-fog came up, and the boat was shrouded from view; those who were on shore or in harbour were glad that they were not upon the sea, which had become discoloured and moaned with premonition of storm. Trelawny had gone to his cabin, but about half-past six was awakened by a sudden tumult. The sea was like lead, and was covered with scum; so sluggish was the water that the heavy thunderdrops spurted from its impenetrable surface, and the wind, passing over, failed to ruffle forth an oily wavelet. At last the tempest came, brief in duration, but fearfully violent. In about twenty minutes the seaward expanse was clear again, but on it was no sign of the *Ariel*. Trelawny was uneasy, but believed she had made Via Reggio by the time the storm had burst.

Three days afterwards Trelawny suspected the truth, and communicated his fears to Byron. Meanwhile, Mrs. Shelley and Mrs. Williams waited at Casa Magni in an agony of suspense, hope and despair alternating until the latter wholly prevailed. More days of dreadful anxiety passed, and at last news came to Trelawny that two bodies had been washed ashore. One had been found at Via Reggio, the other, three miles distant, near the tower of Migliarino, at the Bocca Lericcio. The former proved to be the corpse of Shelley, and the latter that of Williams. The soilure of the sea had so disfigured both that recognition was difficult; the faces and hands were fleshless, and the bodies pitiably frayed. Three weeks later the skeleton of the boy Vivian was washed ashore, but it was not until September that the *Ariel* was recovered; the schooner was found to have been not capsized, but sunk in from ten to fifteen fathoms of water, and was injured by a hole in her stern. There is no doubt that the boat was intentionally run into by a small craft manned by men who thought that the *Ariel* was owned by the rich English "Milord" Byron, who was on board with a large supply of gold. The men did not foresee or had miscalculated the fury of the sudden gale. The *Ariel* sank without the treasure the Italians hoped to find, nor was it till long afterwards that one of the wretched men confessed his share in the crime.

When Shelley's body was found Trelawny noticed that in one pocket was a volume of Sophocles, and in the other a copy of Keats' last volume, doubled back at "The Eve of St. Agnes," as if the poet had been reading there at the moment of the catastrophe.

To Trelawny fell the painful duty of breaking the news to the two waiting wives. It is needless to dwell on their agonised grief, or on the days that followed for them in Pisa, whither their friend had taken them. It had been arranged that Shelley's remains were to be buried at Rome, near his little son William and his friend Keats. The body of Williams was to be conveyed to England.

No one should omit to read Trelawny's vivid account of the cremation of Shelley's remains. The ashes and the heart of the dead were placed in an iron box and conveyed to Rome. Here they were finally interred in a spot in the Protestant Cemetery, selected and purchased by Trelawny. Around the grave his friend planted several cypresses and laurels, amongst whose branches the thrush now calls at morn, and whence in the evening the song of the nightingale is heard.

On the flat gravestone is the following inscription:

PERCY BYSSHE SHELLEY<br>
COR CORDIUM.<br>
NATUS IV. AUG. MDCCXCII.<br>
OBIT VIII. JUL. MDCCCXXII.

> " Nothing of him that doth fade
> But doth suffer a sea-change
> Into something rich and strange.'

That the memory of Shelley is honoured and revered in Italy was shown not long ago by the placing of a bronze wreath upon his tomb by his admirers in that country; also by the erection of a memorial tablet on the Palazzo Verospi, which the poet inhabited when he was in Rome, and in which house he wrote "Prometheus" and "The Cenci."

On the 29th of September, 1894, at Via Reggio, the scene of Shelley's tragic death, a monument was unveiled, which had been erected to his memory. It is situated on the beach and represents the poet at the age of twenty-nine. The eyes are gazing meditatively across the sea, and a pen just laid down appears from under the folds of the cloak. The pedestal is simple, but elegant. On the side away from the sea, encircled by intertwined branches of oak and olive, is a book bearing on its cover the word "Prometeo." Above this is the following inscription: "1894, to P. B. Shelley, heart of hearts, in 1822 drowned in this sea, consumed by fire on this shore, where he meditated the addition to 'Prometheus Unbound,' of a posthumous page, in which every generation would leave a token of its struggles, its tears, and its redemption."

# A Tale of the Fens.

It is a great river that comes to Fevsey Lock. It is broad, it is deep, and it has travelled many miles. It has flowed past great towns where silence is not. It has crawled like a snake through grass and wood. But, ever crawling, it has come at last to the lock. In the summer time, people laugh and say, it is sluggish. But in the autumn and winter, when its wavelets no longer glitter with cheerful sunlight, they hold their breath as they see it swallow up the fields with its muddy waters. It is then that it roars and grows hasty with passionate strength, and that those in the fens watch it with terror.

Of all the locks on the river, the Fevsey Lock is the greatest. There are so many gates to its sluices, and they are so strong. Yet it has only one lock-keeper, Charlie Pendle. And he, he never opens the lock, though he is very careful to raise the sluice-gates when the river grows big with flood. For now no barges come to the lock heavily laden with bricks and timber, with coal and grain. No! not one; the railways have taken their business, and through many an unrepaired lock-gate on the great river, the water is spirtling with white and careless foam. "It is sad, that the river should be so deserted," they say, at the little inn which stands by the side of the lock.

This inn is called "The Dog and Duck." It is situated on the opposite side of the lock and sluices to the little red cottage in which live Charlie Pendle and his old mother. Its landlord is a man named Bagot. He remembers past times, when many barges passed through the lock, and he sold much beer and tobacco. He remembers them with sadness, for he is growing weak from age, and it is difficult to provide food for his wife and daughter with the little money that he earns by eel-spearing, fishing, shooting, and the sale of an occasional pint of beer to a boating party.

The Pendles and the Bagots, they are the only people who live at the lock. And when either family wants bread or one of the household necessaries, it is a five-mile row by river, or when the floods will allow, a three-mile walk by land, to the village of Marsh to obtain it. There is no shop nearer than Marsh, whence it can be procured; nor is there so much as a hamlet or a cot within a three-mile radius of the lone lock and its bridges poised above the rushing river. Each Saturday, then, the families gather in their supplies for the week. Charlie Pendle fetches his own and his mother's—Bagot, or his daughter Annie, those which are required for the "Dog and Duck." But never does Charlie bring Bagot's goods, nor Bagot bring Charlie's. And the village news that is brought back from Marsh, never finds its way from the Pendles to the Bagots, nor from the Bagots to the Pendles. Or, to be quite accurate, very rarely.

The Pendles and the Bagots, they are the only people who live at the lock. But they seldom speak to each other. Mrs Bagot hates Mrs. Pendle. She calls her "rough," and she should know, for she was housekeeper to a "good" family for many years. Mrs. Pendle—whose husband, when he was alive, was lock-keeper before Charlie—calls Mrs. Bagot "stuck up and proud." A river runs betwixt the homes of the old women, but on a calm day their angry voices travel across it; and when it is stormy the rushing water and the rushing wind cannot deaden shrill voices upon the lock-bridge. It is a sad state of affairs. Bagot sometimes thinks so. But Mrs. Bagot is always right, she has seen the great world. And then, that Charlie, he is young, and Bagot likes to *keep himself to himself*. He is a reserved man.

So matters drift on at the lock, till a certain November afternoon.

The sun had set, and left behind it a yellow streak of light in a dull grey sky. Heavy clouds were gradually pressing this remnant of sunshine down upon the horizon, from which the river flowed towards the lock in the solitary grandeur of a long reach. A many foam bubbles were coming swiftly down the centre of the stream. They wound in and out amongst gulping, gurgling eddies. They travelled faster and faster as they came towards the sluices. They hurried with them sticks, pieces of reed, and black objects, at which the eddies sucked with cavernous hunger.

A little breeze sprang up and blew coldly towards the dying light at the horizon. It rippled the watery plains that stretched dimly away from the swirling river. It came from the distant sea, to find a November flood—a flood, that was rising higher and higher, that was pressing savagely upon the locks, that was roaring through the sluices. A flood that was lapping around the small gardens attached to the houses of the lock, and which could only be traversed by boat.

Resting her back against one of the great beams of the lock, sat a young girl upon a pile of rusty chain. A black shawl was pinned tightly across her full bosom to protect it from the chilly airs. But her white arms were bare to the shoulder, and loose locks of her uncovered hair fluttered in the breeze. It was Annie, Bagot's daughter, who had been born in the inn by the lock some eighteen years back, and whose pretty features were glowing with the health which sea and river breezes had brought to them.

It was a mournful and desolate scene that lay before Annie. But it did not sadden her. A life's experience had more than reconciled her to its dreariness. And then—she was very busy. On her lap there lay a white duck, whose neck and head hung limply towards the ground. From its breast, she was quickly plucking the feathers, throwing them by handfuls into the air, and watching the breeze take them greedily away. It pleased her, though she did not know why, to see the feathers rise swiftly towards the grey clouds, to see them hesitate, and then turn and twirl and go rushing with the wind up the long river reach. It pleased her, though she did not know why, to see them sink and fall by ones, by twos, by flights, amongst the foam bubbles that came hurrying down the river.

She had almost finished the plucking of the duck, when the door of Mrs. Pendle's cottage suddenly opened, and there stepped forth a young man. He hesitated for a moment as he caught sight of the young girl seated by the lock; and a doubtful expression passed over his bold, good-humoured face. This expression was like a passing cloud that softens a strong sunlight. It dimmed the boldness of his blue eyes with a tender light that was even beautiful by contrast with the power of his supple and sinewy form. But it passed quickly, and he turned to shut the door behind him, from which came lazily creeping forth a great black cat.

"Make haste, Tinker," said he to the cat, which was the idol of Mrs. Pendle; and he closed the door as Tinker sprang nimbly towards the sluices. This young man was Charlie Pendle, and he was going to raise the sluices yet higher, for the flood was a great one—a greater he scarcely remembered.

Charlie walked to the first of the sluices which were built in a line across the river. But Annie did not hear the noise of his footsteps where she sat by the lock, which was situated at the end of the sluices, and near to the inn. The roar of the hurrying waters was too great. She continued to throw the last of the duck's feathers into the air, and did not look towards him. Charlie took off his brown velvet coat with pearl buttons and laid it by the sluice. Then he took up a crank, and fitting it to the winch began to raise the heavy door. Fiercely and more fiercely boiled the striving water beneath the platform on which he stood, and one after another the rusty cogs of iron shrieked under the strain of the weight that they were compelled to lift. Their screams pierced keenly through the uproar of wind and water to the ears of Annie. She looked in his direction. She watched him as he passed from sluice to sluice, nearer and nearer to her. Now he used a crank, anon he used a heavy crowbar; but he was always strong—very strong. And she liked to watch him. Presently, Charlie stood by her side. He began to open the slides of the lock. But he did not speak to Annie. She believed her mother, she thought that he was rough, and he—he knew that, and was proud to silence.

In a little while Charlie had finished his work. He glanced at Annie. Their eyes met. She tossed her head disdainfully. He turned on his heel, and went back to his mother's cottage. He closed its door behind him with a bang.

A smile rippled the fair face of Annie. It amused her to be disdainful to the shy admiration of Charlie. Then she rose to her feet, and went towards the "Dog and Duck," carrying the plucked duck by its legs. As Annie arrived at the inn door, a white fox terrier ran to her side from the back premises of the inn, and with many wags of the tail, and many barks, sniffed at the duck which she was carrying. It was a troublesome, noisy little dog, but it was the pampered favourite of the inn.

Occasionally, it even had the honour of resting upon Mrs. Bagot's Sunday lap. A high honour, which assured Beauty the old woman's very especial favour and protection. But Annie was beginning to feel the keen chill of the rising breeze. And after tantalisingly holding the duck above Beauty's head, she suddenly opened the door, and passing into the inn, closed it behind her before the excited terrier had time or opportunity to follow.

Beauty sat down with his tail straight out and looked at the door. It was unsatisfactory. He got up again, and placing his head sideways to the ground, he tried to look betwixt door and sill. He fretted and fumed, he scratched and he barked, but the door did not open. A little howl! it did no good, it was lost in the roar of the waters. So he put his tail between his legs and moodily slouched away towards the sluices.

Away in the west the last gleam of yellow light was quickly drowning 'neath the grey clouds. High overhead a long-necked heron was making haste home; whilst down below at the lock, there was only a restless little dog, hunting for a rat—where no rat came—on the sluice bridge.

Mrs. Pendle had just finished her tea. She felt warm and comfortable. She was growing very old, she was over seventy. She felt that she should like to take a nap, but she was first going to draw close the crimson curtains. She stood up from her comfortable arm chair. She looked out from the deep-set window in the direction of the sluice bridge. Then, for one so old, she grew strangely active. She rushed to the door, she threw it open, and she launched forth hatless and jacketless into the bold breeze.

Beauty saw her coming where he was baiting the black and bristling Tinker. He made a hasty rush to close quarters, and secured a mouthful of fur and a scratch on his nose. Then he placed his muzzle low down between his fore-paws, leant back, and barked with joy and excitement. The old woman snatched up a stick and hastened on towards him. Beauty retreated a little way, whilst Tinker, with swollen tail, rushed to the safety of the cottage. Mrs. Pendle came fiercely on. Beauty barked defiantly, and circled around Mrs. Pendle as he barked. She was very angry, but he was very cunning. She could not strike him. Of a sudden she caught sight of a stone. She stooped, and slyly grasping it hurled it with passionate strength at the mocking Beauty. It passed close to his tail, it ruffled the tip, then it went bounding over the bridge, and struck with a heavy thud the door of the "Dog and Duck."

It was a heavy thud, for it caused Bagot and his wife to run quickly to their door to see what was the matter; but Annie did not hear it, for she was upstairs at the back of the inn, dressing the hair that had been so tumbled by the wind. If she had, coming events might possibly have chanced differently, but who can say? As it was, Mrs. Bagot no sooner caught sight of Mrs. Pendle, who was still pursuing Beauty with the stick, than the blood rushed to her head, she shrieked out an incoherency which positively frightened Bagot, and then made all the haste she could to come to the protection of Beauty.

For Mrs. Pendle and Mrs. Bagot—to give and take an explanation in warm blood was an impossibility. They did not attempt it now; besides, Beauty, the origin of the disturbance, retired at once to the "Dog and Duck," having no intention to give evidence in person either for or against himself.

The sole barometer that marked the pressure of the storm of words and gestures which raged between the old women was the blanching face of Bagot. Whiter and whiter it grew, as his quavering voice tried to stem back a personal violence that appeared more imminent that November e'en than ever within his recollection. 'Twas useless. The old women drew closer to one another, and now and again the fringes of their petticoats collided midst the gathering dusk that was indiscriminately falling over lock, river and flooded field.

Minutes—that might have been hours or less than minutes—passed 'midst an excitement that took no note of time. Here, there, swayed the group with its passions of anger and fear. Eye on eye, they took no heed of what was around them, of what was beneath them. 'Twas thus that Bagot stumbled over a rusty bolt and fell heavily upon the rough boards of the sluice bridge.

The shock of his fall shook the slender edifice beneath the feet of the angry women. Terror paralysed their tongues. A moment they stood indeterminate. And then. "Are yer hurt, William?" said Mrs. Bagot, as she nervously stooped over her prostrate husband, and took his hand. Bagot groaned, but did not answer.

"Lord help us," prayed Mrs. Bagot, more and more alarmed.

"Help me up," said faintly the old man. Mrs. Pendle advanced mechanically, and assisted Mrs. Bagot in getting the latter's husband upon his feet.

"Where are yer hurt?" said Mrs. Pendle.

"It is my arm," said the old man, "I think it is broken."

Then, disdaining any further assistance, but groaning bitterly, he slowly made his way, followed by Mrs. Bagot, to the "Dog and Duck."

Mrs. Pendle watched their departure from the bridge, but did not attempt to follow them. She saw the door of the "Dog and Duck" hastily closed. After which she returned quickly to the cottage, and related to Charlie what had happened upon the lock bridge. The young man heard her to the end in silence. Then he sighed. But Mrs. Pendle did not hear him, her ears were still full of Mrs. Bagot's bitter words. Presently he left his mother and strode moodily upon the lock bridge. He was debating in his own mind whether he would risk a rebuff by knocking at the door of the "Dog and Duck" and offering to be of any assistance.

Annie came downstairs just as her father and mother entered the inn parlour. "Why, what is the matter?" she cried, for she had never seen them look so old and feeble.

Bagot groaned for reply as he sank limply into an arm-chair. Annie looked in alarm towards her mother.

"Fetch the brandy," said sharply the latter. Annie, without further question, at once ran for it to the little bar. Returning immediately, she poured some out in a glass and handed it to her father. He drank it off at a gulp. Then rising to his feet, he gently and cautiously felt his arm down its length.

"It ain't broken, I believe," said he. "It is nought but a bad strain. It is better. But it has hurt me terrible."

"What?" ejaculated Annie, quite confused.

It was some little time before Annie fully understood what had happened. Mrs. Bagot was shaking in every limb, and almost speechless with excitement and alarm. And Bagot himself was quite unnerved by the severe shock which he had just experienced. A consecutive narrative was not to be gleaned from them. But this Annie was given to understand from the very first, and clearly, that Mrs. Pendle had behaved disgracefully. Annie was still warm with indignation at the old's woman's behaviour, when she heard a knocking at the outer door of the inn. Thither she repaired to answer it.

"What do you want?" she asked haughtily, as she opened the door and saw Charlie Pendle standing outside.

"I came across to see if I could be of any assistance," said Charlie. "For mother tells me that Bagot has hurt himself." And the young man looked pleadingly at the flushed face of the girl before him.

"No," said Annie, roughly—and she shut the door in his face.

Annie was seriously alarmed and angry with Mrs. Pendle, whom she looked upon as responsible for their trouble, or else it was not in the nature of that good-tempered girl to have behaved so rudely to anyone. She regretted it half-an-hour afterwards. "I was over hasty," she said to herself, "for Charlie, if he is rough, is kindly, and meant well."

Charlie clenched his hands, he bit his underlip. He would have wished to believe that the rough "No" that was still sounding in his ears had not come from Annie's lips. It hurt him. And though the air was dark with falling night, he felt ashamed. Again he crossed the sluice bridge. The first drops of a hurtling rain fell upon his face, as after one wistful glance at the ray of light which streamed from the window of the "Dog and Duck," he entered his mother's cottage.

Faster and faster ran the great river betwixt the Pendles and the Bagots, for the flood was rising. Its white foam rested on black water that hurried beneath black night. Its roar was moody and muffled, for it strove with a strong wind and the hiss of a heavy rain. Faster and faster ran the great river, but steady were the yellow beams of light that shone upon it from the cottages.

The hour grew late.

The light from the Pendles' cottage flickered and vanished. They had gone to bed.

The hour grew later. Suddenly the door of the "Dog and Duck" opened. A broad flood of light spread over the rough wavelets of the river, and mirrored full upon them the dark shadow of a woman as she stood in the doorway. A moment after, she shut fast the door behind her, and fled into the darkness that lay over the rushing river where it roared beneath the sluice-bridge.

Groping her way over the bridge, she came as quickly as she might to the Pendles' cottage. And placing her hand upon its harsh bricks, felt her way to its door. She seized the handle, and shook it fiercely. Then she beat with her hand at the impassive wood.

She was yet knocking when the glare of an ill-struck match appeared at an upper window of the cottage. Just a flash of light and it was gone. But she had seen it and she ceased to knock. Again a light suddenly appeared. It increased, it grew steady. She waited with beating, eager heart, amidst the cold rains. She waited—though she longed to be away, away, for the shadow of death lay over the lock.

At length the door opened. And this time it was Charlie who was within and Annie who was without. Yet Annie did not wait for an invitation to enter. She rushed in like a hunted creature, she stretched out her hands to Charlie and Mrs. Pendle. She sobbed, as the mists of sleep passed from their eyes and Charlie asked her to tell them what was the matter. Slowly at first and word lagging after word, her voice came to her. Then quick, quicker, and with passion, as she begged Charlie for God's sake to come quickly with her.

There was no time to be lost. Mrs. Bagot had been taken seriously ill with something in the nature of a fit, and a doctor must be fetched by boat from Marsh. But to go by boat on such a flood, through such a storm-gripped night, was to brave death. Charlie understood this, even as the girl pleaded before him. Still his heart responded gratefully to her appeal. He determined to go. Yet he hesitated to take action. He was considering whether it was possible for a man by himself to reach Marsh. At length:

"Bagot will come?" he said interrogatively to Annie.

"Father cannot. His arm is powerless after the fall. But I will go with you," she said. "I will steer," she added eagerly.

Charlie thought of the river running, blackly and desperately.

"There is no choice. She must come," he muttered to himself. Whereupon he took down his cap from a nail, and prepared to follow the brave and filial girl.

Mrs. Pendle had been so taken by surprise that she had hitherto kept silence. But the danger that now hung over her son struck her into life and indignation. With tears and threats she tried to dissuade Charlie from risking his life for one who had no claim upon him—who was her enemy.

It was useless. Charlie answered her gently. But—he opened the door.

Mrs. Pendle turned fiercely upon Annie. But the bitter words that she addressed to her were scarcely audible amidst the noise of the rushing wind that entered the cottage through the open doorway. And when the young people stepped out upon the sluice bridge, the bitterness in Mrs. Pendle's heart suddenly left it, and she followed them with a prayer on her lips. She was old, and she dearly loved her son.

Charlie led the way. He carried a lighted lantern in his hand. Passing over the sluice bridge, he stopped before the door of the "Dog and Duck." Annie and Mrs. Pendle drew quickly to his side. All three then entered the inn. Mrs. Bagot lay upon a couch in the back parlour. Her face was flushed, she was insensible and breathing stertorously. Bagot was watching by her side. As Charlie entered the room, he thanked him in a low voice for coming to their assistance. Afterwards, he again fixed his eyes upon his wife's face, and appeared careless of aught else.

It was a sad scene; and it impressed Mrs. Pendle very greatly. She looked at Mrs. Bagot, lying unconscious with never a gleam in her eye, with never a word on her lips. She had never seen her look thus. It was dreadful. It was awful. She pitied her. It was so solitary at the lock, they were so far away from the village. She pitied her. She would like to help her. She, who had quarrelled with her but a few hours back. The dreadful thought!

Charlie perhaps guessed instinctively what was passing in his mother's mind. For, making a sign to Annie, he quitted the room, followed by her, and left Bagot and Mrs. Pendle to keep watch together. Mrs. Pendle saw them go, but she no longer possessed heart or courage to protest against their dangerous venture.

She heard them gently close the outer door of the inn—they were gone!

Below the sluices, and within a few yards of the "Dog and Duck," is a little bay. The river has eaten it out of the mound upon which the inn is built. In this bay, the Pendles and the Bagots have always been accustomed to anchor their boats.

They are quite safe there; they are sheltered from the full wash of the river. It is a little harbour; in summer-time it is quite shallow. Thither, Annie and Charlie now directed their footsteps. The rain had ceased for the moment, and the intense blackness of the night had paled since a storm-shower which had just passed on up the river. Charlie was again carrying the lantern with which he had provided himself at his mother's cottage. Arriving at the bay, he held it out at arm's length. Its rays fell upon two boats and a punt, which were tossing gently in their secure anchorage.

He turned to Annie.

"Hold the lantern," he shouted, for quiet speech was impossible midst such an uproar from wind and water.

Annie took it with a steady hand. He descended the bank, and grasping the painter of one of the boats, drew the rocking skiff to land.

It was a frail boat to entrust with two lives on such a night. But the other, the Bagot's, was of yet weaker construction. And the punt! But who that knew the river would have thought of making use of the punt upon such a flood? With such a depth of water it was impossible. There was no punting pole ever made that would have found bottom that night. To have entrusted themselves to the punt would have been to drift speedily to certain and crashing wreck. Charlie would have laughed at the idea of making use of the *punt!*

In a little while, Charlie had hung the rudder of the boat and cast loose the painter. He rose to his feet. He beckoned to Annie. She stepped quickly down the bank to his side. He took the lantern from her hand, and fastened it in the bow of the boat. He arranged the rudder lines. Then he gripped the side of the boat with both hands, and waited in a stooping posture.

Annie came closer to him. She bent down till her mouth was on a level with his ear.

"Shall I get in?" she said.

"Yes," he answered.

Those were all the words that passed between them. When one is near death, one thinks, but one does not speak.

Annie seated herself in the stern of the boat, and took up the rudder lines. Charlie could not see her face, for the light from the lantern streamed out and away over the bow of the boat. She was in shadow. But he felt that she was brave with the love of a daughter's heart, and that she knew the river and its curves. Then his thoughts left her and went forth to the work in hand.

Cautiously, he pushed the boat from the bank with a scull. It commenced to rock with the waves that came curling into the little harbour. At first, gently, then more roughly as it came closer to the rushing stream, and took to itself some of that strong life. Charlie could feel the frail craft swaying and straining beneath him. But with his hands upon the sculls, and the muscles of his arms rigid, he still controlled and guided it—until, with the rush of a horse that breaks loose from its tether—it started to the unchecked flow of the full current, and burst savagely into freedom.

Below Fevsey lock, the river runs straightly for two hundred yards. Then it turns suddenly and sharply to the left. Annie's heart beat fast as she kept her eyes fixed on the ray of light that beamed forth from the lantern in the bow. So soon as it should fall upon the river bank at the curve, they must prepare to turn or they would be dashed against the obstacle with fearful and dangerous force. Already the roar of the voiding sluices was dulling with the distance that they had travelled. They must be fast coming to the bend. Occasionally the brave girl inclined her head to right or left. Charlie understood, and pressing upon a scull, he would keep the boat's head to the centre of the current from which it was attempting to deviate. So they progressed in the track of the light, as it fell coldly upon a wrath of foam and wave. Nearer, nearer—shrouded in blackness on either side. They must be coming to it! There—no! But *there*—ah, no! There—yes! the light has struck against a high dark bank, and from a narrow beam 'tis spreading into a steady glow—which creeps up the bank—which broadly diffuses itself over great coils of water swirling black and white towards dank earth.

They come. They are there. Charlie pulls for life. He clenches his teeth, for he is fighting, he is wrestling with a cruel strength that would push them to the bank—that yields but to renew the attack—that would toss them into the hungry water, but for the weight of body which Annie and he throw, now this side, now the other of the boat.

He has fought. They have rounded the curve. They have left behind them the roar of the sluices. In their ears, there is nought but the angry hiss of the river, and the voice-shadows of the rushing wind.

And so, again the light clove through the darkness, again the boat followed the light.

Drifting or sculling from danger to danger, Annie and Charlie made rapid progress towards Marsh. In time, there remained between them and the attainment of that village but one peril. Annie almost laughed as she thought of it by the light of those which they had already surmounted. It was a railway bridge, which spanned the river on three piers close to that village. To collide with one of these piers would be to invite an upset. But then, though the river was in flood, though the night was dark, she felt confident that she could safely steer a middle course betwixt the piers. There was sufficient room and to spare. She almost dismissed it from her mind, as Charlie sculled swiftly down the reach which led to it. And in place of the physical fear by which she had been racked, there now came to her the full force of that anxiety which was leading her to Marsh in search of the doctor. She longed that she might find him at home, and that his great boat might be ready for their return journey to Fevsey lock. "Scull faster," said she to Charlie.

Scarcely had the words escaped from her mouth, than they were followed by a booming noise, which came pulsing with a dull energy from the darkness on their right. Charlie started, and looked over his shoulder in the direction whence the noise proceeded. Suddenly, the darkness that veiled its origin was rent asunder by a cloud of swift-travelling light, which swirled onwards, followed by a pale transparency. Right across their track it fled. It was an express train crossing the bridge, which responded to its passage with vacant clangour. For a brief period, its lights flashed and scintillated on the surface of the river, while the two in the boat wistfully thought of the many human beings who were carelessly passing, so swiftly, so safely away from them and the hissing flood. Then it had gone and darkness covered the river again save where the gleam of the lantern pierced it.

Quickly travelled the boat. Presently its light fell upon the gloomy sternness of iron piers. They were a little way ahead, and the river was rushing between them with maddened fury, was spurning them with gouts of white foam.

Annie did not flinch. She strained the rudder strings to their full tension, as she sought with her eye the centre of an arch that came low down upon the swollen waters. Thither, she guided the boat. It passed with a quick smoothness beneath the rim of the arch. Its course was fair. The danger of collision was passed. Annie smiled with relief, for they were hurrying past the iron piers on either hand, and there lay beyond the bridge the safety belonging to the river-bay of Marsh. She smiled. And as she smiled, a shock struck through the timbers of the boat to her heart.

Spasmodically Charlie turned and looked behind him. The bow of the boat was thrusting at the black and glistening trunk of a flood-borne willow tree. It was rolling heavily in the flood from the force of the collision, and its rugged bark had crushed through their bows a passage for water that was spirtling past his feet towards Annie. He saw this. Then, the current took the boat broadside and dashed it with fury against an iron pier. And the lantern, with its light went down beneath the black water, as he threw himself towards Annie and caught her in his arms. One moment he felt her cheek warm against his own : the next the cold water took them to its bosom.

NEIL WYNN WILLIAMS.

# BELGRAVIA ANNUAL.

### CHRISTMAS, 1895.

## The Keystone of the Household.
### BY JOHN STRANGE WINTER.

I MAY as well say at the beginning that I am a married woman, an old-fashioned married woman with no desire to have a vote for anything. I don't want to serve on juries nor to go to coroner's inquests; I don't want to smoke—and, if I did, I know it would make me sick—I don't even want to have a club, and if I did I should think it a piece of useless extravagance (because my husband belongs to the Grosvenor and I can get a cup of tea there whenever I am in the neighbourhood of Bond street, and can look at all the papers interesting to women which I do not take myself). I really have no politics, but I call myself a Conservative. I am an hereditary Conservative—that is to say my father was and my brothers are on that side in politics—and nothing would have induced me to marry a man who was inclined to Liberalism, or still worse to Radicalism. It is a very curious thing that whenever I venture to speak of politics—and I do sometimes—my husband always says, "Really, Jenny, for a staunch Conservative you have the most radical notions of any man or woman I ever knew!" But I think that is only his way of teasing me a little. The real truth is I don't understand politics one little bit, but I am a thoroughly old-fashioned woman with no desire whatever for what is called now-a-days "advancement."

But, all the same, I do believe in a woman being mistress of her own household, I mean in her having a predominating influence in her own household—an influence which should be asserted in wise control, not in petty tyrannies and that kind of thing, such as our mothers and grandmothers were so great at.

Now my mother (who was really one of the most unselfish women in most things that ever existed) had certain privileges as mistress of the house which she permitted no one else to share. One was to always have the first scan of the local weekly newspaper. It came on Saturday mornings, just before breakfast time. My mother always, upon coming downstairs, walked into the kitchen, gave her orders for the day, and glanced at a dish which we had certainly three hundred and sixty mornings out of three hundred and sixty-five which comprised the year—that was fried potatoes. They were not hand-me-downs from the previous day's dinner; no, they were always cooked especially —a good large bowlful of them—the last thing the night before, and were turned out to await the manipulations of the cook. The next morning they were emptied into a frying-pan with a little dripping, chopped up into knobbly pieces seasoned with pepper and salt and set on the fire at least half an hour before breakfast. Those potatoes were always part of the cook's education at home. They had to be of a certain degree of brownness, of a certain degree of greasiness—not too much of that —and to be served piping hot.

On Saturday mornings my mother invariably found the weekly paper awaiting her on the edge of the delf rack; she always put it under her arm, finished her directions to the cook, watched the turning of the potatoes once or twice, and then sailed into the dining room proud in the consciousness of having got the breakfast ready. We were rather a large family and it took some little time to pour out the tea or coffee, whichever we happened to be having; it was a duty which Mother would never relinquish and she always carried it through to the bitter end—but never for one moment did she relax her grip upon the paper. One might be, as some of us frequently were, dying to know who had been at such a dance, what wedding presents such a girl had had, whether there was any news of a certain boat-race, whether anybody we knew was hatched matched or dispatched—it was all one to my mother, she had the first glance at that newspaper under all and any circumstances. I have even seen her—when the breakfast dish happened to be fried bacon—put the paper from under her arm upon her chair and sit on it while she despatched her breakfast; then with the air of one who has satisfied the dictates of a good conscience, she would pour out her second cup of tea and spread out the sheets of crackling paper and proceed to dole out such items of news as came under her observation. I was very much devoted to my mother; but, at the same time, every Saturday morning regularly I used to register an inward vow that, if ever I was mistress of my own house, I would let who will read the newspaper when and how they chose and that I would *not* make that one of my special perquisites of matrimony.

There were other little privileges which my mother never forewent under any circumstances—one was the "parson's nose" of the chickens. I give you my word that until I was married myself I never tasted the "parson's nose" in my life! It is a sweet and succulent morsel, and as my dear George rather dislikes it than otherwise I, during the first years of our married life, felt no compunction and no sense of selfishness in appropriating it to myself. So when our children were growing up it became rather a little joke for George to say "Oh, Mother dear, you haven't had your knob!" Children are very different now-a-days to what we were. It had never occurred to me to dispute the possession of that particular morsel with my own mother; but my own small persons were not long in finding out its special deliciousness. It happened that dear little Kitty hurt herself very much one day at lunch by suddenly falling right off her chair and hitting her head a severe knock on that of the person next to her. George and I both rushed round to the table and we picked her up and made a proper amount of fuss over her. "I would like something," she sobbed.

"Would you darling?" said I; "what is it?"

"I would like Mother's knob if you don't mind, dear."

I have very seldom enjoyed a knob since! The children always ail something, or have some special reason for indulgence when chickens are the order of the day, and they ask for my little portion with a pathetic wistfulness which invariably makes me yield it without a murmur. I often wonder what my mother would think if she could see me, and I sometimes feel that it is as well that she has passed into that land where people live upon milk and honey, for I am sure she would be terribly upset if she could see the way in which I give up all the things which she used to look upon as matrimonial perquisites.

There are times—I suppose every married woman feels the same now and again—when I feel as if my belongings do not care so much for me, as if my mother's harder rule had been the more provocative of affection as well as respect; but then again, there are times when I realise how all-essential I am to my husband and children, to say nothing of the others of the household. Especially do I realise it if ever I happen to spend a day or two in bed. Now, like a great many other women I am subject to the most terrible neuralgic headaches. They generally come on days when I have something a little extra on foot—perhaps I am going somewhere with George, or perhaps I have made up my mind that I will have George's den thoroughly turned out, or that I will go over all the children's summer things and see which will be of use to them during the coming warm weather and which will be only good for giving away to some poor house-mother who is not as well blessed with this world's goods as I am myself. I wake up with a headache. I always feel that my cup of tea will carry it off, because sometimes it does. When it is a real headache it doesn't.

"George," I say, "I have got a most awful headache this morning."

George's answer is always the same. " Poor darling! I would stay quietly in bed."

I always say, " No, dear, I have got a good deal to do to-day. I think I will get up."

Then George says "Now look here, Pussy-Cat,"—oh, yes, he still calls me by names of that kind, even although I am the mother of a family, with long-legged boys and girls with ideas as to jewellery and other things—" Now look here, Pussy-Cat," he says, "don't you be foolish. You just stay quietly in bed and let me send you up a nice little breakfast, and try to eat a nice new-laid egg and a strip of toast and a cup of hot tea; you will feel all the better for it. Stay in bed till lunch time, my dear."

However, I never resign myself; I go on for the next half hour in a dozey state, a state which may end in the throes of a violent headache or which may pass away and permit me to get up with nothing worse than a shattered kind of feeling, as if I had been bashed about the head.

From this I am aroused by a little voice at my elbow. "Mother, Mother darling?"

"Ugh!"

"Mother—dear, I want to ask you something."

I rouse myself with a shake. "Well, what is it?"

"May we have two caramels each?"

I wake with a start. "Yes—yes! Oh yes, you may have two caramels each, but you mustn't eat them before breakfast."

"Oh——h!" in a tone of disappointment. "We do want them so badly."

"Yes, but you mustn't eat them before breakfast. You'll spoil your breakfast." There is a moment's hesitancy on the part of the little applicant. "Where do you keep them, Mother?"

Now to give this information is to give away the hiding-place of my small stock of sweets. However, my head is really aching too much to argue about such a trifle as that. I must find a new hiding-place. "They are in the dressing-table drawer," I reply.

I watch the little figure, in its smart flannel dressing-gown and bedroom slippers, go and carefully count out the caramels for the expectant brood upstairs; then she goes out, leaving the door open. Dear, how tiresome those childen are! I lean out of bed and push the door to. George asks me reproachfully why I did not ask him to do that. The effort of moving has made me disinclined to argue the question, and I say, "Never mind, dear," and settle down among my pillows again.

Ten minutes later the door is once more pushed softly open. It is the boy this time, the one hope of the house—from a family point of view that is. He is dressed, his face shines brilliantly from his morning's scrub, and he comes in on tip-toe. "Dear?" he begins.

"Well, what is it?" I ask.

"Has the post come?"

"Yes."

"Can I have the stamps off the letters?"

"Yes."

They are collecting old stamps with a view to getting a million for which they are going to get three pounds. I have represented to them many times that a certain stamp merchant will sell them a million of used English stamps for a sovereign at any time, and that therefore their grand collection is not of much practical good. They, however, keep on annexing stamps with a faithful persistence which is admirable and may lead them in after life to great things.

Geoffrey annexes all the stamps off the morning's post and then climbs on the bed. "Dear Mummy," he says, "you are very lazy. I have been up ages!"

"Mummy's got a headache," says George.

"Mummy got a headache? Poor darling Mummy—so sorry. You got a headache too, Dad?"

"No, I haven't exactly got a headache," says George, with the grace almost to blush, "but I stayed to keep Mummy company." He doesn't say that he has the newspaper.

Geoffrey goes out. He also leaves the door open. I settle down among my pillows again. George turns over the newspaper. "Balfour made a rattling speech in the House last night," he remarks.

I am absolutely indifferent to Balfour. My head is by this time so bad that I should not be affected in the smallest degree if Mr. Balfour were to suddenly turn Home Ruler and Anarchist.

"I don't think this Government can hold out much longer," says George, and goes into a disquisition on Harcourt lying low, Rosebery doing something else, with a word or two about the "Foundations of Belief." I grunt at appropriate pauses in his remarks; and then there comes a sharp rap-rap at my door.

"Mrs. Hattersley," says a voice, "are you there?"

"Yes—yes, what is it?"

It is the voice of the young lady who to all seeming rules over the fortunes of the house much more than I do. "They have sent round from the cleaner's and Margaret wants to know whether you think those curtains ought to go to be cleaned."

"Curtains?" My dazed brain refused to take in any idea of curtains.

"Yes," says Tippety. She is a small bright creature, this young lady of mine, and I call her Tippety-Witchet out of compliment to her stature. "The curtains out of the spare room—you know. You said the other day that they ought to be cleaned

## THE KEYSTONE OF THE HOUSEHOLD.

again as the laundress did them so badly. Shall they have them?"

"Yes—yes, they ought to have them." I have not the least idea whether they do want cleaning or not, or whether I did say that they did, but it isn't a matter of great moment. Then comes Kitty, my eldest, ready dressed for her school to which she goes in the mornings. "How are you this morning, Mother!" she remarks.

"I have got a headache," I say feebly.

"Headache? Poor darling! Shall I bring you the kitten to keep you company?"

"No, I don't want the kitten, thank you. I don't want anything."

"Well, I am just going down to get my breakfast," she says. "I will come up and say good-bye to you before I go. Oh, what do you want?" she continues as another little person comes into the room. "You are not to come worrying Mother; she's got a headache."

"I shan't worry Mother," says an important little voice. "Mother knows I never worry her. I wouldn't worry her for the world. Dar—ling Mummy, I am so sorry you have got a headache!"

Kitty however hustles little Rosa out with scant ceremony and I hear them go away to the breakfast room protesting vigorously one against another. Then George says with a sigh that he must get up. "Poor old lady," he adds, "it is dreadful having you ill in bed. The whole house seems unhinged. However, I must get up."

He has scarcely departed to his dressing-room when there comes a soft and apologetic knock at the door. It is the housemaid Margaret; she wants to know what I will have for breakfast. By this time I am feeling as if I should never eat breakfast or any other meal again. "Nothing, Margaret," I say.

"Nothing! Oh—but, M'm, you must eat," she says reproachfully. "You will be quite ill if you don't eat."

"Well, I will have a cup of tea—I don't care."

"Will you have a bit of toast, M'm?"

"I don't care—I don't want anything—let me alone, Margaret. I have got a headache."

Margaret coughs discreetly and departs out of the room. In

a few minutes she returns with a very dainty tray on which are a fried egg and rasher of bacon, some strips of toast and a little teapot. I look at it hopelessly. If I had had it half an hour before I might have eaten it all; as it is, I feel as if a single mouthful is an impossibility. Then Kitty comes back to say good-bye. I rouse myself from the contemplation of my own uneaten breakfast to ask if she has had a proper meal herself. "Yes, dear," she says briskly, "we had sausages—lovely!" The mention of sausages finishes me!

Kitty having bade me adieu departs, coming back yet once more to make me a fresh offer of the kitten. The kitten is a little ill-tempered thing which claws in season and out of season; when it doesn't claw, it yells; when it doesn't yell, it squeaks. I thank her, but I decline the kitten. Then I look at the tray once more. Well really I ought to eat something; it is foolish to go on like this—a woman of my age. I know that food will do me good—it is only a nervous headache; so I pour out a cup of tea, but before I can taste it there is another knock at the door. It is Margaret back again. "If you please, M'm, Cook wants to know whether a gentleman wasn't coming to dinner to-night?"

I give a groan. Of course there was a gentleman coming to dinner—that man mixed up with mining, that George thinks such a lot of. Of course! Dear—how stupid of me to forget. "You had better tell Cook to come up to me and I will talk to her about dinner," I replied. "Or she might talk it over with Miss Norman. I am not very well, Margaret."

"No, M'm, I am sure you look dreadful. I thought yesterday you looked dreadful. I said so to Cook then. Shall I ask Miss Norman to come up to you?"

"Yes, I think you had better."

Miss Norman does come up in about five minutes. She sits down on the edge of the bed and contemplates me with pitying eyes. "Dear me, you do look bad! I am sure your head is dreadful. Would you like me to bathe your head?"

I loathe having my head bathed but I cannot say so, but I smile and I say, "No, dear, thank you. It will be better presently if I can only rest."

"Well now," says she, "I will tell you what I will do. It is a lovely morning, I will just arrange for this dinner and then I

THE KEYSTONE OF THE HOUSEHOLD.

*Belgravia Annual 1893.*  *To face page 9.*

will take the children out on the top of the 'bus. It will be a great treat for them and it will keep them out of the way until lunch time."

In my heart I bless Tippety for her happy thought. We arranged the details of the dinner and of one or two things which she is going to do while she is out. She carries away the tray—which I have left in a disgracefully untouched state—gives me a little scent on a handkerchief, lowers the blinds an inch or two—for Margaret always pulls up the blinds when she brings the early tea—and advises me to settle down and have a real good nap. She might as well advise me to settle myself down to become the Empress of China.

Positively they cannot have left the house, or they can only have just left the house, before a barrel organ begins outside. Oh that barrel organ! It plays the Intermezzo from *Cavalleria Rusticana*—plays it at a hand-gallop—and follows it with " Linger longer Lucy," and that again with " Daisy Bell ; " then by some extraordinary lunacy of selection on the part of the maker of the terrible instrument plunges into *Adeste Fideles*. I have by this time reached such misery that I am far too wretched to get up and ring my bell. No, I will lie still and martyrize myself. I will endure this torture ; he cannot be very much longer. Surely the pennies of the neighbourhood will soon be exhausted and then I shall have peace again. Blessed peace ! And the children will be enjoying themselves on the top of an omnibus. There !—he has stopped. I feel so grateful that I would throw him a shilling if I were anywhere near.

In less than five minutes Margaret comes back again. "If you please, M'm, Miss Dodds has sent round to know if you can conveniently let her have your black silk dress to alter ? She finds she can get it done to-day. And have you pinned the skirt just where you wanted that pleat putting in ?"

No, I have not touched it. I send Miss Dodds a message that I am in bed with a very severe headache ; I have not tried the dress on since I saw her, and I cannot let her have it. I know I shall have to wait six weeks now, but still I cannot make an effort and dress myself for the sake of accommodating Miss Dodds. Oh, dear, how bad my head is ! But it is quiet—that is one great thing—and the scent Tippety gave me is very refreshing. I lie back, look at my bedroom and think what a pretty bedroom it is and (in spite of my headache) what a happy woman I am, to feel that husband and children—— But what is that? Oh dear Heaven! "Linger longer Lucy" on a barrel organ or a piano organ—ten times as loud as the one that has just gone away! I am so stunned that I lie listening to "Linger longer Lucy." It is followed by "Daisy Bell" and "Queen of my Heart," then by the *Adeste Fideles*— and I know perfectly well the Intermezzo is coming. I feel as if the beautiful air had turned into some dread ogre. I know that by the time the first tender chords break upon my ears I shall go into raving hysterics. I cannot do anything to stop myself. If only somebody would come! Oh, there is George. "Well, my dear, how are you?" he asks in the hearty voice and with the air of a man who has had a good breakfast.

"I am going mad," I reply.

"What is the matter?"

"Oh—that organ-grinder George."

"The brute! I never heard him. I'll go and stop him."

He comes back presently and tells me that he has given him in charge and that he has also tipped the policeman to keep the square clear for the rest of the morning. "You know, dear, it was a mistake coming to live in a square; we should have done much better in a street. We might have found a street where there was a common garden behind where the children could play. These squares attract all the brutes in the town. All the same, I don't believe even we are as badly off as they are in Queen's Gate. Poor devils! They begin about eight in the morning and they leave off at twelve at night. I am told it is something too fearful!"

Then he too sits down on the edge of the bed. It is a curious thing that if ever I have a violent headache, everybody who comes to see me—excepting of course the servants—sits on the edge of the bed. I don't mind the children much, because I can tell them to get off, but George is a large heavy man and I do mind him. But his intentions are of the kindest so I say nothing, for truly I would not be without them for the world. He asks me if I have had any breakfast and I make him an evasive reply. "Yes, Margaret brought me some bacon and an egg, dear," I say, thinking that he will notice the discrepancy between his question and my answer. But he does not. He tells me that the sausages were really excellent; it was a thousand pities I had not been able to try one; and then he says "Well, I suppose I must go and see Brookbank about that business. It is a ghastly nuisance—I hate leaving you—but you will be all right, won't you?"

I say yes I shall be all right if he will tell the servants to send away any organ-grinders that come. "Then," says he, "I will be back to lunch. Bye-bye, Pussy-Cat. What about Lennox? He was to have dined with us to-night."

"Oh yes, I have arranged all about the dinner."

"You will get up for it, won't you?"

"I will try to," I reply. "If I get to sleep now perhaps I shall be better by dinner time."

"Oh yes, I hope so. It will be horrid if you are not. You don't think I had better put him off."

I tell him I am sure he had better not put Mr. Lennox off. So he kisses me and he takes himself away. He also leaves the door open—it is a family habit of the Hattersleys; no Hattersley born was ever known to shut a door in this world. I think they pride themselves on it! However I am quiet at last and I do get something like a snatch of sleep—not that I feel much the better—and when Tippety comes in to see me she suggests that I shall take a phenacetin tabloid. I do take a phenacetin tabloid and I continue taking them at hourly intervals till five o'clock, when having had a cup of strong tea I make an effort to rise and make a toilet. It is useless. Tippety advises me to stop where I am and I plunge back among my pillows and feel that really life is not worth living.

From this moment till midnight I have no peace. One by one the children come in to tell me the events of the day and I am too ill to have the heart to hustle them out of my room. George comes in to tell me all that he has been doing, and brings with him a whiff of tobacco smoke which is almost the death of me. Margaret comes up with two messages, and Cook sends up at the last minute in a dilemma to say that the asparagus has not come and what is she to do? Then all the children come and say good-night. They have two or three small wrangles over my prostrate body, and then Tippety comes back with three or four letters in her hand. "You won't care about your letters, Mrs.

Hattersley, will you?" she says, sticking them up on the mantelshelf.

Now if I have a craze of any kind it is for reading my letters. I could not exist for ten minutes with an unopened letter in my presence—an unopened letter addressed to me, that is—I simply could not do it. "Oh, I will read them—I will read them," I say feverishly. I do read them. One is an invitation to dinner at a cousin's whom I especially and particularly dislike. We shall not be able to get off going unless we genuinely have a prior engagement, which I am afraid we have not. Another is a bill from my drapers' and demand for payment, the usual thing—"Sorry to trouble you—heavy account to meet next Thursday," you know the kind of thing. Another is from an old lady from whom the children have expectations. She proposes to come to-morrow and spend a long day with us! I feel that if I am able to get out of my bed to-morrow morning I shall be ready for my coffin to-morrow night. Then there is a long gossipy letter from a friend recounting the details of a visit to a large country house. It is an amusing letter enough and it compensates somewhat for the petty annoyances of the others.

Tippety sits down on the edge of my bed. She tells me that she thinks the dinner went off very well in spite of the asparagus being wanting. "Cook is in rather a bad temper," she winds up, "she says she is going to give you notice to-morrow, but I don't think she really means it."

I am indifferent. Cooks may come and cooks may go—even the best of them—but there are times in one's life when their comings and goings do not affect one. Then Tippety too goes to bed and Margaret comes for a final tidying of my room and to find out whether there is anything that I will have. There is only one thing that I want and *that* Margaret cannot give me—I want a peaceful sleep. I feel rather like it—that curious half-numb sense of dreamlessness. I think I really am going to sleep at last—I feel like it—What's that? Oh, it's George coming to bed! He sits down on the edge of the bed, sits down with a plump which shakes me into wide-awakeness in a moment. "Well, Pussy-Cat, how are you feeling? All right by this time?"

I turn my head over without answering. "Bad still? Poor little woman! Is there anything I can do for you? By Jove, I have done good business with Lennox—pulled everything off just as I wanted it. Of course, you know, it was beastly withou you—beastly! He sent you all sorts of messages—hoped you would soon be better and all that. I told him it was only an ordinary headache."

An ordinary headache! "Yes," I say. It is a non-committing little word in some circumstances.

"You are quite sure there is nothing I can get you now? Don't you think a good peg would be best for you?"

"No, I don't think anything will be best for me except going to sleep," I reply.

"Well then, I will tumble into bed at once."

He does tumble into bed. It is a very big bed, bnt it shakes and jars. I say nothing. It is no use complaining—he means well—and in two minutes he is asleep as sound as a top or a church, and I lie wide-awake staring at the dimly-lighted ceiling and my headache is worse than ever. Still a reflection comes to me as I lie that after all I have not suffered this day for nothing. One must pay the price for every position, one must pay the penalty for every pleasure, and to a certain extent the pain of every joy. I am essential to my husband, to every member of my household—the keystone of the whole fabric—and after all what is a headache in comparison with all this? I have had a bad day and I feel broken and shattered now; but, at the same time, I know perfectly well that if I had been left in that undisturbed silence for which my body has been craving since my tea came this morning I should be wretched!

# Noor Mahomed's Bungalow.
## A STORY OF ANGLO-PERSIAN LIFE.
### By M. PECHELL.

"LOOK out, there's something in the way!"

The speaker seized the reins from his companion's hand, and pulled the horse aside with a jerk that made the trap reel and tremble and nearly overbalance as they left the track and went over a sand tussock on the left.

"You'll have the blooming cart over if you don't look out," said Douglas sulkily, resenting the interference with his driving.

"Well, you can't drive over a heap like that, right across the road, too. Wonder what it is?"

"A dead donkey or cow," said Douglas, looking back. "Here, give me the reins, we must get on. I've got to be on duty in that beastly office in half an hour."

"I don't believe it's an animal at all," said Wells, who was long sighted; he jumped off the trap as he spoke and went back to the object, lit up by the brilliant Persian moon. "It's a man!" he exclaimed when he reached the heap, "a white man too! Come here!"

Douglas threw the reins to the syce and went to his companion. The man was lying in a heap upon his face, apparently dead, and the two with some difficulty turned him over.

"Great God, it's Haddon!" exclaimed Wells, as he recognised the features of a fellow clerk, who had formed one of the company at the house they had just left. An hour ago he had been alive and well, the jolliest of the guests.

The three clerks belonging to the Indo-European Telegraph Department, had been dining with some friends in Bushire town. They had kept up the fun till late, or rather early hours, but Haddon had left before the others, declaring he had work to do.

"Is he dead?" asked Douglas, supporting the lifeless head. "Feel his pulse."

Wells searched for the man's wrist.

"No, it's beating," he said, "I can just feel it. We must get him home at once."

They carried Haddon to the trap, and placed him in it in as comfortable a position as they could, and the syce led the horse at a walk.

"How on earth did he get there?" said Wells meditatively.

"He's come a nasty cropper," replied Douglas.

"Cropper! Off the old saddle-back! Why, she's as steady as a rocking-horse. Haddon can ride a bit, too."

"Well, what else can it be?" said Douglas, who by reason of the stirrup cup had become argumentative.

"He's not been robbed," and Douglas pointed to the studs in Haddon's mess jacket, and his gold watch-chain. At the next bend in the road they came across a white mare peacefully browsing upon the scanty turf. The reins were dragging upon the ground and the saddle was twisted underneath her. She made no attempt to escape, and allowed herself to be caught and the gear put to rights, and Douglas rode her home to the telegraph station and aroused the Eurasian apothecary from his beauty sleep. That official discovered a small wound in the back of Haddon's head, deep and ugly-looking, from which the blood still oozed.

"He must have fallen upon a sharp stone," said the apothecary.

"But we found him on his face," objected Wells, who, knowing from long experience the qualities of the old saddle-back mare, was certain that nothing short of an earthquake would startle her into throwing the most inexperienced rider.

"He must have turned round after he fell," replied the apothecary, "I once knew a man who——."

This explanation did not satisfy Wells, but when Haddon was sufficiently recovered to be able to speak, he said that the mare had stumbled and he had lost his seat, and falling against a stone had hurt his head.

The next day Wells made a careful examination of the place where Haddon had been found. It was in a sandy track where the so-called road from Bushire leaves the *maidan*, and continues its way through a small forest of cotton bushes to the telegraph station.

"Soft as a feather bed, and not the ghost of a stone about," said Wells to himself. "I knew he lied. Strikes me that the sooner Haddon clears out of this, the better!" And he remembered a certain scene he had accidentally witnessed a few weeks before.

Haddon did clear out as soon as he was able, he applied for and obtained six weeks' sick leave, and directly he could move he left Bushire by mail steamer for Karachi.

\* \* \* \* \* \* \*

When the Indian government built the telegraph bungalows at Bushire the officials were all bachelors, and with characteristic short-sightedness, the three blocks of houses were laid out in bachelor quarters, only the superintendent being allowed sufficient room for a wife and family.

In those days there was but one white woman in the place —the Resident's wife; but that is all changed now—Love braves everything, even the climate of Southern Persia in hot weather, and married life upon the pay of a telegraphist.

An epidemic of matrimony set in, and in a few years the buildings were so congested that two or three houses had to be hired from natives for the accommodation of married officials, while the Government entered into negotiations for erecting other buildings.

Noor Mahomed's house was one of the first rented; it was within easy distance of the office bungalow, a necessity, where the office hours were twenty-four hours a day, and the work was carried on unceasingly from midnight to cock-crow, and from cock-crow till midnight. When the offer was first made to Noor Mahomed, a well-to-do Persian merchant, for his house, he declined it; he said he intended residing there himself for the rest of his natural life, but a month later, when the Government was still considering his answer, and enveloping it in sufficient red tape to be presentable for the inspection of the Director-in-Chief at Simla, Noor Mahomed changed his mind. He waited upon the Telegraph Superintendent and told him that he, Noor Mahomed, found that his business necessitated his living in Bushire town, and therefore he would rent his handsome, newly-built bungalow to the Feringhees at the ridiculously low rate of 150 *kerans* per mensem.

The superintendent said that the Indian Government would pay 50 *kerans* a month for the house, which was old and out of repair, and after much negotiation the price of 75 *kerans* was agreed upon. This for the house only, and not to include the garden filled with citron and orange trees.

The first refusal of the new bungalow was offered to Sherrad and his newly-wedded wife—and they jumped at the opportunity of exchanging their cramped quarters in the barrack-like buildings, for a roomy house of their own.

So the household gods were transferred. Before the Sherrads had actually taken up residence in their new quarters, some officers from the gun-boat then in harbour invited Sherrad to join them in a shooting expedition up the river, and he, being an ardent *shikari*, after some demur went. In fact it was Mrs. Sherrad who made him accept. He wanted a change, she said, and she would have all the more time to put the new establishment in order.

"Afraid of being left alone! Nonsense! What on earth was there to be afraid of? Plenty of other houses within call and faithful old Carlo" (the Goanese boy, who had been in her husband's service for years) "sleeping in the house."

So Sherrad departed with shooting kit and a light heart; and Mrs. Sherrad busied herself in arranging her new house. Like most Persian houses, it was two stories high, but only the upper storey was used to live in, the lower part being taken up with lumber rooms and go-downs. The largest of these was retained by Noor Mahomed for his own use, and was filled with remnants of all sorts—broken furniture, old saddlery, and rubbish of every description, purchased by Noor Mahomed at divers auctions, and waiting to be tinkered up and palmed upon unwary newcomers.

After dining and spending the evening with friends, Nan Sherrad returned to her bungalow to sleep there. It was the first night she had done so; and after making sure that all the doors were fastened, and Carlo, the cook, at his post, on a *charpoy* at the foot of the stairs, she turned in and lay down. Not to sleep, however, for she tossed restlessly from side to side of the bed, and though beforehand she had been very tired, she could not now keep her eyes closed. A lamp burned dimly in a corner, but it was not needed, for the full moon, like a huge electric light, poured into her room, lighting the remotest parts. Outside, the frogs were holding a concert, and in the distance, some pariah dogs disputed a case.

Presently a long, low, moaning sound arose—first, far distant, then coming nearer till it seemed right under the verandah; a weird, blood-curdling sound, the cry of a creature in torment.

Nan Sherrad shuddered as she heard it, but she tried to persuade herself that it was a jackal or possibly a hyena. It disappeared as it had come, growing fainter and fainter till it died away, and for a space there was silence. But not for long; again the cry arose like a distant wind, and increasing continued till it seemed to enter the room; at first, a voiceless, inarticulate wail, it changed and seemed to speak—words sounded between the agonised shrieks. And Nan distinctly heard: "Frr—ank, Fer—ank."

At the sound of her husband's name, Nan sat up in bed, and looked around with frightened eyes; she didn't at the time remember that there are many Franks in the world. She wanted to escape from the room, but the horror held her bound, and her fox-terrier, from the foot of the bed, growled an angry, sulky growl, while each separate hair of his back bristled. As Nan looked, a shadow came in the doorway, between her and the bright moonlight, a shadow that presently formed itself into a woman's figure. A wild hope arose in Nan's heart that this might be her ayah.

"Fatimeh!" she cried.

But there was no answer, and had she been able to collect her thoughts, she would have known that it was impossible for the ayah (who had gone to her home in the village, hours before) to effect an entrance through the padlocked doors. How long she watched the figure, Nan could not tell, but it seemed hours that the woman stood or crouched against the doorposts. Then slowly she rose, turning her face to Nan's, and the moonlight fell full upon it. The eyes were fixed and sightless. Nan's blood flowed back from her heart, her lungs refused to do their work, she felt as if the end of everything had come, and that there was no future; she could neither move nor speak.

Then the horrible sound recommenced—the long, low wail, beginning softly, increasing in sound, then dying down to a low moaning, and ending with the words:

"Fr—ank, Fer—ank!"

Mrs. Sherrad remembered nothing more until she found herself lying upon the bed next morning. The dawn was breaking and the first golden rays of the sun shone upon the verandah ; the awful night was over. Nan rushed out and leant over the parapet, drinking in the sweet, fresh morning air, and thanking God for the daylight, and that the horror was gone.

Just underneath the verandah stood a man, a real live human being ; and so thankful was Nan for his presence that she could have embraced him on the spot. The man turned to go, and recognising him, she called out :

"Salaam, Noor Mahomed."

The landlord looked up.

"Salaam, Mem Sahib," he replied. "I have come to see if the citrons are ready to be picked."

But he must have wandered out of his way, for there were no citron trees close to the house.

Mrs. Sherrad went downstairs, to where Carlo was folding away his bed.

"Did you hear the noise last night ?" she asked.

"No, Mem Sahib, I hear nothing. Nothing but jackals. They make plenty noise. Plenty jackals here."

"Nothing else ?"

"Nothing, Mem."

This was not remarkable. Carlo had heard nothing, as he had not been there to hear. The night just past was the birthday of one of his fellow cooks, and after ascertaining that his mistress had gone to bed, he had quietly let himself out of the house, and locking the door behind him, joined a festive circle of Goanese boys in the superintendent's cook-house. The whisky was good—so good, indeed, that Carlo did not feel equal to returning home for some hours after sampling it, and the sun was rising before he let himself into the bungalow, and lay down in bed.

A few minutes later the ayah arrived with her mistress's tea, and as soon as she was dressed, Nan Sherrad left the bungalow for ever, and went across to the telegraph buildings to see the superintendent's wife.

"It was awful—terrible," she said, as she concluded her story. "I thought I should go mad. God only knows how I kept my reason."

The story was soon known throughout the station, and Harris, the superintendent, a member of the Psychical Society, and who was on intimate terms with many spirits of high standing, declared his intention of investigating the matter. This he was unable to do for three days, but at the end of that time, he and Wells, in company of fire-arms, whisky and a goodly supply of cheroots, took up their quarters for the night in Mrs. Sherrad's room. She had refused to go near the house again, and the servants had moved her things to the spare room in the superintendent's bungalow. It was ten o'clock when Harris and Wells went to the house, and settled themselves comfortably in long chairs to await what Harris called the "materialization."

"By the way, Haddon returned by to-day's mail, didn't he?" asked Wells.

"Yes, but he's stopping the night in town; he doesn't have to report himself till to-morrow."

They smoked in silence for the best part of an hour, then Wells spoke:

"I wish this spook would hurry up," he said; "it's a trifle monotonous waiting here."

"Listen!" A faint noise arose in the distance.

"A hyena," said Wells.

The noise increased and came nearer and nearer—just as Mrs. Sherrad had heard it, then gradually died away.

"It's uncanny," said Wells shivering, "makes a fellow feel cheap."

"Be quiet," said Harris.

Again the sound arose, howling and shrieking with agony—the agony of a soul in hell. It came nearer till it filled the room. Harris laid his hand upon Wells' arm:

"Look!" he whispered. A shadow appeared in the doorway, hard and distinct, between them and the moonlight; it grew, and resolved itself into a woman's form—a woman cowering and shrinking, as if to ward off a blow. Neither of the watchers moved. The moon grew faint and disappeared behind a bank of clouds, but the light in the verandah remained unchanged, shining upon the figure's sightless eyes.

The wailing, silent for a short space, began again, decreasing slowly, and ending with the words, "Fer—ank, Fer—ank."

"Great God! Zefra."

The reply made the two men start to their feet; the woman's

figure was gone, but another—a well-known figure stood in her place.

"Haddon!" gasped Wells, seizing him.

"Did you see her?" asked Haddon, in a low voice. "Did you hear her?"

"Yes, but how did you come here?"

"I got back to the office just now. Douglas was on duty, and told me the story and how you had come here to watch. I guessed how it was, and I came across. I saw her there and heard her call my name."

"What do you know of it? Who is she?"

"Zefra, I knew the brute had found out, when he nearly did for me that night. By the Lord, he has killed her too. Damn him!" Haddon spoke wildly, but there was method in his words. "Did you see her eyes?" he asked suddenly; "they were blind. He put them out—and she looked at me. It was my fault."

"Who is Zefra?" asked Harris sternly.

"His wife, but I didn't know it. I swear I didn't know it till that night he met me outside Bushire Town. "Oh, merciful God——" And Haddon lapsed into a state of temporary insanity.

The dawn was breaking, and Harris and Wells left the room and went downstairs.

"This is a black business," said Wells, "and there's been murder done, or a pretty good imitation of it. Persians don't stick at trifles where their passions are concerned."

"Does anyone?" enquired Harris. "The question is, what's to be done next. I think—but what's that?" he asked, breaking off suddenly, as a noise attracted his attention. "There is someone in the go-down." And even as he spoke the door opened and Noor Mahomed came forth, followed by two men, bearing something upon a plank. A ghastly thing with rigid outline and upturned face, covered by a woman's *dungaree* veil.

"Look!" cried Wells. "It's the——what we saw."

Harris took Noor Mahomed by the arm roughly.

"You cur—you son of a burnt father!" he said. "What is that?"

"What is that to thee?" muttered Noor Mahomed. "But I will tell thee. It is she who was my wife. Her I am sending to Kerberla, to be buried by the tomb of the Imaum Hussain. The caravan starts at even."

"You dog, you killed her."

The Persian's immobile face grew dark.

"Her hour had come," he replied; "she died the death of the unfaithful. For such has Allah prepared a grievous punishment. I buried her there," pointing to the go-down, "but she gave me no rest, an *afreet* possessed her body, and she could not rest. Therefore I am sending her upon the *Hadj*."

The Persian walked away, followed by the men with their ghastly burden.

"Allah grant that he doesn't see Haddon," said Wells.

"We must get him out of this."

"It's a clear case for the Society," said Harris to himself.

They went upstairs and found Haddon sitting just where they had left him. He took no notice of the two.

"Come," said Harris, touching him, "this is a bad business. You'd better leave by the next down mail. I'll arrange about your transfer."

Then Harris and Wells left the house, arranging the incidents of the past night for reproduction as they went, and Haddon followed them mechanically.

## Fred Alford's Partner.

### By EDITH STEWART DREWRY,

Author of "ONLY AN ACTRESS," "ON DANGEROUS GROUND," etc.

YES, that was it. Six months ago Fred Alford, outside broker, of Old Pence Court, City, had taken unto himself a partner—not a wife you understand. Oh, no, not he; said he wasn't rich enough yet to marry, there was no hurry, as he was only seven or eight and thirty; but it was well known in the City that he was doing very well, and had a good account at his bankers, so that some folks laughed a bit at this excuse, and said, perhaps Fred Alford preferred bachelor freedom, but would some day fall in love and marry all in a rush. "Fred's a nice jolly fellow," said one, "and a capital man of business; but he is rather impetuous in taking likes and dislikes, and is certainly rather susceptible, don't you know, 'quite a masher with the young ladies.'"

"But, my dear fellow, you really do work too hard," was said to him some months back by a man he had met constantly for two years at the restaurant where they lunched—a comfortable, well-to-do City man, typically stout and good-natured, and shrewd, a diamond broker and money-lender too, they said. "You'll be grey as a badger before your time, Alford," added Mr. George Baker. "Why don't you take a junior partner who'll bring a few hundreds, and do a lot of work? Wouldn't keep you so tied by the nose either, eh?—and, by Jove, in these days," and the old cit. dropped his fat voice to a gurgling whisper, "none of us can quite laugh at extra 'sugar.' He, he, he! Think of the idea. I might hear of some one to suit you."

Fred was caught by the idea. "Messrs. Alford and——" too, looked tempting, big, important. His business was really—well, he could do with a junior. By Jove, he would think over the matter seriously. And a few days later he told Mr. Baker that if he could just drop on exactly the right man, he might conclude to take a partner. Did Baker know anyone?

"Bless me! I'd nearly forgotten the matter," said the old diamond broker, opening his round eyes. "Well, I'll see if I can help you. Ah, hum! There is a young fellow I know well. An awfully taking sort of fellow, too; fancy you'd freeze to him, but he hasn't much capital. Still, maybe he and I could arrange if you like him."

Fred was delighted, and it was settled to meet at the restaurant for an introduction on the Friday, this being Tuesday.

The interview duly took place, and Alford was quite charmed with the old diamond broker's young friend, who evidently knew all about stockbroking, but had at present only four or five hundred pounds to invest, but would have more in a twelve-month. Eventually the matter was mutually gone into between the three; further references were given; and, finally, within the month the partnership was concluded, £500 being paid into the business, and £1,000 more to be added in one year. For this last George Baker stood security; his own security being arranged between himself and young Wilmot Clyde.

"*That* part isn't my business," said Fred to a friend when the affair was completed. "Baker's guarantee is safe as the bank, for all his quiet unpretending office in Pence Lane—near my Court, you know."

"Ah, yes, glad to hear it in these shaky days," returned the friend. "I'll give you a look next time I'm near Old Pence Court, and see your partner."

"Do, old chap. Don't be too long either."

But it was nearly three months before Mr. Marling did chance to be in the City; being there then, he went to Old Pence Court as per promise, and made the acquaintance of Fred Arnold's partner. He was a decidedly good-looking young man, of about six or seven and twenty, slight built, and not above medium height; his moustache and thick curly hair were brown; the features well-cut, marked, and a trifle Roman in type, that were quite in keeping with the handsome, audacious, dark eyes. Marling noticed too, that the young fellow's gestures and movements were graceful; his voice pleasant, though not deep, smooth, and well-modulated. Voice, eyes, manner were soft and persuasive; more, there was something curiously seductive about Clyde altogether. Marling was conscious of its subtle influence to attract, even in the short time he was in the junior partner's company, and, therefore, was not surprised that Fred should feel it in three months of daily companionship. He said so to Alford when presently they were alone.

"Yes," said Fred, "that is just it. An awfully winning fellow, and I like him and trust him more and more each week. I think I'm eternally grateful to Geordie Baker for introducing Clyde. Gives one quite an odd sensation sometimes," added Fred, laughing, "that way he's got of looking at one, as if one couldn't resist his persuasiveness. He has quite made himself—unconsciously—a favourite with our clients, not so, primarily, with the feminine ones though, oddly enough; but they seem to prefer my humble self."

"Don't they like him, then? He looks quite a lady's beau, I'm sure."

"Oh, yes, they like him; but it isn't quite the same, somehow, don't you know?"

"Is he a good man of business?"

"Rather," said Fred. "He's clever enough, you bet; and I shall be able to get a nice bit of holiday this Autumn, say three weeks, whilst he takes entire charge. Heigho! That's three months off though, so I mustn't think of holidays now. Where are you going?"

"Well, I've got a rather spiffing invite to a box taken for a shooting party — people named Hilton. I've only recently known them. Don't you remember nearly a year ago, seeing in the papers about a Mrs. Hilton, whose jewels were stolen—by her maid I think it was. At any rate the maid and jewellery did vanish, but as neither could be traced, some folks did hint, I remember, that the robbery was a bit bogus, don't you know?"

"Oh!" said Alford. "What sort of people then are these Hiltons?"

"Oh! well-off nobodies at best—go the pace—live quite up to their means, I should say, and—well, Mrs. H. is the sort who might possibly make such a 'plant,' if she was hard up, to account for the vanishment of the jewellery she had so flourished about. Still, that affair's by the way; it's her concern, not mine; but that's where I'm going. Ta, ta!"

And Marling departed in peace.

Business went on swimmingly with the partners in Old Pence Court, and Alford "froze" to young Clyde more and more; and so did their clients. Indeed, by now Fred more often sent his partner to the bank than himself, to lodge or fetch bonds or scrip in their charge, to be kept or dealt with as might be. Wilmot Clyde was soon well known at Messrs. Three Stars' Bank, and when admitted to their strong room by its guardian would march with prompt familiarity to Alford's safe, whip out the key, and speedily put in or take out what was needed.

"No dawdle about you, Mr. Clyde," said the official one day as he re-locked the solid door of the strong-room, and Wilmot laughed pleasantly.

"Not this child, Mr. Sant. The world soon trips up the dawdlers anyhow; the smart ones haven't such a big chance, without letting Time catch one."

"Ha, ha! Quite true, but *you're* one of the smart ones, though."

"Reckon I am, you bet," laughed Clyde, and with a nod went off about his business.

Fred Alford arranged to take his month's holiday from the 1st of August, and Clyde was to have a fortnight a few days after the senior's return to work.

And Fred went, enjoyed himself hugely, and came back, browned, fresh as a daisy, whilst Clyde looked tired.

"I'm a bit 'autumnified,'" said he, coining a word. "Want my holiday, I suppose."

"Poor fellow, of course you do. Well, we'll set to at once then, so that I shall know what matters are in hand, or out of hand, in my absence. And you can be off to-morrow."

"All right. Thanks. I've got all the books, and my memos, and so forth in order. Of course, as most of our clients are away, business has been dullish."

"Oh, of course. One expects dulness in August."

They had not, however, more than just got to work when they were interrupted by the clerk's coming in to say that two gentlemen wished to see both partners on business.

"Show them in here, Jones," said Alford in his cheery manner, but Clyde, who was standing at the table, shot a vexed—some unkind folks might have fancied a slightly uneasy or suspicious—glance towards the door as the visitors were shown in. Both wore dark morning suits, and were precisely in dress and genteel appearance, of that stamp which, in these pretentious days, the clerk could only announce as "two gentlemen," especially as they might be new clients. The younger man paused by the door, but the elder, a man about fifty, and with an air of quiet authority about him, turned and advanced towards Fred as he rose.

"You are Mr. Alford, I presume, sir?" he asked the senior partner of the firm.

"I am. And this gentleman is my partner, Mr. Clyde," said Fred, half turning, and thinking vaguely that his partner "looked rather odd."

"Ah, yes, sir; thank you." The man stepped forward, lightly touched Clyde's shoulder, and said quietly: "You are my prisoner, on a warrant, on a charge of robbery and fraud—CHARLOTTE THORNE."

Alford sprang to his feet with a cry, staring, breathless and amazed, alarmed beyond measure, from one to the other, as his partner, livid to the lips, said hoarsely:

"There's some mistake. I am not the person you want; this is too absurd!"

"You've been wanted these two or three years," said the officer grimly. "It's no go, my girl, the game's up; and you'd best say nothing, but go quietly with us."

"But, look here, Inspector," interposed Fred, recovering a little, but hot and cold still as he recalled the curiously seductive influence of Clyde, which he and others had so often felt—"there must be a mistake! Good Heaven! it's impossible! He—she—it," cried Fred, getting mixed, "can't be a woman all these months. Why, George Baker, the diamond broker, introduced him!"

The detective at the door grinned behind his upturned hand, the inspector smiled, dryly superior, politely contemptuous of such greenness.

"George has as many *aliases*, sir, as Charlotte Thorne, *alias* Clyde, *alias* Anne Smith, maid to Mrs. Hilton. Lord bless you, sir! he's in custody now at last, and now his accomplice. Those two, sir, are the head, tail and body of one of the most daring gang of swindlers that I've known. I must ask you to look at your bank book, and strong-box, too——"

Alford staggered, though he had expected the blow.

"Good Lord! You don't mean——" he gasped.

"Yes, sir, that's part of the charge against him and the gang. There are bonds worth thousands been stolen and sold, that, with the Hiltons' jewels, we've traced in this direction, belonged to your clients. To-morrow our birds would have flown."

"It's ruin! ruin! ruin to me!" cried Alford, and fell back in his chair.

"You men are all such damned fools when a woman chooses to take you in hand," said the prisoner with a sneering laugh, "even in masculine disguise."

The trial made sensation enough, you may be sure, and the sentences were heavy enough to satisfy the sufferers on that point; but poor Fred Alford told Marling he should emigrate with his wreck of fortune. "He could never show his face in the City again after this. He should never hear the last of his 'partner,' and he couldn't stand the chaff, by Jove! Curse the woman!"

# Bunchie: A Boy's Love.
## PART I.

SHE sat up in the apple-tree, a grotesque little figure, her knees almost on a level with her nose, her golden hair making a bright patch of colour through the shadows of the leaves. A book was on her lap, but her thoughts had wandered far from it, and her great serious eyes were fixed upon the white stretch of road that showed beyond the garden and outbuildings. Not a soul was in sight, but from the meadow came ringing peals of childish laughter. Presently these ceased, and the beautiful silence of the April day brooded over all. A few pink petals, and a tear or two tumbled simultaneously on to the page before Bunchie. She brushed them away hurriedly in a shame-faced manner, forgetting the exquisite beauty of the flowers in the salt-drops that christened them. Bunchie did not often weep, but to-day the promise of the budding world touched her strangely. There was fresh life and hope all round for every thing, for everyone, but herself. Poor little Bunchie! She resolutely wiped her eyes, and the blurred lettering of her book, and was turning her attention once more to the charms of "Sintram and his Companions," when she caught sight of a light cart being driven along the road in the distance. A girl held the reins, and beside her sat a young man, who was pretending that he was not in the least incommoded by the numerous packages at his feet.

Daisy Bennett had driven into Southborough that morning to do the week's marketing for her mother, and while leisurely walking the cob up the steep hill into Melton, she was accosted by a youth, obviously a gentleman, in a dust-coloured tweed suit, and straw hat. This he raised, as he began politely—" Pardon me, but can you tell me which direction I should take for Colonel Bennett's—Melton Priory?"

Three roads crossed before him, and he glanced diffidently from them to the bright sensible face of the girl.

Being a young lady prompt of decision and action, she responded briskly.

"I'm going there. I can give you a lift. Will you come round this side, and jump up?" He did so gladly, for he was both hot and tired, but he made some apology for troubling her.

"No trouble. I live at the Priory. I'm glad to welcome you if you're a new inmate," she answered, glancing pleasantly at him beneath her straight brown brows.

"My name's Charrington," said he. "May I ask if you are Miss Bennett?"

"Daisy Bennett," she corrected. "Then you're the new one. Father didn't expect you till Monday."

"I'm sorry. I hope my coming won't put anybody out. But perhaps before this the Colonel has had my telegram. I wired from town."

"Perhaps," she answered nonchalantly, flicking the flies off "Pimple's" ears. "But the Southborough boys are awfully slow. I daresay your wire'll arrive about the same time that you do."

He was secretly amused at her easy manner. Young as he was, she was one of the first women he had met who ignored his title so completely. It might have been simply "Daniel Charrington" who sat beside her instead of "Sir Daniel."

Turning in at the Priory gates, she trotted "Pimple" sharply up the drive, and stopped before the hall door, gay with westeria flinging its delicate mauve clusters upon the dull red wall above. Daisy sprang down lightly, without waiting to be helped.

"It's lucky you didn't come a week ago," she said laughing. "You'd have found the entrance to our domain in a great mess. We've been having our annual infliction, spring-cleaning, and this year we've actually indulged in a new coat of paint, see? You needn't be afraid, it's quite dry. It wasn't altogether in honour of your arrival," she added, "but stern necessity that drove us to it. Never mind those things, the man will bring them in. Come yourself."

He followed her into the dim cool hall with its white flags, and dark oak panelling. Opening a door at the end, Daisy sent an echoing shout of "Dad" through the house.

"Of course it's a half-holiday," she explained, "else I couldn't do that. We mustn't raise a voice above a whisper in working hours. Come in here, Sir Daniel," with a sudden remembrance of his name, "and sit down."

She led him into a wide, low drawing-room with French

windows which stood invitingly open towards an old-fashioned garden, where a mossy lawn, dotted over with standard roses, was framed by espalier pears white with bloom.

"This is not our tennis lawn. That's in the meadow—too many flowers here," she said, as he strolled towards the window by her side.

They stood a few minutes chatting, Daisy vainly endeavouring to curb her impatience.

"I must go and see after Dad," she said at last. "He's about the place somewhere, I suppose. I know Mother's out, paying calls, but she ought to be in soon too. Make yourself happy with those papers, Sir Daniel," and she went away, putting her head in again at the door to add, "We have high tea at seven, in case no one else tells you." She was gone before he could answer, and he sat down regretfully. Her cheeriness charmed him. He was only twenty and rather shy, although he was a baronet. He had never boarded at a crammer's before, and he had been conjecturing on the journey what sort of an establishment he should find. It promised well, he thought. He could scarcely imagine Daisy's father to be a very formidable person

Just then the Colonel came in. He was a medium-sized man with a round bald head, a tawny moustache, and twinkling blue eyes. He held out his hand, saying genially:

"My dear fellow! Delighted to see you, though I didn't expect you till Monday."

"I know, sir. I haven't put you out, I hope. I did wire. The fact is, I didn't quite know what to do with myself. My mother was away, and I hadn't anything on hand——"

"So you thought you'd come straight on, and settle down a bit? Quite right, quite right. Now let me take you to your room. Oh! Ah! my wife, Mrs. Bennett. My dear, this is our new fellow, Charrington."

Mrs. Bennett, a little plump fair woman, had entered at the moment. She looked up at Charrington's face, nearly a foot above her own, and said kindly:

"Very pleased to see you, Sir—er——"

"Daniel!" responded the owner of the appellation, with a smile.

"Ah! To be sure," added Colonel Bennett, "family name, no doubt. Puritan family, probably, Charrington?"

"Yes, sir, I believe so."

"Well, come and have a wash and brush up, anyway. We'll go to my room, whilst yours is being got ready. We have our next meal at seven."

"But Sir Daniel must surely need a cup of tea or something before then, after his journey and long walk," put in Mrs. Bennett, whose aim it was to supplement the bodily needs of her husband's pupils, as he did their mental ones. "It's only five. The children are just going to tea. Couldn't he join them?"

"Would you mind, Charrington? My youngsters are a very ordinary lot, but they won't bother you if I tell them not to."

The lad replied that he would be very glad. He guessed that Daisy might possibly superintend the school-room tea, so he explained: "I have met Miss Bennett, sir; she overtook me as I was walking out, and kindly gave me a lift."

"Oh! to be sure, Daisy told me. This way then, Charrington."

The children were grouped together in the back-hall, a square oak-panelled room with a table set for tea in the centre. Daisy came down the staircase as the others entered.

"Where's Bunchie? Do any of you know? I can't find her upstairs."

"She's in the apple-tree. I put her there an hour ago," cried a fourteen-year-old school-boy.

"And weren't you going to fetch her back?"

"I hadn't forgotten, but I thought you would. You always go chivvying after Bunchie directly you come in."

"Oh! George! How could you be so careless? And she might have got stiff, and fallen out. Nora, take my place."

Nora, a slim little damsel of twelve, put herself behind the tea-tray, and began filling the cups, while Daisy ran out and across the garden.

Bunchie still sat in the apple-tree. She had twisted a scarlet shawl round her shoulders. There was an ominous cloudiness about her eyes, which Daisy was quick to perceive; she stood below and leaned up into the tree.

"I don't want to come in," remarked Bunchie rather fretfully. "I don't want any tea."

"Let me bring you out a cup, then; but, dear, aren't you tired of sitting there?"

"No," said Bunchie, moving her head restlessly, "I'd rather be left alone."

"So you shall." And with quick steps Daisy flitted across the lawn.

"I'm going to take Bunchie a cup of tea," she explained, appearing with a salver. "She's tired and doesn't want to come in. Plenty of milk, Nora, and another lump of sugar."

Daisy added some buttered scones on a little plate to the tray, and went out. Bunchie had recovered her sweetness of temper, if not her equanimity, and allowed herself to be helped down.

"We have no school-room," Mrs. Bennett was explaining when Daisy returned. "You see there are the class-rooms, and the Colonel must have his private one, and we require two sitting-rooms beside, and so many bedrooms, that really there is not much accommodation to spare. George and Dicky go to school in Southborough, and are only at home from Saturday to Monday. As to the girls, we manage their lessons among us at present. They must go to school of course later on."

Grace and Nora made a furtive grimace at each other, and Hetty remarked in a loud aside to George:

"How *can* you eat so much? You know you're going to have high tea by and bye?"

"You shut up," replied the boy, successfully disposing of another slice of plum cake. "Food was made to be eaten."

Which speech could not be contradicted.

"How's the child now?" inquired Mrs. Bennett, as Daisy slipped in and took a seat beside Nora.

"All right, thank you, mother. She is having her tea in the summer-house."

"Don't let her stay out too long. Although it's such a warm evening, she may get a chill."

This all tended to lead Charrington to suppose that Bunchie was a child. His surprise then was great when he entered the drawing-room a few minutes before seven, to find himself closely followed by a small, weird-looking creature, shrouded in a wealth of golden hair, out of which looked a pale earnest face with aquiline features, and great dark eyes. That there was something wrong about her he could not fail to see, but whether she was child or woman he could not be sure. Mrs. Bennett simplified matters by briefly introducing : " My eldest daughter —Sir Daniel Charrington." And then Bunchie slipped away as usual into the background.

The Colonel came bustling in, followed at intervals by a florid Frenchman and a small spare man—his tutors.

" We call *him* the thin captain," whispered Dicky Bennett at Charrington's side, indicating the spare man. " His name's Dare, but he don't dare a lot with the fellows here. They mostly boss him. Fellows like to boss, you know, whether they are big or little. My ! if he was up at my shop, the chaps there 'ud fairly lam in to him."

" Hush," cried Charrington awkwardly. He had some difficulty in keeping his face from smiles. Colonel Bennett introduced him to his new companions with that *bonhomie* that was peculiar to him.

" M. de Livac ; Captain Dare ; Sir Daniel Charrington ; Lyons, Brakespear, Molyneux, Simmonds——" and so on.

The Frenchman accorded the shy new-comer an elaborate bow. Captain Dare came beside him, and immediately commenced a conversation upon tactics which Charrington mentally voted " shoppy." He was glad when the meal was announced, though he had no experience of high tea, and not the faintest idea what he was about to sit down to. His place was near Mrs. Bennett, and he pleased her by admiring the floral decoration of the table. It was simple. White vases, in which were primroses, mixed with the green of rhibees, and between them were drawn soft billows of pale green art-silk. The primroses looked like white stars in the lamp-light.

" That is Bunchie's work," said Mrs. Bennett, with a quiet tender smile towards her eldest daughter. " We like her to do what she can, she enjoys it. But she is not strong, as you may see."

Bunchie sat next her father. Two bright pink spots burned in her cheeks. Her animation had returned, and she was talking almost gaily with the young fellow upon her other side. Conversation was brisk and frequent, the most silent members of the party being George and Dicky, who sat together, and occupied themselves in quietly getting through sufficient comestibles to last them almost until they came home again.

"Beastly grub up at our's," volunteered Dicky to Charrington, to whom he had taken rather a fancy. "Got to put in ballast when you can."

Being Saturday evening, the young men joined the ladies in the drawing-room, instead of going to work as on other nights. Mrs. Bennett was dozing, and awoke with a start when they entered. Daisy sat, softly strumming. Bunchie was knitting, her long thin fingers flying swiftly in and out with her needles. Charrington drew a chair near her.

"I hope you are rested. You were tired at tea-time," he ventured.

"I am often tired, that's nothing," she responded brightly. "I'm afraid I was out of temper as well. Something had vexed me."

"What was it?" he said unthinkingly.

She hesitated.

"Don't tell me if you don't want to. It was stupid of me to ask."

"I don't mind. It was only such a fine day! Don't you often want things on a fine day that you don't think of when it is dull and rainy? I do. Sunshine makes me want to get out and about like other girls, and you see I can't do that very much. It's stupid of me to mind, when I have such a lot that other girls have not." She gave a quick expressive glance round the room, including her parents and Daisy. "They are all so good to me," she murmured.

"Of course," said Charrington sympathetically. "They'd be brutes if they weren't," was the thought in his mind.

Bunchie deftly changed the subject, and went on talking of other things. She had a soft voice, and her face, when lit up, was charming. Charrington thought he had seldom seen anything more beautiful, but it was difficult to realise that this weird, childish creature, in whose fragile frame seemed pent a soul infinitely too large for it, was really the sister, and the elder sister, of the self-possessed trim young person who was sitting at the piano. A little group was round Daisy, and she had a word and a laugh for all; but she was tired, she declared.

"A day's shopping in Southborough is enough to take it out of any one." And looking across the room, she observed the bent heads of her sister and Charrington. She frowned slightly. "Come, Bunchie, you too must be tired." And rising, she crossed the room.

"I am not," said Bunchie; "don't hurry on my account, dear," but lifting her eyes to her sister's, she caught sight of the troubled expression in them, and at once got up.

"I will come of course, Daisy."

"I think you had better," and Daisy gravely said "good-night" to all, Bunchie following suit. Both girls kissed their father and mother, and Charrington, who was nearest the door, held it open for them. As they passed him, Daisy slipped her arm round her sister with a protecting gesture. Thus, side by side, the physical difference between them was more apparent. Daisy's strong young form, full of health and vigour, showed to advantage near the tiny figure of Bunchie. But there was something singularly attractive about the latter. The quantity of fluffy golden hair which she wore in a luxuriant mass over her shoulders, made her look like a fairy in a pantomime; it was totally unconfined, and reached below her waist. Her dress was of some clinging silky material of pale egg-blue, worn short, and displaying two dainty feet and ankles. Daisy, in a severely simple white frock of regulation length, with closely-twisted coils of brown hair, was a distinct contrast.

The following day was Sunday, and most of the party at Melton Priory went to church in the morning, filling three pews close together. It was a curious little old-world church, with many stained windows, and much fine carving. Both the organist and choir knew their work well, and fulfilled it ably. The result was a rare treat to Charrington, who possessed a music-loving soul. It filled him with the species of intellectual transport that many mistake for a sense of religion.

It was another warm day; the lights of the upper part of the windows were open, and through them could be seen the tops of elm trees waving green and fresh. A thrush sat on one, singing ecstatically. In the pauses of the service his joyous rhapsody could be clearly heard. Bunchie's delicate up-turned profile was set in the direction whence the sound came. The sunlight falling through a yellow pane of glass filtered round her, making the threads of her hair seem like spun gold, and to Charrington's fanciful mood, investing her with the nimbus of some haloed saint. Unbecoming patches of purple and green fell across the faces of Mrs. Bennett and the children, who sat in the front seat, but amongst them Bunchie's picturesque figure shone, hallowed by the golden gleam.

From his seat in the rear, Charrington watched her, lazily half-shutting his eyes, and allowing his imagination full scope.

Presently the hymn was given out. The congregation rose with a subdued rustle. And a less emotional man than Charrington might have noticed the look of rapt longing upon the poor little cripple's sensitive face. The prisoned soul rose to her eyes, and looked through them to the world of blue ether beyond the open windows. It was as though she craved to be gone, whither the notes of the hymn, and the thrush's song were rising.

> "Here in the body pent,
> Absent from Him I roam,
> Yet nightly pitch my moving tent,
> A day's march nearer home."

For the first time Charrington listened to the words rather than to the music only. He seemed to know something of what Bunchie was feeling.

Outside the porch, he went up to her, and taking her books out of her hand, walked home beside her. It nettled him to see Daisy preferred by the other men before her. Bunchie's gentle soul opened like a flower in the sunshine of his shy, unspoken sympathy. She was very quiet during the first part of her walk; the solemnity of the past hour clung about her, and seemed to sweeten and broaden the natural depths of beauty within her. By the time they reached the gates of the Priory, the two were fast friends.

All the party, down to little five-year-old Rowley, sat down to the Colonel's amply-furnished table for the early dinner. It was the only meal of the week which all the children were allowed to share with their elders, and the talk was gay and incessant. Charrington, whose home life had been a narrow one, thought he had never before realised what true domesticity might be.

After dinner the children scampered away on various occupations intent, before their mother should call them for a quiet hour with her in the drawing-room. The young men, who for the most part had acquaintances in the neighbourhood, started in different directions, while some lit their cigarettes, and lounged off to smoke. The Colonel, thinking this a good opportunity to increase his knowledge of Charrington, invited him to come for a walk, and they strolled away to some of the shady lanes about Melton.

The Colonel, however, was neither a young, nor particularly energetic man, and never took more exercise than he found absolutely necessary. Thus it happened that the walk was not a very long one, and a couple of hours later, Charrington, idly wandering through the garden, came upon Bunchie gazing disconsolately into her favourite seat—the gnarled arms of the large old apple tree. Her face brightened at his approach.

"Were you contemplating tree-climbing?" asked he.

"I was wishing I could get up, but I mustn't venture alone," she answered smiling.

"Let me help you. You're not afraid of falling?"

"Not if any one gives me a hand. You see my back isn't strong enough for that sort of thing. But—no, thanks, I won't get up now. Shall we walk on? But don't let me keep you if you were going to do something else."

"On the contrary. I've nothing to do, and shall be very glad if you will let me stay with you. I've been sitting on that granite seat of yours by the gate leading into the meadow. Like the 'gehr-fowl,' 'I was all alone; on the all-alone stone!'"

She laughed.

"So am I, we will keep each other company."

"Where is your sister? She is generally with you, is she not?"

"Yes. Oh, Daisy gives up so much of her time to me, but she is at the Sunday School now. She will be back soon."

There was a quick patter of little feet down one of the paths, and Hetty appeared, hot and breathless.

"Bunchie! Bunchie! Oh! there you are. Mother says, be sure you come in directly you get the least bit chilly."

Bunchie nodded, but the child still stood on one leg, kicking a pebble.

"I was to see if you wanted anything."

"Nothing, thank you, dear; and tell Mother that I won't stay out too long."

When the little girl had run away, Bunchie turned to Charrington. Tears were very near the velvety eyes.

"Aren't they all good to me?"

"I can understand that they would be," he answered rather stiffly.

"They are all so sorry for me."

"But why? And—would you mind telling me why every one calls you 'Bunchie?' It *can't* be your name."

She gave a pretty little laugh.

"Not exactly. You see "—more gravely—" it's because of my figure."

He looked puzzled.

"I don't see anything particular about your figure."

"Don't you? Oh! I *am* so glad. I'm so queer and thick-set, you know, and then I have this hump." She drew aside a long handful of the soft golden hair, disclosing a rising lump between the shoulders.

He now saw that the hair was intended to hide it, which as a rule it did effectually. Pity kept him silent.

"Now you see why I can't do the same as other girls. I don't know how the name grew. But after my accident, when *this* came, everyone called me by it. It seemed just to suit me."

"It wasn't very kind of them to remind you in that way."

"Oh! They didn't mean it unkindly," she answered quickly. "The children began it. It was just fun with them. And then my real name is such a mouthful—Dorinda."

"How did the accident happen?" he asked.

"Oh, when I was quite a little thing. We were playing, and I fell over the banisters."

"Why don't you tell all the truth?" exclaimed a harsh voice behind them. Charrington did not recognise it, and turned quickly. Daisy stood there, her face dark with sudden pain.

"*I* will tell you, Sir Daniel. It was my fault. *I* pushed her. I was always bigger and stronger than she. We were sliding down the banisters, here, in the hall—you know there are stone flags below. And she wouldn't go fast enough, so I pushed her."

"Oh, Daisy, dear!"

Bunchie began to tremble. Daisy drew her arm tenderly through her own.

"There! open confession is good for the soul. Now, Sir Daniel, you know what sort of a girl I am. I have ruined my sister's life."

"It was an accident. And you have been the best and kindest sister to me," said Bunchie eagerly.

"It was an accident," echoed Charrington, but he understood now the motive of the special loving kindness that surrounded the cripple.

## PART II.

THE spring deepened into summer, and that again flushed towards autumn. The golden corn sheaves stood all about the fields of Melton. The world was gay with holiday life to all but the Militia cadets at Melton Priory. They were putting on the last "spurt" of work, for the examination was to be held in September, and many were going up for their final trial. Charrington, although he had only been six months under Colonel Bennett's tuition, had done well, and was now buoyed up with every prospect of success. Yet he was not looking strong.

"The work has begun to tell upon him," said the Colonel to Mrs. Bennett one morning, as they were enjoying one of the rare chats they occasionally permitted themselves, apart from their busy household.

"I know another who looks peaky, and that's Bunchie. I really think I must send her and Daisy away to the sea."

There came a tap at the door.

Mrs. Bennett sighed, and answered regretfully, "Come in."

Daisy stood on the threshold.

"Sorry to disturb you, *madre mia*, but the children want to take their tea to Lyndon Woods this afternoon. I suppose we can go?"

"Certainly, my dear. You had better tell cook to pack what you want, and let her know what time you start. Are you all going? Is Bunchie equal to it?"

"Yes; she wishes it. It's George's idea, and they're all mad to go. Bunchie must drive, of course, and the rest of us will do so in turns."

"Take the phaeton; it will hold more of you."

A shout of jubilation greeted Daisy as she returned to the hall.

"Hooray! Now, girls, look spry."

Dicky sat on the corner of the table, swinging his legs with an air of superiority, while his sisters were busy with their preparations.

"Hollo! youngster. What's the sport?" cried his friend Charrington, who was passing through from one of the class-rooms. "You look uncommonly festive."

"Lyndon! Lyndon!" shouted the boy excitedly, while his brother bounded in from the garden, waving a butterfly net. Dicky began chanting an improvised rhyme:

> "There was a young damsel of Lyndon,
> All of whose garments were pinn'd on.
> When I sighed, Don't they prick?
> She replied, They won't stick,
> So that is the reason they're pinn'd on."

An appreciative roar of laughter from George and Charrington greeted this sally.

"That's just what I've been saying to Daisy in the kitchen. She wears a huge safety-pin hooking up the back of her skirt to her waist-band because it's the fashion! Ugh! Some chap'll be getting his fingers pricked. *You'd* better look out, Charrington! All right—don't kill a fellow," and the boy dodged round the table.

"You impudent young scamp! Your sister would box your ears if she could hear you."

"No, she wouldn't. She'd get as red as a peony, and tell me to stow my twaddle—only she wouldn't put it that way. I have it. Safety pins are made *not* to prick, else she wouldn't wear 'em just there!"

"Shut up, chatterbox, and tell me what all this unseemly hilarity is about."

"Your request is slightly contradictory. However," with a lordly air, "we are going to take the girls and the grub to Lyndon Woods this afternoon."

"What! all of you going? And what are you going to do there?"

"Ratting—if we can get any rats. There are generally loads down near Nettlecombe Farm close by. And catch moths for our collection, and anything else we can find, and have a jolly big tea. Make the girls do the business gipsy-fashion, you know."

"Delightful programme, especially for the girls," laughed Charrington. Dicky caught his arm.

"Oh, I say, Charrington, come too, there's a dear chap. Do now, and you shall boss the show, you shall really. Get the pater to knock you off the afternoon."

"I'm going to knock myself off, if the Colonel doesn't object. I've got a thundering head, and must have a few hours' rest."

"Then come with us. It's the very thing to do you a pot of good."

"I'm not so sure of that," said he doubtfully, when Bunchie came in bent upon some household matter, and jingling a bunch of keys.

She was at once appealed to.

"Here, Bunchie, tell Charrington he's got to come with us this afternoon."

Bunchie looked up, saying as plainly as eyes, as well as lips, could speak, "Do come."

He stammered, and hesitated.

"I'm really afraid, Miss Bennett——"

Dicky broke in with an indignant protest:

"Oh, I say, you *can't* refuse Bunchie."

"I'm sorry to, but——"

Bunchie waited to hear no more. As she turned away, George sprang after her.

"Never mind, old girl. He's an uncivil chap, and we'll have no more to say to him."

"It's no matter to me if he comes or not," said Bunchie with girlish pique, "only I thought he'd like to."

"And so I should. You misunderstood me, Miss Bennett. I was not sure about the Colonel."

It was a lame excuse, but Charrington fell back upon it helplessly.

Bunchie's sweet little face brightened.

"Father won't mind. He was saying yesterday that you needed rest."

Colonel Bennett was not likely to refuse a reasonable request.

"Go by all means, Charrington, and take care of my little girls. They need a steady head amongst them. The boys are but young."

The children were buzzing about the stable-yard like so many happy bees, piling their baskets into the back of the phaeton, and helping, or rather hindering, the man who was harnessing the cob. Daisy came briskly round the corner from the kitchen premises.

"You coming, Sir Daniel?" she said blankly, overhearing her father's last words. He laughed awkwardly.

"Yes, Miss Daisy, if you will allow me. Please don't look so dreadfully disappointed."

She stooped hurriedly to tie a refractory shoe-lace. When she raised her head, the dull red that had suffused her face was slowly melting out of it.

"I shouldn't have thought a function of this sort likely to prove vastly entertaining to you," she remarked rather ungraciously.

Charrington bit his lip. He had half a mind not to go, but he caught a fleeting glimpse of white skirts, and Bunchie appeared, flicking a carriage-whip.

"Now whom am I to have the privilege of charioteering?" she cried.

There was a babel of many voices, as the children began all talking at once. Colonel Bennett settled the dispute. "The girls will drive, the boys will walk—with Charrington."

Hetty, Grace and Nora clambered one after the other into the back seat of the phaeton, while Rowley created a laugh by exclaiming:

"Hadn't you better send one of us wiv ve girls, Faver? Vey can't look after vereselves."

"Hullo! you want to ride, my pigmy? So you shall. Here, Bunchie! Daisy! Can't you squeeze Rowley in between you?"

But Rowley drew back, blushing scarlet.

"I didn't mean *vat*, Faver! I'd *larver* walk, *leally*. Dicky! you go wiv 'em."

"All right," said Colonel Bennett with quick comprehension. "Jump down, Hetty. They can squeeze you up in front. Now, Dicky—George, one of you, get up here. I don't want to hurt the little chap's feelings," he continued, going round to his elder daughters. "But be sure he rides home, it's too far for him to walk both ways."

"Very well, Father, I'll see to that," said Daisy, as she made room for Hetty beside her. Bunchie whipped up "Pimple" and turned his nose out upon the road, echoes of gay laughing voices coming back to the little group in the yard.

"Miss Bennett is not nervous driving?" inquired Charrington.

"Not a bit. Now, boys, it's time you were off. This young man is a brave fellow to look at, but he's not a champion pedestrian as yet, eh, Rowley?"

"I can do seven miles easy, Faver. Hetty could only do five at my age."

"What can you expect of a girl?" put in Dick scornfully. "Come on, Charrington, I know a cut across country. We shall get there as soon as the trap."

It was a pleasant walk over the hills to Lyndon, a village nestling in wide-spreading woods. That part of them that was the destination of the young Bennetts, sloped upwards from the east, until they crowned the cliffs overlooking the sea. Briskly as the three walkers had come, the phaeton had arrived before them, and the girls stood surrounded by baskets, at a gate leading into the woods, while George drove round to Nettlecombe Farm to put up the cob. He came back shouting gleefully.

"There are a lot of rats in the stack-yard, and old Spriggins is going to have out his terriers. Let's get tea over sharp. Come along, girls, earn your living. Not you, Bunchie, don't touch that, it's too heavy for you."

He pushed her aside with rough kindliness, and hurried to and fro with his brothers, carrying the things required into the wood. His sisters had not been idle. In a clearing where the shadows fell deepest, they had tied three poles together, gipsy fashion, and Hetty and Nora, with inflated cheeks, were coaxing the fire into a blaze. Dicky ran off to fill the kettle at the farm, while Grace and Rowley laid the cloth upon the ground, and decorated it with great bunches of heather and foxgloves. Bunchie was quietly unpacking the baskets; Charrington offered to help her; but Daisy stood silently by. She looked and seemed uncomfortable, but it was difficult to be silent or cheerless long, in that merry party, and she laughed out presently, as joyously as the rest. But when tea was over, and the remains of the feast cleared away, and the children were clamouring to go to the farm, she looked up at Charrington, and said, with an apparent desire to make amends for her former ungraciousness:

"There's an awfully pretty view from the top of the cliffs. Do you care to see it?"

"Very much," he responded. "Shall we go? Is Miss Bennett equal to the climb?"

"Oh! Bunchie'll stay here. You'd rather, wouldn't you, dear? You don't want to tire yourself. There's a long drive back."

"I'll stay here," said Bunchie. She crouched down under the bracken, the tall green fronds making an airy pent-house above her golden hair. Charrington looked back at her, disappointed. There were pathetic lines about the little figure that smote him. He yearned to gather it to his breast, and comfort it to strength, and joy, and love. But he followed Daisy up the path. The children were scampering across the field to the farm.

Daisy sent one of her ringing calls after them.

"At half-past six, be back here, remember. George! Nora! You both have watches. Be punctual."

"They won't have much time," remarked Charrington.

"Enough for that delightful pursuit," said Daisy in reply, as she hastened on before him, up the steep path, where the spikes from the pines were thickly strewn, and where an occasional fir-cone fell before them. A clump of wood strawberries attracted her; as she stooped to gather them, her face softened, and she said, holding out some of the fruit on her small sun-burnt palm, "I am singularly caustic to-day, Sir Daniel, you must forgive me. I am haunted by a ghost, the ghost of the Impossible, and it is not pleasing company, and is apt to impregnate one with its own vile spirit of bitterness."

It would have been no compliment to affect to misunderstand her.

"Something is troubling you," he said, quietly. "Can I do anything?"

"Yes, I will tell you what, immediately. You need all your breath for this last pull."

They went on in silence, pushing their way through the underwood, which grew closer near the summit. When they emerged a scene of almost fairy beauty met their gaze. Sheer before them the cliff descended a thousand feet towards the sea, which sparkled in silver and azure far as the eye could reach. Above it, from a bath of molten gold flecked with crimson and rose, poured the rays of the westering sun. Slowly, but surely, it was dipping towards the horizon, breathing warmth and exquisite tenderness in that solemn farewell. It was as though called away, and passing to a fairer but unknown scene, it still lingered, clinging to the world it had known and loved. Charrington and Daisy Bennett stood breathlessly before it. Something in the supremacy of that moment drew their souls out with it, across the littleness of this mundane life, to the grandeur of infinity. It wasn't all, this life. Who could look at such a sea and sky, and believe it were? And somewhere, out beyond there, through the open arms of the west, when the waiting soul should spring beyond them into space, the soothing touch of an unseen hand should smooth the crooked minds and limbs, should waken blinded eyes, and lighten darkened understandings, so that one might know all, and be content. This was partly the thought in each of their hearts. Presently Daisy put out her hand gropingly. It rested upon Charrington's sleeve.

"I want you to do something for me, Sir Daniel, will you?"

"Of course; if I can." His heart sank, though he had no thought of what was coming.

"Your exam. is about the 25th, isn't it? I have heard you say that your mother is abroad, and that you don't much care about going home to an empty house, and that, in fact, you'd stop on here. And I suppose if you happen to have failed, you meant working on with Father for your next shot in March. Well, don't do it, Sir Daniel—that's what I mean, that's what I want. I want you to go away. To go away soon—do you understand?"

Her voice broke huskily, and she turned aside. He thought he understood only too well. There was an awkward silence.

"I must seem very impolite," said Daisy at last stiffly. Then he recovered himself with an effort.

"No, only very candid. But why—oh! why must I? The mischief is gone too far already, but I am man enough to bear it, if it is."

She faced him with flashing eyes in which the tears still lingered.

"Do you imagine that I think of you? It is for *her* sake—*hers*. Do you fancy I can't see how it is with her? My little darling Bunchie. All my life has been spent in trying to screen her from pain and trouble. And now I cannot save her from this most crushing blow of all."

Incredulity strove with keenest delight within him. He caught her by the wrist. "What do you mean? Daisy, you must explain. You can't be saying that——"

"That Bunchie loves you? Didn't you know it? Why, Sir Daniel! You're more of a fool than I took you for. But I—what have I said? I wouldn't have told you for the world, if I hadn't believed you knew."

"How could I know? How could I think such a thing possible?"

"No, it isn't likely, is it? My poor little Bunchie—and I've betrayed her secret. But you'll say nothing to her—you won't let her know? Of course you won't though. I need not ask."

He made no answer, and she continued in a tone of indescribable sadness:

"You see now the burden I bear. Though you do not love her, others might. But for me she might have been well, and strong and happy. As it is——"

"As it is," he echoed mournfully, all his heart crying out with what he dared not give utterance to. Then the words broke out —"I never said I did not love your sister."

She looked at him quickly. Her womanly intuition seemed to comprehend all he could not say.

"It is impossible that she could ever be your wife, Sir Daniel. Think of her, as the mistress of your home, as the mother of your children. No, you may, or may not love her—it matters little. My poor Bunchie!"

He felt the truth of her words, and the iron entered into his soul. In the pain of that moment he almost hated the hapless cause of it, the girl beside him. He followed her again in silence down the hill.

---

## PART III.

FIVE minutes later the wood re-echoed with Bunchie's name. She was not to be found. It was close upon the half-hour, and the children, hot and tired, but happy, came running in from the farm. Their joyous faces changed speedily to dismay, as they, one and all, answered Daisy's quick, concise questions in the negative.

"No, she hasn't been to the farm, I'll take my davy," cried

George, when he came round with the cob, ready to start homewards. "But I say, Daisy, she can't have gone far. Bunchie never could walk a yard. She's got stumped somewhere, and sat down to rest. You take the kiddies home, and Charrington and I will search the wood."

Daisy would rather have remained in the wood all night than have left the place without her sister, but her common sense told her that this was the most sensible plan, and she took her seat and the reins in her hand, while the remaining five younger ones got quietly into the phaeton.

"I shall be back, and Father too most likely, in a couple of hours," she said, with a white anxious face as she leaned over the wheel to speak to Charrington. "Meanwhile, Sir Daniel, you'll search thoroughly, and when you find her, take her into the farm. They will be good to her until we come. Mother wouldn't like the children to stay out; she'd be worrying about all of us, not knowing what had happened, else I would not leave you."

"I will do my best, you may be sure," he answered, and as the phaeton drove away, he and George turned in opposite directions. It was not likely that Bunchie could have gone very far, why indeed should she? The thought of giving trouble would have kept her in the vicinity. And surely no harm could have chanced to her? It was unlikely, but the bare idea filled Charrington with distress. It was maddening to think that she—so fragile, so helpless, could be alone, and in pain or difficulty. His eyes were blurred with sudden moisture, his throat grew dry and aching. He could hear George shouting "Bunchie, hello! Bunchie!" till the wood re-echoed with the little quaint name. He tried to shout too, but he was hoarse, and could scarcely raise his voice above a whisper, so he sped on silently, with wild arms sweeping the bracken and underwood before him. It could not have been long, but to him it seemed hours, when at last, half way up the hill-side, at a spot a quarter of a mile beyond the path by which he and Daisy climbed to the summit, Charrington saw a patch of white upon the ground, and came upon Bunchie lying still and silent, one little foot twisted under her, her hands clenched; the nails had pressed hard, and left their mark upon the soft pink palm. Tenderly he unclasped them, chafing them gently, and speaking to her in tones that he vainly strove to steady. But Bunchie could not hear him; she had fainted, and when he found that she did not recover, he was at a loss to know what to do. Could he leave her, or how else obtain help? He had half raised her in his arms, now he laid her back gently, tearing an arm-full of bracken fronds, and placing it beneath her head, whilst he straitened out the poor crumpled limb. Then he saw that the ankle was much swollen above the little shoe. Carefully but quickly he unlaced this, and drew it off. The girl gave a sigh of relief; her eyelids fluttered. If he could only get some water, he thought, standing up and looking round. As he bent over her once more, she looked up and recognised him. At first she could not speak, and only shut her eyes again, wincing with pain. He suffered almost as much, seeing that he could do so little for her.

"My ankle," she moaned.

"You must have sprained it. If I could only carry you," he cried.

She felt for her pocket. He put his hand in, and found a bottle of smelling salts. These revived her a little.

"Would you mind my leaving you whilst I go and get help?" he asked.

But she shook her head, smiling faintly.

"I shall be all right directly. Don't go."

She leant against him. He supported her with his arm, and for a short time silence—save for the soft sounds of the rustling wood—lay about them. He watched her anxiously. Neither said a word, but in that quiet evening hour heart spoke to heart what lips could never tell. Presently Bunchie's hand slipped into his.

"I am better now, Sir Daniel," she said, struggling into a sitting posture. "Could I stand, do you think?"

"You ought not to try. Let me carry you."

She laughed in her old merry way.

"I am not very heavy. Perhaps you *could* manage it."

"It's just possible, I think," he answered with grim humour. "The question is, will it hurt your foot?"

"No. One moment—I will be brave."

She covered her face with her hands for an instant. When she looked up, there was the usual expression of bright trust upon it.

"Now, Sir Daniel."

He stooped, slipping his arms under her very gently, very tenderly. There was one sharp low cry of pain, which she suppressed immediately. Then he commenced the descent through the wood, stepping carefully, so as not to jar her. The echo of George's voice had long since ceased; the moon had come out, and shone across the valley when the wood opened out before them. It lit up Bunchie's pale face till it showed like a piece of carved ivory against Charrington's shoulder: all about her fell the long, soft golden hair, a strand fluttered across his lips, it was fragrant—silky. He caught his breath and strode on as rapidly as his light burden permitted. Once he looked down at her—only once. Her eyes were closed, and he was glad of it.

When they reached the farm, he laid her down upon an easy settle in the front parlour, and left her with the farmer's wife to attend her, while he went out to call George. The boy was just coming through the gates. He was spent and breathless, but he sprang forward at sight of Charrington.

"It's all right. She's inside. I found her."

"Found her? Oh!" And George leant against the horse-trough and gave way to a sob or two which, though a schoolboy, he was not ashamed of.

"You see, we're all fond of Bunchie," he said apologetically.

Charrington made no answer. He went to look along the road for the first sight of the phaeton. It arrived in a short time, with Daisy and her father inside. A strange horse had been put to the shafts instead of "Pimple."

"We came as soon as we could," said Daisy. "How is she?"

"Better, I think. She has sprained her ankle. You will find her indoors, sir."

Charrington stood by the animal while they brought Bunchie out. Daisy drove, and Colonel Bennett sat beside her, holding Bunchie in his arms, with her foot propped up. George and Charrington got up behind. Nothing much was said upon the way home, only between the moonlight and the shadows, the pale gold-framed face seemed to flit mockingly before Charrington.

"You never told me how it happened," he said a week later. "How did you get up there by yourself?"

Bunchie lay in a long cane chair on the lawn, and Charrington was smoking a cigarette on the grass beside her. She looked whiter, and more wan, her waxen pallor contrasting with the scarlet shawl she wore. She shivered a little, although it was so warm, and coughed before she spoke.

"I don't know. On my feet, I suppose! I wanted to go, and behold my reward! What one wants is always either impossible, or bad for one."

"You said you wouldn't come with us."

"I know, but after you had gone I didn't want to be left alone. Oh! you don't know what it is perhaps, but always—all my life—I have hated it; I have dreaded being left alone—being left out—as it were. It doesn't often happen, because they are all so good to me, but this time I felt it more than ever. Then I got thinking—thoughts are troublesome things sometimes, you know—and it seemed as if I should go mad. Then I tried to walk it off, and I believe I caught my foot in something. I don't remember any more—till you came."

One nervous hand stirred restlessly upon the embroidered *couvrette* across her knees. Charrington had tossed away the end of his cigarette. It was growing dark, and he was very near the little hand. Presently he stooped his lips to it. When he moved, she laid it upon his bared head. There was no need for words.

It was the evening before the examination. Work was practically over, for the Colonel never allowed his pupils to keep it up till the last minute, but presently Charrington was called in about some matter he had to arrange. He was leaving Melton Priory in two days' time. As he stood for a minute beside Bunchie's chair she looked up at him.

"You will do well to-morrow," she said, "I am sure of it."

"I hope so," he answered, "it will make a great difference to me if I do not."

"Not so much as it would to some. You see you haven't only your profession to depend on, like some of the fellows here. Fortune has been kind to you, Sir Daniel. She has given you so much."

"All but the one thing I most desire," he answered quickly, as he turned away. He was half way to the house, when some impulse brought him again to her side.

"Wish me luck, Miss Bennett," he said. "I may not see you in the morning."

Her lips trembled.

"All that is best for you, that I wish you," she said gently.

And he stepped quietly away again across the turf, leaving her alone.

The stars came out one by one, and twinkled down like diamonds upon the hot tears that fell unheeded through Bunchie's thin fingers. Her sacrifice was not complete until that moment, but now in the passionate prayers that went up for him, no thought of self was mingled.

Bunchie's cough kept Daisy awake all that night, and towards dawn the younger girl slipped on her dressing-gown, and ran, frightened, to call her mother. Bunchie lay in agony too great for speech, one hand clutching at her left side. The doctor came, and pronounced it pleurisy.

"She must have caught a severe chill, though perhaps without knowing it. This sort of thing takes five or six days to develop."

"She is not going to be very ill? She is not going to die?" cried Daisy aghast, but with her characteristic straightforwardness, desirous of knowing the truth.

She had stopped the doctor in the passage, on his way from Bunchie's room.

"People are generally very ill when they have pleurisy, but it is not an illness of long duration, unless complications arise. You are all, Miss Daisy, of—h'm!—singularly fine physique and stamina. But unluckily, your sister's lungs are contracted by the malformation of her chest and spine."

Daisy sank against the banisters with a groan. "Again, again," she thought.

"But though her constitution is not such a splendid one as yours, still, cheer up, my dear young lady. With such kind care your sister will do as well as possible, you may be sure."

She scarcely heard him, and shook hands mechanically. She waited for her father to come out of his dressing-room before going to breakfast.

"Dad, none of the fellows know about Bunchie yet. Don't tell them until after the exam. It might upset—some of them."

He patted her shoulder.

"That's my thoughtful girl. You're quite right, Daisy."

So it happened that only when the party returned from Southborough in the evening did they hear of it. Charrington had just entered the drawing-room and noticed the absence of both girls, when he heard what was being said. He stood rooted to the spot, feeling sick with apprehension. Then he crossed over to Mrs. Bennett and asked a few questions. Her motherly instinct, though sharpened by anxiety, was bent only in one direction, or she would have understood him. As it was, when he took her hand to say good night, waiting for the purpose until the others had left, and blurted out awkwardly that he could not go away until he knew that Bunchie was better, that if it made no difference to Mrs. Bennett he would like to stay a few days longer; she answered vaguely:

"It's very kind of you, Sir Daniel. Yes, by all means, stay."

The night after the examination was usually the occasion for a little merriment, but to-night everyone went quietly to their rooms. Only Charrington could not sleep. The next day all the other pupils and the tutors left, and silence, like a great shadow, shrouded the walls of Melton Priory. The children stole in and out on tiptoe. No need to tell them to hush their voices now. Not one could laugh or play happily while Bunchie lay ill upstairs.

Late in the afternoon of the fourth day, Daisy came out into the garden to find Charrington, who was slowly pacing by the old apple tree. He was thinking of his first afternoon at Melton. Daisy came close to him before he perceived her.

"I want to know if you would care to go up," she said; "she is asking for you, and the pain is easier just now."

He hesitated.

"I would like to, but would it be good for her?"

Daisy looked away across the meadow, as she answered:

"It can't do her any harm—now. Go——" she added quickly, as he was about to speak. "She will tell you herself how she is."

Charrington went up. He knew the room; one or two of the children flitted away from the door, where they watched with dog-like devotion. Mrs. Bennett signed to him to come in, and then she went away. Afterwards Charrington could never remember what he had said first. Bunchie lay back on her pillows, herself scarcely whiter than they, her fingers plucking at the frilled coverlet. She smiled, and gave him her hand as he sat down beside her.

"I can't say much. You must do the talking," she said between little short gasps. He tried to, but it was a poor endeavour, and all the time he felt that there was something she wanted specially to say. It came at last.

"You must make haste and get well by that time," he said. They had been talking of the Harvest Thanksgiving service that was to be held at the little church. She looked at him curiously. He felt her eyes upon him, but would not return the look. Instead of that, he watched the line of light fading in the sky, the birds going home to roost. Presently she spoke softly.

"I shall never be well any more. Oh, yes, you must listen to me. It is true. I asked them to let me tell you myself. I thought you would rather. Dan—Dan, don't make it so hard for me, dear."

He was kneeling by her, crying like a child. She stroked the bent head tenderly, till he caught her fingers and kissed them.

"You must get well," he exclaimed wildly, startled out of all self-control. "My little love—my darling, you must—say you will try for *my sake—to be my wife*, Bunchie!"

Her fond eyes brightened, but the next minute she shook her head.

"That couldn't be. Forgive me, dear, but you would never have said those words had I been well, and if I were to get well now, you would wish them unsaid."

"Never, dearest, never."

"I could only be as I was before, Dan, and don't you see, to be your wife, for such as I, is impossible. If it were Daisy now!"

He made no answer. There seemed nothing he could say. Bunchie lay still, her hands in his. Presently she drew closer to him.

"Dan, put your arms round me, dear, closer—so."

He held her in silent agony, his hot lips pressing continually on the little pain-worn face.

"You *do* love me, Dan? I am sure of it."

"My love—my darling!"

It was all he could say.

"Then listen to me. I don't want you to do such a thing to please me, Dan, but for your own sake—for hers—couldn't it be Daisy?"

He did not understand.

"Couldn't what be Daisy, my sweet?"

"Couldn't *she* be your wife?"

Then it became clear to him. But he only held the cripple girl closer.

"You would be glad some day. I don't ask you to pledge yourself now, Dan, only to think of it. Promise me that."

"I promise, dear—I will try—to—think of it—some day. But not yet—oh, not yet, Bunchie."

"No, not yet," she answered tenderly. "You couldn't. But by and bye—and now, Dan, I am quite content."

"Content! and you are leaving me!"

"Can't you understand, dear? Life could never be the same to me as to other girls. Every one is so good to me, but yet the world has never seemed to have quite the right place for me. Perhaps I shall find another one that has."

"Your right place is in my heart, Bunchie."

"I know, Dan, just now it seems so, but by and bye your heart will grow full without me, still, you will always keep just one little corner——"

The twilight deepened and softened in the room. The crimson glow died out in the sky, the birds had all gone home. Mrs. Bennett, weary with anxious watching, had dropped asleep in the next room. Daisy was superintending the children's tea. Thus it happened that not one of those amongst whom she had passed her short life, was with Bunchie at the last. And not even Charrington knew when that moment came. Content, as she had said, because of the love that surrounded her, the soul of the cripple girl passed from the arms that would have held her, to the rest for which none knew how keenly she had longed.

Some one came in presently, and drew her away from Charrington. He was conscious of stumbling out into the passage, where the gas flared into his face. He heard a low sound of weeping; he knew the cause, but failed to recognize it. Bunchie gone? Impossible! Why, only just now she was in his arms, only just now——

He went into one of the class-rooms and sat down, leaning heavily upon a table. He was glad the other fellows were not there. Only the light of the stars came to disturb his privacy. They looked in through the unshuttered windows.

After a time—he did not know whether it was an hour or a year—Colonel Bennett came to him. He did not say much, only took the lad's hands. It seemed to comfort the elder man to do so.

" You will stay on now, till it is all over, Charrington ? "

And Charrington stayed. There seemed a bond between him and these people that nothing could sever. He thought of his handsome home, and his mother—a fashionable woman of the world—they seemed to have belonged to another life.

He clung to the Bennetts, and to Melton Priory; here everything spoke to him of Bunchie.

At the grave-side he looked across at Daisy's white agonized face. He had scarcely spoken to her, and now she did not appear to observe him. All the most sentient part of her seemed going down in the little flower-strewn coffin. At that moment Charrington recalled Bunchie's expressed wish to him about her. Some day perhaps, by and bye, he thought, if it could ever be, but not yet—oh, not for a long time yet.

Suddenly a thrush, forgetful of the season, broke into song from a tree close by. It was the first gay or glad thing to which he had listened for—how long ? A week, a month, a century. And as he listened, he seemed to see again the interior of the little church, the stained windows with the opened lights, the waving foliage, the blue ether beyond, and looking up into it, the rapt face, with the golden halo, of his little saint. The thrush's throat was once more full of melody; his strain of unfettered joy brought the first natural tears to Charrington's eyes, since those he had shed on Bunchie's pillow.

He left the Priory soon after the funeral. There was much before him. He must not neglect the future for the past. Bunchie would not have had it so. One thing he did wish—that she could have known that he had passed his examination. Half the pleasure of doing so was detracted by this, until he remembered that perhaps she did know now, after all. When he was gazetted to his regiment, and ordered abroad, he went, much to his mother's chagrin. She would have had him, her only son, and a baronet, kept as a carpet soldier at home. But Charrington knew better. And on the ocean at night, or on the hot plains of India, camped in Afghan fastnesses, or beside Egyptian rivers, always, through the stars, the eyes of Bunchie seemed to look down, and lead him on.

And by and bye they led him home again.

He went down to Melton Priory. It was early spring-time, and the lanes were sweet with violets, and the meadows gay with daffodils. The tutors were changed; there was a fresh batch of pupils, among them his old friend Dicky, working with a fixity of purpose that spoke well for his success. George was abroad, Rowley at school; of the three little girls, Grace was married, Nora and Hetty were two tall, fine-looking, capable maidens. Daisy still busied herself about the house, but half her occupation had gone with Bunchie, and she found a difficulty in filling that side of her life. And now the little sisters were grown up, and able to undertake all that she did, Daisy felt sadly that home no longer needed her as of yore. Otherwise she was little changed. There were a few grey hairs in the thick brown tresses, for Daisy had known sorrow, and it leaves its mark. But its sign upon her face was an extra sweetness, an extra dignity, a charm that Charrington saw and felt. She welcomed him with almost the old brightness, the cheery *insouciance* that he remembered when he first knew her. But there were times when a pathetic look curved her lips, and dimmed her eyes. At such times she reminded him of Bunchie. Life was rather empty to Daisy Bennett, though she could have filled it, had she chosen, with other, newer interests. Men called her cold; and women wondered why she was Daisy Bennett still, but though her days were not all she could have wished, she bravely went through them, deeming this burden of loneliness but part of her due.

One day, when he had been about three weeks at the Priory, Charrington asked Daisy if he might drive her to Lyndon.

"I have a fancy to go through the woods, the scene of our picnic," he said. "I am sure Mrs. Bennett will spare your company to me for the afternoon."

"Oh! I don't think I shall be wanted. There is always Hetty or Nora. Very well, Sir Daniel, I will come."

And Daisy folded up her work and went to put on her hat and jacket. The cob—"Pimple's" successor—was brought round, and they started at a swinging pace. The chestnut buds hung full and green before them.

"Big with hope," remarked Charrington, lightly tapping one with his whip as they passed underneath.

"Bunchie used to say, I remember, that spring was full of hope for all things except her."

"She hasn't found it so, I'm sure," said Charrington.

"No," said Daisy, looking up with eyes whose faithful love saw more than the grey bank of clouds before her. They put up the dog-cart at the farm, crossed the meadow, and so passed up the steep path through the wood, and came out upon the top of the cliff above. Here they stood still, and for a few minutes neither spoke. The March winds swept stormily over the water, breaking it up into sharp crests of white foam, and whistling eerily in the crannies of the cliffs. The breeze lifted the little rings of hair on Daisy's forehead, and stirred the blood beneath her creamy skin. Charrington looked at her, and took her hand in his.

"Do you remember the last time we stood together here?" he said. "You asked me to go away soon, and I did as you wished—now that I have come back again, won't you ask me to stay, Daisy?"

His meaning was obvious, but she drew back with a little frightened gesture.

"Not because you are sorry for me! Oh, no, Dan, I couldn't bear that."

The little name she always thought of him by, slipped out unawares. He smiled.

"No, dear, but because I love you. Listen, Daisy, I am not going to say that I didn't care for Bunchie. I was little more than a boy then, but I loved her very deeply and truly. Had she lived, I scarcely think that I should ever have asked any other woman to be my wife. The remembrance of her comes as a sweetening and ennobling influence, and I hope it always will, to both of us. But, dear, I am only a man, and I want something more."

It had come then at last. For a moment this wonderful joy almost overwhelmed Daisy. She could not speak. But she laid her disengaged hand, with the other, in his, and lifted her radiant face. Suddenly the grey bank of clouds parted, and a stream of sunlight shot downwards to their feet. It crept softly, clingingly about them, bathing them in tender warmth and glory.

"That is Bunchie's blessing," whispered Daisy, and the sunbeam sealed Charrington's kiss upon her lips.

WINSTON KENDRICK.

# Bessie Thorne's Revenge.
## A STORY.
### By ANNIE THOMAS.

## CHAPTER I.

"To tell you that it was a pleasure to me to be with you for an hour the other day would be but to tell you a small portion of the truth. · I feel now that no enemy either within or without the gates will have the power to make discord between us again. For one thing, my friendship will be less exacting than of old, and for another, you, I think, have greater reliance on the sincerity of that friendship than you had when it tried to absorb you so utterly.—Always your own,

"BESSIE."

This was the way Mrs. Thorne wrote to a man whose power over her from the first date of their meeting had been such that he had gone away for two or three years in order that he might not be led into the temptation of exercising it. Now circumstances had compelled him to come back to look after his houses and lands and property generally, of which an unjust steward had been making ducks and drakes during his absence. The Thornes, his nearest neighbours, were the first to welcome and entertain him. He went to their little dinner in his honour with some misgivings. These were more than justified by the letter he had since received from Mrs. Thorne, which was quoted above.

"She's the dearest woman in the world, but as she's Bob Thorne's wife, I wish there were a thousand miles between us," he said to himself. Then, being a prudent as well as an honourable man, he twisted up her note and threw it into the fireless grate, and forthwith forgot it and her in the absorbing interest of some new works he was carrying out for the better draining of his meadow lands, and irrigation of the uplands.

He was not a beauty man, or even a very fine fellow physically, this Mr. Walter Gilbert, who had unintentionally made himself the centre round which the rest of the world revolved in Mrs. Thorne's estimation. He was simply a strong, straightforward, practical, clear-headed man, with decision and determination marked in every line of his good-looking, aquiline-featured face—in every glance of his steady, penetrating grey eyes, which were quick as a hawk's—and in every action. He never regretted anything, or supinely wished that he had pursued another line than the one he had taken. He never asked anyone's opinion about any matter, important or the reverse. He never took or volunteered advice on any subject, business or social, secular or religious. He never interfered with other people, or told them what he "would do were he in their place." He never sneered or gibed at anyone, though he was outspoken in denouncing as rogues and fools those whom he believed to be these things. And lastly, without effort he swayed men and women equally with an irresistible force that was neither hypnotism nor fascination—for all occult arts were abhorrent to him, and his brusqueness frightened many whom he enthralled. But even the frightened ones excused him and perhaps liked him the better for the brusqueness which was so entirely his own.

Perhaps one of the strongest of his subjugating forces was the intense earnestness with which he pursued everything he took in hand. Every kind of sport claimed him as its own most ardent votary. He would fish for small trout with the same concentrated intensity of purpose with which he would fight, conquer and break in an unruly or vicious horse. He was never frivolous or half-hearted about anything he took in hand, however frivolous in itself that thing might be. It was this combination of physical and moral strength and earnestness which had first impressed Mrs. Thorne. Once impressed by them, and being a dreamily idle woman, she had dwelt upon them until they had assumed such important proportions that they filled her mind, soul, heart and fancy to the exclusion of everything else.

"If Bob had only been like him what a happy woman I should be," she said to herself at the beginning. Then Bob not being a bit like him—Bob being in fact a weak vessel, who could never quite make up his mind what he ought to do or whether he would do it or not, she began to cry out in the innermost recesses of her heart against the injustice of circumstance and the Fates which prevented her having "his" constant companionship.

"Bessie beats the beauties hollow. She has a way with her that no fellow can stand out against," Bob Thorne was wont to assure his men friends—Walter Gilbert among them—in moments of confidence when the wit was out. She was one of those oval-faced, pale brunettes whose dark eyes always droop slightly and look sad. She never tried to take by storm, but just glided softly into your interest and affections with a few softly-spoken words, an expressive gesture or two of the slender hands which, tiny as they were, looked to be quite enough for the delicate wrists to support. For the rest she had a charming supple shape, and her manner when she wished it to be so was one long caress.

It had been one long caress to Bob Thorne from the day she married him until that day ten years after when he had introduced Walter Gilbert to her. It was a necessity of her nature to love and be loved by someone. So, long after Bob Thorne had found out that it was not at all necessary for a fellow to be a devout lover in private, she went on tendering him her pretty flattering homage out of mere force of habit, scarcely noticing, and caring less, whether he responded to it or not.

In public he would play his part of owner proudly enough, boring everyone he could get hold of with, " My wife's opinion," and " My wife's splendid management," the superiority of her boots and gloves, her salads and home-trimmed hats. And Bessie used to writhe under these ill-advised commendatory notices, but still smile at him in her sad, sweet way, and wonder within herself why she had been mad enough to marry such a tactless feeble brother.

He regarded himself as a country gentleman on the strength of being the resident owner of a pretty little house and grounds, but his tastes and pursuits belied him. He was a poor shot, and to ride he was afraid, while the sight of him on the box seat of a dog-cart made strong men weep. But he talked a great deal about shootin', and ridin' and drivin', and fancied he impressed Bessie considerably with his proficiency in these several arts.

To read, and dream, and do beautiful embroideries, and see that her dainty home was always in exquisitely dainty order, and to see as little of Bob as possible, these things had been sufficient for Bessie for ten years. She was not very happy, but on the other hand she was not very *un*happy. Then she met Walter Gilbert and everything was changed. He was like a strong north wind blowing away the relaxing vapours which had hitherto surrounded her. So, simultaneously she grew stronger and weaker.

There was no vice about her. She neither meant nor wished to win his heart or lose her own. Only everything he did and the way he did it interested her more keenly than she had ever been interested in anything before—interested her so keenly in fact that those days were blanks on which she was not hearing or seeing him. It was "all friendship, nothing but friendship," she impressed upon him. But she "couldn't bear that he should have another friend, man or woman, more especially the latter." She was jealous of every moment he gave to anyone or anything else, even his horses she looked upon with jealous eyes, till at last the flattery grew too potent, and he woke suddenly to the fear that the temptation might prove too strong.

So he went away for a time. Now he was home again, and she was more infatuated than ever. Every look that she shot at him betrayed this, but he held out stoutly, and held her in check in spite of herself.

"Bob wants you to dine with us to-night." "Bob wants you to take me to the Parkhurst races, as he can't possibly go himself." "Bob wants you to come and stay a week with us and help him to arrange a big shoot." These and similar missives were fired at Gilbert nearly every day. But still he kept his head honourably, and told himself he would cure her kindly in a short time by marrying some fresh sweet young girl with whom he would fall desperately in love and who would effectually put fascinating Mrs. Bob Thorne out of his head.

But some way or other he did not meet the girl who had the power of doing this, and Time went on after his usual habit.

Bob Thorne had been more than ordinarily trying for several weeks. He had taken a violent fancy to a handsome barmaid, who attracted the gilded youth largely to the "Red Lion," the chief hotel of the neighbouring market town. She happened to be a cool and cute young woman, capable of keeping any number of half-seas-over swains at bay. But Bob Thorne's fatuous generosity touched her, and the possibility of one day ruling as *châtelaine* at his pretty country house appealed to her ambition strongly.

"It's no good, Mr. Thorne, your pretty speeches are windbags that would collapse at a pin-prick," she told him one day when his ardour had led him on to make sundry alluring proposals which would not be legalized.

"Try me," he said eagerly; "test me, Bella. There is nothing on earth that I would not do or sacrifice for you."

"Would you call it a sacrifice to make me your wife?"

"Unhappily, I am cursed with one already," said the weak fool; "otherwise, how proud I should be to call you mine before the whole world."

"Do you mean it?"

"On my sacred word of honour I do."

"Then divorce your wife—any other man would have done it long ago."

"Divorce—! Bessie!!" he stammered.

"Why, yes," she laughed scornfully. "She worships the ground Gilbert treads on, and they're always together. A young man I know—he's my cousin—is his valet, and he brought me a letter of your wife's which you shall see if you like?"

For a few moments the instincts of a gentleman fought against the grossly plebeian temptation—and fought in vain.

"Let me see it," he said hoarsely, and she handed the letter which was quoted at the beginning of this story, to him with a triumphant smile.

\* \* \* \* \* \* \* \*

As Fate willed it, that same day Walter Gilbert met a girl whom he had not seen for years, one who had been his little sweetheart when he was fifteen and she was ten. To have her for his little sweetheart again became his dominating desire. Surely Bessie Thorne would prove her womanhood by releasing him from a bondage that was sinful in thought, though not in deed?

He was always alert and prompt. To remind this girl of old times, to tell her that he wanted her again and meant to have her, was the work of an hour. His power asserted itself over her as instantaneously and overwhelmingly as it had over Bessie Thorne. She was a proud and radiantly happy girl that night when he left her, and all her family seemed disposed to bow down and worship her for having won him.

For two or three days she was in Paradise. Her lover was an ideal lover, openly devoted to her, as far as a man may be devoted to a woman without making an ass of himself. During these few days Mrs. Bob Thorne gave no sign of having received the laconic communication Walter Gilbert had made to her of his engagement to Marjorie Bligh.

At the end of those few days—days which had been full of terror and horror for her—she crept out of the lodgings she had taken when her husband, after confronting her with her own letter to Gilbert, turned her out of her home, and walked in the welcome shade of evening to the house of the man she adored. It was his dinner hour. She would be "sure to find him at home," she told herself, and he would be sure to repair the mischief he had wrought by his careless custody of her letters, by promising to marry her as soon as she was divorced.

His housekeeper met her with an air of greater surprise than welcome.

"Surely not *you*, Mrs. Thorne, out a-walking at this time of night all alone?" she began reprovingly; then struck with the hunted, harassed expression of the lady whom she had never seen in a strait that seemed to crave for pity before, she added: "But come in and rest yourself, Ma'am, if I may make so bold as to ask you to rest and take a cup of tea in my room."

Mrs. Thorne's parched, pinched lips worked nervously for a moment, then she said:

"Mr. Gilbert, I must see him at once. Tell him, ask him——" she paused and fell half-fainting on the stone seat of the porch.

A glass of water and a bottle of lavender salts quickly pulled her round, and she rose and walked into the house, repeating:

"I must see Mr. Gilbert at once—at once!"

"Master is out dining with his young lady," the housekeeper said with distinct coldness.

"With his—*what?*" Mrs. Thorne cried out, putting her hands up as if to ward off a blow.

"His young lady, Miss Marjorie Bligh. Lor', Ma'am, I made sure *you* would have been the first to hear the news of the engagement. Such friends as you and the master are, so all the folks say."

"Engagement! Marjorie Bligh! Merciful God, help me! Bring him back to me, or let me die."

As she sobbed out the last words her strength gave way, and she fell forward in a heap on the floor, where she laid in a state of utter unconsciousness, while the frightened housekeeper ran to seek for sal volatile and a fellow servant's help.

"She's that mad, reckless, that she let the cat out of the bag, poor soul, before she dropped down in this dead faint," the woman explained to the parlour-maid. Then together they lifted Mrs. Thorne up and put her on a couch in the drawing-room, where she remained in a death-like swoon for two or three hours. Just as she was coming to herself, Walter Gilbert came in cheerfully, accompanied by his future brother-in-law, Jack Bligh, who had walked home with him to smoke a last cigar.

## CHAPTER II.

FOR a moment or two they stared at each other in silence. Then she, seeing no one, thinking of no one, caring for no one but him, rose up and faltered towards him with outstretched, imploring hands, crying:

"Walter, Walter, tell me it's *not true*? You are mine, are you not? Not Marjorie Bligh's, or any other woman's; and I shall be all your own now, for Bob is going to divorce me; he has found one of my letters to you, and——"

She stopped short, terrified into speechlessness by the storm that raged in his face.

"You are ill, or hysterical, Mrs. Thorne," he said sternly; "it is impossible that you could receive the tidings of my great happiness in such a way if you were in possession of your senses."

"Your—great—happiness?"

"In having won Miss Bligh's promise to be my wife."

"But you have taken *my* promise that I will be that, if ever I am free. And I shall be free now, for Bob is going to divorce me, to divorce me on *your* account—on account of one of the mad letters I have written to you, believing in your love," she cried wildly.

"By Jove! this is becoming serious, Gilbert; think of Marjorie," Jack Bligh put in. He was a blockhead, but an honourable one, and he had no fancy for seeing his sister thrown over, or dust thrown in her eyes.

"He must think of *me* first," Mrs. Thorne cried furiously.

"If she's mad you had better get rid of her as quickly and quietly as you can," Jack Bligh went on stolidly.

BESSIE THORNE'S REVENGE.

"Mrs. Thorne, control yourself and be reasonable; our friendship has been a happy and honourable one. Why tarnish it now by emotion that you have no right to display?" Mr. Gilbert said collectedly.

"No right to display! When for you I have lost home, reputation, position, everything."

"Most causelessly, as your husband will soon be made to understand," he replied.

"By Jove! she may have heard of the pretty barmaid at the 'Red Lion.' Thorne is dead nuts on her," Jack Bligh suggested thoughtfully.

"Walter, walk back to my lodgings with me," she pleaded; "hear what I have to tell you. You must hear it; you *shall* hear it; your love can't have turned to indifference so soon. Think! I have lost everything for you."

"Order the carriage and tell Robins to drive Mrs. Thorne home," Gilbert said quietly.

"Home! I have no home, I tell you!"

"You will accompany Mrs. Thorne home," Gilbert went on, turning to his housekeeper, "see Mr. Thorne if possible, and tell him I will see him at any place and hour he likes to-morrow."

"I dare not go home," she sobbed, falling on her knees by the couch and burying her face in it. "I have been turned out of it; all my servants saw him turn me out in a fury that made him almost foam. I will stay here, or I will die."

"Then I wish you good-night, Mrs. Thorne. Bligh, I will go home with you. Marjorie must not hear of this from anyone but us two."

She sprang to her feet and flew at him: the gentle, fragile woman was transformed into a tigress.

"She shall hear of it from me," she raved, "she shall hear it when she is happiest. She shall hear everything that a jealous woman can say that stabs."

"Madam, you are mad," he said, turning away, and she shrieked after him:

"Mad with love for you! Love that you won years ago and have held fast ever since. Love that is worth a thousandfold of the poor stuff your Marjorie Bligh can give you!"

"What a shocking scene," said the housekeeper; "do compose

5

yourself, Ma'am, and go home, there's a dear lady, to your own husband."

But Mrs. Thorne refused to stir from the house of the man she claimed. She was indeed mad—or temporarily insane—for love of him.

There was a meeting between the husband (who was betrothed to the barmaid), and the lover (who was betrothed to Marjorie Bligh), the following day, and Bob Thorne had his claws cut in a way he little anticipated.

"I know how you got hold of the letter Mrs. Thorne wrote to me in a spirit of romantic friendship," Walter Gilbert began, without any preface, "you got it from the barmaid at the 'Red Lion,' whom you have promised to marry as soon as you can divorce your wife. Shall I tell you who stole it for the barmaid?"

"It was her cousin who let her see it," Mr. Thorne said, with a pitiable attempt at decision.

"It was my blackguard fellow Rayner who under the pretence of valeting me has been rifling my pockets of cash and letters. He is not your barmaid's cousin; he stands in a far nearer relation to her; he is the father of her child, and she is going to pension him off liberally if he will give her up *entirely*, when she marries you. I got his confession in writing this morning; he was craven enough to make it rather than risk getting eighteen months' hard labour for having robbed me of money and plate, both of which have been found this morning in your barmaid's box. How about your scheme of married happiness with that woman now?"

"Everything is gone from me, my wife, my love, my honour," Bob Thorne groaned.

"Damn it, man, don't sit there and shed maudlin tears over your own confounded folly and your dishonourable practices. What have you done with the letter I wrote to Mrs. Thorne, telling her as a friend and a gentleman in whom she had kindly taken an interest, of my engagement? I entrusted it to Rayner, he gave it into your hands. Take it to your wife now, beg her pardon, and bring her home."

With that parting shot of advice Mr. Gilbert turned on his heel and walked away.

"I'll bet a hundred to one on Bella, still," Bob Thorne

muttered to himself as he rode over to the "Red Lion" half-an-hour after the interview which has just been recorded. "I don't believe about the child, and I know she'll stick to me, though I'm afraid I shan't be able to get rid of Bessie. Confound her! While she was about it, why didn't she write a more criminating letter to the fellow, and why the devil hasn't he given me a scrap of evidence against himself? I won't take Bessie back, that's flat."

He turned into a bye-road as his reflections reached this point, and was passing by a little clump of cottages known as Mount Pleasant, when the sound of a voice he knew—a voice that thrilled him, made him check his horse and listen attentively.

"If you'll take ten pounds, Rayner, and take the child away, and never let me see you or it again, I'll be your friend by cheque as long as I live. He can't marry me, he can't till he has divorced her six months, he says, but as soon as I am his wife you shall have fifty pounds a year, and that's more than you'll ever get by staying here and interfering and persecuting me."

Bob Thorne turned his horse's head and rode back to Mr. Gilbert's house, where he made soft-mouthed enquiries for his wife.

"She's asleep in my room, having cried and sobbed till 'twas pitiful to hear her," the housekeeper told him. "Poor lady! I am sorry for her. I think she must have had a touch of the sun."

"Very likely," Bob said sapiently. "I have had one myself, but I am all right again."

"Of course your lady being here keeps master out of his own house, sir?"

"I'll fetch her this evening," Bob was saying hurriedly, when Bessie, with a tear-stained, swollen face and dishevelled hair and dress, came tremblingly into the room.

"Why have you come?" she asked piteously.

"To take you home, dear; and to give you this letter, which I opened by mistake before I saw that it was addressed to you," he said fawningly.

She read it, her face twitching with agony, her eyes flashing fire with futile jealousy.

"It is true then. He tells me he is going to marry this girl, this baby-faced, bucolic-minded country bumpkin," she said scornfully, crushing the note to a ball in her feverish hand. "Well, I will go back with you if you're weak enough to take me. I must sit down somewhere and rest before I can aid in the completion of his happiness."

"Oh! I'm sure it's a touch of the sun," Mr. Thorne murmured. "I must take her home and look after her well. I hope you don't misunderstand things?" he went on eagerly. "She is really devoted to me when she has her senses about her. She——"

"Oh, don't touch me, and don't attempt to explain," she interrupted. "They know far better than you do what is the matter with me. 'Hell holds no fury like a woman scorned,' and Walter Gilbert has scorned *me!*"

"If you *could* control yourself, Bessie, we would go away for a few years, and all this would be forgotten."

"*Go away!* with *you!*" There was no mistaking the genuine shudder of disgust with which she said this. Through the thick skin of his fatuous conceitedness he was stung by it. But his rage against the barmaid made him tolerant to his wife. Her outspoken abhorrence of him was humiliating, but the barmaid had plotted to defraud him of fifty pounds a year, which was worse.

It was not a pleasant drive home for either husband or wife. He was engaged in speculations as to how much she knew about Bella, of "Red Lion" fame, and she was concentrating all her energies in evolving a scheme of revenge upon Marjorie Bligh for having taken Walter Gilbert away from her. A savage and subtle revenge that should crush Marjorie out of Gilbert's life, and at the same time not render herself, Bessie Thorne, revolting in his eyes. Bob Thorne would have had an easier time of it during that drive had he known how little his wife was thinking of his escapade with the barmaid.

"I will get rid of the servants who saw our little tiff the other night, dear," he said at length, humbly and tentatively.

"Not on my account, I beg," she said coldly. "They will see, and hear, and think no worse of either of us if they stay than they have seen, and heard, and thought already."

"You at least have had no fault to find with me, Bessie. I have always been liberal to you, and indulged your every whim, now, haven't I? It's true I made a little mistake about Walter Gilbert, in fact I am willing to admit I made an ass of myself. But that was because I was so awfully fond of *you*, you know, and it's all over now, isn't it?"

He said all this eagerly, pressing closer to her, trying to take her hand and kiss her, but she shrank into the corner of the carriage muttering:

"Be anything but kind to me—kindness from you I cannot stand. I don't deserve it, and I won't take it."

"By Jove! She hasn't heard about Bella after all. I have her under my thumb," Bob Thorne thought triumphantly, and at that moment they arrived at their own door, and a crowd of eagerly curious servants came forward to meet them.

Days passed on and merged into weeks, and still Mrs. Thorne was unable to mature any plan of revenge on her unconscious rival that should meet all the niceties of the case. Miss Bligh's character was spotlessly unassailable. Her wedding day was fast approaching, and Walter Gilbert was still devotedly attached to her.

It was the commencement of the hunting season, and the opening meet was at Hanging Bridge, and was, as usual, a brilliant and largely attended one. Mrs. Thorne was there in her pony-trap, utterly regardless of the looks askance and whisperings of some of her whilom friends and acquaintances, whose ears the rumour of her mad escapade had reached. Marjorie Bligh was there also, mounted on a young horse, who was as yet unversed in the ways of the hunting field, with her lover by her side.

They soon found and got away in good style on a stretch of open moorland that looked an ideal hunting ground. The short springy turf was seductively green and smooth. But many a horse and rider came to untoward grief upon it, for it was full of pitfalls for the unwary in the shape of rabbit holes. Marjorie Bligh's horse had spent his colthood on this very tract, so he sailed over it at a pace that soon carried her far away from Walter Gilbert's steadier weight-carrier.

There was a check when they came to a thick wood, into which Reynard plunged. Part of the field skirted the wood to a point at which they knew he would emerge, but the master, followed by four or five, rode on straight after their quarry, and among the few who did so was Marjorie Bligh. She rode next to the master, and following her at about ten yards distance came a naval man, who had been more than a little in love with her before the re-appearance of Mr. Gilbert. She turned her head for a moment to call out some blithe remark, the next he saw horse and rider come to the ground with a heavy crash. The fallen bough of a tree concealed by undergrowth stretched across the path. The master's horse had escaped the hidden snare, but Marjorie's had fallen headlong over it, breaking his own neck, and flinging his young mistress to the ground with cruel force.

She was apparently lifeless when they picked up her beautiful young body that had been so full of health and vigour but an instant before. But after a time she opened her eyes and her lips moved, though no sound came from them.

"Someone must go on and tell Gilbert. God forgive me! I can't do it myself," the naval man groaned, and from among the horror-stricken crowd which had gathered about her, one or two came forward and volunteered for the mission of misery and despair.

"Cover my face before he comes," the girl whispered, and then those around her felt that she realised that her fair beauty was marred beyond restoration.

It was an agonising meeting, worse perhaps for the strong man than for the sweet, shattered girl, whose mind soon wandered from the painful present into dreamy labyrinths of imaginary happiness, wherein she strayed for many a long day. When these visions cleared away, she found that her face was seamed and scarred out of all resemblance to the lovely one which had looked back at her the last time she had gazed in the glass, but she was very brave, braver by far than her broken-hearted family. Her voice did not even falter when she asked if "Walter knew?"

"Knows it and loves each scar more than he did the dear little peach-like face you had before the accident," the woman who had helped Marjorie's mother to nurse her the whole time, said cheerfully; "but I mustn't deprive him of the pleasure of telling you this himself."

"Are you Mrs. Thorne?" Marjorie asked wonderingly.

"I am Bessie Thorne," that lady said blushing deeply, "and now Mr. Gilbert shall come in and tell you everything you want to hear."

"I only want to hear him say he loves me still," Marjorie said wistfully.

"And that you shall hear every day of your dear mercifully-preserved life, my own," Gilbert said kneeling down by his loving little love's side, and she was happier than she had ever been in her life before.

But no one ever knew that it was at Bessie Thorne's prayers and solicitations that in the first hours of the awful shock he had clung to his honour and his love. That he did so eventually was the sweetest revenge that her generous, erring, warm heart desired.

# The Lifted Veil.

THE literary executors of the late Hanham Glass, F.R.S., M.D., and late Professor of Physiology at the Institute of Scientists, Esq. desire to make public the following strange narration found amongst his papers after his death. The authorship of the MS. is not to be conjectured, nor is any attempt towards identification possible or desirable at this date; but, from the marginal annotations and expositions, in the doctor's cramped characteristic hand, which figure in profusion throughout the pages of the document, one may assume its commentator's own conviction as to the importance of such evidence in its relation to psychological research. Had he lived longer, Dr. Glass would probably have embodied the record in that new volume of his scientific series which he was projecting at the date of his death, and which was to deal with the pathological analysis of morbid phenomena. Indeed, so much is to be gathered from his notes, which insist, moreover, upon his positive acquittance—in view of the then recent decease of the anonymous writer of the MS.—of any suggestion of abuse of confidence in making public what should be of moment to the entire world of physiologists.

"The tendency to melodrama," he writes, "observable in the course of the narrative, detracts very little, to my mind, from the value of the evidence. The writer was a man of small learning, yet of an order of intelligence supremely susceptible to the picturesque in impressions, and to the stronger contrasts of light and shade that express the abnormal. At the same time, he was possessed of the sturdiest natural instincts, and was most prone to reject evidence, of whatsoever description, that failed to appeal to his common sense. I have no hesitation in accepting, on my knowledge of him, his statement as substantially true in fact. It was put into writing by him at my request, and on the understanding that it should be submitted to outer criticism anonymously, if at all; as the connection of his published name with so equivocal an experience would certainly affect his reputation as a sane man of business."

Such may be deemed sufficient introduction in itself; and it remains only to say that, in view of the strictly technical, if profound and luminous, character of the annotations, where decipherable, it is thought best to print the narrative as it stands, and without more than an occasional reference to Dr. Glass's marginal comments, which, existing as they do merely in embryo, would otherwise both weaken the force of the evidence and, perhaps, fail to convince from their own very immaturity.

The MS. is headed as follows:—

"The experience here set down I testify to be absolutely true, and wishing to remain anonymous for reasons that would be obvious to all who know me for a plain business man, I here, in proof of its *bona fides*, set my mark, which Dr. Glass, who is acquainted with me and my name, will witness."

Hereupon follow the sign and attestation, and, upon an inset of separate paper, some elucidatory matter by the doctor, which serves to introduce him in his first connection with the affair. It runs thus:

"April the 17th, 1884, while acting as *locum tenens* for a fellow practitioner, was summoned to a house in neighbourhood of British Museum, about 9.30 o'clock in the evening. A young man, thirty-five or thirty-six years of age, had died suddenly, while sitting smoking with a companion, from failure of the heart's action. Subsequently a curious statement confided to me by the friend, which I after prevailed upon the latter to reduce to writing."

The MS. then proceeds as follows:

I have attended two inquests only in my life—the first in the capacity of juryman; the second as a witness. The subject of the latter enquiry was, curiously enough, the son of the subject of the former, and an interval of three years separated the two events.

I may say that I dread nothing more than a summons of this description. I am a matter-of-fact and healthy-minded man, but a coroner's court seems to me little better than an official charnel house. For weeks after attending in such a place its atmosphere seems to deaden my social landscape, and take all the breezy relish from life. The world looks to me actually grey, as it does during an attack of nervous dyspepsia. The hideous remains packed for inspection into cheap shells—the sordid surroundings (the court is generally within a court, like disease in a suit of ragged clothes)—the ugly curiosity of my fellow jurymen and of the gloating crowd—the smell of fustian and of cold distempered walls—all these get into my thoughts and my bed and my food, and poison my impressions of familiar life for long after the ordeal is passed, and until the springs of nature freshen in me again with time. And the worst of it is, I know I should be shiftingly uneasy with a sense of damaged self-respect were I to shirk my share of a duty which is a common penalty of the social order we profit by. That is a morbid sensitiveness, perhaps, and akin to that that drives the murderer back to the scene of his crime. Maybe, too, it is a sort of guarantee of something higher than intelligence, if you look at it in the right light—not that *I* of all men need the assurance of an existence beyond the grave. However, facts are better than speculations, and here are mine.

In the winter of the year 1881, I was acting as publishing clerk to a firm in Great Queen Street, and one afternoon I was summoned to attend on a coroner's jury. We were in the parish of St. George's in the Fields, and the court was held in another as unsavoury off Drury Lane; and thither, in a dank November twilight, I trudged through the cold slush of half-melted snow. A hubbub of squalid gutter elfs rose and fell about the door of the building, and in the opening a chilled policeman blew upon his finger tips to warm them. On the dreary brick court walls an oily moisture shone and trickled that seemed to me like a death-sweat from the bodies that lay hidden in the upper rooms. I entered and stood among my unwholesome fellows to await the arrival of the coroner. The room was fairly crowded, and its blank walls re-echoed whisperings from angle to angle. The ghostly influence of the place wrapped me in like a shroud. Life seemed concentrated into one stealthy, monotonous murmur, as though I lay buried beneath the pavement of a church. I tried to give my mind passage to a pleasant memory here, a pictured retrospect there; but it would never work independently of its surroundings.

Presently the coroner arrived and we were ushered upstairs to view the bodies. Three of them there were. One poor wretch, a German, lay in his coffin with shattered skull and a bloody cloth wrapped about it—suicide, the verdict. Another body was that of an old poor woman, shrunken, starved—an ordinary case. The third subject was an aged man with thin white hair and fearful wrinkles about his mouth and middle brow. It is of him I write in this first instance of my story.

He lay in a common coffin, in the common dead room; yet he was a Baronet and possessed of considerable property. He had devoted much of his life to ministering to the needs of the most degraded among the poor, and had latterly volunteered to sit up with a patient suffering from diphtheria, on whom the operation of tracheotomy had been performed. In the dead of night the tube had clogged, and the watcher had sucked it free. A hero's death befell him in consequence and the apotheosis of the mortuary.

At the inquest a strange letter was put in which he had written upon his death-bed, and which was addressed to his only son. The coroner glanced through it, ruled it irrelevant, and it was not made public. Afterwards, however, it was given me to read by him to whom it was addressed, and is now actually in my possession. I quote it here in full.

"My son, whom I cannot claim, I reveal myself to you on my death-bed. At the eleventh hour I throw down the tangled skein of faith and will no more of it. I charge you never to take it up. I charge you to address your mind, your body, your endeavours to sweet and wholesome happiness and the selfishness of unretributive pleasures. I that say this am your father, and for two-and-thirty years I have not looked upon your face, or sought your mother in it, or claimed you mine. Go, when you receive this to the firm of———* They have been my faithful advisers and friends for the last thirty odd years. They have my full instructions, and will make known to you your position, and the position of the father of whose very existence you knew nothing. I charge you again to enjoy to the full the advantages of the new fortune that shall fall to you—to be gay, light-hearted, selfish of your tranquility in its possession—to sacrifice

\* Editorially omitted.

your happiness to no impulse that may resolve itself into a lifelong martyrdom.

"I have latterly written for you the story of my life, which will be handed to you by the same firm.

"Make a happier use of your position than I ever did of mine.

"YOUR DYING FATHER."

Now this, I take it, was fairly strange advice alone from one who had sacrificed some thirty years of his life and the bulk of his annual income to the good of his humbler fellows. But—to quote an odd old lady I know of—"there's nothing so queer as folk." The man was a strange character, and his story, as I came to hear it afterwards from his son's lips, a record of noble madness. I may appropriately outline it here, using his own words where necessary.

The Baronet, Sir——* was, in the year '47 a more or less typical representative of the wholesomer of his class. Refined, cultivated, healthful and well-to-do, he had for some forty years lived a bachelor existence of tranquil pleasures and easy duties that were never so disturbing as to more than ruffle the sunny serenity of his lot. He was a dilettante, a bit of a mystic, a man of many quiet resources, and the vexing waters of toil flowed so far from him as to merely soothe his soul as with a sound of pleasant murmuring. To his self-centred calm, the fact contributed that he was the last of an unprocreative race, and that his Castle of Indolence was unharassed of parasitic relations.

Suddenly, however, all this tranquillity fled to the winds. He fell in love, with all the determined passion of middle age, sunk his ancient distinction of character in a dishonourable connection with a parentless village girl, and married her in time to legitimize their son. Henceforth the fever burned itself through three years, and then the mother died of consumption. He had not conceived the possibility of so fearful an outrage of fate befalling him. Through the latter months of his wife's sickness he had tended her with a slow curious growth of agony in his soul that there was after all no patent of Providence to set him apart from his fellows—that he was born, with the beggar, to

* Editorially omitted.

the mischance of death and the heritage of suffering. Then a morbid horror seized him that his hitherto immunity was the earnest of his moral destruction; that the God of Humanity had indeed set him aside, in his wealth and indolence, as useless to His scheme of regeneration—a toy to be broken and thrown away by-and-by—a worthless pretty gaud to fit the fashion of the times.

For weeks after his wife's death he tramped the streets of London day and night, and never rested; and brick by brick his Castle of Indolence toppled about his ears. He was stunned, bewildered, morbidly fascinated by all he heard and saw and experienced; and when at last his former stronghold was level with its foundations he had resolved upon the course from which he never after swerved to the finish of his life—a self-effacement more stern and complete than that of any ancient royal hermit.

No doubt there was a blot of madness staining the family tree somewhere like a bunch of evil fruit.

He now appointed the firm mentioned in his letter guardians over his baby son, leaving with them minutest detailed directions as to his bringing up. He was to be given an assumed name and to be kept in absolute ignorance of his true position and parentage. What funds were necessary to his good maintenance and training were to be drawn from the income of the estate, and, upon coming of age, he was to be granted an allowance sufficient to keep him in respectability, but not in idleness. But his face his father had ruled himself never to see again. This, the consummation of his irresponsible romance of life, should be his dearest guarantee of its renouncement. It was easier to forego titular and social aggrandisement, and these he sacrificed with his income. With the bulk of the latter he purposed to feed the whirlpool of necessity, and into the same moaning throat to cast the wreck of all his ancient hopes and comforts. He disappeared from the life he had lived in as completely as if he had gone down at sea. His world knew him no more, and the toiling sordid East End woke to the presence of a new grave comforter of substantial influence. His only link with the past was maintained, chiefly through correspondence, with the aforesaid advisers.

And he stuck to it. Such cases do occur occasionally, without doubt—such oblique visions of a vocation that distort the honest face of duty and run perilously close to religious mania. He stuck to it; but with what result to himself let the following passages, gleaned from his communication to his son, show:

"Then I walked from a garden into a desert—blind, staring, hideous. . . . For thirty years have I toiled and suffered in the name of Christ, yielding my all of health, comfort and happiness—and what at last is my reward? The conviction that our self-wrought destiny is death; our doom annihilation; our God an ugly dramatic fiction . . . I have walked amidst suffering till my soul has grown leprous; I have stood helpless by agony unendurable, and heard the priests damn it for blaspheming; I have suffered a hundred deaths . . . No reward can atone for the past; no walls of jasper and onyx shut out the memory of what has been. Great God! What have I not seen and heard in these noisome shambles of Moloch? Let me be wiped out and rest and be forgotten . . . I have no retrospects to soothe the intolerable horror of my vision. I look through the steaming stench of suffering and my past is poisoned. I could recover nothing of the old life by returning to it, for the knowledge of these my neighbours would be with me. The limits of creation could not dim that consciousness . . . I have failed and long for death. Oh, my son—my son, whose natural claims upon me I have forsworn! be true to your best instincts and fastidious in your choice of happiness; crush under the morbid devil in you that *lusts to experience* if ever he shall rear his head! wrap yourself in the enjoyments of life as in flowers, for there is nothing beyond."

What was the life this man had sacrificed with such apparent nobility?

The object of this last solicitude was present at the inquest, but was not called upon for evidence. I saw him, a slender, delicate-looking man of thirty-two, plain in features, with a little ragged, rusty beard and mild large eyes. His thin face was deadly pale—and no wonder. Realize the mine of circumstances sprung upon him—the recent revelations of his history and parentage—his sudden leap from obscurity to wealth and position!

An old, portly man—probably one of his father's advisers—was with him throughout, but left before the jury was dismissed.

As I passed with the crowd through the door and along the pavement without, I found myself behind the newly-elect baronet, and suddenly he reeled and fell into my arms. He had broken down at the last and fainted. I sent for a cab, with assistance got him into it, and drove off with him to my place of business. On the way he partly recovered, and, on reaching our destination, was able to walk with me into my private office where I induced him to sip some weak whisky and water.

This was the beginning of a curious acquaintanceship between us. Our paths in life were of course widely divergent; but he found, I think, a strange moral support in the matter-of-fact side of my character. For he turned out to be a true son of his father—morbid, inclined to mysticism and prone to dark scruples of conscience. What he had done with his crippled life hitherto I could never quite make out; but this I understood —that he had preferred struggling along upon his limited allowance to making any effort to increase it by drudgery. The mystery of his birth he had been content to accept as insolvable, the more so as he feared investigation would prove him illegitimate. He read a great deal at the British Museum, and took a house in Bloomsbury Square to be near it. He was very shy, soft-spoken and retiring, and the nine days' wonder of notoriety that succeeded the inquest was cruelly galling to his sensitiveness. The world left him alone, however, after a time, and he laid himself out to court social neglect.

For the first year of our acquaintance I was frequently in his company. He extended a general invitation to me to drop in of an evening whenever the whim should seize me and smoke a pipe with him. I often availed myself of this. The man interested me oddly; and when his shyness wore off, he proved himself a cultivated and well-informed companion. It was at this time that he made me acquainted with the contents of his father's first and last communication to him. The nature and purport of it were naturally of absorbing moment to him, and in the attempted interpretation of its inner meaning he would often grow moody and, in his speech, to me at least, obscure. He cherished no resentment towards the old man for his treatment of him. Rather he exhibited an unwholesome sympathy with his final despair and a most profound pity of the necessity of his martyrdom. Out of this gradually grew an intense morbid desire to satisfy himself as to the possibilities of a future state. It haunted him day and night, and found frequent expression in his conversation.

"That all should end in this! Iago, the pity of it!" he would say. I combated his gloomy heathenism with the broadsword play of my own breezy confident faith; but I knew all along that I lacked his deadlier weapon, imagination—that petard which, though liable to hoist its own engineer, is invariably the destruction of the little forts of formulæ we plain men throw up. We are no match for the enemy that undermines our conventional beliefs with explosive theories.

In the early Spring of 1883 my friend went abroad, and I saw no more of him for thirteen months; when, upon the 17th of April, in the following year, he entered my room, just as I was in the act of turning the cock of the gas upon my day's official labours, and asked me to return home with him to dinner.

It was a stinging cold evening, and the east wind rumbled in the chimneys, as if the house were flatulent with dyspepsia. Outside, the pavement was grated clean with flying dust, and the jets of the lamps glinted like eyes bright with fever. My companion and I butted the gale with shrugged shoulders and exchanged few words as we made our way towards Bloomsbury Square. I had noticed at his first greeting that thirteen months of Europe had been apparently of small health service to him, and that he was looking ill and prematurely old. Yet his manner had been quietly genial and free from nervousness. Once, while talking to me in the office, he had turned suddenly faint, and I, a little scared, had pressed some stimulant upon him—but he would none of it.

"I don't like these fillips of Dutch courage," he said with a weak smile. "The principle of the moral economy of life is that the soul should exist self-supporting."

"But the perishable frame, my friend—" I began—

"Is subject to the same control," he said. Then his countenance fell. "But is it, is it, is it?" he muttered to himself.

"I have been theorising and experimenting and practising

since I saw you last," he said more cheerfully, looking up into my face.

"Upon what?"

"Upon myself. I find it is possible for the spirit to temporize with the conditions of life without submitting slavishly to their tyranny—possible for it on occasion to hold them in suspension. In the end the exit is voluntary."

"What exit?" said I.

"Death," he answered.

"Well," I said, "I am a plain man of business, and want my dinner."

He laughed and rose and followed me into the street.

At eight o'clock that evening, the meal over, we were sitting in my friend's library smoking. The gas had not been kindled, as we were both wont to fancy the ruddy twilight of a warm fire-crimsoned hearth more conducive to the repose of desultory conversation than the whiter blaze. Sir —— * leaned back in his chair, his face, without the radius of the fire-glow, set in deep shadow. The room in which we sat was at the back of the house and quite undisturbed of the vexing rattle of the streets. It was heavily curtained, and the wall over against the hearth was lined with sombre books. Ancient pictures here and there shot little oily gleams into the darkness, and a shadowy intent bust over the book case took on strange plays of expression in the wavering and jerking of the coal gas.

My companion had been all the evening in a curious frame of mind—morbidly capricious I should pronounce it. He had fallen from mood to darker mood—as a body that plunges into an icy crevasse drops from shelf to shelf—and yet had not plumbed the frozen depths of his imagination. The subject of his dead father's communication, from being uppermost in his mind had come to absorb all its wholesomer impulses, and months of Continental travel seemed only to have intensified the mournful fascination it exercised over him. To-night the string upon which he wearisomely harped was the possibility of forgetfulness in a future state.

"I cannot comprehend it," was the sum of his gloomy discourse. "If what has been, is and must be, memory would

* Editorially omitted.

channel the heart of Heaven like a cancer. Could one forget and remain a pure intelligence? Could one remember and make sport of past horrors that had turned one's human heart grey with agony? To paint over the black of suffering with white is not to erase it."

He sighed and threw the butt of his cigar into the fading fire. The invisible clock on the mantelpiece chimed the half-hour.

"My dead father," he said, "stands before my imagination to-night like Hamlet's. Does he only exist now in mine and others'? A sorry consummation to his awful sacrifice—to be the creature of any common fancy that chooses to recall him. Where is he, Harry, where is he?"

His voice cracked, and he jerked in his chair and drew a deep breath.

I thought it well not to encourage his depressed imaginings and was silent. Suddenly he spoke again, but in an altered voice.

"It is a beautiful, terrible mystery. The earth is but a bead in the sweet rosary of nature's religion. The wonder falls in the dew and sprouts in the flowers that are fragrant in death."

I felt little surprise at his change of tone, but rather welcomed it, with an easing sigh, as indicative of an inclination to healthier moods. I was not unaccustomed to these his rhapsodical ventings of a moral dyspepsia. Only I was conscious that in this instance his words sent a strange shock of happiness throughout me. They impressed me with the sense of an intolerable burden suddenly thrown off. But his speech flowed on with a low soothing sound as of distant waters.

"What little doubts—what petty misgivings in the light of an overwhelming truth! Forgetfulness! Why, who would have it, and forego the pride, the pity and the ecstasy! To have been part of so wondrous a scheme, and to desire degradation to the ranks of the non-fighters—the poor carpet knights! 'Corruption wins not more than honesty!' Oh, Harry, we *can* triumph over suffering!"

And so, in a low eager monotone he wandered on, and I had no desire to interrupt him. For the matter of his discourse was wonderful in the extreme, though such as, half-remembered, would ring but thinly in the repetition. He gave such play to his imagination as I had not thought possible in him, mystic though he was, and enthralled me—the plain, common mind—with interpretations of the inscrutable that presented the solemn mystery of life in a manner to thrill me with the pride of being.

He urged me to be good—to be good!—to be always good and true to the highest instincts in me. He spoke of the pathetic beauty of our world with a divine realism that filled my eyes with unshed tears. He translated to me thoughts—the silent language of knowledge that is Truth beautiful and limitless, of which I had been only dumbly conscious hitherto. He showed my soul the secret of its cage's fastenings, and bade it stretch its wings and soar away into the boundless fragrant heavens.

Twice again did I hear the clock chime — the hour and half-hour—while he spoke thus, and I listened fascinated, and put in no word of my own. Then a little sound came outside the door, and his voice stopped on the instant with a sibilant murmur that reemed to reel up to the ceiling.

His man entered with a tray of glasses and decanters which he placed softly on the table. He then kindled the gas from an electric rod he held in his hand. The leap of white light blinded me for a moment, and in that moment I heard the man gasp and his rod rattle on the floor.

"God Almighty!" he exclaimed in an awful whisper, and took a hasty step towards his master.

I looked, and saw the latter huddled back in his chair, his face of a drawn ashy whiteness, his jaw fallen, his hand trailing limply against the carpet. I rose to my feet with a horrified cry.

"He is dead, sir," muttered the man, half whimpering.

"Impossible!" I said, "he——"

I hurried to him and took his hand—it came up heavy and chilled. I looked into his face—the eyes were partly open, viscous and unspeculative.

"Run—run for a doctor!" I cried.

I knelt by his side while the man was gone, in a whirl of suffocating thoughts and emotions. In ten minutes Dr. Glass entered the room. He made a brief examination and then raised himself upright and addressed me gravely.

"There is nothing to be done," he said.

"He is dead?"

"*He has been dead for over an hour!*"

I stared at him incredulously.

"That is quite impossible," I whispered.

"And why so?"

He inclined his head towards me in some surprise.

"You stake your professional reputation on it?"

"On what?"

"On that—that he died more than an hour ago?"

He shrugged his shoulders slightly.

"You are a little overwrought, sir," he said. "Yes; I stake my professional reputation on that."

He seized me, or I should have fallen. I felt faint and stunned. I begged him to lead me into another room, and not to quit the house till I could speak with him further. For a time I believe I, the man of most Philistine common sense, was feverish and hysterical. When, later in the night I recovered, I made that statement to him, which is here at his request set down in writing.

So ends the manuscript, and what more can be added? At the ensuing inquest the jury, according to Dr. Glass's notes, gave in a verdict of death from disease of the heart, and his friend, the author of the MS., was understood to explain that no doubt the catastrophe had occurred while he (the friend) was unconsciously dozing in his chair.

"This statement, however," the Doctor adds, "was a conventional one, given to evade the responsibility of explanation. To the last the man persisted to me in asserting the absolute truth of his story as here set down."

BEVIS CANE.

# A Hereditary Curse.
## PROLOGUE.

IN the old castle where she was born there she lay dead—the most beautiful and gracious lady in the land. Kind alike to grand and simple. The great gates were closed and within was weeping.

The young Earl, her son, paced the ancestral hall . . . now his, without demur. He had proposed evicting the Countess this very year. Death had spared him the committal of that outrage. A pale, vacuous face his, already stamped with that hereditary curse which had foredoomed successive generations.

And the serene semblance upstairs arranged in state, from which the soul had severed. Through weeks of half-death it had struggled, drawn and distorted the lovely outlines of the sweet countenance, but now they were as they had been when all was well. So marvellously composed they seemed to smile as she had ever smiled in kindly greeting then, now in last farewell.

It was a decade since the late Earl had died. He had been a fond husband even to the moment when his Bacchus-blurred person was entombed in a derogatory grave.

"Wherever you go, Elfrida, you are always the handsomest woman there," he would say to her proudly.

Watford, the present Earl of Shafton and Shafto, was the 12th earl in the peerage of Great Britain and Ireland, and removed by comparatively few heads from the Imperial summit. As he paced the hall his reflections were unenviable.

"*Caed mille failthe*,"

was inscribed over the wide arch dividing the hall, and never was motto more emblematic of the house it adorned. At the extreme end lay the dining-room, corresponding with the drawing-room on this side of the arch, which the young Earl now entered. It was spacious, with beautiful embrasured windows. But alas! the ruin that had overtaken the family was patent everywhere. The once resplendent hangings were reduced to tatters, and the loose coverings of the chairs were dishevelled and forlorn. To the left of the vast old-fashioned grate stood the Chesterfield on which she—his lately-lost mother—so often sat.

Even now, so familiar was the idea of her presence on that couch, the Earl started back imagining that her fragile beauty—like some *haute dame* of the old *noblesse*—with her slender feet peeping forth beneath the dainty frilling of her skirts, ornamented this favoured corner.

Near by was a standard screen bearing an embroidered banner. A biblical picture, representing Jael, wife of Heber the Kenite, as she smote the nail into the temples of Sisera and fastened him to the ground. Beneath were the words:

"The Will of a Wise Woman!"

It had been wrought by one of the family in the remote past, when woman sat and sewed. Doubtless sad thoughts of the terrible heritage were interwoven with each stitch, but in those days, it had not come to the sex to do more than stab the canvas oft moistened with futile tears.

The curse was begotten in this wise.

The first Earl—so created for his effrontery, as the bastard Faulconbridge was made baronet by King John—was a man of extraordinarily dissolute habits. In a lonely cabin on his land he discovered a girl of remarkable beauty; the ancient crone who permitted her to speak to no one was accounted a witch and certainly looked one. The Earl made his first attempt to win her with unusual gentleness. Rendered desperate by failure, he awaited her evening visit to the well for water, when he caught and forcibly detained her, obliging her to drink from a horn he carried until unable to make further resistance. But even as this was achieved, a severe blow from behind obliged him to drop his prey and turn with a cry of pain to receive the curse of the infuriated crone.

"Through you and all the generations that are to come shall run the curse of wine. By the devil by whom you have thought to undo shall you be undone. Never shall the demon of drink die in your veins until the Will of a Wise Woman shall smite it as Jael smote the nail into the temples of Sisera."

As Watford's eyes fell on the screen the story grew vivid. He put his hands to his head with a gesture of despair. It was small wonder reflection but embittered this young man's mourning, intensified the bitterness of natural regret, imbued the memory of yesterday, the yesterdays that had surely begat the misery of to-day with shame—shame that brought the burning colour to his pallid cheek and the shadow of remorse to his aching eyes. He was so young, so terribly young for this hereditary blemish to bristle in his veins. He recalled its ghastly victims—father, grandfather . . . should he prove yet another? She who lay so still and white upstairs, had been done to death by the ruin of all that life held dear, and by fear for his future.

The last scene which had proved just the one straw too much for the loving heart now stilled for ever, recurred persistently. It set his temples throbbing, and flustered his already weakened nerves with a futile repentance.

Have I been wrong to place the result before the reason? . . . Pardon me, for I saw her, Elfrida, Countess of Shafton and Shafto, stretched on the grand bed on which she was born, recalled to the God who gave her life, and she provoked my pity. My loathing of the sin that had poisoned her few years on earth.

Ah, luscious grape and trailing vine! Ah, bloated Bacchus, round whom the rose-decked damsels dance, the day has come when Charon's\* coffers overflow with the wins brought by thy victims.

---

## PART I.

THE country slept under a plenteous mantle of purity—for the snow lay thick. Softly and slowly it descended now. Flake after flake working a wonder of no otherwise witnessed whiteness, worthy of God.

At her open window, Yolande awaited the advent of Christmas. The cold was intense, but physical sensation was quenched by moral suffering.

"I cannot, I cannot," she moaned miserably.

Yet all the while she was conscious that the spider's web held her and there was no way out.

\* Charon was always paid for rowing the shades of the dead across the rivers of the lower world by the coin placed in their mouths before burial.

Christmas Eve had rivetted her contract of marriage to Watford, Earl of Shafton and Shafto. Yet, it was not the great peer that she loathed so much as the devil that sent him reeling from her presence. Since then she had gone down on her knees to her pompous parent, and besought release from the betrothal her soul abhorred and his money had brought about. But this *parvenu* had already accommodated his future son-in-law, and the promised payment was position for his only child. To this end had Matthew Harris dowered Yolande with all that calculating brain and grasping hand had won.

This ambitious man could not foresee how nearly his ships were to be wrecked, as he watched the Earl drive away in his flame-coloured dog-cart, over the white velvet road into the black night. And the snow began to cover him also.

"Hark, Een, do you hear *it*?"

"Surely," acquiesced the girl drowsily, "the stories we heard to-night cultivated our sense of creepy sounds . . . but I am half asleep."

Elfrida, widow of the 11th Earl of Shafton and Shafto, sat up in the old barouche and listened.

When anything untoward threatened the family were warned by the deliberate strokes of a hammer. If the trouble was to pass only the sense of hearing was admonished. If death was imminent vision accompanied sound. It was so now. The Countess beheld the woman Jael smite the nail into the temples of Sisera.

"Dear mother," exclaimed Rowena, love inspiring her with consciousness that something beyond her comprehension was happening, "dear mother, why do you tremble? . . . . Horan and the horses are as steady as Father Matthew's pledge and age can make them."

Horan and the barouche appertained to the friends with whom they had made merry this Christmas eve. There had been every description of carriage in the Shafton coach house, now the young Earl's dog-cart and a jaunting car reigned alone.

"The night the Earl—your father, died——" she broke into low moaning.

The intense nervous tension communicated itself in a less degree to Een, who still held her hand.

"Oh, Rowena," she pursued presently, with a dignity that well became her, and speaking as one speaks who sees beyond our narrow vision: "I saw it—living, vivid—and the stroke of the hammer rings sharp, resolute——"

Their carriage stopped. Poor old rheumatic Horan descended stiffly from the box and came to the window as Een lowered it. He was covered with snow, it lay in heavy flakes on his grizzly beard and drifted in, now smiting the ladies with its icy touch.

"Why do you stop?"

Horan, surprised at the imperious tone of one usually so courteous, attempted to tell her. Before he could enunciate she commanded:

"Open the door. Let me out! I know the Earl is lying dead—thrown from his dog-cart."

"No, no, milady, not the Earl—but the dog-cart."

"I know where my son lies in a shroud of snow. Who should know better?" hysterically.

An instant later, despite Een's protests she was in the road, her rich silken draperies trailing on the pure white carpet which engulfed her slim feet. The strain of mental powers petrified physical suffering, even though the chill of coming death congealed her blood.

The high dog-cart lay smashed to pieces in the centre of the road. The horse had kicked itself free and torn terrified to its stable. To the right, clear of the *débris*, was a snow-crowned mound. Instinctively the mother scattered the snow and discovered Watford. Een and Horan began to chafe his hands; the friction induced him to raise his head and open his eyes enquiringly. His breath was rank with spirits.

"Come back to the carriage now, mother," said Een, almost forcibly compelling her to do so.

Indeed the Countess knew there was no choice. In another moment she would have fainted. The relief of finding her son uninjured overpowered her. With the help of Horan he crept slowly after them, his limbs still benumbed. Then they left the wrecked dog-cart to be sent for, and proceeded homewards.

"Horse shied—saw the bloomin' ghost—suppose Pat followed the horse. I must have been shot out where you found me," explained Watford, adding: "I am just choked. Wish I could get a drink."

"You are a brute, Watford," in low, incisive tones. "This will kill mother."

The Countess lay back in her corner, with closed eyes.

"Goodness knows she should be accustomed to it with father," sulkily. "I did not take much to-night."

"Like Cassio, you have *very poor unhappy brains for drinking*," sneered Een. "As to being accustomed," she glanced towards the fragile figure, "it has sapped her life-blood."

"She wishes me to marry this old plebeian's daughter. I must go to his house—he gives me the best drinks out—brings me to the scratch, ha, ha!"

"Yet I have heard that Miss Harris takes no wine."

"Yolande has never tasted it — her mother was a fanatic on temperance."

"How she must loathe you."

"She does," he laughed defiantly, "would not kiss me; perhaps the day will come when I will not kiss her."

"Love may cure you," she suggested, too young to have given much consideration to the idea of a hereditary curse which neither love nor beauty could uproot.

"I am going to marry her—there is no other course open to me. I am played out."

"I suppose you won't turn mother out of her own home now," sarcastically.

"Yolande does not wish it."

Een checked the exclamation surprise prompted at this mark of deference. As a matter of fact, the Earl lacked audacity to perpetrate this outrage. Every rank would have condemned the extremity of ousting the Countess from her birth-place, albeit a flaw in certain legal documents *re* the heir rendered it practicable.

They involuntarily turned towards the refined face in the corner of the roomy carriage. A tremor passing over it thrilled them, and the hand that lay in Een's clutched and released hers convulsively.

"The Will of a Wise Woman," she repeated twice, "ah, I never had sufficient will and I was never wise."

Her children spoke to her, but she relapsed into a species of torpor. Universally idolized, the Countess had never experienced contradiction except from Watford. Early succession had been pregnant with evil for one inheriting a tendency to drunkenness, though the presence of a parent wanting in self-restraint would have proved a dubious privilege. As soon as Watford was able to hold a glass in his chubby fingers, the father had insisted on his appearance at table.

"He shall be no fool, but learn to carry his liquor!"

A worthy boast! And Elfrida, surrounded by a little court of flatterers, laughed at the baby reveller she had borne at the age of seventeen. It was accounted *devilish clever* of the little scamp when he was found overcome by libations under the table. He would toddle back after the feast and tilt the wine-glasses to obtain the drops left at the bottom.

When on this Christmas morning the heavy carriage lumbered through the great gates and approached the castle—even its dilapidations were beautified by feathery garlands of snow—the first slanting shafts of dawn shot across the picturesque wilderness of lawn and garden.

"Call Molly, Watford," said Een, when they reached the entrance.

But it was unnecessary. The old woman, who had been with the Countess from childhood, hurried forward as the Earl alighted.

"Lord have mercy upon us!" she cried below her breath, as her eyes marked the rigidity of the adored features, "this is more of your work," glowering at him.

This was the beginning of the end. Doctors came and went without result. Here was more than physical hurt. Yet perhaps neither the shock to her nerves, nor the chill to her naturally healthy system obtained when her satin-slippered feet sought her son's side in the snow and saved his life, would have been sufficient to kill her separately. But the combination told on her highly sensitive organization. The strain of suffering that might not permit of sympathy, as she had stood by a husband who drank himself to death, and beheld her son travelling the same road, had—as Een said—sapped her life-blood.

As the beautiful woman lay on her bed to all appearance unconscious, she experienced bitter self-accusation. Neglected duty increased the gloom that lowered above the valley of shadows; but when her spirit supplicated for mercy the terrible decree *too late* was reprieved. Even in this extremity one act of grace was possible. The Countess made a supreme effort and summoned her son's *fiancée* to her presence.

The secret of that death-bed scene is inviolable. Yolande entered on it in trepidation, she left with the birth of awakened responsibility ennobling her expressive features. Watford, who had been in waiting, was held back by that high look—saintlike as the snow-drops that lay secreted by folds of lisse at her throat.

## PART II.

*Cassio.* O, thou invisible spirit of wine, if thou hast no name to be known by, let us call thee devil!

THE magic of gold transformed the lands of Shafton and Shafto, while a still purer currency acted in like manner on their master. Alas! poor, erring human nature found it impossible to believe in good where evil had been dominant. An abstemious Earl of Shafton and Shafto was too prodigious, and while a few kindly souls listened gladly there were more who were out of harmony with such reform. Their own peccadillos had been screened by Watford's elevated position; should he turn Puritan they would suffer exposure.

The Earl and Countess had been absent six months. Meanwhile the keen eye of Matthew Harris had supervised the renovating of castle and grounds. It was a happy home-coming. Yolande had succeeded in drawing into prominence a side of Watford's character never previously recognized. To their mutual joy he found the vice that lowered his moral being, loathsome; freed from its chain life meant so much that was good and useful, and night and morning Yolande felt that the spirit of the dead mother supplemented her cry for help from the cross.

Thus it fell out that the world seemed very good to them as they drove through the entrance up to the Castle, where a new *régime* was to erase a miserable record.

Yet even on this first night there was a preliminary struggle. Old Matthew Harris enjoyed good wine, and being a competent judge, liked to discuss the merits of what he imbibed. Once, very long ago now, he had travelled in wine. His discrimination had formed the foundation of the pile which had attracted the Earl. Perhaps his success in life may be attributed to his non-comprehension of excess, and, like many short-sighted people, what he could not understand he could not tolerate. Total abstinence offended him.

"Yolande," he said pompously, spreading his dinner-napkin over his knees, "you can't keep this up, you know"—indicating a water carafe—"there is a life more valuable than your own to be sustained," with a knowing wink at his son-in-law.

Yolande's clear skin flushed, and Watford gave him a look that warned the old *parvenu* to attend to his fish—the bones of which gave him infinite trouble.

"What, Watford?"—forgetting his manners and speaking with his mouth full in his annoyance—"you must not pass that sherry—you make a mistake . . . there's no brand better calculated to wash down sole. Perhaps you prefer to keep to champagne . . . very well, let us start it now."

"Watford has become my disciple."

Matthew Harris's knife and fork fell with a clatter.

"Well, that scheme won't hold! I suppose, Yolande, you purpose introducing the next earl to the same cold comfort?"

Again the delicate face flushed painfully, and Watford was very angry.

"Look here, sir, if you continue to make allusions that—er—render my wife uncomfortable, I shall be obliged to——"

"But it's preposterous! An earl and not to take his glass!"

"Perhaps it is because I am an earl that I can dispense with stimulants. My forebears imbibed sufficient libations to enrich the blood of all coming generations. Yours were not so circumstanced—pray enjoy your opportunity; and let me act on my own, or rather"—glancing affectionately at Yolande—" your daughter's discretion."

"Hang discretion!" said Matthew Harris, surlily, too thick-skinned to feel the innuendo he had provoked. "It killed your mother."

Tears stood in Yolande's eyes. Only the echo of the late Countess's admonition enabled her to remain at table.

"The Will of a Wise Woman."

She must be resolute. The servants entered bearing a fresh course. Watford addressed himself to her during the remainder of the meal. She tried to include her father in the conversation, but he gave himself up to the delights of the table, and was scarcely conscious of what passed. His chagrin at the Earl's conduct was many-sided. When the Earl drank it sensibly diminished the distance between them. The great gulf between the class to which Watford belonged and the mass from which he had sprung, yawned less aggressively. Indeed, when in the early days of their acquaintance, the young man had drunk heavily, each glass abridged the chasm. The *parvenu* had found it pleasant to despise the peer.

Alas! poor Yolande was to learn that the devil devoted to the development of the hereditary curse was only *couchant.* Wherever it was possible for a wife to accompany her husband, she went, but there were duties incumbent on his position which had to be fulfilled alone. All went well until the apoplectic stroke which killed Matthew Harris occasioned the premature birth of an heir and prostrated Yolande, whose spirit would fain have followed her father and child.

Satan stormed the unguarded citadel. With exquisite cunning insinuating that drink was essential when Watford could not eat.

"A glass or two will sustain you in this hour of trial," asserted the tempter.

Watford acted on the suggestion, and when once spirit had passed his lips all power, all desire to stay his hand vanished. Hours passed. And by-and-bye, where the child had lain drunk after emptying the glasses of his father's guests, there the man dropped down undone by the same degrading demon.

The next morning, without even enquiring for Yolande, he left home for London. He dreaded those crystal-clear eyes; he had no pity for her grief and pain—drink deadens sympathy and scorches hallowed love.

And now, breaking in on her delirium, there reached the deserted wife, the portentous stroke of a hammer—sharp and resolute. No vision visited her. Not death but disaster was impending. She called aloud for her husband—a feeble, fruitless cry. Sleep succeeded exhaustion; from it she awoke sane and free from fever. Still, she was restless and watched the door for Dr. Molloy's appearance. When he came she told him she knew of Watford's absence.

"No one told me," she assured him, as he glanced round enquiring who could have afforded her this disturbing information. "*I felt he had gone.* And now"—beseechingly—"you must come with me to London."

Three days from that time—at the peril of her life, as he told her—Yolande insisted on his accompanying her to her house in Berkeley Square. On arrival, she obediently went to bed, and swallowed a sleeping draught. Dr. Molloy was to be her agent to find out the Earl's address at his club and go to him. He had made arrangements to remain. Her terms were magnanimous, to say nothing of his deep personal interest. How could he have the heart to abandon this fragile but brave woman, knowing in what condition he should find her husband?

So Yolande, knowing that all that could be done was being done, sank to sleep murmuring:

"By the Will of a Wise Woman."

---

## PART III.

*Cassio.* O, God, that men should put an enemy in their mouths to steal away their brains! That they should with joy, revel, and applause, transform themselves into beasts.
—OTHELLO, Act II., Scene 3.

THREE days of riotous liberty told on the unfortunate Earl with rapid retaliation. The night Yolande crossed from Ireland he spent in solitude, conscious that a little more excess meant *delirium tremens*. When in the midst of his misery, the memory of the hereditary curse confronted him, there seemed but one way of escape—suicide. But as he rose with the half-formed intention, the face of his wife started forth from among the surrounding shadows.

The devil within him shrieked.

"I can never return to you!" he moaned, falling back on his bed. "Never touch you! Never pollute your presence after . . ."

Then followed spectres of the coarse vices into which the vinous eyes of Bacchus had lured him. But his good angel had not deserted him, again the beloved face wrought its enchantment . . . . memories of happy days crept into his heart and held him fascinated until he slept. Thus to his surprise, Dr. Molloy found Watford. When he awoke he turned from his visitor ashamed. Then came a poor attempt at bluster—he demanded the meaning of this intrusion. He strove to be defiant. He hurled a string of semi-coherent invectives at the imperturbable Irishman, who understood the situation and waited, immovable. When this aggressive phase had played itself out, Watford's utterance was choked with tears and he whined miserably. The doctor having provided for such a contingency, began his cure. Presently having enjoined the servant neither to quit his post or admit anyone, he left the Earl sleeping placidly.

Yolande broke down on finding she might not immediately see Watford. Thus it befel when Dr. Molloy brought him to Berkeley Square, it was to the side of a sick bed. There he insisted on remaining. *The Will of the Wise Woman* had regained ascendency. Never before, not even by his mother's death, had the hold of the hereditary curse been so shaken. Did he not know that hurried journey to Town, that rush to his rescue, had imperilled Yolande's life?

At length a bright morning dawned. They left London just when the season was at its best, left for Switzerland for the lovely valley of Zermat, at the foot of the Matterhörn. Here presently when Yolande stood amid a wilderness of wild flowers, with a rose-blush on her cheeks and renewed health sparkling in her lustrous eyes, their tongues were loosed.

"Have you forgiven me, darling? You nearly lost your life to save my soul," cried Watford, throwing himself impulsively on his knees and clutching her skirts.

"Nonsense—as for my life—what would it have been, if I knew that the man I loved was drowning everything that was great in him in wine?"

"I have no words," he burst out. "I cannot say what I feel!"

"Do not try," laying a caressing hand on his head. "It was your dying mother's trust—to remember that only by the *Will of a Wise Woman* might the hereditary curse be eradicated. I was never to forget this, in my thoughts by days or my dreams by night, in my prayers and self-communing."

"Ah, if we could only live here it would be easy to be good!" sighing regretfully. "Here virtue was an existent reality, degrading vice a remote possibility. Oh, if I could but die here, Yolande!"

"No! you have to live and—work. To live down tradition, to prove that God is stronger than Fate."

He stood an attentive disciple, thrilled by her low, sweet voice, her child-like faith. When she ceased, the liquid notes of a lark seemed to bear the glad tidings of the return of one more prodigal to his Father's fold.

Under the shadow of the Matterhörn, there is a dainty little church—built by funds raised by Mrs. Bancroft—in its vestry after receiving the Holy Communion, Watford, 12th Earl of Shafton and Shafto, signed a pledge which he never broke. The *Will of the Wise Woman* had conquered.

Good heavens, it was all simple enough. With the Creator everything is simple, the crookedness of man induces complication. Yolande did not sit down and wish to cure this hereditary curse. She resolved and acted, strengthened night and morning by the anointing of the Man of Sorrows, as the flowers are strengthened by descending dew.

PENFOUND CRAWFORD.

## Orazio Calvo.

### By M. P. SHIEL.
#### Author of "PRINCE ZALESKI."

> Le leggi son fatti pei coglione.
> Laws are made for dullards.
> —*Corsican Proverb.*

AT a considerable height above the sea level, in the middle of a chaos of mountains, and not very far from Monte Cinto, the culminating point of the chain which traverses Corsica, stands the Villa Calvo. It is a great pile, half castle, half palace—half northern Italian Gothic, half southern Italian Byzantine—rising sheer from the brink of one of those stupendous ravines which are the commonplaces of the island. The ever-growing tale of tourists who sip absinthe and black coffee in the Hôtel Continental or *al fresco* in the *piazza* at Ajaccio during the early spring, have not seen it. Its solitude, in fact, could not be more complete. In some of its aspects it conveys the impression of a natural outgrowth of the landscape. Around it stretch those primal forests of ilex and laricio pines, which from of old caused the island to be described as "thick, and, as it were, *savage* with wood;"\* and towering above it—nearly always clad in snow—great crags of gneiss, of granite, of porphyry, and of mica-slate. Four miles away, seated lower down on a ridge, and swept in season by the frigid Tramontana wind, dozes the squalid village of Spello, with its white-washed box-houses, gutter tiles, scavenger-army of wild dogs, and windows paned with paper smeared in oil of olives.

The Villa Calvo itself is now the most forbidding of desolate places. The flags of the courtyard are seamed with wild lavender, and cistus, and the rich grasses of the heights; the two gardens are jungles of lentisk and walnut, the scarlet berries of sarsaparilla, and every kind of sub-tropical bindweed; shutters left open by the retainers as they fled from the house still groan to the highland Levante, or rot in the sun; buzzards and ravens, the deadly spider *malmignata*, and the black bat know it well; roofs buried in mosses show a tendency to fall in. The place is the very sanctuary of gloom. It is situated, too, on the more deserted side of the island, called by the Corsicans the "near," *i.e.*, the east or Italian side.

The noble house of the Calvi, Venetian in origin, had established themselves as great territorial *signori* (technical for our "nobleman," and so quite different to the Italian word) in Corsica by means of some one or other of their sons at a very early date. The original stock indeed, after playing a turbulent part in the history of the Republic, extirpated itself by the very exuberance of its own passions, the last of their number perishing by the poisoned dagger of his jealous wife in 1605. The off-shoot, however, found in the still greater insanity of Corsican political warfare a congenial life-element, and grew fat. The fortress-town of Calvi still bears their name in the north-west. Corsica passed under the suzerainty of Pope, Marquis of Tuscany, Pisa, Genoa, France; and with each change the house of Calvi knew how, by its adroitness, to find a stepping-stone to still greater power. From their sinister activities sprang the factions of Red and Black (Banda Rossa and Banda Nera), and taking the Black side, they became the mysterious centre of those intrigues and massacres which for centuries turned the province into a little hell. Considering the proverbial poverty

\* Δασεῖα καὶ ὥσπερ ἠγριωμένη τῇ ὕλῃ.—THEOPHRASTUS.

of Corsica, the revenues of this violent race became enormous; their influence boundless; till at last they grew to be regarded by the peasants with a profoundly superstitious awe. Their power indeed received a check when, joining the popular party in the insurrection of Paoli in '55, they suffered some loss of territories, but most of these were regained under the more favourable *régime* of the earlier period of the Convention. They were till lately regarded in Corsica as the last surviving of the great feudal signori, who migrated from the mainland between the tenth and sixteenth centuries.

It is, however, of the very latest scion of all of this volcanic family that I wish to speak. I first met Count Orazio Calvo in the midst of a bewildering Maelström of light and music and colour at a *masque* in his own Hôtel in the Rue de Rome. All the world was there, and I could not for the life of me imagine why he singled *me* out for the patronage of his talk; I remember, however, that it was his whim to profess a deep admiration for the English, whose language, indeed, he spoke perfectly. I at once set myself to the study of a man whom I saw to be not only remarkable, but unique. To find such a person—a rude Corsican grandee—profoundly *learned*, of course astonished me, though years of Paris failed to add an atom of real polish to his manners, and though his hardly-concealed contempt for all men and things included a contempt for his own acquirements also. Of the license of the Paris of his day he was the high priest, acknowledged and consecrated. He was known to be an atheist, yet he had his religion—the religion of excess; only, the possible excess of a Mephistopheles, not the excess of a Heliogabalus. It was easy to see that he despised what he did, and did it only because he despised it somewhat less than anything else. Yet he was the opposite of *blasé*; for an altogether abnormal energy was written on every feature of his body. His prodigality was in all cases distinguished by a certain *furore* of daring and originality; but the feeling he inspired was not so much admiration as *fear*. His rage was the very rage of the tiger; and though I feel sure he cherished a secret bitterness at the interval which divided him from the rest of men, yet a wise instinct warned the gayest of his satellites in the midst of the wildest Bacchanal never to address him with familiarity. He had a leonine habit of roaming far and wide

7\*

through the slums of Paris in the small morning hours; and stories of mad munificences performed by him at such times were circulated; but his charities, I thought, if they existed, could only be the stony, if prodigal, charity of the gargoyle which vomits for the thirsty. Of lovers' love he knew, of course, nothing; and the possibility of little Cupid coming to shoot baby arrows at such a heart, would have been a notion so exquisitely comic, that, had it occurred to anyone it must have set the entire Calvo Olympus in a flare of quenchless laughter. Round such a man, the *décadents*, the artist-class, the flâneurs and *étoiles*, and all the unfathomable *demi-monde* of Paris flocked—he was too volcanic a rough *Naturkind* to tolerate the *monde*—calling him king. He received in addition the *sobriquet* of *la petite comète*. None of his friends, I was given to understand, had ever seen on the lips of *la petite comète*—a smile.

In personal appearance he strongly resembled several other Italo-Corsicans whom I have met, and was not unlike that specimen of his singular countrymen who happened to become world-famous. He was below the middle height, and not too stout; yet he gave an impression of extraordinary *weightiness*, as though molten of lead. His face was of perfect classical beauty; black hair streaked with grey; skin hairless, and of the dirty olive of waxen effigies not yet painted pink. His brow was puckered into a perpetual frown; eyes cold as moonlight, glancing a downward and sideward contempt; forehead *bastionné*, columnar; jaws ribbed, a hew of graven brass; lips definite and welded; the whole face, the whole man, one, knit, integral—an indivisible sculpture.

Four or five times I met Orazio Calvo in Paris, and always he evinced the same disposition to take me, as it were, by the hand; while I, imagining a distinct element of doubt and even danger in his friendship, rather avoided *la 'tite comète*. I shortly afterwards returned to England, and though rumours of the excessive splendour of his revels sometimes reached me, the count, in the course of some three years had pretty well passed out of my active memories.

Suddenly, one morning, he stood before me in my chambers in London.

He seemed unconscious of my amazement, and informed me with the old air of sultan majesty that he had travelled in his yacht *incognito* and alone to England, and a friend being, for certain reasons, indispensable to him, he had sought me out. *Health* was the jewel which he sought; and, in truth, he looked haggard enough. "The bracing country air of Britain"—could I assure him that under conditions of perfect quiet and seclusion?

Noting in him a tendency to puff and corpulence, I suggested vigorous exercise. Something that I took to be a laugh rattled in his throat. But why not?—I insisted. If he would not walk, had he never heard of such a thing as the bicycle? I myself took an annual tour through parts of England by that means, and should be delighted to accompany him now.

With this suggestion he finally fell in, and we started. It was the beginning of the red-ripe Autumn time. The count, it is true, took somewhat unkindly to his machine, once flying into a hurricane of passion and making it the object of a rain of kicks from his rather short legs. But he quickly began to show signs of the connection between this method of locomotion and bodily well-being. The journey became more and more pleasant, till we reached a delightful retreat in Dorsetshire—a little farm belonging to a widow lady, whom I had long numbered among my friends.

This lady, of comparatively humble social position, was also of that entirely lovable type of English woman characterised by a profound natural piety—sedately gay, puritan, perennially fresh—whose qualities unite to remind one of the wholesomeness and sweetness of home-made bread. The two extremely lovely young ladies, her daughters—Miss Ethel and Miss Grace—added to her odorous home something of the colour and the charm of Paradise.

I may mention incidentally that the two girls were twins, though they possessed none of the resemblances so often accompanying this condition. Grace, with a complexion of dawn-tinted snow, was dark, rather tall, with a superb neck; Ethel was the sweetest flower in the world, fair and winsome.

Into this shadeful and quiet home I, with my friend Orazio Calvo, intruded. I had previously put up for considerable periods at the farm; but our present stay was only timed to last three days. When these had passed, however, others followed, a week, two. My companion showed no disposition to depart. It was the golden season of harvest, and with remarkable gallantry for *him*, the count daily escorted the ladies on their walks in the lanes and fields, entering with them into the life of the country, and watching by their side in the evening the Pan-ic levities of the reapers. His tongue was loosed, and he spoke to them of the world, and its glory. I know not what of misgiving, foreboding, gradually took possession of my mind.

As he sat under the porch by moonlight listening to the pure and simple songs of the ladies, I could see how the cynical man of the world—whose notions of Woman had been derived from the peasant-girls of Corsican villages, and the *étoiles* of the Ambigu and Variétiés—how he, now first in his life's course, realized that an earthly creature may yet be of heaven. I could see him revelling in the transport of an entirely new, a divine impression.

I proposed departure. He refused. I strongly insisted.

"I shall go," I said.

"In which case," he replied, "nothing is so certain as that you go alone."

Then, after a while, a new discovery filled me with new alarm. I believed I could detect in the virgin eyes of both the girls the very abandonment of love for Orazio Calvo.

And one night, after I had retired to sleep, he walked into my room and stood at the foot of the bed, leaning over the rail. The glimmer of a lamp showed me his extreme pallor, the fire that swelled and inflamed his stern eyes. I dreaded to break the long silence between us.

"I *love* them!" he suddenly exclaimed, paroxysmal in passion.

Love *them!* Every nerve in my body rose shuddering in revolt against him. Love *them!* Yet the trill of his voice, the trembling bed-rail, left no doubt of the genuineness, the intensity of his meaning.

"But *which* of them, in God's name?" I asked.

"Which? Miss—Grace—I think."

I *think!*

The enigma utterly confounded me.

But my vague presentiments were laid to rest when, two months later, the dark-haired Grace was led by him to the altar of the village-church hard by. The young wife was immediately carried off to the Continent. From widely divergent points of the earth's surface—from Delhi—from Memphis—her mother heard from her. Finally she took up her residence in the mountain home of her husband's race. Her constant promise to revisit England she never fulfilled.

During the space of two years I received several illegible letters from Count Calvo (the vehemence of his temperament hardly permitted his writing to be read; for a steel nib immediately broke to splinters under his hand; and his attempt to write many a word with the quill resulted in nothing but a thick dash)—and two from his wife, in both of which latter I fancied—though I do not say it was more than fancy—that I could detect a note of deep, and even weird, melancholy.

And once again, at the end of these two years, Count Orazio Calvo stood unexpectedly before me in my house. A glance told me that he was a changed man. Some disease surely—I thought. The hungry eyes, no longer cold, shifted incessantly. His fingers clutched continually at some phantom thing in the palm of his hand. My lips formed the word, "Orestes."

"But the countess?" I enquired.

"Is dead."

"*Dead!*"

"I say it. Dead!"

I shuddered as he uttered the word.

The same hour he proceeded to the farm, I with him. The news of Grace's death had shortly preceded him by letter. He had sent, too, a lock of her hair, several little mementoes. The little home, when we reached it a second time, was a house of woe.

I soon returned to London, leaving the Count behind me. Five months later, I received a letter begging me to go back to the farm on a matter of some delicacy.

Now, I may as well say at once that I am by no means what would be called a *squeamish* person; that in general I regard the notions of Clapham with so much, and only so much, attention as the superstitions of ancient Egypt. Yet, for some reason or other, I now felt impelled to protest with the most heart-felt ardour against the projected marriage of Count Calvo with the fair-haired Ethel. An instinct—illogical, perhaps, but deep—told me of something uncanny, awesome, in the union. Earnestly did I implore the dear mother, now heart-broken and bereft, to interpose her will. She, too, felt all I felt; but dared not, she said, coerce the overmastering inclinations of the girl.

I accordingly accompanied Miss Ethel to Paris, and on a dark

December day, in the gloomy church of St. Sulpice, saw her united to the object of her ecstatic love.

From her, as from a nature more affectionate and sunny than that of her sister, the letters I received came more regularly. They were dated from the various capitals of Europe, and then for some time from Venice; and in them, too, I found—or thought I found—a tone of heart-sickness, of disappointment. But this feeling, if it existed at all, must have been short-lived; for on taking up her residence at the Villa Calvo, her letters became suddenly voluminous and frequent. Ethel, it was now clear, was happy. In one epistle, I received a long and very comical history of the only visit which ever disturbed her solitude, paid by the podestà and staff-general of Bastia; in another, a gay account of the eccentricities of a haughty old Corsican peasant who did duty as butler. Every trifle seemed to make her joyful; and every sentence began or ended with "her dear lord"; his condescending love for her; her worship of him. Quite suddenly the letters ceased altogether.

It may have been a year and a half after the second marriage that I found myself at Marseilles *en route* for Southern Italy. That I felt a certain relief when I entered the station to see my train steaming away is certain; but so secret are sometimes the workings of the Will, that I was only half-conscious of the feeling, nor could I explain it. Half an hour later, however, as I sauntered in la Canabière, I was able to read myself. From this point the harbour is fully visible, and looking westward, I caught sight of a little steamer making her way out from Port la Joliette. I was too salted a *Marseillais* not to know *her*—it was *La Mite*, a boat of the old Valéry line not yet grown into the Compagnie Transatlantique: in eighteen hours she would be lying at anchor in the harbour of Ajaccio. I hastened to the *quai* region; the vessel was then puffing under the guns of St. Nicolas. I accosted a group of propped watermen:

"Tell me—is it at all possible to catch her now?"

They looked lazily at her.

"She's off," said one, "*le bon diable même ne saurait*——"

My desire must have been *very* great, if it was at all equal to my disappointment.

I continued my way eastward; again and again finding it necessary to prove to myself that it was absurd to go out of one's way to visit forgetful friends. Fréjus, Genoa, Pisa—

keeping always to the coast—I reached at last the central point between Pisa and Rome. Here, at Follonica, I stopped short —over-mastered—and travelling by horse, reached the coast village of Piombino, opposite the singular island, tombstone-shaped, called by the Romans Œthalia, and now Ile d'Elbe ; there made terms with the padrone of a small *speronare*, and in twelve hours landed at Bastia. I was bent upon visiting Count Orazio Calvo in his fortress home.

Mounted on a small Corsican pony, and accompanied by a guide on a mule, I turned southward, and began the ascent. The fever-mists of the low-lying east coast hung heavy, and under this pall, interminable stretches of *makis* (thick copse) flamed with arbutus leaves, and the purple of maple fruit, and were aromatic with the myrrh of cisti. Here and there on the dizzy edge of a ravine, a solitary hut ; or in the depths of the wood, the dole of a shepherd's bagpipe ; now the tinkle of goat-bells from afar, now the flap of a raven's wing, or the momentary phantom of a brown wild sheep *(mufri)*. My guttural companion spoke continually on the subject of the brigands. Twice only we passed through mountain villages, and in the afternoon of the second day reached Spello. The short remainder of my upward way I continued in accordance with verbal directions. Before long the Villa Calvo rose sternly before me.

I crossed a dry flat moat, and made fast my animal to a staple in one of the granite pillars of the gateway. Silence pervaded the place. I noticed a decided rankness in the garden on each side of the forecourt. Ascending a flight of marble steps, I rang an iron bell hanging beneath one of the two front porticoes. Its clanging made a sharp break in the stillness. But to my repeated summonses there came no answer. At last I boldly pushed back the unfastened portal, and entered the house.

So long I wandered about, that at last, in a complexity of long velveted corridors and dim chambers, I lost my bearings. The impression wrought on me by the deserted bigness of the mansion was intense. Even my own footfall was inaudible. The evening was now darkening toward night. From where I stood I heard the chirping of a cicada. By an effort I raised my voice and called, but only echoes answered me. In an elliptical apartment, I found a table spread—the white cloth, wines, all the *restes* of a meal, gold and silver plate, faded grapes ; a clock on a pedestal of ebony, it had ceased to tick ; in another chamber I came on a lady's garden-hat on a divan. And over all the dreariness of Gethsemane. Trembling hesitancy to proceed further possessed me.

In a remote wing I came at length to a passage, in the wall of which was a nail-studded Gothic door. It occasioned my surprise, for though it now stood ajar, it was provided *on the outside* with shot- bolts, and from this side a large key still projected. I entered the suite to which it admitted. The rooms were furnished with exceptional splendour, and here a piece of music, there an article of jewellery, seemed to betoken the habitual presence of a lady. Then in the middle of a carpet something chanced to meet my careful outlook which fully confirmed me in this supposition—two very long hairs. At this sight I found it necessary to call up all my courage. With the daring of despair I picked up one of the filaments, and held it to the just dying violet light filtered through the stained glass of the casement. I expected—I must, I think, have *expected*— to find it of the blonde *nuance* of the Countess Ethel's hair. A sob of horror burst from me when I saw it lie on my palm dark as the brown of Vandyke.

Yet another long, heart-torturing search, and in a loftier part of the building I faced a draperied door. On attempting to push it back, I discovered it to be locked. Yet *this* door I determined to open, if I could ; and again I bent all my strength to the effort. It remained closed, hiding its mystery. It was only when on the point of moving away that I noticed, just projecting from under the bottom, a white substance. I stooped and drew it out. It was now dark, but I could see that it was a large envelope, and, peering close, detected my name in the writing of the count. With this in my hand I hurried from the spot—through the vast house of desolation—beyond the bounds of the whole gloomy and terror-haunted domain.

" My friend," thus ran, in the somewhat explosive, Æschylian style so characteristic of him, the all but indecipherable MS. of Count Orazio Calvo—" this document which I address to you will in all probability never reach you. I write it, however, rather by way of monument to my own integrity, than with the hope that it will be read by other eyes.

"My friend, that foul and hellish monster, Pope Clement VII., pronounced in 1525 a curse against the sons of my race. It has been a secret tradition with my uncultured fathers to believe all-unwillingly in its ultimate fulfilment. Perhaps even I myself, in spite of a life of search into the make and meaning of the universe, have been unable wholly to expel some lingering half-credence in this ancient superstition.

"That the malediction has at last overtaken us is now a certainty. With me my race expires. I write this as a protest —and a defiance—against a fate wholly unmerited.

"You cannot doubt that I loved—you could not be so lunatic. And you know, too, that I never withheld my hand from any joy. To desire, with me and the stock of which I come, has always been to possess.

"But soon after realizing my passion, I was confronted by a stupendous problem. In order to solve it I made a leap into the dark, and married—the Countess Grace. I expected happiness. Happiness was far from me. The poor lady, seeing my bitter disappointment, pined. The splendour of her beauty dimmed. After a time I refused to look upon her; to see her face increased my fever. A fire scorched my chest. I traversed the continents, seeking rest; I consulted the greatest physicians; I puzzled them; they pronounced me mad—rabid with the bite of the tarantula. My mysterious malady took only deeper root. I was devoured by the longings of Tantalus—a passion more fervid, *and more pure*, than the holy rage of the seraphim consumed me.

"When my agonies had reached the intolerable degree, I extorted from my wife, who greatly loved and also feared me, a vow to hold no communication with any of her former friends during the space of ten years. On her knees she implored me to pity her mother, her sister, who would suppose her dead. But in her eyes my bare will had by this time acquired the dignity and force of law, and I moreover soothed her with invented reasons which partially satisfied her intellect. Leaving her among the mountains, with desperate resolve I announced her death, and returned to England. I wedded—the Countess Ethel.

"The gross word 'bigamy' perhaps rises to your mind. My friend, it is immaterial. I, too, at the time, was slightly troubled by some such thought. This second marriage I now know to have been the most sacred, just, and essential that was ever consummated.

"And now at least, my friend, I looked for peace; and again —*again*—the mawkish after-taste of the new-awakened glutton filled my mouth. I felt, it is true, some sensible alleviation of my disorder. But my Ethel, observing me still cold, unrestful, grew sad. I found her often in tears. We passed together from city to city, till for a time, we settled in my palazzo on the Canal Grande in Venice.

"The great problem, you perceive, was still unsolved. I loved—with a love of which ordinary men can never dream. But whom?—what? Not Grace, that had been proved. Not Ethel, that was being proved. Then whom? The discovery that waited for me was doubtless accelerated by the wild, brief joy that filled me whenever I left Venice to visit Corsica, or Corsica to visit Venice. Faint glimpses of the truth must have lighted me then; but many months passed before, on a starry night, as a gondola floated me slowly over the Canalazzo, I started up with a shout, my soul flooded with the whole supernal secret of the mystery.

"The very next day I returned to Corsica. My friend, attached to the Villa Calvo is a wing wholly cut off from communication with the rest of the house, save by a single door. It was used in former centuries by some of the women of my race —for periods sometimes of several years—as a place of penitential retreat. These erring souls were careful, however, that their hermitage should be wide and luxurious; the high-walled little garden at the end afforded them a place of exercise; a separate kitchen and staff of attendants compensated for a too rigorous devotion to their rosaries, their *prie-dieu*, and their breviaries; a door bolted on the wrong side guarded them from contact with a world they had too much loved. Into this wing I now introduced the Countess Grace. Her love was thereby tested to the utmost; not, I tell you, without a struggle did my will subdue her high soul. 'Am I then—a free Englishwoman—a prisoner in a Corsican castle?' she asked. 'Aye—a prisoner,' I replied, 'but a prisoner to her prisoner.' Seeing me foam and grovel at her feet, she had pity and yielded. An aged servant of my father, sworn to secrecy, a captive with her, supplied her wants. The other menials, save two, I dismissed. Then I set out for the mainland, and returned to Corsica—with Ethel.

"It was a step bold, but necessary to my sanity. For of the full nature of my passion I was now aware. I did not, as I have said, love the two countesses severally, but——and here was the tremendous secret of my destiny—I loved them conjointly. I write, you think, the drivel of a maniac? If you think so, be sure that the reason is your own shallowness, your own folly. Can it be that you have investigated the nature of things to so little purpose as to imagine that you *know*? Strange births, multiple births; the mystery of chemical combination; of all welding processes, from the welding of metals, to the adhesion of flesh to bone, to the welding of spirits; what is a unity, what a duality; the mystery of the thing named soul—have you then probed these matters? There is none, my friend, wholly dark but him who dreams that he knows! Tell me only this: which of the halves would you love were your wife bisected by a thunderbolt? Neither much, I think? Yet the two together——? So I, too, loved an entity, not either of the parts which composed it. The woman I adored was the woman who would have been born, had the birth of which Grace and Ethel were the product been single and not double. It happened indeed to be double; but do not imagine that that in any way affects the original aggregation either of spirit or of matter. It became clear to me that when the two countesses stood shoulder to shoulder the woman I loved *was there*. They, in respect of me, completed each other. Upon such secrets does the daily sun shine. One—a mystic one, a dual one, if you will —but not two—was my bride. To my soul, now made *clairvoyant* by its passion, they formed, though divided in the flesh, a single being.

"And as the copper and the zinc, kept asunder, remain ineffectual, but put into approximation, evolve the most potent motive in the universe—so they. The effect of rapture which nature had rendered them capable of producing upon me depended, it was clear, upon their physical juxtaposition. So it was in the first instance at the farm, where the impression wrought upon me was an impression not effected by either, but by *both*; and it was this impression which had caused me to *love*. It was therefore essential to my happiness that they should dwell within the same walls—house beneath the same roof—that I should pass straight from the goddess grandeur of the one to the laughter and the love of the other.

"This I accordingly accomplished. And now began a life—for me, for them—of such exceeding bliss as earth contained not beside. No longer could either doubt the genuineness of my passion. My fever vanished. Each revelled in my new-born tenderness. Ah! they loved. Some of the letters written by the Countess Ethel to you at this time I saw; did they not speak of an existence crowned with joy? Grace, too, forgot her repinings, the gloom of her seclusion, in the wealth of the affection I lavished upon her. A shade of anger might cross me if Ethel would revert to the forbidden subject of the decease of Grace, urging me to describe her death-bed. Otherwise all was halcyon. I spent by the side of my Grace those hours of the day during which Ethel supposed me engaged in study; and though my beauteous captive still gently chid me for concealing the secret reasons which moved me to debar her from the rest of the house, she seemed little by little to grow reconciled to my whim, and in her dark eye shone only the light of love and peace.

"My friend, one day in this azure sky the blackness of hell arose.

"I beheld my Ethel stand by night—in the part, too, of the house most remote from her apartments — before the bolted door, and *listen*. Observing my eye upon her, she moved stealthily, guiltily away. I stood rooted—struck by a thunderbolt—to the spot. So then, she knew—*she knew*—that there was something—something hidden, forbidden—behind those bolts and bars!

"This incident unloosed once more in me the demon of gloom. I grew acutely suspicious. Suppose, I whispered to my heart, suppose—— The thought dimmed my eyes. I turned myself into a lynx's eye to watch.

"My moodiness fell straightway upon them both. Grace grew silent, once again resentful, carping; Ethel dreamy, pensive. She ceased to write to you. The laughter was quenched. Weeks passed. I tracked shadows in the dark; I probed to the bottom the creak of a plank at midnight. That vague suspicions, presentiments filled the mind of Grace, I could no longer doubt. One day, throwing off her fear of my anger, weeping on my shoulder, the gentle Ethel boldly questioned me as to what dreadful secret I hid from her '*in the western wing.*' Great God! I silenced her with a reproof.

"But that the catastrophe to happen was inevitable, I should have known. The situation was all too tempting for the forbearance of the Parcæ. Here were all the elements of a disaster, needing but the touch of Fate, the match to the mine, to blow our lives into annihilation. And when the tragedy came, it came with an all-destroying suddenness.

"For as I sat and read in the dead of the night, I knew that a gentle tread went swiftly past my door. I arose and, crouching cat-like, followed. I could discern a bent form in the gloom of the unlighted corridor. God! and now the moonlight streamed in from a window, and beamed athwart a female figure draped in loose attire. I was convulsed with earthquake shocks of rage. Ethel, I hissed to the floor on which I crawled—Ethel again—spying by night! She took the way to her own bedchamber, of old occupied by her sister. And now she reached it—drew open the door—the light from within gushed out upon her: I saw—by the powers of blackest hell!—the arrogant throat, the ponderous cataracts of dark-brown hair — *Grace!* And in that room was Ethel! I rushed forward. For one insensate moment only they stared crazily, crazily into each other's eyes—then from their two throats a shriek so shrill that it must have pierced even to distant Spello—and they flew like maniacs to each other's straining arms.

"It is curious that at this supreme instant, my first unconquerable instinct — the instinct of the Corsican vendetta blood-hound—was to plunge a sword into the bosom of the ancient servant through whose betrayal this woe had befallen us. I crept away in the darkness, and ran towards the western wing, pausing only to take a loaded blunderbuss from the armoury. The bolted door I found secured as usual, and indeed, I alone kept the key; the countess had escaped then through the gate in the wall of the garden, and of this the old man was the guardian. He had thus been either false or careless. As I passed inward, there was light. I noticed lying on an escritoire a scrap of paper. I took it, and read: 'I have chanced to hear a soft sound of singing at nightfall. Whoever you are, try, if you are sorrowful, to escape—to see me. Help, if my help can save, shall not be wanting.' It was unsigned, and the writer, dreading the chance of my eyes, had carefully disguised her hand—yet I knew. With redoubled fury I ran from room to room to find my faithless servant; he presently sighted me, and darted with the alacrity of youth down the steps into the garden, screaming his innocence. He hid among the trees, till marking him well, I fired. Loudly bellowing, he fell. I found later that the others too, hearing the screams and turmoil, and fearing my frenzy, had fled the house.

"I returned to the chamber of the fatal meeting. The two ladies, hand in hand, rose and confronted me. In the gentle eye and the bold eye alike I read my doom—resistance active, resistance passive to my will, even to the death. I know their mother—her quiet but adamantine resolution in matters where the religious *motif* intervenes. And as she, so they. I did not at all doubt that I could sooner turn the sun to ice than move them from their purpose of rebellion.

"'We have no avenger,' said the stately countess Grace, 'but with our own hands we shall protect ourselves from outrage,' and she raised a jewelled dagger as if to strike my breast.

"'Oh, no, no, Grace,' cried Ethel interposing, 'not *him*, my love—strike me.' Then turning to me with tears—'Oh, why, why did you wrong us, who love you, thus?'

"'To your own apartments, madam,' I said to Grace.

"Not yet had my voice lost its intonation of command. Struggling to disobey, with face of ashen hue, she slowly relinquished the hand of her sister—and obeyed.

"And so ended for ever our dream of joy. What further life was now possible for any of us? An hour later, in pity, I waited upon my first-wedded with a goblet of wine. Knowing my meaning, she refused—not angrily, lovingly rather—to drink from my hand; but sweetly yielded up her glorious form when with forceful tenderness I seized it. Alas! the crack, and her sigh, ring like a lunacy in my brain. Ethel, on the other hand, drank without a murmur of the cup I offered, from beneath her lids gazing steadily upon my face with her most blue reproachful eye. She drooped dead upon my breast, smiling, lisping the words: 'Orazio—*husband!*' No *Voceradori* of my land shall wail strange *alalas* over their silence. They lie together on the couch to which I bore them. The first cold grey of the dawning day steals in upon me as I write. The half-emptied goblet is by my side. My friend, their bed is wide! I go—to pass with them—with *Her*—into the Kingdom of Forgetfulness. Farewell!"

So ended the count's narrative.

www.ingramcontent.com/pod-product-compliance
Lightning Source LLC
Chambersburg PA
CBHW031939290426
44108CB00011B/606